Nietzsche, Genealogy, Morality

PHILOSOPHICAL TRADITIONS
(formerly the MAJOR THINKERS series)

General Editor
Amélie Oksenberg Rorty

Nietzsche, Genealogy, Morality

Essays on Nietzsche's
Genealogy of Morals

EDITED BY

Richard Schacht

UNIVERSITY OF CALIFORNIA PRESS

Berkeley   Los Angeles   London

To NANS

University of California Press
Berkeley and Los Angeles, California

University of California Press
London, England

Copyright © 1994 by The Regents of the University of California

Library of Congress Cataloging-in-Publication Data

Nietzsche, genealogy, morality : essays on Nietzsche's Genealogy of Morals / edited
by Richard Schacht.
    p.   cm. — (Philosophical Traditions ; 5)
    Includes bibliographical references.
    ISBN 0-520-08317-2 (alk. paper). — ISBN 0-520-08318-0 (pbk.)
    1. Nietzsche, Friedrich, 1844–1900. Zur Genealogie der Moral.
    I. Schacht, Richard, 1941–   . II. Series.
    B3313.Z73N54   1994
    170—dc20   93-12082
                                                          CIP

Printed in the United States of America

1 2 3 4 5 6 7 8 9

The paper used in this publication meets the minimum requirements of American
National Standard for Information Sciences—Permanence of Paper for Printed
Library Materials, ANSI Z39.48-1984 ∞

CONTENTS

v

ACKNOWLEDGMENTS

I am grateful to Amélie Oksenberg Rorty for her interest in the idea of this volume, and for her encouragement to make this collection an ambitious one; to Scott Mahler and then Ed Dimendberg at the University of California Press for their support and cooperation along the way; to David Blacker, Kevin Hill, James Janowski, and Alexandra Bradner for their invaluable help as research assistants; to Blacker, Annie Pritchard, Jessica George, Alban Urbanas, and Judith Rowan for their work on the translations of the Blondel and Kofman essays; to Cheri Zander, Glenna Cilento, and Judy Short for their secretarial assistance; to the many contributors of essays written expressly for this volume—and for the patience of those who got their essays in long before the volume was ready to go into production; and to the following for their permission to include other essays here that were originally published elsewhere:

To the editors of *Philosophy and Phenomenological Research*, for their permission to reprint Richard White's "The Return of the Master: An Interpretation of Nietzsche's *Genealogy of Morals*," from their volume 48 (1988), pp. 683–696.

To Kluwer Academic Publishers, for their permission to reprint David Couzens Hoy's "Nietzsche, Hume, and the Genealogical Method," from their publication *Nietzsche as Affirmative Thinker*, ed. Yirmiyahu Yovel (Dordrecht: Martinus Nijhoff Publishers, 1986), pp. 20–38. Copyright 1986 by Martinus Nijhoff Publishers, Dordrecht. Reprinted by permission of Kluwer Academic Publishers.

To the editors of *International Studies in Philosophy*, for their permission to reprint Arthur Danto's "Some Remarks on *The Genealogy of Morals*," from their volume 18/2 (1986), pp. 3–15.

To Philippa Foot and *The New York Review of Books*, for permission to reprint Philippa Foot's "Nietzsche's Immoralism," from their 13 June 1991 issue (volume 38, no. 11), pp. 18–22. Reprinted with permission from *The New York Review of Books*. Copyright 1992 by Philippa Foot.

To James R. Langford, Director, University of Notre Dame Press, and to Alasdair MacIntyre, for permission to reprint Alasdair MacIntyre's "Genealogies and Subversions" from *Three Rival Versions of Moral Enquiry* (Notre Dame: University of Notre Dame Press, 1990), pp. 32–57. Copyright 1990 by Alasdair MacIntyre.

To Françoise Laye, of Presses Universitaires de France, for permission to publish a translation of Eric Blondel's "La question de la genealogie," from the PUF publication *Encyclopedie Philosophique Universelle* (tome I).

To T. M. Farmiloe, of the Macmillan Press Ltd., and to St. Martin's Press, Incorporated, for their permission to reprint Alexander Nehamas's "The Genealogy of Genealogy," from their publication *On Literary Theory and Philosophy: A Cross-Disciplinary Encounter*, eds. Richard Freadman and Lloyd Rinehardt (London: Macmillan, and New York: St. Martin's, 1991). Copyright Macmillan Academic and Professional Ltd. 1991.

To Schocken Publishing House Ltd., for permission to use Yirmiyahu Yovel's essay "Nietzsche, The Jews, and *Ressentiment*," from Yovel's book *Hegel and Nietzsche on Judaism*, which is to be published by Schocken.

To Claire Giles, of Journals Rights & Permissions at Blackwell Publishers, for permission to use Bernard Williams's essay "Nietzsche's Minimalist Moral Psychology," from volume 1, no. 1 (pp. 1–14) of *European Journal of Philosophy*, a publication of Blackwell Publishers. Copyright 1993 by Basil Blackwell.

INTRODUCTION

by Richard Schacht

Nietzsche was concerned with morality, value, humanity, knowledge, and the development of our ways of thinking about these matters throughout his career. It was only in the second and final decade of his productive life, however, and indeed only in the last half of it, that he came to a clear realization of how problematic they all are and undertook to address them in the light of this realization. His post-*Zarathustra* works (and notebooks) may be considered his final and most significant attempts to come to terms with these matters. These writings show the lines along which he was thinking about them, and how far he got.

Nietzsche's post-*Zarathustra* writings are as richly suggestive as they are provocative for philosophers and others concerned with these issues today. Had he stopped with *Zarathustra,* that extraordinary work together with his previous writings would have sufficed to earn him a prominent place in the intellectual history of the late nineteenth century. What he went on to do in the few years that remained to him has made him one of the most important figures in the history of modern philosophy, and a looming presence in contemporary philosophical inquiry.

All the concerns mentioned at the outset came together in *On the Genealogy of Morals (Zur Genealogie der Moral),* written in the middle of this brief but remarkable final period, and published in 1887. It had been a dozen years since Nietzsche had written anything in an "essay" style, and this is his only later work written in anything approaching that style (with the partial exception of *The Antichrist*). He had *Zarathustra* behind him, and had published *Beyond Good and Evil* (his "Prelude to a Philosophy of the Future," as its subtitle proclaims) the year before. He also had just written the "fifth book" added to the first four "books" or parts of *Die Fröhliche Wissenschaft (The Gay Science)* in the expanded edition of this work that appeared in the same year as the *Genealogy.* And he further had just completed the series of reflective retrospective prefaces to many of his other pre-*Zarathustra* books (which he had decided to reissue) in the stocktaking year of 1886.

It was at this point that Nietzsche went on to write the three "essays" and preface of which the *Genealogy* consists. Ahead of him lay less than two more years of active life, in which he pursued (in his notebooks) and then abandoned the project of a comprehensive work he planned to call *The Will to Power: Attempt at a Revaluation of All Values* (as he tells us in the Third Essay of the *Genealogy*), and then in a final astonishing burst of productivity completed *The Case of Wagner, Twilight of the Idols, The Antichrist,* and *Ecce Homo.* The *Genealogy* thus came at a crucial juncture, and is in many respects the high point of this last period of his philosophical activity. To borrow some of his own imagery, if the time of *Zarathustra* was his "great noon" (as he himself suggests), when the sun of his intellectual life reached its zenith—following its ascent in the period of *Daybreak*—then the time of the *Genealogy* might be thought of as his "golden afternoon," when that sun's light was no longer dazzling but was still strong (perhaps the best time of day for seeing things clearly), before it cast its last rays in the hours of *Twilight,* and soon thereafter gave way to night.

More prosaically, in the *Genealogy,* along with the virtually contemporaneous fifth book of *The Gay Science,* we encounter the philosopher whom Nietzsche became at the height of his powers and maturity. Here we find him attempting to do at least some of the things he had come to be convinced needed doing in order to pursue the reinterpretive and revaluative tasks of the kind of "philosophy of the future" he had called for and sought to inaugurate in *Beyond Good and Evil.* As he had recognized in his retrospective prefaces of 1886, and as he observes in his preface to the *Genealogy,* his earlier thinking had already been on the way to his thinking here, and is of no little relevance to it. There also are significant connections between what we find him doing and saying here and what he went on to undertake and maintain in his final reckonings with Wagner, Christianity, and the other "idols" he considers in his next and final spate of books. The *Genealogy* may thus serve well as both a focal point and a point of departure for the consideration of much of Nietzsche's thought.

But what is it that he attempts to do here? His announced topic is "*die Moral*"—not necessarily "morality" as such and in general, but in any event several purportedly different and basic types of moral schemes, and certain phenomena associated with them. His announced project in this book is "genealogy"—and more specifically, the "genealogy" of these moral types and associated phenomena. Yet his interest is not merely to understand them, but further and more importantly to use the understanding of them as a springboard to the comprehension of a good deal more. But of what? and how? And how is "genealogy" supposed to help? Indeed, how is it supposed to work? How does it relate to the two basic tasks of Nietzsche's kind of philosopher—(re)interpretation and (re)valuation? What light is shed by what Nietzsche does in the three "essays" making up this book on these tasks themselves?

These are only some of the questions needing to be raised and considered with respect to Nietzsche's efforts and concerns in this pivotal but strange and perplexing book. These questions also lead well beyond the *Genealogy* itself, in many directions. Its importance to the understanding of the "mature" Nietzsche's thinking is obvious; but its import is not. Making sense of it involves bringing a sense of his larger enterprise to bear upon it as well.

Hence the present volume of essays. The idea of such a volume grew out of a symposium held in 1987 (to mark the centenary of the *Genealogy's* publication), under the auspices of the North American Nietzsche Society, at the Pacific Division meetings of the American Philosophical Association, at which earlier versions of some of these essays were presented. Other essays subsequently were invited and selected, in an attempt to make the volume richly diverse in the perspectives and interpretations brought to bear upon Nietzsche's thinking. Some of them have been published elsewhere previously; but the majority of them were written specifically for this volume.

While Nietzsche's *Genealogy of Morals* is the general focus of this volume, the essays written and selected for inclusion here do not all focus directly upon it. Some do, while others bear upon it by way of a consideration of features of Nietzsche's thought more generally. Similarly, while Nietzsche's title suggests that his topic is the "genealogy" of "morals," he restricts himself neither to "genealogy" nor to "morals." The following essays all relate to aspects of what he undertakes to do in the *Genealogy*, but the aspects selected differ, and they are sometimes considered in relation to what he does along these lines elsewhere.

The contributors also differ markedly in their own philosophical orientations, and in their appreciation of what they find in Nietzsche. The volume thus exemplifies the point Nietzsche often makes in terms of "different eyes" and differing "prospectives," both to reject the notion that there is one and only one right way in which to view and interpret something, and to suggest how the understanding of something can best be enhanced. Many different approaches to his thinking are taken here with respect to the matters he discusses in the *Genealogy*, and many different interpretations and assessments are offered. One cannot possibly simply agree with all of them. But one can profit by availing oneself of all of them in order to transcend the confines of narrower perspectives upon what he is doing, and to expand the interpretive resources at one's disposal in one's own attempt to make sense of him and deal with him.

The essays in the first half of the volume deal in various ways with Nietzsche's thinking with respect to the announced topic of his *Genealogy:* "morals"—morality, moralities, and associated phenomena such as pity, cruelty, and *ressentiment.* These essays thus explore aspects of what could quite appropriately be called his moral philosophy and psychology. The first several of them deal with what he himself at times refers to as his "immoralism." Nietzsche's stance with respect to the sort of thing that goes by the general name of "morality" is perhaps second in notoriety only to what he has to say about God and Judeo-Christianity, and is even more disconcerting in the eyes of many moral philosophers associated with the traditional and contemporary mainstream of the discipline. Philippa Foot's essay is a case in point, and expresses deep reservations about Nietzsche's treatment of morality even as it attempts to acknowledge the challenge he poses. It therefore sets the stage very nicely for the rest of the volume, by prompting the question not only of whether Nietzsche does justice to morality but also of whether Foot does justice to him. The essay that follows by Maudemarie Clark pursues the "immoralism" issue, but with a rather different intent, and to different effect.

Arthur Danto's essay is one of several (David Hoy's and a previous essay of Frithjof Bergmann's are others) that appeared some years ago and helped to stimulate further consideration of what Nietzsche is up to in his *Genealogy.* Danto sees a kind of "moral terrorism" in Nietzsche, but discerns something more positive as well. Kathleen Higgins likewise suggests both that "poisons" are at work in Nietzsche's thinking here and that the upshot need not be as harmful as this might lead one to expect.

Richard White's essay goes further in the direction of seeking to discuss a fundamentally positive intent in Nietzsche's juxtaposition of "master" and "slave" moralities, with a view to what might lie beyond his critique. Frithjof Bergmann takes a different approach to the significance of the "master/slave" discussion, using it as a starting point for a consideration of what he suggests to be a basic and important difference between Nietzsche's approach to ethics and that of many philosophers (like Foot) in the analytic tradition.

Robert Solomon offers a much more critical interpretation of Nietzsche's use of the "master/slave" model and an assessment of the phenomenon of *ressentiment* very different from Nietzsche's. Like the next several authors, Solomon tempers his appreciation of Nietzsche's thinking, considering it to be deficient and in need of modification in important respects. Rüdiger Bittner also focuses upon Nietzsche's account of *ressentiment* and argues for the need to modify it to render it more plausible and satisfactory.

Martha Nussbaum directs her attention to Nietzsche's treatment of suffering and pity, and very helpfully places it in a long ethical tradition going back to the early Stoics. While making good and reasonable sense of it, however, she also expresses reservations about it even when properly understood. Ivan Soll in effect approaches the same problem from the other end, taking Nietzsche's unsettling discussion of cruelty as his point of departure. Spreading his compass to include Nietzsche's extension of this discussion to the phenomenon of asceticism, Soll seeks to show how all of this is related to Nietzsche's psychological concerns.

The next two essays follow Nietzsche into several of his most interesting case studies of the kind of moral psychology he seeks to develop (in addition to that of "slave morality") in the *Genealogy* and subsequently. Sarah Kofman examines asceticism as Nietzsche uses the case of Wagner to illuminate it, and offers a fascinating illustration of the power of Nietzsche's moral psychology to shed light on this complex and perplexing phenomenon. Yirmiyahu Yovel looks in a different direction, at anti-Semitism, attempting both to lay to rest the idea that Nietzsche himself exemplifies it and to show that he actually provides an analysis of it that is as illuminating as it is severe. In the final essay of the first part of the volume, using Nietzsche's treatment of the supposed phenomenon of willing as an example, Bernard Williams makes a case for "following a distinctively Nietzschean route towards the naturalization of moral psychology."

The essays in the second half of the volume deal with "genealogy" and its relation to philosophy, as Nietzsche conceives of them and engages in them in the *Genealogy* and related works. David Hoy's essay relates Nietzsche's "genealogical method" to its Humean cousin, and so contributes to the understanding of the extent to which it does (and does not) depart from the classical modern tradition. Alexander Nehamas examines the "genealogy" of the *Genealogy* in relation to Nietzsche's strategy in his early *On the Uses and Disadvantages of History for Life,* and then considers what it means to approach and construe morality "genealogically."

This is Alasdair MacIntyre's concern as well, in the next essay (the second of his 1988 Gifford Lectures). MacIntyre goes on to discuss Michel Foucault after providing an interpretation of Nietzschean genealogical analysis as a fundamentally "subversive" mode of thought—about which MacIntyre has deep reservations. Eric Blondel takes a somewhat similar approach, but in a very different idiom and spirit. He too regards genealogy as the key to Nietzsche's kind of philosophy, with which Blondel is considerably more comfortable. Daniel Conway is in basic agreement with Blondel, construing genealogy as a kind of "symptomatology"—with rather radical implications, which he undertakes to draw out and emphasize. Brian Leiter provides an alternative interpretation centering on a key passage in the *Genealogy* itself, leading to a fundamentally different view of Nietzsche's philosophical aspirations.

The next several essays similarly move in the direction of a broader consideration of Nietzsche's philosophical enterprise, as it relates to the *Genealogy* and as the *Genealogy* sheds light upon that enterprise. Gary Shapiro attempts to show that Nietzsche's central discussion of *Schuld* (guilt/debt) is connected in a deep and important way with his thinking about a problem that may be illuminated by a contrasting consideration of Heidegger on Anaximander and the origin of Western philosophy. Bernd Magnus, Jean-Pierre Mileur, and Stanley Stewart take Nietzsche's treatment of asceticism as their key to a reflection both upon the *Genealogy* itself and upon the kind of thinking toward which they see him moving in it. In my own essay I select yet another of the *Genealogy's* main themes—"the type *Mensch*"—as one of his chief interests here as in his other writings before and after, intimately related to his other concerns with respect to both method and content.

The final two essays have to do with points that may at first seem to be concerned more with form than substance, but which turn out to be well worth considering in thinking about the *Genealogy's* genealogy, and about Nietzsche's later writings more generally. Claus-Artur Scheier has noticed something that seems to connect the form of the *Genealogy* with its substance in a surprising and interesting way. The last word has been given to David Allison, because the stylistic device to which he draws attention (and which Nietzsche came to employ so effectively) is highly appropriate to the conclusion of this volume—which is most emphatically *not* intended to achieve closure. On such a work as the *Genealogy*, and on the topics considered in it, as on the thinking of Nietzsche more generally, there can be no real, definitive, and final last word.

During the past few decades Nietzsche has at last begun to receive the attention he deserves in the English-speaking world, owing in part to larger developments in both American and French philosophy. Several rather distinct styles of Nietzsche studies have emerged along the way, reflecting the differing philosophical sensibilities of those coming out of the modern "analytical" tradition and its earlier and more recent alternatives. It remains to be seen what will become of these differences. While they are not what they used to be, the divergences remain real and substantial, as do the differences of interpretation and appreciation among those whose basic philosophical orientations and styles are rather similar. Yet these divergences are no more to be lamented than are the differences. Both are only to be expected where Nietzsche's thought is concerned. Such divergences of perspective and approach, moreover, contribute more to understanding Nietzsche than any one way of dealing with him can. Indeed, it may well be that the opening up of philosophy itself to these different ways of proceeding is far healthier and more fruitful than the enthronement of any "one way." That certainly would be Nietzsche's view of the matter.

FRIEDRICH NIETZSCHE (1844–1900)

A BRIEF LIFE IN A PRELUDE AND FIVE DECADES

Prelude: Early childhood (1844–1849)
   Firstborn of a Lutheran minister and his wife, living in a small provincial town in what is now eastern Germany.

The precocious youth (1849–1858)
   Bright, serious boy of many talents (musical as well as scholastic), left fatherless at five, raised in an adoring all-female household.

The brilliant student (1858–1869)
   Classics student excelling in his studies, first at an elite boarding school and then at the universities at Bonn and Leipzig; aspiring composer and fine pianist; discovers Schopenhauer and meets Wagner.

The rebellious professor (1869–1879)
   Prodigy in classical philology, a professor at Basel at twenty-four; unconventional interests and writings antagonize his colleagues; an avid Wagnerian (still composing himself); cultural critic becoming a philosopher, while struggling with academic life and debilitating illnesses.

The nomad philosopher (1879–1888)
   Pensioned retiree at thirty-four; plagued with recurring severe health problems; alienated from academic life and nearly everything else; living alone in Swiss and Italian boardinghouses—and proceeding from "free-spirited" reflections to *Zarathustra,* and on toward a "philosophy of the future" and a "revaluation of all values."

The insane invalid (1889–1900)
   Mere shell following a complete physical and mental collapse (probably of syphilitic origin) in early 1889—at the age of only forty-four; a decade of empty madness before the final curtain.

CHRONOLOGY

1844   Friedrich Wilhelm Nietzsche is born on October 15 in Röcken, in the Prussian province of Saxony.

1849   Father dies (at the age of thirty-six).

1858–1864   Attends the classics-oriented boarding school Schulpforta. (Plays the piano and composes on the side.)

1864   Enters Bonn University to study classical languages and literatures.

1869   Associate professor of classical philology (before even completing his Ph.D.) at the Swiss university at Basel.

1870   Full professor at Basel. Enlists as a medical orderly in the Franco-Prussian War, contracting serious illnesses.

1872   First book *The Birth of Tragedy* appears (and is met with scholarly derision)—his only major classical studies publication.

1873–1874   Publishes the first three *Untimely Meditations,* including the essays *On the Uses and Disadvantages of History for Life* and *Schopenhauer as Educator.*

1876   Writes a fourth *Meditation* in homage to Wagner, but his enthusiasm for Wagner cools.

1878   The first volume of *Human, All Too Human* (638 aphorisms) appears. Wagner sends him *Parsifal,* and their estrangement deepens.

1879   Resigns (with pension) from his position at Basel, incapacitated by his health problems. Begins spending his summers in the Swiss Engadine region, and his winters in northern Italy, living in boardinghouses.

1879–1880   Writes two sequels to *Human, All Too Human,* subsequently published as the two parts of its second volume (another 758 aphorisms).

1881   Publishes *Daybreak* (575 more aphorisms). Alternative periods of depression and exhilaration. First summer in Sils Maria, where the idea of "eternal recurrence" comes to him.

1882   The year of his intense but short-lived relationship with
              Lou Salome, which ends badly. Publishes the initial four-
              part version of *The Gay Science* (342 aphorisms and reflec-
              tions).

1883   The first two parts of *Thus Spoke Zarathustra* are written and
              published. Wagner dies. Estrangement from family and
              friends; depression. Resolves against living in Germany.

1884   Completes and publishes the third part of *Zarathustra*.
              Breaks with his sister, unable to endure her anti-Semitic,
              pro-"Teutonic" fiancée Bernard Förster. (She marries him
              the next year, to Nietzsche's disgust and distress, accom-
              panying him to Paraguay where he sought to found a Teu-
              tonic colony.)

1885   The fourth part of *Zarathustra* is written, but is only pri-
              vately printed and circulated. Condition worsens.

1886   *Beyond Good and Evil* (296 aphorisms and reflections in
              nine parts, plus a poem "Aftersong") is published. New
              editions of most pre-*Zarathustra* works are prepared and
              supplied with prefaces.

1886–1887   An expanded second edition of *The Gay Science* is prepared
              and published, with a new preface and fifth part consisting
              of 41 additional reflections, and an appendix of poetry,
              "Songs of Prince Vogelfrei."

1887   *On the Genealogy of Morals* appears, consisting of a preface
              and three "essays" (of 17, 25 and 28 numbered sections,
              respectively). Completes orchestral score for *Hymnus an
              das Leben*. Begins working on *magnus opus*, to be called *The
              Will to Power*.

1888   *The Case of Wagner* is published; and *Twilight of the Idols, The
              Antichrist, Nietzsche contra Wagner, Dionysian Dithyrambs* (a
              collection of poems), and *Ecce Homo* are all written. *The
              Will to Power* project is dropped, in favor of a projected
              four-part *Revaluation of All Values*. Condition deteriorates.

1889   Collapses in early January in Turin, at the age of 44. (Nietz-
              sche never recovers, living his final eleven years in invalid
              insanity in the care of his mother and sister.) *Twilight of the
              Idols* is published in the same month.

1892 First public edition of the fourth part of *Zarathustra* appears.

1893 Sister returns from Paraguay, and—under the name Elizabeth Förster-Nietzsche—assists their mother in the management of her brother's affairs.

1895 *The Antichrist* and *Nietzsche contra Wagner* are published.

1897 Mother dies, leaving complete control of Nietzsche's care—and of his literary estate—to his sister, who exploits his growing fame and fosters the assimilation of his thought to right-extremist political purposes during the next four decades.

1900 Nietzsche dies, on August 25, in Weimar.

1901 Sister publishes an arrangement of selections from his notebooks of 1883–1888 under the title *The Will to Power,* and in his name.

1908 *Ecce Homo* is finally published (twenty years after it was written).

1910–1911 First edition of Nietzsche's collected works is published under the supervision of his sister—including a greatly expanded edition of *The Will to Power.*

1935 Sister dies, triumphant in the knowledge that her brother had come to be regarded by Hitler and Mussolini (and many others) as the philosopher of National Socialism and Fascism—a travesty that would plague Nietzsche's reception for the next half-century.

1967–1984 Publication of the *Kritische Gesamtausgabe* of Nietzsche's works, *Nachlass,* and letters.

NOTE ON TEXTS, TRANSLATIONS, AND REFERENCES

The now-standard German edition of Nietzsche's writings is the recently completed *Kritische Gesamtausgabe* edited by Giorgio Colli and Mazzino Montinari (Berlin: Walter de Gruyter, 1967–1984). *Zur Genealogie der Moral* is to be found in part VI, volume 2 of this edition, along with *Jenseits von Gut und Böse*. Now that a paperback "student edition" of this edition of Nietzsche's writings is readily available, other German editions are seldom used.

The standard English translation of this work is that by Walter Kaufmann and R. J. Hollingdale, *On the Genealogy of Morals,* published together with *Ecce Homo* (New York: Vintage, 1967). Except where contributors have preferred to use their own translations of the passages they cite, or were working from translations into other languages (for example, French), this is the translation generally used in citations in this volume. (Departures are indicated in the contributors' notes.)

Kaufmann and Hollingdale have translated most of Nietzsche's completed works—in some cases together, in others one of them, in others each of them. They also have jointly translated the collection of selections from Nietzsche's notebooks published in his name under the title *Der Wille zur Macht* (*The Will to Power*). For the most part these are the translations used by contributors in their citations; again, see their notes.

Some contributors identify their citations by providing references to the *Kritische Gesamtausgabe* (indicating volume, notebook, and entry numbers) as well as to the specific works. The primary identification of cited passages is usually provided in the standard manner: in the body of the essays themselves, using the customary acronyms derived from the most commonly used English-language versions of their titles (see Reference Key below), followed either directly by Nietzsche's arabic section numbers (where they run consecutively through the entire work) or first by roman numerals indicating main parts and then by the numbers of the section within these parts. (The letter "P" is used to signify "Preface" or other such preliminary portions of the works, which Nietzsche often provided.) In most cases these numberings are supplied by Nietzsche himself, and so are the same in all editions and languages; hence their standard use for this purpose (rather than page numbers, which vary from edition to edition, or volume and page numbers in the *Gesamtausgabe*, which few readers possess). In some cases a bit of stretching is involved, employing roman numerals in place of "First Essay," "Second Part," and so forth; but it usually will be obvious enough what is meant.

In a few cases, however, Nietzsche uses no numbers, and so they have had to be supplied. So, for example, arabic numbers have been assigned (following Kaufmann's numbering) to the speeches or sections in each of the parts of *Zarathustra* to facilitate references to it; and roman numerals have been assigned to the various parts of *Twilight of the Idols* and *Ecce Homo* (as well as the *Genealogy*), within which his arabic numberings begin anew. This expedient is amply warranted by its transparency and convenience, in terms of economy and also of movement between editions and translations. (Many readers find it helpful to write such numberings into their copies of these texts, making it all the easier to interpret and use such references.)

A fairly extensive bibliography of studies of Nietzsche available in English may be found at the back of this volume. See also the bibliographies in my *Nietzsche* (London: Routledge & Kegan Paul, 1983), Kaufmann's *Nietzsche*, 4th edition (Princeton: Princeton University Press, 1974), and Eric Blondel's *Nietzsche*, trans. Sean Hand (Stanford: Stanford University Press, 1992).

REFERENCE KEY
to Nietzsche's Writings
(See Bibliography for publication information)

A   = *The Antichrist* (alternately: *The Antichristian*)
BGE = *Beyond Good and Evil*
BT   = *The Birth of Tragedy*
CW = *The Case of Wagner*
D   = *Daybreak* (alternately: *Dawn*)
EH   = *Ecce Homo*
GM   = *On the Genealogy of Morals*
GS   = *The Gay Science* (alternately: *Joyful Wisdom*)
HH   = *Human, All Too Human* (two volumes, I and II)
NCW = *Nietzsche contra Wagner*
SE   = *Schopenhauer as Educator*
TI   = *Twilight of the Idols*
TL   = *On Truth and Lies in a Nonmoral Sense*
UDH = *On the Uses and Disadvantages of History for Life* (there are numerous alternate translations of this essay)
UM   = *Untimely Meditations* (alternately: *Unmodern Observations*)
WP   = *The Will to Power*
WS   = *The Wanderer and His Shadow* (incorporated into HH II)
Z   = *Thus Spoke Zarathustra*
KGW = *Kritische Gesamtausgabe: Werke*

PART ONE

Morality and Moral Psychology

ONE

Nietzsche's Immoralism

Philippa Foot

In writing about Nietzsche's immoralism I am going to ask a simple question about him, something that is difficult to do: it is hard to hold onto anything simple in the face of this determined joker, who loved masks and hidden things, and whose protean style is sometimes of the most lapidary aphoristic simplicity but often lush and rhetorical. It has been said that *Thus Spoke Zarathustra* should be read as an opera, and it is surely a great shame that we never had a rendition by Anna Russell of those wild journeys between mountain, marketplace, and cave.

Nietzsche thought he could discredit morality; and I want to ask, "Was he right?" I think the question should be asked. It is always respectful to ask of a great philosopher whether what he says is true, and hardly respectful not to ask it. Why do so many contemporary moral philosophers, particularly of the Anglo-American analytic school, ignore Nietzsche's attack on morality and just go on as if this extraordinary event in the history of thought had never occurred? It is true, of course, that it is hard for those of us who belong to the plain-speaking school of analytic philosophers to grapple with his work. We are used to ferreting out entailments, and lines of argument, and building up a theory from individual passages. And I do not think that one can work on Nietzsche quite like that. The unity of his writings—which is most remarkable in spite of their amazing richness and many superficial contradictions—comes from his attitudes, from his daring, his readiness to query everything, and from his special nose for vanity, for pretense, for timid evasion, and for that drive to domination which he finally supposed to be the principle of all life.

One must take account of Nietzsche's attitudes; of the contempt he felt for modern European man, for the "newspaper-reading" public (BGE 263),[1] for democracy, for nationalism, for Bismarck and all things German (save for Goethe, "the exception among Germans" [GS 103]). And account too, of course, of his vituperative attitude to Christianity, which he saw as the religion of pity and weakness but also, at times, as the beneficially tyrannical source of spiritualization in man (BGE 188). One has to remember that Nietzsche was one who wanted to be an *affirmer,* not a caviler, who repeatedly praised lightness of spirit, and wrote much about dancing and laughter. When he put forward his strange theory of the eternal recurrence of all things—round and round again—this was most significantly a rejection of gloomy nihilism and a way of saying "yes" even to his own physically painful, and painfully lonely, life.

All this, and much more, is needed to interpret Nietzsche. But what, then, can he have to offer to the descendants of Frege and Russell, of G. E. Moore and Wittgenstein? What can we ourselves take from the strange Nietzschean symphony of subjectively interrelated attitudes and beliefs? Even in those matters in which there is overlap between his interests and ours, can we assume that he is seriously concerned with the truth? Was it not Nietzsche who saw truth in terms of divergent "perspectives," and who insisted on questioning the value of truth itself? He said all this, and meant it. Nevertheless he saw as a great sign of those things he so much celebrated, "strength" and "life," the ability to face reality as it is. Honesty (*Redlichkeit*) was, he wrote, the one virtue that he and other "free spirits" must take from morality, that they could not leave behind:

> Let us work on it with all our malice and love and not weary of "perfecting" ourselves in our virtue, the only one left us. . . . And if our honesty should nevertheless grow weary one day and sigh and stretch its limbs and find us too hard let us dispatch to her assistance whatever we have in us of devilry. (BGE 227)

Nietzsche may have thought of even his own views as merely *his* truths (whatever exactly that means). But his love of truth was based on one of the strongest things in him, his contempt for evasive falsification. So in spite of all the discouraging omens, I want to ask what truth there could be in the doctrine that makes us name Nietzsche, as he sometimes named himself, "immoralist."

Nietzsche's immoralism! A host of problems and many interpretations live together under this roof. Was he perhaps preaching in favor of a new morality rather than against morality as such? I think not. Nor was Nietzsche simply a run-of-the-mill moral relativist. He branded as "childish" the idea that no morality can be binding because moral valuations are necessarily different among different nations (GS 345). So even his arguments for the subjectivity of moral judgment were idiosyncratic. He saw different moralities as determined by the desires and needs of peoples and generations: at one time the need to control aggressive individuals when they were no longer useful in meeting external enemies; in the long reign of Christianity the desire of the weak and "misbegotten" to brand themselves as "good" and those stronger characters, whom they feared, as "evil"; in modern Europe the longing of the mediocre "to look nobler, more important, more respectable, 'divine' " (GS 352).

Throughout all these changes morality was, Nietzsche insisted, fundamentally a subterfuge by which the weak—the members of the herd—tried to dress up their weakness and their fears as "goodness," a device by which they produced self-doubt and a bad conscience in those who, as nobles, had once unquestioningly called themselves good. The "nobles," the type of the original barbaric Greek and the Renaissance Man, had called "inferior" men bad (*schlecht*) only by contrast to themselves. The "inferiors" on the other hand needed to see dangerous men as "evil" (*böse*) so as to see themselves as good.

In suggesting that different moralities were rooted in the different needs, fears, and desires of different peoples Nietzsche was applying to valuations the characteristically Nietzschean "perspectivism": the interpretation by historical genealogy, and above all by underlying desires, that he applied to all modes of thought. He applied it particularly to abstract philosophies, which he saw as expressing instincts, needs, and fears rather than that will-o'-the-wisp, "pure thought." Thoughts, he said, "are the shadows of our feelings, always darker, emptier, and simpler" (GS 179). But there is, of course, something more specific than this in Nietzsche's insistence that "there are no moral facts" (TI VII:1).

> This problem of the *value* of pity and of the morality of pity . . . seems at first sight to be merely something detached, an isolated question mark; but whoever sticks with it and *learns* how to ask questions here will experience what I experienced—a tremendous new prospect opens up for him, a new possibility comes over him like a vertigo, fear leaps up, his belief in morality, in all morality, falters—finally a new demand becomes audible . . . we need a *critique* of moral values, *the value of these values themselves must . . . be called in question.* (GM P:6)

Nietzsche says that he is going to query the *value* of moral values, which suggests that he has some other value in play. And there is, indeed, a positive side to Nietzsche's ideology. He is affirming a special kind of aestheticism, and attacking morality partly on its own ground but partly in the interest of what he calls the "ascending" type of man. What was to be seen as "good" was the "strong," "fine," "noble," "subtle" type of human being. This free and joyous spirit, subjecting himself to the sternest discipline but accepting no rule from others, was sometimes seen by Nietzsche as the "overman," the superman of Nietzschean popular legend: that is as one who belonged to the future. But actual human beings might be seen as stepping stones or bridges on the way to this future. The important question to ask about any man was whether he represented an ascending or descending type. This was the profound classification, and determined the worth for the particular instance of those elements of character and action that moralists wrongly thought significant in themselves. So egoism, for instance, should not be thought of as either bad or good in all individuals.

> The value of egoism depends on the physiological value of him who possesses it: it can be very valuable, it can be worthless and contemptible. Every individual may be regarded as representing the ascending or descending line of life. When one has decided which, one has thereby established a canon for the value of his egoism. (TI IX:33)

Nietzsche thus, very characteristically, saw our common moral classifications as reflecting reality in a herd-based way that was deleterious to the exceptional man. What was worst about them, and was common to all morality, was the attempt to determine the value of any *kind* of conduct in the case of each and every person. "Good and evil the same for all," he scoffed. There could be no beneficial rules of conduct. "A virtue has to be *our* invention, *our* most personal defence and necessity: in any other sense is merely a danger" (A 11). And again, " 'Good' is no longer good when one's neighbor mouths it" (BGE 43). Thus Nietzsche thinks of value as belonging only to a person who has created his own character in a pattern that cannot be prescribed for others; and it is here that his shift from a moral to an aesthetic form of evaluation becomes clear. Not surprisingly, he is writing of what he himself, as a genius of style and image, knew best. Not for nothing does he say in one place, "We want to be the poets of our lives" (GS 299).

The discipline that he so much stresses for the creation of a splendid individual human being is modeled on the discipline of the artist. For an artist, rules would indeed be beside the point: the goodness of what he or she makes cannot be the same as the goodness of other artists' work, as if there could be a manual for producing what is good. This analogy seems to be an essential element in Nietzsche's aestheticism—in his shift from moral to aesthetic valuation. Theoretically, it is separate from his perspectivism, since, after all, the absence of rules for artistic creativity does not entail the subjectivity of aesthetic judgment. But when the individual himself is both artist and art-work they come together in the fact of his special "interpretation" of the world, the interpretation that determines what he sees as good.

There have been many attempts to see all this as an inspiring call to a kind of joyous paganism that would leave us with all that is best in morals. Can this be sustained? I think not, just because of Nietzsche's attack on the universalism in morality. He insists that there are no kinds of actions that are good or bad in themselves, and this has, it seems, a fatal implication for the teaching of justice. It is justice—understood as one of the four cardinal virtues and as having to do with all that one person owes another—that forbids such acts as murder, torture, and enslavement and brands them as evil, whoever carries them out. Nietzsche, on the other hand, says that there is nothing good or evil "the same for all," and he tells us we must look to see what kind of a person is doing an action before we can determine its "value."

If this implies, as it seems, that not even the most flagrant acts of injustice can be called evil in themselves, then was Thomas Mann not perhaps right in saying that Nietzsche had not faced the reality of evil? Mann said in 1947,

> How bound in time, how theoretical too, how inexperienced does Nietzsche's romanticizing about wickedness appear . . . today! We have learned to know it in all its miserableness.[2]

Mann was writing, of course, soon after the facts about Belsen and Buchenwald, and their images, had come to haunt us. So however much the Nazis had had to distort Nietzsche in order to claim him as one of their prophets, Nazi actions and Nietzsche's reputation may be linked in the way suggested by Mann; that is, in the way his treatment of evil has to look to us in the light of what they did.

It may be argued that this is unfair to Nietzsche. It may be pointed out that neither Hitler nor Stalin were individuals of whom it should be thought for a moment that they embodied his ideals. J. P. Stern is surely mistaken when he writes, "No man came closer to the full realization of self-created 'values' than . . . Hitler."[3] Nietzsche is, after all, vituperative about merely cruel monsters, and while, to be sure, he praises the (as he says) "pranksomely" ruthless "nobles" above the resentful "herd," Alexander Nehamas seems right to say that they do not need to be seen as his ideal for all times.

Nietzsche's defenders may, of course, also remind us of what he said about the need to discipline the passions, which is indeed a central element in his philosophy. For Nietzsche is not at all like Callicles, the immoralist in Plato's *Gorgias*, whose ideal is that of the libertine. Nietzsche preaches hardness and self-mastery. The passions are not to be weakened or extirpated, but used in the creation (once more one thinks "it's like the artist's creation") of the self. Moreover he puts forward a doctrine of the sublimation of the passions (he was one of the first actually to use the term *"sublimieren"*), believing for instance, that the "drive" of cruelty could be turned into a desire for truth. It will be said therefore that Nietzsche did not actually countenance acts of injustice in substituting for morality's canon against such things as murder and oppression his own prescription of self-creation. Did he perhaps believe that no one who truly embodied the Nietzschean ideal would ever find *himself* in such actions? Might the ideal of self-realization turn out in the end to be unshocking?

I am sure that something of all this is true, and that one side of Nietzsche would have welcomed such an accommodation. He speaks of gentleness, in some convincing passages; and he was himself, I would suppose, for all his insistence on the beneficial effect of suffering, actually oversensitive to it in others, really experiencing pity as he notoriously represented it—as "suffering's contagion." The character of the man himself shows too in his heroes and the books he loved. Cesare Borgia was not a hero of his, in spite of his preference "even," as he notoriously said, for him over a mean-spirited member of "the herd." True, he admired Napoleon, but said that he was "half superman, half monster."

Nietzsche's great hero was, it seems, Goethe, whom he praised especially for his molding of sensuality and spirit into a harmonious self. And among the literary works Nietzsche most loved there were not only the novels of Stendhal and Dostoevsky but also two quiet-mannered books, Eckerman's *Conversations with Goethe* and Emerson's *Essays*, a book he "felt at home in" and seems to have kept by him for much of his life. (One gets interesting light on Nietzsche from both of these works.)

Nevertheless there was a side of Nietzsche's deeply pathological psyche that seems to have gloried in the fact that his immoralism allowed, if done by certain people, even terrible deeds. Unlike other proponents of self-realization Nietzsche does not say that these acts could never be a sign of health and of truly "becoming what one is." On the contrary he stresses the fearfulness of his "revaluation of values." He insists that he has set out on a journey over terrifying seas, and, from the time in the early eighties when he first started to attack morality, to the end of his working life, one can find passages that stress the fearfulness of his thought, and seem to license injustice.

In *The Gay Science* of 1882 he writes,

> Hatred, the mischievous delight in the misfortunes of others, the lust to rob and dominate, and whatever else is called evil belongs to the most amazing economy of the preservation of the species. (GS 1)

And again in the same work:

> Some kinds of hatred, jealousy, stubbornness, mistrust, hardness, avarice, and violence . . . belong among the *favorable* conditions without which any great growth even of virtue is scarcely possible. The poison of which weaker natures perish strengthens the strong nor do they call it poison. (GS 19)

Four years later, in *Beyond Good and Evil*, he writes that

> everything evil, terrible, tyrannical in man, everything in him that is kin to

beasts of prey and serpents, serves the enhancement of the species "man" as much as its opposite does. (BGE 44)

And in a note from 1887 included in the *Nachlass* collection *The Will to Power:*

> *When one makes men more evil, one makes them better—* ... one cannot be one without being the other.—At this point the curtain rises on the dreadful *forgery of the psychology of man hitherto.* (WP 786)

Perhaps these passages are not absolutely decisive. Perhaps Nietzsche is talking about "drives" that might be "enhanced" and "strengthened" before being sublimated into harmless actions. But this does not seem at all plausible in the face of his insistence that his doctrine is a fearful one.

In any case I do not think it should be argued that the virtue of justice can be accommodated within Nietzsche's picture of splendid individuals finding each his own values and "his own way." For there is something in Nietzsche's description of this "higher type" of human being that positively tells against it. I mean the way in which the self-guiding person is described as seeing those whom he counts as "inferiors." One simply cannot ignore all that Nietzsche says, approvingly, of the experience, the feeling, the *"pathos"* as he likes to put it, "of distance," of being not just apart from, but higher than, those who belong to "the herd." Nietzsche says at one point that contempt is better than hatred, and of course he thinks the idea of equality utterly despicable.

Now what I wonder is this: whether the practice of justice may not absolutely require a certain recognition of equality between human beings, not a pretense of equality of talents but the equality that is spoken of in a passage of Gertrude Stein's when she says (pretending to be Alice B. Toklas) that she herself had a sense of equality, and that was why people would help her. "The important thing . . . is that you must have deep down as the deepest thing in you a sense of equality." This is particularly striking in Gertrude Stein, who was certainly not one to underestimate her own individuality, talent, or place in literary history. The sense of equality that she is thinking of must, surely, have to do with thinking that one is always, fundamentally, in the same boat as everybody else, and therefore that it is quite unsuitable for anyone to see himself as "grand."

Perhaps I am wrong in thinking of this sense of equality as necessary for the practice of justice. That the two are connected seems, however, to be supported in a certain passage I once came across in which G. K. Chesterton wrote about Charles Dickens. Dickens, Chesterton said,

> did not dislike this or that argument for oppression: he disliked oppression. He disliked a certain look on the face of a man when he looks down on another man. And the look on that face is the only thing in the world that we really have to fight between here and the fires of hell.[4]

Nietzsche's endless talk about inferiors and superiors, and the way he countenances some men looking down on others, together with his own readiness to sacrifice—to write off—the "mediocre," confirms the impression that justice gets short shrift in his scheme of things: that it is quite wrong to see his "aesthetic" as taking nothing we think precious from the morality he attacks. Nietzsche's defenders will rise up, of course, to insist that the "looking down" that he speaks of is nothing so crude as that of which G. K. Chesterton speaks. But the language of contempt is undeniably there. Nietzsche's defenders are like those who say of Wagner that he is better than he sounds.

To our objections on behalf of justice Nietzsche would, no doubt, reply that what should be in question is not whether we want to hold on to a moral mode of valuation, but whether we can do so with honesty. For his contention is that morality is tainted by certain pious falsehoods that are necessary to it: so that morality, in praising honesty, sowed the seeds of its own demise. Therefore we do have to ask ourselves not just what Nietzsche's own system of valuation amounts to but also if morality can withstand his attack.

What were these falsehoods—the "errors" that Nietzsche saw as endemic to morality?

First there is the belief in free will, which he challenged on the ground that will itself, as required for either free or unfree will, is nonexistent. What we call will is, he said, in truth nothing but a complex of sensations, as of power and resistance, and it is pure illusion to think of it as a basis for "moral responsibility." Our actions arise not primarily from conscious motivations but rather from physiological and psychological factors of which we are unaware.

It follows, Nietzsche thinks, that men are totally innocent, as innocent as anything else in the world, though this, he says, is something we hate to accept.

> Man's complete lack of responsibility for his behavior and for his nature, is the bitterest drop which the man of knowledge must swallow if he had been in the habit of seeing responsibility and duty as humanity's claim to nobility. All his judgments, distinctions, dislikes have thereby become worthless and wrong: the deepest feeling he had offered a victim or a hero was misdirected; he may no longer praise, no longer blame, for it is nonsensical to praise and blame nature and necessity. Just as he loves a good work of art, but does not praise it, because it can do nothing about itself, just as he regards a plant, so he must see the actions of men and his own actions. (HH I:107)

The topic of free will and moral responsibility is itself so large that one cannot quickly assess Nietzsche's idea that there is an error on which morality is based. But it may be pointed out that the theory of the will that he attacks would find few defenders today; and of course few would deny unconscious motivation. Nevertheless moral, as opposed to aesthetic, evaluation does require *some* distinction between actions for which we are responsible and those for which we are not responsible. For moral evaluation describes a person in terms of virtues such as courage and justice and charity, and we cannot, of course, ascribe virtues to anyone without knowing first of all which of the things that he did were intended and which unintentional, and secondly which of the unintentional actions were due to lack of care, or to ignorance of that which he could and should have known.

It is not, however, obvious that these distinctions rest on a doctrine of "moral responsibility" that Nietzsche is in a position to deny. He is surely wrong in thinking that we might have to give up thinking in a *special* way about the goodness of men, that we should have to relinquish the concept of a virtue as it applies to human beings and not to plants or to the objects of aesthetic evaluation. The idea of a virtue might even be the correct starting point for a solution to the problem of moral responsibility. For the way in which moral responsibility exists can perhaps be traced precisely by asking how it enters into the concept of a virtue, as shown by the irrelevance to virtue of things done accidentally or in (many cases of) ignorance. And as for unconscious motivation: we might say that this is relevant to moral evaluation (as when we count a person's deep hidden malice against a claim to the virtue of charity) without any implication that the subject is "responsible" for being as he is. So far from destroying morality, Nietzsche's challenge to the possibility of distinctively moral evaluation may actually help us to see what it does and does not require.

Second among the "errors" Nietzsche claims to have found in morality there is the classification of types of actions under the descriptions "good" and "bad." For Nietzsche's objection to this we must go back once more to his scorn for the universality in moral judgment, his scorn for its branding of certain *kinds* of action as good or bad "for all." This was not the commonplace insistence on the relevance of circumstances to moral good and evil. It was not that objection to absolutism which Nietzsche had in mind; he meant rather that moral generalization was impossible because the proper subject of valuation was, instead, a person's individual act. We were to ask not what is done, but rather whom it is done by. He even said that no two actions can be the same, meaning, again, that each individual action takes its character from the character of the one who does it.

His chief defense for this comes, I think, from the skeptical eye that he casts over the motives of the actions that moralists call good. Thus he points out the vanity that is behind many acts of "kindness": the wish to create a good opinion in others by a kindly deed, so as to be able to buy this good opinion back from them. (As T. S. Eliot said, "the endless struggle" to think well of ourselves.) The wish to be a benefactor was, he said, impertinent in

its claims to understanding the one to whom "good" was done, and jealous
in the desire to possess him. Where moralists find altruism Nietzsche sees
various kinds of egoism, self-mistrust, and fear: above all the desire to "live
abroad" with others rather than at home with oneself. Under the heading
"The elevating aspect of our neighbor's misfortune," he says that we gather
to bemoan the ill that has befallen him and "spend an enjoyable afternoon." Nietzsche was a genius at finding hidden motivations, and it is not
surprising that Freud found him so much of a kindred spirit that he deliberately avoided reading Nietzsche until his own work was well advanced.

It is surprising, however, that Nietzsche thought the discovery of the
possibility of dubious motivation behind, for example, acts of "kindness"
to be a count against the moral mode of valuation itself. For it is traditional
in moral philosophy that actions are to be judged not only for the type of
actions that they are but also as individual acts done by a particular agent
at a particular time. Aquinas, for instance, pointed out that a concrete act
could be spoiled, morally speaking, either by what it was "in its kind," as
for example murder or robbery, or by the motive from which it was done,
using for this latter possibility the example of giving alms "for the praise
of men." If Nietzsche extends the range of experience in which the standard of honesty about motives applies, moralists should not take this amiss.

So far, then, Nietzsche seems to be on strong ground in his psychology,
even if mistaken about the import of his psychological observations. It is
not, however, always so, and the next of the "errors" he claims to find in
morality sees him far out in a very doubtful field of psychological speculation. For he believed that he could discern the "drives" (*Triebe*) that
motivate all human action, and could map their dependence on one another. He thought he knew, for instance, that "drives," such as cruelty, that
were branded by moralists as "evil," were the condition of all "good."

Thus, in *Beyond Good and Evil* he speaks of "the reciprocal dependence
of the 'good' and the 'wicked' drives" and the derivation of good impulses
from wicked ones; continuing, in a famous passage, that we

> should regard even the affects of hatred, envy, covetousness, and the lust to
> rule as conditions of life, as factors which, fundamentally and essentially, must
> be present in the general economy of life (and must therefore be further
> enhanced if life is to be further enhanced). (BGE 23)

This was a favorite thought of Nietzsche's: one that he several times
illustrated with the image of a tree which to flourish had to have its roots
in the mud (GS 171). He saw that his views about "evil" drives were inimical
to morality, because morality has to set its face against certain desires; and
he must surely be right about that. But whether there is the least warrant
for the kind of psychological speculations that would support this part of

Nietzsche's immoralism is quite another matter. In the theory of "drives" that finally crystallized into the theory that all "drives" are contained in the Will to Power, Nietzsche seems to have fallen into the trap of working a modicum of psychological observation into an all-embracing theory which threatens to become cut off from facts that could possibly refute it. Nietzsche saw himself as a wonderful psychologist, but the truth is that he was partly a wonderful psychologist and partly a mere speculating philosopher far exceeding any plausible basis for his speculations.

Is no part of Nietzsche's attack on morality, then, convincing? Probably not. It would be wrong, however, to conclude that we analytic philosophers should leave him alone. On the contrary, I think that he should shake us up. For his deepest conviction was that the fact that "God is dead" (so that nothing is guaranteed to us) could not leave our faith in morality unchanged (GS 343). He was particularly scornful of "philosophers"—he singled out George Eliot—who were "fanatics" for morality in spite of their atheism. Nietzsche believed, in effect, that as the facts of human psychology really were, there could be no such things as human virtues, dispositions good in any man; and even if he did not prove it, might he not alert us to the fact that that could be how it is? For if "God is dead" what guarantees that there is a human aptitude for the virtue of justice, given that this requires quite generally that men and women can do certain things—as, for example, pass up great advantage in refraining from murder or theft and moreover do this *in a certain way:* that is without ulterior motive, false elevation, or bitterness? Wittgenstein has taught us to see the existence of some things we take for granted as being a remarkable fact. Should we, perhaps, see the capacity to acquire justice in this light, as depending on certain general human reactions to teaching, somewhat as it is with the capacity to learn to talk or to make calculations?

On grounds such as this, one can well believe that analytic philosophers must lose something if they do not study a philosopher as surpassingly bold and original as Nietzsche, if only because of his capacity to stretch our philosophical imagination. And of course if I am right there is also work to be done in criticizing his theories from the point of view of philosophical argument and truth. This is what I have been just beginning to do here. In a way it is bound to be a somewhat comical proceeding, because it has to be carried out at a schematic level that leaves behind all the riches of Nietzsche's psychological insights and images. So one feels rather like a surveyor reducing a glorious countryside to contours, or like someone telling the Sirens they are singing out of tune. But that is not to say that this rather dry philosophical work can be left undone, especially if, as I think, Nietzschean teaching is inimical to justice. His teaching has been sadly seductive in the past. Who can promise that it will never be seductive again?

NOTES

1. All references to Nietzsche's writings are indicated by the conventional acronyms of their titles in English, together with the relevant part and/or section numbers. (ED.)

2. Thomas Mann, *Nietzsche's Philosophy in the Light of Contemporary Events* (Washington: Library of Congress, 1947).

3. J. P. Stern, *Friedrich Nietzsche* (New York: Penguin, 1979), p. 86.

4. Introduction to the Everyman edition of *Oliver Twist* (London: J. M. Dent, 1907).

TWO

Nietzsche's Immoralism and the Concept of Morality

Maudemarie Clark

Although Nietzsche quite explicitly claims to be an immoralist (for example, EH IV:2–4; BT P:5),[1] many serious and sympathetic interpreters have denied that he is. This is understandable because immoralism is a difficult position to take seriously. An immoralist does not simply ignore morality, or deny its right to our compliance, but claims that morality is a bad thing that should be rejected. Immoralism therefore seems to be defensible only from the viewpoint of a morality, which makes it appear to be as self-refuting as another notorious Nietzschean claim, that truths are illusions. I have argued in my recent book that Nietzsche actually overcame this paradoxical claim about truth in his later works, starting with his *Genealogy of Morals*.[2] But this approach will not work for his immoralism, which is clearly expressed in the *Genealogy* and in later works, and in fact is more clearly expressed in later works than in earlier ones. Nietzsche moved toward, not away from, immoralism over the course of his work. Sympathetic interpreters have therefore usually tried another tack, suggesting that Nietzsche is an immoralist only in a very qualified sense: namely, that he rejects a particular kind of morality (say, Christian morality) or a particular theory or conception of morality, but not morality itself.[3]

There is now evidence of a change of direction on this issue within Anglo-American Nietzsche scholarship. At least three important Nietzsche scholars, Philippa Foot, Alexander Nehamas, and Frithjof Bergmann, have argued that the qualified interpretation trivializes Nietzsche's position on morality. Consider, for instance, his prediction in the preface to the *Genealogy* that one who begins as he did by raising questions about the morality of compassion, but also stays with the issue and learns to ask questions, will experience what he experienced: "A tremendous new prospect opens up . . . belief in morality, in all morality, falters—finally a new demand becomes audible . . . we need a *critique* of moral values, *the value of these values must itself for once be called into question*" (GM P:6). Nietzsche here makes clear that he distinguishes "all morality" from specific moralities—in this case from one he had earlier, under Schopenhauer's influence, identified with morality itself.[4]

The qualified interpretation of his immoralism therefore seems to trivialize what Nietzsche himself wants to say. Those who interpret him instead as a full-fledged immoralist agree that his position is perplexing and confusing. But they also suspect that there is a major issue here that will never get confronted unless we try to understand why Nietzsche thought that morality itself, rather than a specific morality, was the object of his attack. Although Foot certainly does not expect to agree with Nietzsche, she emphasizes that we are bound to receive some enlightenment about morality if we try to confront such a brilliant critic's rejection of it.[5] To do this, we need to try to understand how Nietzsche could find it plausible that he rejected all morality.

That is what I shall begin doing in this essay. I will be concerned not with Nietzsche's arguments against morality but only with his perplexing claim to be against morality itself. I want to make clear, however, that I do not take this as a claim to reject all morality (or morality itself) given every possible understanding of "morality." If, for instance, one counts any set of rules or prohibitions as a "morality," Nietzsche is certainly not claiming to reject all morality. Nor does he do so if one counts as "a morality" any system for evaluating the goodness of persons. Nietzsche himself sometimes uses the word "morality" in such a way that he is not rejecting all morality and thus cannot count himself as an immoralist, for instance, when he praises "noble morality" or insists that "higher moralities" should be possible.

When Nietzsche calls himself an "immoralist," on the other hand, he uses the word in such a way that he does reject all morality. Given this use of the word, I shall argue later, he counts the noble mode of valuation as a nonmoral mode of evaluating persons rather than as a morality. This latter usage—the usage in accord with which he is an immoralist or rejects all morality—is, by far, his most common, especially in the works he published. This is to be explained, I suggest, by Nietzsche's belief that this sense of morality (the sense given that he counts himself an "immoralist") corresponds pretty much to how we primarily use the term "morality" (or, if you prefer, what it would introduce the greatest amount of clarity in what we do say for us to consistently call "morality").[6]

My explanation is supported by BGE 32, in which Nietzsche includes himself among "immoralists" after distinguishing premoral, moral, and extramoral periods of human history. He refers to the second of these as a period that may be called "moral" in the narrower or strict (*engeren*) sense, then asks if we don't stand on the threshold of the third period, "of a period that should be designated negatively, to begin with, as extramoral (*aussermoralische*)." When he then refers to the "overcoming of morality," this clearly means the overcoming of morality in the narrower sense. But why does he call himself an immoralist (at least "to begin with"—that characterization of himself clearly stands or falls with the characterization of the period he wants to inaugurate as "extramoral") if he is only rejecting morality in this narrower sense? Because, as he makes clear in this passage, precisely this is morality in the traditional sense, or, more literally, in the sense "morality" has had until now ("*Moral, im bisherigen Sinne*").

So when Nietzsche occasionally writes of "higher moralities," I take him, in accord with BGE 32, to be using "morality" in a nontraditional and wider sense, which makes it equivalent to "codes for evaluating human beings and their conduct." I take the fact that he uses the term in this wider sense relatively infrequently to reflect his understanding of his immoralism as a rejection of precisely what we have traditionally embraced under the term "morality." My question is how Nietzsche made it comprehensible and plausible to himself that he was rejecting precisely what we have embraced as "morality."

To have a chance of finding a reasonable answer, we must begin by assuming that for Nietzsche what we call "morality" does not exhaust the realm of value. If moral values are to be called into question and found wanting, it must be from the viewpoint of some other species of value. To understand how Nietzsche could have considered himself an immoralist, we then need to know at least what he thinks moral values are, and why he did not take his own values to be moral values. I believe this approach is already implicit in the work of the three philosophers I have mentioned who interpret Nietzsche as an immoralist. However, I do not believe they have given adequate accounts of how Nietzsche understands moral values, or why he does not regard his values as moral values. I will therefore begin with a quick sketch of their views and of the factors that supply *prima facie* reasons to look for an alternative account within the general framework on which they agree.

Foot begins the serious attempt to treat Nietzsche as an immoralist by insisting that valuing a kind of person (or certain traits of character) does not commit one to specifically moral values.[7] Yes, Nietzsche praised and valued strong, independent, courageous people, but Foot thinks his values may be more aesthetic or quasi-aesthetic than moral. For she claims that morality is necessarily connected to the mores or rules of behavior of a society, and that Nietzsche denies that there are any social norms that should be taught to all. True, she says, Nietzsche refuses to praise anyone who is not strong and courageous. However, she thinks that what Nietzsche praises would give rise to an injunction no more specific than "seek your own health," which does nothing to reestablish social norms, and which in any case he would only preach to the exceptional ones truly capable of strength and health.

Foot argues that taking Nietzsche to be an immoralist rather than a special kind of moralist is further supported by the fact that "he was prepared to throw out rules of justice in the interests of producing a stronger and more splendid type of man," whereas morality is "necessarily connected to such things as justice and the common good, and it is a conceptual matter that this is so."[8] But she provides no evidence for this claim, and Nietzsche reserves his highest words of praise in the *Genealogy* for justice and the just person (GM II:11). We therefore have good reason to look for an alternative to at least part of Foot's account.

Nehamas does not mention the justice issue, but seems to accept and be working out the implications of the rest of Foot's account of why Nietzsche is an immoralist. Nietzsche's problem with morality, according to Nehamas, is that it is universalistic or unconditional—that it consists of "codes that are imposed not only on those for whom they are suited but on everyone else as well."[9] It would seem to follow that an immoralist need not reject all codes of conduct, but only all universal codes. There is, however, a problem with understanding morality in these terms. After all, a moralist need not think (and perhaps few have) that everyone has the same obligations or duties. Plato surely thought that the duties of the philosopher-king differed from those of the common person, yet Nietzsche seems right in regarding Plato as a moralist. Therefore, recommending different codes of conduct to persons in different positions or situations would not be sufficient to save Nietzsche from counting as a moralist. Recommending different codes to persons in the same position and situation would be sufficient, but would also render Nietzsche's position unworthy of serious consideration.

Nehamas avoids the resulting problem by insisting that Nietzsche does not teach a code of conduct to anyone. His assumption seems to be that Nietzsche could not recommend a code of conduct without imposing his values on others, thus being a moralist. This, I believe, is why Nehamas is attracted to the view that Nietzsche's books present us with a literary character, the character "Nietzsche," created by the writer Nietzsche. His writings can then function to *show* (some of) us that this character is praiseworthy without *asserting* that he is. Nietzsche can thus have his value stance without being a moralist—that is, without imposing his values on others. One problem with Nehamas's account is lack of evidence that Nietzsche was so worried about imposing his values on others. Further, how could this be so important to him, unless he accepted the moral premise that thou shalt not impose thy values on others? I therefore suspect that

Nietzsche's rejection of morality on the grounds Nehamas suggests would be deeply incoherent.

Bergmann, however, denies what Foot and Nehamas take for granted: that a code of conduct that is supposed to apply to all members of a society must be a moral code or morality.[10] People usually see no hope for Nietzsche's immoralism, according to Bergmann, because they think we need morality to restrain the powerful, and establish justice and control. But perhaps it is a mistake, he suggests, to suppose that all other cultures have a morality. For the Balinese, according to Bergmann, even the most appalling and serious transgression provokes a reaction and judgment that is radically different in quality from what we are accustomed to. Even outrageous violations are interpreted as what we might call "stupidities." The point is not that the judgment made of these violations is milder than moral judgment, but that the underlying conceptions presupposed by these judgments are quite different. Whereas moral judgments presuppose the idea of freedom and a correlative notion of responsibility, according to Bergmann, these are not presupposed by the judgment of a violation as a stupidity. Whereas morality presupposes the idea of a self that is independent and marked off against nature, the other cultures he has in mind take human beings to be integral parts of nature through whom the flow of causally linked events runs.

Now if a code of conduct does not count as a morality unless it presupposes freedom in the radical sense Bergmann has in mind, we can understand why Nietzsche claimed to reject morality, for he clearly rejects the idea that human beings are free in a sense that sets us over against nature. The problem is that Bergmann offers us no reason to think morality *does* presuppose freedom in this sense. Further, there clearly were important philosophers of whom Nietzsche was aware—Hobbes and Hume, for instance—who claim to accept morality but reject radical freedom. So while I am in sympathy with much of Bergmann's account, I do not think he succeeds in explaining how Nietzsche could have convinced himself that he was an immoralist.

The new approach I want to propose for making Nietzsche's claim comprehensible is to look at his own analysis of the concept of morality. Although this may seem fairly obvious, it has actually not been tried by other interpreters. The three I have discussed rely on their own understanding of the concept of morality to make sense of Nietzsche's immoralism. Foot thinks that justice is essential to morality, so she assumes with very little help from Nietzsche's books that he claims to be an immoralist because he rejects justice. Nehamas and Bergmann do the same thing for universalizing one's values and freedom.

This procedure is perfectly understandable, and even necessary, if Nietzsche does not supply his own analysis of the concept of morality. But I believe that he does. This is not obvious to be sure, but I will argue that his *Genealogy of Morals* (or more literally, *Genealogy of Morality*) supplies a very original analysis of the concept of morality as an essential part of a theory of the origin of morality. It may turn out, of course, that this analysis is quite wrongheaded, and that given an adequate understanding of morality, we should count Nietzsche as a moralist. But I do not see how we can seriously confront his thinking about morality unless we try first to understand his immoralism in terms of what he himself has to say about the concept of morality.

My interpretation of the *Genealogy* as a unified theory will seem rather idiosyncratic these days. After all, the book consists of three separate essays, each one evidently devoted to a different moral phenomenon. Kaufmann summarizes the three essays as follows: "The first essay, which contrasts 'Good and Evil' with 'Good and Bad,' juxtaposes master and slave morality; the second essay considers 'guilt,' 'bad conscience,' and related matters; and the third, ascetic ideals."[11] The problem for my interpretation is that Nietzsche makes no explicit attempt to connect up these different essays. Within each essay, the situation is similar: each turns out to consist of several different stories or pieces of stories, and Nietzsche does not seem concerned to patch them together into a unified account.

This has helped encourage the now common view (expressed, for instance, in Alasdair MacIntyre's recent book[12]) that genealogy is a new kind of moral inquiry, an exercise in perspectivism, one that is supposed to let in all sorts of different views without privileging one over others. We are supposed to learn from the *Genealogy* that there are only different stories, some better than others for certain purposes, to be sure, but none containing more truth than others. In an atmosphere pervaded by such ideas, viewing the *Genealogy* as a unified account of the origin of morality will seem bad enough. That I also see it as an extended analysis of the concept of morality will make me seem blind to what Nietzsche is up to, and perhaps deserving of Arthur Danto's recent barb that "to treat the *Genealogy* as though it were precocious analytical philosophy is to have swallowed the bait without having yet felt the hook."[13] I will nevertheless try to convince you that my approach to the *Genealogy* has some merit. I shall begin by discussing the view of conceptual analysis Nietzsche articulates at the very center of the book (in the middle section of the middle essay) in connection with an analysis of the concept of punishment. He begins his analysis of punishment by distinguishing between

> on the one hand, that in it which is relatively *enduring*, the custom, the act, the "drama," a strict sequence of procedures; on the other, that in it which is *fluid*, the meaning, the purpose, the expectation associated with the performance of such procedures. (GM II:13)

Nietzsche adds that "the procedure itself will be something older, earlier than its employment in punishment, that the latter is *projected* and inter-preted *into* the procedure (which has long existed but been employed in a different sense)" (GM II:13). This is an application of the major point of historical method he has been developing in the essay: namely, that "the cause of the origin of a thing and its eventual utility, its actual employment and place in a system of purposes, lie worlds apart" (GM II:12).

I suggest that what Nietzsche calls the "stable element" in punishment is the act of inflicting a harm or loss on a person based on a judgment that the person deserves this loss owing to something he or she has done.[14] Nietzsche's analysis of the debtor-creditor relation earlier in this essay makes apparent his belief that people inflicted harm based on judgments of desert before such judgments became part of punishing. He suggests, in effect, that the stable element in punishment originated in the agree-ment made by debtors that if unable to pay off debts, they would provide a substitute repayment in the form of some harm or physical suffering the creditor would be allowed to inflict on them (GM II:5).

It seems right to deny that such infliction of suffering (for example, the taking of a pound of flesh from the person who cannot repay a debt) constitutes a case of punishment, even though it occurs as a result of a judgment that the debtor owes this suffering (or the opportunity to inflict it) to the creditor. The purpose of inflicting suffering in this case seems to be not to punish the debtor but rather to extract a substitute repayment. The distinction made in civil cases between compensatory and punitive damages also suggests that judgments of desert are not sufficient to make inflicting a loss a case of punishment.

But then what is sufficient? What distinguishes the punitive from the nonpunitive infliction of such harm? Nietzsche answers as follows:

As for the other element in punishment, the fluid element, its "meaning," in a very late condition of culture (for instance, modern Europe) the concept "punishment" possesses in fact not *one* meaning but a whole synthesis of "meanings": the previous history of punishment in general, the history of its employment for the most diverse purposes, finally crystallizes into a kind of unity that is hard to disentangle, hard to analyze and, as must be emphasized especially, totally indefinable. (Today it is impossible to say for certain *why* people are really punished: all concepts in which an entire process is semiot-ically concentrated elude definition; only that which has no history is defin-able.) At an earlier stage, on the contrary, this synthesis of "meanings" can still be disentangled, as well as changed; one can perceive how in each case the elements of the synthesis undergo a shift in value and rearrange them-selves accordingly, so that now this, now that element comes to the fore and dominates at the expense of others; and under certain circumstances one element (the purpose of deterrence perhaps) appears to overcome all the remaining elements. (GM II:13)

In thus denying that "punishment" can be defined, Nietzsche denies that there is an essence of punishing, in the sense of a set of necessary and sufficient conditions that distinguishes the punitive from the nonpunitive infliction of harm. We can say that such harm must be inflicted for a punitive purpose to count as punishment; but Nietzsche's point is that there is no single purpose that constitutes the purpose of punishing—that our idea of punishing is an unstable synthesis of various purposes that have been served by inflicting harm based on judgments of desert. A Nietzschean history of punishment would try to show how different purposes came to be associated with inflicting such harm, and how these purposes replaced or combined with each other to explain the meaning or justification of doing so.

Analyzing the concept of punishment, however, would involve disentangling various of these purposes and exposing how they have been run together or conflated. Nietzsche suggests that concepts influenced by history are like ropes held together by the intertwining of strands, rather than by a single strand running through the whole thing. To analyze such concepts is not to find necessary and sufficient conditions for their use but to disentangle the various strands that may have become so tightly woven together by the process of historical development that they seem inseparable. Such analysis would take place most effectively in conjunction with historical theorizing, because it is the historical synthesis of strands that hides their separability from view, and it is thus by going back and forth between historical and conceptual considerations that one can hope to make progress in either the history or the conceptual analysis. Historical theorizing and conceptual analysis would thus be two sides of a complex theory as to the origin and development of punishment.

Now Nietzsche must believe that this connection between history and concepts also exists in the case of morality. After all, he articulates it in the very middle of a book titled literally *On the Genealogy of Morality*. Kaufmann's translation of the singular "*Moral*" as "morals," while not wrong, has tended to encourage those who deny that the book offers any kind of unified theory. But given the discussion of concepts at the physical center of the book, we should expect Nietzsche's view to be that a unified theory of the origins of morality would uncover the origin and trace the development of different and originally independent strands of morality that history has woven together. This, I believe, is exactly what the *Genealogy* attempts. I suggest that the sometimes disjointed or fragmentary character of the *Genealogy* has nothing to do with telling different stories or allowing in various perspectives, but is due instead to a self-conscious attempt to analyze a concept with a complex history—to disentangle originally independent elements that we can no longer see as such.

Genealogy is nothing mysterious or newfangled. Nietzsche's history of morality is a genealogy because it is the history of couplings. Something that already exists combines with something else that has its own history to give birth to a third thing, which then combines with something else that is also the product of such couplings. Genealogy is simply a natural history. If there is something new in Nietzsche's use of genealogy, it is the suggestion that concepts are formed in the same way as other living things—and, in particular, that this is true of the concept of morality. I will now try to indicate something of the implication of this view for an analysis of the concept of morality.

Consider the First Essay, titled " 'Good and Evil,' 'Good and Bad.' " Following Kaufmann, this essay is usually assumed to be a comparison of master and slave morality, an attempt to distinguish "moralities that originated in the ruling class from moralities that originated among the oppressed."[15] I consider this misleading for two reasons. First, even in the case of good and evil, Nietzsche is not looking at a whole morality in this essay. Standards of right and wrong, for instance, receive no attention. The essay compares not two moralities, but two different ways of determining who is good and who isn't. Further, as I shall argue, Nietzsche's "good/bad" is not a moral distinction.

Nietzsche begins by arguing on philological grounds that "good" originally meant the same as "noble," or "of the ruling class," whereas "bad" meant "common" (GM I:4). But then how could "good" express a value judgment? Nietzsche answers that the nobles' self-affirmation showed through in the words they used to refer to themselves. Happy with their own existence (after all, they had power, wealth, and so forth), they naturally experienced their own lives as preferable or superior to the lives of those they ruled. Nietzsche explains the origin of regarding particular characteristics as "good"—the origin of judgments of virtue—along the same lines, claiming that the nobles called "good" the characteristics they perceived as belonging to themselves and distinguishing them from the commoners. Their self-affirmation or happiness was such that they took any characteristic they saw as peculiar to themselves to be part of their goodness, that is, an aspect of their superiority to the common human being.

At first, they perceived the distinction in crude physical terms, like wealth and power. As time went on, their view of the distinction between themselves and commoners came to center more on traits of soul or character, such as loyalty, truthfulness, and courage. They began to designate themselves as "the truthful," as "distinct from the *lying* common man" (GM I:5). In this process, Nietzsche claims, "good" finally lost all connection to political class, and became identical with superiority of soul. However, it is unclear whether this is supposed to have happened sometime in the past, or is being held out as a possible future development of the good/bad distinction.

In either case, it seems to me that good/bad here is not a moral distinction. Although he does not draw this conclusion, Danto provides the basis for it when he writes:

> From the masters' perspective, those unlike themselves are merely bad humans; that is to say, humans that do not come up to the mark. This is similar to the way bad eggs are low in the scale of egghood. There is nothing *morally* bad in being a bad egg, or, in this usage, a bad human. It is just the way one is. Too bad, then, for the bad. They hardly can be blamed for being what they are; but they are bad.[16]

In other words, calling commoners "bad" is certainly making a value judgment about them, but it is not judging them to be "morally bad" or "immoral." But then it should follow that the nobles are not proclaiming their own moral virtue when they call themselves "good," and that good/ bad does not express a distinction of moral value, a distinction made from the viewpoint of morality. This is most obvious in the earliest stage of the noble mode of valuation. When noble birth, power, and wealth are the criteria for being "good," it is easy to see that goodness is not equivalent to moral virtue. In whatever way the moral point of view is characterized, it is not the viewpoint from which the nobles declare power and wealth to be marks of the good human being.

It may seem less obvious that moral distinctions are not involved when traits such as truthfulness become marks of "the good," and especially when goodness is constituted solely by traits of soul unrelated to political or social position. According to Nietzsche's story, however, there is no change in the point of view from which goodness is judged when it expands to include character traits. It is still merely the natural viewpoint of a group of individuals well pleased with themselves when comparing themselves to a group they would not be happy to be part of. Goodness is still constituted by what members of the self-affirming group perceive as marking themselves off from those they would not want to be.

Further, Nietzsche claims that the German equivalent of the word "bad" had no inculpatory connotations until the time of the Thirty Years' War (GM I:4). We should therefore take him to be using "bad" in such a way that being bad is not something one is to be blamed for, whether it is a matter of being poor and politically weak, or of lying and cowardice. From within the good/bad mode of valuation, the attitude toward the liar is not one of moral disapproval. Instead, Nietzsche claims that the noble feels "contempt for the cowardly, the anxious, the petty, those intent on narrow utility," and "above all, the liars: it is part of the faith of all aristocrats that the common people lie. 'We truthful ones'—thus the nobility of ancient Greece referred to itself" (BGE 260).

Schopenhauer had already distinguished this attitude toward liars from moral disapproval. "According to the principle of knightly honor, the reproach of being a liar is regarded as extremely grave," Schopenhauer wrote, "not because the lie is *wrong*," but because it is taken as evidence of fear and lack of strength.[17] Nietzsche's noble and Schopenhauer's knight "look down on" or feel superior to the liar because lying demonstrates lack of power, and thus the absence of something the nobility spontaneously affirms in its own life. Since this explains why liars are considered "bad" without recourse to moral concepts, we can deny that the distinction Nietzsche calls "good/bad" constitutes a moral distinction, even when made within the realm of character.

Good versus evil, however, is clearly supposed to be a moral distinction. Like good versus bad, it distinguishes superior from inferior people. Unlike bad, evil is equivalent to immoral or morally bad. The main difference seems to be that the evil are blamed or thought deserving of punishment for being the kind of people they are, whereas the bad are not blamed for being bad, any more than the nobles consider themselves deserving of reward for being good. Only when contrasted with "evil" does goodness become something for which it makes sense to think one deserves a reward. By that point, goodness has become equivalent to moral goodness.

According to Nietzsche's theory, this way of judging goodness originated in resentment directed against the nobles and their easy sense of superiority. The resentful call the nobles "evil" and themselves "good." Rather than reflecting the goods' natural sense of their own superiority, these judgments constitute an act of "imaginary revenge" against the nobles (GM I:10). I think this means they involve a sublimated or spiritualized equivalent of burning someone in effigy. As burning in effigy acts out or plays at depriving someone of his life, and in so doing helps satisfy pent-up resentment, calling someone "evil" can satisfy the same kind of feelings by playing at depriving others of their self-proclaimed goodness or superiority.

Calling another "bad" or "contemptible" can sometimes function in the same way, but would not have been very effective against the nobles who in Nietzsche's story possess precisely what the resentful want.[18] This would make very difficult any wide-scale pretense to regard them as inferior. But things change once the idea of blame or culpability is used to transform "bad" into "evil." If they can be *blamed* for what they are, they can be thought deserving of punishment on that basis. And especially since it will then seem natural to regard the good as deserving of reward for being good, it will be much easier for the good to convince themselves that they really are superior and do not want to be like the nobles at all.

If this reading is correct, the First Essay of the *Genealogy* does not compare two different moralities. Instead, it attempts to isolate from the historically conditioned synthesis we call "morality" a particular strand—the idea of moral worth or goodness—and to show how it developed from something that existed prior to morality. The revolt against the noble mode of valuation lies, according to Nietzsche's story, at the beginning of the specifically moral evaluation of persons. The *Genealogy*'s First Essay is an account of how a nonmoral mode of evaluating persons was transformed into a specifically moral mode, of how pagan virtue became moral virtue.

But it would also be misleading to say that this account is supposed to explain the origin of morality. Morality is a very complex affair on Nietzsche's account; and the moralization of virtue could not have taken place without earlier developments that also contribute central strands to our concept of morality—strands left completely out of account in the *Genealogy*'s First Essay. This point can be appreciated by considering the incompleteness of its account of the revolt against the noble mode of valuation. I have so far suggested that it is the idea of blaming people for what they are that transforms the noble mode of valuation into a moral mode. But the practice of blaming people for what they are did not arise out of thin air. Blaming too must have a history, and must already be present in some form to be used to transform "bad" into "evil." One obvious suggestion is that blaming people for what they are probably developed as a transformation of the practice of blaming people for what they do. But blaming people for their actions only makes sense if there are standards for acceptable behavior. Yet Nietzsche's First Essay tells us nothing about such practices and standards, much less where they come from. The rest of the *Genealogy* does suggest answers on both counts—but we must be willing to piece them together for ourselves.

Its Second Essay suggests that the oldest strand woven into the concept of morality is rules or codes of conduct that set out standards of right, of socially permitted and forbidden behavior. For it traces the phenomena with which it deals, "guilt, bad conscience, and the like," to what Nietzsche had earlier called "the morality of mores"—the system of laws and customary practices found in ancient communities (GM II:2).

When he introduced this term in *Daybreak* (D 9), he believed that the mores functioned within such communities as the naturalistic equivalent of moral rules or categorical imperatives that were obeyed not from prudential motives, but from a kind of reverence based on superstition.[19] Nietzsche rejects this theory in the *Genealogy*, claiming that the task of what he had called the "morality of mores" was to create a memory, and that this was done with the use of severe punishments. Through the experience and threat of punishment, Nietzsche claims, "one finally remembers five or six 'I will not's' in regard to which one had given one's promise so as to participate in the advantages of society" (GM II:3). The rules are "I will not's" rather than "ought not's," I presume, because they are kept in place as rules demanding obedience largely by the threat of punishment, and therefore function as hypothetical—rather than as categorical or moral—imperatives. A major (if unspoken) issue of the *Genealogy*'s Second Essay is how rules originally regarded as hypothetical imperatives came to be regarded as moral imperatives.

The big story of the Second Essay is the development of bad conscience, initially characterized as "the consciousness of guilt" (GM II:4). This suggests that on Nietzsche's view the mores become moral rules when they are connected with guilt—when people come to believe that those who violate the rules incur guilt. But where did this idea come from? Nietzsche claims that "the feeling of guilt, of personal obligation" had its origin in the debtor-creditor relation (GM II:8). That is, being guilty originally was nothing more than owing a debt, as is suggested already by the fact that the same German word (*Schuld*) is used to translate both "debt" and "guilt."[20] Originating in the sphere of trade, the idea of having a debt or owing something then transferred itself to the first forms of social organization. The community is viewed as "standing to its members in the same vital relation of creditor to its debtors" (GM II:9). The members enjoy the advantages of community (advantages Nietzsche says we sometimes underrate today), "dwelling protected, cared for, in peace and trustfulness, without fear of certain injuries and hostile acts ... since [they have] bound and pledged [themselves] to the community precisely with a view to injuries and hostile acts" (GM II:9).

What happens, Nietzsche asks, if this pledge is broken? "The community, the disappointed creditor will get what repayment it can, one may depend on that." In the beginning, the criminal is thrown out of the community, back to the savage and outlaw state against which he has been protected, and every kind of hostility may be vented upon him.

> The direct harm caused by the culprit is here a minor matter; ... the lawbreaker is above all a "breaker," a breaker of his contract and his word *with the whole* in respect to all the benefits and comforts of communal life in which he has hitherto had a share. The lawbreaker is a debtor who has not merely failed to make good the advantages and advance payment bestowed on him but has actually attacked his creditor: therefore he is not only deprived henceforth of all these advantages and benefits, as is fair, he is also reminded *what these benefits are really worth*. (GM II:9)

As the society grows stronger, it takes offenses less seriously because they are less dangerous to it. Rather than casting out the criminal and allowing anger to be vented unrestrainedly upon him, the community sets up a system of punishments. Many purposes are served by this, but above all, according to Nietzsche, "the increasingly definite will to treat each crime as dischargeable, and thus at least to a certain extent to isolate the criminal and his deed from each other" (GM II:10). In other words, the person did something that breaks his pledge to the community, and therefore to some extent threatens its stability, angering its members. In the old days, they would have cast him out and treated him as no longer due community protection. But since the community is now stronger, its members no longer feel sufficiently threatened, or angry enough (though the persons directly affected by the crime well may), to need to throw the criminal out. So they set up a system of punishments that allows the criminal to pay off his debt and remain within the community. This is what Nietzsche thinks guilt is in its origins: a debt or substitute payment owed to society for failure to obey the community's rules.

Despite the contempt with which Nietzsche sometimes treats ideas of a social contract, he is clearly working with such an idea here. He rejects the idea that the state begins with an actual contract, an explicit promise that the members make to obey community laws (GM II:17). But he believes that from fairly early times, the relation between individual members and community was viewed on the model of such a contract: If you accept the advantages of the community life, you are in effect making a bargain with the community, agreeing to go along with the rules that make community life possible. You now have an obligation to the community to obey the rules, and if you renege on it, you deserve punishment, that is, "owe" it as a matter of fairness or justice (GM II:9).

It is difficult to find in Nietzsche's discussion here any suggestion that he objects to such judgments of fairness, or any basis he could think he has for doing so. He seems to present judgments of fairness as completely natural to human beings, and in no way based on mistakes or errors. Nor does anything he says suggest that he thinks, or could reasonably think, that human beings will or should eventually outgrow a concern for fairness.[21] But then how can Nietzsche consider himself an immoralist? The only plausible answer I can find for him is that he denies that regarding obedience to the rules as a matter of fairness is equivalent to granting them the status of moral rules.

On textual grounds, I believe that this is in fact Nietzsche's position. As I discuss below, he claims that debt is moralized into guilt, and duty into moral duty, through the development of the bad conscience and of the idea of having a debt to God (GM II:21). But neither of these notions plays any part in or is presupposed by his account of judgments of fairness. Nietzsche evidently believes, therefore, that we can regard obedience to the rules necessary for communal existence as a matter of fairness *without* the help of ideas of moral duty or guilt, and therefore without regarding them as moral rules.

This may seem implausible. It may be thought that a system of rules involving an idea of fairness must have room for acting from conscience, and that conscience necessarily brings with it ideas of guilt. Nietzsche admits the role of conscience, but explicitly distinguishes conscience from "*bad* conscience," the consciousness of guilt (GM II:3–4). Nietzsche's person of conscience obeys the rules that make community existence possible—but not out of fear of punishment. Rather, they are obeyed from an identification with the aims of the community, and from pride in being a person who can be relied on to keep promises—which Nietzsche calls "the proud awareness of the extraordinary privilege of *responsibility*" (GM II:2).[22]

Within the system against the background of which conscience appears, breaking one's promise to obey the rules of society amounts to a failure to pay one's debt to society. Punishment, as a means of substitute repayment, is now the debt one owes to society. But Nietzsche's analysis suggests that this is only what he calls the "very material" concept of debt, which he distinguishes from the moral concept of guilt (GM II:4). One sign of the difference is that a material debt is completely dischargeable. Once you have paid it off, no debt or guilt remains. In the case of moral guilt, however, it seems that we remain guilty of whatever wrongs we have done, even if we have suffered an appropriate punishment. A related point is that material indebtedness, unlike guilt, does not automatically lower one's worth as a person. People of conscience may consider you bad and look down on you because you don't have what it takes to keep your word; but your indebtedness is not itself a matter of your worth, as it clearly is in the case of moral guilt. Indebtedness and worth may be interconnected, but are two separable issues; whereas this is not the case once debt becomes guilt.[23]

If this is correct, the Second Essay of the *Genealogy* tries to show us the possibility—indeed the historical reality—of a nonmoral version of a social contract, involving what we can recognize to be nonmoral ideas of fairness, justice, obligation, indebtedness, and conscience. This suggests that Nietzsche's objection is not to justice or the common good (contrary to Foot), nor to social norms that apply to all (contrary to Nehamas), but rather to the *moralization* of these ideas and norms.[24] I turn now, all too briefly, to his account of how that moralization took place.

There are two evidently independent parts of the story Nietzsche tells about the moralization of debt into guilt. First, he gives an account of the origin of the bad conscience that is very similar to Freud's later one. Nietzsche claims that the bad conscience develops when restrictions on the external expression of hostile impulses becomes so severe that they can be satisfied only through internalization (GM II:17–18). Debt is moralized into guilt, Nietzsche claims, when it is pushed back into the bad conscience (GM II:21).[25] I take this to mean that the moralization of debt into guilt occurs through the taking over of the idea of debt by the bad conscience, the project of internalizing aggression. Debt becomes guilt insofar as people start using the idea of being indebted to inflict suffering on themselves. But how did they do this? And how does using the idea of debt for self-punishment turn it into guilt?

Nietzsche evidently expects us to find our answers in the second part of his story, which concerns the idea of owing a debt to God (GM II:21). The relation to ancestors, he claims, was interpreted along the lines of the debtor-creditor relation (GM II:19). The conviction reigns that the tribe exists only through the sacrifices and accomplishments of ancestors. The tribe therefore owes them a debt that constantly grows greater, since these forebears never cease (in their continued existence as powerful spirits) to accord the tribe new advantages. Eventually the ancestor grows into a god, and finally into God, the God before whom all human beings are guilty (GM II:20).

But why isn't the debt we owe to God just a debt? What makes it a matter of guilt? In Nietzsche's initial telling of this story, the debt owed to God appears to be just a debt, for he suggests that with the dawning of atheism, human beings would get over their sense of guilt and acquire a second innocence (GM II:20). But he then tells us in effect that he has been pulling our leg, writing as if the moralization of the idea had not taken place— whereas the reality is to "a fearful degree otherwise" (GM II:21). If the moralization of the concept *had not* taken place, atheism *would* rid us of guilt, because guilt would just be a debt supposedly owed to God, and given no God, there would be no guilt. Given that moralization, guilt can remain without someone to whom it is owed. We need to understand more about what Nietzsche thinks is involved in this moralization if we are to understand how the bad conscience transformed debt into guilt.

Nietzsche claims explicitly that the moralization of the concepts of debt and duty occurred through the involvement of the bad conscience with the idea of God (GM II:21). I take this to mean that the project of the bad conscience—of internalizing aggression—determined the form the idea of God would take. God was to be understood as pure spirit, the opposite of human beings who are sunk in nature, afflicted by desires, senses, animality. Nietzsche claims, in effect, that one of the major factors behind the transformation of pagan gods who are merely human beings writ large and more powerful into a purely spiritual God was the need for a weapon against the self—a standard of good we could never live up to, and in relation to which we could enjoy judging, condemning, and chastising ourselves and others. The debt we owe to this nonnatural God is one that can never be paid off, and one that is definitely tied to our worth as persons. We owe God a debt not just for what we do, but for what we are.

Nietzsche thus denies that owing a debt to a divine being is enough to make this debt a matter of moral guilt. The material concept of debt was transformed into the fully moral concept of guilt when the divine being to whom the debt was owed was conceived nonnaturalistically or ascetically, as a repudiation of the value of natural human existence. What transforms debt into guilt—makes it unpayable and a matter of our worth as persons—

is the ascetic ideal and its attendant ascetic conception of virtue, which Nietzsche discusses at length in the Third Essay of the *Genealogy*. I do not have time to go into that here, but I hope I have said enough to indicate why he would consider his essay on the ascetic ideal a central part of his account of morality itself. This is because he thinks that through the historical processes he discusses in the *Genealogy* the ascetic ideal became tied to and intertwined with the very concept of morality. Briefly put, rules became moral rules when their violation was thought to incur guilt, and the idea of guilt is a transformation of the idea of debt by means of the ascetic ideal. Further, the noble nonmoral conception of virtue or goodness becomes moral virtue precisely insofar as people are blamed for what they are—that is, are considered guilty.

Despite the incompleteness of my account of the *Genealogy*, I believe that the approach to it suggested here provides the basis for a better explanation than has been given previously as to why Nietzsche believed he was rejecting morality itself. Specifically, I have tried to show that he thinks the ascetic ideal is tightly intertwined with our idea of morality, and I have argued elsewhere that he rejects the ascetic ideal.[26] More generally, I have tried to show that much of Nietzsche's work on morality involves prying apart central components of our concept of morality and showing how these strands came together in the course of human history. This work gives him a basis for insisting that what we call "morality" is not something that has always been with human beings but is instead an extremely complex affair that developed in the course of human history through the multiple coupling of originally separate strands that we can no longer see as independent.

By separating them, I think Nietzsche tries to show us the possibility of tying these strands together differently, and thus the possibility of gaining much of what morality gives us, indeed what we cannot do without, in alternative ways, and specifically without the tie to the ascetic ideal. As an immoralist, he claims that some such alternative is superior to the present synthesis that we call "morality." Explaining this alternative and Nietzsche's arguments for its superiority are complicated matters that I will be working on in the future. Here I have tried only to show that examining his own analysis of the concept of morality helps to make comprehensible why he believed he was rejecting morality itself.[27]

NOTES

1. Nietzsche's books are cited by the initials of their standard English translations, followed by the section number, which is the same in all editions. I have followed Kaufmann's translation of the *Genealogy*, but have made minor changes based on volume 5 of the *Studienausgabe*, ed. G. Colli and M. Montinari (Berlin: Walter de Gruyter, 1980).

2. Maudemarie Clark, *Nietzsche on Truth and Philosophy* (Cambridge University Press, 1990).

3. I would include among those who accept such a qualified interpretation of Nietzsche's immoralism Walter Kaufmann, Arthur Danto, Robert Solomon, John Wilcox, Richard Schacht, and Frederick Olafson.

4. In *Human, All Too Human*, Nietzsche follows Schopenhauer in identifying acting morally with acting unegoistically (of which acting from compassion is taken as a primary example), but had clearly broken from Schopenhauer's narrow construal of morality by the time he wrote the *Genealogy*. I have argued for both of these points in my unpublished dissertation, "Nietzsche's Attack on Morality" (University of Wisconsin, 1976).

5. Philippa Foot, "Nietzsche's Immoralism," *The New York Review of Books* 28, no. 11 (13 June 1991): 18–22. (Reprinted in this volume.)

6. BGE 202 supports this explanation. I take Nietzsche to claim in BGE 202 that we Europeans use the word "morality" so that codes of conduct and valuations he considers "higher" cannot count as moralities. He also proposes a revision in our linguistic practice, so that his higher codes can count as moralities. Why would he propose this? Because he thinks our current use of the word "morality" hides from us our prejudices concerning values, and that if we got over these (or perhaps even got them out on the table), there would no longer be any point in restricting the term in the way we do now. But since we do now restrict the term that way, the least misleading thing for Nietzsche to say is that he rejects morality itself, that he is an immoralist.

7. Philippa Foot, "Nietzsche: The Revaluation of Values," in *Virtues and Vices* (Berkeley, Los Angeles, London: University of California Press, 1978), pp. 81–95. This paper was originally published in *Nietzsche: A Collection of Critical Essays*, ed. Robert Solomon (New York: Doubleday, 1973), and Foot has made its arguments accessible to a wider audience in her "Nietzsche's Immoralism" (reprinted here).

8. Foot, "Nietzsche: The Revaluation of Values," p. 92.

9. Alexander Nehamas, *Nietzsche: Life as Literature* (Cambridge, Mass.: Harvard University Press, 1985), p. 224.

10. Frithjof Bergmann, "Nietzsche's Critique of Morality," in *Reading Nietzsche*, ed. Robert Solomon and Kathleen Higgins (New York: Oxford University Press, 1988), pp. 29–45.

11. *Basic Writings of Nietzsche*, trans. and ed. Walter Kaufmann (New York: Modern Library, 1968), p. 446.

12. Alasdair MacIntyre, *Three Rival Versions of Moral Enquiry: Encyclopedia, Genealogy, and Tradition* (Notre Dame, Ind.: University of Notre Dame Press, 1990). (The chapter in question is reprinted in this volume.)

13. Arthur Danto, "Some Remarks on *The Genealogy of Morals*" in *Reading Nietzsche*, p. 19. (A version of this essay is reprinted in this volume.)

14. It might seem more reasonable to construe the stable element in punishment as the actual procedure for inflicting suffering. Nietzsche discusses such procedures earlier in the same essay (GM II:3), and he would then be making the obviously true claim that techniques for inflicting suffering existed prior to their

employment in punishment. However, it is difficult to see why Nietzsche would equate such techniques of violence with "a strict sequence of procedures," or why he would consider the procedure the "stable element" and the purpose the "fluid" aspect of punishment when there are at least as many different procedures for inflicting suffering as there are purposes for punishing. I therefore suggest that the enduring element, "the custom, the act, the 'drama,' a strict sequence of procedures," he refers to is the sequence of accusing someone of a wrong or violation, judging that the violation has taken place, determining the penalty that is appropriate or deserved, and inflicting that penalty. This amounts to inflicting a penalty as a result of a judgment that the person deserves it owing to something he or she has done.

15. Kaufmann, *Basic Writings of Nietzsche,* p. 440.

16. Arthur Danto, *Nietzsche as Philosopher* (New York: Macmillian, 1965), p. 159.

17. Arthur Schopenhauer, *On the Basis of Morality,* trans. E. F. J. Payne (Indianapolis: Bobbs-Merrill, 1965), p. 162.

18. What this is depends on the person in question. Whereas the people probably envied most the nobles' power and wealth, the priests may well have envied most of all their unquestioning sense of their own worth.

19. I have argued for this interpretation in chapter 1 of "Nietzsche's Attack On Morality."

20. It should be kept in mind that this makes the translation of *Schuld* in the essay difficult, for it is ambiguous between the moral and material concepts Nietzsche distinguishes in GM II:4. Kaufmann sometimes resorts to "guilty indebtedness" in an attempt to capture the ambiguity of "*Schuldgefühl.*"

21. In GM II:10, he does write of the overcoming of justice by mercy. This constitutes an overcoming not of a sense of fairness, however, but only of the need to punish. This is in line with Nietzsche's thought that the stronger the community is, the less threatened it will be by violations of the community norms, and therefore the less in need of causing pain to violators. But the possibility Nietzsche thus entertains of going beyond a concern for justice in this (retributive) sense in no way implies that we can or should overcome the idea that people owe obedience to the rules as a matter of fairness. It only suggests the possibility of giving up holding violators to a particular kind of substitute repayment.

22. Nietzsche does not himself make explicit that identification with community aims is one of the pieces of motivation here. I bring it in because I believe that the motive Nietzsche does make explicit, the pride the conscientious take in the extraordinary privilege of responsibility, makes psychological sense only given their identification with the community and its aims.

23. I want to make it clear that I am not here attempting to determine the essence of guilt, or giving necessary and sufficient conditions for debt being a matter of guilt. I assume Nietzsche thinks this cannot be done. I am suggesting only that we can come up with clear cases of the material concept of debt, on the one hand, and the moral concept of guilt, on the other, and can specify differences between them. The burden of Nietzsche's historical analysis is to specify the processes that led from the obvious case of pure debt to the equally obvious cases of moral guilt.

However, I assume that these obvious cases are the extremes, and that there are many cases in between, and that Nietzsche would deny that there is some exact point at which debt turns into guilt.

24. In the context of Nietzsche's *Genealogy*, "moralization" refers to the process whereby something becomes part of the synthesis we call "morality." There is, of course, no common essence of the process of moralization because different elements become part of the synthesis we call "morality" through different processes.

25. Actually he says pushed back into conscience. But it is clear from what he goes on to say that he means the bad conscience.

26. Clark, *Nietzsche on Truth and Philosophy*, chapter 6.

27. Earlier versions of this paper were read at Colgate University and the University of Pennsylvania. This version has benefitted from helpful comments and discussions on both occasions, and from Brian Leiter's written comments on it.

THREE

Some Remarks on *The Genealogy of Morals*

Arthur C. Danto

The third essay of the three which compose *On the Genealogy of Morals* is, according to Nietzsche's preface to the work, a gloss on its prefixed aphorism, which reads: "Unconcerned, mocking, violent—thus wisdom wants *us*: She is a woman, and always loves only a warrior." What sort of warrior is unconcerned? One, I suppose, for whom the means is an end, for whom warmaking is not so much what you do but what you are, so that it is not a matter of warring for but as an end. There is, he tells us in the first essay, "no 'being' behind doing . . . 'the doer' is merely a fiction added to the deed." So the unconcerned warrior is perhaps best exemplified by the great archer Arjuna, in the *Bhagavad Gita,* instructed by Krishna that unconcern for consequences, hence disinterested participation in the battle, is the path to follow if release is sought from karma: it is not desisting from action, which is in any case impossible as much for the Gita as for Nietzsche, but a certain enlightened view of the metaphysics of action, which wisdom loves.

If this is the recommended morality, what does the warrior mock? Clearly those still locked in the world of goals and purposes, who subscribe to hypothetical imperatives, who fight for causes, rather than those who are categorical fighters, for whom warring is for its own sake. So violence too is not instrumental but the moral essence of the warrior, not something he especially uses to terrorize, but a secondary effect of the martial art. Why should wisdom then love only the anticonsequentialist? The author of the Gita would answer this out of a moral metaphysics in which karmic transmigration is a form of hell, a view finally negativistic and, as we shall see, predicated on a kind of *ressentiment,* since we blame our suffering on karmic pollutions we ourselves are responsible for. These considerations scarcely would have daunted the discoverer of eternal recurrence, hence of the certitude of unending repeated Mahabharatas, in each of which Arjuna fulfills himself by drawing bowstrings and steering chariots; nor would they faze the prophet of *amor fati* for whom the evil to be avoided consists in trying to be something other than what one is. Kant, the other dominant anticonsequentialist, has a metaphysics of morals, in which it is true that an effort is made to derive our duties from our being, *except* that it construes derivation itself to be our characteristic form of action and our essence itself to be reason, and so entraps an opponent as a confirmer, since denial too exemplifies rationality.

So, if you are Nietzsche, you don't deny, you *reject*. And that is what is to be expected from a warrior whose campaigns happen to be philosophical and who philosophizes with a hammer: who does not so much love wisdom as is, like a warrior, loved by wisdom. So not Nietzsche as a philosopher but Nietzsche as *sophiaphilos,* and whose weapons are words, sometimes used as hammers. (Erase the human-all-too-human fraudulence of "the old artilleryman," as he referred to himself on occasion with an affected gruffness.) As one does not argue with an idealist if one does not want to be enmeshed in his web—one instead kicks a rock; or, to cite the practice of one of our most influential contemporary philosophic critics, one does not refute the thinkers one opposes, but instead sneers at them. One puts metaphysics *on ice,* as Nietzsche says in another place: one *mocks*. Mockery is the violence of the metaphysican as warrior. And if one's writings are to be mocking and violent, hence meant to *hurt,* the aphorism is a natural, obvious form to use; for, piercing like a dart the defenses of reason, it lodges inextricably in the mind's flesh, where it sticks as a perpetual invasion: like a barbed arrow, it cannot be extricated without tearing its host.

This aphorism has a complex pragmatics, since it is at once used *and* used to demonstrate what it means to use language in this way, and the commentary, while it does not quite mitigate the pain to philosophical susceptibilities the aphorism may cause—wisdom does not love those who love wisdom—at least reduces the chance of such suffering as it may cause being smothered in *ressentiment* it is also the task of that commentary to dissolve. And in some way its use is meant to have an effect quite opposite to the instillation of an ascetic ideal, as he generalizes upon that concept in the third essay, and so is not meant to transform one into a philosopher, since philosophers are the first to be discussed in that essay as falling under the balefulness of asceticism.

The aphorism is a special use of the language it is also *about,* and it is the second time in two books that he has drawn a joke from the grammar of gender, feminizing wisdom and truth, and both times in order to emphasize a difference between the way he uses language and the ways "philosophers" use it. In *Beyond Good and Evil* he observes that if truth has the attributes of femininity, then she is unlikely to yield her favors to the cloddish and clumsy idiom of philosophers who do not know how to seduce, as he, Nietzsche, does. But in the same way, the aphorism is the way to approach wisdom, epitomized as female in *this* aphorism: wisdom does not bestow herself upon writers who write as philosophers write, hence not from books that are read as philosophical books are read. Rather language must *implant* itself in the reader, and wisdom comes from an experience which is literary only in the sense that it is caused by a book. So it is language used in a way as to bypass the faculties used ordinarily in reading. "An aphorism," he writes aphoristically, "when properly stamped and molded, has not been 'deciphered' when it has simply been read."

In my address to the American Philosophical Association, "Philosophy as/and/of Literature," I argued that by treating philosophy in general as the sort of thing that can be expressed in articles of the sort through which we define ourselves professionally as readers and writers, we misperceive that vast diversity of literary forms the historical bibliography of our discipline displays. Each kind of book has to be read in its kind of way, and just possibly each kind of reader is to be transformed into a different kind of person—the sort of person the philosopher requires the reader to be if the philosophy is to reach him. So we have to realize that in reading Nietzsche we are being attacked; we need some kind of shield or the aphorism will *land* and we lose to the words. One way of fighting back *is* of course to treat him as a philosopher himself: the net, too, is a gladiatorial weapon in the skilled left hand of the *retiarius*. So to cage him into a system of repressive categories, to put his toxin on ice, to slip the manacles of asceticism onto his wrists, to locate him in the history of thought, is like driving a stake through Nero's heart in order to keep his ghost stable.

There is a tendency to divide commentators on Nietzsche into those who portray a hard Nietzsche and those who portray a soft Nietzsche. But it is possible to acknowledge him as hard by treating him as though he were soft; so when Philippa Foot reviewed my book on him with a certain appreciation for the originality of treating him as a kind of linguistic epistemologist, and then raised the question of why, if this was what he was *au fond*, anyone would be especially interested in him any longer, I felt I had won a kind of victory—as though I had transformed him into a minotaur by devising a maze. But certainly there is a Nietzsche who genuinely stands against philosophy rather than illustrating it, and who is dangerous and even terrible: and in this paper I would like to acknowledge the virulent Nietzsche, not this time examining his views on language but his use of language, to see what he must have intended by this use and what his beliefs may have been for such intentions to have been coherent. This approach too is a way of standing aside and at a distance.

The psychology of metaphorical address, since metaphor is a rhetorician's device, is that the audience will itself supply the connection withheld by the metaphor, so that the rhetorician opens a kind of gap with intention that the logical energies of his audience will arc it, with the consequence that having participated in the progression of argument, that audience convinces itself. There is another but comparable psychology for the aphorism, namely that once heard it is unlikely to pass from recollection, so its pointed terseness is a means to ensoul the message it carries, and to counteract the predictable deteriorations of memory. So it is a natural instrument for the moralist. The whole great second essay of the *Genealogy* is precisely addressed to the role of pain in the forging of a moral memory. *Forgetting* is a dimension of animal health, a requisite of mental hygiene— "no mere *vis inertiae* as the superficial imagine." Nietzsche writes: "It is rather an active and in the strictest sense positive faculty of repression." *Consciousness*, in which attention and memory or memorability coincide, is contrary to the animal nature and possibly even a sort of disease—one of the discontents of civilization—a disturbance against which forgetfulness is a preserver of psychic order and peace: "It will be immediately obvious how there could be no happiness, no cheerfulness, no hope, no pride, no present, without forgetfulness."

Nietzsche is speaking of what we might call deep forgetfulness here, a complete metabolization of experience rather than the repressive forgetfulness that Freud's later concept of the Unconscious introduces into mental economy, where what is put there clamors to be made conscious and so is not *deeply* forgotten. In order, then, that this sustaining mental entropy should be arrested or reversed, some mnemotechnic is required. As he puts it, "If something is to stay in the memory it must be burned in; only that which never ceases *hurting* stays in the memory." This, he continues, "is a main cause of the oldest (unhappily also the most enduring) psychology on earth." And, a moment later, "Man could never do without blood, torture, and sacrifices when he felt a need to create a memory for himself." Then, after a catalog of medieval cruelties, he concludes, "All this has its origin in the instinct that realizes that pain is the most powerful aid to mnemonics." We still talk of teaching someone a lesson as a synonym for administering a beating; we still say "this will learn you" as we land a punch. And we all admire Kafka's brilliant image in *The Penal Colony* where the inscription of the crime is the crime's punishment, since it is in the medium of the victim's agony. And, when one comes to it—as we shall in more detail—the entire office of religion has consisted in teaching us that our suffering has meaning, so that the chosen people spontaneously turns to its prophets to explain what lesson it is being taught through the suffering it has come to accept as the avenue of communication.

Nietzsche was too much the classicist not to know that aphorism and remembering are pragmatically complicated, or to be ignorant that the earliest collection of aphorisms was attributed to Hippocrates, and constituted a kind of *vade mecum* of medical praxiology, a body of maxims pointed and polished in order to stick in the intern's mind. Since aphoristic form is prophylactic against forgetfulness, and since pain is the prime reenforcer of retention, aphorism and pain are internally related, and so this form spontaneously presents itself to a writer whose warrior violence must be turned against those he appears to admire: the healthy forgetters, the innocent brutes. So when, in the second essay's discussion of the mnemonics of hurt, he writes, "In a certain sense the whole of asceticism lies here," he is being disingenuous when he inveighs against asceticism while using language specifically framed to scourge. Someone who uses ascetic practices to kill asceticism is engaged in a very complex communication, supposing he is coherent at all, and he would be right that we are missing what is taking place when we merely *read the words*. An apologist for paganism, for the happy instinctive unconscious life of the spontaneously unremembering beast, has no business creating a moral memory in the course of such apologetics, leaving a scar of consciousness against the easy viscosities of the mental life he celebrates: so the apology for paganism must itself be a moral stab, and self-conscious paganism is logically unlivable. So the remarks on paganism are *meant to hurt* in a way in which the memory of happiness becomes, in Dante's scale, the *maggiore dolore* in a general context of torment: it is as though the entirety of the *Genealogy* is a cell of inflictions and instrument of asectic transformation and a very rough book.

"Even those who suppose, erroneously, that *Beyond Good and Evil* is a collection of aphorisms that may be read in any order whatever," Walter Kaufmann wrote, having in mind by "those" specifically me, "generally recognize that the *Genealogy* comprises three essays." This in his view brings the book closest to what we Anglo-American philosophers expect philosophical writing to be, all the more so in that "Nietzsche's manner is much more sober and single-minded than usual." But the manner of the essayist is a marvelous camouflage for the sort of moral terrorist Nietzsche really was, as the essay itself is a kind of literary camouflage for the sharpened stakes of aphorism he has concealed for the unwary, making this in a deep sense the most treacherous book he ever compiled, one almost impossible to read without being cut to ribbons. Flaying alive—"cutting straps"—is itemized in his inventory of ghastly interventions which at last instill "the kind of memory by the aid of which one comes at last to reason!" For how precisely is one to forget what he writes about Jews, slaves, justice, seriousness; about barbarism, morality itself, sensuality, torture, cruelty; about war, women, and will?—even if the book also seems to provide passages of modulating analgesis, enabling him to say, soothingly, that he did not exactly mean what he said, enabling his commentators to reassure us that those who took him at his word had taken him out of context—as though he was after all just to be read. It is like saying the lace handkerchief is the context for the stiletto it hides, or the wine the context for the powdered glass, or the rose an attenuation of the thorn. A man cannot write this way and then stand back in mock innocence and point to the fine print, to the footnote, to the subtle conciliatory phrase written in all but invisible ink, or say that one had expected we were subtle enough to read between the lines!

This book was not written for Nietzsche scholars, capable of handling even deadly poison with the long forceps of *Wissenschaft*. And often Nietzsche tells us as much. At the very beginning, for example, he talks about the English moral psychologists whose interest for us in part lies in the fact that they have written uninteresting books, the question being what were they *doing* by writing such books—"What do they really want?"—hoping we will be clever enough to ask that of this book, take the hint, raise the query as to why he wipes away with his left hand the blood he has drawn with his right, and not pretend that we are not bleeding or that it is our fault if we are. Just by printing on that package the warning against the contents, you have not provided prophylaxis. There is a passage in Wittgenstein in which he explains certain confusions about language as due to "the uniform appearance of words when we hear them spoken or meet them in script or print." "It is like looking into the cabin of the locomotive," he goes on to say; "We see handles all looking more or less alike." But what shows a greater uniformity of appearance than *books?* The *Genealogy of Morals* is of about the shape and heft of *Utilitarianism* or *Foundations of the Metaphysics of Morals*—or for that matter the *Imitatio Christi*. But that does not mean that they are all to be treated the same way, or that reading is a uniform matter—"especially," as Wittgenstein writes, "when we are doing philosophy." To treat the *Genealogy* as though it were precocious analytical philosophy is to have swallowed a bait without having yet felt the hook. After all the subtitle is: *Eine Streitschrift*. So *à la guerre comme à la guerre*: one had better study one's defenses!

In fact the *Genealogy* is in some ways the least analytical of Nietzsche's books, for it contains one of the subtlest discussions of moral predicates I know. For the question must be raised as to who the readers were to be, what was to bring them to this book, and what particularly were they to get from it. And this returns me to the Hippocratic model of the aphoristic collection. Such collections, our sources claim, were regarded as suitable for dealing with subjects to which no scientific or methodical treatment has been as yet successfully applied, such as in particular medicine. I want to claim that the *Genealogy* is in this respect a medical book: etiological, diagnostic, therapeutic, prognostic. I want to underscore *therapeutic* here, for the book is not for other practitioners of the caring art so much as it is for those who suffer from the diseases it addresses. So the assumption must be that the intended reader is sick, if typically in ways unrecognized by him: one learns the nature of one's illness as one reads the book. And part of the reason the aphorism is so suitable a form is that the language has to get past the defenses we bring to the book since the defenses are in a way part of the disease, as in neurosis according to the classic analysis, where the repression of the pathogen is part of the pathogen. As in analysis, a task of the therapist is to bring to consciousness the mechanisms of disassociation and, if there is such a word, of disconsciation. So the reader is as it were being treated as he reads, and a condition of therapeutic success is that he be kept continuously conscious of the disorder the book means to drive out: as Hippocrates says, the practitioner is to be "seconded by the patient." And in a way the patient, or reader here, must be helped by the practitioner to cure himself. In a way, I suppose, there is an analogy to Socratic maieutic, here the point being that only the sufferer can solve the problem of his suffering, the doctor's role consisting in showing him that he is sick. So the book has to be painful. And arguably the cure more painful than the disease, with which, after all, we have grown comfortable.

It scarcely can pass notice how frequently and characteristically Nietzsche here employs the vocabularies of pathology (it would be an interesting scholarly enterprise to see the degree to which the same vocabularies occur in all the main books in this way, or whether each book has its paradigm lexicon, from which the mode of literary address can then be inferred). The period of Nietzsche's great productivity was the great age of German physiology—Johannes Müller, Justus von Liebig, Karl Ludwig, had made Germany the center for physiological investigation in the form it has had ever since, and though in no sense myself a historian of medicine, I am certain that a suitable scholarship would discover among their procedures certain which Nietzsche adapted, transforming them of course through his own special genius. It is still difficult, and it must in Nietzsche's time have been all but impossible, to draw a careful distinction between physiological and physiognomic differences, and to suppose that a certain blue-eyed blondness might not connote a physiological distinctiveness of some importance: or that shortness of stature might not be a physiological defect.

The physiologization of moral concepts, the proposal that in the end moral differences must be physiological differences, or that a certain physiognomical paradigm must be a paradigm of health, all other variants being sick, are among his most reckless and dangerous conjectures. But the shock of Darwinism was still being felt, and he was not immune to the moralization of natural selection that almost defines nineteenth-century thought, which can lead to the view, as we know, that those with different moral beliefs may be contagious, ought to be segregated at least, and at worst may have to be eliminated in the interests of moral sepsis. And they can lead, in the other direction, to the view that those who are physiologically distinctive, and for that matter different, must fall under a different moral order, and need not be treated in the way we treat one another. I imagine that the great movements toward equal rights, equal no matter what one's age, sex, color, competence, or creed, constitute an effort to make physiological differences irrelevant to moral considerations. And while we must not be dismissive since, as Hippocrates says, "art is long, life is short," and there will always be more to find out than we can possibly hope, and no one knows whether criminality is chromosomal—or for the matter generosity genetic—it remains unclear how such discoveries should be responded to morally. It is also doubtful that reading a book of *this* sort could be regarded a significant intervention if it turned out that a certain moral difference *were* a physiological one in that way. But neither would Nietzsche have supposed it were—so the question is what sort of disease could it have been for which he might have thought the book *was* significantly interventive? And here I can say perhaps most of what I have to say about this work.

I think the answer must lie in a distinction between what I shall term extensional suffering and intensional suffering, where the latter consists in an interpretation of the former. As I see Nietzsche's thesis, it is this: the main sufferings human beings have been subject to throughout history are due to certain interpretative responses to the fact of extensional suffering. It is not clear that Nietzsche believes he can deal with extensional suffering. But he can deal with intensional suffering, thus helping reduce, often by a significant factor, the total suffering in the world. For while extensional suffering is bad enough, often it is many times compounded by our interpretations of it, themselves often far worse than the disorder itself.

Consider the example of impotence in the human male, in certain cases genuinely a physiological symptom of an underlying sickness with no clinical identity of its own, due, say, to diabetes, prostate disorder, and the like. For most men, and doubtless for most women sexually involved with men, it is a pretty appalling symptom. But to explain why it is refers us to the complex of ideas connected with the male self-image of adequacy and power, and the extreme vulnerability in the male ego which sexual incapacity opens up. It can lead, it has led, to suicide, depression, despair, divorce. So if we subtracted all this suffering from the sum total of suffering, the actual symptom might not amount to very much in the scale of human agony. Compare it to the other symptoms of diabetes: polyuria, polydipsia, retinopathy, renal malfunction, circulatory problems, propensity to gangrene, susceptibility to fungus, to heart disease, acidosis, coma—and a merely flaccid penis seems pretty minor. But knowing the male temperament I am certain that this morally overcharged symptom would be singled out as the most intolerable effect of this disorder. Very few, I think, attach much significance to the mere fact of hyperglycemia, or would commit suicide over that, or regard themselves as flawed—or sick. It is a good example of moralized physiology, but in any case the disorders addressed by Nietzsche in this book, and which it is his enterprise to help us cure ourselves of, are interpretations of suffering which themselves generate suffering.

They are due, one and all, to bad philosophy, bad psychology, to religion—which in Nietzsche's scheme does not have a *good* form so as to make "bad religion" nonredundant—and of course bad moral systems, such as the one which takes as its primary value-opposition the distinction between good and evil. All of these are in a way modalities of *schlechtes Gewissen,* which I shall persist in translating as "bad consciousness." Bad *conscience*— in English usage at least—is more or less the same as guilty conscience, but guilt is only one of the modalities of badness. Bad consciousness is consciousness of badness, which of course may be illusory, as when someone good falsely seems bad to himself. Any suffering due to false moral beliefs about ourselves is due to bad consciousness, when there is nothing bad about us *except* our consciousness of being bad. And the book might then in part be addressed specifically to the cure of this sort of suffering.

Though at times Nietzsche speaks as though only the extensionally strong and healthy are subject to bad consciousness, in truth it is difficult to see how anyone in our civilization can have altogether escaped it: and even those who in his view really do suffer, really are in his sense "bad"— that is, bad specimens of the species *human*—typically also suffer from misinterpretations of this disorder, and no less than the good may be for this reason subject to bad consciousness. It is possible, of course, that Nietzsche's psycho-historical account is correct, and the particular form bad consciousness takes may be traced back to the pathogens of what he terms *ressentiment,* to which the extensionally bad are subject; even so they themselves suffer from the epidemics of bad consciousness which define the subsequent history of our civilization, that is, not to be coy about it, from Christianity if he is right. So even the bad might profit from dissipation of this sort of intensional suffering, leaving extensional suffering to be treated by those whose speciality it is. After all, identification of the real disease is the first step in medicine.

Let us attend, for a moment, to the concept of *ressentiment.* Nietzsche more or less assumed that anyone in a state of *ressentiment* must also be in some state or other, in his scheme, of actual physiological suffering, for what *ressentiment*—which is only distantly connected to the English word *resentment*—amounts to is a certain sort of interpretive explanation of suffering in the mind of the sufferer. In actual fact it would not matter if the suffering in question were real, that is, physiological, or only believed to be real, as in cases of what used to be called hysteria. Nietzsche's point is put into what one might term an *a priori* of suffering:

> Every sufferer instinctively seeks a cause for his suffering; more exactly an
> agent . . . some living thing upon which he can, on some pretext or other,

vent his affects, actually or in effigy: for the venting of his affects represents the greatest attempt on the part of the sufferer to win relief, *anaesthesia*—the narcotic he cannot help desiring to deaden pain of every kind.

This, which Nietzsche glosses as "the actual physiological cause of *ressentiment*, vengefulness, and the like," could easily have formed a section in the Hippocratic collection. And the implication is clear: sufferers tend to *moralize* suffering by holding someone or something responsible for it: as though mere suffering, undeserved only in the sense that it makes no sense to speak of it as deserved, is simply unintelligible. "Why me, Lord?" is the spontaneous response to sickness; "What did I do to deserve this?"—as though there were no as it were unearned suffering, as though suffering were in every instance a *sentence* of some sort. "Someone or other must be to blame for my feeling ill," Nietzsche puts in the mind of the sufferer—a kind of reasoning "held the more firmly the more the real cause of their feeling ill, the physiological cause, remains hidden." And Nietzsche adds at this point a parade of medical opinion that reflects the state of knowledge of the time, or his state of knowledge, as well as the intention of the text:

> It may perhaps lie in some disease of the *nervus sympathicus,* or in an excessive secretion of bile, or in a deficiency of potassium sulfate and phosphate in the blood, or in an obstruction in the abdomen which impedes blood circulation, or in degeneration of the ovaries, and the like.

Readers of Nietzsche's letters appreciate the degree to which he was a dietary crank; but in any case, amateur diagnostic notwithstanding, it is perfectly plain that the disease he was addressing was not of the sort itemized here, but a metadisease which requires of the sufferer that his illness, as Susan Sontag has phrased it, be metaphorical. In any case *ressentiment* consists in re-feeling suffering as the *effect* of a *moral* cause one may also *resent* if one feels it is undeserved. As in the case of Job, whose classic posture is exactly that of resentment in this form, since he can see no *reason* why God should be causing him to suffer. But even if he did feel he deserved the boils and losses, this would still be a case of *ressentiment* because he moralized his suffering.

Religion, save the rather rare case of Job, abolishes all possibility of resentment; but it scarcely abolishes all possibility of *ressentiment,* since in fact it depends upon it for existence: for what does religion do except to teach us that the suffering we endure we also deserve. Religion redirects *ressentiment,* as Nietzsche puts it, by making the patient the very agent he seeks, informing us that we have brought it on ourselves. Consider the Black Death which swept Florence and Sienna in the fourteenth century. Of course it was physiological, but men alive at that time had no way of knowing how: *b. plagus* was not an available concept. But they immediately assumed they were at fault (as they doubtless were in matters of elementary hygiene), chiefly through their arrogance vis-à-vis God, as shown in their treatment of human subjects in painting after Giotto! So the most rational thing, under prevailing theory, was to change the styles of representation, which have been traced for us by Millard Miess. I don't say this was wholly silly, and the consequences could be benign, as when an outbreak of some epidemic in Venice moved the governing body to commission a church from Palladio. True, this did not help any sufferers, but nothing they knew how to do would have done that anyway, and *Il Redentore* still stands. Religion, then, makes suffering intelligible—but only in the framework of a scheme which makes search after its true causes unintelligible. And this is true even in those cases where we ourselves *have* brought on our own suffering, as in the case of gout or obesity, or venereal disease or cirrhosis of the liver or chronic drug addiction: these disorders are the consequences of, they are not *punishments* for, the excesses that led to them.

Interestingly, Nietzsche observes that "this plant blooms best today among the anarchists and the Anti-Semites." That is, blaming the Jews, or blaming the bourgeoisie, for all social ills, rather than looking more deeply into the social structure for proper etiology, parallels the classic forms of the *a priori* of affect. Admittedly, we may know about as much regarding what affects society as Florentines knew in the Cinquecento what affects the human body, and often in our ignorance we attack as cause what may only be another effect. I tend to think that certain accounts by feminists, in which men as men are blamed for the suffering of women as women, must ultimately yield to a finer analysis in which what coarsely is considered a cause of feminine agony is itself a symptom of the same sickness from which they doubtless suffer. I have often thought no better specimen of *schlechtes Gewissen* can be found than the sort of self-castigation shown by men, say in the weekly column "For Men" in *The New York Times* magazine section, where men boast of their degree of feminization. I have no criticism of this, and nothing but criticism of its opposite, where men vaunt the paraphernalia of *machismo*: but it is a good case of self-despising to illustrate that term in Nietzsche's moral psychology. Nietzsche condenses his general insight in one of his profoundest aphorisms: "What really arouses indignation against suffering is not suffering as such but the senselessness of suffering." And if there is any single moral/metaphysical teaching I would ascribe to him, it would be this: suffering really is meaningless, there is no point to it, and the amount of suffering caused by *giving* it a meaning chills the blood to contemplate.

I of course am not talking about suffering we cause under the name of punishment, where some complex balance must be struck between the suffering caused by the culprit and the suffering the culprit must undergo in order to restore equilibrium. That is a model of justice that must be debated on grounds other than any I want to advance here. What Nietzsche objects to is not so much this model but its total generalization, making *every* suffering a punition and the entire *world* a court of justice with a penitentiary annex. If I am right that this is his view, the final aphorism of the *Genealogy*, "man would rather will the *nothing* than *not* will," does not so much heroize mankind, after all. What it does is restate the instinct of *ressentiment*: man would rather his suffering be meaningful, hence would rather will meaning onto it, than acquiesce in the meaninglessness of it. It goes against this instinct to believe what is essentially the most liberating thought imaginable, that life is without meaning. In a way, the deep affliction from which he seeks to relieve us is what today we think of as hermeneutics: the method of interpretation primarily of suffering. And when he says, in so many places and in so many ways, "there are no facts, only interpretation," he is, I believe, finally addressing the deep, perhaps ineradicable propensities of *ressentiment*. Meaning, *si je peux aphoriser moi-même*, is demeaning.

There is an obverse, which is that in order to accept the consolations of religion, the dubious gift of meaning, as it were, one must accept the anthropology which alone makes religion applicable in the first place, namely that we are weak, defective, and almost defined through our propensity to suffer. The limits of man are emphasized as such that we are unable to release ourselves save through the mediation of a being whose power is adequate to the salvation. Of course, with religions in general, the salvation is often from suffering we would not know we had were it not revealed, to a state abstractly defined through the absence of revealed suffering, by means we again would not understand but for revelation. Who would know we were contaminated by original sin, for instance, that we need to be saved from it, and that the means whereby this might be achieved is if God took on a form whereby he might purge our suffering through his? Leaving everything as it was so far as life itself is concerned, since the suffering we were told was ours was not felt, and the redemption we have been given does not connect with release from any felt suffering. And the limits are finally limits only relative to the scheme of suffering and relief erected alongside the actual schedule of human agonies and joys the scheme itself does not penetrate. Whatever the case, the picture of man as limited and weak, if believed, goes hand in hand exactly with *schlechtem Gewissen*. And to release us from that is to release us from the picture: and that is the therapeutic task of the *Genealogy*, and of Nietzsche's philosophical work as such.

Let me return to hermeneutics. I would concede to the continental theorists that it is the fundamental fact of human being, and hence must be the final datum for the human sciences, that men cannot experience without interpreting, and that we live in a world of intersignification. I am far from certain that the human sciences must themselves reflect the structure of their subject, that science itself is only a form of interpretation of a piece with the interpretations it is supposed to study: hence am far from certain that there is a hermeneutical circle which somehow invalidates such a science: for there may be ways of representing interpretations which are not at all of a piece with the interpretations represented. Even so, we may accept the hermeneutical picture that our *esse est interpretari*. But then the contrast must be perfect between ourselves and the *Bestie*, and it is less their cheerful innocent savagery that Nietzsche applauds in the blond beasts than their absolute freedom from meaning. They live, as he says in his early book on history, as beasts do, "in a happy blindness between the walls of the past and the future." Human existence, by deep contrast, is "an imperfect tense that never becomes a present." It is not so much history as the philosophy of history that robs life of happiness, since the latter seeks perennially the significance of events it would be happiness instead merely to forget or, next best, to take as they came, at a kind of absolute magnitude, without forming a kind of text. Nietzsche's doctrine of Eternal Recurrence, itself the topic of so much speculation and scholarship, must be perceived by everyone, however otherwise divided on its cognitive status, as deeply contrary to any philosophy of history: iteration dissolves meaning, and infinite iteration erases it totally. It is a rock against which history as significance must shatter, and in particular religious history, the history of fall, covenant, sin, redemption, trial, judgment, and hell, where it is an unrelieved anxiety as to where we stand and what we can hope.

When Zarathustra announces the death of God, he goes on to say he died of pity. The implication is that what he pitied us for was him: pitied us for the hopeless disproportion between a being of infinite value and his creatures who must in relationship to him be incalculably worthless. By his disappearing, the ratio is broken and the disvalue which depended upon the disproportion itself vanishes. It is a beautiful gift, that of disappearance: which of the parents among us is capable of it? By comparison sacrificing even only begotten sons is easy: our world is full of gold star mothers and fathers, proud of their distinction. With the death of God we are returned to what Kundera speaks of, alas as unbearable: a certain lightness of being.

It is plain that God did not die in order that something else should take his place: rather, he meant for the place to die with the occupant. The genius of the third essay of the *Genealogy* lies in its inventory of disguises the ascetic ideal takes, so that often positions which define themselves as contrary to asceticism only exemplify it. As a class, these occupants of the position vacated by God impose on their subscribers a network of interpretation of suffering, and project a kind of utopian redemption: science, politics, art, and certainly much that passes for psychological therapy only change the name of the game. There are even ways of understanding the notorious concept of the Superman which vest themselves in the same demeaning armature that Christianity did, another disguise of asceticism. But this could not be Nietzsche's Superman if he has the least consistency. The Superman does not reside in a kind of *beyond* since it is precisely that kind of beyond that Nietzsche is bent on stultifying. The man of the future, he writes at the end of the second essay, is "this bell-stroke of man and the great decision that liberates the will again and restores its goal to earth and his hope to man."

I return to the aphorism I began by interpreting. The *unconcern* that wisdom is supposed to love clearly connects with the will. It is an unconcern with goals which imposes a program of choices on life, where these depend on schemes of meaning it is the goal of Nietzsche's philosophy to demolish. It is not so much the extirpation of the will as its reeducation and redirection: its return to the goals of simply normal life. Nietzsche's philosophical mood is one of lightness, cheer, sunniness, which was also his personal mood, heroic in view of his familiar sufferings. He complains of terrible headaches, nausea, stomach ache: he was afflicted by the cold, the damp, bad food, and of course a sense of isolation and unrecognition. He sought like a cat for a comfortable corner of Europe, and the preposterous exultation of his discovery of the alleged salubrities of Turin are an index to his discomforts. He did not suffer, however, in the way in which, on his view, the bulk of mankind suffer: from meanings which truncate the lives they are supposed to redeem. When we contemplate the sufferings human beings have endured in the century since God made the supreme sacrifice, we wonder at the wisdom of that evacuation. If we were to subtract all the intensional suffering from the history of our century, we would subtract the history of the century.

But that is what Nietzsche would like to have achieved: to subtract all those schemes of disvaluation of the present by reference to an inflated valuation of a future; to make the world the place we live rather than pass through to some higher state; to restore the present to the present; to replace a morality of means with a morality of principle; to act in such a way as to be consistent with acting that way eternally; to stultify the instinct for significance. This is the posture of unconcern, and while it is unclear that it would make us altogether happy, it is perfectly plain that it erases most of what has made for human unhappiness through history: the martyrdoms, the crucifixions, the eggs cracked in the name of political omelettes, man as a means. Not surprisingly it is the only view consistent with human dignity, the only view of man as an end.

FOUR

On the Genealogy of Morals—
Nietzsche's Gift

Kathleen Marie Higgins

NIETZSCHE'S *GENEALOGY* AND JAMES BOND

The obsessions of *On the Genealogy of Morals* are reminiscent of Hollywood's contemporary thrillers. In the *Genealogy* Nietzsche concocts a brew of violence and voluptuousness, complete with sadistic thrills, sexual deviants, and multiple murders. This summary might as well advertise a James Bond movie. The pleasures to be experienced through control over other people's bodies is a central motif of both. Like a James Bond movie, the *Genealogy* presents a multifaceted mystery tale that we readers are invited to unravel. And we are, in Nietzsche's book as in the James Bond movie, the voyeurs of the unabashedly vicious, of those who get away with murder—and are even "licensed to kill."

Why, then, is the *Genealogy* so far from a pleasure to read? Perhaps I speak mostly of myself here: the exhilaration of many of Nietzsche's other writings is for me completely unavailable from this work. But surely I am not alone in this. I have been told by other readers that they find the book debilitating. Why does this work weigh so heavily?

Simone Weil suggests an explanation when she tells us, "Imaginary evil is romantic and varied; real evil is gloomy, monotonous, barren, boring."[1] Clearly, the *themes* of the *Genealogy* are not sufficient to produce a sense of bleakness. The sustained popularity of James Bond and Clint Eastwood movies testifies to that—and it vindicates Weil's first contention. Our movies' fantasies of murder with a good conscience—indeed with honor, glory, and sexual ecstasy attached—are a continual source of pleasure. They are also safe. Part of what delights us in the stories set in exotic and mythic places like the Wild West is that they grant our imaginations a license to kill without qualm, to be gluttons of lasciviousness without responsibility.

But Weil's second contention is more apt for our experience of the *Genealogy*. Nietzsche refuses in this book to license our imaginations. Instead, he ensnares them. And he does so by alluding to the very enticements that delight fantasy. He baits our own sadism and voyeurism, drawing us into mythic scenes in distant historical times. But then he reminds us that these unsavory feelings we enjoy are the root of our actual values and concerns—the very ones we take pride in. And this, I think, is the source of the gloom that many experience while reading the *Genealogy*. It is as if we discover, while riding on a roller coaster, that our lives actually are in danger and that we are trapped in the ride. Emotionally preparing us for safety by initial descriptions of people and places that are distant from us, Nietzsche makes us understand that the dangers he describes are his vision of our real situation. And just as we realize that he has trapped us, Nietzsche leaves us to our own devices.[2] He remarks at the close of the *Genealogy*'s first essay: "Whoever begins at this point, like my readers, to reflect and pursue his train of thought will not soon come to the end of it—reason enough for me to come to an end" (GM I:16).

Nietzsche's *Genealogy* can be seen as a kind of mystery thriller. Superficially, it presents accounts of certain oddities of Christian moral behavior. It makes the reader see this behavior as mysterious, and then offers a key to its significance. This is the level on which the mystery of the *Genealogy* is usually discussed and taught.

But the *Genealogy* is a mystery story in less obvious senses as well. On the one hand, we ourselves are made a mystery. Nietzsche raises our consciousness about the perniciousness of our moral psychology, but he does not explain how we might overcome it. The *Genealogy* lands us in a tangled mystery. We can unravel the mystery only by unraveling ourselves. *We* are the characters, perhaps the pawns of this story.

On the other hand, behind the "mysteries" of Christian moral behavior is another mystery—the mystery of Nietzsche's motive. Why does he lead us onward into darkness, and no further? I will suggest that Nietzsche's rhetorical and literary moves offer clues to this mystery, as well as our own final plight. The key to both mysteries is poison.

A TALE OF MORAL POISONINGS

The monotony that Weil associates with real evil is evident in Nietzsche's diction in the *Genealogy*. Recurrently, the same fate befalls those whom Nietzsche discusses. "Poisoned" and "poisonous" are almost refrains throughout the book. Consider for example, the following passages:

> "If only I were someone else," sighs this glance: "but there is no hope of that. I am who I am: how could I ever get free of myself? And yet—*I am sick of*

myself!" It is on such soil, on swampy ground, that every weed, every poisonous plant grows, always so small, so hidden, so false, so saccharine. (GM III:14)

Morality as consequence, as symptom, as mask, as tartufferie, as illness, as misunderstanding; but also morality as cause, as remedy, as stimulant, as restraint, as poison. . . . (GM P:6)

"Which of us would be a free spirit," this free spirit asks, "if the church did not exist? It is the church, and not its poison, that repels us.—Apart from the church, we, too, love the poison.—" (GM I:9)

This triad of passages suggests the range of victims that the *Genealogy's* poisons afflict. One might see this triad as producing an inverse conjugation of poisonings: *They* are poisoned (passage one); *you* (assuming you take yourself to be moral) are poisoned (passage two); *we* (the free spirits) are poisoned (passage three). That Nietzsche intends to include himself among the poisoned free spirits is suggested by his remark, following the third passage: "This is the epilogue of a 'free spirit' to my speech; . . . he had been listening to me till then and could not endure to listen to my silence. For at this point I have much to be silent about" (GM I:9).

The most palatable contexts in which Nietzsche mentions poison are those in which some third person or group is contaminated. And the *Genealogy* is replete with such suggestions. Its "cool, scientific" accounts of slave morality, *ressentiment*, and asceticism are laced with "poisons" as a metaphor for these conditions.[3] For example, "poison" is the metaphor that a "free spirit" uses to summarize the *Genealogy's* master-slave analysis: " 'The masters' have been disposed of; the morality of the common man has won. One may conceive of this victory as at the same time a blood-poisoning . . .—I shan't contradict" (GM I:9). Similarly, Nietzsche describes the paradigmatic spiritual ascetic, the believer who worships "holy God," as one who aims to poison everything:

> In this psychical cruelty there resides a madness of the will which is absolutely unexampled: the will of man to find himself guilty and reprehensible to a degree that can never be atoned for; his will to think himself punished without any possibility of the punishment becoming equal to the guilt; his will to infect and poison the fundamental ground of things with the problem of punishment and guilt so as to cut off once and for all his own exit from this labyrinth of "fixed ideas"; his will to erect an ideal—that of the "holy God"—and in the face of it to feel the palpable certainty of his own absolute unworthiness. On this insane, pathetic beast—man! (GM II:22)

If we ponder these descriptions even a little, we are likely to doubt that they are only third-person reports. Quite a few of us consider ourselves, if not worshippers, at least moral. Nietzsche's descriptions of the poisoned may hit a bit close to home. And as we shall see shortly, he takes pains to ensure that we recognize ourselves.

Poison abounds, as apparently do its victims. But Nietzsche startles with his admission that he is among the poisoned. Besides his provocative claim about his own need to keep silent, he asserts with respect to "us psychologists nowadays" that "probably, we, too, are still victims of and prey to this moralized contemporary taste and ill with it, however much we think we despise it—probably it infects even *us*" (GM III:20). Before we can ascertain the significance of poison of the *Genealogy*, however, we need to determine what Nietzsche is revealing when he claims that he, too, is probably poisoned.

NIETZSCHE AS POISONED

Nietzsche's *Genealogy* is not the first occasion on which he described himself as infected. The preface to the second edition of *The Gay Science* begins with a depiction of himself as convalescing from a disease, and he describes the experience of disease as a precondition to his understanding of philosophy.[4] In *Thus Spoke Zarathustra*, Nietzsche's depiction of Zarathustra being bitten and poisoned by the tarantula against whom he preaches may suggest that Nietzsche sees himself in the similar condition of sharing the poison of the age he criticizes. This image of being bitten by the tarantula recalls an earlier section in which Zarathustra is bitten by a venomous snake.[5] But in the *Genealogy*, Nietzsche directly casts himself as one who, along with both Christians and free spirits of his age, has ingested poison. What are we to make of this?

Three observations can be made here. In the first place, Nietzsche admits that he is probably poisoned. The details of Nietzsche's inner life are left mysterious, more mysterious here than in most of his other writings. But he allows us to treat his discussions in the *Genealogy* as the products of a poisoned mind. No, it is incorrect to say that he *allows* us an *ad hominem* response to his writing. He *demands* that we respond in this way.

Second, Nietzsche suggests that he has reached his current physical condition deliberately. He casts the entire exploration that has led him to write the *Genealogy* as a Dr. Hyde-type experiment.

> I distinguished between ages, peoples, degrees of rank among individuals; I departmentalized my problem; out of my answers there grew new questions, inquiries, conjectures, probabilities—until at length I had a country of my own, a soil of my own, an entire discrete, thriving, flourishing world, like a secret garden the existence of which no one suspected. (GM P:3)

This strategy itself produced disturbing symptoms:

> Whoever sticks with it and *learns* how to ask questions here will experience what I experienced—a tremendous new prospect opens up for him, a new possibility comes over him like a vertigo, every kind of mistrust, suspicion,

fear leaps up, his belief in morality, in all morality, falters—finally a new demand becomes audible. Let us articulate this *new demand*: we need a *critique of moral values, the value of these values themselves must be called in question.* (GM P:6)

While the infection Nietzsche admits to having is most likely not self-inflicted, the symptoms he describes as the result of his experiment are remarkably akin to those produced by the poisons he considers elsewhere. The "poisoned" resentful gaze into a vertiginous well of suspicions:

The suffering . . . scour the entrails of their past and present for obscure and questionable occurrences that offer them the opportunity to revel in tormenting suspicions and to intoxicate themselves with the poison of their own malice: they tear open their oldest wounds, they bleed from long-healed scars, they make evildoers out of their friends, wives, children, and whoever stands closest to them. (GM III:15)

And suspicion is the medium through which infection is transmitted. In discussing "all men of *ressentiment*," Nietzsche asks when they would "achieve the ultimate, subtlest, sublimest triumph of revenge?" The answer:

Undoubtedly if they succeeded in *poisoning the consciences* of the fortunate with their own misery, with all misery, so that one day the fortunate began to be ashamed of their good fortune and perhaps said to one another: "*It is disgraceful to be fortunate: there is too much misery!* " (GM III:14)

But a third observation should be made about Nietzsche's description of his own situation in the *Genealogy.* He insists that his "subterranean" experiences have been a strange good fortune.[6] He concludes his description of the "secret garden" that he has constructed with the exclamation, "—Oh how *fortunate* we are, we men of knowledge, provided only that we know how to keep silent long enough!" (GM P:3). The admonition to keep silent here is reminiscent of alchemy, with its aim of self-transformation. Silence is essential to alchemic methodology, for it ensures the damming up of tremendous pressure, which provides energy to be used in the metamorphosis. But silence is also the harbor of suspicions. A suspicion confessed can be confronted and questioned; but a secret suspicion grows according to its own entelechy. And elsewhere Nietzsche (through Zarathustra) describes this development as itself a poisonous thing: "All truths that are kept silent become poisonous" (Z II:12).

Nietzsche's method here sounds like a recipe for magic of a double sort. One is reminded that the magician's potions include herbs that are both poison and healing, depending on how they are used.[7] What results they have depends on the magician's intentions and power. What kind of sorceror is Nietzsche?

NIETZSCHE THE POISONER

Let us consider the sorcery Nietzsche works upon us. That Nietzsche means to meddle with the reader's psychophysical condition is evident in *Ecce Homo*'s self-congratulatory review of the *Genealogy*. There Nietzsche emphasizes his intention of luring the reader into experiences that are genuinely unnerving:

> Regarding expression, intention, and the art of surprise, the three inquiries which constitute this *Genealogy* are perhaps uncannier than anything else written so far. Dionysus is, as is known, also the god of darkness.
>
> Every time a beginning that is *calculated* to mislead: cool, scientific, even ironic, deliberately foreground, deliberately holding off. Gradually more unrest; sporadic lightning; very disagreeable truths are heard grumbling in the distance—until eventually a *tempo feroce* is attained in which everything rushes ahead in a tremendous tension. In the end, in the midst of perfectly gruesome detonations, a *new* truth becomes visible every time among thick clouds.[8]

Nietzsche describes himself in the *Genealogy* as a malicious musician. He "detonates" his verbal tones as one might detonate a hand grenade, and he manipulates us by means of rhythm, through our very physiology. Although, like a detective writer, Nietzsche draws various threads together into an ultimate tangle, he does not unsnarl it. And the knot we are left with is made up of our own nerves.

At first glance, Nietzsche appears to speak with the voice of demystification in the *Genealogy*. But he describes his analyses' beginnings as "calculated to mislead." They mislead us, I suggest, by concealing the fact that we are being poisoned as we read. We are being poisoned, that is, by Nietzsche.

Of course, much of the manifest content of the *Genealogy* concerns the ways in which our orientation has been poisoned by the worldview of our Christian tradition. I do not intend by what I say here to mitigate the force of this analysis. But I do wish to probe Nietzsche's authorial motive in presenting it. For the analyses of the *Genealogy* are not aimed merely at altering the reader's belief. It will not do simply to accept the fact that one's moral orientation is malignant, any more than it would do simply to accept that one has ingested poison. The only reasonable response is to attempt to undo the damage. If one is poisoned, one is in urgent need of an antidote. Nietzsche obviously intends that readers recognize the urgency of their position.

But instead of offering antidotes, Nietzsche seems bent on further infecting the reader. While tracing the progress of various moral poisons throughout the course of human history, the *Genealogy* contributes to the reader's disease.

In the first place, Nietzsche implicates us in the poisonous projects he describes. Whatever Nietzsche touches here turns to blood. We can avoid indulging our own sadism only be rejecting what is described as distant from us. But to do so is to fall into Nietzsche's trap, to indicate that we ourselves can observe cruelty only with a bad conscience. And if the *Genealogy* describes an earlier history when good conscience accompanied joy in cruelty, its reminders of our own guilt make good conscience, the basis of the desirable master morality, all the farther from us. No enterprise is spared contamination by blood pollution. Our most spiritualized desires were paid for with somebody's blood.

But in arousing the reader's guilt feelings, Nietzsche also effects a second degree of poisoning. For he incites our defenses by attacking us so aggressively. We internally pursue defensive trains of thought that might counter what Nietzsche has told us. But we are unlikely to think our way out of the trap he sets. He has foreseen the strategies we will use to evade his accusations, and seen to it that our strategies themselves will demonstrate the very force of what he alleges. In this, Nietzsche himself seems to instantiate the cruel voyeurism he considers a symptom of Christian hatred. He seems to take pleasure in envisioning the efforts we will make to extricate ourselves from the psychological morass he describes, only to succumb again to some other part of it.

Let us consider the ways we get stuck in the *Genealogy*'s various accounts. Reading the First Essay, we want to deny that we are slavish in our morality. We are inspired to introspect, in an effort to demonstrate that ours is not a slave morality. But as soon as we do so, we are succumbing to slavish tendencies. We care too much what Nietzsche says about us. Moreover, our attempts to deny his charge are likely to conform to the very behaviors that Nietzsche associates with the slave mentality: we compare ourselves to others in order to feel better about ourselves; or we attempt to beat Nietzsche's rap by means of cleverness or concealment.

Nietzsche's accusation in the First Essay itself spurs us to display the very traits that he accuses us of. We see our orientation through his frame, and in this way we see ourselves as impotent. We see ourselves as trapped in patterns dictated by others—and we see ourselves this way by virtue of Nietzsche's own discussion.

We have already considered how Nietzsche makes us see ourselves as guilty as we read the Second Essay. We are guilty of cruelty; for presumably we do discover guilt when we read Nietzsche's lurid, sadistic depictions.

> It seems to me that the delicacy and even more the tartuffery of tame domestic animals (which is to say modern men, which is to say us) resists a really vivid comprehension of the degree to which *cruelty* constituted the great festival pleasure of more primitive men and was indeed an ingredient of almost every one of their pleasures. (GM II:6)

It seems to me that this is tantamount to telling us not to think of elephants. Lest our own imaginations be too cautious, Nietzsche suggests some colorful possibilities.

> In any event, it is not long since princely weddings and public festivals of the more magnificent kind were unthinkable without executions, torturings, or perhaps an auto-da-fé, and no noble household was without creatures upon whom one could heedlessly vent one's malice and cruel jokes. . . . Without cruelty there is no festival: thus the longest and most ancient part of human history teaches—and in punishment there is so much that is *festive!*—" (GM II:6)

Our awareness of our own guilt seems to be part of what Nietzsche is after. By baiting our sadism, he induces us to expose ourselves to our guiltiness. As readers we want to distance ourselves from the bloodthirstiness that he insists characterizes our ancestors and our species. But as soon as we deny the characterization, we are falling into the pattern that he associates with modern humanity: we deny our animal natures; we seek justifications and meanings in every case of pain-affliction that we endorse; or we feel guilty, we turn our lust for cruelty inward. Again, we respond to Nietzsche's accusation by exhibiting to ourselves the very traits of which he accuses us. As soon as we deny our own viciousness, we are impaled by his analysis.

The Third Essay similarly incites us to feel trapped by the ascetic ideal. The reader who has borne with Nietzsche thus far is likely to be one who is willing to entertain "modern" ideas and inclined to scoff at superstitious beliefs and practices. Such an individual might read the beginning of this analysis with some pride, pleased to be immune from the ascetic reasoning that Nietzsche inveighs against. But Nietzsche is again unwilling to let the reader off easily. Already in the passage cited earlier from the First Essay, he has reminded us that the "free spirits" who have denied the church have not escaped its poisonous patterns of thinking. In the Third Essay he is more pointed in his insistence that "modern men" who are enthralled with *Wissenschaft* and its debunking of earlier myths are themselves ascetic in their tenacious faith in knowledge. Those who have turned to *Wissenschaft* in lieu of religious faith are still victimized by the same framework.

> Physiologically, too, science rests on the same foundation as the ascetic ideal: a certain *impoverishment of life* is a presupposition of both of them. . . .
> No! this "modern science"—let us face this fact!—is the *best* ally the ascetic ideal has at present, and precisely because it is the most unconscious, involuntary, hidden, and subterranean ally! (GM III:25)

We may, as readers, try other dodges. But by the end of the essay, Nietzsche has linked every form of fixed idea to the ascetic ideal. He even obstructs the dodge that the self-convicted guilty are apt to take: repentance and the resolve to "never do that again." The psychological value of this move is obvious—one need no longer identify with the guilty "doer of the deed"; one declares that one is no longer the pawn caught in a destructive pattern.

But Nietzsche's retort is that by swearing off our fixed ideas, we've only given in to another absolutism, which amounts to another ground for asceticism. Insofar as we demand some unconditional basis for anything and will sacrifice our own pleasure to this faith, we are ascetics. And insofar as we are forced to recognize ourselves as ascetics, we are again convicted by Nietzsche's analysis. And if we attempted to resist this conclusion (as I think we are bound to do), we have again displayed the very behaviors of which he accuses us.

THE PURPOSES OF POISON

Nietzsche, the self-styled manipulator behind his *Genealogy*, has constructed an ingenious labyrinth for his reader, in which our struggles to escape lead only to our exhaustion. Our struggles, moreover, are efforts of thought. Trains of disturbing realizations are unleashed within us, and we are not given any opportunity for catharsis. These trains of thought themselves become poisonous, secret thoughts that we wish to conceal from everyone, including ourselves. Why has Nietzsche heightened our discomfort? What motivates him as a poisoner?

Poison has many possible uses. It can be a great equalizer, as when a fire ant bites a relatively gigantic human being. With poison, the small can have influence on the great (to put it in Nietzschean language). Is Nietzsche being vindictive here, taking revenge for the resentment that he often acknowledges feeling? This seems a possible but insufficient explanation, particularly since Nietzsche presents himself as sharing the problem of being poisoned. It may be a gain to share his "secret garden" with others. But he himself is bound to be in quest of an antidote—something that sharing poison does not secure.

Perhaps a clue can be found in the temporal character of poison. Poisons have different life spans, and these determine the sorts of use to which the poisons may be put. A fast-acting poison may be used to secure an instant death. But one that is slow in its impact can be used over time to various effects, ranging from torturous to innocuous, and some of which may even be pleasant. Alcohol and other drugs in small amounts can produce a span of pleasant feelings. Certain poisons can even be used medicinally.[9] Moreover, a slow-acting poison, even if deadly, might be neutralized if proper steps are taken.

Clearly, the poisons encountered in Nietzsche's *Genealogy* are slow-acting. The entire history of Christianity is part of the story of the poisoning of

Western consciousness. And Nietzsche has conducted a lengthy experiment of internalizing poisonous trains of thought, the results of which the *Genealogy* records. Moreover, the time it will take us to unravel the various themes of the book and their impact on us is considerable. As Nietzsche puts it, we will "not soon come to an end."

Time, I am convinced, is the key to what positive suggestions emerge from the *Genealogy*. I do not mean that time will "heal the wound" produced by the book. Time is not the typical antidote to the effects of poison. And the slow-acting character of the poisons Nietzsche describes does not offer much hope that thinking it over will resolve the problem.

Nietzsche is suggesting something very different about the value of time for our urgent spiritual problems. Our usual treatment of time, when we operate as thinkers, is to use it as a means to get something secure. But Nietzsche suggests here that this treatment itself is part of our problem. We have allowed ourselves to become poisoned because we have ignored the temporal character of our moral habits. We have become habituated to patterns of thought and behavior that are increasingly poisonous.

Nietzsche may not be entirely benevolent in writing the *Genealogy*. But to the extent that he is screaming "Stop!" in response to our moral habits, his attempt to poison our thinking about ourselves makes sense. He forces us to recognize the poisonous character of our moral perspective by abruptly heightening it. In other words, he plays with our awareness by manipulating our temporality: for the harshness of his accusations moves us to escalate our defense mechanisms so much that we become conscious of them. And having secured our attention to ourselves, Nietzsche has forced us to take the first step toward altering our moral habits. Before we seek an antidote, we need to be aware of the problem.

While I am convinced that this is Nietzsche's chief authorial motive in the *Genealogy*, I think that he offers some suggestions for how we might proceed. Again, he does not spell out particular thoughts that he wants us simply to embrace. But he exerts some influence on our habits by suggesting alternative orientations for our thinking. I shall consider two hints he makes in this direction, both of which concern the importance of temporality for our understanding of ourselves and our resolution of the problematic of the *Genealogy*.

TAKING ONE'S TIME

The first of Nietzsche's hints is that we would do well to become *aware* of temporality, of process in our thinking. This suggestion is the focus of the first remarks he makes in this book. The preface to the *Genealogy* begins with some remarks on our ignorance of ourselves and our experiences. Berating present-day "men of knowledge," Nietzsche insists that "there is one thing alone we really care about from the heart—'bringing something home.'" In other words, we treat the activities leading up to the present as having value only to the extent that they give us some secure bit of knowledge that we might nestle with as we sip a cup of tea in the evening. The product is what counts for us, not the process.

Nietzsche goes on to claim that we don't really even have experiences. "Whatever else there is in life, so-called 'experiences'—which of us has sufficient earnestness for them? Or sufficient time?" (GM P:1). This sounds like an absurdist joke. If we don't have time for our experiences, what *do* we have time for? But this, precisely, is the riddle. We don't *have* time, in that we entirely ignore it. And as a result, we do not come to know ourselves.

> Present experience has, I am afraid, always found us "absent-minded".... Rather, as one divinely preoccupied and immersed in himself into whose ear the bell has just boomed with all its strength the twelve beats of noon suddenly starts up and asks himself: "What really was that which just struck?" so we sometimes rub our ears *afterward* and ask, utterly surprised and disconcerted, "What really was that which we have just experienced?" and moreover: "Who *are* we really?" and, afterward as aforesaid, count the twelve trembling bell-strokes of our experience, our life, our *being*—and alas! miscount them.— So we are necessarily strangers to ourselves. (GM P:1)

What is Nietzsche after? It takes time, he claims, to have a real experience. And it is his own experience that Nietzsche aims to pass along, not his conclusions. We can recall his claim that "whoever sticks with it and *learns* how to ask questions here will experience what I experienced." An experience of genuine self-awareness requires that we recognize what habits have grown up with us. The *Genealogy*'s analyses concern precisely such habits—habits of taking pleasure in cruelty by means of morality; of feeling guilty and slavish in our self-assessments; of affirming the ascetic ideal, however "modern" one is in one's disguises. And these are not the kind of projects that one can simply step out of by adopting "better" beliefs. These habits are slow-working poisons that can be overcome only through the practice of constructing better habits. But this is a process that we must "have time" for. Nietzsche, by wounding us, gives us a sense of the time.[10]

Thus the trains of thought he incites, cruel as they may be, are essential if we are to have any hope of recovering from poison. And in order to understand what must be done, we need to engage in the process of digesting whatever our systems will tolerate. Nietzsche overtly discusses what is required to digest our experiences thoroughly: "Something for which one has almost to be a cow and in any case *not* a 'modern man': *rumination*" (GM P:8).

But digestion, Nietzsche also points out, is something that does not need to enter consciousness. Active repression, forgetfulness, is essential to the psychic process of digestion. This forgetfulness is what forges a "present" for us. And without it, a person "cannot 'have done' with anything" (GM II:1). Digestion is indeed the ideal way to deal with disturbing insights, including the unsightly truths that Nietzsche forces to our awareness. "All of this is interesting, to excess, but also of a gloomy, black, unnerving sadness, so that one must forcibly forbid oneself to gaze too long into these abysses" (GM II:22). The ultimate goal, then, is to "have done with them."

But at this point, Nietzsche's own poisoning project gets in the way. Our consciousness aroused, we are not easily able to just "have done with" the traumatic trains of thought now whirling in our minds. What we cannot get over by thinking requires another remedy. The antidote necessary is one toward which Nietzsche hints at odd moments in the *Genealogy*, and again it involves a conscious awareness of temporality. This odd antidote is comedy.

THE MORAL COMEDY

Nietzsche closes his preface with some comments on the difficulty some readers may have with the *Genealogy*, and concludes that "the fault . . . is not necessarily mine" (GM II:22). He proceeds to mimic Schopenhauer by demanding that his readers be prepared for this work by already having digested all his previous writings.[11] But he also suggests a motive for giving the book the time he requires. Of the problems of morality, he submits,

> there seems to be nothing *more* worth taking seriously, among the rewards for it being that some day one will perhaps be allowed to take them *cheerfully*. For cheerfulness—or in my own language *gay science*—is a reward: the reward of a long, brave, industrious, and subterranean seriousness, of which, to be sure, not everyone is capable. But on the day we can say with all our hearts, "Onwards! our old morality too is part *of the comedy!*" we shall have discovered a new complication and possibility for the Dionysian drama of "The Destiny of the Soul"—and one can wager that the grand old eternal comic poet of our existence will be quick to make use of it! (GM P:7)

Are we actually supposed to see a hint of comedy in all this? Even the possibility that something might be funny here? Nietzsche does tend to associate comedy with hilarity. In *The Gay Science* he had compared tragic ages, when people seek purposes, to comic ages, characterized by "waves of uncountable laughter" (GS 1). And indeed he insinuates this possibility again at the end of the *Genealogy*:

> Enough! Enough! Let us leave these curiosities and complexities of the most modern spirit, which provoke as much laughter as chagrin. . . . All I have been concerned to indicate here is this: in the most spiritual sphere, too, the ascetic ideal has at present only *one* kind of real enemy capable of *harming* it: the comedians of this ideal—for they arouse mistrust of it. (GM III:27)

Nietzsche's sense of humor in such remarks seems more than a little odd. Even as serious as he always seems to be, the *Genealogy* is abnormally sullen. What could he possibly see as funny here?

The tone of his remarks actually suggests that he *doesn't* see anything very funny here. For he speaks hopefully of "one day" taking these things cheerfully. Nietzsche himself is, as he confesses, poisoned and still digesting. But he is also like Moses seeing the Promised Land—he knows which way to lead.

And the direction Nietzsche suggests we travel is in the direction of comedy. He might not be able to do this himself, as he still stares down abysses. But he suggests that after ruminating and thereby opening our own abysses, we suddenly stand back from our previous experiences and their disturbing patterns and recognize their nonsense. And indeed, the *Genealogy* prepares us to consider our moral habits nonsensical. To the extent that Nietzsche has forced us to recognize in ourselves the traits he analyzes in the book, he has given us a preliminary experience of their nonsense. We see that they are self-sabotaging, and that they motivate us to ludicrous and self-perpetuating extremes of slavishness, guilt, and asceticism.

Our way out is not, as it might seem, thinking our way further into the labyrinth. We have to think in order to recognize the extent of the problem; but thinking is not the ultimate means of our escape. Instead, we must step back from the whole span of time over which we've developed our pernicious habits—laughing at their foolishness.

Again, tactic is a matter of consciously attending to the temporal character of our moral development. The ludicrous pattern emerges only when we recognize the repetition of the same self-destructive motifs through a whole span of experience. We need to see ourselves behaving through time in order to have the one experience that really involves stepping out of time: the experience of laughter.

Laughter is the ultimate cathartic that can alleviate our overly poisoned systems. Having himself contributed to our excessively poisoned state, Nietzsche leaves us to laugh it out. Only by creating distance from our previous temporal habits can we begin new ones. And only laughter will achieve for us the position from which we can, like *Zarathustra*'s child (Z I:1), mirthfully begin again.[12]

NOTES

1. Simone Weil, "Evil," in *Gravity and Grace*, trans. Emma Craufurd (London: Routledge & Kegan Paul, 1952), pp. 62–63.

2. See *On the Genealogy of Morals*, trans. Walter Kaufmann and R. J. Hollingdale (together with *Ecce Homo*, trans. Walter Kaufmann) (New York: Random House, 1967), third essay, section 24. There Nietzsche describes his meditations on the

motto of the Order of the Assassins, "Nothing is true, everything is permitted," as "labyrinthine."

3. *Ecce Homo,* trans. Walter Kaufmann (together with *On the Genealogy of Morals,* trans. Walter Kaufmann and R. J. Hollingdale) (New York: Random House, 1967), p. 312.

4. *The Gay Science,* trans. Walter Kaufmann (New York: Random House, 1974). "A philosopher who has traversed many kinds of health, and keeps traversing them, has passed through an equal number of philosophies; he simply *cannot* keep from transposing his states every time into the most spiritual form and distance: this art of transfiguration *is* philosophy" (GS P:3).

5. *Thus Spoke Zarathustra,* in *The Portable Nietzsche,* trans. and ed. Walter Kaufmann (New York: Viking Press, 1968), p. 214 (Z II:7, "On the Tarantulas"). This is not the only instance of Zarathustra's being bitten and poisoned. In the section "On the Adder's Bite" in Part I of *Zarathustra,* an adder bites Zarathustra while he is sleeping. The adder in this case responds to Zarathustra's scolding ("But take back your poison. You are not rich enough to give it to me.") and licks the poison out of the wound (Z I:19, pp. 179–180). In Part II of *Zarathustra,* where the section "On the Tarantulas" appears, Zarathustra does not fare so well. For a consideration of Zarathustra's relationship to Nietzsche's own psyche, see C. G. Jung, *Nietzsche's Zarathustra: Notes on the Seminar Given in 1934–1939,* ed. James L. Jarrett, 2 vols., Bollingen Series 99 (Princeton: Princeton University Press, 1988).

6. See GM P:7, where he describes his procedure as having involved a "subterranean seriousness."

7. Compare Jacques Derrida, "Plato's Pharmacy," in *Dissemination* (Chicago: Chicago University Press, 1981), pp. 70–75.

8. EH III, p. 312.

9. Again, see Derrida, "Plato's Pharmacy," pp. 70–75.

10. Arthur Danto analyzes Nietzsche's methodology as one of wounding in order to ensure remembrance. See Arthur C. Danto, "Some Remarks on *The Genealogy of Morals,*" in *Reading Nietzsche,* ed. Robert C. Solomon and Kathleen M. Higgins (New York: Oxford University Press, 1988), pp. 13–28. (A version of this essay may also be found in this volume.)

11. Schopenhauer similarly insists, in the preface to volume 1 of *The World as Will and Representation,* that in addition to being familiar with his *On the Four-fold Root of the Principle of Sufficient Reason,* the reader should read the present book twice, since the beginning's sense depends as much on the end as vice versa.

12. See also GS 382 and 383, the "Epilogue" of the fifth book of GS—written just prior to GM. (Ed.)

FIVE

The Return of the Master
An Interpretation of Nietzsche's
Genealogy of Morals

Richard White

I

Nietzsche has taught us to be wary of origins, and to despise every account which recalls "the origin" as the ideal moment of some essential value or truth. In the very first aphorism of *Human, All Too Human*, for example, he exposes the glorification of the origin as a metaphysical subterfuge: for he claims that one evades all the complex problems of historical emergence— "How did reason come from unreason, or altruism from egoism, or disinterested contemplation from out of covetous desire?"—when one assumes the conceptual and historical priority of the favored term as a privileged origin which precedes all dissociation.

In *On the Genealogy of Morals*, Nietzsche tells us a story of masters and slaves to describe the origin of our most basic moral values. But given his earlier strictures against "the origin," I think we have good reason to maintain an ironic distance from Nietzsche's account. Even though Nietzsche seems to praise the master far more highly than the slave, we cannot read the *Genealogy* as if it were a straightforward historical narrative which laments a lost origin. Nietzsche certainly does use the conflict of master and slave as an analogue to specific historical situations—where, for example, the triumph of Christianity over the classical ideal is said to embody the triumph of the slave. But as I will suggest, in a deeper sense the terms "master" and "slave" refer to basic modalities of individual existence, and in this respect they are "types" which still concern us all.

In fact, Nietzsche makes it clear from the very beginning of the *Genealogy* that in this inquiry the issue of the origin is entirely subordinate to the issue of value. And so he poses his guiding question as follows:

Under what conditions did man devise these value judgments good and evil? *And what value do they themselves possess?* Have they hitherto hindered or furthered human prosperity? Are they a sign of distress, of impoverishment, of the degeneration of life? Or is there revealed in them, on the contrary, the plenitude, force, and will of life, its courage, certainty, future? (GM P:3)

Such fundamental questions require us to re-view the whole horizon of morality "as if with new eyes." Nietzsche must wrench us free from our established perspectives, and confound all our moral prejudice. Precisely because of this, he returns to the "origin" of morality—not to legitimate contemporary values ("in the fashion of the English"), but, as he says, to pose them as a problem for the very first time.

In this respect, Nietzsche *uses* the story of the master and slave in order to suggest a *double* origin of value: the master is the one who celebrates life as it shines forth in his existence, by consecrating his instinctual power as something "good"; the slave is the one who suffers this discharge of strength, though he finally revenges himself in the revaluation of all active instincts as "evil," and his own passivity as "goodness." Following the guiding thread of his philology, Nietzsche suggests that there cannot be an "original" or "true" designation of value since the master and the slave must always evaluate the world in entirely different ways.[1] Then, in the rest of the *Genealogy*, Nietzsche goes on to detail the history of the West as the history of the slave's triumph, in which all the "active" forces of life have been negated or suppressed. As he comments: "The masters have been disposed of; the morality of the common man has won" (GM I:10). Indeed, he argues that the master has not only been defeated: Because he has lost his original voice the master has been condemned to silence, and this means that the very possibility of "mastery" has been forgotten. Thus, everything now hides the *exclusion* of the master: art, religion, morality, even science, which comprehends the world with entirely "slavish" categories like "reaction" and "adaptation," "struggle" and "universal law."[2]

In what follows, I will show how in describing the victory of the slave, Nietzsche's strategy in the *Genealogy* is to force us to undertake a *recollection* of the master. This is not to say that the *Genealogy* must be understood as a careful work of scholarship which simply aims to put the record straight. In the Third Essay, Nietzsche rejects all scholarly pretensions when he suggests that interpretation is always a matter of violence, "forcing, adjusting, abbreviating, omitting, padding, inventing, falsifying and whatever else" (GM III:24). He also describes himself as "the comedian of the ideal," and though he uses the mask of the scholar it is only to explode the sober horizons of all traditional scholarship. Instead, I think it is more helpful to understand the *Genealogy* as a type of "performative critique," where in accordance with the second *Untimely Meditation*, Nietzsche uses his reading of the past in order to direct us towards a particular vision of the future.[3] Nietzsche uses genealogy to recall the forgotten position of the master; he describes the logic of history which suggests the imminence of the slave's final victory; and he attempts to inspire us with an urgent longing for "the master's return."

In this interpretation of *On the Genealogy of Morals*, I will first discuss the proper significance of Nietzsche's account of masters and slaves. I will then examine the details of the slave's triumph, to see how this has been achieved through the "artistry" and cunning of the priest. Finally, this will allow me to consider Nietzsche's own position vis-à-vis the *Genealogy* as a philosopher and legislator of the future. And in this respect, I will attempt to determine what the *return* of the master might *mean*, and how, according to Nietzsche, it provides us with an alternative ideal which can overcome the historical dominion of nihilism.

II

Nietzsche's profound veneration of the heroes and philosophers of Ancient Greece gives place, within his writings, to the distinction between masters and slaves as examples of basic types of the Will to Power. This is by no means an "exact" criterion, but it allows Nietzsche to consider an individual like Goethe as a master-type, insofar as the latter achieved complete sovereignty in the organization of all his natural impulses; while it allows him to condemn someone like Eugen Dühring as the prototypical slave, who is driven by disaffection and longing for revenge.[4] Similarly, though on a larger scale, the Attic culture of tragedy is held to represent the true "nobility" of culture, as the controlled expression of all the powers of life within the unifying context of Apollo and Dionysus; while the triumph of Christianity, or the French Revolution, represent the vengeance of the slave as the annihilation of all difference and privilege of soul.

In the First Essay of the *Genealogy*, Nietzsche clarifies this basic typology of masters and slaves within the context of a mythical prehistory. Here, he describes the noble master as a man of "overflowing health," who celebrates all of the instinctual powers of life in the constant turmoil of "war, adventure, hunting, dancing, war games, and in general all that involves vigorous, free, joyful activity" (GM I:7). Such an individual, living "in complete trust and openness with himself," does not seek to preserve or justify his life. Indeed, when he is free of the usual social constraints he abandons himself to the ferocious forces inside him, and discharges all of his strength in "a disgusting procession of murder, arson, rape, and torture . . . as if it were no more than a student's prank" (GM I:11). As the victim of these unconscious cruelties, the slave is one of the peace-loving herd who simply does not have the power to resist. Because he lacks every outlet, his suffering feeds upon itself as he is forced to experience his own weakness over and over again; until eventually, such *re-sentiment* is established as memory, which allows him to calculate his own revenge.

Having established this distinction, Nietzsche then demonstrates how in a variety of different languages the words which are used to designate "good" and "bad" are all derived from words which express the self-affirmation of the master, or his indifferent contempt for the slave. The Latin *bonus*, for example, is said to derive from *duonus*, which signifies a man of war, while *malus* stems from *melas*, which designates the common man as "the dark-colored one." Likewise, the German *gut* means "godlike" or "the man of godlike race," which probably signifies the original significance of the Goths; while in Gaelic, the word *fin* came to mean "good" through its apparent association with "the fair-haired," who were the Celtic conquerors of the native dark-haired population (GM I:4, 5). By multiplying such examples, Nietzsche's ultimate aim is to show that value can have another meaning than one of simple utility. We may be accustomed to thinking of "the good" as equivalent to whatever is "useful," or perhaps to what all men could affirm without contradiction. But if we accept Nietzsche's philology, it now appears that at the very start of history, or the origin of language itself, "good" is the name and celebration of life as it appears in its most powerful exemplars. Hence, in a complementary section of *Beyond Good and Evil* Nietzsche insists that this "protomorality" is not oriented toward the self-preservation of the individual but the self-glorification of life: "The noble type of man experiences *itself* as determining values, . . . it knows itself to be that which first accords honour to things; it is *value-creating*. Everything it knows as part of itself it honours: such a morality is self-glorification" (BGE 260).

But how are we to understand this parable of masters and slaves? If Nietzsche's philology is correct then it *is* the forgotten master who expresses the most primordial meaning of value: and in this way he *recalls* us. And yet, while the noble master is an attractive and compelling figure in many respects, it also seems clear that Nietzsche deliberately *destroys* the possibility of our identification with him, by stressing his most horrible aspect as a murderous "beast of prey." Similarly, though the servility of the slave invites our contempt, Nietzsche also reminds us that without the slave, man would have remained an entirely stupid creature, and that all the achievements of our culture actually derive from the internalization of his suffering. In short, we must conclude that neither the master nor the slave are intended as simple ideals.

In a significant passage, Nietzsche suggests elsewhere that the democratization of Europe represents nothing other than the irreversible *mixing* of master and slave races: "In accordance with the slowly arising democratic order of things (and its cause, the intermarriage of masters and slaves), the originally noble and rare urge to ascribe value to oneself on one's own and to 'think well' of oneself will actually be encouraged"; and he concludes, "It is 'the slave' in the blood of the vain person, a residue of the slave's craftiness—and how much 'slave' is still residual in woman, for example!—that seeks to seduce him to good opinions about himself" (BGE 261). While in a similar sense he once declared that it would be "the surest sign of commonness" to be related to one's parents.[5] Clearly, in such passages Nietzsche is using the language of race and heredity in order to describe something which transcends the narrowly biological. And indeed, I would suggest that the whole dialectic of master and slave must also proceed along the same "psychohistorical" or "psychodramatic" register: Of course, there are *no* pure masters and slaves, because the races have been mixed, and probably they *always were* mixed. Nevertheless, Nietzsche wants to isolate and typify these two principles, because the conflict between master and slave must always continue within the individual life as well as in history itself.

Thus in section 18 of the Second Essay, Nietzsche actually describes the creative imposition of form upon one's own animal nature as exactly similar to the master's own unconscious imposition upon the unfortunate slave:

> Fundamentally it is the same active force that is at work on a grander scale in those artists of violence and organizers who build states, and that here, internally, on a smaller and pettier scale, directed backward, in the "labyrinth of the breast" . . . creates for itself a bad conscience and builds negative ideals—namely the *instinct for freedom* (in my language: the Will to Power); only here the material upon which the form-giving and ravishing nature of this force vents itself is man himself, his whole ancient animal self—and *not*, as in that greater and more obvious phenomenon, some *other* man, *other* men. This secret self-ravishment, this artists' cruelty, this delight in imposing a form upon oneself . . . eventually . . . this . . . brought to light an abundance of strange new beauty and affirmation, and perhaps beauty itself. (GM II:18)

Once we allow ourselves to go beyond the fable of a *literal* prehistory—though as Nietzsche says, "this *is* present in *all* ages"(GM II:9)—the guiding question is no longer, "How can the individual abrogate his own conscience and attachment to society in order to recover himself as a spontaneous and instinctual being?" but "How can the individual reaffirm and celebrate the original happiness of the master, given a society which has always been the effective instrument of the slave's success?" Through attention to etymology, Nietzsche has reawakened the essential possibility of the Master—and now we are called to confer a meaning upon the master's return, to change the direction of history with the meaning of our slavish life.

In fact, if we read the story of the master and slave on this psychohistorical level it is relatively easy to comprehend them as the fragments of a single identity. In an obvious respect, for example, the master is simply the embodiment of pure *activity*—as Nietzsche remarks: "[His] work is an instinctive creation and imposition of forms," (GM II:17) while the slave seems purely suffering and *passive*. But more crucially still, I think we can also understand the master as the expression of an ideal and unmediated *autonomy:* the master creates and affirms himself in everything he does, but exactly like Kant's God, he is not commanded to good actions because everything he does is *ipso facto* a creation of "the good."[6] In like manner, the slave is supposed to be powerless and ruled by *ressentment*, and this implies that his actions are entirely determined by a principle of sensibility. His revenge against the master, and his denial of the active powers of man suggest that he is the embodiment of "heteronomy," insofar as his will is always determined from outside itself.

If we follow this suggestion, then the question of the master's return becomes equivalent to the question of autonomy—not within its Kantian context of "reason" and adherence to the categorical imperative, but in a broader "Nietzschean" context of "life." So that, given the victory of the slave, and Nietzsche's diagnosis of "the degeneration and diminution of man into the perfect herd animal" (BGE 203), our guiding question becomes: "How can the individual affirm himself as an *autonomous* individual, given a society that has steadily suppressed all active forces, and thus established will-lessness, or *self*-denial, as the dominant moment of contemporary life?" In order to answer this, however, we must first rehearse the details of the slave's revenge, since this will illuminate Nietzsche's alternative ideal. More specifically, we must consider the tactics of the "priest," who as the guardian and director of the slave establishes himself, within the *Genealogy,* as Nietzsche's own counterprinciple, and his most dangerous enemy.

III

In the Second and Third Essays of the *Genealogy,* Nietzsche seeks to show how the historical dominion of the slave has been strengthened and brought to its most incredible forms through the supreme artistry of the Judaco-Christian priest. And, as a necessary moment of his own "counterartistry," Nietzsche exposes the various strategems which the priest has used in order to maintain the most complete enslavement of man—characterizing Christianity in general as "a great treasure house of ingenious means of consolation, . . . a collection of refreshments, palliatives and narcotics" (GM III:17). Nietzsche argues that while the priest has seduced the slave by providing some meaning for his suffering, all of his so-called "remedies" have only weakened the slave, and ensured his continued enfeeblement.

To make us fully aware of the priest's own cunning and artistry in guilt, Nietzsche provides us from time to time with the elements of a "natural history of society," which functions within the *Genealogy* as a kind of ideal correlate.[7] In the first sections of the Second Essay, for example, he claims that the proper *result* of society is the "sovereign individual," and that this "autonomous" individual is capable of commanding his own nature because he has learned how to promise himself, in sustaining his will over a period of time. Nietzsche argues, moreover, that such an individual can only emerge after a long process of social training in which the *slavish* qualities of memory and calculation are steadily branded into his soul. Similarly, he stresses that "the bad conscience," is the inevitable outcome of man's confinement within society, and the consequent redirection of his cruelty against himself. Though as we have seen, he describes this happening as an *active* bad conscience, and he suggests that it is the origin of all beauty, and even justice, since it can lead to the overcoming of *ressentiment* (GM II:11). It is clear, then, that Nietzsche does not regard society itself as an "original evil," for both here and in *Beyond Good and Evil* he valorizes the submission to law as "the categorical imperative of nature," and the only means by which individual sovereignty is achieved.

On the other hand, when Nietzsche considers the *priestly appropriation* of bad conscience—as a morbid consciousness of guilt before God and total self-disgust—he argues that it is precisely *this* which has produced "the most terrible sickness that has ever raged in man." According to Nietzsche, the priest turns the individual will against itself, not in order to bring about a sovereign self-control, but rather self-laceration and the mortification of the will through guilt. As he comments:

> This man of the bad conscience has seized upon the presupposition of religion so as to drive his self-torture to its most gruesome pitch of severity and rigor. Guilt before God: this thought becomes an instrument of torture to him. He apprehends in "God" the ultimate antithesis of his own ineluctable animal instincts; he reinterprets these animal instincts themselves as a form of guilt before God (as hostility, rebellion, insurrection against the "Lord," the "father," the primal ancestor and origin of the world); he stretches himself upon the contradiction "God" and "Devil"; he ejects from himself all his denial of himself, of his nature, naturalness, and actuality, in the form of an affirmation, as something existent, corporeal, real, as God, as the holiness of God, as God the Judge, as God the Hangman, as the beyond, as eternity, as torment without end, as hell, as the immeasurability of punishment and guilt. (GM III:22)

In this respect the story of Christ the Redeemer must be considered as a real "stroke of genius." For if Christ's sacrifice is a debt that can *never* be repaid, then it must follow that we are all eternally guilty. Henceforth, we have to consider ourselves as the creatures of sin, and the only possible release from our suffering and guilty existence is through ascetic denial or the destruction of our individual will. In effect, the priest directs us to use our power to destroy our power; he explains the "meaning" of our unhappy suffering (when the latter is just the impotence of the slave and his basic physiological depression); and his "ministry" is to make us forget this pain, by forgetting ourselves.

In the Third Essay, Nietzsche goes on to describe the whole variety of ascetic ideals and practices which the priest has promoted to preserve a declining life, and to ensure its continued sickness. Thus he relates the "innocent" forms of the ascetic ideal which tend toward "self-narcosis" and allow the slave to avoid the reproach which his own existence offers him. In this category are the hermit's fasting and withdrawal from life, complete immersion in some form of mechanical activity like work, and "petty devotion to others"—an involvement in the communal life of the herd which allows the individual to forget "himself" in the shadow of something grander. More dramatically, Nietzsche then reviews the "guilty" forms of asceticism: the penitent's scourge, the hair shirt and starving body, and the dancing epidemics of the Middle Ages. He claims that all of these "remedies" sought to deaden man's secret suffering through the production of an orgy of feeling—although their final effect has only been to weaken man even further.

At the end of the *Genealogy*, Nietzsche turns to the state of contemporary scholarship, to argue that in modern times yet another version of the ascetic ideal has become dominant: one that is manifest by the scholar's unselfish devotion to the "truth," for which he is ready to sacrifice anything, including himself. Thus he talks of "the proficiency of our finest scholars, their heedless industry, their heads smoking day and night, their very craftsmanship," and he comments: "How often the real meaning of all this lies in the desire to keep something hidden from oneself! Science as a means of self-narcosis: do you have experience of that?" (GM III:23). We should notice, however, that the ascetic ideal of the scholar is definitely *not* a function of his religious belief. Indeed, in several passages Nietzsche emphasizes that such a total devotion to "the truth" eventually leads every good scholar *away* from the lie which supports belief in God; and in this respect, the will to truth brings about the complete self-overcoming of Christianity and Christian morality.[8] Hence, in promoting *this* form of asceticism, Nietzsche's priest must survive the abandonment of explicitly religious forms. It follows that he is more than the representative of a particular religion, or even the avatar of religion as such. And, while Nietzsche uses the *Genealogy* to uncover various strategies and disguises which the priest has used in the past, we are brought to realize that we cannot expect the latter to appear in the same (religious) masks he has always worn before. In this way, Nietzsche suggests the necessity for a continual "revision" of the *Genealogy*, for the priest can always assume new masks, though the ultimate effect of his machinations will always be the same.

Finally, then, as the heirs to all of the priest's disastrous remedies, Nietzsche gives us to understand that the overall tendency of the priestly ideal has actually been to "diminish" man completely, and to turn him into a "timid" herd animal. And he concludes that the continual suppression of the individual will has its issue in "will-lessness" as the basic characteristic of modern life:

> We can no longer conceal from ourselves *what* is expressed by all that willing which has taken its direction from the ascetic ideal: this hatred of the human, and even more of the animal, and more still of the material, this horror of the senses, of reason itself, this fear of happiness and beauty, this longing to get away from all appearance, change, becoming, death, wishing, from longing itself—all this means—*a will to nothingness*, an aversion to life, a rebellion against the most fundamental presuppositions of life. (GM III:28)

And again,

> the diminution and leveling of European man constitutes *our* greatest danger. . . . We can see nothing today that wants to grow greater, we suspect that things will continue to go down, down to become thinner, more good natured, more prudent, more comfortable, more mediocre, more indifferent, more Chinese, more Christian—there is no doubt that man is getting "better" all the time. Here precisely is what has become a fatality for Europe—together with the fear of man we have also lost our love of him, our reverence for him, our hopes for him, even the will to him. The sight of man now makes us weary—what is nihilism today if it is not that?—*We are weary of man.* (GM I:12)

Genealogy has revealed the will to nothingness as the fundamental will of history, and Nietzsche equates this will to nothingness, this "last will of man," with the progress of *nihilism* which now becomes explicit. In other words, the meaning of nihilism is nothing other than the triumph of the slave and the continued destruction of the individual as such. And, as the artist of such a history the priest is finally revealed as the world-historical agent of nihilism itself.

It follows that "the *return* of the master" corresponds to the overcoming of nihilism, with the destruction of the priest in history, and the slave within ourselves. For in the celebration of an *active* will to self-empowerment, the master provides us with a new ideal that opposes the will to nothingness, and may even reverse it. And, as this conflict continues—with Nietzsche against the priest, the master against the slave, and *Dionysus versus the Crucified*—I shall turn, finally, to Nietzsche's attempt at a legislation of the future.

IV

I have argued that for Nietzsche the essential meaning of nihilism is the destruction of the individual will as an active and distinctive power. In the final analysis, nihilism is to be identified with the will to nothingness—and this is a will not to have to will, which craves its release from willing. Hence, Nietzsche's ideal of "autonomy" may be understood as the most extreme counterthought to nihilism, since the autonomous will, the will of the master, is precisely the one which celebrates and affirms itself in the joy of self-creation. Simply put, if nihilism is the will *not* to will, then autonomy is nothing but the will to will.

Of course, Nietzsche was fully aware of the antipodal nature of these themes, primarily in the symbolic opposition of master and slave, but also in his continual exhortation of the individual will in the face of a growing will-lessness. In *Beyond Good and Evil,* for example, he diagnoses the sickness of modern Europe as a "paralysis of will" suggesting that as the modern individual grows ever "smaller" and more similar, his will becomes the victim of "a new European Buddhism." For Nietzsche, writing as a "philosopher of the future" and not merely as a cultural critic, the only possible remedy is to recreate those conditions which might produce a *sovereign* will.[9] And in this respect, his analysis of history is itself an attempt to force the direction of the future.

Thus, as we have seen, in the *Genealogy* Nietzsche envisages the bearer of this sovereign will—or the "sovereign individual"—as the longed-for justification of history: through the long and bloody training of culture, a will is created which must eventually appropriate its slavish presuppositions, and achieve the total commandment of its own existence. And Nietzsche argues that such a will finally secures the freedom of "autonomy":

> If we place ourselves at the end of this tremendous process, where the tree at last brings forth the fruit, where society and the morality of custom at last reveal *what* they have simply been the means to: then we discover that the ripest fruit is the *sovereign individual,* like only to himself, liberated again from morality of custom, autonomous and supramoral (for "autonomous" and "moral" are mutually exclusive), in short, the man who has his own independent, protracted will and the *right to make promises*—and in him a proud consciousness, quivering in every muscle, of *what* has at length been achieved and become flesh in him, a consciousness of his own power and freedom, a sensation of mankind come to completion. (GM II:2)

This "sovereign individual" is the one who orders and overcomes all of that brutal "accident" which constitutes his own prehistory or past. In this respect, he is capable of pledging himself as the master of his own future; for as the one who possesses a *commanding* will, he alone has acquired the right to "make promises."

Now we may accept that for obvious reasons, Nietzsche's only direct presentation of the master's return is through such fragments and moments of evocation as the passage quoted above. Indeed, it could be argued that any account of autonomy is necessarily "suggestive" and incomplete, since autonomy, as the sovereignty of the individual as such, is precisely that which must exceed all conceptual determinations. Following Nietzsche's earlier work, Zarathustra comes to realize that the commander of a new will can only teach by the example of his own life, but never by prescription. Even so, there is still another important objection, for at first glance it seems that Nietzsche's account of history gains its most compelling power through a "dialectical" sleight-of-hand: First, the powerful master tyrannizes the slave and makes him suffer; then the calculating slave subdues the master through the ploy of a revaluation of values; and finally, now that the slave's triumph is almost complete, we are made to anticipate the master's return as the final synthesis of two opposing moments—following exactly the same logic of *The Birth of Tragedy*, where the "music-practising Socrates" is scheduled to appear only when spiritual conditions in Europe have reached their lowest ebb.

Such a reading, however, would only obliterate the very deep awareness that Nietzsche had of the complete chance and fortuity of human events and human history. As he says, the creation of the bad conscience was "a lucky dice throw," and the domination of the ascetic ideal an incredible "accident" which only occurred because no other ideals were proposed over the past two thousand years. In this sense, Nietzsche writes of history as "a game in which no hand, and not even a finger, of God took part as a player" (BGE 203). Thus, if there is any kind of "teleology" in the *Genealogy*, I would have to say that it belongs to Nietzsche's counterartistry, as a strategy to compel us toward the recollection of the master, but always within the deliberately *irreal* context of a mythological history.

On the other hand, it is also clear that there is no *final* teleology or destiny at work in this text. For just as Nietzsche gave us a double origin of good and evil at the beginning, so at the end he offers the possibility of two different conclusions to our history, which allow us to choose how the story will end. The first suggestion is that we must be headed for the final victory of the slave; as the triumph of the tame man, the "maggot man" who has destroyed every distinction of "rank." Here, Nietzsche suggests that the spur of ideals will soon become unnecessary as everyone will be "content" with his lot; and the utter will-lessness of the last man will thus inspire only nausea and pity: "Suppose these two were one day to unite, they would inevitably beget one of the uncanniest monsters: the 'last will' of man, his will to nothingness, nihilism. And indeed a great deal points to this union" (GM III:14).

In opposition to such a gloomy prediction, however, Nietzsche uses a figure like "the sovereign individual" in order to awaken us to the possibility of a different future. And this is his evocation of the master's return:

> This man of the future who will redeem us not only from the hitherto reigning ideal but also from that which was bound to grow out of it, the great nausea, the will to nothingness, nihilism; this bell-stroke of noon and of the great decision that liberates the will again and restores its goal to the earth and his hope to man; this Antichrist and antinihilist; this victor over God and nothingness—he must come one day. (GM II:24)

Nietzsche clearly believed that with the "unraveling" of the death of God, and the questioning of all ideals that have hitherto inspired us, mankind stood at a crossroads. The logic of history suggests his final decline, but the *Genealogy* shows that another outcome is possible. Indeed, Nietzsche's text is itself an attempt to produce that different future: it is a *performative* critique insofar as it aims to inspire the individual with the promise of the master's return.

In this respect, I would suggest that Nietzsche's philosophical activity in the *Genealogy* corresponds exactly to the model of "the philosopher of the future," which he describes in *Beyond Good and Evil*:

> *Genuine philosophers—are commanders and legislators:* they say, "*Thus it shall be!*" . . . With a creative hand they reach for the future, and all that is and has been becomes a means for them, an instrument, a hammer. Their knowing is creating, their creating is a legislation, their will to truth is—*Will to Power.* (BGE 211)

Without any context these descriptions would be difficult to grasp. But now that we have traced the scope of Nietzsche's artistry and suggested the subtle mechanics of his performative critique, the essential activity of this philosopher of the future is much easier to understand. One final quotation may help to explain:

> Toward *new philosophers;* there is no choice; toward spirits strong and original enough to provide the stimuli for opposite valuations and to revalue and invert "eternal values"; toward forerunners, toward men of the future who in the present tie the knot and constraint that forces the will of millennia upon *new* tracks. To teach man the future of man as his *will,* as dependent upon a human will, and to prepare great ventures and overall attempts at discipline and cultivation by way of putting an end to that gruesome dominion of nonsense and accident that has so far been called "history." (BGE 203)

In the *Genealogy* Nietzsche *revalues* and *inverts* the established values. His genealogy is an attempt *to force the will of millennia upon new tracks* by recollecting all that was *nonsense* and *accident* in our history, and showing how it may be redeemed with the return of the master, or the sovereign individual, as the fulfillment of the individual life. In this way Nietzsche suggests that the slave may free himself from the cancer of *ressentiment,* for the will loses "its ill-will against time," when, as a sovereign will, it finally becomes capable of embracing every stage of its accidental history as a necessary moment of its own self-appropriation. And hence, on both the individual and world-historical levels, Nietzsche's topology of masters and slaves is a performative critique, since it promotes the possibility of a *transformation* of types.[10]

NOTES

1. Underlying such differing conceptions of value, it would seem that at the very start of history Nietzsche sets before us two different versions of the will to power—the one that belongs to the master, who experiences power as an active expression of self-affirmation and strength, and the one that belongs to the slave, who only knows power as something that is used to dominate and constrain. He exclaims in the Third Essay, "The will of the weak to represent some form of superiority, their instincts for devious paths to tyranny over the healthy—where can it not be discovered, this Will to Power of the weakest!" GM III:14, p. 123.

2. See GM II:12, p. 79: "One places . . . 'adaptation' in the foreground, that is to say, an activity of the second rank, a mere reactivity; indeed, life itself has been defined as a more and more efficient inner adaptation to external conditions. Thus the essence of life, its *Will to Power* is ignored."

3. See Nietzsche, *On the Uses and Disadvantages of History for Life*, trans. R. J. Hollingdale (Cambridge: Cambridge University Press, 1983), section 6, p. 94: "When the past speaks it always speaks as an oracle: only if you are an architect of the future and know the present will you understand it."

4. See GM III:14 and TI IX:48.

5. From a passage Nietzsche intended for inclusion in *Ecce Homo* but that was later suppressed: "I don't understand it, but Julius Caesar could have been my father—or Alexander, this embodied Dionysus." A full translation of this passage may be found in T. Strong, "Oedipus as Hero: Family and Family Metaphors in Nietzsche," *Boundary 2* 9, 10 (Spring/Fall 1981): 259ff.

6. This comparison is forcefully made by W. Hamacher in his article, "The Promise of Interpretation: Reflections on the Hermeneutical Imperative in Kant and Nietzsche," in *Looking After Nietzsche*, ed. Lawrence A. Rickels (Albany: State University of New York Press, 1990), pp. 19–48.

7. This is pointed out by G. Deleuze in *Nietzsche and Philosophy*, trans. Hugh Tomlinson (New York: Columbia University Press, 1983), p. 111ff.

8. See Nietzsche, *The Gay Science*, trans. Walter Kaufmann (New York: Vintage, 1974), section 344, p. 283.

9. It is in this sense that we should understand Nietzsche's general speculations about the future of Europe, and in particular the promise of Russia: "There the strength to will has been long accumulated and stored up, there the will—uncertain whether as a will to negate or a will to affirm—is waiting menacingly to be discharged" (BGE 208: 131).

10. See Deleuze, especially pp. 114–116 for an account of Nietzsche's typology, and the possibility of such a transformation.

SIX

Nietzsche and Analytic Ethics

Frithjof Bergmann

> "A confrontation with Nietzsche is a difficult thing to arrange."
>
> PHILIPPA FOOT, "Nietzsche: The Revaluation of Values"

> "We are contrasting ethical and egoistic considerations. . . . What sorts of considerations bear on action but are not ethical considerations? There is one very obvious candidate, the considerations of egoism, those that relate merely to the comfort, excitement, self-esteem, power, or other advantage of the agent. The contrast between these considerations and the ethical is a platitude."
>
> BERNARD WILLIAMS, *Ethics and the Limits of Philosophy*

I

It is strange and startling. In many respects the wall between "continental" and English-speaking "analytical" philosophy has obviously come down— but a genuine exchange or serious meeting of the minds between Nietzsche and the mainstream of current ethics has not yet occurred. This is stranger still, considering the recent wave of Nietzsche's popularity, which is now tidal. Nonetheless, the two enterprises stubbornly remain in a state of non-communication, despite the fact that there is a weird and remarkable co-incidence of subject matter. For in the evolution of analytic ethics, the question concerning the nature of morality as an institution has gradually become more central; and it is this very question that is perhaps the single most important topic in the whole of Nietzsche's writings.

One could suppose that this lack of dialogue, this silence prevailing between Nietzsche and analytic ethics, is only one more curiosity of the contemporary intellectual scene. This, I shall be arguing, would be a superficial conclusion—even a downright mistake. The citation from Philippa Foot puts it *exactly* right, and it is extraordinarily suggestive. We need to understand, however, why an encounter or confrontation with Nietzsche is so difficult to arrange. Between Nietzsche and the enterprise of analytic ethics there is an obstacle blocking communication which proves troublesome to identify and even harder to remove.

Could it be that analytic ethics (or at any rate a large part of it) rests centrally on the premise that Bernard Williams expresses more flatly and overtly than other philosophers have? If so, we could say that this assumption—that we are basically egoistic—serves as a wall dividing Nietzsche and mainstream ethics and impeding a meeting between these minds.

I am suggesting that Nietzsche in no way subscribes to the dichotomy that places egoism on one side and morality on the other, making of them two forces in fundamental opposition. Indeed, the crux of what I hope to show is that it is utterly impossible to understand his writings if one approaches them with this assumption in mind. That a fruitful dialogue has not yet begun may, therefore, be anything but a strange and puzzling accident. The silence may have a very interesting and revealing reason—a reason so out of the ordinary and compelling that understanding it may at long last break down the wall, and make it possible to arrange the encounter in which conversation between Nietzsche and analytic ethics might finally begin.

II

The classic statement of Nietzsche's criticism of morality—which has an awesome power, and the very force needed to lift us out of the deep ruts worn by long-established habits, almost *rituals*, of thought—is contained in the first essay of his *Genealogy of Morals*. Nietzsche asks there what is by now a famous question: How was it that humility and meekness, modesty and denial of the flesh—and, in a way, the wholesale denial of the self—were turned into *values*? How can one explain that these became the compass-setting gauges by which people steered the courses of their lives?

To avoid missing the entrance into Nietzsche's basic way of thinking—really, his world—one has to pay attention to the *tone* with which he asks this question. It is not a philosopher's detached wondering, nor a mere scratching at the passing itch of a curiosity. The tone in which it is asked makes Nietzsche's question more an outcry in dismay and alarm that one might utter in the presence of a sudden, great calamity; it shouts urgently that the cause of this disaster must be exposed and *understood!*

Nietzsche's most elementary perception is that values, in their foundational intention, were simply meant to designate the *valuable*—the precious, the sunny, the golden, the encouraging, and the health-giving—but came then to be perverted into their precise opposites: into the self-denying, the self-emaciating, and hence the self-destroying. The recognition of that patent inversion strikes Nietzsche as a shocking affront; and his question voices his appalled reaction to the danger of that perversion. One can read the answer to his question on a superficial level as a story, for which Nietzsche provides much evidence, insisting on its truth. But the story also has a mythic quality; and we might begin by reading it as follows.

In primordial times, the world was divided between what Nietzsche provocatively calls the "masters" and the "slaves." It must be emphasized, to see his basic starting point correctly, that these designations are intended to sting and to disturb. (Here Nietzsche is like Freud, who threw down a glove to his Vienna when he insisted on speaking of the "sexuality" of babies—and of their "*oral* sexuality" at that!) The lines along which Nietzsche's thought unfolds do not come into view unless one understands that the "masters" in Nietzsche's use are emphatically not a race, a people, or a nation. They are an aristocracy—but not in the customary sense; and they therefore are not identical with any ruling group. Their superiority, their elevation, derives directly from the generosity with which nature treated them when she handed out her gifts.

Nietzsche conceives the *range* of these gifts very broadly. The "masters" are those who received bountifully from the enormously diverse and splendid mass of happy and desirable attributes. They are those who are creative and able to invent and improvise, but also those who have great stamina and a resilient, speedily recovering health. The masters are also those who are engaging, especially skilled or charming, aesthetically attractive, or of course (and importantly for Nietzsche) just plain strong—and hence not fragile, not easily subdued. Moreover, the ambience of Nietzsche's writing, the lighting of the stage on which his drama will be played, enhances the *delight*, the sensuous pleasure, the sheer gusto with which the shower of these presents is enjoyed.

On the other side are Nietzsche's "slaves," who are (again) not a demarcated group or class, or straightforwardly the poor, nor simply the oppressed, though all of this is suggested and plays a role. More specifically they constitute the masters' symmetrically corresponding opposite numbers: they are those who were "treated niggardly by nature," who received only a pittance when others were endowed with abundance. They are— and here Nietzsche's vocabulary is particularly various and stinging—the "dregs," the "superfluous," the "pale," the "sickly," the "many-too-many," the "inferior" and the "low." If one wanted to filter out the offensiveness, the edge that Nietzsche added to needle and draw blood, then one could substitute Frantz Fanon's phrase "the wretched of the earth," and capture with it much of the remaining meaning. For the kind of human beings Nietzsche has in mind are indeed the "poor," but by no means primarily in gold or money. They are the poor in every conceivable and hence also heart-rending respect: the collectivity of the untalented and ungifted, in the most encompassing and saddening sense. They are "poor" in stamina and health, poor in energy, vitality, and spirit, poor in physical and sexual attractiveness; the shapeless, the unformed, the indifferent—whose decomposition starts at birth.

The slaves, not surprisingly, are burdened with a far more difficult, discouraging existence than that enjoyed by their counterparts. Their lives, not graced with nature's gifts, must be seen as gradually wearing and exhausting, a stupefying grinding down. They lack the gifts that offer *sustenance*, which feed and give strength, spell comfort and endurance. Those nature has treated opulently, who have been lavished with all her splendors, will have vastly easier, far less arduous and painful lives. Here it is crucial to note (since it goes directly against the grain of some of the grimmest and most inveterate presumptions about Nietzsche) that the lives of the gifted are far more desirable than those of the ungifted because their talents enable them to *give delight to others*. Nietzsche likens this capacity to that of a magic fountain, from which both they as gift-givers and others as gift-receivers can forever drink. It is therefore part of the pallor and harshness of the lives of Nietzsche's "slaves" that they *cannot* give such delight, that even that succor is denied them. This should raise the general apprehension that their lives are too frugal and too harsh, so that if a time should come when even their final sustenance—their religion, their belief in God—is taken from them, they will not be able to endure. In exasperated outrage and maddened desperation, they will, instead, "rebel against life."

To picture the "masters" and the "slaves" as like two Shakespearean armies, facing each other in the night, would be a sophomoric mistake. Quite differently from this, one has to imagine them in a close but inflamed and forever irritating coexistence. A large portion of the suffering of the "slaves" would hence be *internal*. The worst of it would be the knowledge of their hopeless inferiority. For the permanent confrontation with their lacks gives rise to painful and humiliating envy—but not only that. More aggravating (in a characteristically Nietzschean perception) is the cyclical, reenforcing, downward spin that this envy engenders. For jealousy and hatred make for self-detestation, which corrodes and decomposes—like acid on flesh—the substance of the self. This injured, weakened sense of self then in turn intensifies and further heats the anger, until the process of one twist following another devolves downward into a frantic, Dostoyevskian rage!

Essential to the core of Nietzsche's novel idea of resentment is the insistently proposed contention that the simple knowledge of what one lacks is able to produce an escalation of dismay, which can jack upward until its pitch becomes hysterical and shrill, until even the horrific and normally unthinkable presents itself as the most natural relief—as no more than the cooling hand for a hot fever. Prior to Nietzsche the concept of resentment did not exist on our intellectual maps. He placed it there in part by showing that much that we associate with envy and self-hatred runs to far higher extremes than we previously had imagined, and that it does so in every possible direction. Its ramifications are thus far more pervasive than we had previously supposed. In that respect, Nietzsche did with resentment what Freud a little later did with sex: he unearthed it and showed it to us in nooks and crannies in which we had never before thought to look. When he was done, the world as we had seen it prior to him seems sterile and naive.

The ubiquitous presence of resentment, however, is only one of its dimensions. Just as important—prompting no less a change in our self-understanding—is Nietzsche's demonstration of the frightful pitch to which "mere" envy is capable of rising. What Nietzsche does in this regard suffices to upend our former sense of what rational or sensible creatures we might be. For the havoc we produce around us, and the egregious self-destructiveness to which the ever-wounded sense of our inadequacy drives us, are so appalling that the dismay is bound to spread—until one questions in a new and different fashion the very function of our sensitivity, and of our consciousness and knowledge. One is left wondering (as Nietzsche did through great portions of his writing) whether those faculties are not ultimately afflictions and dis-abilities that weaken and distract us. This is far indeed from the self-satisfied Aristotelian assurance that we humans are the sole animal distinguished, privileged, and singled out for our ability to reason.

But what of Nietzsche's story? It has its beginning in the primordial morality first created by the masters. Characteristic of their code was the utter directness, simplicity, and crude anything-but-aristocratic obviousness of its design. This is true even of the two main categories employed by the masters, which were straightforwardly and without further ado no more than "good" and "bad." The same simplicity and directness is evident in the fact that the word "good," in the master's use of it, did not transform or alter anything. The word "good" itself did not perform an *action*: it represented a mere summing up, a bracketing together. It was no more than a flat, uninformative, and general *summative* term for the amplitude of attributes in which the masters took delight.

So too with the opposite of "good": "bad," the way the masters said it, was just a sad, regretful expletive that signaled the disappointment and deflation that come with "the absence of the good" (as Aristotle had put it). "Bad," therefore, does not properly refer to a quality at all; it comes at the end, when the search for happy attributes has failed, and comes up empty-handed. More than anything it expresses the recognition of a lack, the conclusion that both you and I and all of us have *less* and are poorer because this object or that act or yonder person is *unfortunately* bad.

That tone of regret should, however, not deceive us. It should not suggest that the master morality was mild, permissive, flexible, or (as we are wont to say) "nonjudgmental." Nothing of the sort! With the master categories it was entirely natural and easy to pronounce a thing to be *wanting*, and to judge that it had seriously and fundamentally *failed*. One could be intolerant, harsh, and even "absolute" in this pronouncement.

Consider now the slaves, who are not strangely shaped or colored, but who are merely the patently ungifted—and who, therefore, could be *us*. How would they fare under the master's dispensation? If Nietzsche is right, life for them would be harrowing, demeaning and self-undermining in ways that would relentlessly drive them toward the point where all scruples drop away. That is important: for the slaves perpetrated an action (whether imagined at the end of a protracted and exhausting struggle, or pictured as occurring sooner) that was bizarre and mad—an action enough to spin and disorient and derange the mind.

What, in essence, did they do? In the large frame of Nietzsche's total thinking, they "turned against life." Their deed is reminiscent of tales from the Middle Ages, in which as an ultimate act of vengeance against an oppressor or an enemy, those faced with defeat "poisoned the wells" on which both depended. How did the slaves do this?

This is the crux of Nietzsche's entire story. It is the answer to his question of how self-effacement, humility, and meekness were elevated to the status of high values. The slaves took hold of the old master's idea of the "good," and not merely imposed a different coloration upon it, but converted it into its diametrical *opposite*. More precisely: they distilled an altogether strange idea out of their own bile, and with it blotted out the old idea of "good." The idea was that of "evil," and it was with this idea that they covered over what formerly had been called "good." These same qualities—the obviously valuable, the nourishing and healthy—the slaves now cursed with their malediction: they exorcised and damned them, and pronounced them "evil!"

The slave idea of "evil," which now designates what formerly was "good," is at the same time (as one would expect) deeply different from the master's idea of the "bad." In an essential way, what renders something "evil" is not as plain and visible as was true with the former "bad." For "evil" conjures up a sense of threat, connotes dark, demonic forces set out to defile all purity. "Evil," from the start, introduces a hidden and mysterious element—sinister insinuations, with vile and monstrous spirits in the wings. (For philosophy, this will have momentous and unending consequences; for the *validation*, the proof of that "evil"—but also of the new "good," which is its novel and surprising counterpart—will not be in the same way "natural" and obvious as were the master's "good" and "bad." To contrive a "justification," a legitimating base or a foundation for the "evil" and "good" of the "slaves," became the great conundrum that was to occupy much of the energy of philosophy for two millennia to come.)

The word "evil" is, therefore, not merely an expression of regret, nor simply the complaint that there is less in the world to celebrate. Whatever the details of the story, the word "evil" evokes a drama of fear and rage and perhaps horror. It does not just indicate the absence of the good, but has a distinct, dangerous, and vile quality of its own. In crucial contrast to the expression "bad," the invocation of evil is a call to *resist*, to muster one's defenses, and to go into battle—to *"extirpate,"* to kill off and utterly extinguish the "enemy of the good."

This brings us to the core of Nietzsche's answer to his own iconoclastically asked question: the "pale" values of meekness, humility, and self-effacement were enshrined in the course of a great, truly world-historical act of deception. Yet the elevation of these values was a by-product, an afterthought, a side effect. The first strike in the battle was the superimposition of the idea of "evil." First there came the disparagement and deprecation of the fortunate, the distinguished, and the noble. The sowing of that self-doubt, the transformation of the excellent and admirable—*out of resentment*—into the wanton and the vile, was the cunning Trojan horse contrived by the slaves and brought into the city dominated by the masters.

The elevation of the common, impoverished, and ordinary was a *secondary* consequence: as one side of the scale sank, the other had to rise. The slave morality's conception of the "good" that resulted from this sequence of substitutions was, predictably, different down to the root from what formerly had been designated by that word. It now was severed from the vigorous and virtuous and strong, and "good" was no longer just a label, a mere summative appellation. It too—like the word "evil"—now performed an *act*, a masking and transfiguration. If the word "evil" was meant to degrade the proud possessions of the masters; if it represented the slaves' last desperate way of reconciling themselves to the lack of their endowments—namely by *damning* the very gifts and talents they craved, and casting upon them a curse in order finally to douse the flames of their intolerable envy, to make loathsome the very goods that they found themselves so wretchedly without—then likewise now the word "good." The slaves affixed that word to the plain, the poor, the common and the modest, and surrounded these qualities with a new nimbus; and it is this that gave us the slave's idea of "good." "Good" are now the long-suffering and patient, the sweet and saintly and forgiving, the gentle and the mild. So mild, in fact that the "good" become incapable of exerting force, and end up purifying themselves utterly out of this world—like Parsifal the innocent and blissful fool, or like Dostoyevski's saintly, epileptic prince.

III

Let me now ask a perhaps unexpected question. What is the most *common reaction* to Nietzsche? And here I mean not that of the aficionado, and even less that of the "specialist," but rather the typical reaction of those who encounter him fortuitously—for example, the average undergraduate.

Usually the small drama of such encounters is left to the side. By the prevailing canons of what deserves serious attention, it is relegated to the margin. Now this is precisely what I would like to end. Indeed, I will go to the opposite extreme: I propose to lay hold of the general type of these unassuming, seemingly inconsequential episodes, move this type into the very center of the stage, and examine it there under the very brightest lights. For it repays study, and is as revealingly instructive as a body without clothes.

Central to the typical initial reaction, in my experience, is the recognition that the morality we practice is a hoax, and that we therefore have been pursuing a useless and debilitating fool's errand. However—and it is crucial that this should be properly observed and noted—this recognition does *not* bring in its train the sort of response that our stereotypes would lead us to expect. What happens next does *not* fit Dostoyevski's often-quoted "everything now is permitted." For most people there is no drifting: they are not unmoored, not lost and tumbling, without direction, in empty space. Far from it! The core of their experience of losing faith in their morality is neither lofty nor metaphysical.

On the contrary: the core of it is a mad and flaming rage. They feel *duped* by the trick contraption of morality, which in their own eyes made them bland and timid and reserved. Now that the morality that transformed them into lamblike dolts has turned out to be only wool that had been pulled over their eyes, they burn and cry out in horror at how much they have *missed*. The thought of how much of their lives they have permitted to drift past, as if it were mere flotsam on a river, fills them with panic. But strangely, they are also controlled, almost methodical, and mainly move in one quite definite direction. Their thought is "to catch up," to "make up for lost time." The idea that hammers in their brain is that now it is to be "*their* turn!" Their hour has come, and they will seize it!

In direct reaction to their previously excessive forbearance and considerateness, they now "steel themselves" against all others—though it is not exactly "steel," but only a crust of callouses and dead skin. Feeling they have been duped, they now barge ahead with nothing but their own advantage on their minds. *Not* to be vulnerable any longer, but to be armor-plated in mailcoats of insensitivity, is all that counts.

Now ask: Where will this lead? What is apt to happen? Having painted it so luridly makes it easy to divine the answer. *Obviously*—it will not go well! If you imagine someone acting out this monomaniac Me-ness for any length of time (for a few days, or weeks, or months), then predictably he will encounter a crescendo of withdrawals, irritations, and hostilities. Soon a wall of these reactions will mount around the person; and not much later he may find himself pummeled with retaliations, caught in the return cross-fire of the offended and the violated. That, quite naturally, will bring on a miring, a slowing and sinking, as in mud or in deep snow. Usually it is the realization that one is "stuck," stumbling into a blind alley, that initiates a period of *reconsideration*. Think of this as the next phase—the hour of second thoughts.

The downpour of displeasure, hatred, and aversion will inescapably evoke a private and internal side. One can hardly fail to pose questions and wonder about oneself. What ghastly force did I unleash? Can I still esteem or have affection for myself, or do I feel only loathing and disgust? And then the next question: Why am I doing this? What is my purpose, gain, or motive? And further: If I continue, and allow this new persona to become yet more exacerbated and extreme, where will it *end?* In what fiasco will it terminate? For that this down-spinning is doomed to reach a final cataclysm seems evident already. So why not stop and end the masquerade? Why not search for the torn threads, and with their help find my way back to my old demeanor, to the sweeter and more harmless person that I was before?

These questions and these reappraisals, however, are likely to be mere preliminary stepping stones; they lead upward to a new plateau, a place where one comes to rest with definite and settled new conclusions. Two thoughts, or two convictions, stand like a gateway to this plain: and the two balance and support each other like the two sides of an arch. These now need to be looked at closely, for in them lies the substance of what I hope to say with this entire essay.

The first is the idea that the raw and brutish roughness with which one has been behaving is representative of how people in general *would* be acting, if they had no morality. One might elaborate this in picturesque detail, and invent all manner of different scenes in which this brutish coarseness displays itself—usually, of course, to grim or horrible effect. With larger or smaller steps one may eventually generalize from these examples until one settles into the conclusion that without morality life would be (in Hobbes's immortal phrase) "nasty, brutish, and short."

Given this first step, the second step is already preordained. One decides that morality has a very definite and even crucial purpose after all: namely, to assure that the world is NOT like this! Morality is designed to guarantee a life less nasty, less brutish, and considerably longer. Moreover, one may feel confident of the basic ways in which this is accomplished: on one hand, morality restrains the presumptuous and the overbearing; and on the other side it safeguards and protects the disadvantaged, weak, and frail.

Settling into these two thoughts typically spells sudden disenchantment with Nietzsche, and the abrupt end of one's intense initial relationship to him. In retrospect the episode seems like a brief and passionate affair that to one's surprise collapsed abruptly. One looks back, and it seems difficult even to remember why every encounter was previously so taut with meaning. Now everything seems grey. One's mouth seems filled with ashes. With bitterness, one reinterprets the relationship that has just ended: it was just an escape, a mere adventure, a little fling.

This is the meaning many give to their relationship to Nietzsche as they part company with him. But a decisive role is played here by a grotesque misunderstanding of him; and it is part of the essential purpose of this essay to show that this is so. *Why* one's relationship to Nietzsche so often collapses at this point is something that must be made utterly explicit and clear. For it would be disastrous to leave it vague, and ascribe it merely to the normal cooling of emotions, or to the comedown from the heights of Nietzsche's poetry to our (academic) prose. So what is it, at this precise confluence of ideas, that causes the disillusionment and disenchantment with Nietzsche that so many undergo?

It seems to me of pivotal importance that the first of the above ideas (i.e., the conviction that coarse brutishness represents how people in general would act if morality did not constrain them, and that this brutishness is therefore a picture of *human nature*) has everything to do with a major fact concerning our culture: namely, with the depth and power with which *we believe in egoism.*

That there is a connection should be evident. It is as if this cultural belief stood ready, waiting for us, like a niche. It seems that without effort, merely by allowing ourselves to slide, we naturally slip into the idea that without morality the world would be a chaotic, grim, and ghastly place—*because* we have believed in egoism all along.

That we indeed believe in egoism (at least in many settings), that this is a fact about our culture, seems to be incontrovertible and patent. One need only recall the ready assent given to the ubiquitous references to the "materialism" of what we call "ordinary people"—most particularly, of course, in the context of consumerism, but also in that of practical affairs generally. Consider how commonly "idealistic" (and, significantly, in our culture this normally is taken to *mean* "altruistic") proposals are dismissed with a perfunctory allusion to the overridingly supreme status of "number one!" Remember the "science" of economics—which takes it to be axiomatic that human beings invariably seek to "maximize their gains." And last, but certainly not least, think of capitalism and of the entire rhetoric of competition and *material* incentives.

The next step, however, is not so obvious. We should ask ourselves explicitly: Why is it that these ideas bring on disenchantment with Nietzsche, and specifically with the at first so entrancing and so liberating train of thoughts that he offers in his *Genealogy of Morals?* Why does settling into these convictions tend to bring one's attraction to Nietzsche to such a dismal, abrupt end? The answer has to do with one's realization that if a world in which life would be "nasty, brutish, and short" really is a danger, then morality is NOT a hoax, a deception, a lie, a trick-contraption, or a Trojan horse. On the contrary, morality in that case performs a patent, urgent, and most vital function.

To go over this more slowly: the ideas we are discussing lead us, in a large circle, back to our pre-Nietzschean beginnings. We find ourselves again in the old, only too familiar, landscape. It would seem that the values of self-denial, self-effacement, deference, modesty, meekness, and forbearance have to be enforced and practiced after all, since the world otherwise would be a raw, cruel, and blood-drenched place. And it further may come to seem that the essence of morality really is to protect the poor, the wretched, and the disadvantaged. But these are patently the very beliefs in which we were *raised*. So we only took a brief vacation from them, and are back at the very spot from which our journey started. If anything we will now be even more entrenched and dug in deeper—harder, older, and grimmer.

Is it any wonder if one then suffers from a dismal sense of horrible deflation? Does anything remain of Nietzsche's thoughts? What is their point, or relevance, or bearing? What do they have to teach us? If the slaves indeed "invented" the morality with which Nietzsche credits them, then who could blame them? Did they not "invent" precisely what was needed—indeed, a cultural tool of the most inestimable value? And if so, is the word "invent" not a gratuitous and empty slur when applied to it? From the perspective of "the stronger" (recalling Plato's Thrasymachus) it plausibly represents a *device*, but not from the point of view of the weaker. Nothing devious is being perpetrated: the slaves needed forbearance, patience, and protection—and they said as much. So indeed, where does this leave us?

IV

Let me recapitulate: the idea arises *first* that the boorish ego-maniac behavior in which many people typically engage when morality appears to them to be a hoax is representative of human nature. It is *secondly* decided that, if this is so, the world without morality would indeed be a ghastly place, and that morality therefore is urgently needed to give us some order and humanity. And *thirdly*, we discerned that our cultural belief in egoism is crucially implicated in the first two of these steps.

Now, it is easy to imagine an initial, quick, and intemperate reaction to what I have been describing. One might exclaim that this is preposterous; for how could anyone imagine that the behavior which was so patently a *reaction* to a very specific and esoteric set of circumstances is representative of *human nature?* Nothing about it suggests that this behavior is either general or neutral, or independent of individuating cultural variables. On the contrary, this is a reaction to the specific discovery that a particular morality is a tactical contrivance. Nothing justifies an inference to humanity in general. Even if just the morality in question had been different, the reaction might not have been the same. Crucially, this morality extols altruism, arguably to an excessively high degree; and the episode of behavior described thus was directly triggered by the recognition that one had been duped. So it is not a neutral symptom of human nature in its general condition.

To make the invalidity of this inference quite visible was one main reason for the above detailed description of the twists and turns that the reaction to Nietzsche often takes. To the extent that this disparity can now be seen, these efforts have paid off. But a more important point is that the width of this very gulf is one more measure of how credulous our belief in egoism really is. For egoism was the bridge on which we crossed this gulf. It was our belief in egoism (possibly even a distant echo of Hobbes's famous phrase) that allowed us to move so precipitously from our own reaction to humanity as such.

This, unsurprisingly, has another side: the power and strength of our belief in egoism also means that we are not easily dissuaded from it. And even if the previous paragraph has opened a small chink, much remains to be done before we see fully how very questionable, dubious, and down-right *strange* this belief is. In order to accomplish this, I shall make what might appear to be a detour, and go back briefly to Hegel to offer a sketch of what his critique of egoism—if he had written it explicitly—might have been like. It goes far deeper than those to which we are accustomed. And it is highly relevant to the present case. For here (at least) Hegel and Nietzsche are allies.

To gain a first approach to Hegel's unexpected disagreement with egoism, we could imagine him listening (of course in modern dress) to what has become the most usual of conversations on this topic. All of us have participated in these debates, and know the well-worn tracks on which they run. Whoever defends the contention that we all invariably pursue whatever is in our own best interest, and that at bottom we are all hopelessly selfish in our core, usually has the upper hand, and prevails with conspicuous ease. The advocate of altruism normally begins with plausible everyday examples in which decent people, on the face of it, seem to sacrifice their immediate advantage for the greater benefit of someone else. However, that strategy proves quite astonishingly *ineffectual*. For the defender of egoism can always and easily come up with some sneaky, selfish motive that lies concealed beneath the surface. A familiar logic then propels the conversation toward illustrations that grow ever more wayward and extreme. This happens in part because the contest narrows itself down to the search for one exception, one solitary case that will break the interminable chain of egoistic actions! That makes it natural to go on escalating, with inventions growing ever more far-fetched and contrived.

This is likely to continue until the ultimate, last-throw example turns out to be an utterly weird story of the following type. "Imagine a nun who nursed nine lepers, all of whom were covered with ghastly smelling sores, and that this nurse washed and bandaged her patients down somewhere in the horrible wet sewers beneath Paris. (She must be hidden in the darkness, so that her vanity can not take pleasure being seen.) These sewers in addition crawled with large rats who pinched and bit the saintly nun's toes and feet while she ministered and served. Surely *this* would count as a genuine case of altruism."

We know that the defender of universal egoism will be able to reply as nonchalantly as he did before. He need only observe that such examples merely prove how very devious the twists and turns of our egoism indeed are; and what is truly amazing is simply the fact that some human beings do indeed derive their satisfactions in such extraordinary ways. Such tales, he might continue, therefore do not begin to refute egoism. More closely considered, they do the exact opposite. The very extravagance of this example boomerangs. It ends by supporting the opposite of what the advocate of altruism had intended: it merely demonstrates that egoism may appear even in the most unlikely guises, and it thus illustrates still further how ubiquitous and ineluctable it actually is.

We can now imagine Hegel joining the debate—not with an example still more esoteric and bizarre, but on the contrary, with an at first startling and strange reproach: that the very *attempt* to prove, with one example, that we sometimes do not seek to maximize our own advantage, is hopelessly misguided and off base. It is misconceived because it is founded on a wholly erroneous *assumption* about what we are normally and usually like: the premise namely, that the *normal, neutral* starting point is that of seeking our own advantage, while it is our deviation from this that is the rarity and the exception that requires proof.

Since this may sound puzzling and cryptic, we need a different example: not one to illustrate that altruism does sometimes occur, but one that makes concrete this Hegelian contention. One domain from which that sort of illustration could be easily derived is the world of *therapy.* Imagine a client who has been seeing his therapist regularly, once a week for years. Picture him arriving one day for his session in great excitement. "In the last week," he almost shouts, "after the long, humiliating sequence of my defeats, I finally took a delicious, catapulting leap forward! It was in the middle of the week, on Wednesday, exactly at three o'clock, when I felt for the first time in years NOT cowed by the grey ghost of my father, and was not intimidated by all the other ghosts that have been haunting me. And, although I also felt the pressure of the expectations that my admired teacher would have had for me in this situation, I did not bow to him either. Likewise with all the others—even my wife and children. For once, at last, I surrendered to none of them. I was only too aware of what *they* wanted and expected me to do. But no, this time I shook myself like a wet dog, and these obligations and demands and hesitancies flew away like drops in all

directions. Incredible as it may seem, I stopped, and wondered what I myself in this great moment deeply and seriously *wished to do*. I looked and
saw it with more clarity then I had ever seen before, and after that it was
effortless and easy. Think of it, *me*, the eternally evasive, vacillating, forever-
turning needle on the dial—*I* decided, and *I* acted, and *I*, this one ground-
breaking time, did what I seriously wanted, desired and was determined to
do!"

This example is meant to be much more than a story. It is intended to
provide a vivid glimpse of a radically different general worldview—a view
deeply opposed to the entire configuration of assumptions that formed the
framework for seventeenth and eighteenth century thinking: in short, a
first hint of Hegel's systematic and coherent philosophical position, which
fought with all its might against a coterie of foundational assumptions of
which egoism is one prime representative. Hegel insisted, in many different
ways, that we are *not* isolated, and are *not* like self-sufficient atoms; that we
are on the contrary exposed and sensitive and vulnerable—so much so,
that this indeed may be the one most telling difference between us and
other animals. We are moved and influenced and feel the power of forces
far subtler, and far more distant than the forces that impinge on a horse
or on a cow.

Hegel developed this general orientation, moving from the periphery
of life gradually toward the center, in a whole panoply of different domains.
In its furthest reaches it involves a different conceptualization of the basic
problem of knowledge; for in the sharpest contrast to Descartes, Hegel held
that we know the distant, outer world far better than our own selves and
minds. That same perspective set the stage for his discussions of religion,
art, culture, history, and politics and much else.

Of foremost importance for us is the wholesale *inversion* we find here.
In the Hegelian view we are not always and inescapably driven by our own
egoistic desires. Far, far from this. Indeed, the exact opposite. We are exposed, and vulnerable, and "open" to the outside world, to the world of
other people and of culture. We are in fact very weak and frail and unde-
veloped, with very little sense of *ourselves*; and we are therefore controlled
and moved and driven by all manner of different forces that lie *outside* of
ourselves. We are like small pieces of wood, tossed helplessly in the surf of
powers far greater than ourselves; or like Gulliver, fettered and tied down
by a thousand threads. We are not as a rule autonomous agents calling the
shots at the helm of our lives. The typical, normal action is therefore *anything but egoistic*. The average case is exactly like that of our client's past life:
we are like marionettes, moved by the strings of *other* people's expectations,
of *other* people's threats and hopes and offers of reward. Many, indeed,
spend their entire lives in this condition.

Acts done by ourselves and on our own behalf, acts of egoism, are therefore *not* the norm. On the contrary, they are the rare, the unusual, and indeed the marvelous exception. As in the case of our client, we are anything but doomed to an inescapable, inevitable egoism. It may take years of work, long episodes of therapy and of self-transformation, and even luck or fortuitous circumstances, until we are able to perform one single act that is truly what *we* have decided, and what *we* want.

Let me pass on to a second illustrative example, which is meant to advance the argument by another major step. It also is intended to approach the subject under consideration from a direction opposite to the usual one. I shall draw it from my own experience. One of my assignments, in the philosophy department in which I teach, happens to be the counseling of seniors who are about to graduate. My conversations with these students tend to follow an amazingly persistent pattern; like carts, they run along exactly the same tracks. The same mood, even the same metaphors recur again and again.

Listening to these young men and women, the underlying theme is always that they are about to leave—but they feel *expelled*. They constantly invoke the image of a fear-inspiring, horribly blank, white space that they are facing; or of a seemingly bottomless, icy, black crevasse into which they are about to fall. They talk as if an irresistible, ominous force presses them every day closer to the edge. In their minds the day of graduation approaches like a nightmarish, awful fall. What shall they do with their whole lives—after they leave college? Naturally, I ask whether there is something they look forward to, if not with excitement, then at least with some anticipation, or some hope. But upsettingly enough, the answer is very often: No! As we go on to explore, it becomes evident that they have already considered many possibilities: this is not their problem. The difficulty is that regardless of where they turn or look, *nothing appeals* to them! They feel jaded, stale, and weary. It seems telling to me that even the most cautious and gentle persistence on my part often causes an abrupt, almost violent change in their mood. Some show signs of anger, a few break down and cry, and many quickly find some excuse to leave.

Why is the question, "What is it that you really *want?*" so powerful and so upsetting? A part of the explanation may be that the search for one's serious or deep desires can be driven by a kind of *panic*. Many feel that they should *at least* be able to locate or identify their *wants!* Trying to do so represents a last resort, an attempt to find a final narrow foothold. If a genuine sense of who one is, of what one's "true" identity or self is like, is unavailable, if ideals for which one stands are nowhere to be found, and if even mere convictions are not there to be discovered, then—at the bottom of the barrel—there should at least be *wants!* Desires seem far more elementary, more basic than values, or beliefs. So, if one suddenly confronts an emptiness, a white space, or a black hole, even when one is searching for one's own *desires*, then it is very natural to feel panic. The experience is very like that of falling down into a shaft. Here, if ever, one comes to recognize what Heidegger and Sartre have in their different ways at length described: namely, the possibility that in one's inner essence is a Nothing, a Negativity, an Absence, a palpable and flagrant *Lack!*

In a different language: the syndrome from which these students suffer could also be described as a *Poverty of Desires*. And that fact could be a metaphor, a condensed, emblematic representation of an otherwise dispersed array of Hegel's abstract philosophic views. The phrase "Poverty of Desires" captures and makes concrete the general Hegelian orientation in which the self, in the beginning, is not merely unknown (though that is crucial—and in the sharpest possible contradistinction to Descartes). More than that: to begin with, the self literally *does not exist!* Indeed, the entire arduous process of history and culture, with all its turbulences and frustrations, is required gradually and piece by piece to build and construct the self that we eventually may come to possess. If one extrapolates from this general perspective to the more specific domain of the desires, one immediately comes to the conception that desires, too, are in the beginning weak and frail, and indeed unformed and almost nonexistent—and that (in sharpest contrast to our usual convictions) much arduous labor and long cultivation may well be needed to turn the green seedling of a passing whim into the full-grown tree of a passionate desire!

To connect this now with what has gone before: for our purposes the central point is the juxtaposition, the polarity between the idea of egoism and the conception of the Poverty of Desires. In a nutshell: we could not possibly be further than we are from *always* acting on our own desires; and we are still further, an immense distance, from *invariably* aiming at our own greatest advantage. Indeed, the aptness of the idea of the Poverty of Desires is one measure of how distant we are from this condition. Or, conversely: we very rarely—and then often only after a prolonged and arduous struggle—reach a stage of self-development in which we at last act on our own serious and deep desires. (Attaining this condition of self-determination is a large part of what Hegel means by freedom.)

The two examples provided above are meant to be two complementary halves. The first is intended to show that the external world has enormous power over us; while the other example is meant to illustrate the weakness, the frailty, and the immaturity of our internal world. Both together cumulatively reinforce the view that we are *not* driven entirely by our own desires. There is far more that could further be said against egoism. One could bring out how implausible it is even from a biological perspective, since ants or bees are unmistakably not egoistic, but rather are "socialized perfection." (In that connection one could ask: Whatever possessed us to create a self-image of ourselves that places us so far *below* the animals?) One could also underscore the mind-numbing sheer monotony of egoism, the grey sameness of always seeking nothing but one's own advantage—which among other things seems almost willfully unaware of our inveterate and flamboyant tendencies to self-destruction.

One could also go on to show how the Hegelian perspective anticipates major themes that have been taken up by feminism—the ideas that assertiveness needs to be trained; that many women are far *too* eager to subordinate their own advantage to that of their men; that not a few are afflicted with a desire *not* to succeed, to mention only a few of the most obvious parallels. More detailed elaboration of these and other ideas of feminism would add to the plausibility and force of the Hegelian view; but for present purposes we have said enough.

V

The main results to which this essay have been the stepping stones can now be stated swiftly and succinctly. If one reads Nietzsche—and in particular his most basic injunction concerning what he most urgently wants us to do—taking for granted the assumption of egoism and the image of human nature that such egoism generates, Nietzsche simply *does not make sense!* What sense could it make to preach to those already possessed by a monomaniac self-centeredness—by only one divinity and worship, namely that of their own greatest benefit and advantage—that they should *"become themselves"*? Why proclaim to them that they should take possession of who they are? And even more hyperbolically, that they should create an emblem, a higher version, an overimage of themselves? No motive! No rhyme nor reason! Why ask for more where there is already far too much? But also literally: there would be no *sense* to this! For how could one go further than an already unsurpassable outer limit? That is on one side.

On the other side: the premise of egoism creates a need, an expectation, or even a full-fledged *demand* that Nietzsche has no intention—and also no inclination whatever—to satisfy. Let me explain. If human beings really are compressed and pent-up quantities of sheer rapaciousness, or fundamentally little atomic incarnations of greed, which if left to themselves would devour each other, then there is an imperative need for some power to restrain and tame their demonic impulses—and this would almost have to be *an authority* with enough clout to impose order and control. But Nietzsche demonstrably goes out of his way to underscore that the higher sort of "morality" he envisions does *not* involve authoritarian "*oughts*", that in its very conception it is not a "*law*", that it does not invoke sanctions and threats and rewards—least of all sanctions that have their foundation above or beyond this life. And there is the rub: for to those who believe in egoism, what Nietzsche offers is *irrelevant*. It is a toy, a trinket of no useful service in the human predicament. But this is only a predicament ironically created by their own *belief,* in their own minds.

We now have dug up one of the keystones of the answer to the question we posed at the start: Why is a genuine encounter and a serious exchange between analytic ethics and Nietzsche so difficult to arrange? Fundamentally, this is because much of the enterprise of analytic ethics *presupposes egoism.* I do not have the space here to show the full extent to which this is so; but I might at least add one broad hint to the quote from Bernard Williams I cited at the outset as an epigraph. Let me suggest that even the emphasis on the impersonality and the impartiality of the moral point of view, which are often taken as definitional of the moral, invoke this very assumption and polarity. One insists on the *im*partial and the *im*personal because one believes that, "in our natural condition," we are far *too partial* and *too personal*—in other words, fundamentally far too egoistic!

For those who make this assumption, as so many analytic philosophers do, the cardinal message of Nietzsche's work is pointless and without any sense; while what Nietzsche offers is not in any way designed to meet the needs that *this assumption* creates. If one believes in egoism, one will feel a need for an authoritarian (or at least a firm) moral law. Nietzsche emphatically does not offer this—but he does not do so *because* he does not believe in the universality of an insatiable egoism that presupposes that each and every one of us from the outset is (or has) a unitary and clearly individuated self that is capable of seeking its own advantage. The upshot is a double-crossed purposiveness. What philosophers in analytic ethics look for, or want, Nietzsche does not give; and what he does give seems to them to be of no use. Even worse, it conjures up for them the picture of the glorification of a horrific, ghastly, purely egoistic world. This explains why the encounter between them is so "difficult to arrange."

The sense of disenchantment, of one's first excitement giving way to disillusionment and disappointment, can be understood along exactly the same lines. It is not only analytic philosophers who believe in the ubiquity of egoism. On the contrary, this is a belief that is widespread and deeply endemic in our culture. Therefore many students—and also many who write books and essays about Nietzsche—read and interpret him through the lens of this assumption. If so they have predictably a similar twofold experience. On the one hand, they find that Nietzsche advocates a self-development that sometimes seems strange (or just too strenuous) to them, but that more often conjures up for them the image of a frightful and nihilistic world: a world in which rapaciousness is celebrated. But once again, it is the assumption of egoism that conjures up the fantasy of such a world. On the other hand, they do not perceive what Nietzsche offers as having to do, properly speaking, with *"values"* at all. Nietzsche's ideas or proposals do not have the (supposedly) requisite commanding—and above all, constraining—force; they do not reassure those who read him through the lens of egoism that this rapaciousness will be controlled, and if need be punished and suppressed. Hence the horrible deflation—the shocking disproportion between what one initially saw in Nietzsche, in one's first excitement, and what one now upon reflection finds left in one's hands.

All of this changes in the most drastic and thoroughgoing way if one substitutes for the premise of egoism the inverse picture of human nature which I have here derived from Hegel—and for all his differences with Hegel, Nietzsche's image of humanity corresponds very closely to Hegel's in this respect. If human beings really are initially and fundamentally incomplete, frail, and timid, if in the beginning they are buffeted about by external causes like leaves in a strong wind; if they do come into their own slowly, and only through arduous exertions and with small steps may approach the condition of having at least *some* control, becoming only gradually and to *some degree* "the architects of their own lives"—*then* the main core of Nietzsche's message makes immediate and obvious sense. *Then* it is vital, and urgently needed. If the cardinal difference between human creatures and the rest of nature is the fearful and horrifyingly dangerous incompleteness with which we are born, if our physical unfinishedness at birth is a metaphor for how raw and embryonic the rest of our being is through much of our life—*then* the task of working on oneself, of shaping and transforming the "raw material" of which we are made, of "giving style to oneself," and of creating oneself "as if one were a work of art" is needed and appropriate.

The same is true in the matter of philosophic expectations: if we reverse prevailing assumptions about human nature, if people are not basically rapacious, but are instead are too mild, and bland, and above all passive— then the last things needed are organs of repression, and curtailment, and control. Then the shoe plainly pinches on the other foot. Then the worry is not that pandemonium and chaos are ready to erupt. Then the sanctity of moral values is not most urgently needed to hold them back and the maintenance of stability and social order need not be the object of our most anxious concern. For in that very different world, the forces of control—or of lethargy—are too strong already. Here an imposing (and preferably metaphysically sanctified) *"law"* is not what is required. What is needed is the very opposite: newly imagined devices of individual encouragement, enticement, and inspiration—conceivably images like that of Nietzsche's "overman," designed to give people the heart and stamina, but also the irreverence and the sheer truculence needed to persist in the awesome task of peeling themselves out of their pulp.

SEVEN

One Hundred Years of *Ressentiment*
Nietzsche's *Genealogy of Morals**

Robert C. Solomon

> . . . an act of the *most spiritual revenge*. . . . It was the Jews who, with awe-inspiring consistency, dared to invert the aristocratic value-equation (good = noble = powerful = beautiful = happy = beloved of God) and to hang onto this inversion with their teeth, the teeth of the most abysmal hatred (the hatred of impotence), saying "the wretched alone are the good; the suffering, deprived, sick, ugly alone are pious, alone are blessed by God . . .—and you, the powerful and noble, are on the contrary the evil, the cruel, the lustful, the insatiable, the godless to all eternity, and you shall be in all eternity the unblessed, the accursed, and damned!" (GM I:7)

Nietzsche's *On the Genealogy of Morals,* perhaps together with *Beyond Good and Evil,* is one of the five or six seminal works in secular ethical theory. It is also the most outrageous of those seminal works in ethics. Plato gives us the perfect society; Aristotle gives us a portrait of the happy, virtuous life; Kant provides an analysis of morality and practical reason; John Stuart Mill gives us the principle of utility with its benign insistence on collective high-quality happiness. Nietzsche, by contrast, offers us a diagnosis in which morals emerge as something mean-spirited and pathetic. What we know as morality is in fact "slave morality," so named not only because of its historical origins but because of its continuing servile and inferior nature. The basis of slave morality, he tells us, is *resentment* (he uses the French *"ressentiment"*), a bitter emotion based on a sense of inferiority and frustrated vindictiveness. He contrasts slave morality with what he calls "master" morality, which he presents as noble and self-secure. His descriptions leave little question which of these two "moral types" he (and consequently we) find preferable. Nietzsche's "genealogy" of morals is designed to make the novice reader uncomfortable with his or her slavish attitudes, but it is also written to inspire a seductive sense of superiority, the urge to be (if

* An earlier version of this essay was presented at a meeting of the North American Nietzsche Society in December 1984. Some of the arguments have now appeared elsewhere, in my "Nietzsche, Postmodernism, and Resentment," in Clayton Koelb, *Nietzsche and Postmodernism* (Albany: State University of New York Press, 1990), and in chap. 6 of my *Passion for Justice* (Reading, Mass.: Addison-Wesley, 1990).

not the confidence that one is) a "master." These are dangerous attitudes, quite opposed to the edifying moral support we usually expect from ethical treatises. They are also (as in most seductions) extremely misleading, both as a moral guideline and (we suspect from some of his other writings) as an expression of Nietzsche's own intentions.

Nietzsche's "genealogy" is, in fact, only a small part genealogy; it is much more a psychological diagnosis. It does include a very condensed and rather mythic account of the history and evolution of morals, but the heart of that account is a psychological hypothesis concerning the motives and mechanisms underlying that history and evolution. "The slave revolt in morality begins," Nietzsche tells us, "when *ressentiment* itself becomes creative and gives birth to values" (GM I:10).[1] Modern critics might well dismiss such speculation as yet another version of the genetic fallacy: the real question (they might say) is not the genealogy, genesis, or motivation of morals, but rather only (in neo-Kantian terms) the *validity* of our current moral principles. Traditional moral theorists and Nietzsche expositors thus often talk past one another, the former focusing on arguments concerning the form and justification of moral precepts, the latter exposing the ulterior motives that underlie these supposedly noble, impersonal, and necessary ideals. It is a large and still largely unanswered question how genealogy and psychology can best engage the concerns of current morality and moral philosophy.

In this essay I would like to focus only on the more particular question raised by Nietzsche in the *Genealogy*—the ethical dimensions of resentment and the implications of resentment for ethics: How does resentment give rise to ethical judgments, and what does this imply about those judgments? Is resentment as such a "bad" emotion, and does its diagnosis therefore suggest the inadequacy of a morality based upon it? Max Scheler raised similar questions about the relationship between resentment and Christianity many years ago. His intention was to protect Christianity from Nietzsche's harshest accusations.[2] I have no such ax to grind here; but I do have mixed feelings about the Nietzschean campaign against morality and *ressentiment*, which will be evident in what follows. Like most novice readers, I too once was persuaded (or seduced) by Nietzsche's master-and-slave, strength-and-weakness dichotomy; but as a philosophy teacher and Nietzsche commentator, I also have promulgated it and held onto it longer than I should have.[3] There is no denying the power of Nietzsche's self-styled "polemic"—but we philosophical lambs should remain cautious in our respect for birds of prey, however "noble" they may be.

IS GENEALOGY A GENETIC FALLACY?

Historical refutation as the definitive refutation.—In former times, one sought to prove that there is no God—today one indicates how the belief that there is a God could *arise*, and how this belief acquired its weight and

importance: a counter-proof that there is no God thereby becomes superfluous. . . . In former times . . . atheists did not know how to make a clean
sweep. (D 95)

Is Nietzsche's "genealogy" in fact nothing but a sophisticated version of
the so-called "genetic fallacy"—the conflation of something's value and its
origins?[4] We should not dismiss this dismissive view of contemporary moral
theory too easily. It is certainly true—as Nietzsche says—that the genealogical argument is much more "interesting" than the often vacuous ratioci-
nations concerning the various forms of the categorical imperative. But it
would not be altogether advantageous to praise Nietzsche for placing a
collective *ad hominem* argument at the center of moral philosophy—and in
one obvious sense this is just what the genealogy of *ressentiment* does for us.
On the other hand, if Nietzsche's "genealogy" is really more psychology
than history (albeit presented in a specific historical context), then the
charge of "genetic fallacy" may be quite beside the point. It is hard to
argue, despite the still heavy Kantian bias in ethics, that the content of
ethical analysis should not include the motives of those who practice (let
alone create) an ethics. Indeed, Kant himself would insist that one cannot
evaluate the "moral worth" of an action without considering as central the
intentions (or the "will") behind it; and as Kant also points out, the distinction between the formal intentions (or maxims) of an action and the
motives behind it may in practice be undeterminable.[5] The genealogy of
morals is, first of all, a thesis about the motivation of morality.

The substance of ethics is not to be found only in the circumstances and
consequences of acts and judgments; and of course we no longer expect
to find it in mere maxims and their formal generalization. The past decade
has seen a welcome resurgence of an ancient paradigm of ethics—now
often called "virtue ethics." (Aristotle's *Nicomachean Ethics* is typically cited
as the prime example.) The core claim of virtue ethics is the importance
of moral character and virtues of character in determining moral worth.[6]
In the evaluation of character, a person's motives and emotions in acting
are surely essential. An action performed out of noble sentiments is a noble
action, even if the act itself is rather petty and inconsequential. An action
expressing vicious sentiments will be vicious, even if (through error in judgment, chance, or an overly subtle sense of irony) the act itself has benign
consequences. At least in part, the content of ethics is made up of what
one might generically call "feelings"—or better, what Kant called the "in-
clinations"—which would include not only such Kantian *Gefühle* as respect
and a sense of duty, and the sweet Humean sentiments of sympathy and
compassion, but also the nasty negative emotions of envy, anger, hatred,
vengeance, and resentment.

Where do these motives and emotions fit into an ethical analysis? One
familiar suggestion is the idea that they actually serve not only as motives

but to define ends; their satisfaction is the aim of moral (as well as non-moral) behavior. Adam Smith's supposedly "impartial" gentleman acts not only "out of sympathy" but also in order to satisfy the demands of that sympathy. ("How selfish soever man may be supposed, there are evidently some principles in his nature, which interest him in the fortune of others, and render their happiness necessary to him, though he derives nothing from it except the pleasure of seeing it."[7]) The utilitarian acts not only because of the desire for pleasure but in order to maximize pleasure as a matter of principle ("the principle of utility"). But if the utilitarian insists that ethics must be based on the pursuit of pleasure (or happiness), and the moral sentiment theorist suggests that morality depends on such sentiments as sympathy, the door is already open to the suggestion that an ethics might be based on any number of other motives or sentiments—including resentment.

It remains to be seen what these other ethics might amount to, and whether we do in fact live for pleasure (or, as Nietzsche quipped, whether only the English utilitarian does). But it is by no means an unreasonable hypothesis that we live for power rather than pleasure, and ultimately prefer a sense of self-importance to mere satisfaction. And resentment is, above all, an emotion concerned with power—or rather, with the lack of it. But we have to be very careful how this idea is developed. Lack of power is not the *cause* but the *content* of resentment; and resentment in turn is not merely the cause but the content of morality, as Nietzsche envisions it. It is not the soil from which morality springs (one of his routine metaphors) but rather the structure of morals as such—the consciousness of one's own vulnerability. ("Do unto others as . . .")

Of course, a sufficiently formal or narrowly focused account of morality might be able to ignore this—for example, by concentrating only on the logical features of the categorical imperative, or on consequences of an action rather than on its psychological content. But at the very least, as dozens of ethicists have recently (and not so recently) argued, these formal or focused accounts leave out much that is crucial.[8] Nietzsche's genealogy of resentment, accordingly, is not an instance of the genetic fallacy, but may be a substantial moral insight.

But does the grounding of morality in resentment render our morals merely pathetic, servile, herdlike, or inferior—inferior, in particular, to some more aristocratic morality? Whatever his occasional claims to the contrary, Nietzsche's genealogy of resentment is itself an ethical thesis. The study of moral "types" is not value-free, and "revaluation" is itself evaluative, not just descriptive. Whether or not there might be such a dubious discipline as "value-free" anthropology, any description of the values of one's own society is bound to be permeated with the very values described. (Claude Lévi-Strauss: "When I witness certain decisions or modes of behavior in my own society, I am filled with indignation and disgust, whereas if I observe similar behavior in a so-called primitive society, I make no attempt at a value judgment. I attempt to understand it."⁹)

To put the point differently: metaethics or moral philology is itself a way of doing ethics, though often indirect, subversive, even fraudulent—the familiar rabbit-out-of-the-hat trick in philosophy. A substantial normative conclusion is miraculously derived from a purely formal analysis of the "grammar" of ethical language, or the meaning of "good," or certain formal assumptions about rationality. What often makes metaethics appear to be ethically neutral, of course, is its seeming lack of content, its dry banality, its emphasis on the trivial and the obvious (in the guise of the technical and the obscure). Nietzsche's philology, by contrast, wrings spectacular results from what supposedly is merely social science. But the mask of neutrality is neither plausible nor appropriate; and when he insists that he is providing only historical descriptions, much as Heidegger and Sartre later insisted that they are providing phenomenological ontologies and not an ethics, we would be foolish to believe them.

But in Nietzsche's case, even more than in the work of his two illustrious successors, it is clear that there is much more to ethics than categorical imperatives and specific advice. Just as the jargon of "authenticity" or "own-ness" (*Eigentlichkeit*) has its unmistakable if nonspecific moral imperatives, the unavoidable message of the diagnosis of resentment and the pathology-laden language that surrounds it is that slave morality is *bad*. True, the supposed neutrality of Nietzsche's genealogical diagnosis might also reflect his uniform disdain for (and an implied distance from) all things human. Like his moral revolutionary predecessor Jean-Jacques Rousseau (whom Nietzsche of course despised), he was a misanthope who translated his disgust with humanity as he found it into an inspiring portrait of humanity (or superhumanity) as it once was and again may be. Master morality—albeit in refined and more artistic form, and not as primordial brutishness—is not only good but in some sense more natural, healthier, and truer to our ideal nature(s). Master morality is the "original" morality; slave morality is a reaction, an inversion, a corruption.

But Nietzsche, like his predecessor Rousseau again, insists that "we cannot go back," that more than twenty centuries have had their beneficial as well as deleterious effects. We have become more spiritual, more refined, largely under the auspices of slave morality and Christianity. What we should aspire to, therefore, is no longer what he described as "master morality," though it is notoriously unclear what Nietzsche's "legislation" of morals for the future ought to look like. The *Übermensch* is clearly beyond us, and even the best of the "higher men" are still "human, all too human." And so we seem stuck with our "slave" or "herd" morality, albeit in "bad conscience." The unrelenting contrast of the *Genealogy*, between what is natural and noble and what is reactionary and born of *ressentiment,* makes it hard for us to avoid the uncomfortable acknowledgment that, yes, morality does protect the weak against the strong; and, yes, it does sometimes seem to be the expression of resentment; and, yes, it is often used to "put down" or "level" what is best in us, in favor of the safe, the conformist, the comfortable. (The Kantian discomfort with the "supererogatory"—virtue above and beyond the call of duty—is suggestive in this regard.) Given a warrior perspective—the view that Nietzsche absorbed from the *Iliad,* and that so many American college students are taking away from *Rambo* and *Conan the Barbarian* movies (*Ninja Turtle* cartoons for their younger siblings)—our everyday conception of morality does indeed seem limp and timid, conducive to civility, perhaps, but not to spontaneous self-expression or heroism.

> With noble men cleverness can easily acquire a subtle flavor of luxury and subtlety—for here it is far less essential than the perfect functioning of the regulating unconscious instincts or even a certain imprudence, perhaps a bold recklessness . . . , or than enthusiastic impulsiveness in anger, love, reverence, gratitude and revenge. (GM I:10)

We have learned to distrust the prejudices that underlie and motivate those seemingly formal moves in moral theory; but we should also distrust any reductionist argument that claims neutrality while undermining some cherished ideal by showing its origins—of whatever kind—in something slimy, smarmy, or suspicious. Nietzsche sometimes denies that he is passing judgment on morality; but one has to be a fool to think that there is nothing discouraging or demeaning about the suggestion that we should understand our current moral "prejudices" as "slave" or "herd" morality, or that one can accept any such suggestion without looking upon morality with a kind of revulsion or embarrassment.

> Supposing that . . . the meaning of all culture is the reduction of the beast of prey "man" to a tame and civilized animal, a *domestic animal,* then one would undoubtedly have to regard all those instincts of reaction and *ressentiment* through whose aid the noble races and their ideals were finally confounded and overthrown as the actual instruments of culture. . . . Rather is the reverse not merely probable—no! today it is *palpable!* These bearers of the oppressive instincts . . . represent the regression of mankind! . . . What today constitutes *our* antipathy to "man"? . . . *Not* fear; rather that we no longer have anything left to fear in man; that the maggot "man" is swarming. (GM I:12)

Nietzsche's characterizations of *ressentiment* are anything but ethically neutral ("the hopelessly mediocre and insipid man"), nor could they be so—given the self-demeaning ethical content of the emotion itself. Walter Kaufmann is in one sense undoubtedly right when he reminds us that "it is not Nietzsche's concern in the *Genealogy* to tell us that master morality is good, while slave morality is evil"; and indeed, Nietzsche insists that we overcome our childish tendency to think of all valuation in terms of Manichean "opposite values"—good and evil, in particular. But in the last line of the First Essay he reminds us again that this rejection of "good and evil" does not entail the rejection of "good and bad"—and it is Nietzsche, not only his Manichean readers, who suggests that the polemical polarity of "master and slave" defines the whole of ethics.[10] It may be true that Nietzsche "wants to open up new perspectives" on morals; but this does not subtract from the overwhelming impression, not just owing to Nietzsche's hyperbolic rhetoric, that morality as such is something disgraceful, pathetic, despicable—and those who "invented" it were contemptible (even if they were also diabolically clever).

> The man of *ressentiment* . . . loves hiding places, secret paths and back doors, everything covert entices him as his world, his security, his refreshment; he understands how to keep silent, how not to forget, how to wait, how to be provisionally self-deprecating and humble. A race of such men of *ressentiment* is bound to become eventually cleverer than any noble race; it will also honor cleverness to a far greater degree. (GM I:10)

Nietzsche's attack on morality and its philosophical justifications is not, however, an attack on morals and values as such. It is, on the contrary, an attempt to save values and a concept of the virtues from what only appears to be their philosophical defense, in Kant and his successors and some of his predecessors as well. Alasdair MacIntyre, in his attack on the entire "enlightenment tradition and its project," has argued that modern metaethics is a nihilistic form of compensation (or resignation) for the loss of social consensus; and he makes an equally biting accusation concerning the loss of content in ethics.[11] He too argues that the essential missing ingredient is an adequate concept of the virtues and the kindred concepts of character and culture. Nietzsche's emphasis on character and his sketch of moral typology, I have argued[12] and will argue again here, help to supply this missing ingredient.

I find it surprising, therefore, that MacIntyre identifies Nietzsche as a nihilist, the "last word" on the enlightenment project, and juxtaposes him *against* Aristotle. It would rather seem that Nietzsche should be one of MacIntyre's main allies, together *with* Aristotle. Whatever else it may be, Nietzsche's emphasis on nobility and resentment is an attempt to stress character and virtue (and with them, tradition and culture) above all else in ethics. A "master morality" of nobility is an expression of good, strong character. An ethics of resentment is an expression of bad character—whatever its principles and their rationalizations. This is why abstract ethical theories, allegedly logical notions of universalizability, and most models of practical reasoning are all suspect; they distract us from concrete questions of character, and in addition often provide not only a respectable facade for faulty character but an offensive weapon for resentment as well. Reason and resentment have proven themselves to be a well-coordinated team in the guerilla war of everyday morality and moralizing.

But does resentment lie behind morality as such, as its underlying motive and definitive characteristic? Is what we call "morality" in fact a "slave" morality, based on and an expression of weakness? This is much the same defensive question asked by Max Scheler, and my answer will be much the same too: Nietzsche had a series of powerful psychological insights, but characteristically overstated and oversimplified them. There are aspects (and uses) of morality (and Christianity) that do indeed invite a diagnosis of resentment; but it is wrong to think that the condemnation is therefore global, much less "the definitive refutation." There are indeed "herd" and servile aspects of morality, and the motivation of morality may indeed (in part) be based on *ressentiment*—but even *ressentiment* has its uses.

RESSENTIMENT, RESENTMENT, AND THE POWER OF EMOTION

> While the noble man lives in trust and openness with himself (*gennaios* "of noble descent" underlines the nuance "upright" and probably also "naïve"), the man of *ressentiment* is neither upright nor naïve nor honest and straightforward with himself. His soul squints. (GM I:10)

Resentment is a familiar if uncomfortable emotion. It is always aimed at others (sometimes individuals, sometimes groups or institutions, in odd if not pathological cases divine or inanimate objects). "This *need* to direct one's view outward instead of back to oneself . . . is of the essence of *ressentiment*: in order to exist, slave morality always first needs a hostile external world; it needs, physiologically speaking, external stimuli in order to act at all—its action is fundamentally reaction. The reverse is the case with the noble mode of valuation: it acts and grows spontaneously" (GM I:10). It is a bitter emotion, typically a reaction to an injury or slight (whether intended or not); and it is often linked up with frustrated fantasies of revenge. So Nietzsche speaks of "that falsification perpetrated on its opponent—*in effigie* of course—by the submerged hatred, the vengefulness of the impotent" (GM I:10); and again, of "the submerged, darkly glowering emotions of vengefulness and hatred" (GM I:13). Of course, the frustration of those fantasies further feeds the resentment, which stimulates increasingly drastic fantasies for vengeance, and so on. By way of contrast, "should [*ressentiment*] appear in the noble man, [it] consumates and exhausts itself in an immediate reaction, and therefore does not *poison*" (GM I:10).[13]

Because resentment is thus frustrated as action and in its expression, it becomes most pronounced as a *feeling* (from the Latin "*resentire,*" to feel)—

a strong, often bitter feeling that also indicates sensitivity and vulnerability. So too the German *Empfindlichkeit* suggests a "reactionary" emotion, a form of sensibility ("*empfinden*," to feel; "*Empfindlichkeit*," sensibility, sensitivity, irritability). Why does Nietzsche so often use the French term? Arthur Danto suggests that the French "*ressentiment*," although it covers a broad range of feelings and sensibilities, encourages the distinction between vulnerability and merely imagined vengeance on the one hand and an aristocratic sense of honor on the other. The resentful man has deep feelings; the noble man acts. Then again, Danto suggests, "It may have been one of those expressions that civilized people simply used,"[14] and in any case both the origin and the meaning of the word in French seems close enough to both the English and the German.

Resentment in any language suggests a feeling, a sensitivity, and it is not particularly pleasant nor flattering. Resentment means vulnerability, and implies a reaction to an offense (real or imagined, local or global), which includes (mostly imaginary) schemes of revenge. In this, one might note, the analysis of resentment resembles Aristotle's classic account of anger in his *Rhetoric*, except that revenge intended in anger is typically part of the expression itself (e.g., in an outburst of abuse); if it is not so expressed, anger tends to turn into resentment. Thus one might say that frustration lies at the heart of resentment, and this is what distinguishes it from effective anger.

Resentment—I will dispense with the knowing tone of the French in favor of the more familiar and more easily typeset English word—is an emotion that is distinguished, first of all, by its concern and involvement with *power*. It is not the same as self-pity, with which it often shares the subjective stage; it is not merely awareness of one's misfortune, but involves a kind of blame and personal outrage, an outward projection, an overwhelming sense of injustice. But as I argued above, neither is it just a version of hatred or anger, with which it is sometimes conflated; for both of these presume an emotional and expressive power base, which resentment essentially lacks. Resentment is typically obsessive; "nothing on earth consumes a man more quickly," Nietzsche tells us. But its description often embodies such metaphors of duration and consumption as "smoldering," "simmering," "seething," and "fuming"—rather than "raging," which would quickly burn itself out.

Resentment is also notable among the emotions for its lack of any specific desire. In this, it is not the same as envy—another kindred emotion—which has the advantage of being quite specific and based on desire. Envy *wants*, even if it cannot and has no right to obtain. If resentment has a desire, it is the desire for revenge; but even this is rarely very specific—for example, as the abstract desire for the total annihilation, preceded by the utter humiliation, of its target (though the vindictive imagination of resentment is such that even that would probably not be sufficient—if it were possible, which, of course, it is not). So too, resentment is quite different from spite, into which it occasionally degenerates, for resentment is nothing if not prudential, strategic, even ruthlessly clever. It has no taste at all for self-destruction; to the contrary, it is the ultimate emotion of self-preservation (we are not talking about mere survival) at any cost.

Contrary to the most familiar accounts of Nietzsche's ethics and many of his own uncompromising condemnatory statements, Nietzsche has mixed feelings about resentment. If creativity is one of the highest virtues— and it certainly seems to be for him—then resentment would seem to be one of the most virtuous emotions; for it is certainly among the most creative, perhaps even more so than inspirational love. (Compare the schemes of Iago and Richard the Third with the witless reactions of Othello and Orlando, for example.) Insofar as language and insight, ruthless criticism and mastery of irony are skills worth praising (and Nietzsche is perfectly willing to build an entire self out of them[15]), then resentment would seem to be one of the most accomplished emotions as well—more articulate than even the most righteous anger, more clever than the most covetous envy, more critical than the indifferent spirit of reason would ever care to be. Not surprisingly, our greatest critics and commentators are men and women of resentment. Nietzsche is surely right, that our most vocal and influential moralists are men and women of deep resentment—whether or not this is true of morality as such. Our revolutionaries are men and women of resentment. In an age deprived of passion—if Kierkegaard is to be believed—they alone have the one dependable emotional motive, constant and obsessive, slow-burning but totally dependable and durable. Through resentment, they get things done. Whatever else it may be, resentment is not ineffectual.

Resentment may be an emotion that begins with an awareness of its powerlessness; but by way of compensation, or what we call "expression," resentment has forged the perfect weapon—an acid tongue and a strategic awareness of the world, which in most social contexts (excepting a few bars in Dallas and San Bernardino) guarantees parity if not victory in most social conflicts. Thus the irony, the dramatic turnaround of fortunes, as defensive resentment overpowers defenseless self-confidence and a sense of inferiority overwhelms its superiors. The neo-Nietzschean stereotype is too often portrayed as the cultivated, noble master and the miserable, illiterate slave; and the descriptions in Nietzsche's *Genealogy* certainly encourage such a reading. But the typology that counts in the genealogy of resentment and morals is the articulate slave and the tongue-tied, even witless master. It is the slaves who are sufficiently ingenious to do what even Nietzsche despairs of doing; they invent new values. And it is the masters, not the slaves, who become decadent and dependent, and allow themselves to be taken in by the strategies of resentment. Hegel had it right in the *Phenomenology*; so did Joseph Losey in his 1963 movie *The Servant*.

Speech is the swordplay of the impotent; but in the absence of real swords it is often overpowering. Language may be the political invention of the "herd" (as Nietzsche suggests in *The Gay Science*), but it is also the medium in which real power is expressed and exchanged. Irony is the ultimate weapon of resentment; and as Socrates so ably demonstrated, it turns ignorance into power, and personal weakness into philosophical strength. It is no wonder that Nietzsche had such mixed feelings about his predecessor in the weaponry of resentment, who created the "tyranny of reason" as the successful expression of his own will to power. Nietzsche used irony and "genealogy" as Socrates used dialectic, to undermine and ultimately dominate others and their opinions.

Nietzsche famously tells us that certain emotions "drag us down with their stupidity"—but resentment is surely not one of them. There is no emotion more clever, more powerful, more life-preserving, if not life "enhancing," no emotion more conducive to the grand act of revenge that Nietzsche himself wishes to perpetrate on modernity and the Christian world. Resentment creates its own power, which displaces its own targets and (even despite itself) satisfies its desire for revenge. Thus the victory of the slave over the master in Hegel's *Phenomenology*. Thus the victory, writ large, of slave morality. The felt impotence of resentment should not be confused with its expression, which is a kind of arrogance, or with the practical results of resentment, which sometimes tend to be powerful and effective indeed. Thus what Nietzsche despises about resentment—and an ethics built out of resentment—cannot be its ineffectiveness; for he often acknowledges and even admires its success (as in GM I:16, where he comments: "The Jews were the priestly nation of *ressentiment par excellence*, in whom there dwelt an unequaled popular-moral genius").

The expression of resentment, when ineffective, may be pathetic but is rarely worthy of comment. When it is effective, it may be vicious and destructive, insensitive to and uncaring about the needs of others even if it is overly sensitive to its own sense of slight or offense. But, in any case, it is hard to find Nietzschean grounds for an attack on viciousness or a defense of pity—another emotion Nietzsche obviously loathes. Masters as well as slaves can be (and sometimes ought to be) cruel, so it is not cruelty as such that he abhors. Nor is it vengeance, which he sometimes demeans as an inferior form of justice, but also praises—when quick and efficient—as the antidote to resentment (GM I:10–12). Indeed, although Nietzsche is sometimes suspicious of cruelty, in GM II:5–7 he discusses the cruel historical spectacles that were part of every festival—and he does so with remarkably little disgust or criticism. Indeed, he even notes that "without cruelty there is no festival," and says: "To see others suffer does one good, to make others suffer even more: this is a hard saying but an ancient, mighty, human, all-too-human principle" (GM II:6).

One might argue, of course, that the means that resentment employs in obtaining power are hypocritical: one gains power by denying one's power, and one advances one's self-interest by appearing to be indifferent to one's self-interest (for example, by pointing to "the rules" or defending one's action strictly in the name of some "principle"). "The man of *ressentiment*" is devious. "His soul *squints*; his spirit loves hiding places, secret paths and back doors, everything covert entices him as his world, his security, his refreshment; he understands how to keep silent, how not to forget, how to wait, how to be provisionally self-deprecating and humble" (GM I:10). But it is not clear that such duplicity and deception is hypocrisy rather than just smart strategy. "A race of such men of *ressentiment* is bound to become eventually *cleverer* than any noble race" (GM I:10).

Despite its display of indifference and disdain for power, resentment exemplifies the obsession with power. But isn't this what "the will to power" is all about—or is there supposed to be some further (moral) prohibition, "power, yes, but not by hook or by crook"? So, what is it about resentment that Nietzsche so despises? True, resentment is essentially a "reaction"—but why should we give so much ethical weight to the *au courant* (and, I believe, mistaken) dualism of the "active/reactive" in Nietzsche?[16] Why should "spontaneity" be such an exceptional virtue, or the overly Kantian virtue of "autonomy"? Why should the "poison" that fueled his genius be the source of such (self-?) contempt for him? How did Nietzsche think himself to be escaping the vicious psychological circle involved in resenting his own resentment—a dubious form of "self-overcoming" or "undergoing" in any case?

We can readily appreciate the temptation here to dismiss the whole performance as "just another perspective" or another great display of clever irony, even "a polemic."[17] But the problem of what is wrong with resentment cuts very deep into Nietzsche's philosophy. As an expression of the will to power, it cannot invite his scorn. As an ingenious and deceitful expression of the will to power, it would seem to invite his praise. And so what I have come to suspect is that it wasn't resentment that was at fault at all, nor its expression, nor its presumption in making supposedly universal moral judgments. What was despicable and pathetic to Nietzsche, it seems, was the underlying weakness, the presupposition of resentment rather than the emotion itself.

EAGLES AND LAMBS, MASTERS AND SLAVES: METAPHORS OF STRENGTH AND WEAKNESS

That lambs dislike great birds of prey does not seem strange: only it gives no ground for reproaching these birds of prey for bearing off little lambs. And if the lambs say among themselves: "These birds of prey are evil; and whoever is least like a bird of prey, but rather its opposite, a lamb—would he not be good?" there is no reason to find fault with this institution of an ideal, except perhaps that the birds of prey might view it a little ironically and say: " *We* don't dislike them at all, these good little lambs; we even love them: nothing is more tasty than a tender lamb." (GM I:13)

Among human beings, at least, contempt for weakness is not an unusual sentiment, even among the weak. Servants not infrequently express their loathing for servants, patients for patients, derelicts for derelicts, failures for failures, losers for losers. As such, the contempt for weakness lends itself to self-contempt, even self-loathing. Strength—whether as independence or as health or as social status or as success or as victory—becomes a good in itself. Of course, what counts as "strength" and as "weakness" varies considerably from example to example. But it is not unusual (as with other such central evaluative terms) to generalize quickly and (too) confidently over the entire range of meanings; and what Nietzsche particularly despises so much about resentment is just that generalized sense of impotence— the germ (not the soil) from which the whole plant grows. It is weakness itself that is "bad" and pathetic, not its effects or its expressions.

But the criteria for strength and weakness are by no means obvious or consistent in Nietzsche; and it is not even obvious, for example, that weakness is a lack of strength. Sometimes the descriptions in the *Genealogy* suggest that social status and class alone determine strength and weakness; aristocrats, by virtue of their breeding and education, are strong. Because of their servile positions, slaves are weak, whatever physical or spiritual strength they might possess. The analogy of the lambs and the eagles (an overly American interpretation of the text, but shorter to type than "birds of prey") takes the difference to its extremes, as a biologically determined, obviously irreversible species difference between prey and predators. So to speak of strength and weakness—natural plunderer versus perpetual victim—is, to put it mildly, to stack the deck from the beginning. (Consider, for example, Hobbes's no more benign but obviously more plausible assumption of basic equality—the simple fact that even the most powerful of men is vulnerable to the right kind of conspiracy, stealth, or weapon.)

Sometimes Nietzsche seems to be using a quasi-medical ("physiological") criterion; strong means healthy, weak means sickly. But even this, we shall see, is by no means consistent; and some of what he says would even imply that it is the slaves who are strong, not the masters. More than anything else, he seems to see strength and weakness in *aesthetic* terms, harking back, no doubt, to his famous earlier injunction that one should live one's life like a work of art.[18] Masters are a delight to behold; it would be even more of a delight to be one, to experience that sense of spontaneity and self-confidence. Slaves, to put it politely, are banal and boring. Their demeanor is servile and timid. They protect themselves with humorless, submissive smiles, without character.[19] When backs are turned, they snarl. It is Othello who provides the nobility in the play that bears his name. Iago provides only the plot, after proving himself already hateful to the audience. But then again, we should remember Simone Weil's well-placed warning, that the vices that make good theater are intolerable in life, and the banality of goodness on the stage is no argument against the virtues.[20]

Again, Nietzsche sometimes says that he is giving us mere descriptions, linguistic analyses, "two types" of moral creatures. But his preference for "the masters" is suggested in dozens of different ways. Notice, for example, that in his notorious "lambs and eagles," Nietzsche describes the lamb's conversation in the third person but the eagles' irony in the first person. A small symptom, but a significant one. I think that there can be little doubt that Nietzsche admires power, takes it to be a value in itself (second only, perhaps, to the value of "increasing one's power"). Some philosophers love neatness and order. Their typically static philosophies are, ultimately, an homage to domesticity. Nietzsche has an obsession with power, with energy and expression. (*Ad hominem* ironies abound, of course.) His philosophy, accordingly, is an homage to the virtues of potency, strength, robustness. And this is so even when he is not (*especially* when he is not) explicitly praising "the will to power." Indeed his very *style* is an obvious expression of a spectacularly robust and powerful philosophical mind. What Nietzsche despises about resentment is not the emotion but its presupposition of impotence. What he despises about impotence is its lack of energy and robustness. What he loathes about slave morality is not its deceitfulness, or even its hypocrisy, but rather its meekness and timidity.

Of course, this raises one of the perennial questions about Nietzsche's philosophy: What is "power" (*Macht*)? I want to sidestep this difficult question, however, and continue to pursue the simpler pair of questions (not the same by any means, but more manageable): What is strength? And what is weakness? It is all too easy to think in Homeric warrior metaphors—the strength of an Achilles or a Hercules, the broken servility of a captured slave. Of course, there were all those Christian gladiators and the Jews at Masada, and there were those generations of effete and all-but-defenseless mutually resentful Roman emperors and aristocrats. (Poison isn't exactly the weapon of choice for a warrior.) But physical and military prowess is not the "power" that Nietzsche is endorsing; and one of the most effective responses to Roman military might, it turned out, was the rather masterly practice of "turning the other cheek." In our own times, this is the strategy of "nonviolent resistance" practiced by Gandhi and Martin Luther King. Is there any sense in which this is an expression of weakness? Does the unwillingness to fight indicate weakness? Or doesn't it rather display great courage, strength, and self-certainty, even superiority? The refusal to fight does not entail the inability to fight; and it is not essential to the question of whether cheek-turners could in fact physically defeat their rivals (a popular loss of conviction displayed in many a country song and cowboy movie).

It may matter, of course, whether the cheek-turning is the expression of an ideology or some deeper strategy, or just an attempt to avoid a fight; but even in the latter case, is it necessarily an expression of weakness? Is the presence or absence of fear a consideration here? And if so, in what amounts? (Aristotle, for instance, insists that courage is not the absence of fear, but rather its presence in appropriate amounts.) Does it matter who ultimately wins? Are self-confidence and self-esteem the ultimate measures of strength, whatever the strategy and whatever the outcome? Indeed, isn't "strength" ultimately a *moral* notion? Of course, "moral" here need not mean "defined by morality," but rather may mean (in the more general sense assumed by Aristotle) "practical"—having to do with social behavior, and so being not merely theoretical or personal. Nor need we assume (in Kantian terms) any problematic distinction between moral and nonmoral virtues. It is here, I think, that we see the kind of "strength" that Nietzsche praises (and envies) in the "masters" of the *Genealogy*—that spontaneous personal confidence that is comparatively free from self-doubt, that feels not so much superior as self-satisfied and independent. It is worth noting how much at odds this enviable sense of self-satisfaction is with the advocacy of self-doubt, even self-contempt, and "going under" that marks one of *Zarathustra*'s major moral themes. But it is also easy to see how it would be a virtue. Moral fortitude is a virtue in its own right, quite apart from its particular intentions and its consequences.

The measure of strength may have seemed happily straightforward in those mythical days when "men were men" and all struggles and competitions were settled through physical combat. There we have the stripped-bare, even less-than-Spartan landscape described by Hegel in the *Phenomenology* as the confrontation of "two self-consciousnesses." (So too we might think of the meeting of "unencumbered" but fully rational beings in John Rawls's "original position," except that strength in that odd circumstance would lie wholly in one's negotiating abilities.[21]) But once we introduce such messy complications as an already existing society with an established "pecking order" and classes and social status and the ordeals of civility, the measure of strength (and weakness) is by no means so obvious. In *End of the Road* John Barth's college teacher (Jacob Horner) asks his students: Who is more free, the person who flaunts the rules or the person who lives within them? We can simply change the word "free" to "strong" and appreciate the paradox that civility imposes on the seemingly natural notions of strength and weakness.

Nietzsche, of course, is not defending civility as such; but it is worth noting that his own list of "the four cardinal virtues"—honesty, courage, generosity, politeness—not to mention the descriptions we have of his own behavior from Lou Salome,[22] sounds about as civil as one would expect of a nineteenth-century German gentleman. But even in "the state of nature," two male wolves settling their turf disputes often seem not to notice that one is in fact three times the size of the other, and the confrontation is almost always settled by bloodless compromise. And, according to Jane Goodall, alpha male chimps (models of Nietzsche's "master"?) are not always (or even usually) the strongest or the smartest males, but rather those with the most *chutzpah* (a technical term in primate studies).[23] Here too these potentially vicious animals rarely kill or harm one another, and civility (what else would one call it?) rules. Accordingly, Nietzsche rightly insists (though not consistently) that strength is not to be measured by any such confrontation at all, much less by physical strength and prowess, and that strength is an intrinsic and not a competitive quality.

It is with this in mind that I want to go back to Nietzsche's famous dualistic and no doubt overly simplified typology of "two moral types: master and slave." Even sticking to his own descriptions, there are a variety of ways of characterizing the two types. There is, first of all, the initial, quite biased description that so readily lends itself to envy of the original masters and disgust with slave morality. According to this portrait, masters are self-assertive, creative, and self-confident. They have all the advantages of birth, good breeding, good upbringing, power, and wealth. They enjoy themselves, think well of themselves, and do great things. Slaves, by contrast, are miserable, threatened, and forced to do the bidding of others. They are impoverished, often unhealthy, cowardly, inhibited, and mutually dependent. We picture them pathetically huddling together, plotting and scheming. They are not too bright, but are bitterly vindictive. They reject those desires they cannot hope to satisfy, plot against those who do satisfy them, and call both the desires and those who satisfy them "evil." Nietzsche's contrast between the noble bird of prey and the pathetic little lambs makes the picture quite graphic. Notice also his conflation of master morality with social superiority and all of the advantages of power. Slave morality, by contrast, is not just a moral perspective but the entirety of a miserable, pathetic life. Who among us, then, would choose to be a slave?[24]

Even in the context of ancient history, however, this portrait is simpleminded and inaccurate. Anyone who keeps up with the news or is a regular viewer of "Life-Styles of the Rich and Famous" will not be surprised to hear that the powerful are often uncreative, belligerently undereducated, shallow, pathetically dependent, defensive, and narcissistic. Should we really believe that Sardanapulus was otherwise? And in the ancient world, the best educated were more often than not the slaves—who shared (rather than rejected) their masters' way of life. But, of course, this isn't the point of Nietzsche's caricature. The point is simply that master morality (what now would probably be recognized as self-actualization) was first and unproblematic; while slave morality could only come into existence as a *reaction* based on resentment—the resentment of some slaves, not of all, and then originally only of the most clever and resentful among them. But this raises the question, with regard to these ingenious rebels, whether they deserve to be identified with the herd, or rather to be celebrated as champions of the downtrodden—and whether resentment, accordingly, should be recognized as nothing less than the basic heroic prompting of a general sense of injustice.[25]

So here is a very different description. Master morality is represented by those who had the good fortune to be born well and raised with many advantages—not the least of which is that self-confidence bordering on arrogance that, at its best, breeds bold achievement, but (not even at its worst) may express itself in that unearned and typically pompous posture of superiority that one expects to see through the windshield of any Corvette. Masters pursue their own desires, and their satisfaction, and they treat most inhibitions and prohibitions as something quite foreign, not applicable to them. They are not particularly ambitious, for ambition is already a sign of insecurity and lack of mastery. They may think of themselves as superior as a group; but this shared sense is about all there is to their sense of community. Masters do not think much about justice, both because they lack any motive to do so, and because any reasonable standard of justice makes them (at least) uncomfortable. I think it would not be far-fetched to say that such beings, far from representing some proto-ubermenschly ideal, come rather closer to Christopher Lasch's description of contemporary narcissism.

Consider, then, the so-called slaves—those who are group-oriented, mutually dependent, ambitious, but frustrated by obstacles not of their own making. The slave has an ideal image of the world—perhaps even an ideology—which (not surprisingly) emphasizes some of one's own (perceived) virtues and raises general (rather than merely personal) narcissism. They have legitimate, justified complaints about the state of the world and their own position in it—complaints that include systematic features (if not universal principles) encompassing others who may be much worse off than themselves. Consequently, they become envious, rebellious, and resentful. They *react* against a world that they did not make, which is not just, which is ruled by people who—even by the standards they themselves espouse—do not deserve their advantages. Like Camus's Sisyphus, they may continue in their duties, made tolerable by "scorn and defiance." Yet they recognize not the absurdity but the *injustice* of their situation.

This is the crux of my doubts about Nietzsche's thesis—his refusal to acknowledge resentment as an essential ingredient in our sense of justice (and his corresponding restriction of "justice" to a virtue of the powerful and privileged). (More on this in the final section.) There are, to be sure, certain moralities that drain or squander our energies with needless inhibitions, moralities that distract us or demean our bodily needs and delights; and much of Nietzsche's attack—especially his well-focused critique of asceticism in the Third Essay of the *Genealogy*—is (like the work of a corporate time-study man) designed to lay their inefficiencies bare. But the sense of oppression and injustice—no matter how "reactive"—can be a powerful source of energy and well-directed vitality; and thus at least one form of slave morality and resentment would seem to escape his harsh and one-sided critique.

The metaphors Nietzsche most often uses in talking about strength are medical metaphors, health and sickliness, "physiological" images. Master morality is healthy; slave morality is sickly. Strength as health is clearly a personal and not a competitive virtue. It has much to do with one's metabolic fund of energy, expressed in a spontaneity that is not so much thoughtless or carefree as robust. Weakness as sickliness is above all a lack of energy, a lethargy caused by exhaustion. But Nietzsche's vision here is often of a very different kind; and it is not health as such but the response to ill-health that is the measure of strength. His famous (but clearly false) comment that "what does not overcome me makes me stronger" is emblematic of a certain way of thinking about strength and heroism, manifested recently in all of those made-for-television movies about brave souls with AIDS or cancer, or a child tragically ill with leukemia.

One need not speculate or search very far for the personal origins of Nietzsche's concern about health and his rather complex conceptions of the proper response to illness. Having sampled the gamut of such reactions ourselves during a week-long bout with a virulent flu, most of us can easily understand how such mixed and obsessive feelings are possible. But they don't add up to a philosophy, much less a consistent criterion of strength. That which does not overcome me typically leaves me weaker, no matter how noble and stalwart my resistance has been. It is all well and good to desire good health; but, as Aristotle noted, health is a presupposition of virtue and not itself a virtue that deserves admiration. It is certainly admirable that Nietzsche defied ill-health and insomnia and wrote ten brilliant pages a day; but this is hardly the mark of the spontaneously healthy "master" that emerges in those pages. The medical metaphor, accordingly, is a rather bewildering place to look for his conceptions of strength and weakness.

Sometimes Nietzsche seems to indicate that strength lies in one's sense of *independence* (not to be confused with the more Kantian notion of autonomy). Weakness, by contrast, is identified with dependency—that same dependency that Rousseau so despised and opposed to the natural independence he called "freedom." The identification of weakness with mutual dependency is more obvious in the designation of "*herd* morality" than in "slave morality"; but again, this raises a great many problems (some of which Nietzsche surely shares with Rousseau). Bernd Magnus has commented that what Nietzsche intends by his unflattering collective noun "the herd" is what most of us mean by "community." And as soon as one probes the alleged "weakness" of interdependency, one discovers, I believe, far more virtues than vices.

It is true that a person who is "attached" to his or her friends and loved ones is thereby vulnerable, not only to loss but to moral accusations of lack of consideration and, worse, betrayal. But why should vulnerability be considered to be a weakness, and not rather a strength? Compare Nietzsche's discussion of "parasites" in the Second Essay, where he makes it quite clear that one's strength should be measured by how many of them one can endure. But if parasites, why not friends, family, and lovers? And why think that such relationships can or ought to be unidirectional only? What is so admirable about so-called independence? True, one can be devastated by the loss of a close friend (and Nietzsche's own relations with his friends were, one can reasonably say, often devastating). Even if one has many friends, the loss of one can be catastrophic; but the implied alternative of affectionate indifference or Zarathustra-like hermitage is hardly the solution. Nietzsche does not dismiss the moral importance of friendships. Indeed, he personally and occasionally in his works gave friendship a place in his ethics comparable only to Aristotle's rich discussion in books eight and nine of the *Ethics* (e.g., in *Human, All Too Human*). But in the *Genealogy* and too often elsewhere the attachments and dependencies of mutual need and affection are given too short *schrift*; and the implication is that interdependence is itself a product of resentment, and therefore servile and degrading. (Lambs like and need other lambs; eagles tend to be singular, and prey particularly on those lambs whose misfortune it is to wander off alone.)

However strength and weakness are to be understood, resentment presupposes some *sense* of impotence and vulnerability. Thus it is important to distinguish between any number of more or less "objective" criteria for strength and weakness on the one hand and this personal sense of weakness on the other. It is often thought that Nietzsche's claim is that only the weak feel resentment; but the text of the *Genealogy* makes it quite clear that this is not so. The strong feel resentment, too, for they also find themselves facing a world that is not always in their control or to their liking. The most illuminating cases of resentment are to be found not in the pathetic digs of the underclass but in the highest rings of power. In the Washington White House, for example, we have seen the spectacle of the most powerful politician on earth seething with resentment, every act expressing a sense of frustration and impotence. Agamemnon was capable of resentment, though he would also seem to be a paragon of ancient master morality. And then there is Achilles, sulking and fuming in his tent. Napoleon, Nietzsche's timely exemplar of master morality in the *Genealogy*, was a cauldron of simmering resentment, probably because he was Corsican rather than because he was short. Or, to take a more modern example: Pete Rose, once of the Philadelphia Phillies and more recently of Las Vegas, still displayed a sense of bitter resentment even when he was one of the most physically powerful and successful men in America. (It has been pointed out that Rose was quite short in his formative years, and he never lost that sense of defensiveness even when he filled out to size later on.)

Resentment, in other words, is based on an original perception of oneself, not—as Nietzsche sometimes seems to argue—on any natural or socially objective criterion. And so too the weakness he so despises is neither the natural vulnerability of the lamb nor the social inferiority of the slave, but rather a kind of self-contempt—a refusal to accept or acknowledge oneself, a kind of self-torture that in Nietzsche as well as in those ascetics he attacks gets passed off as a kind of virtue, even as virtue itself.

Nietzsche insists that the difference between the weak and the strong is not the occurrence of resentment but its disposition and vicissitudes. A strong character may experience resentment but immediately discharges it in action; it does not "poison" him (GM I:10). But it then becomes clear that objective strength or success cannot be the issue; the poison of resentment works only on those who have frustrated ambitions and desires, whose self-esteem depends on their social status and other measures of personal worth and accomplishment. Thus it is easy to see the wisdom of the Zen master and the Talmudic scholar, who are never poisoned by resentment because they never allow themselves those desires and expectations which can be frustrated and lead to resentment. One also finds great strength and acceptance (not just resignation) among the most abused and downtrodden members of society. ("I have found strength where one does not look for it: in simple, mild, and pleasant people, without the least desire to rule—and, conversely, the desire to rule has often appeared to me as a sign of inner weakness." What would Nietzsche have thought of "the Blues"?[26]) Here, of course, we remember Nietzsche's bitter criticism— "only the emasculated man the good man"—but the difference between what he himself praises as discipline and self-mastery and the harsh accusation of *apatheia* (despite its lineage as the highest philosophical praise) is not always easy to make out. It seems to me that we need a far more subtle ethics of emotion than some crude scale of the intensity of desire and its frustration.

The man of resentment is hardly devoid of passion—even intense passion; his is the ultimate passion, which burns furiously without burning itself out. But what fuels that resentment is a raging sense of wounded self-esteem; and a plausible hypothesis is that the most demanding people, not the most impotent, will most likely be the most resentful. In two of Camus's most famous novels, one might compare and contrast Meursault (in *L'étranger*) and Jean-Baptiste Clamence (in *La chute*). Meursault has no expectations, no emotional attachments, virtually no thoughts, no morals, no more than a momentary sense of embarrassment or shame, no fears, hopes, or anxieties; and even as he is being condemned to death in an absurd mockery of a trial, he is not the least bit resentful. Clamence, on the other hand, has been "on top of the world," a great success in his career and in his life in the liveliest city in the world; but he harbored an outrageous presumption, the presumption of his own innocence. He is high on his own self-esteem. He believes he *deserves* his success. He thinks himself to be perfect. And when we meet him sipping cheap Dutch gin in a seedy bar in Amsterdam, we recognize him as one of the most resentful characters in modern literature. Indeed, Camus's own characterization of "the Absurd" as a confrontation between our "rational" expectations and an "indifferent universe" says a lot about the human foundations of resentment.

If our morality is an ethics of resentment, therefore, it should not be concluded that it is thereby an ethics of weakness, an expression of weakness, or a devious attempt to protect the weak from the strong. Indeed, it might be something quite different. It might be important, for example, to know *who* among the ancient Zoroastrians, Hebrews, and Christians was most responsible for the revolution in morals that Nietzsche describes. A good educated guess would be that, just as modern revolutions tend to be led by the middle- and upper-middle class—and then when circumstances are improving rather than desperate—moralities of resentment tend to be created by the comparatively well off, who want but are blocked from more power, just when they are in fact already ascending in society. Not slaves but freemen and scholars, not the martyrs but the Christian administrators, brought about the slave revolt in morals.

POWERS OF THE WEAK: MASTERS, SLAVES, AND THE ORIGINS OF JUSTICE

Justice naturally derives from prudent concern with self-preservation. . . . Men have forgotten the original purpose of so-called just, fair actions, and for millennia have been taught to admire and emulate such actions. Hence it has gradually come to appear as if a just action were unegoistic. (HH I:92)

As for Dühring's proposition that the home of justice is to be sought in the sphere of the reactive feelings, one is obliged for truth's sake to counter it with a blunt antithesis: the last *sphere to be conquered by the spirit of justice is the sphere of the reactive feelings!* (GM II:11)

One must be careful not to conflate envy and resentment. For resentment is a moral feeling. If we resent our having less than others, it must be because we think that their being better off is the result of unjust institutions, or wrongful conduct on their part. Those who express resentment must be prepared to show why certain institutions are unjust or how others have injured them.

JOHN RAWLS, *A Theory of Justice*, p. 533

In the Nietzschean context, we are so accustomed to thinking of resentment in its seething, vicious, most nasty and "squinty" embodiment and expression that we fail to see that the same emotion invites a very different sort of interpretation. (Scheler, for instance, never took Nietzsche to task for being unfair to resentment; he only wanted to insist that Christianity and Christian morality were not necessarily based on this admittedly repulsive emotion.) Resentment is an extremely philosophical emotion. It is aware of the larger view. It has keen eyesight (the more Aristotelean analog of Nietzsche's much-celebrated sense of smell). It is quite conscious of not only how things are but of how they might be—and, most important, of how they ought to be. True, resentment always has a personal touch; one is always to some extent resentful *for oneself.* Yet resentment has not only the capacity but the tendency to open itself up to more general considerations—namely, those we call compassion (literally "feeling with," not just empathy). And, most important of all, it is the gateway to a sense of justice— or, more accurately, a sense of injustice—from which our sense of justice is derived.[27] It is a harsh and one-sided analysis indeed that insists that the camaraderie of the resentful is only that of the "misery loves company" variety.

What is also true is that the sense of injustice is contagious, and that justice is a concept that is never merely personal. Miserable people made aware of the systematic structures of their oppression are bound to generalize, schematize, and conspire—not for the sake of mere commiseration but for the sake of corrective action. It is true that one all-too-familiar expression of resentment (much cited by Nietzsche) is mere *Schadenfreude*, the vicious delight in other people's misfortunes. But a very different expression of the same emotion can be a call to action combined with mutual support and solidarity ("fraternity" and "sisterhood" are common metaphors for a shared sense of oppression). Resentment is, above all, this sense of oppression and the renewed appreciation of politics and political strategy that goes along with it; and this presupposes, as a matter of strategy if not also compassion, that the oppression and thus the resentment are shared.

The sense of oppression may be as general as a reasoned but burning dissatisfaction with the way the world is—the "scorn and defiance" so celebrated by Camus in his *Myth of Sisyphus*. But the sense of oppression may also turn itself into an insatiable curiosity about the institutional structures that are responsible for one's fate, thereby taking that fate upon oneself— for example, in the more political existentialism of Jean-Paul Sartre. It is no surprise that both brands of "existentialism" found an enormous audience in the confusion following the Second World War; nor is it a surprise to find that both philosophers elevated resentment (though not by that name) to a philosophical principle of sorts. Resentment lies at the very heart of democracy—Nietzsche was right about that—but that is not an argument against it. Resentment is no mere "reaction" but a keen sense of injustice, which is, in turn, the foundation of our sense of justice and the interpersonal linkage—no matter how fraught with tensions and disagreements—that ties our society together.

Many philosophers, including not only Nietzsche but Socrates too, have contrasted resentment and vindictiveness with justice. But resentment plays a spectacular role both in the evolution of justice and in the recognition of injustice. Granted, resentment always begins with a sort of self-absorption if not outright self-interest, as well as some bitter sense of disappointment or humiliation. But it then tends to rationalize and generalize, and so project its own impotence outward as a *claim*—even a theory—about injustice in the world. It is from this sense of being unfairly treated, along with a consequent feeling of vengefulness (and, one hopes, a countermanding sense of compassion and other more generous sentiments), that our overall sense of justice—based on a prior sense of injustice—develops.

Indeed, even Rawls, who works so hard to make justice out to be a matter of practical reason, acknowledges the significance of resentment in the psychological origins of justice. He notes that resentment is already the recognition that someone else's "being better off is the result of unjust institutions, or wrongful conduct on their part,"[28] and he construes that emotion as if it already contains within it the demands usually leveled against philosophical argument: "Those who express resentment must be prepared to show why certain institutions are unjust or how others have injured them." I think that "must" is out of place here; resentment as such is not under any particular academic or conversational obligations. But it is true that resentment, in its urge to generalize and project itself and in its aim to undermine the status quo, tends to be quite articulate and outspoken, full of reasons if not reasonable or rational in the usual sense of dispassionate objectivity. Indeed, if justice really did depend on Rawlsian rationality, it is not hard to imagine that there would be no justice at all.

Of course, there are those people whose sense of justice is almost wholly obsessed with resentment, whose sense of "oppression" far outweighs any sense of compassion and eclipses any possible empathy with "the oppressor." And there are those for whom the slightest slight and most minimal offense are cause for petty *ressentiment*. (It *does* sometimes sound more sarcastic *en français!*) But even then, resentment rarely remains mere personal bitterness and almost always thinks of itself in terms of some larger injustice—not only to oneself but, typically, to an entire group of fellow-sufferers. This is not to say that resentment has embodied within it any principles of justice; but it certainly may contain such principles and, in any case, it involves some appeal to expectations or implicit standards of fairness.

These may be as simple and concrete as (in the case of my two sibling puppies) "that's for me, not you!" or as complex and abstract as "no one should get an ambassadorship on the basis of party politics alone" (when I, a foreign service professional, have just been passed over). Resentment always has a personal basis, though not a person-focus or personal scope. One always feels somehow deprived or slighted oneself (or feels this *for* someone else, with whom one identifies); but the focus of one's complaint is the nature of the slight rather than just the slight itself. And the scope of the complaint is, at least in articulate "rational" animals such as ourselves, the whole class of deprivations and slights that have been instantiated here in this one. Resentment, one might say, is the class action suit among the emotions. Thus even if self-absorbed, it typically becomes a social emotion, embracing others (even if with a snarl). One might say that it is resentment, not misery, that loves company. And with enough company and a little bit of courage, it can even start a revolution. It often has.

Nietzsche's attack on the familiar sense of justice is an attack on the purely vindictive, "reactive" emotions by which the weak and incompetent tried to "get at" those who were strong and successful. He takes it to have consisted more of envy than resentment, and more of petty vindictiveness than retribution or even revenge. It thus has become an instrument of "leveling," of equal distribution, of denying differences. What Nietzsche prefers to call "justice," by contrast (though not what most of us would recognize as "justice"), is that superior sense of being "above" all slights and beyond resentment, envy, and vindictiveness.

Justice as we usually understand it tends to turn on such notions as "getting even" and making sure that each person gets his or her due. A sense of justice properly understood, according to Nietzsche, is very much akin in its expression (though not in its motivation) to the Christian virtues of mercy and forgiveness. But as so often, he turns these virtues inside out as he defends them. One is merciful and just not because one does not feel the right to judge or punish, nor because one ought rather to appeal to some greater court of justice, and emphatically not because one is afraid of the consequences of one's actions. It is rather that one has much more important things to do with one's life than worry about the past and about those whom Nietzsche refers to with his usual flattering vocabulary as "parasites." As for the worry that each person should get his or her due, he insists that justice so considered is not intended as a defense of the weak, but rather has to do with the cultivation and expression of one's own best virtues. (He allows, however, that those who are so virtuous have a "duty" to help the weak.[29])

One might draw a very cautious parallel between Nietzsche's very elitist view of justice and the view that one finds today in some libertarian writings; for example, Robert Shaeffer's recent *Resentment Against Achievement,* where the author distinguishes between a "morality of achievement" and a morality of "resentment against achievement." Of course, Nietzsche would have little tolerance for the obsession with "rights" that preoccupies so much of libertarian thinking; and he would be the first to point out the bitter resentment of many such authors against those who supposedly "resent achievement." But his emphasis on personal excellence and his condemnation of reactive mediocrity would strike a sympathetic chord in this quarter. What Nietzsche presumes, along with a great many conservative thinkers, is the relative stability of character and abilities, as well as sharp differences between individuals. There are those who have the talent and energy to achieve, and those who do not. People don't change (although the rhetoric of bootstrap "self-improvement" often disguises this sense of fatalism under a mask of personal responsibility); and it is as absurd for a talented person to deny those talents as it is for an untalented person to claim the privileges of the talented. (The lambs and eagles analogy in the *Genealogy* makes this point as brutally as is imaginable.)

Nietzsche frequently lambasts those whom he sarcastically calls "the improvers of mankind," and often seems as annoyed with those who would try to improve the human condition as with those who would "level" it to the lowest common demoninator. (The *Übermensch,* remember, is meant to *replace* us mere humans, not merely serve as our new role model.) Thus we can understand (but hardly applaud) Nietzsche's nearly total lack of sympathy with what many modern writers would call "social justice." Justice requires taking resentment seriously. But resentment doesn't make sense unless we also acknowledge the warrant of its essential freedom and central negativism: the world could and should be other than it is, with those at the top no longer on top, and those on the bottom no longer at the bottom. And here, as Nietzsche often acknowledges, resentment is not impotent but dangerous.

What bothers many readers of the *Genealogy,* even those who are persuaded by its central characterization of and attack on "slave morality," is Nietzsche's apparent determinism—not in the now-established technical sense, to be sure, but in the more ordinary sense in which "people are the way they are, and there is little that they can do to change." His sarcasm regarding "the improvers of mankind" is one familiar reflection of this attitude (see TI VII, especially 2); and the analogy of eagles and lambs explicitly suggests that the difference between the strong and the weak is one of basic biology, not a matter of choice.

A far darker interpretation of the "improvers" that Nietzsche attacks, accordingly, is to be found not in the naïve reformer of society but in its most cruel and uncompromising tyrants—who might all too easily be considered "masters" in Nietzsche's simple-minded dualism. Such modern monsters as Stalin and Pol Pot come to mind as brutal examples of men who had a vision—an "ideology"—about what humanity might be as opposed to the miserable and deluded creatures that they are in present society; and so they set about systematically decimating entire populations, turning their values upside down (as George Orwell straightforwardly argued in *Animal Farm*, including "strength is weakness"). With such an interpretation in mind we should be thoroughly shocked when Nietzsche tells us, at the end of a discussion in which he is centrally concerned with resentment and the "revaluation of values," that one is not responsible for one's predatory ways, any more than one is responsible for one's weaknesses. That a person is responsible and capable of change, he argues, is purported to be an illusion fostered by centuries of Christianity, and more recently by Kant. That in turn undermines the validity of resentment and moral judgment:

> No wonder if the submerged, darkly glowering emotions of vengefulness and hatred exploit this [Kantian] belief [in the changeling subject] for their own ends and in fact maintain no belief more ardently than the belief that the strong man is free to be weak and the bird of prey to be a lamb—for thus they gain the right to make the bird of prey *accountable* for being a bird of prey. (GM I:13)

I have always found Nietzsche's peculiar brand of fatalism (*amor fati*) troublesome at best; but combined with his scornful dichotomy of weakness and strength, and his biological determinism, it becomes a hateful thesis indeed. Of course, his determinism is not as such the same as *amor fati*. There is no doubt that the latter is an important and attractive thesis for him, as well as one of the admirable traits of the so-called masters of the *Genealogy*. It represents a carefree, nonjudgmental attitude, even "a bold recklessness" that he clearly envied. And though it is not a thesis that survives extensive probing, it is an attitude that we, too, can readily appreciate.[30] But Nietzsche's biological determinism is quite a different matter. It emerges, most notoriously, in his overly abused enthusiasm for genetics and racial stereotyping. It emerges, more philosophically, in his denial and mockery of "free will" and "the changeling subject," and in his rather restricted insistence on the cultivation of one's inborn virtues. His famous instruction to "become who you are" has been read (and read well) as an "existential imperative"; and it has been read—equally well—as a mode of discovery and reinterpretation.[31] But the dominant impression—at least in the *Genealogy*—is that one can do very little to change one's basic being, much less to "improve mankind." In particular, whether one is strong and noble or weak and pathetic is not a choice of existential options but a kind of "given," in terms of one's social origins and upbringing and at the core of one's character, perhaps even in one's genes. When Nietzsche insists in the *Genealogy* that an eagle can no more become a lamb than a lamb can become an eagle, we are forced to wonder—*à la* Kant—what all the fuss about morality could possibly be about.

It is this quasi-biological deterministic thesis that has always disturbed me more than any other in the *Genealogy*. This is not because I want to believe in the transmutation of avian and mammalian species, or in the easy possibility of thoroughly changing one's character by a mere act of "will." Rather, it is because this too readily suggests that weakness and strength as such are singular, concrete characteristics—as fixed and un-ambiguous as eye color, and as all-encompassing as the defining character-istics of a biological species. Kant was certainly right: there is no point in preaching if one cannot do otherwise, and there is no point to ethics if our behavior is predetermined. It makes no sense being resentful if we are not also free to change our situation.[32]

Of course, there may be a great deal of latitude in the cultivation of our innate abilities; and this will depend not only on our genes but on our environment, nourishment, and even, to a modest extent, on our "will power." So, too, such virtues as generosity and courage can be cultivated, more or less; and the activities that manifest those virtues can be practiced to become something of an art form. But the very possibility of such virtues, according to Nietzsche, seems to be something already determined; and a person cruel or miserly by nature is not only condemned but permitted (having no other choice) to be cruel or miserly. "Become what you are," on the deterministic reading, is neither an existential imperative nor a plea for interpretation, but a kind of *license*. Birds of prey have no reason to worry about the legitimacy or justice of their activities, and should not be held accountable for them. Of course, the lambs too cannot but become who they are—vulnerable, frightened, and prone to idealize their own meekness. But then it is clear to whom Nietzsche is addressing his suppos-edly "neutral" descriptions: not to the lambs but to readers who identify with the "master" and want to be eagles. They may well suffer (or seem to suffer) from what he calls "bad conscience," but the problem more likely is the usual adolescent rebellion against the suddenly burdensome impositions of social conformity, peer pressure, and morals.

For such readers, Nietzsche can be a liberating experience. (Too many contemporary students seem to be getting the K-Mart version from Ayn Rand instead.) They feel pressured to conform and perform, they feel inhibited, guilty, constrained, and he loosens the constraints for them. But is the message of the *Genealogy*—that they should discover their own superior and noble natures—an inspiring and usually benign message for undergraduates? Or is he encouraging them to adopt a particularly unattractive, even mean-spirited elitism toward their less fortunate fellows, a feeling of superiority by way of the contrast? Is he urging them to make some sort of choice, or is it simply to adopt a certain kind of attitude? Of course, where determinism is in question we typically try to have it both ways, presupposing determinism when it suits our moral prejudices and denying it when it does not. Our talents and achievements are our own accomplishment; our faults and failures were beyond our control.[33] The deterministic attitude allows those who accept it to be highly uncritical of themselves. (It has been argued, for example by Melvin Lerner in a book on how we rationalize injustice, that determinism is one of the premises of a variety of phony arguments about our own self-worth and the just desserts of others.[34])

On the other hand, Nietzsche's seductive writing style makes it all too easy for his readers simply to assume that they share his contempt for the pitiable and his affinity with the noble. Whenever I hear academics praising his elitism, it always strikes me with a kind of horror that they consider themselves—without self-doubt or the least bit of humility—to be among the elite themselves (sometimes just by virtue of having read him). In not just a few cases, this is irony indeed: a lamb (or skunk) who imagines himself a noble bird of prey. Was Nietzsche himself guilty of this bit of arrogance? I think not. His self-deprecating remarks—and his constant appeal to other philosophers, future philosophers, higher men and other (often parenthetical) suggestions—are geared to block that reading. But then again, he did not go out of his way to emphasize his own humility (except, perhaps, in the fictitious person of Zarathustra), and in certain of his moods.

The most interesting interpretation of the master-slave relationship is one that Nietzsche suggests but does not adequately pursue: the uncomfortable coexistence *in a single soul* of "master" and "slave"—that is, the urge to spontaneity and self-expression, on the one hand, and on the other the often proper inhibitions of civilized society. It is this inner duality that makes possible the rather complex processes of self-undermining, self-overcoming, and undergoing. It is what accounts for Zarathustra's rather odd behavior, and what in more modern guise explains the bizarre seductiveness of the "judge-penitent" Clamence in Camus's *The Fall*. In each of us, to varying degrees, there is that familiar mix of exhibitionism and inhibition, desire coupled with guilt, anxiety, humility, and pity. But once we even begin to spell out this tug-of-war between the antagonistic forces that determine our character and behavior (Freud is waiting in the wings), we ought to stumble on the poetic wisdom of Hermann Hesse, who caricatured Nietzsche's theory in his masterpiece *Steppenwolf*. Why suppose that the number of forces fighting for our souls is so impoverished, and why suppose that the soul is not itself the totality rather than the victim of the many forces (from any sources) that define us? Could not the obsession with mastery and noble superiority—"spontaneity" on command—constitute an inhibiting force as brutal as any of the inventions of slave morality? And doesn't the uninhibited emphasis on *amor fati* suggest a world that is all but unthinkable, devoid of caring as well as pity (as in Hesse's "magic theater")?

What Nietzsche ignores—in part because of his own sense of biological determinism, but also, I suspect, because of his own sense of rootlessness and social impotence—is the legitimacy of the sense of oppression, the proper resentment toward an unjust world and the felt need to change it. The sentiment of resentment is not the voice of mediocrity or incompetence but the passion of justice denied. None of this is to say that resentment isn't nasty. Of course it is. It looks enviously at those who are on top, who have the power. It is vindictive. It wants to pull them down. But it does not follow that resentment is mediocrity undermining excellence, the losers tripping up of the winners.

Nietzsche separates what he calls "justice" from the "reactive emotions," defending justice as a rare and unusually noble sentiment, while attacking such emotions as resentment for their impotence. This is no less questionable. But we need not therefore disagree when he objects to the abuse of justice as a facade for the defense of one's own interests, whether in the name of "rights" or equality; and we need not endorse the consequent "leveling" effect of enforced mediocrity. In the name of "justice," for example, one may adopt an egalitarian standpoint, but look only in one direction. The French bourgeoisie during the French Revolution only looked up at the aristocrats they wanted to replace, but they never looked down at the rest of the "third estate" who were much worse off.

The hard question is whether there is any "neutral" social position (other than our position as outside observers) that would provide a proper standpoint for making such evaluations. Justice always begins as situated, with the self and its personal passions; but it need not therefore be selfish, and resentment need not be petty or opposed to a noble sense of generosity and compassion. Indeed, given that we are not Nietzsche's fantasized *Übermenschen*, wholly satisfied and in charge of our world, it is hard to even imagine what justice—and for that matter morality—would be without resentment and the modicum of selfishness that makes it possible. Perhaps Dühring was right: the home of justice *is* to be sought in "the sphere of the reactive feelings."

CONCLUSION

It has not been my aim to be perverse—to argue in Orwellian fashion that strength is really weakness and weakness is really strength, or that Nietzsche really (or should have) liked resentment, or was confused about its true nature. I think what Nietzsche says about resentment and ethics is powerful and persuasive; but I also want to insist that his attitude toward resentment and questions of strength and weakness—like his attitudes to Socrates, Jesus, and Judaism—was quite complex, and too often has been expressed in one-sided momentary polemical insights that we at our peril interpret as bits of theory or a single coherent philosophical perspective. The existential question (do we choose strength or weakness, or does it "choose" us?) is left open; and the rigid historical (etymological) dichotomy of master and slave is as misleading as it is exciting. An ethics of resentment is not just a matter of good character/bad character or good emotions and bad emotions. It is also—contra Nietzsche (and MacIntyre)—a question of justification, of the political and social context and the legitimacy of motives and emotions. Resentment, indeed, is the emotion of legitimacy—the emotion that more than any other prompts the "slavish" demand of the "herd" (that is, the socially responsible insistence of the community) for justice and justification.

NOTES

1. Nietzsche, *On the Genealogy of Morals,* trans. Walter Kaufmann (New York: Random House, 1967).

2. Max Scheler, *Ressentiment,* 1912, 1915 (New York: Free Press, 1961).

3. I owe this bit of confession and implicit apology to the promptings of Professor Kathleen Higgins, who was a recipient of my early promotion of Nietzschean arrogance (in *From Rationalism to Existentialism* [New York: Harper & Row, 1972]).

4. Nietzsche himself argues against the genetic fallacy in the *Genealogy.*

5. For example, *Groundwork of the Metaphysics of Morals,* trans. Herbert James Paton (New York: Barnes and Noble, 1967), p. 64; original German edition, p. 396.

6. See, for example, the various essays in Peter French, et al., eds., Midwest Studies in Philosophy 13, *Ethical Theory: Virtue and Character* (Notre Dame: Notre Dame University Press, 1988); also S. Hauerwas and A. MacIntyre, eds., *Revisions* (Notre Dame: Notre Dame University Press, 1983).

7. Adam Smith, *Theory of the Moral Sentiments* (London: George Bell and Sons, 1880), book I, i.

8. For example, G. E. M. Anscombe, "Modern Moral Philosophy," *Philosophy* (1958): 1–19; Michael Stocker, "The Schizophrenia of Modern Ethical Theories," *Journal of Philosophy* 73 (August 1976): 453–466. An earlier diatribe against both Kantian formalism and nascent utilitarianism is Arthur Schopenhauer's *On the Basis of Morality*, trans. E. Payne (Indianapolis: Bobbs-Merrill, 1965). And then, of course, there was Aristotle, who argued against the Platonists and hedonists of his own day, especially in book I of his *Nicomachean Ethics*.

9. Claude Lévi-Strauss, Interview, 1970, quoted in R. Solomon, *Ethics: A Brief Introduction* (New York: McGraw-Hill, 1984), p. 9.

10. *Beyond Good and Evil*, section 260.

11. Alasdair MacIntyre, *After Virtue* (Notre Dame: Notre Dame University Press, 1981).

12. See my "Nietzsche's Affirmative Ethics," *From Hegel to Existentialism* (New York: Oxford University Press, 1987).

13. See Kathleen Higgins on Nietzsche and poison, elsewhere in this volume.

14. In correspondence, 1987.

15. Alexander Nehamas, *Nietzsche: Life as Literature* (Cambridge, Mass.: Harvard University Press, 1985).

16. See, notably, Gilles Deleuze, *Nietzsche and Philosophy*, trans. H. Tomlinson (New York: Columbia University Press, 1983).

17. Compare *Ecce Homo*, in the same volume with the *Genealogy*, Kaufmann translation, p. 236.

18. Compare *The Birth of Tragedy*, trans. Walter Kaufmann (New York: Random House, 1967).

19. The protective, submissive evolutionary origins of the smile have become something of a major debate in sociobiological circles in recent years. The "smile" of the submissive pack animal in response to the alpha male, for example, is part of the "don't hurt me; you win" posture that is essential to peace-keeping among competitive social animals. But whether or not this thesis holds up as sociobiology, it has great plausibility as social phenomenology. The smile of the sycophant can hardly be read in any other way.

20. Simone Weil, "Evil," *Gravity and Grace*, trans. Emma Craufurd (London: Routledge & Kegan Paul, 1952).

21. Of course, Rawls would insist that such abilities, like all other individual advantages, must be placed behind "the veil of ignorance" (*A Theory of Justice*, [Cambridge, Mass.: Harvard, 1971].) It has often been pointed out, accordingly, that Rawls's rational negotiators are not in fact "unencumbered" at all, but in fact presuppose the skills and knowledge of first-rate social scientists and decision theorists—if not the strategic know-how of a good divorce lawyer.

22. The four cardinal virtues are listed by Nietzsche in *Daybreak*, section 556. Lou Salome offers a different list: "quiet, pensive, refined, and lonesome." *Nietzsche* (New York: Doubleday-Anchor, 1973). (Quoted in *Nietzsche*, ed. R. Solomon [New York: Doubleday-Anchor, 1973].)

23. On wolves and chimps, see my *A Passion for Justice* (Reading, Mass.: Addison-Wesley, 1990), chap. 3. See also Jane Goodall, *In the Shadow of Man* (Boston: Houghton-Mifflin, 1971).

24. Compare Frithjof Bergmann on slavery and freedom, in *On Being Free* (Notre Dame: Notre Dame University Press, 1977).

25. It is certainly worth reminding ourselves, in this context, that Nietzsche insists that master and slave morality can coexist within the same personality—no doubt an accurate self-assessment.

26. Kathleen Higgins suggests that he sings them himself in *Zarathustra*. The quote is from *Daybreak* 413 (quoted in Kaufmann, p. 252).

27. I have argued this thesis at some length in my book, *A Passion for Justice*. A similar defense of the idea that injustice is primary while the more celebrated concept of justice is (at best) derivative is Elizabeth Wolgast's *A Grammar of Justice* (Ithaca: Cornell University Press, 1987).

28. Rawls, *A Theory of Justice*, p. 533.

29. *Antichrist* 57.

30. Our (albiet vicarious) love of sports, adventure, and gambling are mundane expressions of our desire for a life less secure and more exciting; but Bernd Magnus's recent second thoughts about the *Übermensch* reflect our proper resistance to any such *laissez-faire* attitude toward the moral state of the world. (See, for example, "Perfectibility and Attitude in Nietzsche's *Übermensch*," *Review of Metaphysics* 36 (1983): 633–658; and "Nietzsche's Philosophy in 1988: *The Will to Power* and the *Übermensch*," *Journal of the History of Philosophy* 24 (January 1986): 79–98.)

31. Bernd Magnus, *Nietzsche's Existential Imperative* (Bloomington: Indiana University Press, 1978). Nehamas, *Nietzsche: Life as Literature*.

32. This "transcendental" argument, interestingly enough, has recently emerged in Anglo-American analytic philosophy in the work of P. F. Strawson, who argues that resentment presents us with a kind of "proof" of our freedom. "Freedom and Resentment," *Freedom and Resentment and Other Essays* (London: Methuen, 1974).

33. Rawls canonizes but disguises this popular prejudice in the labyrinth of *A Theory of Justice*, where he argues both that we have no right to claim "merit" on the basis of those talents we were lucky enough to inherit (and lucky enough to develop, too) and that our overall place in society should be considered *as if* we had negotiated and agreed to the social institutions in which those talents and their development take on their significance.

34. Melvin Lerner, *Belief in a Just World* (New York: Plenum, 1980). Of course, it also provides premises for a number of extremely sophisticated arguments, for example, John Rawls's dismissal of the notion of "merit" in justice, on the grounds that no one deserves credit for their natural advantages. (*A Theory of Justice*, pp. 106, 310f.)

EIGHT

Ressentiment

Rüdiger Bittner

"Too long the earth has been a madhouse," Nietzsche exclaims in one of the most powerful passages in his writings (GM II:22). Indeed, this is a central impulse of his later work: the experience of a mad world. No wonder that this man wrote the way he did—loud, hurried, overblown. For all the talk of aristocratic virtues, there is nothing noble in his style, no "pathos of distance" (BGE 257), just a desperate ferocity.[1] But there is nothing to blame in that. The style answers the world. Nice distinctions or comfortable eloquence are out of place. If the world is a madhouse, you had better scream to say that it is.

But let us try to keep our head above water: In what does the alleged madness consist? Summarily speaking, in "guilt, bad conscience and their kin" (GM II). It is madness that we are ridden with feelings of guilt; that we grant authority to the demands of traditional morality; that we punish offenders to make them recognize their failings. It is madness, too, to believe in a God embodying all the perfection we find lacking in ourselves; to assume that there is a real world beyond the vagaries of our experience; and to cling to the notions of substance, subject, transcendental freedom and other cherished ideas of traditional philosophy. Nietzsche is less clear about the relations of kinship connecting the various pieces of madness. But that is not the question to be pursued here. Let us suppose without argument that Nietzsche is right here: these attitudes form a package, traditional morality and metaphysics. And let us suppose he is right in this, too: traditional morality and metaphysics are indeed madness through and through.

The question to be pursued here is this: Given that the earth has long been a madhouse, how did it become one? This is a serious question for Nietzsche, for he is clearly convinced that madness arose in man, it is not coeval with him. The "knowledge of the conditions and circumstances in which moral values grew" (GM P:6), that is, the knowledge sought for in the *Genealogy*, is evidently knowledge of conditions coming to hold and circumstances arising at some time.[2] It is not knowledge of conditions and circumstances belonging to the human predicament. But if moral and metaphysical madness have been with us, not always, but for a long time only, it is worth wondering how humans of "flourishing, abundant, even overflowing health," of "vigorous, free, joyful activity" (GM I:7) got infected by the disease. Nietzsche's Greeks, taking as foolishness, not as sin, whatever terrible thing they had done, nonetheless asked themselves how such foolishness could have befallen them in the particular case (GM II:23). So we should ask how the much greater foolishness befell us to stop thinking of our misdeeds in terms of foolishness.

Nietzsche's answer in the First Essay of the *Genealogy*[3] is: The change was brought about by a slave revolt in morality (GM I:7,10). The idea comes straight from BGE 195, this being one clear instance of the *Genealogy* serving as a "clarification" of *Beyond Good and Evil*, as the note on the reverse side of the title page puts it.[4] But the *Genealogy* serves as a "supplement" to it, which is the other term Nietzsche uses there, in explaining how the slave revolt in morality itself came about. It came about, Nietzsche says, through *ressentiment*.

First to get the linguistic facts straight: There is no English word "ressentiment." I use the expression as proxy for the German word *"Ressentiment,"* much the same way that writers on Greek philosophy often use expressions like "phronesis" in English texts. The German word in turn needs to be distinguished from the French word spelled and pronounced alike, which is also its source. The words need to be distinguished because they differ in sense—if only because the German word has, and the French word lacks, the connotations of a word of foreign origin. Actually, however, it seems that both "to resent" in English and *"ressentir"* in French suggest a more straightforward annoyance, less of a grudge than the German word does. But be this as it may, the concept conveyed in Nietzsche's use of the word is the present topic.

Ressentiment is a psychic mechanism. To put it more agreeably perhaps, it is a pattern in people's reactions to certain experiences. As such a mechanism or pattern, *ressentiment* explains the slave revolt in morality and thereby, indirectly, our current madness. The slaves, introducing the slave morality under which we are laboring still, were driven by the mechanism, or were reacting in accordance with the pattern, of *ressentiment*.

> The slave revolt in morality begins when *ressentiment* itself becomes creative and gives birth to values: the *ressentiment* of natures that are denied the true

reaction, that of deeds, and compensate themselves with an imaginary revenge. (GM I:10)

So this is how *ressentiment* works. There are those who are worse off than the others, inferior or suppressed in some way—Nietzsche's talk of slaves should be understood in a broad, metaphorical sense, not restricted to what is called "slavery" in economic history.[5] They wish to better their situation, but they cannot, because those better off are powerful enough to prevent it.[6] So they set up values instead—slave values, that is. Judged by these, the slaves turn out to be well off, the masters badly, which is what the slaves wanted. To be sure, the values are imaginary: the slaves are actually still inferior, the masters superior. Still, the establishment of this valuation has real, indeed momentous, effects. The valuation gains adherents and finally it wins (GM I:7), eradicating both the appreciation of human splendor and that splendor itself (GM I:16); and this is madness reigning.

On this account, it takes two for *ressentiment*. It is not because the slave finds himself badly off, but because he finds himself worse off than his master, that he takes his imaginary revenge and at least condemns him to hell. Nietzsche emphasizes this point in the sentences immediately following the one just quoted (GM I:10): the action of *ressentiment* is reaction; negative reaction, that is, to the human flourishing it encounters. This is also in accordance with common usage. Ordinarily, you cannot have *ressentiment* all by yourself, you have to direct it against someone or some people, however vaguely specified.[7] A few years earlier, however, in Zarathustra's discourse, "On the Afterworldly," Nietzsche described a mechanism similar to *ressentiment,* but dispensing with the envied other. People who were sick and withering away, Zarathustra tells us, "wanted to escape from their misery and the stars were too far for them. So they sighed: Oh that there were heavenly paths to sneak into a different being and happiness!—so they invented for themselves their sneaking ways and potions of blood" (Z I:3).

Here, then, one need not be inferior to someone else in order to invent heaven. It suffices to be sick, that is, deprived of well-being according to one's own standards. And one may invent the poisonous medicines of heaven for one's own use. As Zarathustra says, "*da erfanden sie sich ihre Schliche und blutigen Tränklein,*" they invented their sneaking ways and bloody potions *for themselves.* It is true, the present passage, and others in *Zarathustra* describing the same reaction,[8] do not employ the word *"ressentiment."* Thus Nietzsche's point that *ressentiment* is always reactive stands unaffected. But it becomes merely a verbal point, given that otherwise the mechanisms described in the *Genealogy* and in *Zarathustra* are the same. I am going to depart, then, from Nietzsche's and from common usage and will employ the term *"ressentiment"* as covering both the reactive case considered in GM I:10 and the solitary case considered in "On the After-worldly."

In the broader sense, then, *ressentiment* is at work where people who are unhappy, who wish to improve their lot and who are incapable of doing so, invent a story according to which they really are well off. In the case at hand, the story is metaphysical or moral or both. In morality people tell themselves that, however miserable their life may be, they really are well off, since on the standard that truly counts—the moral one—they come out as good. In metaphysics they tell themselves that, however they may be suffering in this world, there is a true and lasting world beyond and in that world happiness lies in store for them. But the mechanism of *ressentiment* is not restricted to cases of grand metaphysical or moral stories. On the contrary, Nietzsche's account of current metaphysical and moral madness in terms of *ressentiment* has explanatory value precisely because *ressentiment* is (or appears to be) a familiar phenomenon in ordinary life, where people tell themselves small lies, just fudging the facts enough to make themselves appear better off than they are.

La Fontaine's fox is a case in point. He sees the grapes, they are vermil-ion, visibly ripe, and he would love to have them. But he cannot reach them. So he tells himself that they are green. On this story he is better off than he really is. True, grapeless he stands in either case. But in actual fact his desire for the grapes is aroused, and in this desire he is frustrated. In his story he does not desire them: no fox worth his salt desires grapes that are not ripe. So he does not suffer frustration, in addition to his hunger. The fox, then, represents all the elements of Nietzsche's account of *ressen-timent*: unhappiness, wish for improvement, inability to reach it, and the false story that makes one appear better off than one really is.[9]

But such an account runs into a difficulty. It is hard to understand why people should in these circumstances produce a false story of that sort. They know that it is a mere story. After all, they make it up themselves. As Nietzsche says, they "invent" their heavenly ways; or (in GM I:10) *ressenti-ment* is "creative" in setting up values. So they know as well that telling the story will not help. Everybody knows that to be happy and to figure in a story in which one is happy are two things. So how could anyone, failing the former, settle for the latter? To acquire metaphysical and moral mad-ness in this way one would have to be pretty mad to begin with.

It will be replied that this is simply the phenomenon and cannot be disputed. There are human foxes, and indeed plenty of them. La Fontaine's fox owes his fame precisely to the fact that he is understood to be an ex-emplar of a large subspecies of mankind. And similar phenomena abound. For instance, daydreaming: people heartily, if furtively, enjoy telling them-selves stories of their imaginary successes. They know all the while that nothing of the sort is true, yet they enjoy it. Or the opposite: it is just great to abuse people with whom we are in a rage. True, we sometimes do it to harm them by denigrating them in others' views, and sometimes we do it because it is just fun to let go and shout and use vile language. But sometimes none of this applies and we silently tell ourselves what a piece of shit that person is, knowing full well that the case is just an ordinary one, of conceit, narrow-mindedness, or negligence. The cartoons drawn under the desk in class and shown around probably served a similar purpose. It is fun to express what this horrible guy looks like, while knowing nonetheless that he doesn't really look like that. So the phenomenon invoked by Nietzsche is perfectly common. To acquire metaphysical and moral madness in the way he suggests, one does not have to be mad from the start: one only has to be like ordinary humankind.

The trouble is that to be like ordinary humankind begins to look pretty mad itself. That is to say, the reply misses the point. There is no denying that there are those whom we are accustomed and inclined to describe as foxes, daydreamers, abusers. The difficulty is to understand them, and for that it is no help to insist that the phenomenon is a common one—so much the worse! To say of the fox, for example, that because of their inaccessibility he thinks the grapes are sour while knowing that they are sweet, is not to understand him. It is to fall into contradiction. We do not understand what it means to say of a person that he knows something and believes just the opposite. But neither of these we can give up, it seems. If the fox does not think the grapes sour, but only says to others that they are—trying, say, to cover his defeat—then the problem disappears. But that is not the story we are told here, nor is it the story we are familiar with in our experience. Our fox is honest. He means what he says: the grapes are sour. Also, if he were just lying, we should not understand how he can draw comfort from his story. On the other hand, there is no problem either if the fox does not know that the grapes are ripe. But that again would seem to be a different story. The skin of the grapes has turned vermilion, and it would be a poor fox who failed to realize what this means—that the grapes are just perfect. But to say both that he knows the grapes are ripe and that he thinks they are not does not make sense. The point here is not that people just are not as irrational as that. The point is that so to describe them is unintelligible. Not the rationality of people, but the rationality of what we say about people needs defending here. Without such a defense, Nietzsche's *ressentiment* story will be an explanation of the obscure through the more obscure.

The difficulty has received a lot of discussion in recent years.[10] People have tried to escape the problem by introducing various finer distinctions—between different agents in the person, different kinds of beliefs held, or different ways of processing them. To cut what would have to be a very long story short, these attempts have failed. They have failed primarily because they failed to clarify and to justify the invoked distinctions themselves. The original contradiction persists; and so one of the two claims has to go. What should go is the claim that the fox knows the grapes to be ripe. This is what should go, because in the end there is no denying his sincerity in calling them sour. He may be lying sometimes; but that he *always* is in such cases cannot be true, given the honesty in what he says and does. So the fox does think the grapes are sour, and he does not know that they are ripe.

But now it needs to be explained that he does not know that they are ripe—and explained other than by stupidity or inexperience, of which the story gives no evidence. That *can* be explained: he does not know that the grapes are ripe because he desired and could not reach them. Not that his desire distorted his perception. Rather, he is incapable of thinking that there are grapes he both desires and cannot reach. Since that idea just will not go into his head, he settles for the next best account of the matter: the grapes are green, and he does not desire them.

His inability to entertain the idea of desirable but inaccessible grapes may in turn be explained in a variety of ways; here we would have to know more about our fox's life so far. Just as an example, the fox may be a spoiled child who hasn't learned to live with the idea that something desired may definitely escape him.[11] But whatever the precise explanation, the point is that any idea needs learning to entertain it. Thinking is not the unresisting medium it was taken to be in the tradition, receptive for anything we are not too dull to pick up. It's lumpy. True, with many ideas we live easily—mathematics, the classical instance of the learnable, being for most people the prime example. But some ideas we are constitutionally unable to harbor; constitutionally not by nature, but by what we have become in our lives.[12]

It is a Nietzschean point after all. Early and late in his writings Nietzsche insisted on the subordination of intellect to life.[13] But if the intellect is subordinated to (that is, dependent on and in the service of) life, it clearly isn't able to grasp everything that comes along. This is not because things are in themselves unknowable. The point is, rather, that someone may not have grown in his life to accommodate some ideas.

Things are similar with respect to the other phenomena mentioned. Daydreamers believe the story they tell themselves; it is not true that they know better. After all, that is one reason they are called so: dreamers normally don't know better either—we are mostly honest dreamers. Unlike foxes, daydreamers may not be incapable of entertaining a certain idea: for example, that there isn't much to them. They may simply forget that, carried away by images of what they are going to do; as one forgets the watch on one's wrist when reaching the lake to go swimming. Thus daydreamers are short-term foxes: temporarily closed to certain ideas. Likewise, in abusing people we often do believe our story. That person *is* a piece of shit (metaphorically speaking to be sure), and not just the ordinary jerk; and the caricature tells the truth (metaphorically again) about what the guy is really like. To be sure, we sometimes retract when challenged. But we did not therefore know better all along. It may have been the challenge that brought us to reconsider our opinion. And often we are dishonest in retracting, just giving in to how the world speaks.

Things are similar, finally, with respect to *ressentiment*. The slaves, Nietzsche says, "compensate themselves with an imaginary revenge" (GM I:10); and the sickly, according to Zarathustra, "invented sneaking ways and bloody potions for themselves" (Z I:3). But they cannot actually compensate themselves with a revenge they themselves consider imaginary, and potions that are to give actual comfort cannot be simply invented. They can imagine a revenge and invent a story of how to sneak into heaven. But they cannot expect relief through the revenge they imagine, and they cannot expect happiness in the invented heaven. Conversely, they may indeed come to feel better, and so compensate themselves, by taking a revenge, which unbeknownst to them is imaginary, and by swallowing a placebo. But then they did not also invent the revenge and the potion.

As before, one of the two has to go—the compensation or the invention. And as before, it is the invention that goes. Compensation cannot go. After all, they are suffering, and merely to invent a story of comfort which does not comfort is no help for them. Besides, if our metaphysical and moral convictions are so deeply entrenched in us as Nietzsche says they are, it is hard to believe that in the last resort they derive from a cooked-up story only. Finally, slaves capable of fabricating the whole compensation story and getting the world to believe it, without thereby achieving any compensation for themselves, would be remarkably free spirits—contrary to the hypothesis.

So there is no slave revolt; *ressentiment* is not creative; and the revenge is imaginary, but not known to be so. This does not mean that the slaves must have received their mad beliefs and valuations from others. Beliefs and valuations need not be either invented or taken over. They may have dawned on the slaves and grown on them, without ever having been set up expressly. So revised, the theory explaining the origin of metaphysical and moral madness comes to this. People who are suffering and eager, but unable, to change their condition are liable to develop (as one develops a symptom) the metaphysical and moral convictions which in spite of being false still dominate our lives. Simply: people go mad from suffering. Too long the earth has been a madhouse, true. That is because too long it has been a prison.

The difference between Nietzsche's original theory and the present revision is this. On Nietzsche's account, the slaves did it. Suffering without hope, they poisoned the wells. They succeeded. The metaphysical and moral madness they started spread over slave and master, sick and healthy alike. But their victory did not improve their lot. Indeed it brought "fresh suffering with it, deeper, more inward, more poisonous, more life-destructive suffering" (GM III:28). Yet they had their revenge in getting their masters to suffer too. But also they debased mankind, perhaps irretrievably (GM I:7, 9, 11, 12). On the revised account, it is the same story—only the slaves didn't do it. Nor did anyone else. Madness just grew from suffering, and as it brings fresh suffering with it, what we have is just suffering proliferating. Metaphysical and moral notions did debase mankind, perhaps ruinously. But it is an illness, not a poisoning.

Nietzsche clearly rejects the proposed revision. He never gave up the idea that valuations spring from a creative act, and presumably this holds for metaphysical beliefs too, closely tied as they are to moral valuations. "Evaluation is creation," Zarathustra teaches (Z I:15);[14] and if that is so, something very much like Nietzsche's story is bound to be true. The madness of traditional metaphysics and morality was created—but given its mad content it couldn't have been created from an abundance of life, of "vigorous, free, joyful activity" (GM I:7). It could only have arisen from a lack of such: it arose from something like *ressentiment*. But the premise of this reasoning, "evaluation is creation," is doubtful—indeed, doubtful on Nietzsche's own terms. "A thought comes when 'it' wants to come, not when I want it to come," he writes (BGE 17); and it is natural to extend this idea from thoughts to values, and from what crosses an individual's mind to what becomes part of the common outlook of a whole population.

A second reason against Nietzsche's pathos of creativity is his insistence that the subject is an invention. "A quantum of force is equivalent to a quantum of drive, will, effect—more, it is nothing other than precisely this very driving, willing, effecting. . . . There is no 'being' behind doing, effecting, becoming; 'the doer' is merely a fiction added to the deed—the deed is everything" (GM I:13). If this is true, there is no creation. The idea of creation requires a creator distinct from the creative act. If this is true, it is strong support for the idea that values grow on us. The deed is their rising in our minds, and that's all there is: no one made them rise. So for both of these reasons Nietzsche's idea of *ressentiment* becoming creative involves him in difficulties. That raises the question of why he stuck to it.

There are several reasons. One can be gathered from the context of the last quotation from "On the Thousand and One Goals": "Truly, men have given themselves all their good and evil. Truly, they did not take it, they did not find it, it did not descend to them as a voice from heaven" (Z I:15). To deny that God gave values to man, Nietzsche affirms that man gave them to himself. But that is to overshoot the mark. To contradict the traditional belief he need not affirm the contrary one. Affirming it, he fails to get out of Exodus. For him, it still takes a Moses to bring tables of values down from some Mount Sinai, even if God did not write them. Wedded to that framework, he overlooks the possibility that values may not be given (created) at all, by God or by anyone else. They may simply emerge in history. In human history, to be sure; but there is no other.

A second, connected reason is Nietzsche's exalting the role of individuals in the formation of history.[15] Accordingly, if by the nature of the case no great individual can be found who is responsible for a morality excluding human greatness, other individuals must have done it—un-great ones, slaves. That important things happen in history which are not the intended outcome of individuals' actions is an idea that is not close to Nietzsche's mind.

A third reason, connected again with the previous one and perhaps the most important of all, may be suspected. Nietzsche insists on the slaves' creativity in bringing about metaphysical and moral madness because in this way he has somebody to hold responsible for it. His own diagnosis may apply to him: " 'Someone or other must be to blame for my feeling ill'— this kind of reasoning is common to all the sick, the more so as the real cause of their feeling ill, the physiological cause, remains hidden." Now the real cause may not remain hidden once it is recognized that it is not a physiological cause, like "a deficiency of potassium sulfate and phosphate in the blood" (GM III:15), but a social one, like hunger or real slavery. But whatever the real cause may be, it is quite understandable that those who are sick wish to lay their misery at someone's door. Once it can be imputed to some particular person or persons, the misery no longer appears ingrained in what the sick have become, physiologically or historically—and that is a more hopeful, hence more agreeable, thought.

This can be applied to Nietzsche's own case. He is saying: man has tortured himself through his madness up to this day. But it is the slaves' fault that this is so. Thus it is an accident—a huge but nevertheless avoidable mistake. It is not *what we are*. Thus, behind or before a debasement of mankind that may be irreparable, there appears an image of man untainted. Nietzsche's idea of the slave revolt, of a human act ruining humanity, is the story of a fall.

> From time to time grant me—supposing there are granting heavenly goddesses, beyond good and evil—grant me the sight, grant me but one sight of something perfect, accomplished, something happy, powerful, triumphant, in which there is still something to fear. Of a man who justifies man, a lucky hit of man, fulfilling and redeeming, for the sake of which one may hold to one's belief in man! (GM I:12)

This is how Nietzsche gives vent to "a sigh and a last hope" (GM I:12). There being no heavenly goddesses beyond good and evil to grant his request, Nietzsche helped himself to that "sight." It is the vision of man who has not yet created, and might not create, the values of *ressentiment*. He needed this vision too dearly, because his belief in man depended on it. This is the belief that the liberating man, who is to redeem the world from the ruling ideal and from its inevitable result, nausea, "must come one day" (GM II:24). As "must" instead of "will" suggests, this is the sort of belief that is maintained against the odds. It is indeed a last hope: one that transcends our world. To keep up that hope, Nietzsche needed the vision of man before the fall. Only what we have been in the beginning holds out the promise of the better life to come. Fulfillment is return. No redemption without paradise.

Nietzsche was not nihilist enough. He needed the idea of *ressentiment* becoming creative to insulate the disruption in man, and so to preserve the idea of a human substance unaffected. But that idealism turned out to be as destructive as any other. It not only involved him in the difficulties mentioned a few paragraphs back. It also led him to side with the masters, to glorify their violence, to extol aristocratic values—doctrines the horror of which has been amply demonstrated by some of his readers, who did not entirely misunderstand him. He was led to these doctrines because, once the source of the disease ravaging mankind has been located in the slaves, the masters—whoever they are—come to carry that hope beyond all hopes. They are invested with the glory of man unseen.

There is something of the Catholic in Nietzsche, in the sense that he keeps trying to lay his hands on what would be truly divine: undistorted humanity. He is not too fastidious here. Sometimes Roman values embody "the salvation and future of the human race" (GM I:16). More often the Greeks appear in this role (GM II:23);[16] and sometimes it is only Nietzsche's chosen individuals—Caesar, Goethe, Napoleon—who represent man's highest potential. But somewhere with us it must be.

This is not so on the proposed revision of Nietzsche's theory of *ressentiment*. Suffering bred madness and continues to do so—but all over the place. There isn't anyone who brought about the disease; and there is no one who is exempt from the infection either. Free human beings we have not seen. It is not that they are invisible. The historical fact is that none have been around, in all this time. Nietzsche would find this picture dismal: no pledge of eventual relief, no redeeming feature in all the madness. But dismal is only the account of what we are, and not of what—without pledge and redemption—we may become. A humanity of the future, liberating the will and victorious over God, may not be something that "must come one day" (GM II:24). But we can try.

NOTES

1. At times Nietzsche himself is aware of this. Referring to GM, he writes to Overbeck, 3 February 1888: "In the position of a bow bent to the point of breaking, any affect does you good, provided it is violent. At present, nobody should expect 'nice things' from me."

2. For instance, GM I:7 ascribes "a history of two thousand years" to the slave revolt in morality; GM I:16 mentions a struggle going on "for thousands of years" between "good and bad" on the one hand and "good and evil" on the other; GM II:2 knows of "a long story of how responsibility originated"; GM II:16 remembers the beginning of "the gravest and uncanniest illness, from which humanity has not yet recovered."

3. A different answer is offered in GM II:16–17, and it is not clear whether the two are compatible.

4. The note, not contained in the manuscript Nietzsche sent to the publisher, may have been put in its present place by the latter. However, if so, he followed Nietzsche's statement in his letter of 8 November 1887: "That this polemic stands in a necessary relation to 'Beyond Good and Evil,' serving as its supplement and clarification."

5. In GM I:7 the slaves are described by the following series of attributes: the wretched, poor, impotent, lowly, suffering, deprived, sick, ugly. Since the extensions of these predicates obviously do not coincide, Nietzsche means by a "slave" probably anybody falling under one or the other of them.

6. This is the implication in Nietzsche's saying that the slaves are "denied" the true reaction, that of deeds, and a bit further on, that the impotent let loose their revenge on their opponents—"*in effigie* of course" (GM I:10).

7. This is a point about usage: we do not call *ressentiment* what is not directed against someone else. Nietzsche sometimes holds a corresponding material point: " 'Someone or other must be to blame for my feeling ill'—this kind of reasoning is common to all the sick" (GM III:15). This is an interesting hypothesis. If true, it would help in explaining nationalism, chauvinism, anti-Semitism, and the like.

8. See in particular the discourse "On the Despisers of the Body" (Z I:4).

9. The fox gained philosophical prominence through Jon Elster's work, *Sour Grapes* (Paris: Cambridge University Press, 1983). But Elster misdescribes him in a curious way. According to Elster, the fox adjusts his preferences to what is possible. He perceives the grapes to be out of reach, and that causes him to desire them no more. But in this account the alleged sourness of the grapes—the point of the story after all—has dropped out of the picture. If the fox adapts his preferences to what is possible, he may as well continue to believe and to say that the grapes are ripe and sweet, for even so they don't attract him, inaccessible as they are. Furthermore, this fox would be, contrary to our suspicion, a reasonable animal indeed. Only fools, Aristotle tells us, desire the impossible (*Nicomachean Ethics* 1112 a 20, b 24–26).

10. The discussion focused on Elster's treatment of "sour grapes," on the one hand, and on ascriptions of self-deception, on the other. With respect to the latter, see Uma Narayan's bibliography in *Perspectives on Self-Deception*, ed. B. McLaughlin, A. O. Rorty (Berkeley, Los Angeles, London: University of California Press, 1988), pp. 553–558.

11. Margret Kohlenbach sketches a story of this sort in the case of Eduard in Goethe's *Wahlverwandtschaften,* in "Error or Self-Deception?" *Perspectives on Self-Deception,* pp. 515–534.

12. This is developed at greater length in my article, "Understanding a Self-Deceiver," *Perspectives on Self-Deception,* pp. 535–551.

13. This is a prominent theme in the early unpublished essay on truth and lie, underlying the argument of the second *Untimely Meditation,* "On the Use and Disadvantage of History for Life," coming to the fore in Zarathustra's discourse "On the Despisers of the Body," reappearing in GM III:12. Of *Nachlass* fragments see for instance KGW VIII 2[190], 5[31], 7[60].

14. "On the Thousand and One Goals." See also GM I:14: it is taken for granted here that ideals come into existence by being fabricated.

15. See, for example, D 20; GS 4, 362; KGW V 4[197]; VII 14[2].

16. See also HH II:I:220 and GS 139.

NINE

Pity and Mercy
Nietzsche's Stoicism

Martha C. Nussbaum

I

Nietzsche objects to pity. No fact about his critique of morality is so widely known—or so variously understood. The fact of the objection is itself plain enough, or so it would seem. Already in *Daybreak,* pity is attacked as a weakness that leads to a loss of self and increases the amount of suffering in the world (D 134). Zarathustra consistently teaches the inadequacy of pity as a response to human misery. "All creators," he insists, "are hard" (Z II, "On the Pitying")[1]; and he himself finds his inclination to take pity on the higher men a final temptation that he, as creator, must overcome. "My pain (*Leid*) and my pity (*Mitleid*)—what is the importance of that! Do I then strive for happiness? I strive for my creative work!"[2] With this exclamation, he reaches the climax of his long spiritual development; with the rejection of pity he becomes "glowing and strong, like a morning sun that rises up from the shadowy mountains" (Z IV, "The Sign").[3] Finally, in *On the Genealogy of Morals,* Nietzsche announces that his central and most difficult problem is "this problem of the value of pity and the morality of pity," and that we urgently need a critique of this morality: "The value of these values must itself . . . be called into question" (GM P:6). And in the rest of the work (as in related passages of *Beyond Good and Evil*), he does indeed subject the "morality of pity" to withering scrutiny, connecting it with shame, nausea, and an absence of creative self-command.

This attack on pity has been interpreted in two radically different ways, with major consequences for the overall assessment of Nietzsche as an ethical thinker. On the one side, we have what we might call the "boot-in-the-face" portrait of Nietzsche. Moral philosophers such as Philippa Foot and Jonathan Glover have insisted that the historical linkage between Nietzsche and fascism is not altogether mistaken.[4] For, as they understand the critique of pity and the praise of hardness, these are indeed injunctions to cultivate a callous indifference to the fate of one's fellow human beings, and to take pleasure in displays of violence and cruelty that manifest this indifference. On the other side, we have the portrait of Nietzsche as noble and innocuous quasi-Christian moralist. In this picture, associated above all with the ground-breaking work of Walter Kaufmann,[5] Nietzsche's attack on pity does not mark him as a figure in any way startling or shocking within the tradition of Western ethical thought; he is simply continuing a line of reflection familiar from the works of the Greek and Roman Stoics, Spinoza, and Kant. And his attack on Christianity is itself an attack only on what is insincere or imperfectly consistent in Christian ethical practice, a recalling of Christianity to the true doctrine of the Gospels.

I shall argue here that neither of these portraits does justice to Nietzsche's project—which is, I shall claim, to bring about a revival of Stoic values of self-command and self-formation within a post-Christian and post-Romantic context. This project, as I shall argue, does not make Nietzsche a boot-in-the-face fascist, since the attack on pity is itself intimately linked—as it is in the Stoics—with an attack on the roots of cruelty and revenge. A true self-creator has no need and no reason to lord it over others; his hardness is more like the hardness of a disciplined dancer than like that of a thug. Yet it seems to me that Kaufmann is wrong to suggest that the morality with which Nietzsche leaves us is innocuous or uncontroversial. For it does, I think, assail the roots of the deepest sorts of human love. And it also embodies a deliberate assault on the foundations of political socialism and democracy—above all as these were constructed by Rousseau, in his eloquent writings on pity as the basic moral sentiment. But to see all this we must, I believe, examine the tradition of debate about pity—especially in the ancient thinkers—more closely than any of these interpreters has done.[6]

Before we can do this, however, we need to say something about terms. At least seven words figure in Nietzsche's thinking about what I am calling pity: Greek *eleos* and *oiktos*, Latin *misericordia*, French *pitie*, German *Mitleid*, and English *pity* and *compassion*. These words have, to some extent, different nuances: thus, when he wants to bring out the fact that pity involves a concomitant suffering on the part of the pitier, Nietzsche is likely to focus on *Mitleid*, and even (as we saw above) to play on the relation between *Leid* (pain) and *Mitleid*. When, by contrast, he wishes to focus on the suggestion of condescension toward the sufferer contained in pity, *pitie* and *pity* are likely to be his focus (as in *Daybreak*). Yet Nietzsche is perfectly clear that, for him, these words form a single family, connected to one another through the translational processes of the Western philosophical tradition; and in this, it seems to me, he is correct. In what follows I myself shall continue to use "pity," mentioning the specific terms in Nietzsche's text only where it seems important to his argument. But I use the word simply as a translation of the various terms in the tradition—and to that extent I ask the reader to disregard any connotations it may have that are not the common stock of the tradition itself—to which I now turn.

II

Priam comes to Achilles to ask for the return of Hector's corpse.[7] He asks Achilles to pity him in his loss, reminding him that he too has a father who may be suffering in his old age. Achilles is stirred to grief—for his father, for Priam, for the loss of Patroklos; the two men draw close in recognition of the ways in which loss, affliction, and age can come to any human being. Shortly after this, Achilles tells Priam the story of the two urns from which Zeus capriciously hands out fortunes to mortals, mixing the good and the bad. Now able to see his enemy as a human being like himself, with possibilities similar to his own, Achilles agrees to return the corpse and permit the funeral.

Similar in structure, opposite in outcome, is a case from the *Odyssey*. Disguised as a beggar in his own house, Odysseus approaches the suitors' table. He asks their leader Antinoos to take pity on him, telling him that he too once enjoyed the prosperity that Antinoos now enjoys, but came to grief through no fault of his own. But Antinoos refuses to see in the beggar's current state possibilities for his own life, for human life in general. "What spirit brought this pain upon us, to spoil our feasting?" he exclaims, evidently considering himself above all that. Instead of the expected conclusion, generous giving, we have the beggar's dismissal from the table—and our knowledge, as readers, that Antinoos's impending punishment will be a just one.

These two examples display the cognitive structure of the emotion of pity, and its alleged social benefits. The cognitive structure is made explicit by Aristotle in the *Rhetoric,* and I shall follow his analysis; but it is clear that he accurately records a much older tradition that lies deep in Greek ethical thinking and in Homeric and tragic poetry.[8] Pity is a painful emotion directed at another person's pain or suffering. It requires, and rests upon, three beliefs: first, the belief that the suffering is significant rather than trivial; second, the belief that the suffering was not caused by the person's own fault; and third, the belief that one's own possibilities are similar to those of the sufferer, that the suffering shows things "such as might happen" in human life. The first point is obvious: we do not go around pitying someone who has lost a toothbrush or a paper clip—or, to anticipate a Stoic image, someone whose skin has merely been lightly grazed. The occasions for pity enumerated by Aristotle are also the ones on which tragedy focuses: loss of friends, loss of city, loss of opportunities for effective action, sickness, old age, impending death, childlessness, loss of children, having bad children. The assumption behind his entire discussion is that such losses are in fact of deep importance for the person's whole project of achieving a flourishing human life. (His ethical writings develop this point, denying that virtue is sufficient for a flourishing life.)[9]

The second point is also straightforward: insofar as we think that people have come to grief through their own fault, we will blame them and judge them, rather than pitying them. Insofar as we do pity, it is either because we think the person without blame for the loss or impediment or because, though there is an element of fault, we believe that the suffering is out of all proportion to the fault. Thus, for Aristotle, pity is addressed to the tragic hero under the description "unworthy" of the reversal and its attendant suffering.[10] And the tragic tradition supports this; characters who appeal for pity almost always seek to establish their innocence at the same time— or, as is the case in Euripides' *Bacchae,* the fact that their extreme suffering goes well beyond any just penalty that might have been assigned for their fault.[11]

The third point is the most subtle and controversial, but it is one on which the ancient tradition emphatically insists. The claim—made implicitly in the structure of literary appeals for pity, explicitly in Aristotle and later thinkers who follow his lead—is that one will not respond with the pain of pity, when looking at the suffering of another, unless one judges that the possibilities displayed there are also possibilities for oneself.[12] If, like Antinoos, one thinks that one is (as a king) a breed apart, and invulnerable to the ills that the beggar's lot displays, then one will not feel anything at all when looking at the beggar. And insofar as one does feel pain at the suffering of others, it is a pain that is closely linked to an acknowledgment of one's own vulnerability and incompleteness. (This is why pity is so closely linked to fear, both in the literary tradition itself and in Aristotle's faithful reconstruction of it.)[13]

Unlike the other two claims—which seem to be points about the logic of pity, attempts to define it and to distinguish it from other emotions— this claim appears to be a psychological claim about the causal mechanisms of other-directed concern.[14] The point seems to be that the pain of another will be an object of my concern only if I acknowledge some sort of community between myself and the other—to the extent that I am able, in imagination, to see that suffering as a possibility for me and to understand, on the basis of my own experience, what its meaning might be for the person who has it. Only then will I know enough about it to react to it with concern. Without that sense of commonness, I will react with sublime indifference or intellectual curiosity—like a Martian scientist, or a certain sort of god.[15] The point is that such strangers cannot help being indifferent and unconcerned, insofar as they have no idea at all what it means to be in pain, to be mortal, to risk life itself for those one loves. If they have no inner, experiential sense of the importance of these matters, they can't help looking a bit clumsy, and even callous, when they deal with them.

Pity, as the pro-pity tradition sees it, has certain distinct advantages for human social life. First of all, the beliefs that ground it are (as this tradition sees it) true: for it is true that human beings are needy, incomplete creatures who rely on circumstances beyond their control in many ways for the possibility of flourishing and complete life, and who can therefore come to grief should those circumstances prove adverse. Pity acknowledges this, and it is good to acknowledge the truth. Second, the acknowledgment contains a reminder that being rich and powerful does not remove one from the ranks of humanity—that one is still a mortal, needy, incomplete being to whom terrible things may happen. This too is true—of Antinoos as of the beggar he disdains. And it is good for kings and heroes to remember and acknowledge what is true—both because it is true and because one will act more appropriately if one remains aware at all times of the sort of being one actually is. Third, and perhaps most significant, in pity one acknowledges as important for all human beings certain external things that society can arrange to distribute to those who need them: and the acknowledgment of the importance of these things, coupled with the acknowledgment that one might be in a position of need oneself some day, works to ensure a more equitable distribution of these goods. The position of the pitier (or of the tragic spectator *qua* pitier) is not unlike the position of the party in the 'original position' in John Rawls's theory of justice.[16] For he or she, looking at the represented action, is aware that goods such as food, health, citizenship, freedom, do all matter—and yet is uncertain whether she will be (or remain) one of the privileged ones in the society of the future. She is reminded that the lot of the beggar might be (or become) hers. The tendency, then, will be to arrange society in such a way that the lot of beggars, people defeated in war, and so on, is as good as it can be. Self-interest itself promotes the selection of distributive principles that raise society's floor. The floor does not get very high up in Homer, where the beggar gets a handout rather than equality; but later versions of the tradition become more and more egalitarian, I think—at least within the narrow (male, freeborn) confines of the ancient democratic imagination.[17]

This fact about the ancient tradition is fully grasped by Rousseau, who accordingly makes pity the cement of the egalitarian society he wishes to promote.[18] In *Emile* (book IV) he argues that pity is the first and most important emotion to be cultivated in the future citizen. Taking as his epigraph Dido's statement from the *Aeneid*—"Not inexperienced in suffering, I learn how to bring aid to the wretched"—he explains, in very classical terms, why a citizen who lacks pity is likely to be harsh and ungenerous, lacking in compassion for the poor and weak:

> Why are kings without pity for their subjects? It is because they count on never being human beings. Why are the rich so harsh to the poor? It is because they do not have fear of becoming poor. Why does a noble have such contempt for a peasant? It is because he never will be a peasant. . . . It is the weakness of the human being that makes it sociable, it is our common sufferings that carry our hearts to humanity; we would owe it nothing if we were not humans. Every attachment is a sign of insufficiency. . . . Thus from our weakness itself, our fragile happiness is born. (*Emile*, book IV, my trans.)

With this in mind, the teacher now undertakes to give the adolescent Emile—who does not yet have any understanding of the pain of others— some lessons in human finitude, beginning with the difficult task of showing him what death is, and what it means for people who endure the loss of a loved one, or face their own. The general emphasis of the teaching is on the importance of the external goods that fortune controls, and on their extreme undependability: "Make him understand clearly that the fate of the unhappy can be his own, that all their ills are beneath his feet, that a thousand unforeseen and unavoidable events can plunge him into those ills at any moment." This, the teacher argues, will lead Emile to be a generous and beneficent citizen, favoring social arrangements that secure the basic needs of life to all citizens alike.

III

But for Socrates, a good person cannot be harmed.[19] And Socratic thinking about virtue and self-sufficiency inaugurates a tradition of reflection that opposes pity as a moral sentiment unworthy of the dignity of either the pitier or the recipient. According to Socrates, one's own virtue is entirely sufficient for a flourishing human life, or *eudaimonia*. This virtue is thought to be always within one's own control: thus, the only way to be damaged with respect to *eudaimonia* is to make bad choices or to become unjust; and the appropriate response to such deliberate wickedness is, of course, blame, rather than pity. As for the events of life that most people take to be objects of pity—losses of loved ones, loss of freedom, ill health, the impending loss of one's own life—these events are now redefined as of only minor importance. For the historical Socrates, they can perhaps make a difference to the degree of one's *eudaimonia*.[20] The later Stoics, as we shall see, do not go even this far. In any case, they can never make the difference between being *eudaimon* and not being so; and since *eudaimonia* is usually understood to be bound up with notions of sufficiency and completeness, the

Socratic understanding is that a virtuous person is truly complete in him or herself, whatever the world around him is doing.

To a person with such views, the usual appeal to pity will be repugnant for several reasons. First, because the cognitive structure of the emotion is false: pity acknowledges as important what has no true importance, as seriously bad what is not seriously bad. Furthermore, in so doing pity insults the dignity of the person who suffers: it implies that this person really needs the things of the world, whereas in fact, if the person is virtuous and self-commanding, he or she emphatically does not. Finally, pity diminishes the dignity of the person who pities: it implies that this person, too, is such as to be vulnerable to terrible losses through no fault of his or her own. But no virtuous and self-sufficient person is fragile in this way.

This position on pity is already implicit in the *Apology*, where Socrates rejects the usual practice of bringing one's children into the courtroom, connecting this with the claim that a good person cannot be harmed by being put to death.[21] It is brought out far more explicitly in the *Republic*, where Plato makes these arguments the basis for his rejection of tragedy from the ideal city. The events that tragedy depicts—deaths of loved ones, one's own impending death—are really not terrible evils, though they are supposed to be so. A good man will not lament for the death of a friend, calling out for pity, since such a man is "most of all sufficient to himself with reference to living well, and exceptionally more than others he has least of all need of another. . . . Least of all, then, is it a terrible thing to him to be deprived of a son or brother or money or anything of that sort" (387DE). Accordingly, speeches of lamentation and requests for pity must be, if retained at all, assigned to inferior characters, such as women, so that the young citizens will come to regard such responses with contempt. Book X takes an even stronger line, completely censoring all speeches expressive of pity, on the grounds that they "nourish the element of pity in us, making it strong." The only literature that will remain is literature praising the goodness of good gods and heroes: for even the usual tension and drama of literary plot must go, since it is complicitous with pity, suggesting, falsely, that circumstantial changes have real importance for the course of one's life.[22]

But it is in the moral thought of the Greek and Roman Stoics that the assault on pity finds its most sustained and careful philosophical development. And it is the Stoic tradition that is the primary source for later assaults on pity—including those of Descartes, Spinoza, and Kant and, as I shall argue, Nietzsche's own. The Stoics take Socrates as their exemplar, insisting that our moral norm should be his calm, self-sufficient demeanor in misfortune, rather than the undignified and unworthy wailings of tragic heroes.[23] They accept as their basic starting point the Socratic idea that virtue is sufficient for *eudaimonia*. But they make several important additions to the Socratic tradition.[24] First of all, they argue that virtue is not only sufficient for *eudaimonia*, but actually identical with it. One's virtuous willing and reasoning is the only thing of intrinsic worth; and the activities of will and reason in a person simply are what it is to live well. Second, they develop in connection with this thesis a conception of the good person as a self-commanding person—one who, rather than being the slave of fortune, is truly free just because she doesn't care for the things that fortune controls. Commanding herself, she commands all that is important for living well; she is thus a person of real power and command in a world in which most people value things—such as money and political authority—that appear to offer power but really offer slavery. (Hence the famous Stoic paradox that the wise person is the only truly free person, though he be a slave; the others, though they may be freeborn, are slaves in reality, if they care about lording it over others or augmenting their store of possessions.)

Finally, the Stoics base their denunciation of pity on a detailed and systematic analysis of the passions and their interrelationships with one another. According to this analysis, not pity alone, but all the major emotions—including fear, grief, anger, gratitude, love, envy, and yet others— are based upon evaluative judgments that ascribe extremely high value to "external goods" that are in the control of fortune. Thus, according to Stoic moral theory, all are based on judgments that are false, and that will be removed by the acceptance of correct philosophical teaching. To grieve at a death is to acknowledge the importance of that person for the course of one's life; to fear an impending event that one cannot control is to ascribe importance to that event. To love is to give hostages to fortune. And there will be no occasions for either anger or gratitude for a person who does not entrust her *eudaimonia* to the care of others. If I value only my virtue, which nobody else can either damage or produce, I will see the events that are the usual occasions for anger as beneath me, unworthy of a passionate response.[25]

What Stoic analyses bring out again and again is that the repudiation of pity is not in the least connected with callousness, brutality, or the behavior of the boot-in-the-face tyrant. In fact, we might say that on this picture it is pity itself, not the absence of pity, that is closely connected with anger and cruelty. For the pitier acknowledges the importance of certain worldly goods and persons, which can in principle be damaged by another's agency. The response to such damages will be pity if the damaged person is someone else; but if the damaged person is oneself, and if the damage is deliberate, the response will be anger—and anger whose intensity will be proportional, the Stoics believe, to the intensity of the initial attachment. The soft soul of the pitier—Stoics are very fond of using images of softness and hardness to contrast vulnerability to external conditions with the dignified absence of such vulnerability[26]—this soft soul can be invaded by the serpents of envy, hatred, and cruelty.[27] When Seneca writes to Nero reproving the emotion of pity,[28] he hardly has in mind the project of making Nero the sort of person he apparently did become, cruel and callous to the wrongs of others. On the contrary: his project is clearly the project of getting Nero to care less about insults to his reputation, about wealth and power and status generally. This project is explicitly said to be motivated by the desire to make him a gentler and more merciful ruler. Not only is this project not hindered by the removal of pity, it demands it, because it demands the removal of the attachments to external goods that are the basis both for other-directed pity and for anger. Nero, that budding tragic actor who loved to sing the role of Agave in Euripides' *Bacchae,* is not to be trusted with the fate of his people as long as he continues to indulge in tragic weeping over the vicissitudes of life. Cruelty, according to Seneca, is not the opposite of pity; it is an excessive form of anger, which is, in turn, simply a circumstantial inflection or modality of the same evaluative beliefs which, in other circumstances, have pity as their inflection.[29] So pity is cruelty's first cousin, and the difference between them is made by fortune. In short, Stoic hardness is not tyrannical, but a source of gentle forbearance; it is a softness, not hardness, that we should fear.[30]

What will the attitude of the good and self-sufficient person be toward the misfortunes and the bad behavior of others? Here we arrive at an innovation in Roman Stoicism that will be of great importance for Nietzsche's arguments. When others suffer loss the good Stoic will, of course, not pity them; he will concern himself, and try to get them to concern themselves, with their further development toward virtue and self-command. When others commit damaging or evil actions, his attitude will remain one of concern for their development and their well-being. Not angered on account of his own personal damage, not feeling himself dragged down by the bad acts of another, the good Stoic will be free to ask what punishments are most likely to do good for society as a whole, and for the criminal's life as a whole. And Seneca argues in *On Anger* and *On Mercy* that such punishments will be free from the harshness and cruelty that he connects with anger's uncontrolled vulnerability. They will be as judiciously selected as are a doctor's prescriptions; and frequently they will be merciful. Mercy is understood to involve the selection of a penalty milder than the one appointed by law for the offense; and this bending or waiving of punishment will often be preferred by the good person for several different reasons. First, it is expressive of his own strength and dignity; it shows that he does not need to inflict pain in order to be a whole person. Second, it displays an understanding of the difficulties of human life, which make it almost impossible not to err in some respect; and it also displays the awareness that the punisher is himself an imperfect person, liable to error. Third, it is socially useful, since it awakens trust and affection for the emperor, rather than fear and antagonism.[31]

What we see here, in effect, is a translation of the cognitive structure of pity into the terms appropriate to a Stoic conception of virtue. For in Seneca's mercy (*clementia*) we have, as in pity, an acknowledgment of the difficulties and struggles peculiar to human life, coupled with an acknowledgment that one is oneself a fellow human being of the one who receives mercy. But pity takes as its focus chance events that virtue does not control; in giving these importance it lies about the human good. Mercy, by contrast, takes as its focus the uphill struggle to be virtuous and to perfect one's will. It places the accent in the right place, and ascribes importance to what really has importance. It still says, as pity does, that to live well is difficult for a human being, and that it is highly likely that a person who makes reasonably good efforts will come to grief somehow. But pity focuses on occasions where the coming to grief was not the person's fault; according to Stoicism there are no such cases, since either it is not real coming to grief or it is one's fault. Mercy focuses on fault, and refuses—as Seneca emphasizes repeatedly—ever to let the person off the hook for that fault. Mercy is analogous to mitigation in sentencing, not to a not-guilty verdict. Mercy simply says: Look, I don't need to hurt you; and you were probably having a tough time being good, since it is very hard to be good. So I will, like a good doctor (or a good parent) tell you firmly that you are bad, but punish you lightly. And it is this lofty, affectionately parental attitude, according to Seneca, that will hold society together far better than pity does, inspiring a genuine mutual gentleness that is not tinged with fearfulness or a gnawing sense of one's own need.

Notice that in mercy, unlike pity, there is no incentive to the redistribution of socially distributable goods. In fact, just the contrary. For if the only truly free person is the one to whom external conditions don't matter, then it really doesn't matter whether one is a slave in circumstances, so long as one is free within; it doesn't matter whether one is poor or rich in circumstances, so long as one's moral will is whole. (And Stoics typically deny that economic circumstances are necessary for the development of moral virtue.) It is no big deal to be poor; but it's also no big occasion for worry to be rich, as Seneca, sitting around in his luxurious villa, is fond of pointing out.[32] Why worry about giving it away, if the goods don't matter to those who would receive them? Nero, learning mercy, learns a certain attitude toward the moral being of his subjects; he learns nothing at all about what economic conditions would be just or unjust, good or bad. In fact, in reality, he learns that none of these things matters at all to justice and injustice, the good and the bad. We might say that from the point of view of the assault on pity, any very strong interest in democratic freedom or equality would be morally suspect, as putting the emphasis on the wrong things. For what can be wrong with existing distributions, if they don't prevent people from achieving a flourishing life? Thus, although anti-pity thinkers such as Spinoza and Kant, who follow the lead of the Stoics, are able to point out that the removal of pity also removes the bases for much strife and rivalry in human affairs, they have more difficulty showing that, and how, their Stoical agents will be committed to material beneficence and to anything like equality.[33]

IV

Nietzsche's classical education focused intensively on Stoicism. Among his first scholarly publications were three studies—still valuable—of Diogenes Laertius's *Lives of the Philosophers,* one of our major sources for Stoic thought.[34] And the works of Seneca and Epictetus are among the most heavily read and annotated in his library.[35] His first sustained discussion of pity, in *Daybreak,* begins with a reference to "the great men of antique morality, Epictetus for instance" (D 131), and challenges the imagined interlocutor: "—You say that the morality of pity is a higher morality than that of stoicism? Prove it!" (D 139). In the Preface to the *Genealogy* he alludes, more broadly, to pre- and post-Stoic exemplars of the anti-pity argument, citing Plato, Spinoza, La Rochefoucauld, and Kant (GM P:5). On the pro-pity side, he is obviously well aware of Rousseau's political doctrine of pity, referring prominently both to French discussions and to the connection of pity with socialism and democracy (for example, D 132); and he is also very familiar (though contemptuously so) with Schopenhauer's attempt to make pity the basic moral sentiment (for example, D 132–133). But throughout his work it is above all, I think, the well-developed arguments of the Stoic tradition—especially the Roman Stoics—that influence him, though, as well shall see, he adapts these arguments to a specifically post-Christian and post-Romantic context. And his opposition is, therefore, no mere local or recent perversion of Christian values (as Kaufmann sometimes suggests); it is the foundations of the tragic tradition itself, and the sense of life on which it is based. This assault on the tragic is not, I believe, consistent throughout Nietzsche's entire career;[36] and even in the works on which I shall focus—*Daybreak, Zarathustra,* and the *Genealogy*—there remain tensions within his thought that I shall discuss in my concluding section. But for the most part and on the whole he sides, I shall argue, with Seneca and against Aristotle.

I shall now describe six arguments that appear prominently in several texts; then, turning more intensively to the *Genealogy,* I shall argue that the discussion of punishment and mercy in that work makes Nietzsche's anti-pity argument even more profoundly a Stoic argument, one that takes its stand against cruelty and in favor of self-command.

1. *Pity is an acknowledgment of weakness and insufficiency in the pitied.*
Nietzsche's central and most frequently stressed objection to pity is that it
is an acknowledgment of human insufficiency and frailty, and thus a diminution of the dignity of the object. "To offer pity is as good as to offer
contempt," he argues in *Daybreak* (D 135). A suffering person whom one
respects will, if an enemy, be regarded with admiration for the fortitude
with which he bears his suffering; if a friend, he will be regarded with a
delicate respect for his pride and a concern for fostering the friend's ability
to continue creating himself. "All great love is even above all its pity; for it
still wants to create the beloved," speaks Zarathustra (Z II, "On the Pitying"), and concludes, "But all creators are hard."[37] Part IV of *Zarathustra,*
which begins with an epigraph from Part II's "On the Pitying," shows us
that the last temptation that Zarathustra must overcome as a friend and
teacher is his tendency to have pity for the sufferings of the "higher men."
This is a defect in his relation to himself, as we shall shortly see; but it is
also a defect in his relation to them. He must learn to take up the attitude
characteristic of both Seneca and Epictetus, who, while not lacking in concern for the pupil's self-development, foster that development by refusing
to have pity. "Wipe your own nose," Epictetus rudely tells the all too passive
pupil.[38]

This argument can actually be seen to be a family of closely related
arguments. First, pity makes a statement that the person's own efforts are
not sufficient for that person's flourishing; this is an insult to that person's
efforts. Second, it makes a statement that the conditions of the world, the
conditions that cause the suffering, are of great importance—of so much
importance that they dwarf the person's own efforts; this is not only false,
it is an inappropriate exaltation of worldly goods. Third and finally, pity
has for these reasons bad consequences: the pupil whose nose is too often
wiped will not wipe her own nose, the child whose parents' love is too
smothering will not become a mature adult, the recipient of too much pity
will never become capable of creation and self-command.

In the *Genealogy*, as to some extent already in *Zarathustra*, Nietzsche focuses on a particular variety of pity that he connects closely with the Christian depreciation of the body and this world. Christian pity thinks the human being a low and pathetic being, low above all because of his shameful
bodily nature and his animal instincts. When one pities the suffering of
such a being, that pity lies very close to shame and disgust. Thus in the
preface to the *Genealogy*, Nietzsche, referring to Schopenhauer, claims that
"the instincts of pity, self-abnegation, and self-sacrifice" became that philosopher's way of saying no "to life and to himself":

> It was precisely here that I saw the beginning of the end, the dead stop, a
> retrospective weariness, the will turning against life, the tender and sorrowful

signs of the ultimate illness: I understood the ever-spreading morality of pity
that had seized even on philosophers and made them ill, as the sinister symptom of a European culture that had itself become sinister, perhaps as its bypass to a new Buddhism? to a Buddhism for Europeans? to—nihilism? (GM
P:5)

It is at this point that Nietzsche mentions the arguments of the anti-pity
tradition, announcing his affiliation with them. And in the body of the work
he does indeed develop this line of thought further, connecting pity with
shame and disgust at the physical conditions of our existence (GM II:7),
and with a nausea that turns away from all earthly life as poor and worthless
(GM III:14):

What is to be feared, what has a more calamitous effect than any other calamity, is that man should inspire not profound fear but profound *nausea*; also
not great fear but great *pity*. Suppose these two were one day to unite, they
would inevitably beget one of the uncanniest monsters: the "last will" of man,
his will to nothingness, nihilism.

2. *Pity is an acknowledgment of weakness and insufficiency in the pitier.* In a
number of texts Nietzsche stresses, following the pro- and also the anti-pity
traditions, that pity is connected with a sense of our "impotence" and of
"human vulnerability and fragility in general" (D 132). By contrast, the
attitude of Stoicism is connected with an awareness of oneself as powerful—
over oneself and, as Stoic texts so often stress, over the vicissitudes of fortune as well. In Aphorism 251 of *Daybreak*, entitled "Stoical," Nietzsche
writes, "There is a cheerfulness peculiar to the Stoic: he experiences it
whenever he feels hemmed in by the formalities he himself has prescribed
for his conduct; he then enjoys the sensation of himself as dominator."
This sense of power and sufficiency is at the other remove from the feelings
of the pitier; it is also, obviously enough, very far removed from the sort of
"power" that needs to lord it over others or strike out against others. It is
this that Nietzsche puts in the place of pity:

What in the end distinguishes men without pity from those with it? Above
all—to offer only a rough outline here too—they lack the susceptible imagination for fear, the subtle capacity to scent danger; nor is their vanity so
quickly offended if something happens that they could have presented (the
cautiousness of their pride tells them not to involve themselves needlessly in
the things of others, indeed they love to think that each should help himself
and play his own cards). They are, in addition, mostly more accustomed to
enduring pain than are men of pity.... Finally, they find that being soft-
hearted is painful to them, just as maintaining a stoic indifference is painful
to men of pity; they load that condition with deprecations and believe it to
threaten their manliness and the coldness of their valour—they conceal their
tears from others and wipe them away, angry with themselves. (D 133)

Here we have an eloquent portrait of a Stoic agent right out of Epictetus, wiping his own nose, pursuing his own perfection. And thus Zarathustra's enterprise in Part IV should be seen not just as an other-directed enterprise but as a self-directed one as well. When he finally gets rid of his pity, only then is he able to reject the aspiration to happiness in the sense of worldly contentment, and to devote himself adequately to the task of creation: "My suffering and my pity for suffering—what is the importance of that? Do I then strive for happiness? I strive for my creative work." This point is recapitulated in the second and third essays of the *Genealogy*, where Nietzsche stresses the connection between pitying others and having disgust before oneself and one's own humanity. The human being who "holds his nose in his own presence" (GM II:7), the "inward-turned glance of the born failure" who exclaims that he is sick of himself" (GM III:14)—this is the human being who will, Nietzsche argues, result from the dominance of the morality of pity in his time.

3. *Pity is not really altruistic, but rather egoistic.* In a third argument, Nietzsche takes on the internal claims of the morality of pity, insisting that its claim to be altruism is in any case highly suspect. The pitier is pained at the sight of the suffering of another, and his deed of pity is an attempt to get rid of his own pain (D 133, 145). This thought of oneself may be unconscious, and may take a very subtle form: for example, our act may serve not so much to remove a particular feeling of suffering as to reassure us that we have defenses lined up against the world's assaults (D 133). But it is egoistic nonetheless, in the sense that it is based (as the pro-pity tradition acknowledges) on the fear one has for one's own life.

4. *Pity does no good: it simply increases the amount of suffering.* Daybreak stresses that to give way to pity is to augment the number of the sufferers, and thus to add to the total "amount of suffering in the world: if suffering is here and there indirectly reduced or removed as a consequence of pity, this occasional and on the whole insignificant consequence must not be employed to justify its essential nature, which is, as I have said, harmful" (D 134). It does good, Nietzsche adds, only where, as in Indian philosophy, it functions as an antidote to suicidal disgust with existence, in the sense that it substitutes for that disgust the cognitive goal of knowing human misery as fully as possible. The point seems to be that in pity one at least comes to understand something, and if one is already low enough one may find this understanding a pleasure and a seduction to existence. "In the eyes of such men of *inherited* pessimism *pity* at last acquires a new value as a *life-preservative* power—it makes existence endurable, even though existence may seem worthy of being thrown off in disgust and horror" (D 136). But Nietzsche stresses that this is so only in rare cases, and only as the result of an antecedently terrible condition of the spirit.

5. *The things for which we pity people are, on the whole, things that are not bad*

but good for them. In the *Genealogy* above all, Nietzsche turns to the central evaluative claims of Stoicism, concerning the value of "external goods" such as money, status, friendships, family, marriage, and material comforts of all kinds. And he goes far beyond Stoicism, in a direction suggested by Romanticism, in holding that these "goods" are, on the whole and for the most part, not valueless (as the Stoics, with some qualification, hold) but actually *bad.* True philosophers are in a certain sense ascetics: "Poverty, humility, chastity"—in these they find "the most appropriate and natural conditions of their best existence, their fairest fruitfulness" (GM III:8). Nietzsche here famously argues that marriage and children are damaging distractions to the philosopher; solitude, material hardship, obscurity, friendlessness, are all not impediments but actually "an optimum condition for the highest and boldest spirituality and smiles . . . to the point at which he is not far from harboring the impious wish: *pereat mundus, fiat philosophia, fiat philosophus, fiam!*" (GM III:7). A roughly contemporaneous fragment of *The Will to Power* makes the same point in even more graphic terms:

> *Type of disciples.*—To those human beings who are of any concern to me I wish suffering, desolation, sickness, ill-treatment, indignities—I wish that they should not remain unfamiliar with profound self-contempt, the torture of self-mistrust, the wretchedness of the vanquished: I have no pity for them, because I wish them the only thing that can prove today whether one is worth anything or not—that one endures. (WP 910, 1887)

In *Zarathustra* similarly, Nietzsche depicts a philosopher who welcomes chastity,[39] solitude, and the incomprehension of the crowd as necessary conditions of true creativity: "Go into your loneliness with your love and with your creation, my brother. . . . I love him who wants to create over and beyond himself and thus perishes" (Z I:17, "On the Way of the Creator").

Here, as I say, Nietzsche goes beyond Stoicism, though in a direction strongly suggested by it. The ideal philosopher of the Hellenistic schools is frequently depicted as unmarried,[40] undistracted by worldly cares, poor, simple in diet, obscure in status. And in the Cynic tradition, which strongly influenced the major schools, a virtue is made of extremely meager and even squalid conditions, as a sign of one's indifference and self-sufficiency. (The Cynic sage shows his indifference to worldly opinion by not washing, his radical independence of others by public masturbation.[41]) Stoics on the whole reject this extreme interpretation of self-sufficiency. Epictetus carefully defends bathing, and Roman Stoics in general defend marriage and child-rearing, all as fully compatible with a philosopher's appropriate pursuit of philosophy. Nietzsche's philosopher is partly a Cynic, in his radical rejection of comfort and close affiliation with the dominant culture; partly a Christian, in his praise of chastity and his failure to consider the Cynic alternative; partly a Romantic, in his connection of loneliness and its pain with creativity. In any case, the net effect of these moves is to undermine still further the claims of pity in human life.

6. *Pity is connected with revenge, and even with cruelty.* Like the Stoic tradition, Nietzsche observes that pity is very closely linked to the desire to retaliate; for once we ascribe significance to the events of life that others can harm, we have no end of occasions for envy and resentment against those who cause *us* to suffer in one way or another. This argument is most fully made in the Third Essay of the *Genealogy.* Here Nietzsche argues that the "veiled glance" of pity, which looks inward on oneself with "a profound sadness," acknowledging one's weakness and inadequacy—this glance of the pitier is the basis of hatred, directed against a world that makes human beings suffer, and against all those, in that world, who are self-respecting and self-commanding: "It is on such soil, on swampy ground, that every weed, every poisonous plant grows. . . . Here the worms of vengefulness and rancor swarm . . ." (GM III:14). Or, as Zarathustra puts it: "The spirit of revenge, my friends, has so far been the subject of man's best reflection; and where there was suffering, one always wanted punishment also" (Z II:20).

This material shows more clearly than anything else the extent of Nietzsche's acceptance of the full Stoic position regarding the extirpation of passion. For, like the Stoics, he sees clearly that in order to remove the motives that lead to revenge he must also remove the attachments that are the basis of more apparently innocuous attitudes, such as pity, and even gratitude.[42] For the attachments, and the excessive importance they ascribe to external goods, *are* the motives for revenge.[43]

V

This last argument brings us directly to the heart of the Second Essay of the *Genealogy,* with its eloquent critique of the motives that produce punishment and its corresponding praise of mercy.[44] The essay develops an account of the original motives to punish that conforms closely to Stoic antecedents—especially, perhaps, to the arguments of Seneca's *On Anger.* The claim is that punishment is a form of exchange, in which the injured party is paid back for his pain and suffering by the pleasure of inflicting suffering on the original wrongdoer, and by the additional pleasure of being allowed to "despise and mistreat" the person who has at one time had him in his power (GM II:5–6). Nietzsche, like Seneca, holds that this way of looking at things frequently leads on to a good deal of cruelty, as the one who had been put down by the offense revels in the chance to put the offender down. "And might one not add," he comments, "that, fundamentally, this world has never since lost a certain odor of blood and torture?" (GM II:6). In certain ways Nietzsche prefers this simple revenge-morality to a morality based on the idea that the human being is, as such, worthless and disgusting (GM II:7). But he is quick to point out, as does Seneca, that the interest in taking revenge is a product of weakness and lack of power—of that excessive dependence on others and on the goods of the world that is the mark of a weak, and not of a strong and self-sufficient, human being or society. (Thus, we can see that it is closely linked to pity and shares its evaluative foundation.) Then, in a most important passage, he argues that the interest in revenge will, in a strong and self-sufficient person, eventually overcome itself in the direction of mercy:

> As its power increases, a community ceases to take the individual's transgressions so seriously, because they can no longer be considered as dangerous and destructive to the whole as they were formerly. . . . As the power and self-confidence of a community increase, the penal law always becomes more moderate; every weakening or imperiling of the former brings with it a restoration of the harsher forms of the latter. The "creditor" always becomes more humane to the extent that he has grown richer; finally, how much injury he can endure without suffering from it becomes the actual measure of his wealth. It is not unthinkable that a society might attain such a consciousness of power that it could allow itself the noblest luxury possible to it—letting those who harm it go unpunished. "What are my parasites to me?" it might say. "May they live and prosper: I am strong enough for that!"
> The justice which began with "everything is dischargeable, everything must be discharged," ends by winking and letting those incapable of discharging their debt go free: it ends, as does every good thing on earth, by overcoming itself. This self-overcoming of justice: one knows the beautiful name it has given itself—mercy; it goes without saying that mercy remains the privilege of the most powerful man, or better, his—beyond the law. (GM II:10)

Nietzsche does not here explicitly connect the repudiation of pity with the praise of mercy; the same is true of Seneca—who, but for a brief connecting text in the *De Clementia*, tends to treat the topic of mercy together with that of anger and revenge, and to make the connection between pity and anger using separate arguments. But since we have followed the connections in Nietzsche's argument up to this point, we can ourselves observe how close the connection is. The pitied and the pitier both need to take revenge; the strong and self-commanding person does not. Since the offenses of others do not threaten the core of his being, which is secure, he can afford to be indulgent to them, letting them go free. Like Seneca, Nietzsche stresses that the merciful response to an offense is not an injustice; it does not say that no offense has taken place, and it does not rewrite the law governing offenses. It simply decides not to hold this person to the letter of the law, not to exact the strict punishment mandated in the law. Mercy (*Gnade*) is now called the "self-overcoming of justice": the suggestion is that justice is still there intact, in the merciful deed, but a justice that, springing from a powerful and secure nature, is able to dismiss the pleasure of inflicting pain.

A parallel passage in *Daybreak* adds one more piece to the Stoic picture. Here Nietzsche makes the same argument, that it would be a good thing to move beyond a morality based on injury and revenge:

> At present, to be sure, he who has been injured, irrespective of how this injury is to be made good, will still desire his revenge and will turn for it to the courts—and for the time being the courts continue to maintain our detestable criminal codes, with their shopkeeper's scales and the desire to counterbalance guilt with punishment: but can we not get beyond this? What a relief it would be for the general feeling of life if, together with the belief in guilt, one also got rid of the old instinct for revenge. . . . Let us do away with the concept sin—and let us quickly send after it the concept punishment! May these banished monsters henceforth live somewhere other than among men, if they want to go on living at all and do not perish of disgust with themselves! (D 202)

And in connection with this, Nietzsche introduces the medical conception of punishment that is Seneca's answer to this problem in *On Anger*: we should aim at an attitude that treats the offender as sick, and we should bend our efforts toward curing him, making his future life as good as it can possibly be. Sick people, too, he comments, take a lot of time and use a lot of social resources: "Nonetheless, we should nowadays describe as inhuman anyone who for this reason desired to take revenge on the invalid." Primitive societies did so; and, Nietzsche asks, when will our society be ready for the opposite move, namely to treat the criminal as we treat sick people? Here we see a further extension of mercy: the offender is not simply let go, he becomes an object of the strong person's devotion and care.

VI

I hope to have shown by now that Nietzsche's views about pity are, on the one hand, far subtler than they have sometimes been thought to be, and far less connected with callousness and harshness; on the other hand, like the Stoic views they follow, they are highly controversial, and not the bland platitudes that Kaufmann sometimes suggests. The full assessment of these views would require nothing less than a complete account of the human good: for one would need to decide how much worth persons and things and events outside ourselves actually have in the planning and conduct of our lives; what needs we actually have from the world and to what extent those needs can be removed by a new attitude of self-command toward and within oneself. These questions obviously cannot be answered here; and yet I want to give some suggestions about where I think the evaluator of Nietzsche should begin in thinking about them.[45]

Two brief remarks, first, about two of Nietzsche's minor arguments. His claim that pity simply increases the amount of suffering in the world, without doing any good, seems to me to be the weakest of his claims. For the tradition has advanced powerful arguments showing that the suffering of pity does in fact lead to deeds of beneficence, and to the construction of societies in which the worst off do better than they otherwise would have done. It is possible that the same benefits could be effected without pity, say by some Kantian (or Stoic) sentiment of respect for humanity; but the burden of argument is, I think, on Nietzsche to show that, and how, this is possible. He does not shoulder the burden.

The argument that pity is at bottom egoistic is of greater interest—but still, I believe, seriously flawed. Nietzsche correctly notices that pity contains a thought experiment in which one puts oneself in the other person's place, and indeed reasons that this place might in fact be, or become, one's own. To that extent, the reasoning in pity, like the reasoning of the parties in Rawls's "original position," is prudential reasoning. But in this structure of prudential reasoning is contained a model of what is most fundamental in the moral point of view: namely, a decision to acknowledge the suffering person as one like me, one who counts as I count, one I might be. In pity one treats the other as one would wish in similar circumstances to be treated oneself; and this, I think, is not even compatible with using the other as a means to one's own security or satisfaction.[46] So, once again, Nietzsche has a lot more work to do before he can convict altruistic moralities of a fundamental inconsistency.

But it is obvious that the important arguments in the attack on pity all revolve around the question of weakness and need, the question of whether the acknowledgment of neediness is ever a good thing, either in the pitier or toward the pitied. As I have said, this question ultimately demands a more exhaustive treatment than can be given here, but several points, at least, can be made.

First, it is important to see that the pro-pity tradition is not prevented from judging that some instances of pity are inappropriate, some occasions for pity illegitimate. Indeed, the tradition is largely preoccupied with judging which of the reversals of life really do have serious importance; and Aristotle, for example, goes to some lengths to criticize those who attach too much importance to money, status, or pleasure, seeing them as things without which no life could flourish. An Aristotelian will appropriately be pitied for losses connected with friendship, children, family, personal health, citizenship, the necessary conditions of action; but a mere change in financial status that falls short of damaging citizenship or action will not be an appropriate occasion for pity. Thus Aristotle agrees with Nietzsche that people should not find weakness everywhere they turn, or weep over any and every reversal; on the whole, they should value above all their own inner resources.[47] The pro-pity and the anti-pity tradition are thus not completely at odds, as Nietzsche sometimes suggests.

Nor is the pro-pity tradition prevented from also endorsing, as of great importance, the attitudes of self-respect and respect for the dignity of others that Nietzsche fosters and values. The ethical thought of Aristotle shows this clearly. Pity and respect do not address themselves to the very same objects: a person will be respected for that which he or she chooses, does, or controls, and pitied for a reversal of an especially severe sort in a sphere of life that he or she does not control. There is nothing odd about combining the two attitudes, even toward the same person in the same calamity. Aristotle stresses that when a person is "dislodged" from *eudaimonia* by chance reversals of a very severe sort, this merits pity; nonetheless, even in such catastrophes the person's nobility of character may still "shine through" in the way misfortune is borne; and this would merit our respect.[48] Thus, once again, Nietzsche seems to have oversimplified the contrast between the pro-pity and the anti-pity traditions, suggesting—falsely—that a pitier cannot also show respect, that a pitied person cannot also win respect.

We now turn to the heart of the matter, the role of "external goods" in the good human life. And here we encounter a rather large surprise. There is no philosopher in the modern Western tradition who is more emphatic than Nietzsche is about the central importance of the body, and about the fact that we are bodily creatures. Again and again he charges Christian and Platonist moralities with making a false separation between our spiritual and our physical nature; against them, he insists that we are physical through and through. The surprise is that, having said so much and with such urgency, he really is very loathe to draw the conclusion that is naturally suggested by his position: that human beings need worldly goods in order to function. In all of Nietzsche's rather abstract and romantic praise of solitude and asceticism, we find no grasp of the simple truth that a hungry person cannot think well; that a person who lacks shelter, basic health care, and the basic necessities of life, is not likely to become a great philosopher or artist, no matter what her innate equipment. The solitude Nietzsche describes is comfortable bourgeois solitude, whatever its pains and loneliness. Who are his ascetic philosophers? "Heraclitus, Plato, Descartes, Spinoza, Leibniz, Kant, Schopenhauer"—none a poor person, none a person who had to perform menial labor in order to survive.

And because Nietzsche does not grasp the simple fact that if our abilities are physical abilities they have physical necessary conditions, he does not understand what the democratic and socialist movements of his day were all about. The pro-pity tradition, from Homer on, understood that one functions badly if one is hungry, that one thinks badly if one has to labor all day in work that does not involve the fully human use of one's faculties. I have suggested that such thoughts were made by Rousseau the basis for the modern development of democratic-socialist thinking. Since Nietzsche does not get the basic idea, he does not see what socialism is trying to do. Since he probably never saw or knew an acutely hungry person, or a person performing hard physical labor, he never asked how human self-command is affected by such forms of life. And thus he can proceed as if it does not matter how people live from day to day, how they get their food. Who provides basic welfare support for Zarathustra? What are the "higher men" doing all the day long? The reader does not know and the author does not seem to care.

Now Nietzsche himself obviously was not a happy man. He was lonely, in bad health, scorned by many of his contemporaries. And yet, there still is a distinction to be drawn between the sort of vulnerability that Nietzsche's life contained and the sort we find if we examine the lives of truly impoverished and hungry people. We might say, simplifying things a bit, that there are two sorts of vulnerability: what we might call *bourgeois vulnerability*—for example, the pains of solitude, loneliness, bad reputation, some ill health, pains that are painful enough but still compatible with thinking and doing philosophy—and what we might call *basic vulnerability*, which is a deprivation of resources so central to human functioning that thought and character are themselves impaired or not developed. Nietzsche, focusing on the first sort of vulnerability, holds that it is not so bad; it may even be good for the philosopher.[49] The second sort, I claim, he simply neglects—believing, apparently, that even a beggar can be a Stoic hero, if only socialism does not inspire him with weakness.[50]

In this neglect, Nietzsche once again follows Stoicism—which, while holding that the soul is a physical entity through and through, is committed to denying that the physical goods of life are necessary conditions for *eudaimonia*.[51] And thus Stoics are committed to holding that people who are severely deprived, and even imprisoned or tortured, can still retain *eudaimonia*, so long as they are virtuous and self-commanding. But Stoic thought on this issue is subtler than Nietzsche's is: for Stoics at least give the "goods of nature" a certain sort of worth or value, holding that in general it is appropriate for an individual to pursue them, and for society to concern itself with their distribution. And they also hold that sufficient deprivation of material goods makes life not worth living and gives reason for suicide.[52] Thus, although they often do shirk the question of political and material support for human functioning in much the way that Nietzsche does, they need not do so; and certain Stoic thinkers do have a developed political theory.

Finally, we arrive at what is perhaps the deepest question about the anti-pity position: is its ideal of strength really a picture of strength? What should we think about a human being who insists on caring deeply for nothing that he himself does not control; who refuses to love others in ways that open him to serious risks of pain and loss; who cultivates the hardness of self-command as a bulwark against all the reversals that life can bring? We could say, with Nietzsche, that this is a strong person. But there clearly is another way to see things.[53] For there is a strength of a specifically human sort in the willingness to acknowledge some truths about one's situation: one's mortality, one's finitude, the limits and vulnerabilities of one's body, one's need for food and drink and shelter and friendship. There is a strength in the willingness to form attachments that can go wrong and cause deep pain, in the willingness to invest oneself in the world in a way that opens one's whole life up to the changes of the world, for good and for bad. There is, in short, a strength in the willingness to be porous rather than totally hard, in the willingness to be a mortal animal living in the world. The Stoic, by contrast, looks like a fearful person, a person who is determined to seal himself off from risk, even at the cost of loss of love and value.

Nietzsche knows, or should know, this. For a central theme in his work is that Christianity has taught us bad habits of self-insulation and self-protection, alienating us from our love of the world and all of its chanciness, all of its becoming. On this account we have become small in virtue, and will remain small, unless we learn once again to value our own actions as ends, and our worldly existence as their natural home. I think that in the end Nietzsche fails to go far enough with this critique. He fails, that is, to see what the Stoicism he endorses has in common with the Christianity he criticizes, what "hardness" has in common with otherworldliness: both are forms of self-protection, both express a fear of this world and its contingencies, both are incompatible with the deepest sort of love, whether personal or political.

I want to end with a passage—not unlike quite a few others in *Zarathustra*—where Nietzsche seems to me to endorse a worldly risk-taking sort of life, contrasting it to a Stoic life that (as Seneca would put it) stays at home with its own virtue. It is from the section "On the Famous Wise Men," in which Zarathustra confronts certain comfortable professors of philosophy in German universities and teaches them about the difference between security and true happiness:

> Spirit is the life that itself cuts into life: with its own agony it increases its own knowledge. Did you know that?
> And the happiness of the spirit is this: to be anointed and through tears to be consecrated as a sacrificial animal. Did you know that? . . .
> And you have never yet been able to cast your spirit into a pit of snow: you

are not hot enough for that. Hence you also do not know the ecstasies of its coldness. . . .

You are no eagles: hence you have never experienced the happiness that is in the terror of the spirit. . . .

Have you never seen a sail go over the sea, rounded and taut and trembling with the violence of the wind? Like the sail, trembling with the violence of the spirit, my wisdom goes over the sea—my wild wisdom.

But you servants of the people, you famous wise men—how could you go with me?

Thus spoke Zarathustra. (Z II:8)

Here, with characteristic stylistic exuberance,[54] Nietzsche draws on many of the central images for the riskiness of human functioning in the pro-pity tradition: the eagle, the boat in the wind, the sacrificial animal. He glosses them, as so often, in a typically Romantic manner; and yet there is no doubt that he is, in a sense, aligning himself with the view of the moral depth and importance of contingency that animates the defense of pity in the Greek literary and philosophical tradition. But Nietzsche, like the famous wise men, is in the end too comfortable by half. Like them, he really doesn't see what the life of a beggar is, what it is really like to lose your only child, what it is really like to love someone with all your heart and be betrayed. These experiences, and their depth, are at the heart of the pro-pity tradition; and I don't think that Nietzsche could make that sort of risk central to his thought without endorsing pity (as the tradition does) as a morally valuable response. But he is determined to have it both ways: to play-act at romantic risk-taking while retaining Stoic hardness; to have as his spokesman a character who makes nice speeches about eagles and boats and risk-taking and solitude—but who never seems to endure a moment's human grief or thirst or hunger, wrapped up, as he is, in his own self-commanding thought and speech; to make a rhetorical gesture in the direction of the contingencies to which pity is a response, while repudiating pity in favor of self-sufficiency.

This comes about, I think, because Nietzsche is really all along, despite all his famous unhappiness, too much like the "famous wise men": an armchair philosopher of human riskiness, living with no manual labor and three meals a day, without inner understanding of the ways in which contingency matters for virtue.[55]

NOTES

1. In general, I follow Walter Kaufmann's translations of the relevant works; for an exception, see note 2 below. For *Daybreak* I use the translation by R. J. Hollingdale (Cambridge: Cambridge University Press, 1982).

2. "Trachte Ich denn nach *Glücke*? Ich trachte nach meinem *Werke*!" Kaufmann

translates this as: "Am I concerned with *happiness?* I am concerned with my *work.*" But this misses the implication of the German that it is the direction of Zarathustra's *striving* or *aspiring*—not some more inert concern or attention—that has altered; and the English "work," unqualified, suggests German *Arbeit,* rather than *Werk,* which connotes an artistic or creative endeavor.

3. Again, my own translation.

4. Philippa Foot, "Nietzsche's Immoralism," *New York Review of Books* 38, no. 11 (13 June 1991): 18–22 (reprinted in this volume); Jonathan Glover, in "Never Such Innocence Again," (manuscript).

5. Walter Kaufmann, *Nietzsche: Philosopher, Psychologist, Antichrist* (Princeton: Princeton University Press, 1950; 3d rev. ed., Vintage Books, 1968).

6. In what follows, I shall be drawing on work on the ancient traditions that I have also developed more fully elsewhere. See especially, *The Fragility of Goodness: Luck and Ethics in Greek Tragedy and Philosophy* (Cambridge: Cambridge University Press, 1986): *The Therapy of Desire: Theory and Practice in Hellenistic Ethics* (Princeton: Princeton University Press, 1994), the most relevant portions of which, for these purposes, have been published as "The Stoics on the Extirpation of the Passions," *Apeiron* 20 (1987): 129–164, and "Serpents in the Soul: a Reading of Seneca's *Medea,*" in *Pursuits of Reason: Essays in Honor of Stanley Cavell,* ed. T. Cohen, P. Guyer, and H. Putnam (Lubbock: Texas Tech Press, 1993); "Tragedy and Self-Sufficiency: Plato and Aristotle on Fear and Pity," in *Essays on Aristotle's Poetics,* ed. A. Rorty (Princeton: Princeton University Press, 1992), and, in a longer version, in *Oxford Studies in Ancient Philosophy* 10 (1992); and also, "Poetry and the Passions: Two Stoic Views," in *Passions & Perceptions,* Proceedings of the Fifth Symposium Hellenisticum, ed. J. Brunschwig and M. Nussbaum (Cambridge: Cambridge University Press, 1993).

7. This example, and in general the Greek poetic tradition on pity, are discussed at greater length in my "Tragedy and Self-Sufficiency." The examples are from *Iliad* 24.503 ff., and *Odyssey* 17, 415 ff.

8. See Aristotle, *Rhetoric* 1385b13 ff. On pity and fear, see also the excellent discussion in Stephen Halliwell, *Aristotle's Poetics* (London: Duckworth, 1986).

9. On the connection between Aristotle's view of tragedy and his ethical views, see *Fragility of Goodness,* chap. 11 and interlude 2, and "Tragedy and Self-Sufficiency."

10. See *Poetics* 1453a4, 1453a5; *Rhetoric* 1385b14, 1385b34–1386al, 1386b7, 10, 12, 13.

11. Euripides, *Bacchae,* 1244, 1259, 1324, 1346. Other tragic examples are given in "Tragedy and Self-Sufficiency," and in Halliwell, *Aristotle's Poetics.*

12. *Rhetoric* 1385b14–15, b21–2, b31. Within the literary tradition, see especially Sophocles, *Trachiniai,* 1271 ff., where Hyllus contrasts the *suggnomosune* ("concern-along-with") of the human characters who view his father's unjust suffering with the *agnomosune* ("lack of concern") of the gods who heedlessly caused the suffering.

13. On the link, see especially Halliwell, *Aristotle's Poetics.*

14. This is suggested in Aristotle's discussion, in which he first defines pity with reference to undeserved and serious pain, and then goes on to make observations about the conditions under which pity is likely to be produced. The distinction is,

in effect, a distinction between those beliefs that are necessary (and possibly also sufficient) conditions of pity, and the sort of person who is likely to form such beliefs.

15. Some portraits of the Olympian gods make them rather like this—especially, perhaps, the Sophoclean portraits; others, insisting on a kind of familial commonness and/or the possibility of divine suffering, do not. Plato will hold that any conception that is truly a conception of divinity, hence of invulnerable perfection, has no room in it for pity. For helpful discussion of this issue, I am indebted to Stephen Halliwell.

16. John Rawls, *A Theory of Justice* (Cambridge, Mass.: Harvard University Press, 1971).

17. A very interesting example, in this development, is Sophocles' *Philoctetes* in which pity dictates that a homeless diseased outcast not only be restored to the community but be treated with respect and told the truth. On Sophoclean criticisms of the class bias and elitism of traditional morality, see Mary Whitlock Blundell's fine study, *Helping Friends and Harming Enemies: A Study in Sophocles* (Cambridge: Cambridge University Press, 1989).

18. This material is discussed more fully in the long version of "Tragedy and Self-Sufficiency." All translations from Rousseau are my own.

19. See Gregory Vlastos, *Socrates: Ironist and Moral Philosopher* (Cambridge: Cambridge University Press, 1991), and my review in *The New Republic*, September 1991.

20. This interpretation is defended in Vlastos, *Socrates*.

21. *Apol.* 41D, and cf. 30CD.

22. For fuller discussion, see "Tragedy and Self-Sufficiency" for an excellent treatment of the texts and the issues, see Stephen Halliwell, "Plato and Aristotle on the Denial of Tragedy," *Proceedings of the Cambridge Philological Society* 30 (1984): 39–71; and also Halliwell, *Plato: Republic X*, trans. and comm. (Warminster: Aris and Phillips, 1989).

23. See my "Poetry and the Passions: Two Stoic Views." On the role of Socrates as *exemplum*, see also A. A. Long, "Socrates in Hellenistic Philosophy," *Classical Quarterly* 38 (1988): 150–171.

24. For a more detailed discussion of all these elements of Stoicism, see *The Therapy of Desire*, and its previously published pieces, especially "The Stoics on the Extirpation of the Passions."

25. For this argument, see especially Seneca's *On Anger* (*De Ira*).

26. For one good example of this, see Seneca, *Moral Epistles* (*Epistulae Morales*) letter 15.

27. For this imagery, see Seneca's *Medea*—and other tragedies as well. There are good discussions of this in Charles Segal, "Boundary Violation and the Landscape of the Self in Senecan Tragedy," *Antike und Abendland* 29 (1983): 172–187, and in D. and B. Henry, *The Mask of Power: Seneca's Tragedies and Imperial Rome* (Warminster: Aris and Phillips, 1985). I analyze the serpent imagery of the *Medea* in "Serpents in the Soul."

28. Seneca, *On Mercy* (*De Clementia*).

29. For this argument, see Seneca, *On Anger* and *On Mercy*, the view is discussed in "Seneca on Anger in Public Life," chap. 11 of my *Therapy of Desire* and in my "Equity and Mercy," *Philosophy and Public Affairs* 22 (Spring, 1993).

30. There are particularly graphic and horrifying images of this in Senecan tragedy. Medea, since she has permitted herself to be soft, and thus susceptible to the
entry of love, can (she imagines) rid herself of the pains of love only by violence to
others. She imagines the murder of her children as an assault on the roots of love
in her own body; and her fantasy of triumph is the fantasy of restored virginity.
Oedipus, who has, similarly, been entered by desire, imagines that the only way to
rid himself of this incursion is to rip open his eyes and dig his fingers into his brain.
For references and further discussion, see Segal, "Boundary Violation," and my
"Serpents in the Soul."

31. See *On Anger* (especially II.9–10), and *On Mercy.*

32. The role of external goods in Stoicism is highly complex. For some qualifi-
cations, see the last section of this paper. It is clear, however, that Stoics are committed to denying (a) that external goods have any intrinsic value; and (b) that they
are necessary for *eudaimonia.* For a very good recent treatment of the problem, see
Glenn Lesses, "Virtue and the Goods of Fortune in Stoic Moral Theory," *Oxford
Studies in Ancient Philosophy* 7 (1989):95–128.

33. I am not, of course, denying that beneficence is central to Kant's ethics; I
am simply claiming that there is a tension between the Stoic element in his thought
(including a very strong repudiation of *Mitleid,* in *The Doctrine of Virtue*) and his
interest in duties of beneficence.

34. See his "De Laertii Diogenis fontibus," *Rheinisches Museum für Philologie,* new
series, no. 23 (1868): 632–653 and no. 24 (1869): 181–228; "Analecta Laertiana,"
Rheinisches Museum für Philologie, new series, no. 25 (1870): 217–231; and *Beiträge zur
Quellenkunde und Kritik des Laertius Diogenes* (Basel: Carl Schultz, 1870). All three
publications may be found in KGW II:1, *Philogische Schriften 1867–1873.*

35. See Max Oehler, "Nietzsches Bibliotek," *Vierzehnte Jahresgabe der Gesellschaft
der Freunde des Nietzsche-Archives* (Weimar: 1942).

36. *The Birth of Tragedy* shows, as one might expect, a greater sympathy to tragic
values. (On the argument of that work, see my "The Transfigurations of Intoxica-
tion: Nietzsche, Schopenhauer, and Dionysus," *Arion* NS 2 [1991].) And several
sections of *The Gay Science* show a critical stance toward Stoic hardness that is not, I
believe, replicated in any other mature works (see esp. 99, 326, 359). I shall return
to some of these passages in my concluding section.

37. Maudemarie Clark suggests to me that Nietzsche does not altogether condemn pity in this section, since he offers advice concerning the restraint with which
a friend should pity a friend. But I think that the context makes clear that he says
this only because he recognizes how extremely difficult it is to get rid of pity entirely:
"If I must pity . . . it is preferably from a distance." The true goal of the pitier,
however, should be a more thoroughgoing extirpation of pity, even with a friend:
"If you have a suffering friend, be a resting place for his suffering, but a hard bed
as it were, a field cot: thus will you profit him best."

38. Epictetus, *Discourses* 1.6.30: " 'Yes, but my nose is running.' 'What have you
hands for, then, slave? Isn't it so that you can wipe your own nose?' "

39. Z I, "On Chastity," counsels the avoidance of chastity only for those for
whom it would be a burden and a distraction: "Not a few who wanted to drive out

their devil have themselves entered into swine." But those who can be chaste in an unburdened and uneffortful way (like Zarathustra) are praised. And Zarathustra perceptively here links his adherence to chastity with a rejection of tragedy, and tragic pity: "Do you love tragedies and everything that breaks the heart? But I mistrust your bitch. . . . Is it not merely your lust that has disguised itself and now calls itself pity?" Here we have clear evidence of Nietzsche's adherence to a Senecan analysis of the relationship between pity and sensuality.

40. Diogenes the Cynic, being asked what was the right time to marry, replied: "For young men, not yet; for old men, no longer" (Diogenes Laertius, VI.54). For Epicurus's position against marriage (because of the distractions that both marriage itself and child-rearing cause for the philosopher, a very Nietzschean argument), see the review of the evidence in C. W. Chilton, "Did Epicurus Approve of Marriage?" *Phronesis* 5 (1960): 71–74. Roman Stoics argued that the philosopher ought to be married, because of his duties to the larger political community. But he was emphatically not to feel either love or strong sexual desire for his spouse; and he was to have intercourse for reproductive purposes only. See especially the fragments of Seneca's *On Marriage* (*De Matrimonio*), ed. F. Haase in *L. Annaei Senecae Opera Ouae Supersunt*, 3 vols. (Leipzig: Teubner, 1897–1898); and Musonius Rufus, *On the End of Marriage*, ed O. Hense in *C. Musonii Rufi Reliquiae* (Leipzig: Teubner, 1905).

41. See Diogenes Laertius's life of Diogenes, VI.20–81. The following extracts give the general idea: "Once when he was masturbating in the marketplace, he said, 'I wish it was as easy to relieve hunger by rubbing an empty stomach.'. . . When someone scorned him for being an exile, he replied, 'But it was through that, you unhappy man, that I became a philosopher.'. . . He once begged for a handout from a statue, and, when someone asked why he did that, he said, 'I am getting practice in getting turned down.'. . . Seeing some women hanged from an olive tree, he said, 'Would that every tree bore such fruit.' " Nietzsche's misogyny has evident connections with this Cynic tradition; these connections should be further investigated. Another connection is with Nietzsche's position on the philosopher's independence of patrons and their demands: compare *Genealogy* III.5 (on the poets as "too-pliable courtiers of their own followers and patrons") with Diogenes Laertius's life of Diogenes, VI.58: "Plato saw him washing lettuce, came up to him, and said quietly, 'If you had paid court to Dionysius, you wouldn't now be washing lettuce.' He answered, equally calmly, 'And you, if you had washed lettuce, would not have paid court to Dionysius.' "

42. The connection between gratitude and revenge is a central topic of Hellenistic passion theory, stressed in Epicureanism and Stoicism alike; see *The Therapy of Desire*, chaps. 7, 10, 11. Nietzsche insists on the connection in several texts, for example, EH I.5, and HH 44, which concludes, "Swift remarked that men are grateful in the same proportion as they cherish revenge."

43. Thus, though I find Michael Green's analysis of Nietzschean pity helpful and suggestive (in "Nietzsche on Pity and *Ressentiment*," read to the North American Nietzsche Society at the Central Division Meeting of the American Philosophical Association, April 1991), I disagree with his claim that the pitier *rejects* the value of the external goods that the person pitied has lost (and is therefore, Green claims,

inconsistent with himself, in that his very sadness is at the same time a tacit acknowledgment of the worth of these goods). I think that pity's logic is much more consistent—and, from Nietzsche's point of view, more thoroughly flawed.

44. It must be emphasized once again—although this is something that Kaufmann's book should have laid to rest once and for all—that the Masters mentioned in the *Genealogy* Essay I are not in the least Nietzsche's heroes. Their thoughtless cruelty and their freedom from constraint are in fact condemned by Nietzsche in no uncertain terms (esp. I.11); and they are said to lack not only the discipline that is a necessary prerequisite of Nietzschean virtue, but also the inner self-awareness and self-critical reflectiveness that is a central mark of the virtuous, and even of the "interesting."

45. I discuss some contemporary applications of the Stoic idea of self-command in chap. 9 of *The Therapy of Desire*.

46. On the connection between callousness toward others and a failure to make the judgments of similarity that ground pity, see in particular Raoul Hilberg, *The Destruction of the European Jews* (New York: New Viewpoints, 1973), who gives a fascinating account of the ways in which Nazi treatment of the Jews was psychologically supported by self-deceptive stratagems that denied Jews the status of similar human beings, portraying them as animals or inanimate objects; and of ways in which, when a sharp access of empathy in a particular case cut through these fictions, conduct was, albeit temporarily, altered.

47. For further discussion of this, see *Fragility*, chap. 11, and "Tragedy and Self-Sufficiency."

48. See *Nicomachean Ethics* I.11, and the discussion in "Tragedy and Self-Sufficiency."

49. One reason why this is an oversimplification is that Nietzsche holds that some forms of what I call bourgeois vulnerability—for example, the pains due to romantic love and intense attachments to other individual persons—are not actually good for philosophy, and should be avoided. In this, too, he is a Stoic; and his account of friendship has striking similarities with the Stoic-inspired accounts of friendship in Emerson and Thoreau. (I am indebted to Eric Klinenberg and Marco Lau for excellent seminar papers that advanced my understanding of this topic.)

50. It is in this light that we should read Zarathustra's announcement, "But beggars should be abolished entirely! Verily, it is annoying to give to them and it is annoying not to give to them" (Z II:3, "On the Pitying"). In the context, Zarathustra has invited the poor to help themselves to what philosophy offers; here he is, then, not saying that the poor should be done away with, but, rather, that they should help themselves, and then they will, by definition, no longer be beggars. Here and elsewhere, Nietzsche's views may be usefully compared to those of Ayn Rand.

51. For the evidence, see Lesses, "Virtues and the Goods of Fortune."

52. For discussion, references, and bibliography, see *The Therapy of Desire*, chap. 11.

53. Nietzsche himself sees this point in *The Gay Science*, especially 359, an attack on Christian versions of Stoicism, and above all 326, "The physicians of the soul and pain." Here Nietzsche concludes with a question: "Is our life really painful and burdensome enough to make it advantageous to exchange it for a Stoic way of life

and petrification? We are *not so badly off* that we have to be as badly off as Stoics."
Here Nietzsche achieves an insight that he does not stably retain—perhaps because
he would then have to rethink his position on pity, something that he is willing to
do. And even in this aphorism, he rejects the Stoic position only to the extent of
saying that, after all, the pains of life are not so very great—which is, itself, a version
of the Stoic position.

54. The relation of Nietzsche's style to Stoicism would itself be the topic for a
very interesting study. On the one hand, we see in passages such as the one before
us a very non-Stoic Dionysian sort of exuberance; on the other hand, this exuberance often all too quickly resolves itself into a praise of hardness and self-sufficiency.
And the polemical style of *Zarathustra* owes a large debt to the *Discourses* of Epictetus
and the *Moral Epistles* of Seneca. We might even see in the more apparently emotional passages something comparable to Senecan tragedy.

55. I am very grateful to students in two courses at Brown (on Nietzsche and on
Aristotle) for listening to these ideas and making many valuable suggestions, both
textual and philosophical. I hope I shall be forgiven if I have not managed to cite
by name everyone who had some input into the product. I am also grateful to the
audience at the meeting of the North American Nietzsche Society at the American
Philosophical Association Eastern Division, 29 December 1991, for a stimulating
discussion. For discussions that helped me with the issues, and for valuable comments on an earlier draft, I am indebted to Maudemarie Clark, Jonathan Glover,
Steven Hales, Stephen Halliwell, Eric Klinenberg, Marco Lau, Richard Posner, Richard Schacht, Cass Sunstein, and Robert Welshon.

TEN

Nietzsche on Cruelty, Asceticism, and the Failure of Hedonism

Ivan Soll

ON THE GENEALOGY OF MORALS: BEYOND GENEALOGY AND MORALS

The nominal subject of Nietzsche's *On the Genealogy of Morals* is the investigation of the origins of our moral values. While the book tenaciously pursues the topic of its title without disintegrating into a loosely related collection of aphorisms (as some of Nietzsche's other books tend to do), it nevertheless deals with more than morality, and more than genealogy. Like Nietzsche's work in general, this book repeatedly returns to issues and hypotheses that constitute a fundamental and integrating core of his entire philosophic enterprise. One aspect of this enterprise is the construction of a theory about the ultimate goal of human behavior. The central thesis of this theory that a *will to power* is the deepest and most general motive of human behavior, that the *ultimate* goal of *all* human striving is the acquisition and increase of power.

Nietzsche's theory of the will to power is not only psychological but axiological: the will to power is put forward not only as the ultimate motivation of all human behavior but also as the ultimate source of all human values. Nietzsche also takes for granted that whatever constitutes the ultimate object of our desires ought to be considered not only in accounting for the development or "genealogy" of our systems of moral values but also in assessing and revising them, in the project he calls the "revaluation of all values." But though the will to power is an essential component of Nietzsche's theory of values, it is obviously meant to be considered in its own right as a psychological hypothesis.

In the *Genealogy*, the general psychological hypothesis of the will to power forms the implicit, yet omnipresent, backdrop for Nietzsche's analyses of the genealogies of moral systems that constitute the core of the book. Because this hypothesis is not explicitly advanced and advocated here, one might easily come to view it as a tool or method, developed and justified elsewhere, and brought to bear in this work upon the specific subject matter of morals without any further critical scrutiny or argument. This is a natural but overly narrow and unfruitful way to approach the will to power in Nietzsche's *Genealogy*. One should keep in mind that the application of previously argued general hypotheses to specific problems inevitably constitutes a further test or confirmation of these hypotheses. And though the *Genealogy* neither directly nor explicitly advocates the underlying psychological thesis of the will to power, which Nietzsche considered one of his two major ideas,[1] the book contains Nietzsche's fullest treatment of the issues that are crucial to his case for it. In the *Genealogy*, as in much of his other work, Nietzsche not only applies but also indirectly argues for the psychological theory of the will to power.

The significance of this theory for Nietzsche lay not only in its elegance and explanatory power, as a theory enabling us to understand all of human behavior as the varied expression of one basic drive, but also in its provision of an original and importantly different alternative to *psychological hedonism*—the theory that the deepest motive of all human behavior is the attainment of pleasure and the avoidance of pain. The latter theory in one form or another has long dominated our thinking about human behavior. The alternative psychology of will to power was offered not only for its explanatory superiority but also for its potential to liberate us from a broadly and deeply rooted error.

There is ample evidence that Nietzsche, in offering his analyses of the origins of moral values in the *Genealogy*, was concerned with what he took to be the prevalent and erroneous view of psychological hedonism. The first of the book's three parts begins with a discussion of "these English psychologists," who had proposed utilitarian accounts of the genealogy and current meaning of moral values (GM I:1–3).[2] In rejecting their accounts, Nietzsche is also mounting a broader attack upon that tradition of English utilitarianism in which an action's value is derived from its "utility," which is taken to be determined by the degree of human happiness (or unhappiness) it creates, with the degree of happiness defined in turn by the amount of pleasure and pain (or displeasure) experienced.

Thus the utilitarianism of "these English psychologists," which concerned Nietzsche at the outset of the *Genealogy* and in his other works, is also a *eudaemonism* (a theory in which the ultimate motives of human beings or their ultimate values are said to derive from considerations of happiness)—which is in turn a *hedonism* (a theory in which these ultimate motives or values are defined by considerations of pleasure and the avoidance of pain). This linkage of utilitarianism with eudaemonism and hedonism is not conceptually inevitable; utility need not be defined in terms of happiness, nor happiness in terms of pleasure and pain. But in our philosophic tradition they have commonly been so linked.[3]

NATURALISM BEYOND FALLACIES

I have characterized utilitarianism, eudaemonism, and hedonism as theories about "ultimate motives *or* values" to call attention to the fact that each can be offered either as a psychological theory or as an ethical theory—either as a theory of what in fact *does* motivate our behavior or as a theory of what *should* motivate it. Nietzsche's theory of the will to power, like some of the classical statements of utilitarianism it seeks to replace, is offered as both. In Mill's utilitarianism, as in Nietzsche's theory of the will to power, it seems to be taken for granted that this double duty is an unproblematic norm—the value of actions and their results obviously being a function of what it is that we really want.[4]

This melding of psychological and ethical theory has been seen by many as a confusion—a "naturalistic fallacy," the mistake of trying to derive prescriptive statements from descriptive ones, of benightedly trying to make logical inferences from statements about what we in fact want to statements about what we ought to want, of ignoring Hume's injunction that one can never "derive an *ought* from an *is*." And this fallacious inference is taken to arise from a confusion between what is desired and what is desirable— that is, between what we in fact desire and what we should desire. But it is far from clear that either Nietzsche or Mill was attempting to make inferences from descriptive statements to prescriptive ones. Both were of the opinion, however, that what has true value for us can only be what corresponds to our deepest and truest needs and what ultimately satisfies our most general and ineluctable desires.

With respect to a plurality of specific and competing desires, what one wants can easily be something other than what one should want. But with respect to what is proposed as the one universal, ultimate, and necessary goal of all desiring (pleasure and the absence of pain in Mill's utilitarianism, power in Nietzsche's philosophy), we cannot, in the same sense, want something other than what we should want. The specter of a "naturalistic fallacy" that fails to respect the difference between what one in fact wants and what one ought to want dissolves in the context of theories that propose, as do Nietzsche's and Mill's, that all human behavior has only one ultimate and ineluctable motivation. Only where there is a plurality of possible goals can one choose the wrong one, for only in such contexts is there any choice at all. In the context of a theory like Mill's or Nietzsche's, in which such a plurality of drives is viewed as the varied and superficial expression of a single fundamental drive, there exists choice (and thus the possibility of incorrect choice) only in choosing from among the superficial plurality of drives, but not with respect to the one fundamental drive that they are all supposed to represent.

Nietzsche's "naturalistic" grounding of his "revaluation of all values" in what he takes to be the true nature of human desires thus rests in part upon his success in showing the vast variety of human striving to be the varied expression of a single basic drive—the will to power. This point can be generalized: any such naturalism in ethics, aesthetics, or general value theory is similarly shielded from the objection that it is fallaciously attempting to derive an *ought* from and an *is,* insofar as: (1) it is combined with a reduction of the variety of human wants to one basic drive; and (2) the value theory, ethics, or aesthetics is directly grounded in this basic drive and not in the plurality of wants that are purportedly derivatives of it. The combination to be found in both Nietzsche's and Mill's philosophies, a naturalism in ethics or value theory entwined with a reductive motivational monism in psychology, is anything but fortuitous.

The dependence of the plausibility of such naturalistic theories of value upon the accompanying reductionistic theories of drives has not been adequately appreciated. The confluence of psychology and value theory has often been misunderstood as a gratuitous union deriving from an infelicitous confusion, which it would be better to dissolve, so that each may be treated separately.

My exploration of the psychological aspect of Nietzsche's theory of the will to power in the *Genealogy,* a work devoted to the analysis of values, should not be taken as subscribing to these common but misguided separatist tendencies. While insisting on the important connection between the axiological and psychological aspects of Nietzsche's theory of the will to power, I should like to point out that their relationship is asymmetrical, the ethics being grounded in the psychology and not vice versa. Given this relationship it is not surprising that Nietzsche, even when most consistently pursuing ethical topics, continues to argue for his psychology of power. It also suggests that Nietzsche's psychology of power can be examined in isolation from the value theory this psychology is used to support, while his value theory can less easily and legitimately be treated apart from the psychology in which it is grounded.

CRUELTY AND ASCETICISM AS PROOFS OF THE WILL TO POWER

Hedonistic utilitarianism and the theory of the will to power confront each other as the two major proposals for the ultimate motive of all behavior and consequently the source of all value.[5] To supplant the prevalent view of psychological hedonism with the hypothesis of the will to power, Nietzsche must find behavioral phenomena that are more illuminatingly and convincingly accounted for by a psychology of power than by a psychology of pleasure. Phenomena particularly recalcitrant to explanation in terms of seeking pleasure and avoiding pain can be expected to receive his special attention. Any desire or action that does not seem directed toward the increase of pleasure and avoidance of pain presents a problem to the psychological hedonist and, correspondingly, an opportunity to the proponent of any competing view. Any behavior that appears not only to make no effort to avoid pain but even to seek it out provides particularly important problems and opportunities of this sort. To exploit such opportunities the advocate of the competing view must, of course, show that his theory can better account for these problematic cases.

Cruelty and asceticism, I shall argue, present just such problems for hedonism and corresponding opportunities for Nietzsche's psychology of power. His extended treatment of these phenomena in the *Genealogy* is due not only to what he takes to have been their crucial role in the development of moral values but also to their crucial role in his advocacy of the theory of the will to power.

CRUELTY AND THE OTHER PROBLEM OF OTHER MINDS

Cruelty, hedonistically conceived, finds its satisfaction in the suffering of others: actions motivated by cruelty aim at making others suffer; a cruel person is one who desires and enjoys the suffering of others. But why should we derive enjoyment from the suffering of others—as we often clearly seem to do? For that matter, why should we derive pleasure from the pleasure of others? Is there an account contained in hedonism—and not merely consistent with it—that explains why the hedonic states of others should affect my own, and why there should be any intrinsic connection between the happiness or unhappiness, the pleasure or pain, the psychological well-being or ill-being of others and my own?

That some utilitarians have insisted upon the ethical importance of considering the happiness of all human beings and not just one's own happiness is a moral, not a psychological thesis, and thus is irrelevant to our question.[6] It may be morally reprehensible to enjoy the suffering of others and even worse to attempt to bring it about, but it is something that human beings often do. It therefore needs explanation. That some hedonists have also insisted on the psychological thesis, that the happiness or unhappiness of others is crucial to our own, is only to acknowledge this phenomenon, not to account for it.

Why should another's happiness or unhappiness produce a similar state in me? The way in which one consciousness is separated from another seems to preclude one person's directly experiencing another's pains and pleasures. Consequently, our reaction to the pains and pleasures of others has to be really a reaction to our beliefs about their experiences of pain and pleasure. Still, why should our beliefs about the pleasures and pains of others produce pleasures and pains in ourselves?[7] Any appeal to an innate and further unanalyzable tendency to empathize with our fellow human beings simply generalizes the phenomenon to be explained. It does not explain why we are empathetic creatures. Moreover, while an appeal to empathy addresses the issue of why we rejoice and suffer along with what we perceive to be the joys and sufferings of others, it only makes our cruel enjoyment of the suffering of others even more puzzling.[8]

It might be maintained that psychological hedonism need not contain within itself an account of why and how the hedonic states of others affect my own. Hedonism can certainly describe the various possible and actual combinations in its own terms. Hedonistically construed, empathy or sympathy is the taking of pleasure in another's pleasure or suffering pain because of another's pain; envy, jealousy, or *ressentiment* are the suffering of pain because of another's pleasure; cruelty is the taking of pleasure in another's pain.

Hedonism offers a language in which these phenomena can be clearly described. Why must it do any more? Why must our empathy, cruelty, and jealousy, which naturally result in our wanting others to experience pleasure or pain, be themselves explicable in terms of our seeking pleasure and avoiding pain? Could the phenomena in question not simply be the consequences of conditions of our existence not generated or governed by the pleasure principle? But inasmuch as psychological hedonism aspires to offer an account of the ultimate motivation of all human behavior, it cannot turn its back on this problem. It must account for *every* sort of behavior, including those in which one's pleasures and pains depend upon those of others, by appeal to the pleasure principle.

CRUELTY AND POWER

Confronting the proponents of psychological hedonism with the shortcomings of their theory regarding those types of behavior that seem to find satisfaction in the well- or ill-being of others, Nietzsche attempts to demonstrate that his theory does not suffer from these same shortcomings. As part of his project, he tries to show that the hypothesis of the will to power can supply a much more satisfying explanation for the widespread occurrence of human cruelty than can the pleasure principle. As we have seen, psychological hedonism offers a language in which cruelty can be described as a type of character or behavior that finds its pleasure in the pain of others. But it offers no analysis of the *infrastructure* of the satisfactions of cruelty, no account of the *mechanism* by means of which cruelty tempts and gratifies us.

An advocate of psychological hedonism might be forced to maintain that the pleasure many of us often take in the displeasure of others is simply an unanalyzable given; it is simply a fact that people sometimes enjoy the suffering of others—a fact that can be used to explain behavior but is not itself amenable to further explanation. If another account of cruelty could be produced, however, which explained this mechanism—that is, which provided an analysis of the underlying structure of the satisfactions of cruelty—the alternative theory would offer a deeper and more satisfying account. This is exactly what Nietzsche undertakes and, to some extent, accomplishes.

This account of cruelty in terms of power occurs principally in the second of *Genealogy*'s three essays, " 'Guilt,' 'Bad Conscience,' and the Like." Nietzsche locates the origin of the ideas of justice, guilt, and punishment in early forms of commerce—specifically in relationships between debtors and creditors. He derives the notion of guilt (*Schuld*) from that of debts (*Schulden*). Punishment, he argues, originated as a practice to compensate creditors for unpaid debts. The unpaid creditor claims or is awarded as compensation the right to punish the defaulting debtor, and "this compensation, then, consists in a warrant for and title to cruelty" (GM II:5).[9]

In order for a punishment to serve as compensation for an unpaid debt, the debtor's suffering must be viewed as a fitting substitute for the original form of payment. This in turn requires, first, that the various types of goods and services that can be owed are convertible into a common currency of pleasure and pain, and second, that the debtor's pain provides pleasure and satisfaction to the creditor.

Nietzsche indeed hypothesizes just such a genealogy for the notion that pleasure and pain constitute a universal currency in which all types of goods can be assigned an equivalent value:

> Through the greater part of human history punishment was imposed . . . from anger at some harm or injury, vented on the one who caused it—but this anger is held in check and modified by the idea that every injury has its *equivalent* and can actually be paid back, even if only through the pain of the culprit. And whence did this primeval, deeply rooted, perhaps by now ineradicable idea draw its power—this idea of an equivalence between injury and pain? I have already divulged it: in the contractual relationship between *creditor* and *debtor,* which . . . points back to the fundamental forms of buying, selling, barter, trade, and traffic. (GM II:4)

To offer a genealogy of the idea that pleasure and pain constitute a universal currency is not to offer a justification of its claim to truth. On the contrary, there is reason to think that this idea is untrue—even if a convenient illusion. Nietzsche approaches what he takes to be a manifestly implausible idea with curiosity about the reasons for its astonishing prevalence. His description of the idea as "perhaps by now ineradicable" suggests that it may deserve to be eradicated because of its implausibility, but cannot be eradicated because it has long served a crucial function in legal and ethical theory and practice.[10] Nietzsche is here supplying, without much fanfare, a genealogy of an idea that makes psychological hedonism and utilitarian ethics possible. But to do this is as little to accept or justify these views as his genealogy of "slave morality" indicates an acceptance or justification of it. In Nietzsche's philosophy, to produce the genealogy of an idea is certainly not tantamount to producing a justification for it.

The idea that quantities of any kind of goods can be converted into corresponding quantities of pleasure makes it possible for the creditor to be paid in pleasure for the unpaid debt owed to him in other sorts of goods. Still, it does not explain how this pleasure can be found in the suffering of the debtor. The pain of the debtor is supposed to compensate me for damages because this pain is supposed to bring me pleasure; but we are still confronted with the question: Why should *someone else's* pain constitute or produce *my* pleasure?

Nietzsche's explanation, as one might expect, is made in terms of the will to power. The "warrant for and title to cruelty" allows me to make the debtor suffer. The satisfaction then consists more in *my power to make him suffer* than in the mere occurrence of his suffering. Nietzsche's explanation consists in a removal of the locus of the satisfaction of cruelty away from the occurrence of the suffering in the other (and even from my own consciousness of or belief in this suffering), and its relocation in my feeling of delight in being able to make him suffer, that is, in my enjoyment of my own power. He describes punishment as a "recompense in the form of a kind of *pleasure*—the pleasure of being allowed to vent one's power freely upon one who is powerless, the voluptuous pleasure *'de faire le mal pour le plaisir de le faire'* [of doing evil for the pleasure of doing it], the enjoyment of violation" (GM II:5).[11] On this account, our satisfaction in making others suffer derives from *making* or *doing* something, rather than from the content of what is made or done. It is not the mere occurrence of suffering in others that gratifies me but my being able to make them suffer.

> To ask again: to what extent can suffering balance debts or guilt? To the extent that to *make* suffer was in the highest degree pleasurable, to the extent that the injured party exchanged for the loss he had sustained, including the pleasure caused by the loss, an extraordinary counterbalancing pleasure: that of *making* suffer. (GM II:6)

The hedonist cannot explain how the suffering of the debtor or wrongdoer even appears to make up for the debt or transgression. Why indeed should the suffering of another be any recompense to me? Why should the pleasure or pain of another constitute or cause any pleasure or pain in me?

Nietzsche calls attention to this problem, admitting that "the depths of such subterranean things are difficult to fathom, besides being painful," and continues:

> Whoever clumsily interposes the concept of "revenge" does not enhance his insight into the matter but further veils and darkens it (—for revenge merely leads back to the same problem: "how can making suffer constitute a compensation?"). (GM II:6)

Nietzsche's rejection of an appeal to the motive of revenge in explaining why we want to hurt those who have hurt us is paradigmatic, importantly illuminating his general conception of an adequate psychological explanation of human behavior. Ascribing our wanting to harm those who have harmed us to a general human desire for revenge simply gives a name to the desires and behavior at issue; it does not offer a satisfying psychological account. The same sort of critique could be applied to the notion of empathy or sympathy when adduced to account for our experiencing pleasure at the pleasure of others and pain at the pain of others, or to the notion of envy as an explanation of our experiencing pain at the pleasure of others.[12] The notion of cruelty itself could conceivably be brought into the discussion of why we enjoy the suffering of others as a putative explanation as well as the phenomena to be explained. In general, appeals to empathy, envy, revenge, and cruelty as explanations of behavior, desires, and experiences of satisfaction and dissatisfaction can all be rejected as question-begging redescriptions of the phenomena they are supposed to explain.

A central enigma concerning the satisfactions derived from punishing and cruelly treating others depends once again upon the question of why my hedonic states or my state of general well-being should be linked to those of others. An acceptable account of these satisfactions will have to show how my states follow from those of others. On a hedonistic account, it seems more plausible to derive the satisfactions of cruelty not from the suffering of others per se, but from our beliefs that they are suffering. It is, after all, not plausible that the pleasures and pains experienced by others of whose existence and psychic vicissitudes I am unaware, regularly produce pleasures and pains in myself. By relocating the source of my cruel satisfaction in my own mental states (that is, in my beliefs about the suffering of others), the puzzle of how the mental states of others affect my own has been addressed—or more accurately, avoided. By representing the satisfactions of cruelty as arising from certain beliefs of the same person who enjoys these satisfactions, the problem of the mysterious linkage among the hedonic states of different people is obviated. It still remains a puzzle, however, why my beliefs about another's pleasures and pains give rise to pleasures and pains in me.

An analysis in terms of power better accounts for the connection between the suffering of others and my own cruel satisfaction by presenting their suffering—or actually my beliefs about it—as naturally producing in myself feelings of powerfulness, which *constitute* my satisfaction. While feelings of power can be plausibly presented as constituting a satisfaction, beliefs can at best be viewed as causing or giving rise to states that are themselves satisfactions. To ground the satisfactions of cruelty (or anything else) in beliefs, one must show how the beliefs—which are not themselves mental states of a sort that are intrinsically satisfactions or dissatisfactions—result in mental states that are. On the other hand, to the extent that we can show that cruelty involves feelings of power, we have thereby already accounted for its satisfactions.

AN INVITATION TO A BEHEADING: SPECTACULAR MALICE; OR, WHAT FANS THE CRUELTY OF FANS

Nietzsche's account faces a major difficulty, however. It is offered as a general theory of all cruelty, but it seems to be supported by a consideration of only one particular type of cruel enjoyment, that in which the one who enjoys the suffering of others is also the one who imposes this suffering upon them. What does or can Nietzsche say about the myriad cases in which one person cruelly enjoys the suffering of others that he himself does not—either directly or indirectly—bring about?[13] The satisfaction derived from those cases in which I punish or make someone suffer may be accounted for by my feeling of power at *making them* suffer, but what about those cases in which I enjoy their suffering although I am not the agent of their suffering?

Nietzsche clearly wants to include such cases in his account. With allusions to the cruel entertainments prevalent in human history, he asserts: "To see others suffer does one good, to make others suffer even more: this is a hard saying but an ancient, mighty, human, all-too-human principle. . . . Without cruelty there is no festival" (GM II:6). Nietzsche is obviously aware that there was cruel enjoyment for the spectators at gladiatorial contests as well as for those who triumphed and meted out pain to others in doing so. While he can locate the enjoyment of the gladiator who "makes others suffer" in a feeling of power, how can his psychology of power account for the indisputable fact that it also "does one good," that is, sometimes provides a less than admirable but nevertheless real satisfaction simply "to *see* others suffer?"[14]

While acknowledging and even insisting upon the prevalence and naturalness of cruel spectacles, Nietzsche shows no awareness that his analysis apparently fails to account for the satisfactions of the spectator at such spectacles. He admits only that witnessing the suffering of others is not as satisfying as bringing it about. It remains puzzling, however, how on his account the cruel spectacle would afford any satisfaction at all.

Although Nietzsche does not specifically address this problem in the *Genealogy*, it is not difficult to see how someone with his theoretical commitments might argue the case if he were to deal with the issue. Anyone committed to a general psychology based upon a will to power will have to construe the satisfaction provided by cruel spectacles—by the mere witnessing of the suffering of others—as constituted by a feeling of power deriving from that experience. Where the one who enjoys another's suffering is also the cause or agent of that suffering, his enjoyment can easily be located in a sense of power over the other. Where the person who enjoys the suffering of another is not also the agent of that suffering, the satisfaction can be located in a sense of power only to the extent that the spectator can *identify with* the perpetrators of the suffering.

Even when the cruel pleasure is experienced by the agent of the suffering, it depends upon the agent's consciousness or identification of himself as such, not merely upon the fact of the matter. If I am the agent as well as the spectator of your suffering but am unaware of my agency, how I derive a feeling of power from the situation is as opaque as it would be if I were not the agent. Clearly one can be the agent of another's suffering and not be aware of it, but how can one who is not the agent of another's suffering identify himself with this agent? One possibility is that the person mistakes himself for what he is not. If this were the only possibility, the satisfactions of the cruel spectacle would appear to rely upon the implausible commission of a rather gross error by multitudes of otherwise reasonably clearheaded people. While it might be morally comforting to think that the enjoyment of cruelty depends on a serious lack of cogency, this seems not to be true.[15]

More promising is the notion that the person who cruelly enjoys the suffering of others can identify with the actual agent of this suffering in a way that does not entail a false belief that he in fact is that agent. The mechanisms by which an individual identifies with other individuals, groups of individuals, and even with nonhuman entities is complex and difficult to analyze. But it seems almost beyond dispute that such identification is extremely common and does not necessarily involve the mistaken belief that one literally is the person (or thing) with whom one identifies. We regularly identify with people who share some common traits and experiences with us (nationality, gender, sexual orientation, age, schooling, occupation, ethnic background, and so on) without ever forgetting that we do not share all our traits with them. We identify with others as extensions of ourselves or as co-members of a variety of cohorts without obliterating the distinction between us and them.

It is arguable that a great part, if not all, of our enjoyment of the suffering of others that we do not bring about relies upon some sort of identification with the people (and perhaps even with nonhuman and nonsentient forces) who actually bring—or at least appear to bring—that suffering about. Consider a spectator at a boxing match who wants to see the "other guy" beaten to a pulp and enjoys his pain and humiliation: Does he not identify with the boxer who metes out the punishment? In situations in which suffering is likely—in contests and conflicts of various sorts, whether in war or in sport—do we not tend to identify with individuals or groups with whom we have something in common, encouraging them to inflict humiliation, pain, and defeat upon their opponents? Is it not possible that our interest and enthusiasm from the sidelines for the defeat of the "others" stems from our experiencing a sense of power though identification with the apparent agents of the suffering?

It remains open how far this kind of analysis can be extended from the cases in which the satisfactions of cruelty can plausibly be understood as the agent's enjoyment of his own power to effect suffering in others to those cases in which a spectator's enjoyment is seen as arising from a process of identification with the agent. This seems, however, the most obvious and promising way to extend the scope of an analysis of cruelty using a psychology of power.

CRUELTY'S SPECIAL SATISFACTIONS

The prevalence of cruelty and, more specifically, of the predilection of many for the satisfactions of cruel behavior suggests not only that cruelty provides some sort of satisfaction but also that it might supply a satisfaction of a particularly intense sort, or of an irreducibly distinct kind. In connection with such considerations, Nietzsche's account of cruelty appears to be potentially problematic. By identifying the satisfactions of cruelty with the feeling of power derived from being able to make someone suffer, does he not simply reduce the satisfaction of cruelty to the feeling of power involved in making anything happen to someone else? And is this feeling of power anything other than an instance of the still more general phenomenon of the experience of power associated with making anything at all happen? Can a power analysis account for the particular satisfactions to be found in cruelty? Or does it simply show cruelty to be a species of behavior, like many others, which allows us to experience our efficacy in the world and hence our power? In showing that the satisfaction of making someone suffer lies primarily in *making* something happen to another, does it become a matter of complete indifference that what we bring about is *suffering*?

I think not. An analysis of the satisfactions of cruelty in terms of the feelings of power that come from treating others cruelly allows, and even suggests, that there is a special enjoyment to be experienced in causing others to suffer. Although the experience of effecting anything in particular is at the same time an experience of our general efficacy, and the experience of making others do or undergo anything is an experience of our power to affect them in general, it can be argued that the experience of making them suffer supplies a particularly intense awareness of our power. For in making them suffer we are making them undergo something that they normally do not want—or at least something that we believe they do not want—to undergo.[16]

Being able to manipulate the events, beliefs, or emotions of others so that they have experiences that are welcome to them also allows us to experience our power. That part of our sexual satisfaction that flows from our being adequate—or more than adequate—lovers derives no doubt at least in great part from the experience of our power to satisfy our partners. In general the satisfaction furnished by the performing of "altruistic" actions can, at least to some extent, be attributed to the feelings of power engendered by our ability to make others happy. But in making others suffer we are made aware that we are making them experience things *against their will*—that we have *power over them* in the special sense that our wills have triumphed over their wills.

This aspect of making others suffer, this overcoming of their resistance, which is not present in all the ways we affect their lives, could be used by a proponent of a psychology of power (like Nietzsche) to explain the special attraction of cruel behavior, and the unusual intensity of its pleasures. The special attractions of human cruelty lie in that particular kind of power one feels in making others do or experience what they do not want. Indeed, suffering, analyzed in terms of a will to power, is tantamount to having to do or experience something you do not want. Making people suffer entails overcoming their resistance, and, as Nietzsche often argues, one's own power is typically (if not always) experienced in overcoming some sort of resistance. It is only to the extent that resistance is overcome that an action can provide us with the proof and experience of our power. Inasmuch as the satisfactions of cruelty involve overcoming resistance, they are similar to the satisfactions derived from the successful completion of any difficult task.

Explaining the satisfactions of cruelty as an instance of the satisfaction of overcoming resistance, and so of accomplishing what is difficult, raises the question of whether a psychology of power can account for the special quality of cruel satisfactions. Can a psychology of power explain the particular attraction of hurting others that is arguably different from that of performing other prodigious and rigorous feats of mind and body not involving cruelty? What differentiates cruelty from other behavior that involves overcoming difficulties is that cruelty involves overcoming the opposed and resisting will of another person. If the advocate of a psychology of power feels the need to define the attraction and satisfaction of cruelty more specifically, he can emphasize the special feeling of power and thus delight in overcoming an obstacle that is itself a will in opposition to one's own. The joys of cruelty become the joys of the triumph of the will over other wills, of interpersonal domination.

SUBLIMATION AND THE TRANSCENDENCE OF CRUELTY

A psychological account of cruelty is in itself not a justification of cruel behavior, but rather an explanation of the attractions of cruelty, and consequently of its prevalence in human life. But Nietzsche argues further that our tendency to be cruel and to dominate is universal and ineluctable, and therefore should not simply be dismissed as an immoral and avoidable aberration. To show a tendency to be natural and necessary seems tantamount to justifying it, and Nietzsche has been understood as both excusing and recommending cruelty. His analysis of cruelty is not, however, tantamount to a simple acceptance and approval of cruelty.

Nietzsche's emphasis on "sublimation," the process through which fundamental and unavoidable drives and desires are able to find less objectionable and more powerful forms of expression and satisfaction, points the way to an ideal resolution of the problem of cruelty. It opens the possibility of removing the more objectionable aspects and forms of cruelty without unrealistically denying cruelty's essential place in the inventory of human traits and desires. In locating the impetus of cruelty in a drive toward the sense of power achieved in overcoming the will of others, it allows for the satisfaction of the drive in types of behavior that are less repugnant than some of its cruder and more abhorrent expressions.[17]

To the extent that any human need or drive is construed as an instance of a broader one, it is conceived as admitting the possibility of alternative expression or gratification and thus of sublimation. Inasmuch as Nietzsche presents cruelty as an instance of the will to power, cruelty is presented as amenable to sublimation into other expressions of the will to power—some of which do not entail making others suffer. Correspondingly, to the extent that cruelty is a *uniquely gratifying* form of the will to power that involves dominating the wills of others, it cannot be replaced by just any experience of power. Yet substitute gratifications are possible in which others are dominated but not humiliated, and in which the opponent is made to suffer some sort of defeat but not any further physical or psychological pain.

Nietzsche had long emphasized and approved of the importance to the ancient Greeks of the *agon*, the contest, as an essential mechanism for furthering human development and happiness. Victories of the will over other wills occurred in the athletic games and artistic competitions of ancient

Greece as well as on its bloody battle fields. He makes much of the concept of the *agon,* and the related distinction between the good and bad *Eris* (strife). Nietzsche finds them to have been salient in classical culture, but unfortunately obliterated since then. They are the key to his often overlooked construction of a theoretical framework that allows for and even encourages the transcendence of cruelty—at least in its more objectionable forms.[18]

THE PARADOX OF ASCETICISM: PAIN THAT IS PLEASURE

Asceticism presents an even more acute problem for psychological hedonism than does cruelty. Whereas cruelty raises the question of why the pleasures or pains of others should be pleasurable or painful to me, asceticism, hedonistically characterized, seems simply *self-contradictory.* Both cruelty and asceticism are presented as finding satisfaction in the creation of pain. The satisfactions of cruelty conceived in this way raise the issue of why another's pain should be pleasurable to me, while those of asceticism pose the far greater enigma of how my own pain can be pleasurable to me. In moving from the problem of cruelty, which is a central theme of the second part of the *Genealogy,* to that of asceticism, which is the main topic of the third, Nietzsche is moving from a phenomenon that, hedonistically conceived, is a *surd* to one that is simply *absurd,* from mystery to paradox.[19]

Hedonistically described, asceticism is characterized by behavior that finds its satisfaction in its own suffering, by desire that finds its pleasure in its own pain. Yet in psychological hedonism pleasure is normally conceived of as the opposite of pain, and the avoidance of pain is taken to be a fundamental aspect (sometimes the fundamental aspect) of the pleasure principle.[20] If the avoidance of pain is a basic part or aspect of what we really, most profoundly, and ultimately want, how can there ever exist behavior that has as its goal the suffering of pain? Since ascetic (and masochistic) behavior seems to demand oxymoronic description when described in hedonistic terms, a nonhedonistic reconceptualization of asceticism seems called for, and the adequacy of psychological hedonism as a general theory is thereby seriously called into question.

Nietzsche finds both the prevalence and paradox of ascetic behavior remarkable and requiring explanation. Speaking of the ascetic who "treats life as a wrong road . . . as a mistake that is put right by deeds—that we ought to put right," Nietzsche wonders at the ubiquitousness of asceticism:

> What does this mean? So monstrous a mode of valuation stands inscribed in the history of mankind not as an exception and curiosity, but as one of the most widespread and enduring of all phenomena. Read from a distant star, the majuscule script of our earthly existence would perhaps lead to the con-

clusion that the earth was the distinctively ascetic planet, a nook of disgruntled, arrogant creatures filled with a profound disgust with themselves, at the earth, at all life, who inflict as much pain on themselves as they possibly can out of pleasure in inflicting pain which is probably their only pleasure. For consider how the ascetic priest appears in almost every age; he belongs to no one race; he prospers everywhere; he emerges from every class of society. (GM III:11)

The ubiquitousness of asceticism is particularly puzzling in light of what Nietzsche recognizes as its highly paradoxical nature:

> Here an attempt is made to employ force to block up the wells of force; here physiological well-being itself is viewed askance, and especially the outward expression of this well-being, beauty and joy; while pleasure is felt and sought in ill-constitutedness, decay, pain, mischance, ugliness, voluntary deprivation, self-mortification, self-flagellation, self-sacrifice. All this is in the highest degree paradoxical: we stand before a discord that *wants* to be discord, that *enjoys* itself in suffering. (GM III:11)

For Nietzsche there are actually two sorts of paradoxes involved in the phenomenon of asceticism to which he alludes without separating them sharply. First, there is the *hedonistic paradox* of pleasurable pain as the goal of ascetic behavior. Second, there is the *vital paradox* of a form of life that strives against (the natural aims of) life—and moreover survives, prospers, and prevails. Inasmuch as asceticism is directed against the natural aims of life, "ascetic life is a contradiction" (GM III:11).

The vital paradox of "life *against* life" is for Nietzsche "a simple absurdity" (GM III:13). Without further examination of related doctrines in his philosophy, this denial of the possibility of drives and desires inimical to the preservation and enhancement of life seems shallow and dismissive—based on a description of ascetic ideals and practices that is gratuitously oxymoronic. After all, Freud later considered the possibility of a basic drive toward death—a "death instinct"—in his *Beyond the Pleasure Principle.* Can one simply reject Freud's hypothesis as being incoherent?

Nietzsche's rejection of the notion of basic drives inimical to life, however, is not based solely on the formulation of them as "life *against* life." His reasons are rather systemic, being rooted in some of his other philosophical positions. Nietzsche could not admit to the possibility of any human drive that aimed at diminishing life, because he tended to equate the will to life with the will to power, and to use these as alternative expressions of the one basic human drive.[21] Inasmuch as the will to life is the will to power, the basic motivation of *all* human action, no action can have goals contrary to it.[22]

Whatever his reasons for taking asceticism conceived as "life *against* life" to be a "simple absurdity," Nietzsche clearly finds the self-contradictory nature of the phenomenon understood this way to be ample reason to reject this way of conceiving it:

> It [asceticism understood as life against life] can only be *apparent*, it must be a kind of provisional formulation, an interpretation and psychological mis-understanding of something whose real nature could not for a long time be understood or described *as it really was*—a mere word inserted into an old *gap* in human knowledge. (GM III:13)

Contrary to a long entrenched tradition of reading Nietzsche as some-one who is not at all concerned about making his own ideas consistent and who does not consider consistency a necessary requirement for philosophy or even one to which we should aspire, his approach to this apparent self-contradiction shows that consistency was indeed one of his concerns. His resolution of the vital paradox of asceticism consists in viewing it as a con-voluted strategy of an instinct for the preservation and enhancement of life that, because of internal debility or external obstacles, cannot pursue its natural goals directly:

> Let us replace it [the paradoxical conception] with a brief formulation of the facts of the matter: *the ascetic ideal springs from the protective instinct of a degen-erating life* which tries by all means to sustain itself and to fight for its existence; it indicates a partial physiological obstruction and exhaustion against which the deepest instincts of life, which have remained intact, continually struggle with new expedients and devices. (GM III:13)

The working out of this hypothesis—that asceticism, despite appear-ances and interpretations to the contrary, actually serves the will to life—depends upon identifying the will to life with the will to power. What Nietz-sche intends to show is that asceticism is ultimately a strategy for the pres-ervation and enhancement of power.

Approaching asceticism as a strategy of a fundamental drive for power also supplies a solution to the hedonistic paradox presented by asceticism. Nietzsche finds that in asceticism understood hedonistically, "pleasure is felt and *sought* . . . pain . . . voluntary deprivation, self-mortification, self-flagellation, self-sacrifice." And he concludes that "all this is in the highest degree paradoxical." His solution to these hedonistic paradoxes of asceti-cism consists of two related steps: first, he reinterprets and reconceives the relevant behavior in terms of power instead of pleasure; and second, he complements this shift of perspective with the complete rejection of the major principle of psychological hedonism, the pleasure principle, denying any ultimate importance to pleasure and the avoidance of pain as ultimate motives of human action.

This reinterpretation of ascetic behavior is a reprise of the way in which he handled the phenomenon of cruelty: asceticism is construed as a case of being cruel to oneself. The satisfaction of hurting oneself is located, as it was in the case of hurting others, in *the sense of power entailed by being able to make someone suffer.* It is just that in ascetic behavior this someone turns out to be oneself. Nietzsche characterizes ascetics as creatures who "inflict as much pain on themselves as they possibly can out of the pleasure of inflicting pain—which is probably their only pleasure" (GM III:11). The satisfaction of asceticism is located in *the inflicting* of pain upon oneself, not simply in the experience of pain that is thereby inflicted.

Even if we allow that there is satisfaction in being able to make someone suffer (even when it is oneself who is made to suffer), a bundle of related problems remains to be addressed: Would the appeal of being able to make someone suffer not be to some degree negated or neutralized, in the special case of asceticism, by the expectation of *having to suffer?* Is not the attraction of the prospect of the experience of power to be attained in ascetic practices diminished by the prospect of pain? Should we not expect that the pull of asceticism would generally be weak, the feeble result of opposed forces that to a large extent cancel each other out? If so, how can we then account for ascetic tendencies that are overwhelmingly strong? Should we not expect ascetic tendencies to become weaker as the prospect of our own pain becomes greater? How could we then account for those cases in which the attraction of ascetic actions increases with the intensity of the prospective pain?

Nietzsche has implicitly addressed and dissolved this set of problems by totally rejecting the efficacy of the avoidance of pain as an ultimate motive of human behavior. Since pleasure and the avoidance of pain are "epiphenomenal" and not the real motives of human behavior, they do not have any real weight in our strategies of pursuing power. We are, in Nietzsche's view, ready to accept any amount of pain for an increase in power. The attractions of the power to be experienced by making someone suffer are not *at all* reduced in the case of asceticism by the fact that we ourselves shall have to suffer to experience this power. To handle issues raised by the phenomenon of asceticism, Nietzsche not only has to reconceptualize its satisfactions in terms of power but also must reject psychological hedonism flatly and deny any ultimate efficacy for the pleasure principle. To account adequately for aceticism Nietzsche must not only analyze it as a manifestation of a will to power but also view the will to power as replacing, and not just supplementing, the pleasure principle. And this is exactly what he does.[23]

Nietzsche's remark that the ascetic's inflicting of pain upon himself is probably his only pleasure suggests that he viewed the ascetic as one who introjects a cruelty whose primary object is making others suffer. He is willing to hurt himself when he cannot hurt others. Following this suggestion, asceticism is presented as a mode of behavior resorted to only when external avenues of cruelty that supply feelings of power are blocked, as what Freud later called a "substitute gratification."[24] Nietzsche takes the natural, initial object of cruelty to be the other rather than oneself. He does not say why he believes this to be so; but it is perhaps because cruelty to others does not involve ones own suffering. But even if Nietzsche is here allowing the prospect of pain to provide some reason for initially preferring cruelty to others over cruelty to oneself (and this is far from clear), he continues to present it as a superficial concern clearly superseded by considerations of power.

So far we have seen how Nietzsche accounts for the attractions of ascetic behavior despite the suffering it entails. He also explains how asceticism is particularly satisfying precisely because it involves hurting oneself. Just as cruelty to others is seen to be particularly satisfying because it provides a special sense of power in making others suffer (i.e., in making others experience what they do not want to experience), cruelty to oneself provides a special sense of power in being able to make oneself suffer what one normally wants to avoid.

Again the case of asceticism presents special problems. In making myself suffer, I feel powerful as the one who is able to overcome an opposing will—in this case my own. On the other hand, it is my will that is overcome, and this defeat should produce a sense of powerlessness. Issues arise with respect to this case that are analogous to the ones just considered with respect to power and pain. How do these opposing senses of power and powerlessness interact? Would we not expect them to neutralize each other, producing attitudes of indifference or weak preference toward asceticism? And given this expectation, how can we account for the strong attraction that ascetic practices often exert upon us?

Nietzsche's answer to all these questions is that we simply identify with that part or aspect of the self that makes the suffering occur, disassociating ourselves from the part that is forced to suffer. We identify with the aggressor and not with the victim in ourselves, with the agent of the suffering and not with that which suffers. Assuming the possibility of such a division of the self to explain how we can revel in the power of subjugating ourselves without suffering the impotence of the subjugated seems unproblematic to a theorist (like Nietzsche) who generally holds that the purported unity of the self is, in any case, only a frail illusion.[25] Because Nietzsche holds the self to be more like a society of many selves than a unity, he naturally analyzes the reflexive acts that constitute asceticism—acts such as self-discipline, cruelty to one's self, and self-denial—on the model of interpersonal discipline, cruelty, and denial. He takes the cruelty involved in ascetic practices to be imposed by some members of the intrapsychic "society" of sub-selves constituting the self upon other members of that same "society."[26] This sort of analysis resolves the philosophic problems attending the notion of reflexive acts of cruelty by ultimately removing their reflexivity.[27]

BEYOND PLEASURE AND POWER

Through this analysis of asceticism in terms of power, Nietzsche attempts to remove the paradoxes that arise from the standard hedonistic accounts of this phenomenon. To the extent that his accounts of both cruelty and asceticism as motivated by a will to power are more satisfying than those that try to account for them as motivated by a drive to maximize pleasure and minimize pain, he supports his case for a psychology of power against the prevalent view of psychological hedonism. Since his *On the Genealogy of Morals* presents the fullest discussion of these two pivotal topics, it must be viewed as an essential part not only of Nietzsche's theory of value but also of his psychology, which, as I have argued, constitutes the basis for his "revaluation of all values." Nietzsche's psychology of power is arguably the richest and most profound expression ever produced of one of the most fruitful hypotheses concerning the ultimate motivations of human behavior.

Nietzsche's argument that a better account of cruelty and asceticism can be given in terms of power than in terms of pleasure, if sound, would remain of interest and value even if his general hypothesis, that all behavior is motivated by a will to power, finally proves to be unacceptable. His argument would still reveal notable deficiencies of the competing and prevailing hypothesis of psychological hedonism. Even if it does not convince us to follow Nietsche's in denying all motivational efficacy to the seeking of pleasure and the avoidance of pain, his argument might still point the way to the abandonment of both psychological hedonism and the will to power as monistic theories of motivation. It might incline us to favor pluralistic theories that allow for more than one irreducible motivation, and that go beyond both pleasure and power considered as singly sufficient and exclusive alternatives.

NOTES

1. The other being *"die ewige Widerkehr des Gleichen,"* the eternal return or recurrence of one's life and the history of the world.

2. Friedrich Nietzsche, *On the Genealogy of Morals*, in *The Basic Writings of Nietzsche*, trans. Walter Kaufmann (New York: Modern Library, 1968) First Essay, sections 1–3. Henceforth indicated by the abbreviation "GM."

3. John Stuart Mill's classic statement of utilitarianism clearly exemplifies this linkage: "The creed which accepts as the foundation of morals 'utility' or 'the greatest happiness principle' holds that actions are right in proportion as they tend to promote happiness; wrong as they tend to promote the reverse of happiness. By happiness is intended pleasure and the absence of pain; by unhappiness pain and the absence of pleasure. . . . Pleasure and freedom from pain are the only things desirable as ends; and that all desirable things . . . are desirable either for pleasure

inherent in themselves or as means to the promotion of pleasure and the prevention of pain" (*Utilitarianism* [1861; Library of Liberal Arts Press: Indianapolis and New York, 1957], chap. 2, p. 10).

4. An example of an attempt to base what is desirable—that is, worthy of desire— in what is in fact desired can be found in Mill's dictum that "the sole evidence it is possible to produce that anything is desirable is that people actually do desire it" (*Utilitarianism*, chap. 4, p. 44). This has seemed to some a confusion of what is worthy of desire (desirable) with what is in fact desired. What one in fact desires (it is argued) may not be worthy of being desired, and so may not be desirable.

5. There are not many things that present themselves with any plausibility as the possible ultimate motives of all human behavior. In addition to pleasure and power, which are the most prominent alternatives, some theorists seem to have proposed autonomy. Hegel's *Phenomenology of Spirit* seems to argue for such a theory. (See my *An Introduction to Hegel's Metaphysics* [Chicago and London: University of Chicago Press, 1969], especially chap. 1.) Hegel's theory is echoed in Sartre's *Being and Nothingness*, especially in Sartre's notion that the "project" of all human action is to become an *"en-soi-pour-soi"* (in-itself-for-itself), "the ground of its own being." Carl Jung posits a drive to perfection as the ultimate motivation of behavior.

6. Mill, for example, explicitly extends the object of relevant ethical considera- tion to the happiness of all human beings (*Utilitarianism*, especially chap. 5). This extension has a certain appeal; but Mill's argument that such an extension is implicit in the principle of utility itself is unconvincing.

7. This is not the traditional Cartesian "problem of other minds" concerning the possibility of having knowledge of the minds of others. It is instead a problem about the somewhat mysterious way in which the happiness or unhappiness of others affects our own.

8. The hypothesis of emphatic tendencies in human beings similarly lends added mystery to those phenomena that, hedonistically described, represent the converse of cruelty: suffering because of the happiness of others. These include jealousy, envy, *ressentiment*, and *Schadenfreude*, which, like cruelty, are topics much discussed by Nietzsche.

Whether appeal to an innate tendency toward empathy successfully accounts even for our empathetic reactions themselves is also doubtful. It no more explains our empathic reactions than does the infamously fatuous appeal to a dormitive virtue explain the soporific effects of a drug.

9. For an explanation of this and all other such references, see note 2 above.

10. Nietzsche soon after refers to the "attempts to discover equivalents" in the suffering of the malefactor for every possible malfeasance (GM II:10), not to the actual finding of them. He describes this process as that of "contriving equiva- lences" (*"Äquivalente ausdenken"*), suggesting that such equivalences do not really exist, waiting to be discovered (GM II:8). He also approves of the Roman view that it is a matter of indifference how much of the debtor's body was cut off in compen- sation for his debt. He takes it to be an "advance" over a prior system in which an appropriate bodily equivalent was sought, suggesting perhaps that the advance lay in part in overcoming the illusion that there can be any such equations (GM II:10).

11. Despite Nietzsche's use of the word "pleasure" in his analysis of cruelty, he

is actually offering an alternative account to the standard hedonistic one. He is using it here to designate whatever it is that satisfies or gratifies our drives and desires. In this use—as an "internal accusative" of the verb *to want*—pleasure is conceptually tied neither to any feeling of pleasure nor to the absence of suffering or pain, as it is in the standard theories of psychological hedonism. Used this way, to suggest that some "pleasure" is found in the experience of power is simply to say that what supplies the satisfaction is a feeling of power. When Nietzsche contrasts pleasure and power, however, he is employing a notion of "pleasure" conceived of in terms of a *sui generis* and further irreducible type of experience which entails the absence of pain. His point in doing so is usually to reject pleasure as the ultimate object of human behavior and true source of satisfaction. His inconsistent use of "pleasure" is potentially confusing; but his position with respect to these matters is generally consistent and comprehensible.

12. While there are significant differences among the concepts of revenge, cruelty, and *Schadenfreude* (malicious joy), they all share the same hedonistic description as psychological phenomena in which satisfaction is found in the suffering of others.

13. Whether the one who enjoys another's suffering is the immediate agent of this suffering or brings it about through the manipulation of intermediate agents is not a crucial issue. I can derive a sense of power from the proceedings whether I myself wield the whip or arrange for someone else to do so.

14. To the extent that the spectators at Roman gladiatorial contests had the power to determine the fate of the loser by voting with their thumbs for death or mercy, they became the (indirect) agents of the suffering, and not just spectators. But such power is not generally enjoyed by spectators who nevertheless enjoy other cruel spectacles, such as our boxing matches.

15. The satisfactions of cruelty viewed this way would seem to rest upon a prevalent fallacy of confusedly taking powers that reside in others as being our own. This fallacy would appear to be something like the obverse of the "pathetic fallacy" of projecting our own feelings onto sentient and nonsentient objects of our experience (for example, viewing landscapes as gay, sad, tormented, and so on). The purported fallacy here would involve not the projection of our own states onto objects in the outside world, but rather a false introjection—a misidentification of qualities belonging to other beings as our own.

16. There are, of course, cases that deviate from the norm. The recipient of the punishment may actually want to be punished. This state of affairs does not affect the cruel enjoyment of the punisher as long as he is unaware of it. Upon becoming aware that the punishment is desired, and hence in some sense not really a punishment, the one who seeks the satisfactions of cruelty should be expected to seek another punishment, one that runs counter to the desires of his victim. ("Beat me!" pleads the masochist. "No, I won't," replies the sadist with glee.) We would expect the seeker of the satisfactions of cruelty to inflict what he *believes* to be contrary to the will of his victim.

There are also cases in which someone may not want to experience a particular pleasure in a particular context. In these cases, bringing about the pleasure in the other, through force or manipulation, threat or seduction, against the will of the other, may be understood as a form of cruelty. If causing pleasure against the will of its recipient can plausibly be construed as cruelty, this possibility constitutes a further argument against a hedonistic construal of cruelty as the causing of pain in others. It constitutes another powerful argument in favor of a psychology of power.

17. While Nietzsche does not object to cruelty on utilitarian, hedonistic, or moral grounds, that is, because of the suffering it causes to others per se, he does object to it solely from the standpoint of power. In section 13 of *The Gay Science* ("On the Doctrine of the Feeling of Power"), he allows that "benefitting and hurting others are ways of exercising one's power upon others." He then argues that "pain is a much more efficient means to that end than pleasure; pain always raises the question about its origin while pleasure is inclined to stop with itself without looking back." Despite this superiority of exercising one's power over others by hurting them rather than by helping them, he still criticizes hurting others (that is, cruelty) as a sign of powerlessless: "Certainly the state in which we hurt others is rarely as agreeable, in an unadulterated way, as that in which we benefit others; it is a sign that we still lack power, or it shows a sense of frustration in the face of this poverty; it is accompanied by new dangers and uncertainties for what power we do possess, and clouds our horizon with prospects of revenge, scorn, punishment and failure."

18. Nietzsche's best discussion of the historical and philosophical importance of the *agon* and the distinction between good and bad strife is to be found in his early essay, *Homer's Contest*.

Whether one views such sublimations as cases of completely transcending cruelty or only of transcending its more obvious and cruder forms depends, of course, upon whether one categorizes the sublimated forms of the domination and defeat of others as being forms of cruelty at all. While noting their kinship through similarity of motivation, we could still choose to deny that defeating one's opponents in athletic, intellectual, or artistic competitions should be classified as cruelty. In this kind of case, one could claim that it is possible to transcend cruelty completely. If, on the contrary, such sublimated forms of domination were categorized as refined forms of cruelty—but nevertheless *as cruelty*—then only a transcendence of certain *forms* of cruelty would be possible, not of cruelty itself. On either construal, however, a way is allowed to avoid those types of cruelty that are most objectionable.

The notion of sublimation also supplies the key to the solution of another related problem posed by Nietzsche's position in the first essay of the *Genealogy*. There, the currently prevalent "slave morality" of the Judeo-Christian tradition is contrasted with a more ancient and noble "master morality," which, though presented as being much more attractive than slave morality, is nevertheless fraught with cruelty and domination. The notion of the sublimation of cruelty allows for the possible transcendence of this master morality—which, though arguably preferable to slave morality, still seems unacceptable—or at least for its transformation into a more attractive, less objectionable form.

19. Nietzsche's discussions of the difficulties of accounting for what he calls "cruelty" and "asceticism" prefigure Freud's belabored and inconclusive attempts to account for "sadism" and "masochism." Though there are differences of nuance and context of use between the Nietzschean and Freudian concepts, their hedonistic analyses coincide: both cruelty and sadism take pleasure in the pain of another, while both asceticism and masochism take pleasure in one's own pain. Freud's no-

torious troubles with these topics are largely attributable, I believe, to his general (though wavering) commitment to a hedonistic framework of explanation.

20. The notion that the avoidance of pain is the fundamental aspect of the pleasure principle finds expression in the classical recommendation to emphasize the avoidance of pain over the seeking of positive pleasure in order to achieve happiness, for example, in the Stoic strategy for living the good life. It is also contained in the idea that pleasure is nothing but the absence or reduction of pain— an idea to be found in Arthur Schopenhauer's *The World as Will and Representation* (New York: Dover, 1969), vol. 1, chap. 58. A similarly negative conception of pleasure is entailed by Freud's notion of pleasure as being nothing but a reduction of tension or pain (see his *Project for a Scientific Psychology*, Standard Edition, vol. 1, ed. and trans. J. Strachey [1895; London: Hogarth Press, 1966], pp. 281–397).

21. Nietzsche equates the will to life with the will to power in two steps. First, he distinguishes between the will to the preservation of life and the will to the enhancement of life. He argues that the latter is often to be gained only through the sacrifice of the former, and that a gain in the intensity of life sometimes entails a curtailment in its duration. Second, he identifies the will to the enhancement of life with the will to power. This equation is discussed and documented in my essay, "The Hopelessness of Hedonism and the Will to Power," *International Studies in Philosophy* 18 (1986): 103–106. See also BGE 259 and WP 692.

22. The emergence of this vital paradox with respect to the description of asceticism in terms of a will to life is probably one of the reasons why Nietzsche gradually shifted from the idiom of a "will to life" to one of a "will to power."

23. "Whether it is hedonism or pessimism, utilitarianism or eudaemonism—all these ways of thinking that measure the value of things in accordance with *pleasure* and *pain*, which are mere epiphenonomena and wholly secondary, are ways of thinking that stay in the foreground" (BGE 225). And from *Twilight of the Idols,* "Maxims and Arrows": "Man does *not* strive for pleasure; only the Englishman does" (TI I:12).

24. Compare GM II:16 on the "internalization" of "all instincts that do not discharge themselves outwardly," and Nietzsche's discussion of the *Genealogy* in *Ecce Homo,* in which he alludes to "the instinct of cruelty that turns back after it can no longer discharge itself externally" (EH IV:GM). This idea is often echoed by Freud, notably in *Civilization and its Discontents.* "Aggression is introjected, internalized, but really sent back to where it came from, which means it is turned against one's own ego" (section 7).

25. Compare BGE 12: "One must also, first of all, give the finishing stroke to that other and calamitous atomism which Christianity has taught best and longest, the *soul atomism.* . . ."

26. "There is a defiance of oneself among those to whose most sublimated expressions some forms of asceticism belong. For certain human beings have such a great need to exercise their force and lust to rule that, lacking other objects, or because they have always failed elsewhere, they finally have recourse to tyrannizing parts of their own nature, as it were sections or stages of themselves. . . . In every ascetic morality man adores part of himself as God and to that end needs to diabolize the rest" (HH 137).

27. Resolving the special problems presented by the reflexive cruelty of asceticism by removing its reflexivity allows us only to account for asceticism as well as we
can account for cruelty. It is, therefore, an interesting strategy for a power theorist,
like Nietzsche, only inasmuch as he seems to have provided a convincing explanation of cruelty. Insofar as hedonism, on the contrary, seems not to provide an adequate account of cruelty, the removal of the reflexivity of asceticism through a division of the self still would not enable hedonism to offer a satisfying analysis of
ascetic behavior.

ELEVEN

Wagner's Ascetic Ideal According to Nietzsche*

Sarah Kofman

NATURE DOES NOT ABHOR A VACUUM

This essay does not claim to examine the relations between Nietzsche and Wagner in all their complexity. It simply provides a reading of the first few paragraphs of the Third Essay of *On the Genealogy of Morals,* which Nietzsche dedicates to the ascetic ideal of the artist.

As *Ecce Homo* would have it, each of the three essays announces "truths" which, by their scandalous novelty, appear explosive, untimely, sharp as a flash of lightning.[1]

The "truth" of the First Essay concerns the psychology of Christianity. In this essay Nietzsche denounces the mystification inherent in morality and religion. The former presents itself as a collection of facts, although it is merely an interpretation of certain phenomena; while the latter promotes the view that Christianity is born of the holy "Spirit," although it is merely born of the spirit of *ressentiment*—a reactionary movement against the domination of aristocratic values.

The "truth" of the Second Essay pertains to the psychology of moral conscience. Beyond the mystification involved when moral conscience (and all phenomena resembling it) pretends to be the voice of God in man, the genealogical method sniffs out and revivifies the smell of blood that has been hidden: a cruelty that is intolerable to modern—feminine, all-too feminine, hysterical—sensibilities.

The "truth" of the Third Essay is a response to the following paradox: the ascetic ideal created by *ressentiment* and bad conscience is especially powerful, although especially noxious, since it is the very ideal of deca-

---

* Translation by David Blacker and Jessica George, revised by Alban Urbanas and by the editor and Judith Rowan.

dence and its will is a will to nothingness. The solution to the paradox consists in demystifying the popular belief that divine omnipotence is responsible for the power of the ascetic ideal—whereas its power actually merely derives from its not yet having been challenged by any other ideals. Such is the case even despite the ascetic ideal's negative goal; for it is better to will nothing than to fail to will for lack of a goal, making it impossible for the will to exercise its power. The will to nothingness is not a nihilation of will—quite the contrary—and it is therefore not the "nothing," the "vacuum" that nature abhors, but rather the inability to exercise its will for lack of a goal.

The three essays are comparable to prolegomena to a "psychology" of the sort needed for any future revaluation of values, whose precondition is the ability to oppose to the ascetic ideal a counter-ideal capable of displacing it through its own power.

It is the impious Zarathustra—to whom Nietzsche gives the last word in paragraph 25 of the Second Essay—who, because he is young enough, strong enough, and beautiful enough, can propose to overturn the reigning ideal: the ascetic ideal that wages war on all that is natural, the enemy of life and slanderer of the world—a perverse ideal in the worst taste. He puts forward a wholly different ideal: one that only true warriors can treasure—those who fear neither adventure, danger, nor pain; neither the mountain, nor the bracing air of peaks and glaciers—because they possess "great health," and the sublime mischievousness that is characteristic of it. Zarathustra is the veritable Messiah, the true Redeemer. He announces a great love for Man along with contempt for present-day man. He alone will be able to free mankind from the curse with which the prevailing ideal has burdened it: the great disgust and nihilism, both necessary consequences of the ascetic ideal. Nietzsche only heralds the coming of this antichrist and antinihilist, conqueror of God and/or nothingness, who will give men a goal and a hope. The three essays prepare the ground that will make possible the coming and reception of Zarathustra and his good news.

First condition: to show that the ascetic ideal (and this is one of its mystifications) is not limited in its impact to a single restricted domain—that of priests or saints. The ideal's power lies, *inter alia,* in its ability to spread itself everywhere. There is no single essence of the ascetic ideal, but a plurality of possible meanings. Artists, women, philosophers, scholars, invalids, priests, saints, and so on are just so many forces that can appropriate it. Nothing allows one to decide *a priori* upon an original meaning. Nevertheless, the plurality of meanings does not preclude a typological unity: every force that seizes upon this ideal wills nothingness, a will to nothingness that is always a mask—the necessary response of a distinctive kind of life to specific conditions of existence, a subtle and indirect manner that life still has of affirming itself. This is the paradox: the will to nothingness is a strategy of life to maintain itself as life. It is the still-alive part of a living being in the process of degenerating and dying, which remains able either to invent this ideal or to appropriate it for its own use in order to continue to exercise its will to power. Such is the case even when the ascetic, for example, claims to restore this will completely to God, and literally to will nothing more. The Nietzschean suspicion reveals that, far from exhibiting a nihilation of will, the ascetic is an extraordinary case of willing. One therefore must not confuse a nihilation of will and a will to nothingness.

Among the forces capable of using the ascetic ideal as a mask and a strategy for life, Nietzsche makes special mention of artists. That an artist should seize upon such an ideal, however, seems an extraordinary and relatively atypical phenomenon, since art and the ascetic ideal appear fundamentally incompatible. Art, through its will to mendacity, playfulness, and the unreal, its "good will to appearance,"[2] is opposed to the will to truth which animates the ascetic ideal. Through its will to illusion,[3] art "imitates" a life that lives in illusion, thereby reaffirming life and willing it once again. Art, as the cult of the untrue, alone makes bearable to our probity the ubiquity of the untrue, mendacity, frenzy, and error as the conditions of what adorns itself with the good name of science,[4] and which wrongly believes itself to be opposed to art in claiming "to see that which is"[5] and to be realistic.

In fact, far from being faithful to nature, "realism" is only the way an impoverished, anti-artistic instinct saps the strength of everything it grasps. In contrast, the artist's "idealism" consists in transforming things until they reflect his power, giving him a feeling of perfection and beauty. Thanks to his rejection of the will to see or hear everything, the artist eliminates certain details, adds others and masks certain parts, giving to everything a surface, a skin, which is not completely transparent. Art is a cult of surfaces, and it educates man to will playfulness[6] and illusion, not "reality" or truth.

From *Das Philosophenbuch* on, Nietzsche distinguishes two types of men: the *scholar*, in whom conceptual activity dominates and where the artistic instinct manifests itself only masked; and the *artist*, in whom this instinct, called "metaphoric," allows itself free rein in lies, dreams and myths—or, in a word, in art. Supposing this to be so, how can we understand an artist's seizing upon an ascetic ideal which, far from willing to repeat life, wills nothingness—an ideal which, far from willing appearance, illusion, and playfulness, wills truth and its weightiness, and is precisely responsible for the hierarchical opposition of real and apparent, "truth" and error, and all of the metaphysical oppositions which, together with them, constitute a system?

Nietzsche's answer is found in the physiology of art, as he practices it. It reveals that the artist is no more sheltered from pessimism and nihilism than anyone else, and that certain physiological premises may give birth to a decadent art—as others may to a flourishing one.[7] Aesthetics as "applied physiology" allows for the establishment of a typology that differentiates one artist from another, and an artist from himself over time, when his physiological constitution is transformed. Certain determinate conditions—those of a physiological decadence—allow us to understand that an artist needs to seize upon the ascetic ideal for his own use. This is why, to the question posed at the outset of the Third Essay (i.e., "What does the ascetic ideal mean for the artist?"), Nietzsche responds at once that it means either nothing or too many things for it to be taken seriously.

The single example chosen by Nietzsche is that of Wagner.

WHY DID THE MUSIC OF WAGNER BECOME GOOD FOR SWINE?

The example of Wagner is a "case" with which Nietzsche, doctor *par excellence* of famous diagnostic skills, has been very familiar for quite some time. He has often been consulted regarding this patient, who himself professes to be the right physician for cases of hysteria. Doctor Nietzsche, however, for his part, defends an opposing view: to wit, that this patient is a most nefarious danger to the health of women and young people. Has the doctor "been" consulted? Well, rather, he consulted himself; for behind the case of Wagner, and furthermore that of Socrates (between which cases multiple parallels could be drawn), lies the case of Nietzsche: of the mad admiration he first manifested for Wagner, whom, in the correspondence of his early period,[8] he calls his master and father, and to whom, in the manner of a dutiful son, he never failed to send birthday greetings; and then of the final rejection, marked in *The Case of Wagner* and *Nietzsche Contra Wagner* by Wagner's reduction to a typical artist of decadence—a veritable calamity for music, who sickens all that he touches.

Wagner thus becomes the "Cagliostro of modernity": actor, buffoon, neurotic, and hysteric, whose power of seduction reaches prodigious levels. This power alone explains how Wagner—like that other seducer of the grand style, Socrates[9]—was able to charm Nietzsche enough for him to be caught in his snares; for him to fail at first to see the actor in him (or pretend not to see it);[10] and for him to have taken seriously Wagner's panegyric to chastity—his ascetic ideal, of which chastity is one of the three cardinal virtues.[11] Thus subjugated, Nietzsche did not understand at first that, as in the case of every artist, nothing in Wagner was to be taken seriously.

Taken seriously, the panegyric Wagner makes to chastity in his old age is, for Nietzsche the doctor, a grave symptom of disease: seizing upon the ascetic ideal by these means, Wagner becomes, in effect, the very antithesis of the artist he had been up to this point. He becomes the opposite extreme of the artist—and, at the same time, the opposite extreme of Nietzsche (at least in one of his evaluative schemes).

Yet if Wagner offered such a panegyric only in his old age, nothing but a transformation in the organization of his drives can explain how a man could have become his own opposite, to the point of giving a radically different meaning to his life. The question Nietzsche asks himself about Wagner is the same one he posed in *Philosophy in the Tragic Age of the Greeks* concerning Parmenides. And in both cases the response is the same. How could Parmenides, a Greek living in the most flourishing age of Greek history, have abandoned his first philosophy in favor of the second, that of Being—a most abstract philosophy in which the perceptible is pure illusion? And how could Wagner, an artist, have come around to praising chastity? For in both, it was the moral imperative of their nature that required their transformation. This imperative demanded, when Parmenides became old, that he take refuge in a cob-webbed castle in order to weave a philosophy devoid of all sense and of all blood, as anemic as its author. It is this same imperative that demanded that Wagner, at the end of his life, address a panegyric to chastity to the avid throng of Bayreuth—to his essentially feminine public. Lying behind the imperative of chastity addressed to all is a moral imperative of nature (the nature of an old man) which found itself, *de facto*, turned into music.

Unless one thinks that Wagner should not be taken seriously, that he was not diseased himself, but only shrewd enough to exploit a public that needed a morality of chastity.

Whichever hypothesis one accepts, by espousing an ascetic point of view Wagner signed his own death warrant as an artist and musician; for he wanted music for something other than itself—that is, to bring chastity on stage for its praises to be sung.

To Nietzsche, this panegyric by an artist seems so alien that he incessantly asks: Why did this reversal occur in Wagner? And for whom did it occur? To whom is this music addressed? To what type of listeners? To the first question Nietzsche initially responds: Because he became old and betrayed himself—what he had been and might have been. But clearly this response is unsatisfactory: while old age may favor chastity, it does not necessitate a panegyric to it. Wagner might have written a completely different type of music—as he had done earlier, in the strongest, most joyous, and courageous period of his existence,[12] when he accepted life in all its forms, along with man's animality and sensuality. Then he had the courage to see that sensuality was not the opposite of chastity, and that it was possible to praise both. A panegyric to one or the other, where both are viewed as antinomic, is grounded in the ascetic ideal and its most basic opposite, sensualism, with which it forms a system: a philosophy worthy of swine that demands music worthy only of swine. Consequently, the question becomes: Why at the end of his life does Wagner show such an interest in swine?

There was indeed a time when Wagner was not absorbed in the asceticism/sensualism, chastity/sensuality opposition: namely, when he took interest in *The Wedding of Luther.* And while he never gave it the form of an opera, one finds an echo of what this nuptial music might have been later in *Die Meistersinger* (1867). What fascinated Wagner about Luther was precisely his courage to refuse the sensuality/chastity opposition: after having lived it as a monk, he recognized it as a hoax—and demonstrated this revelation by his marriage. *Peccas fortiter, ama fortiter.* The union of these two "opposites" marked his divorce from the ascetic ideal: salvation is not so much secured by deeds as by grace, which can come to even the greatest of sinners. Man is also an animal, and he had better know it, lest while making himself out to be an angel he find himself metamorphosed into a swine, more swinish than an actual one.

> They abstain, but the bitch, sensuality, leers enviously out of everything they do. Even to the heights of their virtue and to the cold regions of the spirit this beast follows them with her lack of peace. And how nicely the bitch, sensuality, knows how to beg for a piece of spirit when denied a piece of meat! And this parable too I offer you: not a few who wanted to drive out their devil have themselves entered into swine. Those for whom chastity is difficult should be counseled against it, lest it become their road to hell—the mud and heat of their souls.[13]

So writes Nietzsche, retaining the lesson of Luther: the lure of angelism and chastity (since the truly chaste also poke fun at chastity, knowing it to be mere vanity)[14] only results in a transformation into swinehood, leading the "ascetic" to roll in the filth. The tendencies to perdition and salvation are not opposed. If Luther was the first to denounce this false opposition, it is because he had the courage to affirm his sensuality, as did Wagner when he planned *The Wedding of Luther.*

According to Nietzsche, Wagner's "beautiful period" was from 1841 to 1868. In his works of this period he expresses a conception of the complete man, in which the natural side is not eliminated. The third act of *Die Meistersinger* is a hymn to Luther and to the Reformation. In *Tannhäuser,* the hero declares that love implies sensuality, and there is a satire on chaste love. The break from this perspective came in 1870; and in *Parsifal* (1882) the panegyric to chastity in opposition to sensuality is triumphant.

Nietzsche's own account again takes up and generalizes the consistent truth of the first Wagnerism: all good marriages, all passions of the heart are beyond the chastity/sensuality opposition. Already in *The Gay Science* (GS 71, "On Female Chastity"), he showed how pernicious it is for women to have an education which, imposing complete chastity upon them until marriage, drives them to hysteria upon the brutal discovery of sensuality at the moment of marriage—a contrast in which women's extreme philosophy and skepticism is anchored. Nietzsche is grateful to the young Wagner for having had Luther's courage; and he regrets that Wagner, when he later showed his gifts for theatre, did not bring the life of Luther to the stage to make sensuality pleasing in the eyes of the Germans—who, as Luther recognized, had so repressed their sensuality that they could not accept it save under the delicate, effeminate name of "evangelical liberty."[15]

Yes, Wagner would have done well to produce a comedy making fun of the serious German of the ascetic ideal who introduced the tragic opposition between chastity and sensuality. Against the German love for tragedy and all that breaks the heart,[16] Nietzsche wants above all to show that if there is opposition or rupture between chastity and sensuality, it must not be thought of as tragic. According to Hegel—for whom it is tragic for there to be an opposition between two equally legitimate principles—the opposition is reconciled in the *denouement*, the moment of *Aufhebung*, when it turns out to be dissolved and superseded in a third term. Still under the forceful influence of Hegel (as he avers in *Ecce Homo*), the Nietzsche of *The Birth of Tragedy* understands it thus: tragedy consists in the opposition between the two aesthetic principles (the Apollinian and the Dionysian) and their reconciliation. Later, Nietzsche erases the tragic opposition between these two principles, which he conceives as two different forms of will: one symptomatic of an impoverished life, the other of an overabundance of life. Between the two, no reconciliation or dialectical supersession is possible—only eternal conflict. Nietzsche distinguishes tragedy from drama—a typical example of the latter being Bizet's *Carmen*, a drama affirming life in all of its cruelty and sensuality, one that returns love to its rightful place in nature and in life.

Now life differs from tragedy in that it admits neither opposition nor dialectic, but only conflict among divergent forces. Life establishes a relation of supplementarity rather than of opposition between sensuality and chastity. Chastity is a "supplementary attraction" that life furnishes to sensuality. It is a stimulating ingredient in sexual life, giving it all of its salt and spice. When a woman, that fleshly animal, seizes upon the ascetic ideal, this "*morbidezza*" gives her a new charm. Such is the response invented by woman to the morbidity of man who, in a hypercivilized age, no longer tolerates the image of the fleshly woman—an image that hardly excites him any longer. As a sexual strategy and stimulant to modesty, feminine chastity is part of a certain vital balance between the angel and the animal in man. Goethe[17] and Hafiz[18] had already understood this.

The ascetic ideal's point of view, that of tragic opposition, is the point of view of the swine[19] which seeks only to satisfy its needs—completely ignorant of desire and its unlimited character, and so of the play and simulation that is necessary for this infinity of desire not to be suppressed. It thus ignores the necessary supplementarity between chastity and sensuality. This is why an unsatisfied swine turns toward the adoration of chastity construed as the strict opposite of sensuality. This is why "saints," after rolling around in the filth, turn the violence of their drives against themselves: the violence of opposition—tragic opposition—is but the symptom of the violence of the repression of sensuality.

Why then did Wagner, toward the end of his life, put chastity to music and stage this tragic opposition? Why did he henceforth produce a music agreeable only to "the pitiful animals of Circe,"[20] that witch who changed the companions of Ulysses into beasts (but not Ulysses himself, whose true love for Penelope protected him from seduction)? We know that elsewhere[21] Nietzsche calls morality "the great Circe of philosophers": she seduces and attracts them through her divine glitter; because she is a party to all the hierarchical oppositions, including that between chastity and sensuality, she transforms men into swine. Whether she represents sensuality or morality, Circe, with her magic wand, always effects the same metamorphosis.

Why, then, did Wagner, toward the end of his life, place his art in the service of swine? What could they have mattered to him?

THE CONVERSION OF WAGNER: *PARSIFAL*

In *Parsifal* Wagner's ascetic ideal triumphs; one hears its final hatred of life.[22] Parsifal is the innocent, the chaste. Kundry gives the following etymology of his name:

> Foolish and pure I will name you
> Foolish Parsi
> Pure and foolish "Parsifal"
> Parsifal: child of foolish purity.

Kundry, under the power of the sorcerer Klingsor, tries to bewitch and seduce Parsifal. She is sensual, yet nostalgic for salvation. In Parsifal, by contrast, love and desire are divorced: he can only save Kundry by remaining chaste. In short, Wagner transforms the child of nature into a Catholic: thus he renounces the "evangelical liberty" of Luther.

It appears incredible to Nietzsche that Wagner could have been interested in a character with so little virility. And in order to avoid reaching the hasty conclusion that the musician is inherently decadent, he offers the hypothesis that *Parsifal* is a parody, a purely satiric drama. Wagner's way of nobly leaving the stage would be through an excessive parody of tragedy— one involving his simultaneous departure from both tragedy and himself. In this way, Wagner would have overcome the grossest form of counter-nature preached by the ascetic ideal, since to urge chastity is a provocation against nature and a surreptitious assault on the first condition of life.[23]

If Wagner had indeed ended his life and work by taking this distance with regard to himself, he would have been a great and accomplished artist—true greatness and nobility implying this distancing and ability to laugh at oneself.[24] Once again, by this hypothesis Nietzsche makes the same gesture as in the case of Socrates. Before deciding upon the typical decadence of Socrates and Wagner, he suggests that perhaps the former's words and the latter's music should not be taken seriously. Socratic irony, by the distance it establishes concerning his belief in the omnipotence of reason, allows for the suspicion that Socrates knows very well the power of instinct, and that he is making fun of himself and others when he prescribes reason as a cure for the passions. The role of Socratic irony in Wagner would be performed by satyric parody. Nevertheless, Nietzsche will not retain this saving hypothesis for either of these identifying models; in the end, both Socrates and Wagner will be classified as decadent types.

But if *Parsifal* is not a parody and must be taken seriously, it is altogether a bad opera, symptomatic of a hatred for knowledge, spirit, and sensuality. It marks a return, or a conversion to obscurantist and morbid ideals—a conversion more Catholic than Protestant. It marks neither the apotheosis of the artistic life nor the summit of art, but rather an artist's renunciation of himself and his ideals, which had until then linked together the spirituality and sensuality in his art and his life.

This conversion, which is not to be explained by a special divine intervention, leads Wagner to return to Christianity, and to turn his back upon the philosophy of Feuerbach that he had followed in his youth. At that time, for Wagner, redemption was to be found neither in the word nor in the blood of Christ, but in Feuerbach's panegyric to sensuality. Feuerbach's panegyric shows, in effect, that there are only oppositions between alienated forces. By taking the point of view of nature, man can reconquer the forces alienated from his by his customs. The conflict between chastity and sensuality lies only within alienation. Wagner recalls these themes in his music. Opera is not yet for him, in 1848, an end in itself; and he does not yet consider himself a priest. In 1848 he is looking for a unity of dance, word, and music in relation to the eternally human, opposed to all convention. Thanks to Feuerbach, this Wagner has a conception of nature that permits him to denounce false oppositions.

Thus it appears that Wagner, in the end, was converted, and underwent a radical change of perspective: in his life, art, and teaching he became a Christian, a Catholic. He began to believe in oppositions and became a pessimist. This infused him with an agony he could not rid himself of save through a renunciation of will. He consequently became a follower of Schopenhauer, for whom appeasement lies in a negation of will.

The Wagnerian conversion is a complete phenomenon. Symptomatic of the perversion of his instincts, it marks a reversion to the Middle Ages, a return to a pre-Reformation age, a loss of self-confidence and, as a consequence, the distancing of disciples. Wagner sends them elsewhere, and backward, to look for salvation. He no longer offers them redemption in sensuality and life, but rather in the blood of Christ. All of his final texts—troubled, shrivelled, and bewildered—are signs of a loss of courage in the face of life, a loss of the virility of the instincts. Hatred of life triumphs in Wagner.

One can therefore understand Wagner's interest in such a weak creature as Parsifal, and his making a Catholic of him. But this interpretation no longer allows us (as it had previously with Gottfried Keller) to laugh at the spectacle of *Parsifal*. For this work is henceforth seen as a spiteful and vengeful attack against life. Goethe would have pronounced it dangerous, "suffocating of the rumination of moral and religious absurdities."[25] While Wagner only uses terms of loyalty, purity and chastity, and while he presents himself as a doctor and a savior (again in the manner of Socrates), he is really more of an invalid than a physician. His medicine, because it sends one back to Christ for redemption,[26] is more dangerous than redeeming.

The "final word" of Socrates[27] had allowed Nietzsche to understand that the one whom he had taken for a joyous and courageous soldier was only a pessimist, sick of life, and that he had always been so (even though this pessimism had been masked by the irony of his character). In the same manner *Parsifal* revealed to him that at bottom Wagner was always haunted by the theme of redemption—the veritable *leitmotif* of all his work. Wagner's work is pervaded by heroes and heroines who seek in one way or another to be saved:

> In *Tannhäuser*, innocence saves the sinner.
> In *The Flying Dutchman*, an errant Jew finds his salvation in becoming a stay-at-home through marriage.
> In *Parsifal*, Kundry, an old and corrupt woman, desires to be saved by chaste youths.
> In *Lohengrin*, hysterical youths are saved by their doctor.
> In *Die Meistersinger*, beautiful young girls are saved by a knight.
> In *Tristan and Isolde*, a wife is saved by a knight.
> In *The Ring*, an old god is saved by an immoralist.[28]

And in the epilogue to *The Case of Wagner,* Nietzsche declares that the need for redemption is the truest expression of decadence—its most sincere and grievous affirmation in sublime symbols and practices.

THE PERVERSION OF WAGNER

The Third Essay is less harsh in its criticism of Wagner than is *The Case of Wagner.* In it Nietzsche hesitates to label Wagner as a decadent type; decadence is diagnosed only beginning with *Parsifal,* and only supposing that the opera was indeed the product of a serious intention. This means, on the one hand, that Wagner did not intend to be parodic (a pleasant hypothesis, but one that Nietzsche does not retain) and, on the other hand, that Wagner might have identified with his character, taking himself seriously in taking himself for Parsifal.

Now the vague impulse to identify with a character is a typical symptom of the artist. It is an impulse corresponding to a weariness with one of the artist's most basic characteristics—his will to the unreal, to be removed from the world. Identifying with a character provides the artist a means every now and then of escaping "unreality" and the falseness of his life—a means of trying to be a real being, and so of willing that which is most prohibited to him. Such would be Wagner's last "will/impulse," as though in growing old he had lost the strength to hold fast to his characteristic will to appearance, illusion, and unreality.

On this hypothesis, Wagner's conversion to the ascetic ideal is caused by his impulse to identify with one of his characters. And according to Nietzsche, this is exactly what marks the artist's perversion. For the true artist, only his work matters: it alone is real and should be taken seriously—and it can be taken seriously only if the artist does not take *himself* seriously. Nietzsche uses two metaphors to describe the relationship between the artist and his work. First, "the soil": the work, like all plants,[29] depends upon its soil. But even so, this soil must not mistake itself for the tree for which it is but the condition of existence. The soil has both positive and negative connotations: it is the medium that allows the work to grow; yet sometimes it is manure—fertile, but nauseatingly smelly. In order to rejoice in the art work's beauty, it is best to forget its genesis—the disgusting and repugnant conditions of its existence. There is no art without the "Apollonian" veiling of the intolerable, of the "Dionysian" that renders it possible—which smells awful.

Nietzsche does not reproach artists for ignoring the constitutive genesis of art as such.[30] It is for the genealogist, the physiologist, to concern himself with the biological premises of works of art, conducting a vivisection that releases the fertilizing manure—and not needing to wash his hands after having touched it.[31] From the point of view of this "applied physiology"[32] Wagner, handed over to the vivisector, appears as the modern artist *par excellence,* who has locked within himself a balance of contradictory values: "He has within his body values, words, phrases and morals of contrasting origins." In physiological terms, he is false, "always sitting on the fence,

with one breath saying 'yes,' and with another 'no.' " He is, in total innocence, biologically duplicitous.

Nietzsche is grateful to Wagner for allowing him to see into himself so
clearly—but not for having so bewitched him that he did not at first understand how much of a seducer Wagner was, and see that his music was a
veritable Circe: *Parsifal* being precisely the height of Wagner's seductiveness—a "masterstroke of seduction"[33]—a work that Nietzsche admires
(and would have liked to have done himself), and that attains perfection
by refining the alloy of beauty and disease.

Considered in this light, Wagner was never more inspired than at the
end of his life. All that followed would be too luminous, too wholesome.
But the danger of this seduction is that it creates a reversal of values, leading
one to mistake light for shadow, and vice versa. It drives one mad, enervates
the spirit, makes one forgetful of "the virility under a rose bush." Wagner
works like a wizard—or rather, like a witch. This is why, despite all the
admiration that he professes for the work, the philosopher/physiologist
must extirpate the manure from it. He must display the biological conditions which, in this instance, are those of an invalid afflicted with a general
illness of the entire organism—an overexcitement of the whole nervous
system, a modern sickness *par excellence* of which third-rate theatrics is one
of the manifestations, the symptom of a physiological degeneration, a form
of hysteria.[34] But in order to love the work, the artist (like the public) must
on the contrary "forget" its genesis.[35]

The soil metaphor is complemented by a second: according to Nietzsche, the artist is the maternal breast of his work, and must be nothing
more. He procreates the work and nourishes it with his own blood; but he
is not the work, and he must exist for it alone, as a mother for her child.
Just as the mother who, in order to take joy in her child, must forget the
unpleasantness of the pregnancy (her distastes, her peculiarities, a sign of
her "hysterical" refusal to give life to a child, to be a simple condition of
its existence), so must the artist "forget" his work's genesis in order to be
able to regard it favorably, and to love it enough to refuse to identify with
it (thereby accepting its separate existence).

For an artist to identify with his character is sheer intellectual perversion,
since in doing so he distorts the natural goal of childbirth (for artists are
"male mothers").[36] This natural goal, in effect, implies a break between
mother and child. If the mother is made only for the child, the child is
more than those who created it.[37]

Corresponding to the perversion of the woman who cannot avoid showing her repulsion at bringing into the world a child who is detached from
her, is the spiritual perversion of the artist who, through a type of association by contiguity, takes himself to be what he was capable of representing,
imagining, and expressing: for if the artist were his character, he could not

and should not have invented him. Homer is not Achilles, and Goethe is not Faust.[38]

Thus Wagner was able to convert himself by virtue of having forgotten to forget that he was only the manure or the mother of his child. His conversion results from his perversion, from his being absorbed in a character who drove him to regress into medieval oppositions. Keeping his distance from all true elevation and discipline of the spirit equally drove him to an intellectual perversion and a general reversal of values. "Wagner perverted everything." In the matter of taste, he causes rhythmic feelings to degenerate; while where ideas are concerned, he becomes an idealist, considers himself above science, and poses as a philosopher. He perverted nerves.[39]

Nietzsche therefore laments the fact that at the end of his life Wagner, breaking with the will to unreality typical of the artist, wanted to take the place of his child, and with *Parsifal* abandoned his art and his public in this equivocal fashion, allowing nihilistic, ascetic (Schopenhauerian) values to triumph.

It remains to discover why, in this manner, the artist put himself in the service of a philosophy—and, more precisely, why he needed to become Schopenhauer's ventriloquist.

SCHOPENHAUER'S VENTRILOQUIST

If Wagner needed to become another's spokesman, it is because in the case of an artist the ascetic ideal means either nothing or so many different things that they convey no determinate meaning. The artist is not serious enough, or real enough, to have his valuations taken seriously. He can only express the valuations of another force which he seizes upon and serves. He is always a servant—whether of a morality, a philosophy, or a religion. Like a child, he cannot face the world alone. He always needs a bulwark, a buttress, an already established authority.

All the terms of the text underline the artist's dependent status: he is a servant, a courtesan, and an opportunistic flatterer of authority old or new.[40] He does not take a solitary path; if he takes his role seriously, he can only express himself by wearing the mask of other forces, which guarantee his own seriousness by virtue of their authority. Thus Wagner felt the need for the Schopenhauerian guarantee of seriousness, which commanded respect and held a dominant position in Europe in the 1870s.

One may wonder what the ascetic ideal means when it is seized upon and paid homage by a philosopher, described by Nietzsche as a man with a steely gaze, independent, virile, not feeling the need to see his valuations ratified by any authority, human or divine. If the philosopher has the courage to be himself, why does he need to don the mask of the ascetic ideal (a much more serious question for him than for the artist)? In subsequent paragraphs of the Third Essay, Nietzsche tries to respond to this question, in part by showing that this mask corresponds to the optimal conditions of existence for the philosophic animal at the beginning of his development. But this constitutes an altogether different problem. Let us limit ourselves to examining the oblique route that led Wagner to place himself under Schopenhauer's banner.

It was the poet Herwegh[41] who first converted Wagner to the philosopher's conception of art. From 1870 on, Wagner expresses a point of view apparently opposite to the one he expressed in *Opera and Drama* (1851), especially with regard to the hierarchical position he accorded to music. In his first conception—and this is a paradox for a musician—Wagner made of music a simple medium subordinated to drama: a simple woman who needed a man in order to blossom (at least if one accepts the Aristotelian conception of woman as passive matter, an indeterminate force of opposites necessitating the virile form in order to find meaning and determination).[42] He derived all of music's meaning from drama, to which music was entirely submissive, as drama itself was subordinated to the actor Wagner. As a man of the theater, Wagner was an actor *par excellence* as much as he was a musician. In *Nietzsche Contra Wagner,* Nietzsche—who believes that a true artist can have nothing but disdain for theater, the perfect art for the masses[43]— does not cease to denigrate the preeminence Wagner, manifesting his perverted taste, gives to it.[44] In fact, music for Wagner served only to accentuate, reinforce, and internalize the dramatic gesture and surface of the actor. In symptomatic fashion Wagner repeats again and again that his music signifies more than just music. For Wagner, as Hegel's heir, music is subordinated to drama, and so also to the "idea": "It was not with his music that Wagner conquered them [German youths], it was with the 'idea'—it is the enigmatic character of his art, his game of hide-and-seek with a hundred symbols, the polychromy of his ideal that draws these youths to Wagner."[45]

When Wagner submits himself to the authority of Schopenhauer, the hierarchical status given to music changes. The philosopher grants music its sovereignty.[46] It becomes an independent art which, unlike other arts, does not reflect phenomena, but is rather the language of will, the most spontaneous and original revelation of the abyss.[47] Actually, as a follower of Schopenhauer, Wagner continues to be a "woman," continues to be submissive to a theory, to a philosophy. Further: to elevate music to the highest rank is not to make it independent and wanted for itself, since it is thought of as the agent of the will. Thus it remains in the service of the Idea, even if the "idea" is no longer the same. What then does Wagner gain by his conversion to Schopenhauer?

The benefit is that he is able to take himself seriously, to feel "real" by becoming an oracle, a priest, a spokesman for the in-itself, a telephone line to the Beyond. He pours out not only music, but God. As Schopenhauer's Ventriloquist, he is God's ventriloquist, and the spokesman for ascetic ideals. It is at the very moment in which he espouses the most negative ideal that, paradoxically, he can best affirm his power and "reality"—even if this causes a break with his artistic nature which would constrain him to obliterate himself before the only reality willed for itself: the reality of music.

In the final analysis, Wagner's ascetic ideal is only a mask he dons in order to affirm at last the reality of his existence.

CONCLUSION

In conclusion I shall emphasize three points.

1. If one grants the Nietzschean position that a decadent artist is always the servant of a philosophy, a morality, or a religion, does this mean that such an art is always condemned to be subordinated to ends other than itself? Would "art for art's sake" in contrast be the distinctive feature of a flourishing art?

There is nothing to that. In an aphorism entitled "*L'art pour l'art*" in *Twilight* (TI IX:24), Nietzsche shows how the phrase "art for art's sake"— which fights against moralizing tendencies in art by declaring deep enmity to morality—is simply a reversal of the opposite phrase, and in fact signifies the power of moral judgment. Pure passion would remove all goals from art, rather than assign to it a moral goal. For even if the goal of moralizing and ameliorating men is excluded from art, it still does not follow that art should be absolutely without an end or goal, and so deprived of meaning. This would be tantamount to forgetting that art depends upon the artist, that it fortifies or weakens certain valuations, and that the faculty of *power* in the artist is art's first condition.

This is why the artist's most profound instincts lead not to art, but to the meaning of art—that is to say, to *life* and to the desire for life: "Art is the great stimulus to life: how could one understand it as purposeless, as aimless, as *l'art pour l'art*?" Against the pessimistic outlook of Schopenhauer and his evil eye, one must call upon artists themselves in order to understand that art's true meaning lies in the glorification and affirmation of life. This is why the ascetic ideal is so fundamentally antiartistic. When an art says "yes" to life, it is because it has nothing to do with such an ideal: "If Raphael said 'yes' to life, it is because he was not a Christian."

Also, when at the end of the Third Essay Nietzsche questions whether any ideal can counterbalance the dominant ideal's power, he shows that it is art, far more than science, that could play this role:

> Art, in which the *lie* is sanctified and the *will* to deception has a good conscience, is much more fundamentally opposed to the ascetic ideal than is

science: this was instinctively sensed by Plato, the greatest enemy of art Europe
has yet produced. Plato versus Homer: that is the complete, the genuine
antagonism—there the sincerest advocate of the "beyond," the great slanderer of life; here the instinctive deifier, the *golden* nature. To place himself
in the service of the ascetic ideal is therefore the most distinctive *corruption*
of an artist that is at all possible; unhappily, also one of the most common
forms of corruption, for nothing is more easily corrupted than an artist. (GM
III:25)

2. The Nietzschean position, which makes the artist above all a "creator
of affirmation of life" rather than just a creator, prevents the return of the
religious to art in the guise of a sacralization of the artist, rival of God—
nay, God himself—or in the guise of the sacralization of art, erected as a
new absolute (in the manner of Malraux, whose atheism in fact is only a
disguised and displaced theism).

On this point Nietzsche and Freud concur. Freud in his own way also
opposes a theological conception of art, by showing that what we call artistic
"creation," "gift," or "genius" ultimately derives from a play of forces and
a certain destiny of drives. Art's enigma is the same as that of life which,
from its beginning unto death, is abandoned to the random play of forces
and their encounter. Each individual's life is only one of the multiple ex-
periments that life—the only true artist—realizes in its game. In place of
the idolatry of the artist (his veneration as a great man), Freud substitutes
only respect for Nature, which eternally creates and destroys without reason. The Freudian conception allows for a break with the religious illusion
that through art as antidestiny, man can succeed in triumphing over death.
Nietzsche's view is similar, since to define the artist as a creator of affirmation of life is to say that he wills life, with its joys, but also with all that
is terrible and unbearable in it. None of this contradicts the cult of appearance and surface to which the artist is devoted and which alone allows
for *amor fati*. For it is only through the lens of the ascetic ideal that "appearance" and "surface" are opposed to "reality" and "depth."

3. A final question: Does not the vague impulse of the decadent artist to
identify with his characters, in order to feel "real," equally apply to Nietzsche? And in speaking of Wagner, was Nietzsche ever speaking of anyone
other than himself?[48] Did he not spend his life identifying with Wagner,
Schopenhauer, Socrates, Heraclitus, Empedocles, with all the historical figures who are all fictions,[49] characters of his own creation?

In the preface to *Human, All Too Human*, Nietzsche admits to having
wittingly closed his eyes to Schopenhauer, and to having deceived himself
over the incurable romanticism of Richard Wagner, feigning that it was a
beginning and not an end. Likewise over the Greeks; likewise over the
Germans and their future—one might continue with a long list of such
"likewises." It is a degree of superior vigilance (his instinct for preserva-

tion) which needed such falsity "in order to permit the luxury of his truth-fulness":

> Thus when I needed to I once also *invented* for myself the "free spirits" . . . : "free spirits" of this kind do not exist, did not exist—but, as I have said, I had need of them at that time if I was to keep in good spirits . . . : as brave phantom companions with whom one can laugh and chatter . . . , spectres and phan-tasms to a hermit's liking, who will perhaps exist one day. (HH I:P:2)[50]

Wouldn't the typical general impulse of Nietzsche—a decadent artist in this way—have been to be able to feel real, at last, by identifying with these multiple characters of his own creation? But didn't the multiplicity of iden-tifications lead rather to a radical dispossession—to what one calls Nietz-sche's madness?[51]

NOTES

1. From very early on, Nietzsche mentions "lightning" as a "nonethical liber-ating force." (For example, 7 April 1866 letter to Gersdorff.)

2. *The Gay Science,* trans. Walter Kaufmann (New York: Vintage, 1975), section 107 (henceforth, for example, GS 107). See, however, note 49 below.

3. "Art is entirely based upon humanized nature, a nature enveloped by and interwoven with errors and illusions, of which no art may be free." (*Nachgelassene Fragmente, Ende 1876—Sommer 1877*), in *Nietzsche Werke: Kritische Gesamtausgabe,* ed. Giorgio Colli and Mazzino Montinari (Berlin: Walter de Gruyter, 1967), 23 (150).

4. "At times we need a rest from ourselves by looking upon, by looking *down* upon, ourselves and, from an artistic distance, laughing *over* ourselves or weeping *over* ourselves. We must discover the *hero* no less than the *fool* in our passion for knowledge; we must occasionally find pleasure in our folly, or we cannot continue to find pleasure in our wisdom" (GS 107).

5. "To see *what is*—that is the mark of another kind of spirit, the antiartistic, the factual." *Twilight of the Idols,* trans. Walter Kaufmann, in *The Portable Nietzsche* (New York: Viking, 1982), ninth part ("Skirmishes of an Untimely Man"), section 7 (henceforth, for example, TI IX:7).

6. For the instinct of play proper to the artist, compare also the famous text on Heraclitus in *Philosophy in the Tragic Age of the Greeks.*

7. "Aesthetics is tied indissolubly to these biological presuppositions: there is an aesthetics of decadence, and there is a classical aesthetics—, 'the beautiful in itself' is a figment of the imagination, like all of idealism.—" *The Case of Wagner,* trans. Walter Kaufmann, with *The Birth of Tragedy* (New York: Vintage, 1967), "Epilogue" (henceforth CW).

8. See, for example, the letters to Wagner of 22 May 1869, 21 May 1870, and 20 May 1873: three birthday letters. In the last one which begins, "Beloved Master," one reads: "I always tremble with fright when I fancy that I might not have known you, in which case life would truly not be worth living." Finally, on 20 May 1874: "I can do nothing other than honor you as a father. In celebrating your birthday, at the same time I also celebrate my birth."

9. See my *Socrate(s)* (Paris: Galilée, 1988). (The chapter on Nietzsche has been published in an English translation under the title "Nietzsche's Socrates: 'Who' is Socrates?" *New School for Social Research Graduate Faculty Philosophy Journal* 15, no. 2 (1991): 7–29.

10. This is what he suggests in the *ex post facto* (1886) Preface to vol. 1 of *Human, All Too Human*.

11. When Nietzsche speaks of the ascetic ideal of artists, only chastity is taken into consideration. Poverty and humility, by contrast, will intervene as well in the ascetic ideal of the philosopher, the priest, the saint, and invalids.

12. Nietzsche speaks in the same terms of Socrates—that joyous warrior full of courage, until he was reduced to pronouncing final and all-too-many words revealing his illness, his profound pessimism in regard to life, which until then he had disguised very well. Compare with GS 340.

13. *Thus Spoke Zarathustra*, trans. Walter Kaufmann, in *The Portable Nietzsche*, "On Chastity" (Z I:13).

14. Ibid.

15. On the role Kant plays in repressing the overflow of German sensuality, see BGE 11 and "Kant, a Doctor in Spite of Himself," a chapter in my *Nietzsche et la scène philosophique*, 2e édition (Paris: Galilée, 1968), to be published in English by Humanities Press International.

16. Compare "On Chastity" in *Thus Spoke Zarathustra*. "Do you love tragedies and everything that breaks the heart? But I mistrust your bitch" (Z I:13).

17. In *The Twilight of the Idols*, in an aphorism dedicated to Goethe, Nietzsche declares that Goethe is the last German for whom he has any respect (TI IX:51). But Goethe to him was European rather than German. He represents a grandiose endeavor to conquer the eighteenth century through a return to the state of nature, to elevate it to the natural state of the Renaissance (compare TI IX:49).

18. A Persian lyric poet.

19. One might recall here Book II of *The Republic*, in which, after Socrates has described to Glaucon a just city founded according to the needs of each class, Glaucon responds: "But it is a city of pigs, Socrates, that you have just described" (Plato, *Plato's Republic*, trans. G.M.A. Grube [Indianapolis: Hackett Publishing Co., 1988], 372 d [as cited by the author in French—Ed.]). Luxury, dangerous supplementarity, and mimesis are introduced along with human desire. What Plato presents as a second moment in evolution corresponds in fact to the structure of desire always already there in man, who is precisely not a swine (that is to say, a being with fixed needs). As Rousseau puts it in *Emile*, in the animal world, "once the hold is full," the female rejects the male. Woman, however, is never satisfied.

20. Compare *Nietzsche Contra Wagner*, trans. Kaufmann, in *The Portable Nietzsche*, "Wagner as the Apostle of Chastity," section 2. The text is nearly identical to that of the Third Essay (henceforth NCW).

21. Compare with *Daybreak*, P:3.

22. In NCW Nietzsche associates Wagner, in respect of this hatred, with Flaubert.

23. Compare also NCW, "Wagner as the Apostle of Chastity," section 3.

24. Compare BGE 207.

25. CW 3.

26. The theme of redemption is fundamental in *Parsifal.* For example, Parsifal says:

> I hear the grievous cry of the Savior
> I weep, alas, he weeps
> Over the betrayed sanctuary
> Redeem me
> Save me from these hands soiled by imperfection
> Thus cried the lamentation of God
> Terribly, to the very depths of my soul
> And me, the coward, me the fool
> I flee toward childish adventures
> Redeemer! Christ savior! Prince of peace!
> How do I atone for such sin?

Kundry later refers to Parsifal as a redeemer come to save her. At the end of the opera he baptizes her:

> As the first act of my ministry,
> Receive the baptismal water and believe in the Redeemer.

The last word of the Libretto is *redeemer.* While Kundry falls dead at his feet and Parsifal contemplates the Grail, all together sing:

> Miracle of the supreme grace
> In his turn the Redeemer is redeemed.

27. GS 340.

28. Compare CW 3.

29. Nietzsche also uses this metaphor in *Philosophy in the Tragic Age of the Greeks* to describe the relation of philosophical systems to their authors.

30. See *Human, All Too Human,* I: 145, 162, 252.

31. See CW 5–7 and the "Postscript," the "Second Postscript," and the "Epilogue."

32. "My objections to the music of Wagner are physiological objections" (NCW, "Where I Offer Objections").

33. See CW, "Epilogue."

34. "Everything that ever grew on the soil of *impoverished* life, all of the counterfeiting of transcendence and beyond, has found its most sublime advocate in Wagner's art" (CW, Postscript). "If anything in Wagner is interesting it is the logic with which a physiological defect makes move upon move and takes step upon step as practice and procedure, as innovation in principles, as a crisis in taste" (CW 7).

35. One can find the same position in Marcel Proust. Compare what Norpois says about Bergotte: "Ah! there's a man who justifies the wit who insisted that one ought never to know an author except through his books. It would be impossible to imagine an individual who corresponded less to his—more pretentious, more pompous, more ill-bred. Vulgar at times, at others talking like a book, and not even like one of his own, but like a boring book, which his, to do them justice, are not— such is your Bergotte." *Remembrance of Things Past,* vol. 1: *Swann's Way, Within a*

Budding Grove, trans. C. K. Scott Moncrieff and Terence Kilmartin (New York: Vintage Books, 1982), p. 404.

36. GS 72.

37. See Z I:20, "On Child and Marriage"; Z I:18, "On Little Old and Young Women."

38. See HH I: 211.

39. See the "Postscript" to CW.

40. Perhaps Nietzsche is here taking revenge against the period in his youth when the press spoke of him as Wagner's "lackey scribe." (See letter to Erwin Rohde, 25 October 1872.)

41. German poet (1817–1875).

42. Does Nietzsche himself have such a conception? In any case, he makes use of it to describe the relationship Wagner establishes between music and drama. This is in any case not innocent, even if the Nietzschean conception, as we know, is very complex and does not "reduce itself" to the Aristotelian. Compare Jacques Derrida: *Éperons. Les styles de Nietzsche* (Paris: Flammarion, 1978); Sarah Kofman, "Baubô," in *Nietzsche et la scène philosophique,* translation in *Nietzsche's New Seas,* ed. Tracy Strong (Chicago: University of Chicago Press, 1988).

43. "Whatever is perfect suffers no witnesses. In the theater one becomes people, herd female, pharisee, voting cattle, patron, idiot—*Wagnerian:* even the most personal conscience is vanquished by the leveling magic of the great number; the neighbor reigns, one becomes a mere neighbor" (NCW, "Where I Offer Objections").

44. "*Theatocracy*—the nonsense of a faith in the *precedence* of the theater, in the right of the theater to *lord it* over the arts, over art. . . . The theatre is a revolt of the masses, a plebiscite against good taste" (CW, Postscript).

45. CW 10. This is also the conception Nietzsche has of music at the time of *The Birth of Tragedy.*

46. See Arthur Schopenhauer's *The World as Will and Representation,* trans. E. F. J. Payne (New York: Dover, 1969):

> 'What is life?' Every genuine and successful work of art answers this question in its own way quite calmly and serenely. But all the arts speak only the naïve and childlike language of *perception,* not the abstract and serious language of *reflection;* their answer is thus a fleeting image, not a permanent universal knowledge. Thus for *perception (Anschauung),* every work of art answers that question, every painting, every statue, every poem, every scene on the stage. Music also answers it, more profoundly indeed than do all the others, since in a language intelligible with absolute directness, yet not capable of translation into that of our faculty of reason, it expresses the innermost nature of all life and existence (III:34).

> That in some sense music must be related to the world as the depiction to the thing depicted, as the copy to the original, we can infer from the analogy with the remaining arts, to all of which this character is peculiar. . . . The (Platonic) Ideas are the adequate objectification of the will. To stimulate the knowledge of these by depicting individual things (for works of art are them-

selves always such) is the aim of all the other arts (and is possible with a corresponding change in the knowing subject). Hence all of them objectify the will only indirectly, in other words, by means of the Ideas. As our world is nothing but the phenomenon of appearance of the Ideas in plurality through entrance into the *principium individuationis* (the form of knowledge possible to the individual as such), music, since it passes over the Ideas, is also quite independent of the phenomenal world, positively ignores it, and to a certain extent, could still exist even if there were no world at all, which cannot be said of the other arts. Thus music is as *immediate* an objectification and copy of the whole *will* as the world itself is, indeed as the Ideas are, the multiplied phenomenon of which constitutes the world of individual things. Therefore music is by no means like the other arts, namely a copy of the Ideas, but a *copy of the will itself,* the objectivity of which are the Ideas. For this reason the effect of music is so very much more powerful and penetrating than is that of the other arts, for these others speak only of the shadow, but music of the essence.

That this is the origin of the song with words, and finally of the opera. For this reason they should never forsake that subordinate position in order to make themselves the chief thing, and the music a mere means of expressing the song, since this is a great misconception and an utter absurdity. Everywhere music expresses only the quintessence of life and of its events, never these themselves, and therefore their differences do not always influence it.

For, as we have said, music differs from all the other arts by the fact that it is not a copy of the phenomenon . . . and therefore expresses the metaphysical to everything physical in the world, the thing-in-itself to every phenomenon. Accordingly, we could just as well call the world embodied music as embodied will. (III:52)

47. See my study *The Childhood of Art* (New York: Columbia University Press, European Perspectives Series, 1988).

48. This is what he avers in *Ecce Homo* about "Richard Wagner in Bayreuth" (the fourth of the *Untimely Meditations*). See also Nietzsche's letter to Erwin Rohde of 9 December 1868: "Listening to Wagnerian music is for me a jubilant intuition, indeed an astonishing self-discovery."

49. On the figure of Democritus, for example, he writes in a letter to Erwin Rohde of 9 December 1868: "I feel a powerful attraction to the figure of Democritus—of course I have completely reconstructed it for myself, since our historians of philosophy have been able to do justice neither to him nor to Epicurus."

50. [When the author's French version of this and other Nietzsche texts cited differs significantly from the Kaufmann translation of these texts, the former has been followed, in view of the relation of what the author is saying to the material cited.—Ed.]

51. A French version of this essay appeared under the title "Nietzsche et Wagner: comment la musique devient bonne pour les cochons," *Furor* 23 (Lausanne, May 1992).

TWELVE

Nietzsche, the Jews, and *Ressentiment*

Yirmiyahu Yovel

In a volume dedicated to Nietzsche's *Genealogy* there is no need to dwell on the meaning of *ressentiment*. My aim in this essay is to see how this key concept (together with another, "self-overcoming") functions when applied by Nietzsche to both Jews and anti-Semites. These two polarities haunted Nietzsche throughout his creative life, and occupy a more central place in his thought than is usually recognized.[1] Liberally using quotes, I shall organize this essay as a kind of case file, somewhat following Nietzsche's own handling of Wagner.

First, a few methodological remarks: (1) My interest focuses on Nietzsche's own thought, not on its various uses, abuses, vulgarizations, and the like (although these are of great interest and importance when studying empirical history), nor on what is called "Nietzscheanism." (2) I am addressing Nietzsche as philosopher; that is, I consider his view of the Jews in its links with the rest of his thinking, rather than as a fleeting or occasional reflection that any intellectual, artist, writer, or scientist might have framed about the Jews. (3) While examining Nietzsche's words in their philosophical context, attention should also be given to their *rhetorical context* and to how they sound among the other voices coming from Nietzsche and from others. (4) Nietzsche is commonly described as "ambivalent" about the Jews (but the term itself is left ambiguous). I shall try to explicate the *structure* of that ambivalence and clearly bring out its precise components.

To do this we shall have to make certain distinctions: first, between Nietzsche's attitudes toward *anti-Semitism* and toward *historical Judaism*. Second, within historical Judaism three further phases are to be distinguished: Old Testament Judaism, whose "grandeur" Nietzsche adored: the "priestly" Judaism of the Second Temple, which he profoundly despised and condemned as the parent of Christian culture; and the post-Christian

Jews in the Diaspora and modern times, whom he defended, admired, and saw as a healing ingredient for his "new Europe."

To understand this complex relation—a seeming paradox—we must recognize a major methodological point. When Nietzsche attacks the anti-Semites or defends the Jews, he has in mind concrete entities: the contemporary Jewish communities living in Europe, and the actual anti-Semitic movement working against them. By contrast, when criticizing ancient Judaism, Nietzsche approaches it as a psycho-cultural (or "genealogical") *category*; it is for him a qualitative feature deeply ingrained in Western culture, whose psychological structure Nietzsche—as the "genealogist" of that culture—is out to analyze and expose.[2] Hence the characteristic gap between his critique of second temple Judaism and his defense of contemporary Jews. Unlike the anti-Semitic theorists, both vulgar and subtle—and also unlike many Jewish apologists—*Nietzsche avoids carrying over his negative analysis of ancient Judaism into his attitude toward contemporary Jews.* This methodological *epoche*, a self-disciplinary move (and a hallmark of his uncommon psychology), allows Nietzsche to be—at the same time, and with the same passionate ardor—both an anti-anti-Semite and a critic of ancient Judaism, the cradle of Christianity.

ANTI-SEMITISM AS A PROBLEM IN SELF-OVERCOMING

> I have never yet met a German who was favorably inclined to the Jews; and however decided the repudiation of actual anti-Semitism may be on the part of all prudent and political men, this prudence and policy is not perhaps directed against the nature of the sentiment itself but only against its dangerous excess, and especially against the distasteful and infamous expression of this excess of sentiment;—on this point we must not deceive ourselves. (BGE 251)

As in the cases of other such testimonies (another example is Sartre), I think we may accept Nietzsche's words. It is plausible to expect virtually any child exposed to a Christian upbringing to have absorbed some anti-Jewish sentiment. The question is what one does with this sentiment in maturity. Does one make a theory of it? Contend against it? Allow it to persist but, for "political" reasons of the kind Nietzsche mentioned, restrain its more brutal manifestations, and yet let some "soft" or "subtle" anti-Semitism permeate one's life?

Speaking for himself, Nietzsche hints that "I, too, when on a short daring sojourn in very infected ground, did not remain wholly exempt from the disease" (BGE 251).[3] For a brief but intense time, as we know, he was close to Wagner, a rabid anti-Semite; and in Basel Nietzsche came under the influence of another anti-Semitic thinker, Jacob Burckhardt, the famous historian of the Renaissance, whose master-figure hovered problematically over Nietzsche to his last lucid days. And of course, Nietzsche had the "infected territory" even much closer to home in the form of his sister Elizabeth and her future husband, Foerster. However, as I shall suggest, the intimacy of Nietzsche's complex relations with these figures served as a lever for a powerful self-overcoming and for inner reinforcement of his stand as an *anti*-anti-Semite.

Self-overcoming is the key concept here. It not only is central in Nietzsche's philosophy in general but also describes what Nietzsche seems to have realized in his own personal case concerning the Jews. The "new philosopher's" self-overcoming entails surmounting the decadent culture in which he or she has been bred—and that includes not only rationalistic metaphysics and Christian morality but also lesser deformations such as nationalism and anti-Semitism, which equally derive from a deviant will to power and ressentiment. Nietzsche had to—and to a great extent did—overcome *both* the "Jewish" (Judeo-Christian) element of his upbringing *and* anti-Semitism.

The Jew is embedded in Christian consciousness as an archetypal negative figure, his image so deeply incised as to be almost ineradicable. There is a sense of the death of God for which the Jew is held responsible. He is God's murderer, who by rejecting the Savior had justifiably been deprived of his election and historical mission; his due is to be outcast and downtrodden. Yet the Jew stubbornly persists in his error, protests his outcast status and, full of hatred, seeks revenge against the Gentiles.[4]

The primal Jewish consciousness, on the other hand, perceives the Gentile Christian as alien and hostile—an unreachable "other" representing the world of negation, who vainly pretends to supplant the Jew and usurp his divine history and election. On top of this, of course, are the bitter memories of persecution and torture.

Given such powerful primary images, self-overcoming is the only way. Nietzsche, of course, does not mean liberal civility or simple "political" restraint, nor is he talking about "good will" and "tolerance" as universal values. These are fragile shields that the first volcanic outburst will destroy. Self-overcoming as Nietzsche conceives it is an act—or rather, a process—which penetrates and reshapes a person's inner drives and urges, rather than merely imposing external rational restraints or censorship upon them. This process requires personal strength, and a kind of hard honesty toward oneself that ordinary psychology does not provide, and which cannot therefore be expected from the greater public. Nietzsche's solution, here too, seems suitable only for a minority.

Furthermore, in order for one to mobilize the power required for an inner transformation of one's drives, an energy-boost is needed—which (as Freud, a semi-Nietzschean, suggested in his theory of transference) a person's privileged relationship to another person might generate. In

Nietzsche's case, his intimate relations and intense grappling with his sister and the others mentioned above could have provided some of the energy needed for overcoming the temptations of anti-Semitism.

THE ANTI-ANTI-SEMITE: QUID FACTI

To first establish the textual case—a kind of *quid facti*—I shall cite a sampling of Nietzsche's comments on anti-Semitism. I have drawn these comments from four different types of text: (1) Nietzsche's publications; (2) his intimate letters—to his sister, mother, and close friends; (3) an ironic correspondence with Theodor Fritsch, a renowned anti-Semitic propagandist; and (4) Nietzsche's last letters written in mental twilight.

The Published Works

A strong statement against anti-Semitism appears, not surprisingly, in the *Genealogy,* the same work in which ancient priestly Judaism is also condemned—and for the same genealogical reason. "They [the anti-Semites] are all men of *ressentiment,* physiologically unfortunate and worm-eaten, a whole tremulous realm of subterranean revenge, inexhaustible and insatiable in outbursts against the fortunate and happy" (GM III:14).

In *Beyond Good and Evil* Nietzsche chides the anti-Semites who seek to curb Jewish immigration to Germany:

"Let no more Jews come in! And shut the doors, especially towards the East (also towards Austria)!"—thus commands the instinct of a people whose nature is still feeble and uncertain, so that it could be easily wiped out, easily extinguished by a stronger one. The Jews, however, are beyond any doubt the strongest, toughest, and purest race at present living in Europe; they know how to succeed even under the worst conditions (in fact better than under favorable ones) by means of virtues of some sort, which one would like nowadays to label as vices—owing above all to a resolute faith which does not need to be ashamed before "modern ideas"; they alter only, *when* they *do alter,* in the same way that the Russian Empire makes its conquests—as an empire that has plenty of time and is not of yesterday—namely, according to the principle, "as slowly as possible." (BGE 251)

In contrast to the young and artificial nations now arising in Europe, Nietzsche adds, the Jews are a stable and ancient race, of the sort that exists forever. Then he makes a significant observation, which I cite here for its tone and timbre (expressing clear empathy for the Jews) no less than for its content:

It is certain that the Jews, if they desired—or if they were driven to it, as the anti-Semites seem to wish—could now have the ascendancy, nay, literally the supremacy over Europe, that is certain; that they are not working and planning for that end is equally certain. Meanwhile they rather wish and desire, even somewhat importunely, to be insorbed and absorbed by Europe; they long to be finally settled, authorised, and respected somewhere, and wish to put an end to the nomadic life, to the "Wandering Jew";—and one should certainly take account of this impulse and tendency, and make advances to it (it possibly betokens a mitigation of the Jewish instincts): for which purpose it would perhaps be useful and fair to banish the anti-Semitic bawlers out of the country. (BGE 251)

This passage, which clearly defends the Jews, should be read in conjunction with another, high-sounding passage on the Jews, from *Daybreak*, which says among other things:

> The psychological and spiritual resources of the Jews today are extraordinary. . . . Every Jew possesses in the history of his fathers and grandfathers a great fund of examples of the coldest self-possession and endurance in fearful situations, of the subtlest outwitting and exploitation of chance and misfortune; their courage beneath the cloak of miserable submission, their heroism . . . surpasses the virtues of all the saints. . . . They themselves have never ceased to believe themselves called to the highest things, and the virtues which pertain to all who suffer have likewise never ceased to adorn them. . . . They themselves know best that a conquest of Europe, or any kind of act of violence, on their part is not to be thought of: but they also know that at some future time Europe may fall into their hands like a ripe fruit if they would only just extend them. To bring that about they need, in the meantime, to distinguish themselves in every domain of European distinction and to stand everywhere in the first rank. . . . And whither shall this assembled abundance of grand impressions which for every Jewish family constitutes Jewish history, this abundance of passions, virtues, decisions, renunciations, struggles, victories of every kind—whither shall it stream out if not at last into great men and great works! (D 205)

Close to his proposal to expel not the Jews but the "anti-Semitic bawlers," Nietzsche gives pointed expression to his view of anti-Semitism itself. In *Nietzsche contra Wagner* he cites this offense as one of the worst signs of decay: "Since Wagner moved to Germany, he had condescended step by step to everything I despise—even to anti-Semitism" (NCW 8:1). And in *The Antichrist*, another late work, speaking of the anti-Semites' "inner conviction," he says:

> Long ago I posed the problem whether convictions are not more dangerous than lies as enemies of truth. . . . "Respect for all who have convictions!" I have heard that sort of thing even out of the mouths of anti-Semites. On the contrary, gentlemen! An anti-Semite certainly is not any more decent because he lies as a matter of principle. (A 55)

The published texts speak for themselves. Of even greater significance are Nietzsche's intimate letters—especially those written within the family circle, where he cannot be suspected of "politic" caution. These letters reveal the pain Nietzsche suffered from the infection of his own family by anti-Semitism.

Personal Letters to His Sister, Mother, and Overbeck

To Overbeck:

> This accursed anti-Semitism . . . is the reason for the great rift between myself and my sister. (BW, III, 503)[5]

To his sister (upon her engagement to the virulent anti-Semite Foerster):

> You have gone over to my antipodes. . . . I will not conceal that I consider this engagement an insult—or a stupidity which will harm you as much as me. (BW, V 377)

To his mother:

> Because of people of this species of men [anti-Semites], I couldn't go to Paraguay [where members of Foerster's anti-Semitic circle had set up an experimental colony]. I am so happy that they voluntarily exile themselves from Europe. For even if I shall be a bad German—I am in any event a *very good European*. (BW, V, 443)

Again to his sister, several years later:

> You have committed one of the greatest stupidities—for yourself and for me! Your association with an anti-Semitic chief expresses a foreignness to *my* whole way of life which fills me ever again and again with ire or melancholy. . . . It is a matter of honor to me to be absolutely clean and unequivocal in relation to anti-Semitism, namely *opposed*, as I am in my writings. I have been persecuted in recent times with letters and *Anti-Semitic Correspondence Sheets*; my disgust with this party (which would like all too well the advantage of my name!) is as outspoken as possible . . . and that I am unable to do anything against it, that in every *Anti-Semitic Correspondence Sheet* the name of Zarathustra is used, has already made me almost sick several times. (BW, V, 479)

The Fritsch Affair

One of the anti-Semites Nietzsche had in mind in the previous letter—those who "persecuted" him in the hope of winning his favor—was Theodor Fritsch, editor of a sheet called *Der Hammer* and author of virulent, best selling anti-Semitic tracts.[6] Complaining about Nietzsche's "perverted judgments" of the Jews, Fritsch had suggested they were due to Nietzsche's personal relations with Jewish friends (such as Paul Ree). The anti-Semitic material he sent Nietzsche contained a pamphlet by Foerster, Nietzsche's brother-in-law, which praised other well-known preachers of anti-Semitism as follows: "Those who deal with the Jewish question from the most exalted

moral point of view are . . . Richard Wagner, Paul De Lagarde, Eugen Dühring, and Adolphe Drumont. Their writings must serve every anti-Semite as
an indispensable weapon, just as the Talmud serves the rabbis."

The dull-witted Fritsch could not have been any more off target. The
"authorities" he cited could only arouse Nietzsche's ridicule and contempt
or, in Wagner's case, aversion. In his first reply (dated 23 March 1887)
Nietzsche was still ironic, even relatively polite:

> Very Dear Sir,
>   Your letter, which I have just received, accords me such great honor that
> I cannot but direct your attention to yet another place in my writings which
> deals with the Jews, be it only in order to give you a redoubled right to speak
> about my "perverted judgments." Please read *Daybreak*, page 194. (BW, V,
> 819)

Nietzsche here refers Fritsch to the famous section 205 in *Daybreak* cited
above (which Nietzsche clearly understands as pro-Jewish and irritating for
an anti-Semite). Then he goes on:

> Objectively, the Jews are more interesting for me than the Germans: their
> history raises many fundamental questions. And in such serious matters I am
> used to ignore sentiments of sympathy or antipathy, as is required by the
> scientific spirit and its ethics, its training—and, in the final analysis, its *sense
> of taste*.
>   In addition I must confess that the "German spirit" of our times is so alien
> to me that only with great impatience can I observe its [idiosyncratic] man-
> nerisms, among which I especially include anti-Semitism. To the "classic lit-
> erature" of that movement, which your pamphlet lauds on page 6, I owe
> several entertaining moments: if only you knew how much I laughed last
> spring when reading the works of that crooked-minded sentimentalist known
> as Paul de Lagarde! I evidently lack that "most exalted moral point of view"
> referred to on that page.
>   All that remains for me now is to thank you for having courteously sup-
> posed that "it is not out of some consideration for society" that I have arrived
> at my "perverted judgments" [concerning the Jews]; and perhaps it will help
> assuage your mind if I say, finally, there are no Jews among my friends. But
> neither are there any anti-Semites.——
>
> > Your most devoted servant,
> > Prof. Dr. F. Nietzsche
>
>   A request: Please publish a list of German scholars, artists, poets, writers,
> actors, and virtuosi of Jewish extraction or intraction! That will be a valuable
> contribution to the history (and criticism!) of German culture. (BW, V, 819)

The final witticism: "There are no Jews among my friends. But neither
are there any anti-Semites" clearly mocks the well-known protest of anti-
Semites: "Many of my best friends are Jewish." In saying that he, on the

contrary, "does *not* have Jewish friends," Nietzsche is ironically dissociating himself from the anti-Semites, just as he does in the second phrase ("But neither are there any anti-Semites"), now spoken seriously.

It seems that, meanwhile, the post delivered Nietzsche more anti-Semitic material from Fritsch. Six days later (29 March 1887) Nietzsche wrote Fritsch another letter, more caustic this time and with cruder irony:

> I hereby return your three *Correspondence Sheets* with gratitude for the trust that enabled me to get a glimpse of the concoction and confusion of principles upon which this strange movement of yours is founded. That being the case, I request that you no longer continue to privilege me with these mailings: I do fear finally for my patience. Believe me: that nauseating desire of naïve dilettantes to have their say about the value of peoples and races; that submission to "authorities" whom any intelligent mind would reject with abhorrence (such as A. Dühring, R. Wagner, Drumont, de Lagarde ...), those constant and absurd distortions of vague concepts: "Germanic," "Semitic," "Aryan," "Christian," "German"—all that is liable to rouse my ire seriously and for long, and to extirpate from my heart the generous irony with which I have so far observed the gyrations of hypocrisy of the Germans of our time.
>
> Finally, what do you think I feel when Zarathustra's name is borne in the mouths of anti-Semites?
>
> Yours submissively,
Dr. F. Nietzsche[7]

Nietzsche's Twilight Letters

Early in January 1889 Nietzsche collapsed on a street in Turin. He was taken to his lodgings and after regaining consciousness he wrote many letters in a few days—to his close friends (Franz Overbeck, Peter Gast, Erwin Rhode), to Jakob Burckhardt, August Strindberg, Malwida von Meysenburg, and others. Most of the letters are signed "The Crucified" or "Dionysos," which calls to mind the conclusion of Nietzsche's last book, *The Antichrist,* where he says: "Did you understand me?—Dionysos against The Crucified." There is no contradiction here: Dionysos has come to oust the Crucified but is himself a new Crucified of sorts. Similarly in his twilight letters, Nietzsche sees himself cast in the role of God's son, a demi-God who recreates the world and culture, and shapes totally new values. Even his suffering, perseverance, and power, are Christ's. He is the Antichrist *as* a new Christ; or he is Dionysos come to unsettle Christianity but thereby fills a role like that of the founder of Christianity himself. A characteristic example:

> *To my maestro Pietro* [Peter Gast, a musician]:
> Sing to me a new song: The world is transfigured and all the heavens are glad.
> The Crucified One (*Unpublished Letters,* no. 71)

To friend Overbeck and wife:
> Although so far you have demonstrated little faith in my ability to pay, I yet hope to demonstrate that I am somebody who pays his debts—for example, to you. I am just having all anti-Semites shot.
>
> Dionysos (BW, V, 1249)

Perhaps the longest letter was addressed to Jacob Burckhardt, the old cultural historian who had influenced the young Nietzsche in Basel, and with whom he sustained a complicated relationship. Burckhardt, a pessimistic humanist and student of the Renaissance, was then at the end of his career and lived in fear of a great cultural eruption that would shake Europe. Although compared to his contemporaries he was relatively free of bigotry, Burckhardt did persist in one prejudice—against the Jews, who will, he thought, be the only beneficiaries of the looming European catastrophe (a cruel irony in retrospect). There is no doubt that Nietzsche, like many others, regarded him as an anti-Semite. In the dim last hours of his active life, Nietzsche wrote to Burckhardt:

Dear Professor,
> In the end I would much rather be a Basel professor than God; but I did not dare push my private egoism so far as to give up the creation of the world on its account. You see, one has to make sacrifices. . . .

Nietzsche goes on to describe his life in Turin in concrete detail: how he does his shopping, the room he rented, how he suffers from torn shoes—as if alluding to Jesus as an earthly God. He also identifies himself with various figures in the news, and through them projects again his image as an inverted son of God, or a Dionysos functioning as the Antichrist. His signature—or farewell—is unusually personal and warm: "Cordially and lovingly, Your Nietzsche." However, in a postscript he adds: "I had Caiaphas put in chains . . . , Wilhelm Bismarck and all anti-Semites deposed" (*Unpublished Letters*, no. 75).

Here Burckhardt too gets his due as an anti-Semite—and from the hand of the Crucified himself, who at the same time takes his revenge against Caiaphas, the high priest who recommended his crucifixion. This is confused, but not without sense. In his waning hours Nietzsche lashed out especially against the nationalist and anti-Semitic Germans, against the ideology of the new Germany. In his frenzied state he put forward a plan for the unification of Europe under his scepter—and sent letters ordering the king of Italy and the Pope to organize the necessary congress on January 8. However, he demanded that the representatives of unified Germany—"Wilhelm, Bismarck and all anti-Semites"—be excluded from the congress, and gave the other German princes a good shepherd's advice: "My children, it is never good to join in friendship with those madmen from the house of Hohenzollern . . . —The Crucified" (BW, V, 1255).

Thus his final remarks before he sank into darkness bring into the open—in distorted but instructive relief—some of the deepest motifs in Nietzsche's mind: the inversion of the existing world, the creation of a new culture, his role as Dionysian prophet and Antichrist—and also the political unification of Europe, to renew its decadent culture. All these drives and ideas are now thrust outside and illumined by the high beam of madness. His mental twilight thus has considerable hermeneutic importance in providing clues to Nietzsche's inner mind as it was also during his sanity.[8] It shows that his opposition to anti-Semitism, and the German nationalism with which it was connected, were among the most powerful negations agitating Nietzsche's mind.

We may find it significant that Nietzsche obliterates Caiaphas in the same breath as the anti-Semites: the Jewish priest not only sent Christ to his cross but, in a deeper sense, begot him. Thus Christianity stems from the same distortion that later made anti-Semitism possible. So Caiaphas, the Jewish priest, Bismarck, the German nationalist and state-worshiper, and the modern anti-Semites, all have the same genealogical ancestor, *ressentiment.* In the next section we shall see that Nietzsche makes this clear in saner and more systematic texts, especially the *Genealogy.*

"I am just having all anti-Semites shot"; "Wilhelm Bismarck and all anti-Semites deposed"—that is not an incidental cry issued by Nietzsche as his mind was fading out. Rather, as Podach says, it expresses a challenge to and struggle "against those Nietzsche holds responsible for the corruption of German culture, and thereby of the culture of Europe as a whole."

The four types of text I have cited show that Nietzsche had no ambivalence in his rejection of anti-Semitism; that he did not mildly despise or oppose it as a liberal, but fought against it with intensity, as against the "antipode" of his entire nature; and that, far from being marginal, this issue was central to him both theoretically and psychologically. No less univocal is his defense of and admiration for *contemporary* Jews. But what are his theoretical grounds? Having answered the question *quid facti,* we must, so to speak, now ask: *quid juris?* What is it in Nietzsche's *philosophy* that makes anti-Semitism both so central and so antipodal?

THE SOURCES OF NIETZSCHE'S ANTI-ANTI-SEMITISM: *QUID JURIS*

When dealing with an existential thinker like Nietzsche it is, of course, difficult to sever completely the personal from the theoretical. As I have suggested, his overcoming of anti-Semitism must have been assisted by his struggle with such figures as Elizabeth, Wagner, Burckhardt, and by refashioning his love-hate relationships and overt and covert conflicts with them. However, even outside the psychological arena, there is sufficient philosophical anchorage in Nietzsche for his active anti-anti-Semitism.[9] I shall enumerate the main points and illustrate each one with a quotation or two.[10]

A New Slave Revolt

Anti-Semitism is a mass movement, ideological and vulgar. As such, it is a popular neurosis that affects weak and insecure people, who are deficient in self-confidence (in contrast to Nietzsche's *"Übermensch"* or Dionysian individual); and it presents a new kind of "slave revolt." A mass movement generally derives its strength from the coalescence of weak individuals[11] joined by an object of common hatred. Moreover, despite his sense to the contrary, the weak individual sinks even lower in the crowd, because he draws a semblance of strength from *outside*—from the faceless mass within which he has let the remnants of his personality be submerged. His originally petty, insecure spirit is not redeemed within the crowd but rather compounded. Through a veil of self-deception, he acquires a sense of counterfeit power (political, not existential) which he cannot sustain otherwise than by projecting it negatively against his "other."

Furthermore, the anti-Semitic movement as Nietzsche understood it was not even the decline of an originally strong and creative position. Rather, already from the start and in the mouths of its originators, it expressed mass psychology in its direct and most primary form. If the image of a "herd" has meaning in Nietzsche, its derogatory connotations apply most distinctly to the anti-Semitic movement, as a modern embodiment of "herd" and "slave" mentality, though without its original creative power.

The Nationalistic Neurosis

Especially in Germany, anti-Semitism was the other Janus face of nationalism, which Nietzsche also opposed as madness and neurosis. Nietzsche attacked both nationalism in general and, in particular, the new German nationalism of his time, then reaching an exalted climax through the unification of Germany under a Prussian Kaiser and Bismarck's *Reich*. In exposing nationalism as another modern form of the "herd mentality," he also identified the context within which German anti-Semitism functioned and from which it drew much of its motivation and negative energies.

In place of nationalism in its various guises, Nietzsche favored *Europeanism* as an ideal—not in today's basically economic form but as the product of "a grand politics" that would overcome all petty and aggressive nationalisms and set forth a supranational culture, fused with a "Dionysian" quality and a "revalued" sense of life. The Jews were to have a constitutive role in the new Europe, which would set the normative tone for the rest of the world. (In that respect Nietzsche remained parochial and Eurocentrist.)[12] A textual illustration:

A little fresh air! This absurd condition of Europe shall not go on much longer! Is there any idea at all behind this bovine nationalism? What value can there be now, when everything points to wider and more common interests, in encouraging this boorish self-conceit? And this in a state of affairs in which spiritual dependency and disnationalization meet the eye and in which the value and meaning of contemporary culture lie in mutual blending and fertilization! (WP 748)

Owing to the morbid estrangement which the nationality-craze has induced and still induces among the peoples of Europe, owing also to the shortsighted and hasty-handed politicians who with the help of this craze, are in present in power . . . , the most unmistakable signs that Europe wishes to be one, are now overlooked, or arbitrarily and falsely misinterpreted. (BEG 256)

It should be noted that, in conventional terms, Nietzsche's attack on nationalism would be classified as coming "from the Right" (though in a cultural sense rather than a political one). Today nationalism is linked with right-wing politics; but in the early nineteenth century, especially under the repressive "Holy Alliance," it drew much of its vigor from the liberal "Left" which demanded the liberation of ethnic peoples as the condition for liberating the individual, too, within his or her genuine identity. Nationalism was later transformed into a chauvinistic, right-wing movement; and Nietzsche, living under Bismarck, was witness to that transformation. But he was aware of its earlier career, and continued to see it as part of the "modern ideas" originating in the Enlightenment (liberalism, democracy, socialism, equality, utility, and the like), all of which he opposed as the offspring of Christianity, enhanced by the modern culture of the masses, and thereby as belonging to the same genealogical family.[13]

The Cult of the State—the New Idol

Anti-Semitism is also objectionable because it reinforces the German Reich and the cult of politics and the state—especially the modern national state, which Nietzsche denounces as a "new idol" (Z I:1). He is entirely opposed to the apotheosis of politics, and to letting it dominate all other dimensions of life. The modern nation-state, and the German Reich in particular, are venerated for doing precisely that, and thus have become the objects of idolatry and fetishism. Observing them, Nietzsche calls himself the "last nonpolitical German" (EH I:3). For him politics is the enemy of culture, and its lowest form. The politization of Germany has led to the destruction of German spirit and the decline of its culture.[14]

I wish to be just to the Germans. . . . One pays heavily for coming to power: power makes stupid. The Germans—once they were called the people of thinkers: do they think at all today? The Germans are now bored with the spirit, the Germans now mistrust the spirit; politics swallows up all serious concern for really spiritual matters. *Deutschland, Deutschland über alles*—I fear that was the end of German philosophy. (TI VIII:1)

Even a rapid estimate shows that it is not only obvious that German culture is declining but that there is sufficient reason for that. . . . Culture and the state—one should not deceive oneself about this—are antagonists. . . . All great ages of culture are ages of political decline: what is great culturally has always been unpolitical, even antipolitical. . . . (TI VIII:4)

To this, in stylized wrath, Zarathustra too joins his voice:

State is the name of the coldest of all monsters. Coldly it tells lies too; and this lie crawls out of its mouth: "I, the state, am the people."

Every people speaks its tongue of good and evil. . . . But the state tells lies in all the tongues of good and evil. . . .

Everything about it is false; it bites with stolen teeth, and bites easily. Even its entrails are false. . . .

Where the state ends—look there my brothers! Do you not see it, the rainbow and the bridges of the overman? (Z I:11)

This too is part of the context in which to understand Nietzsche's opposition to anti-Semitism: namely, as a component of the cult of the German Reich. The adoration of the German nation projects itself into the idolatry of the German Reich, and depends on anti-Semitism for its mass hysteria and fire.

Racism and the New Europe

Anti-Semitism also depends on racism—meaning the defense of racial "purity." Nietzsche's theory admits the *concept* of race, but rejects *value* differences linked to biology alone; and it calls for an amalgamation of the races in a new European synthesis. This means that, while adhering to a dubious scientific theory about races, he rejects *racism* as a normative doctrine and ideology. Admitting races as a fact, he does not clearly distinguish between them and "peoples." Moreover, he seems to believe that a race's historical experiences can become embedded in its biological inheritance. According to this semi-Lamarckian view, races have the capacity to interiorize their past experiences, imprint them in their "blood," and thus pass them on to new generations (compare WP 942).

However, that makes it desirable to achieve a *blend* of many races rather than to segregate them. The Jews in particular have trained themselves for centuries in self-overcoming and discipline. Now they carry in their "blood" a long and profound history of faithfulness to their identity, which makes them a most desirable candidate and invigorating ingredient in the new European mix. Thus while Nietzsche's stand on *races* is questionable and confused, his stand on *racism* is clear and rather unequivocal.

On occasion, genealogy is found to be more fundamental than race differences. For example, the "priestly" mental-form is more fundamental than "Semitism" in engendering Christianity:

> A lot is said today about the *Semitic* spirit of the New Testament: but what is called Semitic is merely priestly—and in the racially purest Aryan law-book, in Manu, this kind of "Semitism," i.e., the *spirit of the priest,* is worse than anywhere else. The development of the Jewish priestly state is *not* original: they learned the pattern in Babylon: the pattern is Aryan. (WP 143)

The link between Nietzsche's negation of racism, nationalism, and the nation-state as three factors of his anti-anti-Semitism, is well expressed in a section of *Human, All Too Human* entitled "European Man and the Abolition of Nations." Nietzsche explains his choice to be a "good European" rather than a nationalist, and continues:

> Incidentally, the whole problem of the Jews exists only in nation states, for here their energy and higher intelligence, their accumulated capital of spirit and will, gathered from generation to generation through a long schooling in suffering, must become so preponderant as to arouse mass envy and hatred. In almost all contemporary nations, therefore—in direct proportion to the degree to which they act up nationalistically—the literary obscenity is spreading of leading the Jews to slaughter as scapegoats of every conceivable public and internal misfortune. As soon as it is no longer a matter of preserving nations but of producing the strongest possible European mixed race, the Jew is just as useful and desirable an ingredient as any other national remnant. (HH I:475)

This passage covers a good part of the intellectual ground on which Nietzsche's objection to anti-Semitism was born. His four negations—of racism, nationalism, anti-Semitism, and the cult of politics and the nation-state—are interrelated and reinforce one another.

The Underlying Pattern: Ressentiment

Underlying all the above points is a common psychological pattern: fear, a weak "slave" mentality, and above all, *ressentiment*—that vengeful animosity toward the "other," usually a person of higher worth, which mediates the inferior person's sense of selfhood and makes it possible. In the anti-Semite's case, his fervor conceals a profound lack of self-confidence. His primary position is not the celebratory affirmation of his own being and worth, but the negation of the Jew, conceived as his absolute other—and, under the shroud of his inferiority, sensed as feeling himself (and probably being) superior. Only through such negation is the anti-Semite able to recognize and affirm himself too—which he does in an inflated manner, relying on the counterfeit power of the masses, and substituting the arrogance of petty moralizing for existential self-confidence.

No wonder, then, that it is precisely in the *Genealogy* that we read the following passage linking anti-Semitism and *ressentiment*: this linkage is the genealogical basis for all the rest. No less noteworthily, Nietzsche attacks the anti-Semites as the modern "Pharisees" (whom he confounds with the "Jewish priests").[15] I have already cited part of this passage at the beginning of this essay; here it is in full:

> This hoarse, indignant barking of sick dogs, this rabid mendaciousness and rage of "noble" Pharisees, penetrates even the hallowed halls of science (I again remind readers who have ears for such things of that Berlin apostle of revenge, Eugen Dühring, who employs moral mumbo-jumbo more indecently and repulsively than anyone else in Germany today: Dühring, the foremost moral bigmouth today—unexcelled even among his own ilk, the anti-Semites). They are all men of *ressentiment*, physiologically unfortunate and worm-eaten, a whole tremulous realm of subterranean revenge, inexhaustible and insatiable in outbursts against the fortunate and happy. (GM III:14)

Thus in an ironic turn of events, the anti-Semite becomes the legitimate heir of the ancient Jewish priest, from whom he took over as the modern paradigm of the psychology of *ressentiment*. In the meantime Judaism, fortified by its long trials and self-overcoming in exile, has become a storehouse of positive power which modern Europe badly needs—and which, Nietzsche hopes, will fuel the creation of a higher cultural synthesis in Europe.

What distinguishes the anti-Semite as a *modern* phenomenon is not only *ressentiment* but its fusion with the psychology of the masses. The modern mass society compounds the power of *ressentiment* and provides a new terrain for its expression. The ancient Jewish priests, when performing their revolution in values, worked in relative privacy. Their subtle vengeance against pagan Rome was profound but tacit, almost underground; and its bearers, the early Christians, were a repressed minority with no public voice. In Nietzschean terms, they should therefore be deemed stronger spirits than their genealogical cousins, the modern anti-Semites, who must project their *ressentiment* into vulgar mass movement as a further (second) precondition for the anti-Semite's ability to affirm himself. Modern anti-Semitism *depends* on the imaginary power emanating from a crowd united in hatred against an "other."[16] This also means that it must eventually become externally repressive: pogrom and holocaust are its natural expressions.

All of this makes Nietzsche an enemy of the anti-Semite, though not necessarily a "philo-Semite." Characteristically, the *Genealogy* also contains some of Nietzsche's most critical attacks against Judaism—more precisely, against its Second Temple "priestly" phase, from which Christianity was born. This leads to the second part of my study, which I can only sketch here.

THE CRITICISM OF ANCIENT JUDAISM[17]

Nietzsche's criticism of ancient "priestly" Judaism is as severe and uncompromising as is his attack on modern anti-Semitism. He directs his diatribe, however, not at real individuals nor at a concrete historical group, but against Judaism as a genealogical category embedded within Christianity. And he does not let his critique of ancient priestly Judaism project into a negative attitude toward contemporary Jews. On the contrary: for contemporary, post-Exile Jews he has great admiration and hopes, just as he admires the Jews of the Old Testament. His violent attacks against Judaism concentrate on the second, "priestly" phase in Jewish history. While anti-Semites accuse the Jews of having killed Christ, Nietzsche scolds them for having begotten him.

The Jewish priests excelled in *ressentiment* and, moved by it, took subtle revenge upon pagan Rome. They distorted all natural values. They spread false ideas about sin, punishment, guilt, a moral world order, compassion and love for one's fellow man as fundamental values. The humble and weak are the good and may expect redemption; all people are equal in their indebtedness to the transcendent God and in relation to the values of love and compassion that He demands. (Nietzsche frequently reads Christian doctrine *directly* into priestly Judaism, even without acknowledging the gap that separated them.) Yet beneath their doctrine of compassion the priests insinuated the vengefulness of the weak-spirited, whose will to power cannot be expressed except in the distorted way of *ressentiment* as analyzed in the *Genealogy*. In them, moreover, *ressentiment* became creative, a value-engendering power: it revolutionized Roman (Western) culture by investing it with the values of the "slave morality" that Christianity embodied and made everyone internalize. Henceforth, the strong and noble person sees himself as sinner not only through the eyes of the other but in his own eyes as well. His very being inspires him with guilt.

> On such utterly *false* soil, where everything natural, every natural value, every *reality* was opposed by the most profound instincts of the ruling class, *Christianity* grew up—a form of mortal enmity against reality that has never *yet* been surpassed. (A 27)

The Three Phases of Judaism

By linking priestly Judaism and the psychology of *ressentiment*, Nietzsche locates his criticism of historical Judaism at a focal juncture of his philosophy. His attack on the Jewish priests provides the genealogical base for his critique of the Christian component in Western culture, both in its religious form and in its secularized versions at work in "modern ideas" like liberalism, democracy, and the Enlightenment. It is therefore crucial to Nietzsche's philosophical enterprise as a whole. At the same time, he distinguishes between three periods in Judaism (apparently influenced here by Wellhausen, the famous Biblical scholar and critic).

(1) *The Old Testament period,* which inspires Nietzsche's admiration and in which he seems to discern a "Dionysian natural" sense compatible with his philosophy. For example:

> In the Jewish "Old Testament," the book of divine justice, there are men, things, and sayings on such an immense scale that Greek and Indian literature has nothing to compare with it. One stands with fear and reverence before those stupendous remains of what man was formerly. . . . (BGE 52)

> I find in it [the Old Testament] great human beings, a heroic landscape, and something of the very rarest quality in the world, the incomparable naiveté of the *strong heart.* (GM III:22)

(2) *The Second Temple period* and its priests, a period of decline and degeneration as analyzed above. The concept of "priestly code" (*Priesterkodex*) had gained currency among Protestant theologians and scholars; and Nietzsche uses it in relation to the Second Temple phase in Judaism. It is characterized by the New Testament, of which he says:

> To have bound up this New Testament, (a kind of rococo of taste in every respect), along with the Old Testament in one book . . . is perhaps the greatest audacity and "sin against the spirit" that literary Europe has on its conscience. (BGE 52)

> In the New [Testament] . . . I find nothing but petty sectarianism, mere rococo of the soul, mere involutions, nooks, queer things, the air of the conventicle. . . . Humility and self-importance cheek-by-jowl; a garrulousness of feeling that almost stupefies. (GM III:2)

(3) *The Jewish Diaspora* again invokes Nietzsche's admiration (see BGE 251, cited above). The Diaspora cured much of the Jews' proto-Christian decadence, because in their many centuries of exile they manifested an extraordinary power to affirm life in the face of adversity. They have accumulated diverse and profound historical experiences, practiced self-overcoming, showed great discipline, courage, self-mastery, and toughness toward themselves. These are "Nietzschean" values which outweigh and override the fact that the Jews were still worshipers of a transcendent God. Nietzsche rejects their religious *doctrine,* but is attracted by the Jews' *existential* qualities—especially the extraordinary process of *breeding* which their long history in exile has provided, and which nothing else in Europe seems to match.

As a result of that history and breeding, the Jews have become the most powerful race in Europe. They could even dominate Europe (says Nietzsche in the famous passage in *Daybreak* [205] cited above); yet contrary to the widespread anti-Semitic myth, the Jews do not wish that. Their demand is rather for admittance and assimilation—which Nietzsche regards as a possible sign of weakening, while yet insisting that the Jews be allowed this entry. Jewish strength and spiritual treasures will then flow into the new Europe, and the Jews will excel in all walks of life. They might indeed become dominant—not politically but culturally, by renewing European values and setting its normative tone.

Nietzsche welcomes that prospect as appropriate compensation for the harm inflicted on Europe by the Jews' priestly ancestors. To fulfill their new role, the Jews must give up their uniqueness and seclusion and mix with the other races in creating a Dionysian Europe, freed of Christian culture. If that should happen, the Jews too will be redeemed of their barren isolation and the vestiges of *ressentiment* that cling to them, and "Israel will have transformed its eternal revenge into an eternal blessing for Europe." Nietzsche in his enthusiasm goes on to envision that even as the re-creation of the world itself (just as he did later in his twilight letter to Burckhardt!) and flies into the following crescendo: "[Then] the ancient Jewish God may *rejoice* in himself, his creation, and his chosen people—and let us all, all of us, rejoice with him!" (D 205).

Nietzsche thus made himself an advocate of Jewish emancipation and assimilation, for reasons that have nothing to do with liberalism or the Enlightenment, but rather derive from his own "Dionysian" philosophy of power. The anti-Zionism implied in his proassimilation plan also derives from his wish that the Jews "repay their debt to Europe." Nietzsche supports modern Jews for the same reason he attacks their "priestly" ancestors: his concerns remain centered on *Europe* and its culture. The Jews had corrupted Europe in the past; they are now needed to heal it. (It is noteworthy that Nietzsche's view of the Jews always assigns them some major historical role, whether negative or positive, as befits the theological idea of a "chosen people"—or its Nietzschean secularization.)

Nietzsche, who did not pretend to be an empirical or "scientific" historian, took as many liberties with Jewish history as he did with ancient Hellenism. His characterization of the three periods in Jewish history is debatable. Yet it does illustrate a major point: *For Nietzsche there is no constant "Jewish essence," either attached to race or to any other eternal substance.* Jewish history is a changing, evolving entity, and has known radical shifts and several shapes. The metaphor of "genealogy," too, must not be taken as indicating an irreversible destiny; for genealogy is not hereditary conditioning. Peoples and individuals can *overcome* the genealogical traits that their earlier life manifests; they can evolve and adopt new depth-preferences and positions. Nietzschean genealogy points to a *psycho-existential* "ancestry" of a person's or a group's life-form, rather than to a historical or biological one (though the two may overlap on occasion). It looks for the *psychological* origin of our covertly preferred kind of life, action, and thought, not for its literal genetic origin. Thus the Jews, too, while accumulating and transmitting many historical experiences, are not bound by a single genealogical pattern. Rather, the psycho-existential (genealogical) pattern underlying their mind and form of life has taken several turns in the course of their long journey—which also enables Nietzsche to judge it differently according to its several shapes.

POSTSCRIPT: NIETZSCHE, FASCISM, AND POLITICS

Combined, Nietzsche's four negations—of nationalism, anti-Semitism, racism, and the cult of politics and state—forcefully exclude the fascist and Nazi ideology that later claimed Nietzsche and used him. At the same time, he did provide fascism with other themes; and his flamboyant pen, his love of rhetorical shock and aphorism, his self-intoxication with the process of free thinking and the art of the unexpected, produced a corpus of texts which, next to the Bible, lends itself to as many uses and abuses as interest and imagination can produce. Among his abusers, the fascists had the further advantage that Nietzsche, like them, though in a different and "antipodal" way to theirs, was also a right-wing revolutionary who rejected democracy, human rights, and other basics of the Enlightenment. They also capitalized on the fact that he promoted a too-loosely-defined notion of "power" which fascism could use against the grain of his own philosophy.

No less importantly, *fascism benefitted from Nietzsche's failure to provide an adequate theory for the masses* (or the "multitude") compatible with the spirit of his own Dionysian revolution. This lacuna made his philosophy vulnerable, and indeed impotent with regard to politics. It left a vacuum into which the fascists could enter, pretending to "apply" Nietzsche to the masses, though in fact—and partly thereby—manipulating and distorting his own ideas.

Nietzsche might well have expected this. A master of linguistic and hermeneutical maneuvers, he could not have been blind to the dangerous possibilities he invested in his kind of text. Moreover, he must have been aware that his theory *cannot* be vulgarized, and yet *will be*. It is incompatible with the new mass society—and yet the latter was so pervasive that it could prevail, in which case a "vulgarized Nietzscheanism" could not be avoided, and the only question will be: *Who* was to shape it? Since Nietzsche himself didn't—or couldn't—he left the field open to others, including the fascists.

In this respect Mussolini, and even Hitler, although they were Nietzsche's grotesque "antipodes," were nevertheless two possibilities that the Nietzschean texts—and the cunning of history which Nietzsche refused to consider—could partly have held in store. In other words, *genealogically* the fascists were not even Nietzsche's bastards, let alone his legitimate offspring; yet *historically* their advent may have been assisted by something coming from him.

This serves to prove again that genealogy and history are not the same. Genealogical enemies may be historical allies. Nietzsche seems to have been blind, or indifferent, to that possibility. He had no special message for the multitude, and considered vulgarization too base and impure for the philosopher to worry about. Yet the multitude *is there*. It is the real power in modern history, and will vulgarize the philosopher's work for him.

In a word: Nietzsche's purism, and overriding concern with genealogy, caused his theory to miss the train of real history—and, combined with the author's intemperate pen, made him a ready candidate for abuse.[18]

NOTES

1. This essay is based on part of a larger work in progress, *Hegel and Nietzsche on Judaism* (Tel Aviv: Schocken, forthcoming).

2. Nietzsche writes of the ancient Jews much as the "contract" theorists have written of the "state of nature" and its overcoming—the style of historical narrative serves and covers the analysis of an embedded *structure*.

3. From the context it is not quite clear whether anti-Semitism alone is meant here, or other forms of xenophobia as well (against the French, the Poles, and others).

4. The latter idea is manipulated by Nietzsche himself in his anti-*Christian* campaign: Christianity, he says in *The Antichrist* (58), is the subtle revenge of the Jewish priests against its humiliation by Rome. That attributes to Christianity the nature of its most despised antagonists. Nietzsche even capitalizes on his audience's inbred anti-Semitism to chide the Christians for bowing to "three Jews and a Jewess" (Jesus, Peter, Paul, and the Virgin Mary). Here, the anti-Semitic sensibilities buried in Nietzsche's own mind allowed him, I think, to come up with that rhetorical trick.

5. BW is an abbreviation for Nietzsche's *Briefwechsel*, ed. Giorgio Colli and Mazzino Montinari (Berlin: Walter de Gruyter, 1975). Unless otherwise specified I give my translations.

6. *The Anti-Semites' Catechism* (25 editions, 35,000 copies); *Handbook on the Jewish Question* (29 editions, 75,000 copies); *My Proofs Against Yahweh*; and *The False God* (9 editions, 53,000 copies). He also produced some thirty additional anti-Semitic tracts and pamphlets, including *The Protocols of the Elders of Zion* and a tract on the Beilis blood libel.

7. BW, V, 823. This letter and the others to Fritch cited here were published in 1926, in the silver jubilee volume of the *Der Hammer*. Its editors had to be very thick-headed indeed to publish these texts, which in fact are slaps in their faces. Perhaps they sought to preen themselves on an association with so famous a personality as Nietzsche had in the meantime become, even if the association was negative or failed to materialize. This too is part of the history of the vulgarization of Nietzsche and of the abuse to which he was subjected by various parties.

8. Remember, for example, the end of section 205 of *Daybreak*, where the same

idea as in the twilight letter to Burkhardt, the Pope, and others—creating the new European culture, with the decisive participation of the Jews—is likened to the re-creation of the world itself: a task which Nietzsche, in great exaltation, assigns met-aphorically to the "ancient Jewish God." In the twilight letters (especially to Burk-hardt), speaking as "The (Dionysian) Crucified," Nietzsche takes the same task upon *himself*, and again makes it conditional upon the participation of the Jews—by demanding to exclude their enemies, the anti-Semites and German nationalists. That reveals great coherence under the veil of insanity (here) and exaltation (there).

9. Since we are not dealing with a systematic rationalist, what we are after is not a deduction but a clarification of a growth-context—that is, the ingredients of an intellectual setting from which Nietzsche's opposition to anti-Semitism was born and in view of which it makes sense.

10. As mentioned, the present section summarizes a more detailed chapter on the same topic.

11. I use Nietzsche's adjective "weak" as meaning: *psychologically* too weak to assert oneself without first negating another, or to face up to certain "Dionysian truths," such as the tragic side of existence, or the inexorable immanence and transience of all there is. We may call it *existential* weakness, which is not necessarily physical or political and may coexist with political success and control.

12. However, Nietzsche did not envision a European nationalism molded as sim-ply an enlargement of German or French nationalism. It is, among other things, by overcoming nationalism that Europe will set a dominating example: its new values will become universally diffused.

13. At the same time, it is very difficult—indeed, in my view impossible—to attribute any political theory to Nietzsche. My main point is that, by rejecting the culture and politics of the masses, he put himself theoretically beyond relevant modern politics. It is inherently impossible to universalize—that is, vulgarize—the rare psychology destined for the happy few, and the system of values based upon it. Unlike Aristotle and Spinoza, Nietzsche did not have a special theory adapted for the public domain and multitude as such (like Aristotle's "practical reason" or Spinoza's theory of semi-rationality), nor one for treating the mutual relation be-tween the multitude and the elite (as in Pareto, Carl Schmitt, and others). Nietzsche left the "multitude" as merely a passive matter, neither a political agent of any kind nor a philosophical problem *per se*; yet politics is primarily a theory of the multitude.

Nietzsche can also give some support to "left-wing" politics because of his rejec-tion of chauvinism and similar forms of other-hatred based on *ressentiment*. He could also be used to support pluralism and tolerance based upon the multifaced nature of the world and its possible interpretations. Yet here too, these political applications are fragile for lack of *fundamental* support. A Nietzschean "noble" person could easily negate the Other and even destroy him or her—not in the mode of *ressenti-ment*, but in a spontaneous flow of self-affirmation. He might sometimes be ex-tremely cruel to the other, at other times generous, but never egalitarian: the other can make no *claim* of him, and there is no *rule*, claiming universality, which forbids a nonresentful negation of others. Nietzschean pluralism, too, does not imply that all life-styles and interpretations have the right to exist; again it is pluralism without *rights,* and with no universal rule by which the competing parties can have a claim on each other. Thus it seems incompatible with the deep-structure of left-wing politics. At the same time Nietzsche's "right-wing" affinities are too revolutionary to be conservative, and too indefinite to allow a coherent political theory.

I am therefore, despite learned efforts to the contrary (one of them, a brilliant thesis by Peter Berkowitz, written under my own supervision), unable to see Nietzsche as a political thinker in any orientation. It is easier to see what he rejected, and why, than to attribute a coherent positive political theory to him. Even the "grand" politics he allows—his unquestionable support of European unity—cannot have a precise meaning in his writings in the absence of a broader, coherent political context. Thus his Zarathustra does not really come down to the people, and the analogy with Plato's cave does not really work. (See also the Postscript to this essay.)

14. This shows again, incidentally, that Nietzsche's positive concept of "power" must not be confounded with political control, just as his "aristocracy" is not necessarily the title-bearing hereditary nobility. "Noble" for him is an existential and mental posture, and so is "power" in its primary, or genuine, sense. Even when he speaks of social domination, in many contexts Nietzsche means setting the cultural tone and values rather than holding the reins of government.

15. Actually, the Jewish priest-establishment around Jesus' time were mostly the enemies of the Pharisees. Despite their clerical office, they were associated with the mundane elite whom both Jesus and the Pharisees combated and often belonged to the Sadducees, the party that opposed the Pharisees.

16. I say "imaginary" (and said above: "counterfeit") power, using the concept of power in Nietzsche's sense. Of course the multitude can gain political influence, control, or other forms of pragmatic strength, which in Nietzsche's phenomenology may rather express a weak personality and a self-repressive stream of life. I take this (terminological) point as granted within a Nietzschean field of discourse.

17. As mentioned, the present paper is based on a larger manuscript in which the contents of this summary are spelled out in detail.

18. I thank Ettel Weingarten for her editorial help in preparing the manuscript of this essay.

RELATED WORKS

Continuo, A. C. "Nietzsche's Critique of Judaism." *Review of Religion* 13 (1938/9): 161–166.

Duffy, M. F. and W. Mittelman. "Nietzsche's Attitude toward the Jews." *Journal of the History of Ideas* 49(2) (1988): 301–317.

Eisen, A. M. "Nietzsche and the Jews Reconsidered." *Jewish Social Studies* 48(1) (1986): 1–14.

Golomb, J. "Nietzsche on Jews and Judaism." *Archiv für Geschichte der Philosophie* 67(2) (1985): 139–161.

Lonsbach, R. M. *Friedrich Nietzsche und die Juden.* Bonn: Baurier Verlag, 1985.

Neuman, H. "Superman or Last Man? Nietzsche's Interpretation of Athens and Jerusalem." *Nietzsche Studien* 15 (1976): 1–28.

O'Flaherty, et al., eds. *Studies in Nietzsche and the Judaeo-Christian Tradition.* London: The University of North Carolina Press, 1985.

Stern, A. "Nietzsche and Judaism." *Contemporary Jewish Record* 8(1) (1945): 31–42.

Talmon, J. L. "Nietzsche's Jewish Aspects in Historical Perspective" (Heb.). *Ha'aretz* (daily) 12 (September 1969).

Yovel, Y. "Perspectives nouvelles sur Nietzsche et le judaisme." *Revue des Etudes Juives,* 138 (1979): 483–485.

THIRTEEN

Nietzsche's Minimalist Moral Psychology

Bernard Williams

NIETZSCHE, WITTGENSTEIN AND THE EXTRACTION OF THEORY

Nietzsche is not a source of philosophical theories. At some level the point is obvious, but it may be less obvious how deep it goes. In this respect, there is a contrast with Wittgenstein. Wittgenstein said repeatedly, and not only in his later work, that he was not to be read as offering philosophical theory, because there could be no such thing as philosophical theory. But his work was less well prepared than Nietzsche's to sustain that position posthumously. There is more than one reason for this.[1] Wittgenstein thought that his work demanded not only the end of philosophical theory but the end of philosophy—something associated, for him, with the end of his demands on himself to do philosophy. That association, of the end of philosophical theory with the end of philosophy, does not deny the idea that if there is to be philosophy, it will take the form of theory; indeed, it readily reinforces that idea. Moreover, the topics on which Wittgenstein wanted there to be no more philosophy—the topics, for him, of philosophy—were traditional topics of academic philosophy. It is not surprising that those who continue theoretical work on those topics still look for elements in Wittgenstein's work itself from which to construct it.

No doubt many who do this lack a suitable irony about what they do to Wittgenstein's texts, but their attitude is not in any important sense a betrayal: less so, in fact, than the attitude of those who think that Wittgenstein did bring to an end philosophical theory on those topics, and themselves sustain an academic activity that consists of reiterating that very thing. Among those who think that there is room for ongoing philosophical theory on those topics, and that Wittgenstein contributed to it, someone owes Wittgenstein an account of why he had ceased to see that this was so. But such an account might be given, and we might come to understand that if Wittgenstein could no longer see the edifice of an intellectual subject, his sightlessness was not that of Samson, but rather that of Oedipus at Colonus, whose disappearance left behind healing waters.

Wittgenstein's posthumous texts, though not designed to express or encourage theory, are not actually mined against its extraction. With Nietzsche, by contrast, the resistance to the continuation of philosophy by ordinary means is built into the text, which is booby-trapped, not only against recovering theory from it, but, in many cases, against any systematic exegesis that assimilates it to theory. His writing achieves this partly by its choice of subject matter, partly by its manner and the attitudes it expresses. These features stand against a mere exegesis of Nietzsche, or the incorporation of Nietzsche into the history of philosophy as a source of theories. Some think that these features stand against the incorporation of Nietzsche into philosophy as an academic enterprise altogether, but if that is meant to imply the unimportance of Nietzsche for philosophy, it must be wrong. In insisting on the importance of Nietzsche for philosophy, I mean something that cannot be evaded by a definition of "philosophy." In particular, it cannot be evaded by invoking some contrast between "analytic" and "continental" philosophy. This classification always involved a quite bizarre conflation of the methodological and the topographical, as though one classified cars into front-wheel drive and Japanese, but besides that and other absurdities of the distinction, there is the more immediate point that no such classification can evade the insistent continuities between Nietzsche's work and the business of what anyone calls philosophy. At least in moral philosophy, to ignore them is not simply to adopt a style, but to duck a problem.

I agree with a remark made by Michel Foucault in a late interview, that there is no single Nietzscheism, and that the right question to ask is "what serious use can Nietzsche be put to?" One serious use is to help us with issues that press on any serious philosophy (in particular, moral philosophy) that does not beg the most basic of its own questions. Nietzsche will not help if he is taken to impose some one method on us. I have already said that I find his texts securely defended against exegesis by the extraction of theory; but it does not follow, and it is important that it does not follow, that when we are trying to put him to serious use our philosophy should contain no theory. This is because the insistent continuities between his questions and our business run in both directions. Some of the concerns to which he speaks are going to be better met—that is to say, met in a way in which we can better make something of them—by quite other styles of thought, and perhaps by some theory of other origins: certainly not by theoretical, or again antitheoretical, incantations supposedly recovered from Nietzsche himself.

NATURALISM AND REALISM IN MORAL PSYCHOLOGY

There is some measure of agreement that we need a "naturalistic" moral psychology, where this means something to the effect that our view of moral capacities should be consistent with, even perhaps in the spirit of, our understanding of human beings as part of nature. A demand expressed in some such terms is perhaps accepted by most philosophers, apart from some *anciens combattants* of the wars of freewill. The trouble with this happy and extensive consensus, however, and no doubt the condition of it, is that no one knows what it involves. Formulations of the position tend to rule out too much or too little. The position rules out too much if it tries reductively to ignore culture and convention; this is misguided even on a scientific basis, in the sense that to live under culture is a basic part of the ethology of this species.[2] It rules out too little if it includes many things that have been part of the self-image of morality, such as certain conceptions of moral cognition; a theory will scarcely further the cause of naturalism in this sense if it accepts as a basic feature of human nature the capacity to intuit the structure of moral reality. It is tempting to say that a naturalistic moral psychology explains moral capacities in terms of psychological structures that are not distinctively moral. But so much turns on what counts as explanation here, and what it is for a psychological element to be distinctively moral, that it remains persistently unclear whether the formula should be taken to be blandly accommodating, or fiercely reductive, or something in between.

The difficulty is systematic. If a "naturalistic" moral psychology has to characterize moral activity in a vocabulary that can be applied equally to every other part of nature, then it is committed to a physicalistic reductionism that is clearly hopeless. If it is to describe moral activity in terms that can be applied to something else, but not everything else, we have not much idea what those terms may be, or how "special" moral activity is allowed to be, consonantly with naturalism. If we are allowed to describe moral activity in whatever terms moral activity may seem to invite, naturalism excludes nothing, and we are back at the beginning. The trouble is that the very term "naturalism" invokes a top-down approach, under which we are supposed already to know what terms are needed to describe any "natural" phenomenon, and we are invited to apply those terms to moral activity. But we do not know what those terms may be, unless they are (uselessly) the terms of physics, and this leads to the difficulty.

In this quandary, we can find in Nietzsche both a general attitude, and some particular suggestions, that can be a great help.[3] I shall say something later about what I take some of his suggestions to be. The general attitude has two relevant aspects, which have to be taken together. First, to the question "how much should our accounts of distinctively moral activity add to our accounts of other human activity?" it replies "as little as possible," and the more that some moral understanding of human beings seems to call on materials that specially serve the purposes of morality—certain conceptions of the will, for instance—the more reason we have to ask whether there may not be a more illuminating account that rests only on conceptions that we use anyway elsewhere. This demand for moral psychological minimalism is not, however, just an application of an Occamist desire for economy, and this is the second aspect of the Nietzschean general attitude. Without some guiding sense of what materials we should use in giving our economical explanations, such an attitude will simply fall back into the difficulties we have already met. Nietzsche's approach is to identify an excess of moral content in psychology by appealing first to what an experienced, honest, subtle and unoptimistic interpretor might make of human behavior elsewhere. Such an interpretor might be said to be—using an obviously and unashamedly evaluative expression—"realistic," and we might say that what this approach leads us toward is a realistic, rather than a naturalistic, moral psychology. What is at issue is not the application of an already defined scientific program, but rather an informed interpretation of some human experiences and activities in relation to others.

Such an approach can indeed be said to involve, in Paul Ricoeur's well-known phrase, a "hermeneutics of suspicion." As such, it cannot compel demonstratively, and does not attempt to do so. It invites one into a perspective, and to some extent a tradition (one marked by such figures as Thucydides, for instance, or Stendhal, or the British psychologists of morals whom Nietzsche described as old frogs), in which what seems to demand more moral material makes sense in terms of what demands less. The enterprise can work, however, only to the extent that the suspicion it summons up is not a suspicion of everything. Writers on Nietzsche typically pay most attention to his claims, or what appear to be his claims, that every belief about the relations of human beings to reality are open to suspicion, that everything is, for instance, an interpretation. Whatever may need to be said at that level, it is equally important that when he says that there are no moral phenomena, only moral interpretations, a *special* point is being made about morality. This does not mean that we should simply forget, even in these connections, the larger claims. We need to get a deeper understanding of where these points of particular suspicion are to be found, and it may be helpful to work through larger claims on a path to getting a grasp on more limited claims. This is particularly so if we bear in mind that "claim," for Nietzsche is in fact rarely the right word. It is not only too weak for some things he says and too strong for others; we can usefully remember, too, (or perhaps pretend) that even when he sounds insistently or shrilly expository, he is not necessarily telling us something, but urging us to ask something.

In the rest of this paper, I shall try to assemble some of Nietzsche's suggestions about a supposed psychological phenomenon, that of willing. I shall leave aside many interesting things that Nietzsche says about this concept, in particular about its history. My aim is to illustrate, through a schematic treatment of this central example, the way in which a method of suspicion—the search, one might almost say, for a culprit—can help us to achieve a reduced and more realistic moral psychology.

ILLUSIONS OF THE SELF

Speaking seriously, there are good reasons why all philosophical dogmatizing, however solemn and definitive its airs used to be, may nevertheless have been no more than a noble childishness and tyronism. And perhaps the time is at hand when it will be comprehended again and again *how little* used to be sufficient to furnish the cornerstone for such sublime and unconditional philosophers' edifices as the dogmatists have built so far; any old popular superstition from time immemorial (like the soul superstition which, in the form of the subject and ego superstition, has not even yet ceased to do mischief); some play on words perhaps, a seduction by grammar, or an audacious generalization of very narrow, very personal, very human, all too human facts. (BGE P)

The general point that Nietzsche makes here (one shared with Wittgenstein, and indeed J. L. Austin, about the extraordinary lightness of philosophical theories) is directed to a particular idea, that the ego or self is some kind of fiction. Later in the same book (BGE 17) he follows Lichtenberg in criticizing the *cogito* as the product of grammatical habit. Elsewhere, he makes a similar point more specifically about action. He quotes a sceptic:

"I do not in the least know what I am doing. I do not in the least know what I ought to do." You are right, but be sure of this: *you are being done* [*du wirst getan*], in every moment. Mankind at all times has mistaken the passive for the active: it is their constant grammatical mistake. (D 120)

Many ideas might be drawn from this complex, some of them uninviting; for instance, that we never really do anything, that no events are actions. More interestingly, Nietzsche can be read as saying that *action* is a serviceable category of interpretation, but a local or dispensable one. This seems to me hardly less implausible, but some have accepted it.[4] If people perform actions, then they perform them because they think or perceive certain things, and this is enough to dispose, further, of a crude epiphenomenalism which might be found in some of Nietzsche's sayings—perhaps in his suggestion that all action is like willing the sun to rise when the sun is just about to rise. (D 124)

Nietzsche's doubts about action are more usefully understood, I suggest, as doubts not about the very idea of anyone's doing anything, but rather about a morally significant interpretation of action, in terms of the will. The belief in the will involves for him two ideas in particular: that the will seems something simple when it is not, and that what seems simple also seems to be a peculiar, imperative, kind of cause.

> Philosophers are accustomed to speak of the will as if it were the best-known thing in the world. . . . But . . . willing seems to me to be above all something *complicated*, something that is a unit only as a word—and it is precisely in this one word that the popular prejudice lurks, which has defeated the always inadequate caution of philosophers. (BGE 19)[5]

He goes on to explain that what is called "willing" is a complex of sensations, thinking, and an affect of command. He points to the consequences of our being both the commanding and the obeying party, and of our "disregarding this duality."

> Since in the great majority of cases there has been an exercise of will only when the effect of the command—that is, obedience; that is, the action—was to be *expected*, the appearance has translated itself into the feeling, as if there were a *necessity of effect*. In short, he who wills believes with a fair amount of certainty that will and action are somehow one; he ascribes the success, the carrying out of the willing, to the will itself, and thereby enjoys an increase of the sensation of power that accompanies all success. (BGE 19)

What exactly is the illusion that Nietzsche claims to expose here? It is not the idea that a certain experience is a sufficient cause of an action. He does indeed think that the experiences involved in "willing" do not reveal, and may conceal, the shifting complex of psychological and physiological forces that lies behind any action, the constant, unknown, craving movements that make us, as he puts it, a kind of polyp (D 119). But it is not that the experience sets itself up as the cause. Rather, the experience seems to reveal a different kind of cause, and suggests that the cause does not lie in any event or state of affairs—whether an experience of mine or otherwise—but in something that I refer to as "I." Such a cause seems to be related to the outcome only in the mode of prescription, through an imperative; and since this stands in no relation to any causal set of events, it can seem to bring about its outcome *ex nihilo*.

Of course, any sensible theory of action, which allows that there is indeed action, and that thoughts are not merely epiphenomenal in relation to it, will have to allow that the consciousness of acting is not the same as a consciousness that a state of mind causes a certain outcome. This follows merely from the point that the first-personal consciousness that one has when involved in action cannot at the same time be a third-personal consciousness of that very involvement. But the first-personal consciousness which an agent necessarily has does not in itself have to lead to the kind of picture that Nietzsche attacks; action does not necessarily involve this understanding of itself.[6] The picture is a special one, particularly associated with a notion such as "willing," and when it is present, it is not merely a philosophical theory of action, but can accompany many of our thoughts and moral reactions. So where does it come from, and what does it do?

Part of Nietzsche's own explanation is to be found in the course of one of his most famous passages:

> For just as the popular mind separates the lightning from its flash, and takes the latter for an *action,* for the operation of a subject called lightning, so popular morality also separates strength from expressions of strength, as if there were a neutral substratum behind the strong man, which was *free* to express strength or not to do so. But there is no such substratum: there is no "being" behind doing, effecting, becoming; "the doer" is merely a fiction added to the deed—the deed is everything. The popular mind in fact doubles the deed; when it sees the lightning flash, it is the deed of a deed: it posits the same event first as cause and then a second time as its effect. (GM I:13)

There are two helpful ideas in this account. One is that the picture under attack involves a kind of double counting. The self or I that is the cause is ingenuously introduced as the cause *of an action.* If my agent-self produces only a set of events, it may seem that I shall not have enough for my involvement in the action: I shall be at best the "pilot in a ship" to which Descartes referred. The same result follows from the idea that the mode of causation is that of command: obedience to a command consists of an action. But commanding is itself an action. The self can act (at one time rather than another, now rather than earlier) only by doing something— the thing it does, willing. In making action into something that introduces an agent-cause, the account has a powerful tendency to produce two actions.

The second helpful thought to be recovered from Nietzsche is that such a peculiar account must have a purpose, and that the purpose is a moral one.

THE TARGET OF BLAME

The purpose of the account can be read from the way in which it associates two ideas, which contribute to its incoherence and together compound it. One idea is that there is a metaphysically special unit, a real action, unlike anything else that can be individuated among the world's processes. The other is that this stands in an unmediated relationship—something like being an effect *ex nihilo*—to something of quite a different kind, again unique—a person, or self, or agent. There is an idea that needs items standing in just such a relation: it is a certain purified conception of blame.

Blame needs an occasion—an action—and a target—the person who did the action and who goes on from the action to meet the blame. That is its nature; as one might say, its conceptual form. It does not need these things in the pure and isolated form implied by the account of the will. The Homeric Greeks blamed people for doing things, and whatever exactly went into their doing so, it was not all this. Rather, this version of the occasion and the target will be demanded by a very purified conception of blame, a conception seemingly demanded by moral justice. It is important that the mere idea of just compensation does not make this demand, nor every idea of responsibility. If A has been damaged by B's careless action, B may be held responsible for the loss and reasonably required to compensate A, though the loss to A formed no part of what B willed. A very exact concentration on B's will, and the purely focused conception of blame that goes with it, are demanded not merely by responsibility or demands in justice for compensation, but by something more specific.

It is not hard to find an explanation of the more specific demand. It lies in the seeming requirement of justice that the agent should be blamed for no more and no less than what was in his power. What the agent brought about (and for which, in the usual order of things, he may be asked to provide compensation) may very well be a matter of luck, but what he may be strictly (as these conceptions say, "morally") blamed for cannot be a matter of luck, and must depend in a strict and isolable sense on his will. It is appropriately said that what depends on his will is what is strictly *in his power*: it is with regard to what he wills that the agent himself has the sense of power in action to which Nietzsche refers. As agents, and also as blamers under justice, we have an interest in this picture.

The needs, demands and invitations of the morality system are enough to explain the peculiar psychology of the will. But there is more that needs to be said about the basis of that system itself. Nietzsche himself famously suggested that a specific source for it was to be found in the sentiment of *ressentiment*—a sentiment which itself had a historical origin, though hardly one that he locates very precisely. I shall not pick up the historical aspect, but I think it is worth suggesting a brief speculation about the phenomenology of focused blame, which is a close enough relation to Nietzsche's "genealogy," perhaps, to be a version of it.[7]

If there is a victim with a complaint for a loss, there is an agent who is to blame, and an act of that agent which brought about the loss. The anger of the victim travels from the loss to the act to the agent; and compensation or recompense given by the agent will acknowledge both the loss and the fact that he was the cause of the loss. Suppose the agent brings about a harm to the victim, and does so intentionally and voluntarily; where "intentionally and voluntarily" is not supposed to invoke the special mechanisms of the will, but merely means that the agent knew what he was doing, wanted to do it, and was in a normal state of mind when he did it. Suppose that the agent is not disposed to give compensation or reparation, and that the victim has no power to extract any such thing from him. In refusing reparation, the agent refuses to acknowledge the victim or his loss; it is a peculiarly vivid demonstration of the victim's powerlessness.

These circumstances can give rise, in the victim or in someone else on behalf of the victim, to a very special fantasy of retrospective prevention. As victim, I have a fantasy of inserting into the agent an acknowledgment of me, to take the place of exactly the act that harmed me. I want to think that he might have acknowledged me, that he might have been prevented from harming me. But the idea cannot be that I might in some empirical way have prevented him: that idea presents only a regret that it was not actually so and, in these circumstances, a reminder of humiliation. The idea has to be, rather, that I, now, might change the agent from one who did not acknowledge me to one who did. This fantasied, magical, change does not involve actually changing anything, and it therefore has nothing to do with what, if anything, might actually have changed things. It requires simply the idea of the agent at the moment of the action, of the action that harmed me, and of the refusal of that action, all isolated from the network of circumstances in which his action was actually embedded. It involves precisely the picture of the will that has already been uncovered.

Much can grow from this basic feeling. It lays the foundation for the purest and simplest construction of punishment, and it is very significant how the language of retribution naturally deploys teleological notions of conversion, education, or improvement ("teaching him a lesson," "showing him") while insisting at the same time that its gaze is entirely retrospective and that, inasmuch as it is purely retributive, it does not look to actual reform.[8] But the construction is at least as much at work when it is not a question of any actual punishment, but only of the purely moral conceptions of guilt and blame, and it then involves a further abstraction; it introduces not only retribution's idea of retrospective causation, but morality's idea of an authoritative but sanctionless law, of a judgment that carries no power except that judgment itself.

CONCLUSION

This is, of course, only a sketch of a possible account, drawn (fairly directly) from Nietzschean materials. The most important feature of it, for the present purpose, is its structure. We start with a supposed psychological phenomenon, willing, associated with the conception of the self in action. The phenomenon seems recognizable in experience, and it seems also to have a certain authority. Its description already presents difficulties and obscurities, but proposals merely to explain it away or to ignore it seem typically to have ignored something important, even to leave out the essence of action. Reminded both that different pictures of action have been held in other cultures, and that the notion of action itself is less than transparent, we can be helped to see that the integrity of action, the agent's genuine presence in it, can be preserved without this picture of the will. The process by which we can come to see this may be complex and painful enough for us to feel, not just that we have learned a truth, but that we have been relieved of a burden.

Since the picture is neither coherent nor universal, yet has this authority, we need to ask where it comes from and what it does. It is not itself manifestly tied to morality, offering rather a picture of voluntary action in general, but there is a moral phenomenon, a certain conception of blame, which it directly fits. This conception, again, is not universal, but is rather part of a special complex of ethical ideas which has other, and related, peculiar features. The fit between the special psychological conception and the demands of morality enables us to see that this piece of psychology is itself a moral conception, and one that shares notably doubtful features of that particular morality itself. In addition to this, we may be able to supply some further psychological conceptions which help us to understand the motivations of this particular form of the ethical. Those conceptions, as presented by Nietzsche under the name of *ressentiment,* certainly lead out of the ethical altogether, into the categories of anger and power, and it cannot be a matter simply for philosophy to decide how much those categories will explain. Other explanations may be needed, and it may be that they will prove to be more basically linked to notions of fairness, for instance. But in laying such explanations against one another, and in diagnosing the psychology of willing as a demand of the morality system itself, we shall be following a distinctively Nietzschean route toward the naturalization of moral psychology.

NOTES

1. Even when we leave aside the point that there is only one work by Nietzsche (*The Will to Power*) that is not a work by Nietzsche, the later works of Wittgenstein are, as whole books, very variably his.

2. I have discussed this point at greater length in "Making Sense of Humanity" in *The Boundaries of Humanity: Humans, Animals, Machines,* ed. James J. Sheehan and Morton Sosna (Berkeley, Los Angeles, London: University of California Press, 1991).

3. It will be obvious that Nietzsche's interest is located by the present discussion mostly in terms of his more "skeptical" works, rather than in (for instance) his ideas of self-overcoming. This is not to deny that they, too, can have their uses. In any case, there is no hope of getting anything from those ideas without setting them against his accounts of familiar morality.

4. For example, Frithjof Bergmann, "Nietzsche's Critique of Morality," in *Read-*

ing Nietzsche, ed. Robert C. Solomon and Kathleen M. Higgins (New York: Oxford University Press, 1988). Bergmann includes "individual agency" (along with such items as selfhood, freedom, and guilt) in a list of concepts allegedly special to our morality; he takes himself (wrongly, I think) to be following Clifford Geertz in the claim that it was not known in traditional Bali. Similar errors have been made about the outlook of Homeric Greece: see below, note 9. The idea that *action,* in our ordinary understanding of it, is a dispensable and indeed mistaken conception is shared by a very different kind of philosophy, eliminative materialism; in that case for scientific reasons.

5. The whole section is relevant.

6. This is clearly illustrated by the treatment accorded by some scholars to the Homeric conception of action; not finding in Homer this picture of action, they have thought that the archaic Greeks either had no idea of action, or had an imperfect one, lacking the concept of will. I discuss this and related misconceptions in *Shame and Necessity* (Berkeley, Los Angeles, Oxford: University of California Press, 1993); see in particular chap. 2.

7. A Nietzschean genealogy typically combines, in a way that analytical philosophy finds embarrassing, history, phenomenology, "realistic" psychology, and conceptual interpretation. The historical stories, moreover, strikingly vary from one context to another. Some of Nietzsche's procedures are to be seen specifically in the light of Hegel's *Phenomenology,* and of his recurrent amazement that there could have been such a thing as Christianity. Some are certainly less helpful than others. But the mere idea that we need such elements to work together is surely right. We need to understand what parts of our conceptual scheme are, in what degree, culturally local. We understand this best when we understand an actual human scheme that differs from ours in certain respects. One very important way of locating such a scheme is finding it in history, in particular in the history of our own. In order to understand that other scheme, and to understand why there should be this difference between them and us, we need to understand it as a human scheme; this is to understand the differences in terms of similarities, which calls on psychological interpretation. Very roughly speaking indeed: a Nietzschean genealogy can be seen now as starting from Davidson plus history.

8. A particularly illuminating example is Robert Nozick's discussion of retributive punishment in *Philosophical Explanations* (New York: Oxford University Press, 1984), pp. 363 ff. His heroic attempt to express what pure retribution tries to *achieve* (as opposed to what, in actual fact, it does) reveals, it seems to me, that there is no logical space for it to succeed.

PART TWO

Genealogy and Philosophy

FOURTEEN

Nietzsche, Hume, and the Genealogical Method

David Couzens Hoy

Genealogy is for Nietzsche a way of doing philosophy that shows not only the inadequacy of traditional metaphysics or "first philosophy" but also the prospects for nonmetaphysical philosophy. In the preface to the *Genealogy of Morals* (§4) he says his own adaptation of the method of genealogy was motivated by his reaction to Paul Rée's *Origin of the Moral Sensations*. This "upside-down and perverse species of genealogical hypothesis, the genuinely *English* type," is criticized for being too unhistorical, haphazard, or random. What is perverse is Rée's social-Darwinian hypothesis that the most recent product of human evolution is, because of the survival of the fittest, also the highest product of human evolution. Nietzsche parodies Rée cruelly in laughing at the idea that the fittest and highest human type is the modern "moral milksop" (*Moral-Zärtling*, GM P:7) who thinks of morality as "selflessness, self-sacrifice, or sympathy and pity" (GS 345). Equally perverse and "English" is Rée's own "refined indolence," his inability to take the problems of morality seriously.

In a manner that English-speakers tend to find typically "German," Nietzsche insists on taking *extremely* seriously the problems of morality, or more accurately, morality itself as a problem. I will assume that when Nietzsche criticizes Rée for being too much like the English psychologists, Nietzsche has the doctrines of Englishmen like Herbert Spencer in mind.[1] But the method of inquiring into the "origins" of moral ideas is presumably a general one, and more notable British philosophers are also genealogists. To show this, I take David Hume as a prime example. Commentators like Arthur Danto and Mary Warnock have noted similarities between Nietzsche and Hume on epistemological topics, but there is a more general methodological kinship between the two, particularly when their views on morality are considered as well.[2]

Nietzschean genealogy is like British genealogy in being a form of what Hume called "experimental reasoning," formulating hypotheses about what causes could have led to given effects. The method for Hume provides a common basis for doing both epistemology and ethics, and the *Treatise on Human Nature* is subtitled *An attempt to introduce the experimental method of reasoning into moral subjects.*[3] Comparing not their moral theories so much as their applications of the method to particular examples, however, there is an obvious difference in that Nietzsche does not imitate Hume's detached, observational tone or the British pretension to neutral, value-free description. On the contrary, Nietzsche wants genealogy to be as value-laden as possible. Not only does he want genealogy to investigate the question of the value of morality, he also intends for it to come up with a definite valuation of the traditional moral virtues and principles. In particular, he plans it to be not simply a descriptive but also a prescriptive (or at least critical) inversion of *both* the good-natured "English" pessimism of Rée and the world-weary German pessimism of Schopenhauer.[4]

Since Rée was already using the genealogical method, and since Nietzsche implies Rée was simply borrowing that method from the English, Nietzsche is not claiming to be the first to discover and use genealogy. Yet he does suggest in section four of the preface to the *Genealogy* that hitting on this method allowed him to bring together in a coherent framework points that were scattered in previous works. The method thus enables him to synthesize not only his views about the nature of morality, as in this work, but also his other systematic views insofar as they were to be unified by the hypothesis of the will to power as the principle for the application of the genealogical method.

Since the validity of genealogy as a method does not necessarily depend on the soundness of the theory of the will to power, however, in this essay I discuss two features of the method which undermine any pretensions of the will to power to be a quasi-metaphysical doctrine. I maintain that genealogy need not be affirmative in the sense of asserting specific substantive doctrines but in the sense of being heuristically feasible. First, drawing on recent French poststructuralist readings of Nietzsche (but with critical reservations), I will be considering how genealogy is a philosophical tool that is at once antimetaphysical and nonmetaphysical. Since the preface of the *Genealogy* singles out Schopenhauer as the crucial test of the method, the analyses of Schopenhauer's ascetic ideals in sections 4–8 of the third essay are of particular importance. Nietzsche there uses the method wittily to bring out the extent to which Schopenhauer's metaphysical longings and ideals were a product of sexual desires, of what Schopenhauer called "the vile urgency of the will" (GM III:6). Without supplanting Schopenhauer's metaphysics of the will with yet another metaphysics, then, Nietzsche will use genealogy to destroy metaphysics altogether. Genealogy itself becomes a way to do nonmetaphysical philosophy.

Hume's own method of experimental reasoning is also intended to consign metaphysics to the flames, and to show reason to be the product of bodily instinct. The method allows him to inquire into the origin of morals without assuming as his contemporaries did that the virtuous dispositions were implanted in all of us by a divine creator. The degree of methodological similarity between Hume and Nietzsche is thus the second feature to be considered. In both cases the method is hypothetical, tracing ideas back to psychological impressions, and finding like causes for like effects. Perhaps an even better example of how close Nietzsche's use of the method comes to Hume's is the "genealogy" of religion offered by Hume's character Philo at the conclusion of his *Dialogues Concerning Natural Religion* (part XII). There Philo traces the ideas and practices of religion back to the impression of terror, produced in states of illness and depression. Religion, suggests Philo, has little force and relevance in normal health and in the cheerful conduct of everyday affairs, Hume's insistence on which Nietzsche would again consider typically British. Of course, Nietzsche takes particular pains in the preface to distinguish his genealogies from those of the British, and he is especially right about Hume in remarking on the unhistorical character of their psychological studies. Nietzsche's own genealogies, however, do not provide the detailed historical studies the preface calls for, and I cannot see that they are less psychologically speculative than Hume's.[5]

METHODOLOGICAL SELF-JUSTIFICATION

When Nietzsche attempts to justify his new method metaphilosophically, he sometimes claims that genealogy cuts through deceptive appearances until it sees the phenomena as they really are. This realist claim appears to fall back into metaphysics when the principle of will to power is posited as that which lies behind every phenomenon. Nietzsche sometimes makes this claim by drawing an analogy between genealogy and philology, where by philology he means close, accurate reading. In the preface to the *Genealogy* he states that the third essay is a paradigm of his own method of reading, and thus an example of how to read him. Presumably the readers of a genealogical analysis will themselves have to practice genealogy in the act of reading. Nietzsche may have developed his own aphoristic style because it requires readers to practice the genealogical method of reading:

> An aphorism . . . has not been "deciphered" when it has simply been read; rather, one has then to begin its *interpretation*,[6] for which is required an art of interpretation. I have offered in the third essay of the present book an ex-

ample of what I regard as "interpretation" in such a case. . . . To be sure, one thing is necessary above all if one is to practice reading as an *art* in this way, . . . something for which one has almost to be a cow and in any case *not* a "modern man": *rumination.* (GM P:8)

This passage shows the intimate connection for Nietzsche between genealogy and the process of reading and interpreting in general, a connection that is anticipated by sections 373 and 374 of book five of *The Gay Science.* Here he attacks both Spencer's moral philosophy and materialist, mechanistic philosophy of science. He thinks both divest existence of its "rich ambiguity" by trying to reduce it to frameworks that not only are simplistic and "meaningless" but also fail to recognize that "science" is only one possible *interpretation* of the world, and a "*most stupid*" one at that (GS 373).

What grounds does Nietzsche have, however, for preferring his own readings and interpretations to those of Spencer and the positivists? He wrestles with this question in section 374, "*Our new 'infinite'.*" Here he raises all the difficulties his genealogical theory of reading implies, but elusively and without taking the stand we would expect. After rejecting the reductionists who insist that "mechanics is the doctrine of the first and last laws on which all existence must be based as on a ground floor," he asks whether we need to think that there is any ground floor for our perspectives or interpretations. Since we could not get out of our own conceptual framework to ask how reality would be independent of that framework, he infers that whether reality exists independently of our interpretations, or even whether the very idea of uninterpretable reality makes sense "cannot be decided." That is, we cannot decide either that "existence without interpretation, without 'sense,' " is " 'nonsense,' " or that all existence is interpretive in essence.

Why does he insist on this undecidability when he seems already to have decided? That there is no ground floor to interpretation, but only interpretation all the way down, should be a liberating thought. He knows, however, that to claim the essence of existence is such that there are only interpretations would be tantamount to saying paradoxically that the essence of things is not to have an essence. Moreover, if we cannot say anything about things as they are independently of our interpretations, then he recognizes that a Kantian would insist that we also cannot deny that the things might involve relations other than those we attribute to them. The next few lines give us a clue to why he lets himself get caught in the Kantian dilemma when he clearly believes in the richly interpretational character of our cognitive and moral capacities. Instead of speaking mainly about interpretations in these lines, he speaks about perspectives, thus suggesting (mistakenly, I will argue) that the terms perspective and interpretation are interchangeable with no significant differences. He says first that we are trapped in our own human perspectives: "The human intellect cannot avoid seeing itself in its own perspectives, and *only* in these." From the thought that we cannot get out of our own corner I would have expected him to narrow down the possibilities of interpretation to our best-confirmed hypotheses, and thus to avoid relativism. Instead he insists we shun the "ridiculous immodesty that would be involved in decreeing from our corner that perspectives are permitted only from this corner."

Why, however, should we *not* embrace this immodesty? Nietzsche is hardly a person to praise modesty. Is immodesty here really ridiculous? For some people to refuse to recognize the possibility of other people having some different perspectives could, of course, be narrow-minded and dogmatic. In this passage, however, the question is about perspectives other than those a *human* intellect could possibly have. Yet the idea of a conceptual scheme other than the human is difficult and perhaps impossible for us to render intelligible,[7] Nietzsche could have insisted more strongly that positing an uninterpretable reality independent of our sense-making faculties indeed cannot make sense, and that for something to count as making sense it must first be part of an interpretation.

Nietzsche seems to have been led by his notion of perspective into a logical corner. He expresses the dilemma characteristically well: "Rather has the world become 'infinite' for us all over again, inasmuch as we cannot reject the possibility that *it may include infinite interpretations*. Once more we are seized by a great shudder . . ." (GS 374). Interestingly enough, Nietzsche is himself sometimes interpreted today, especially in France, as the proponent of the possibility of infinite interpretations.[8] Yet here the thought leads to a shudder, and to the recognition that if the infinity of interpretation cannot be rejected, it also cannot be so easily accepted. Why is there a shudder? The passage suggests two reasons. First, there would be too many possibilities of interpretation, which is itself a nauseating possibility because it includes so many nauseating interpretations. Second, there would be no grounds for rejecting interpretations just because they were nauseating, since they could nevertheless be right.

The worry here is that the idea of an infinity of perspectives on reality makes reality not only unknowable but also unintelligible, because contradictory interpretations would be equally possible. This idea is itself indigestible, even after long rumination. Notice that Nietzsche speaks of "our *new* 'infinite,' " of the world becoming infinite for us "*all over again*." He realizes that the thought of infinite interpretations could tempt us to "deify again after the old manner *this* monster of an unknown world" (Nietzsche's emphasis).

The problem of the unknowability of the world arises because a perspectival theory of knowledge usually involves thinking of the mind as representing reality. On this representational model the only way to question the accuracy of representations is to represent the initial representation. This process of representing representations can go on without limit, and we would still not have proved the correspondence of our representations to reality as it is independently of our representations. The shudder is thus a logical one, and results from the threat posed by this infinite regress.

A possible psychological reaction to this logical difficulty is to resort to metaphysics and posit reality as a nonphenomenal domain that is unknowable but at least harmonious with our own purposes. Nietzsche thinks this Kantian tactic is now bankrupt, since metaphysics could not claim to know that the unknowable is unified, single, and harmonious rather than multiple, incoherent, and horrible. Probably reflecting on Schopenhauer's substitution of blind, chaotic will for Kant's rational, holy will, Nietzsche concludes that the unknown so construed could include infinite interpretation in the sense of "too many *ungodly* possibilities of interpretation," "too much deviltry, stupidity, and foolishness of interpretation."

An alternative to the logical and metaphysical shudder is suggested by Nietzsche's own images, but in a way he does not exploit in section 374. If we should conclude that we are necessarily confined to our own corner, then it ceases to be a corner. We can decide *both* that there is no uninterpretable reality and that there is no unintelligible infinity of interpretations. For if existence is not unknowable (or at least, not uninterpretable), but indeed exists only insofar as it is interpreted, then only an intelligibly finite and not an infinite range of interpretation is really possible for us.

Of course, narrowing down the range of possible interpretations from infinity would not help much if the range turned out to be finite, but indefinite. The insistence on infinity is one form of methodological, "Pyrrhonian" skepticism, since it says that the range of interpretations is unbounded in principle. That is, interpretations are not constrained in any identifiable respects by that which they interpret. On this view, our present interpretations could be succeeded by completely incommensurable ones. A more *modest* skepticism would recognize that future interpretations would not be total revisions of our current ones, but would incorporate much of what is taken as true in the current ones. However, these interpretations could themselves be succeeded by further ones that had only the vaguest family resemblance to present ones, until finally interpretations were produced that had little in common with present ones. Two arguments against skepticism are required: one that the range of interpretations is not infinite, and another that it is not indefinite. I think infinity of interpretation is in principle impossible, but I do not know of an *a priori* argument that indefiniteness is any more than improbable in practice. However, if indefinite proliferation is practically improbable, as I will argue, that suffices to block these skeptical and nihilist worries.

GENEALOGY AS HERMENEUTICS

While Nietzsche's rhetoric sometimes leads him into logical corners he knows he should avoid, his understanding of genealogy contains other ways of avoiding such corners. What I wish to argue is that if he had fully developed his account of the nature of interpretation, he would have come up with the notion of the hermeneutic circle. And since circles have no corners, he could not have backed into the logical difficulties he encounters when he tries to provide metaphilosophical justifications of his genealogical method.

Let me proceed by drawing a sharper contrast than Nietzsche does between the notions of perspective and interpretation. To someone trained in the "English" philosophical tradition with its empiricist background, the term perspective connotes a visual relation between a perceiver and a thing perceived. The thing perceived is itself usually thought of as a medium-sized physical object. Nietzsche's appeal to perspectivism then appears as an antidote to the rationalist tendency to project an aperspectival, godlike comprehension of the whole. In contrast to the metaphysical belief that there is only one correct description capturing reality in its own terms, perspectivism implies that there can be many different perspectives on the same thing. Since Nietzsche's perspectivism extends beyond simple epistemological cases to scientific theories and even to moral systems, however, the original connection between the point of view and the comprehended reality becomes metaphorical and tenuous. The reason that the perception of medium-sized physical objects under normal conditions seems unproblematic is that the verification procedures are reasonably well satisfied simultaneously with the act of perception. But Nietzsche's perspectivism does not imply that these verification procedures serve to validate all knowledge. On the contrary, verification procedures are both internal and relative to the particular kinds of perspectives. There is no general epistemology to specify a single verification procedure that any particular perspective would have to satisfy.

I think this account of what Nietzsche is saying is standard, and its obvious paradoxes are fully exploited by him. What is not so obvious is the sense in which perspectivism preserves what it appears to negate. Let me use a term of Hilary Putnam's and call the view that is usually contrasted with perspectivism "metaphysical realism."[9] This is the view that reality may be different from the way it appears to us, and that our scientific terms refer only to these phenomena, not to the things as they are in themselves. A consequence of metaphysical realism is that our best-confirmed physical theories could be completely wrong, even in the long run. But perspectivism also leads to this skeptical conclusion. Perspectivism is often construed as implying that there is a thing that can be validly grasped from different perspectives, and is thus independent of any particular perspective. More problematically, the idea of different perspectives implies that *from within* a given perspective, especially a complex, long-standing, and heuristically successful one, there are respects in which the perspective would inevitably be inadequate, distorting, and even wrong. Furthermore, since verification procedures are internal to perspectives, there would be no way ever to rectify these deficiencies.

What I have just described is close to Hume's position that we will never get in touch with the "secret springs" of the world. How he even knew there were secret "springs" if causation is only a subjective and never an objective property is, of course, the question Kant raised. I think that genealogy ought not to be defended by appeal to perspectivism. Perspectivism is too weak a justification for genealogy, because the genealogist does claim to be capturing the phenomenon as it really is. Genealogy is *not* simply another perspective. How the genealogist could make this claim as a perspectivist is not clear. Why would the genealogist need to think of the genealogical discovery as another perspective? Only, I think, as the result of some metaphilosophical reflection whereby the genealogist is asked to justify the outcome of the analysis. A thoroughgoing genealogist could avoid metaphilosophy altogether by suggesting that the only way to challenge the results of one genealogical analysis would be to produce another genealogical analysis either of the original phenomenon or of the initial genealogical account itself. Genealogy is not easy to do successfully, and I see no *a priori* reason to believe there is an infinite regress here. The challenge is a practical one, and in practice there would have to be strong motivation to attempt a genealogy of a genealogy. Even with strong motivation, moreover, the second-order genealogy will not necessarily succeed. If it does succeed, then we will be concerned with the substance of its concrete findings, and metaphilosophical justification will be unnecessary.

As two French Nietzsche scholars, Jean Granier and Sarah Kofman, have both brought out, Nietzsche sometimes offers an alternative account of genealogy.[10] Instead of thinking of genealogy as a perspective, he often suggests that it is simply good, rigorous philology. The *Genealogy*'s third essay, the paradigm case of genealogy, is thus construed not as incorrigible perception, but as close reading. One advantage of this way of thinking of genealogy is that metaphilosophical justification is beside the point if the genealogical analysis appears compelling. Another advantage of this more hermeneutical and less epistemological understanding of the genealogical method is that Nietzsche thereby avoids the paradoxes of perspectivism and the metaphorics of vision by construing the phenomenon not as a physical object but as a text. Traditional problems about how the senses can be known to be in touch with the object, or how the mental hooks up with the physical, are now circumvented. A text is a physical object in some minimal sense (black marks on a page, for instance), but that is an uninteresting sense. We do not read black marks on a page, we read sentences. Texts come to be only in readings and have no existence independent of readings. Of course, the same text occurs in different readings, but there is no special problem as there was for the empiricists in explaining what "same" means. To know two interpreters are talking about the same text even though they read it somewhat differently is just to know that despite their differences, their readings agree for the most part on much of what is going on in the text. The text is the product of a reading, and in the hermeneutical process of reading, interpreting, and understanding there is no mental-physical dichotomy, as well as no problem about a gap between our knowledge and the given.

GENEALOGY AS CRITIQUE

I think it is significant, then, that in the preface to the *Genealogy* Nietzsche avoids the earlier problems of *The Gay Science* and does not suggest that his genealogy of morals is just a perspective. Calling genealogy an art of reading and interpretation rather than a science does not mean that "anything goes." On the contrary, he says "no" to every aspect of Paul Rée's genealogy, thus implying he believes genealogies can be wrong, and that his own is better than any alternatives of which he knows. Of course, there are different ways for genealogies to be wrong. They may be wrong by not corresponding to the facts, but they may also be wrong by being shallow and leaving important questions unexplained. For instance, Rée and Spencer take for granted the value of altruism, without asking the question *why* altruism should be morally valued. Nietzsche's criticism of Rée is reminiscent of Kant's complaint that teleological, heteronomous moral theories (like Hume's, for instance) do not explain *why* helping others is moral. Hume's genealogy of morals traces our moral beliefs back to personal sentiments, such as sympathy for our fellows, and then argues that these sentiments are universal. Thus, Hume's genealogy of morals goes into great detail about how moral qualities are useful to ourselves and others. His genealogy itself will have some effect on our moral actions, since by having a clearer idea about the origin of our actions we may decide to cultivate certain qualities rather than others. For example, in describing virtue according to the degree of usefulness, Hume says we may be inclined to give money to beggars because of our desire to help them, but may cease giving money if we find out that we are not really helping but hurting them by encouraging habits not really useful to them.[11]

Although this example is not one of Hume's more felicitous ones, I cite it because it is especially susceptible to Nietzsche's criticisms of the utilitarians. In *Daybreak* (230) Nietzsche complains against the utilitarians that sentiments crisscross, and what seems useful to one person will seem wrong to another for that same reason. Genealogy thus cannot stop with identifying what is useful, but must identify that in terms of which we can say something is genuinely useful or not. Neither utility nor pleasure are stable and informative enough to provide a ground floor for a universal ethical theory.

While this objection to Hume echoes Kant, Nietzsche is equally critical of Kant's universalistic moral theory. Kant's conception of moral personality points beyond the phenomenal world to a noumenal or intelligible world we supposedly inhabit as well, and from which we give ourselves our moral laws. Nietzschean genealogy follows Hegel's and Schopenhauer's criticisms of this idea of reason as an autonomous law-giver. Genealogy undercuts the motive behind metaphysics by showing that Kant's projection of a two-world view as the presupposition of morality can itself be explained as an attempt to escape the recognition that the phenomenal world is for us the only intelligible world.

Although Nietzsche shares Kant's rejection of Hume's appeal to utility and pleasure, Nietzsche's "method of ethics" goes beyond both Hume's and Kant's. Kant's arguments are transcendental ones. That is, they start from some feature of experience we take as essential and then argue that if we are to speak, think, and act as we do, we must also believe certain other features also obtain. Thus, for the Kantian if we make moral judgments, we must believe we are free; and since as phenomenal beings we are not free, we must believe we are free in some other world than this one. While Nietzsche's critical arguments are sometimes transcendental in form, their *purpose* differs from that of these conceptual ones. Nietzsche's arguments do not simply confirm that our ways of speaking, thinking, and acting are intelligible in the same terms in which we describe them to ourselves. Genealogy tends to find an incoherence in our own self-understanding (for instance, between our various self-descriptions, or between the way we think and the way we act) and then to show how that incoherence is produced from within us. Rather than confirm the adequacy of our present self-descriptions and the coherence of our practices, genealogy makes us more intelligible to ourselves by showing us the *inadequacy* of our present self-understandings and practices, and then giving an interpretation of how such an inadequacy could have come about.

I stress that Nietzsche is giving an interpretation, not an explanation of the sort that would deduce a single necessary conclusion from universal principles and observable facts. Furthermore, there are counterfactual elements in the interpretation. To understand how something could have come about implies that a different outcome was also possible. But even Hume's genealogies do not result in interpretations in this sense. He calls his reasoning experimental, in that moral ideas can be traced back to moral sentiments we can identify in ourselves. He believes further that a sentiment such as sympathy is universal, and constant enough to constitute the basis for generalizable moral judgments. There is thus an important difference in both form and content between Hume's and Nietzsche's use of the hypothetical method. In content, placing *ressentiment* rather than Hume's universal sympathy at the origin of morality leads Nietzsche to reject the universal status of ethics. A distinction like that between the values of the noble and the values of the slavish calls into question Hume's claim that there are natural (psychologically universal) as well as artificial (socially useful) virtues. If the virtues of the nobles are more natural than those of the slaves, they are not invariable features of human nature since slave morality can corrupt and replace them.

The arguments against the utility of particular virtues will also be different in form. Nietzsche says, for instance, that asceticism is the result of willing nothingness rather than not willing (GM III:28). Such a claim is both weaker and stronger than Hume's. It is weaker in that it does not claim to be identifying psychological facts. We are not aware psychologically of willing nothingness, and Nietzsche's suggestion that we are willing nothingness although we are not aware of doing so is just an interpretation of what we are willing. The psychological fact is that we think we are willing something. The interpretation is that contrary to what we think, we are really willing nothingness.

But in another respect Nietzsche's claim is stronger than Hume's. As in Kant, there is some logical consideration involved, for supposedly we *must*, on reflection, come to accept Nietzsche's interpretation rather than our own of what we are doing. For instance, the claim is that we are willing nothingness rather than doing something else, namely, not willing. But of course it is impossible not to will. We could perhaps try not to will, knowing that trying is already willing, and therefore that in trying not to will, we fail in not willing. But Nietzsche follows Kant in believing that it is irrational to try to do the impossible. So the alternative of not willing is inevitably counterfactual. Willing nothingness turns out to be an alternative that is *forced* on the ascetic. But a lifetime of willing nothingness is impossible in practice, and would be self-defeating. Nietzsche thus derives what Kant called an *absurdum practicum* to show the incoherence of the attempt to put a certain theory into practice throughout a life.[12] While different in purpose from Kant's use of transcendental arguments in ethics, Nietzsche's arguments nevertheless share with them this kinship in structure.

THE FEASIBILITY OF GENEALOGICAL INTERPRETATIONS

Because Hume's genealogies, in contrast to Nietzsche's counterfactual ones, are factual and experimental, they are defeasible. The inductive generalizations can be falsified. Thus, if we found a tribe of human beings (for instance, the Ik) lacking the sentiments of humanity and sympathy, Hume's hypothesis of the universality of moral sentiment would have to be discarded (unless he is allowed to salvage his theory with the *ad hoc* stipulation that the repugnant mores of the Ik are caused only by extreme scarcity).[13] Nietzsche's genealogical hypothesis that the will to power is at the basis of all formations of the will cannot be similarly falsified. For one thing, will to power is not equivalent to a psychological state. Even people who conceived of themselves as out for power could be mistaken. For another, showing people that their moral values really express, say, *ressentiment* rather than Humean sympathy, is not likely to be confirmed by their agreement. They are probably going to find the interpretation implausible, and even if they were to assent, that assent would itself have to be interpreted in turn to see if it was motivated by *ressentiment*. How a Nietzschean genealogy of a particular case could be confirmed or disconfirmed is not at all clear. If the confirmation is itself only a further interpretation, then there seems to be no end to the task. Nietzsche's shudder suggests he does not accept that result willingly, so we must look elsewhere for the answer.

One point to notice is that what is being interpreted is itself an interpretation. This is not to say there are not some facts. There are facts that any interpretation would have to take into account. These facts would be, for instance, the psychological ones about the self-descriptions of the agents. But those facts themselves are only part of an interpretation, namely, the agent's self-interpretation. The facts might be the sorts of sentences the agent utters about itself, and the self-interpretation would be the reconstructed account of how these utterances fit together systematically into a coherent self-understanding. Other facts might include the social actions of the agents of a particular society, and a social self-understanding could also be constructed. But the genealogist need not accept either the individual agent's or the group's self-interpretations as the last word. The genealogist can try to build an interpretation that will take account of the agents' self-interpretations and at the same time explain what the genealogist takes to be a further fact, namely, that there are basic incoherencies in these self-interpretations. The genealogist can even explain why these incoherencies were themselves not explicit for the agents. That is, the genealogist's interpretation makes plausible *both* why the agents did not understand themselves the way the genealogist does, and nevertheless why they *could* have understood themselves as the genealogist does.

For Nietzschean genealogy it is thus not entirely right to say there are no facts, only interpretations. There are facts, but only insofar as they inhere in interpretations. The interpretation will determine what counts as a fact. Thus, the ascetic moralist will believe certain things to be valuable, and will have an interpretation, whether implicit or explicit, of why these beliefs are reasonable. For the genealogist there is another interpretation of these beliefs that is more reasonable than the moralist's own interpretation and that explains both why the beliefs were believed at one time, and why they are no longer believed.

So interpretations are defeasible, although not because particular beliefs can be shown to be false in isolation from any interpretation. Interpretations can be shown to be superior to other interpretations if they explain features of these interpretations that could be perceived as problems for the interpretation from within, but for specifiable reasons are not so perceived. Hegel, of course, had used this strategy before Nietzsche, but Nietzsche demurs, as far as I can see, from any attempt to show a dialectical transition between the earlier and the later interpretations, such that the earlier necessarily evolves into the later. As detailed cultural analysis Nietzschean genealogy could establish empirical plausibility, but not logical or dialectical necessity. Genealogy is not dialectical, and does not assert a general teleology (even though there may be *internal* teleologies, as, for instance, in the devolution of Platonism first into Christianity and then into explicit nihilism).

What, however, is the test for the critical dimension of Nietzschean genealogy? Even though by avoiding an epistemological doctrine like perspectivism Nietzsche could avoid many familiar epistemological problems, there are other kinds of problems with a hermeneutical reformulation of the genealogical method. Most troublesome is how the genealogist is to justify the inference that some interpretations are better than others. The genealogist is forced to have preferences. For instance, genealogical philosophy is preferred to metaphysical (or "first") philosophy that seeks to ground certainty through presuppositionless foundations or incorrigible axioms. If every philosophical theory (counting *both* genealogy and metaphysics as philosophical theories) is an interpretation, what is the basis for preferring the hermeneutical view that there are no noninterpretive theories over the dogmatic view that there must be only one right theory? The attempt to construct a theory that is not just another interpretation is not obviously incoherent even if so far it has not been successful.

The genealogist has preferences for certain sorts of theories and values but ought not to smuggle these preferences into the genealogical analysis by presupposing *a priori* schemas or moral standards. Sarah Kofman accounts for the genealogist's preferences of some interpretations over others by distinguishing the conditions holding for first-order interpretations from those holding for second-order ones.[14] The first-order interpretations are the immediate result of the instinctual need to make life intelligible. The second-order interpretations of these first-order ones often mask the interpretive character of the first.

This suggestion is a fruitful one, and I would like to take it one step further by noting how Nietzsche's insistence on honesty can be converted into a methodological principle for rationally preferring some interpretations to others. A strict philology should be honest with itself, and this means two things. First, it should present its interpretation explicitly as an interpretation. This recognition might seem implicitly relativistic or even nihilistic insofar as it seems to be an admission of the arbitrariness of the genealogical account. However, the second feature of methodological honesty is that the relation between the interpretation and that which is interpreted should *not* be arbitrary, or at least it should be supportable by rational argument. What is being interpreted is itself a given interpretation, and the second-order interpretation is asserting itself to be a nonarbitrary and indeed valid account of the advantages and disadvantages of the first-order interpretation.

Kofman, however, takes her own interpretation yet another step further, and in so doing, I think, goes *beyond* Nietzsche. Kofman thinks a satisfactory middle ground between dogmatism and relativism is pluralism. What distinguishes healthful from sick (life-affirming from life-abnegating) interpretations on her account is that the former are deliberately an active "multiplying of perspectives" to enrich and embellish life.[15]

On *Nietzschean* grounds there are two difficulties with this pluralism. First, it obscures the basic difficulty about preferring an interpretation to another. For to say that the life-affirming interpretations are those that multiply rather than inhibit the formation of other interpretations is simply *to prefer* pluralistic interpretations of interpretation to nonpluralistic ones. Insofar as multiplying perspectives or interpretations is only a criterion for discriminating among *second-order* interpretations, it does not serve the genealogist in critically evaluating the *first-order* interpretations. So although I think Kofman is right to suggest that the will to power is not asserted by Nietzsche as a dogmatic "truth," but only as an interpretive hypothesis, I think something must also be said about how hypotheses are tested and how one determines their utility. She suggests that Nietzsche's hypothesis of the will to power has the advantage of "permitting an indefinite interrogation and an indefinite multiplicity" of further hypotheses (p. 380). I would agree that a good hypothesis will lead to the formulation of *some* other determinate hypotheses, but I think that a hypothesis that led to an *indefinite* (i.e., endless and boundless) multiplicity should be rejected *for that reason alone.*

Second, I think Kofman (like Derrida, Foucault, and Blanchot) does Nietzsche an injustice by suggesting that genealogy leads to an infinite proliferation of interpretations. This reading of Nietzsche loses an essential feature of Nietzsche's claim that genealogy reveals various forms of will to power. Although it is true for him that no one project is the best manifestation of will to power, and that will to power is "multiple," it does not follow that the point of genealogy is only to multiply interpretations. On the contrary, genealogy must criticize some interpretations, and it does so by discriminating between healthful and sick manifestations of the will to power. Nietzschean genealogy is thus *not* akin to recent methodologies maintaining either that anything goes (Feyerabend), or that interpretations are undecidable (Derrida). Nietzsche would see the defenses of sheer proliferation and of undecidability as hidden *ressentiment* of a sickly indecisiveness.

I think Nietzsche would insist that interpretations conflict and compete, and that some *must* be preferred to others. The principles of proliferation and undecidability are too thin to account for this feature. They cannot be used to decide which interpretations are better, but at most only to reject a specific second-order interpretation of interpretation, namely, the dogmatic theory requiring a single correct reading. The pluralists' principle of proliferation cannot even be used to reject dogmatic first-order interpretations asserting of any given text that it must be read in just this way. In fact, pluralism seems forced to controvert its intentions by saying, "The more of these dogmatic readings the better." The pluralists' principles of proliferation and undecidability thus lack survival value, and this in itself provides a Nietzschean reason for rejecting them.

NIETZSCHE AS AFFIRMATIVE THINKER?

A crucial question in thinking about the feasibility of Nietzschean genealogy today, then, is how the genealogist can argue for and against particular interpretations, both first-order and second-order. In Nietzsche's terms, how can the genealogist discriminate critically between healthful and sickly interpretations? I wish to draw a positive conclusion from my reflections on proliferation, pluralism, and undecidability. A minimal condition of such critical discrimination is that healthful interpretations be those that set out the conditions for finding their own inadequacies, and the strategies for revising themselves.

To put the point in this methodological way is not to go beyond Nietzsche's own metaphors of health and sickness, but simply to express them in another way. In sections 120 and 382 of *The Gay Science*, for instance, Nietzsche makes clear that what counts as health is something that must continually be called into question and challenged. Health can be acquired only gradually, and only by risking it and even giving it up. Health and sickness are different not in kind, but merely in degree. Furthermore, there is no universal criterion for health. Health is instead relative to the individual's goals and make-up. These medical metaphors I interpret as implying that the standards for what makes an interpretation a live option are internal to the interpretation, and that a sickly interpretation would be one that refused to investigate itself and to raise the question of its own viability.

In the remarkable second section of the preface to the second edition of *The Gay Science,* Nietzsche sketches a genealogy of the will to philosophize and traces that will back to a sickness of the body. This move back to the body is typical of both Hume's and Nietzsche's use of genealogy. Hume recognizes, for instance, that there are apparent counterexamples to his claim that the feelings of "humanity" and benevolence are universal. Characteristically he thus tries to explain away a misanthrope like Plutarch's Timon by asserting that Timon did not really lack the feeling of humanity, but was simply suffering from a bad spleen.[16] Nietzsche differs from Hume, however, in that Hume accepts most people's feelings at face value and has to explain away a few exceptional cases, whereas Nietzsche often seems to be making the exception the rule by explaining away entirely the generally accepted explanations of behavior.

While neither Nietzsche nor Hume, as skeptics, assess constructive philosophy highly, Nietzsche goes beyond Hume in saying that any philosophy that is "affirmative" is probably the result of a sickly will: "Every philosophy that ranks peace above war, every ethic with a negative definition of happiness, every metaphysics and physics that knows some *finale,* some final state of some sort, every predominantly aesthetic or religious craving for some Apart, Beyond, Outside, Above, permits the question whether it was not sickness that inspired the philosopher" (GS P:2). Nietzsche does not *want* to be an affirmative thinker in this sense, but he also does not want to be simply a critic, as his tirades against critical (Kantian) philosophy make clear. This paragraph calls for a "philosophical *physician.*" The goal of this physician cannot be simply to cure him- or herself, but "to pursue the problem of the total health of a people, time, race or of humanity." Hence, the physician will be offering an interpretation that will prove its use only insofar as it exposes what counts as both sickness and health, and shows the "patients" how to move away from sickness toward health. But the physician must be aware that the diagnosis could itself be motivated more by sickness than by health, and its prescriptions must be monitored continuously and changed when they appear to do more harm than good. The medicines themselves are poisons when used in extremes. In the second *Untimely Meditation,* for example, the sickness of too much history is said to be controllable with touches of the unhistorical and suprahistorical, even though if these antidotes began to dominate they would themselves become the sickness.

Nietzsche's medical analogy shows, therefore, that to be healthful and feasible, an interpretation must be defeasible. Furthermore, since the conditions for an interpretation's defeasibility are internal, it will be "honest" about itself only if it makes these conditions explicit. If I am right in this rendering of the special Nietzschean virtue of honesty, then doubts arise about the honesty of applications of genealogy which find sickness everywhere, but never health. Nietzsche was wise not to publish his own thought that will to power could be found everywhere, not only in people, but in the world as such (WP 1067). The claim that everything is will to power explains nothing. To avoid the vacuity of this level of generality, commentators like Kofman stress that the concept of will to power is only a hypothesis and a diagnostic tool, not a metaphysical principle. What must also be recognized, however, is that Hume was right not to make the exception the rule. Genealogy would be methodologically defective if it always discovered only *degenerate* manifestations of will to power. Nietzsche's metaphor of the philosophical physician clearly implies that not everything is sickly, for even to make the diagnosis of sickness there must be a contrasting conception of health. Unlike traditional philosophical methods, genealogy is not aprioristic. Hence, the genealogical physician should not prescribe in advance the same diagnosis and fatal prognosis for every possible patient.

NOTES

1. Nietzsche mentions Spencer favorably a few pages later in the *Genealogy* I:3, but for a typical tirade against Spencer for doctrines similar to Rée's see *The Gay Science* 373. Walter Kaufmann in a footnote to this paragraph, but also in his *Nietzsche: Philosopher, Psychologist, Antichrist*, 4th ed. (Princeton: Princeton University Press, 1974), p. 274, notes that William James in his 1884 essay, "The Dilemma of Determinism," caricatured Spencer much as Nietzsche did.

2. See Arthur Danto, *Nietzsche as Philosopher* (New York: Macmillan, 1965), especially chap. 3; Mary Warnock, "Nietzsche's Conception of Truth," in *Nietzsche: Imagery and Thought*, ed. W. Pasley (Berkeley, Los Angeles, London: University of California Press, 1978).

3. In *Hume's Moral Theory* (London: Routledge & Kegan Paul, 1980) J. L. Mackie suggests that the subtitle signifies that the *Treatise* "is an attempt to study and explain moral phenomena (as well as human knowledge and emotions) in the same sort of way in which Newton and his followers studied and explained the physical world" (p. 6).

4. In the *Genealogy* Nietzsche does not seem to be aware of the methodological problem of the genetic fallacy, which he does mention in *The Gay Science* 345, where he sees clearly that the question of the *value* of morality is independent of morality's *origin*: "Even if a morality has grown out of an error, the realization of this fact would not as much as touch the problem of its value."

5. The contrast Nietzsche's preface wants is perhaps better illustrated by some recent *French* practitioners of genealogy. A book like Michel Foucault's *Discipline and Punish: The Birth of the Prison*, trans. Alan Sheridan (New York: Vintage Books, 1979), which reads like a historical case study of the theory of punishment in the second essay of the *Genealogy*, is perhaps a better example of historical genealogy than Nietzsche's own work.

6. I have used "interpretation" for *Auslegung* instead of the translators' term "exegesis."

7. See Donald Davidson, "On the Very Idea of a Conceptual Scheme" (1974),

reprinted in his *Inquiries into Truth and Interpretation* (Oxford: Oxford University Press, 1984); Richard Rorty, "The World Well Lost" (1972), reprinted in his *Consequences of Pragmatism (Essays: 1972–1980)* (Minneapolis: University of Minnesota Press, 1982); Alexander Nehamas, "Immanent and Transcendent Perspectivism in Nietzsche," *Nietzsche-Studien* 12 (1983):473–490; but contrast Ralph C. S. Walker, *Kant: The Arguments of the Philosophers* (London: Routledge & Kegan Paul, 1978), pp. 30–41.

8. See Michel Foucault, "Nietzsche, Freud, Marx," in *Cahiers de Royaumont, Philosophie,* Numero VI: *Nietzsche* (Paris: Les Editions de Minuit, 1967); Maurice Blanchot, *L' Entretien infini* (Paris: Gallimard, 1969); Jacques Derrida, *Spurs: Nietzsche's Styles,* trans. B. Harlow (Chicago: University of Chicago Press, 1979).

9. Hilary Putnam, *Reason, Truth and History* (Cambridge: Cambridge University Press, 1981); see chap. 3.

10. Jean Granier, *Le problème de la vérité dans la philosophie de Nietzsche* (Paris: Seuil, 1966); Sarah Kofman, *Nietzsche et la métaphore* (Paris: Payot, 1972).

11. David Hume, *An Inquiry Concerning the Principles of Morals* (New York: Bobbs-Merrill, 1957), section 2 ("Of Benevolence"), part 2, p. 13.

12. On the *absurdum practicum* see Kant, *Lectures on Philosophical Theology,* trans. Allen W. Wood and Gertrude M. Clark (Ithaca: Cornell University Press, 1978), pp. 122–123.

13. On the African tribe of the Ik, who appear to take pleasure in the suffering of one another, see Colin Turnbull, *The Mountain People* (New York: Simon and Schuster, 1972); cited by Raymond Geuss, *The Idea of a Critical Theory: Habermas and the Frankfurt School* (Cambridge: Cambridge University Press, 1981), pp. 49–54. Geuss gives a succinct characterization of the criticism of Christianity in the *Genealogy* to show how it exemplifies critical theory:

> This criticism . . . appeals to a purported fact about the "origin" of Christianity—that Christianity arises from hatred, envy, resentment, and feelings of weakness and inadequacy. . . . How do we know that these motives are "unacceptable"? . . . Since it is a central doctrine of Christianity that agents ought to be motivated by love, and not by hatred, resentment, envy, etc., Christianity itself gives the standard of "acceptability" for motives in the light of which it is criticized. If Nietzsche's account of its "origins" is correct, Christianity "requires" of its adherents that they not recognize their own motives for adhering to it. (GM44)

Genealogy thus ought to be a form of immanent rather than external criticism, one that also explains the fact of the blindness of the agents to their own real motives and interests.

14. See in particular, Kofman, *Nietzsche et la métaphore,* pp. 120–145, 173–206.

15. Kofman, *Nietzsche et la métaphore,* p. 378. For further discussion see my article, "Philosophy as Rigorous Philology? Nietzsche and Poststructuralism," *New York Literary Forum* 8–9 (1981): 171–185.

16. David Hume, *An Inquiry Concerning the Principles of Morals,* section 5, p. 53.

FIFTEEN

The Genealogy of Genealogy
Interpretation in Nietzsche's Second
Untimely Meditation and in *On the*
Genealogy of Morals

Alexander Nehamas

Though it is often vague, naïve, nostalgic, and sometimes cloying, Nietzsche's *On the Uses and Disadvantages of History for Life* (UDH), his second *Untimely Meditation,* which denounces history as long as it is not made to "serve life," must still be taken seriously—for two reasons.[1] First, because of its virtues, which we must not allow its vices to obscure and which, if Nietzsche is right in agreeing with Goethe that "when we cultivate our virtues we at the same time cultivate our vices" (UDH F), may be intimately connected with them. Second, because the essay addresses the question of the relationship of our past to our present and future: "If you are *to venture to interpret the past* you can do so only out of the fullest exertion of the vigour of the present. . . . When the past speaks it always speaks only as an oracle: only if you are an architect of the future *will you understand it*" (UDH 6).

This essay thus addresses the most central theoretical question concerning interpretation: Is meaning discovered or created? Better put: Can meaning be discovered at all if it is not at the same time being created? And since the ultimate product of this question is Nietzsche's genealogical method, the second *Untimely Meditation* provides us with the material for a genealogy of genealogy itself. But if that is the case, then we certainly must not be deterred by its vices. As Nietzsche had already written, "Everywhere in all beginnings we find only the crude, the unformed, the empty and the ugly";[2] or, as he was to write later, "All good things were formerly bad things; every original sin has turned into an original virtue" (GM III:9).[3] Thus UDH has its own importance for the history of Nietzsche's ideas—and perhaps, if genealogy is correct in identifying history with essence, for their nature as well.

In his foreword to UDH, Nietzsche urges "German youth . . . to serve history only to the extent history serves life" (UDH F). As always, he is intolerably vague about what "life" is supposed to be. Part of his point is that although human beings are the only animals that live historically, aware of and conditioned by their past, nevertheless we must also develop what he calls an "unhistorical" attitude if we are to engage in genuinely new action. Complete knowledge, he believes, renders action impossible because, he seems to be convinced, in reality

> the past and the present are one, that is to say, with all their diversity identical in all that is typical and, as the omnipresence of imperishable types, a motionless structure of a value that cannot alter and a significance that is always the same. (UDH 1)

"Forgetting," accordingly,

> is essential to action of any kind. . . . There is a degree of sleeplessness, of rumination, of the historical sense, which is harmful and ultimately fatal to the living thing, whether this living thing be an individual or a people or a culture. (UDH 1)

Too much attention to history, in all its three forms—monumental, antiquarian, and critical—is dangerous in five ways: It produces a conflict between thought and action; it fosters the view that we today are more just and civilized than the people of earlier ages; it forces the disruption of spontaneous, "instinctive" activity; it creates the sense that one is a latecomer and has little of value to contribute to the world; and it generates an ironical and cynical attitude toward oneself and the world. All of these were attitudes Nietzsche thought he detected in Bismarck's Germany.

The central point of these accusations is that an overemphasis of history encourages us to think of ourselves not simply as the end point of a long process, but also as its product. It is, of course, possible to feel that such a product is actually the crowning achievement of the process, not unlike the young Sartre, who in *Les mots* defined progress as "that long, steep path which leads to me." Such an attitude can easily lead to a self-satisfied complacency. But the very same sense that we are the products of our past can easily become the sense that we are *merely* the products of our past and that we therefore do not exist as sovereign agents.[4] Since everything that makes us what we are has already occurred, and since the past is something over which we no longer have any control, we also seem to have no control over what we are and over what we can do. As epigones, we can at best understand what made us what we are: we have nothing of our own to introduce into history.

I am particularly interested in such an attitude because I think that it corresponds in a number of ways to views now current in debates over literature, the arts, and the very idea of interpretation. In the arts, originality is often identified with, or forsaken for, allusion and rearrangement.

And the main object of criticism is sometimes no longer taken to be the development of interpretations of literary works, but rather the investigation of how those interpretations we do possess have come about: "To engage in the study of literature is not to produce yet another interpretation of *King Lear* but to advance one's understanding of an institution, a mode of discourse."[5]

It is precisely in order to forestall such attitudes, I believe, that Nietzsche writes that "forgetting is essential to action of every kind" (UDH 1). In this, he marvelously anticipates Borges's story, "Funes the Memorious," whose hero, almost in recompense for becoming completely paralyzed, develops total recall. Funes

> knew by heart the forms of the southern clouds at dawn on the 30th of April, 1882, and could compare them in his memory with the mottled streaks of a book in Spanish binding he had only seen once and with the outlines of the foam raised by an oar in the Rio Negro the night before the Quebracho uprising. These memories were not simple ones; each visual image was linked to muscular sensations, thermal sensations, etc. . . . Two or three times he had reconstructed a whole day; he never hesitated, but each reconstruction had required a whole day.[6]

Incapable of action, Borges's character "was also not very capable of thought. To think is to forget differences, generalize, make abstractions. In the teeming world of Funes, there were only details."[7] Funes died at twenty-two, of congestion of the lungs. Remembering every breath you have ever drawn leaves no room for drawing new ones. The story is a perfect metaphorical illustration of the Hegelian view that when reason finally achieves absolute self-consciousness, history is effectively over. When absolute knowledge is reached, reason finally "consists in perfectly knowing itself, in knowing what it is." Such a situation involves an awareness, and presupposes the accomplished occurrence, of all genuine new possibilities. Rearrangement remains the only option.

Hegel's view is directly connected with our discussion. In the second *Untimely Meditation,* Nietzsche argues that history has no immanent meaning, no meaning that has been or that can in principle be discovered; history does not involve a rational process to which all particular historical episodes make some contribution and of which they are parts:

> Close beside the pride of modern individuals there stands their ironic view of themselves, their awareness that they have to live in a historicizing, as it were a twilight mood, their fear that their youthful hopes and energy will not survive into the future. Here and there one goes further, into *cynicism,* and justifies the course of history, indeed the entire evolution of the world, in a manner especially adapted to the use of us moderns, according to the cynical canon: as things are they had to be, as human beings now are they were bound to become, none may resist this inevitability. (UDH 9)

But despite the suspiciousness Nietzsche here expresses toward Hegel, he ironically shows himself to be more of a follower than he might have been willing to admit. "We moderns," he writes,

> race through art galleries and listen to concerts. We feel that one thing sounds different from another, that one thing produces a different effect from another: increasingly to lose this sense of strangeness, no longer to be very much surprised at anything, finally to be pleased with everything—that is then no doubt called the historical sense, historical culture. (UDH 7)

This is a Hegelian passage to the extent that it envisages the possibility that the arts at least have played their history out: Not that new artworks (or interpretations of them) will no longer be produced, but that such works will only be variations on originals that already exist. History ends not because nothing happens but because nothing genuinely new *can* occur; the possibilities have been exhausted. Nietzsche is afraid that, having convinced ourselves that this is in fact the case, we shall in fact bring such a situation about. But he hopes that we shall not; and the very purpose of his essay on history is to incite "youth" into the performance of truly "new deeds." Yet in offering this as a true description of his culture's frame of mind, Nietzsche anticipated Arthur Danto, who in his own Hegelian essay, "The End of Art," writes:

> It is possible that . . . art as we knew it is finished. . . . The age of pluralism is upon us. It does not matter any longer what you do, which is what pluralism means. When one direction is as good as another direction, there is no concept of direction any longer to apply. Decoration, self-expression, entertainment are, of course, abiding human needs. There will always be a service for art to perform, if artists are content with that. Freedom ends in its own fulfillment. A subservient art has always been with us. The institutions of the art world—galleries, collectors, exhibitions, journalism—which are predicated upon history and marking what is new, will bit by bit wither away.[8]

Whereas Danto bewails this already actual posthistorical, postmodernist free-for-all, Nietzsche believes that we are in danger of creating such an age for ourselves and hopes that we shall not: "No, the *goal of humanity* cannot lie in its ends but only *its highest exemplars*" (UDH 9).

According to the view Nietzsche alludes to in this sentence, any significance or meaning history has is not inherent in it, but is bestowed upon it by the activities of particular individuals. But this immediately raises the question: Do these "highest exemplars" of humanity introduce something genuinely new into history or do they only seem to do so, in reality leaving history fundamentally unchanged?

I believe that at the time he wrote his *Untimely Meditations* Nietzsche thought that in reality history is simply the succession of chance events which essentially lack an order, a meaning, or a purpose; that there is a pattern in history, but that this pattern is itself meaningless. In reality, history is a causal sequence of events, and this causal sequence constitutes its pattern. But these events occur for no reason, and this deprives it of meaning. Whatever his great individuals accomplish, therefore, is bound to be illusory. This is exactly why forgetting is necessary for action of any kind. To forget is to falsify, to repress what is in fact there. If one were to become aware of the forgetting, of the illusion on which all action depends, one "could no longer feel any temptation to go on living or to take part in history" (UDH 1). Such awareness gives rise to the attitude Nietzsche calls "suprahistorical" and according to which, as we have already seen, "the past and the present are one."

A person with this attitude, I now want to suggest, is the historical analogue of the Dionysian character who, in *The Birth of Tragedy*, is said to resemble Hamlet in that "both have once looked truly into the essence of things, they have *gained knowledge,* and nausea inhibits action; for their action could not change anything in the eternal nature of things" (BT 7).[9] The connection between the two works is established beyond doubt by Nietzsche's writing that the suprahistorical attitude reduces one "to satiety, oversatiety and finally to nausea ... to ... nausea and ... wisdom" (UDH 1). In both cases Nietzsche claims that true wisdom is incompatible with action because, in their real nature, neither the world nor history can ever be altered. What meaning they have, which is no meaning at all, is already there. At best, through forgetting in the present essay and through the illusion of tragedy in *The Birth of Tragedy,* one can fool oneself into action by forgetting that change is really impossible: What is accomplished is insignificant, but the effort remains.

The connections between the two works are actually even deeper. Paul de Man has argued that, in claiming that illusion is necessary for action and for understanding, *The Birth of Tragedy* puts itself into question as well.[10] For the work seems to want to make its readers understand that nothing can be fully understood; it appears to state the truth that the truth cannot ever be known, or stated. It thus undermines its own message. Understanding is produced only through an illusion, and an illusion can produce only the illusion of understanding. Forgetting, I think, plays a parallel role in the essay on history. The work aims to convince "German youth" to the performance of "great and high deeds," but it states clearly that only by forgetting that such deeds are in reality impossible can the young engage in the effort to perform them. But how can this be something of which one can hope to convince one's audience, who, if convinced, will remember the lesson and will be unable to forget just what they need to forget if they are in fact to learn it?

De Man used his reading of *The Birth of Tragedy* to support a radically revisionary interpretation of Nietzsche's philosophical development. He argued that since the view he found in this work is identical with the ironic view of Nietzsche's later works (and since, insofar as this is possible, that view is correct), the traditional picture of Nietzsche's development must be abandoned. For that picture attributes to Nietzsche a more or less naïve, dogmatic, and metaphysical view in his early works, and finds a sophisticated, ironic, ante-deconstructive approach only in the works of his "maturity."

De Man's reading is too subtle and his conclusions too far-reaching for me to be able to deal with them fairly here. Very briefly, it would not be inaccurate to say that his reading and his conclusions about Nietzsche's development have been broadly accepted by literary critics, while philosophers, who generally reject his conclusions, have also disagreed with his reading. By contrast, I want to be free to reject de Man's conclusions even if his reading of *The Birth of Tragedy* proves to be correct. For even if Nietzsche accepts the position de Man locates in his earlier works, he certainly rejects it in the works that follow *Thus Spoke Zarathustra*.[11]

Moreover, the view de Man attributes to Nietzsche is itself dogmatic and metaphysical. For it holds that the character of the world, or of history, or of a text (of any object, that is, of action or understanding) is in reality beyond our reach, impervious to all efforts to affect it. De Man distinguishes explicitly between "the teleological domain of the text" on the one hand and "nature" on the other. And he believes that "no bridge, as metaphor or as representation, can ever connect the natural realm of essences with the textual realm of forms and values."[12] But the later Nietzsche, who begins by writing, "What is 'appearance' for me now? Certainly not the opposite of some essence: what could I say about any essence except to name the attributes of its appearance!" (GS 54)[13] could never countenance that idea.

But de Man's contrast between nature and our representations of it is clearly evident, again transposed in historical terms, in UDH. In coming to terms with our past, Nietzsche writes:

> The best we can do is to confront our inherited and hereditary nature . . . , combat our inborn heritage and implant in ourselves a new habit, a new instinct, a second nature, so that our first nature withers away. It is an attempt to give oneself, as it were *a posteriori*, a past in which one would like to originate in opposition to that in which one did originate.

But a contrary current in Nietzsche's thought is manifested by his going on to claim that

> here and there a victory is nonetheless achieved, and for the combatants, for those who employ critical history for the sake of life, there is even a noteworthy consolation: that of knowing that this first nature was once a second nature and that every victorious second nature will become a first. (UDH 3)

This intriguing passage seems to cast doubt on the solidity of the distinction between "first" and "second" nature. It suggests that there is no such thing as an absolutely first nature, that everything seemingly fixed has been at some point introduced into history and that the distinction between first and second nature is at best provisional—between a second nature that has been long accepted and one that is still new. And this of course casts doubt on the idea of a second nature as well. What Nietzsche here calls "critical" history begins to appear as the unearthing of an infinite chain of second natures with no necessary first link.

Here, then, we have one of the elements out of which genealogy eventually emerges. For genealogy is a process of interpretation which reveals that what has been taken for granted is the product of specific historical conditions, an expression of a particular and partial attitude toward the world, history, or a text that has been taken as incontrovertible.

In UDH Nietzsche also prefigures another element of genealogy:

> To what end the "world" exists, to what end "mankind" exists, ought not to concern us at all for the moment except as objects of humour: for the presumptuousness of the little human worm is the funniest thing at present on the world's stage; on the other hand, do ask yourself why you, the individual, exist, and if you can get no other answer try for once to justify your existence as it were *a posteriori* by setting before you an aim, a goal, a "to this end," an exalted and noble "to this end." Perish in pursuit of this and only this—I know of no better aim of life than that of perishing, *animae magnae prodigus*, in pursuit of the great and the impossible. (UDH 9)

Here as well two conflicting ideas are conjoined. If there is to be a purpose in life, Nietzsche claims, it will have to be a purpose *constructed* by each particular individual and capable of redeeming the life that was lived, and perhaps lost, for its sake. But such a purpose can never be fully achieved, insofar as it aims to effect a real change in the world—hence Nietzsche's description of it as "impossible."

It is out of these two sets of conflicts, I would now like to suggest, that Nietzsche eventually develops the view of interpretation and of our relationship to our past that characterizes *On the Genealogy of Morals*. The step most crucial to this development was his coming to give up the view that the causal description of objects and events in the world corresponds to their true nature. He therefore no longer had to believe that interpretation or reinterpretation, which cannot really affect such causal sequences, cannot possibly change the events in question and thus introduce something genuinely new into the universe. If the causal description of the world is not a description of its real nature, if in fact there is no such thing as the world's real nature, then reinterpretation need not be, as Nietzsche had believed when he composed his earlier works, falsification.

The *Genealogy* contains a sustained effort on Nietzsche's part to show that morality is a subject fit for interpretation, that we can ask of it, as we usually put the point, "What does it mean?" This is in fact the very question Nietzsche asks of the asceticism, the denial of the common pleasures, that has been traditionally associated with philosophy. Traditionally, the fact that philosophers have tended toward asceticism has been considered natural. Nietzsche, instead, sees it as a question. "What does that *mean?*" he asks, and continues: "For this fact has to be interpreted: *in itself* it just stands there, stupid to all eternity, like every 'thing in itself' " (GM III:7).

The great accomplishment of the *Genealogy* is the demonstration that morality in general and asceticism in particular are indeed subjects of interpretation, that they can be added to our interpretative universe. Now, how is it, in general, that we can show that something can in fact be interpreted? In the first instance, we can only show it by actually offering an interpretation. That is, in order to establish a new subject of interpretation, we must produce an *actual* interpretation of that subject: we must in fact establish it *as* such a subject by means, moreover, of an interpretation that makes some sort of claim to the attention of others.

Nietzsche, I believe, offers such an interpretation of morality. The first and perhaps the most important feature of that interpretation is that, as Nietzsche emphasizes throughout this work, morality itself is an interpretation to begin with. And this establishes at least a partial connection between genealogy and the discussion of history in the second *Untimely Meditation*: morality, that is, something that we have considered so far as absolutely basic, solid, foundational, is shown to be a particular reaction to a preexisting set of phenomena; a first nature, as it were, is shown to be a second nature whose status has been concealed.

The notion that morality is an interpretation is absolutely central to Nietzsche. "There are altogether no moral facts," he writes, for example, in *Twilight of the Idols;* "morality is merely an interpretation of certain phenomena—more precisely, a misinterpretation."[14] Where others had previously seen merely a natural development of natural human needs, desires, and relationships, where others had "taken the value of [moral] values as given, as factual, as beyond question" (GM P:6), Nietzsche saw instead what he described as a system of signs. Such a system, naturally, like all systems of signs, remains incomprehensible until we know what its signs are signs of and signs for. In order, then, to show that morality can be interpreted, Nietzsche actually interprets it; and his interpretation involves a demonstration that morality itself is an interpretation to begin with.

We have just seen that Nietzsche considers that morality is a misinterpretation. He is therefore obliged to offer an alternative account of the phenomena morality has misconstrued, or (as he would prefer to put it), has construed in a manner that suits it. This account depends crucially on his view that one of the most important features of the moral interpretation of phenomena is the fact that its status *as* an interpretation has been consistently concealed:

> Morality in Europe today is herd animal morality—in other words, as we understand it, merely *one* type of human morality beside which, before which, and after which many other types, above all higher moralities, are, or ought to be, possible. But this morality resists such a "possibility," such an "ought," with all its power: it says stubbornly and inexorably, "I am morality itself and nothing besides is morality." (BGE 202)[15]

Let us then suppose (a considerable supposition!) that morality is an interpretation. What is it an interpretation of? Nietzsche's general answer is that it is an interpretation of the phenomenon to which he refers as "human suffering." His own attitude toward this phenomenon is very complex. In one mood, he debunks it. He attributes it not to a divine cause (as, we shall see, he claims that morality does), not even to anything serious, but to the lowest and crudest physiological causes. Such a cause, he writes,

> may perhaps lie in some disease of the *nervus sympathicus,* or in an excessive secretion of bile, or in a deficiency in potassium sulfate and phosphate in the blood, or in an obstruction in the abdomen which impedes the blood circulation, or in degeneration of the ovaries and the like. (GM III:15)

For years, I considered this as one of those horribly embarrassing passages that Nietzsche's readers inevitably have to put up with in defensive silence. Then I realized that Nietzsche was actually making a joke, that he was reducing one of the "highest" expressions of being human—our capacity for suffering—to one of the "lowest." And, having seen the passage as a joke, I realized that it was after all serious or, at least, that it was a complex joke with a point to make. For the list of ailments Nietzsche produces is not haphazard. A disease of the (nonexistent) *nervus sympathicus* could well be supposed to be the physiological analogue of the excess, even of the existence, of pity—the sentiment that is the central target of the *Genealogy,* which takes "the problem of the value of pity and the morality of pity" (GM P:6) to be its originating concern. "Excessive secretion of bile," of course, traditionally has been associated with malice and envy, which are precisely the feelings those to whom the *Genealogy* refers to as "the weak" have always had for those who are "strong," while weakness and, in general, lassitude and the inability to act are in fact a direct effect of potassium deficiency. Impediments to the circulation of the blood are correlated with the coldness, ill will and lack of sexual potency Nietzsche associates with the ascetic priests, and such impotence, along with infertility, whose spiritual analogue would be the absence of any creativity, may well be the psychological/moral correlate of ovarian degeneration (whatever that is).

In another mood, Nietzsche attributes the suffering to which we are all inescapably subject to necessary social arrangements:

> I regard the bad conscience [this is one of his terms for referring to suffering] as the serious illness that human beings were bound to contract under the stress of the most fundamental change they ever experienced—that change which occurred when they found themselves finally enclosed within the walls of society and of peace. . . . All instincts that do not discharge themselves outwardly *turn inward*—this is what I call the *internalization* of human beings: thus it was that we first developed what was later called our "soul." (GM II:16)

It is very important to note at this point that Nietzsche, though he offers in this work an interpretation of morality according to which morality is an interpretation of suffering, never characterizes his own accounts of suffering as themselves interpretations. Only the moral approach to suffering, but none of the explanations he offers, is an interpretation:

> Human beings, the bravest of animals and those most accustomed to suffering, do *not* repudiate suffering as such; they *desire* it, they even seek it out, provided they are shown a *meaning* for it, a *purpose* of suffering. The meaninglessness of suffering, *not* suffering itself, was the curse that lay over mankind so far—and the ascetic ideal offered them meaning. . . . In it, suffering was *interpreted*. (GM III:28)

What is it, then, that makes the moral account of suffering, but not Nietzsche's own, an interpretation? My own answer, in general terms, is the following. According to Nietzsche, the ascetic priests take the fact of suffering, the existence of the bad conscience which *he* considers as "a piece of animal psychology, no more," and claim that it is prompted by, perhaps equivalent to, a sense of guilt produced by sin. "Sin," Nietzsche writes, "is the priestly name for the animal's 'bad conscience' (cruelty directed backward)." Convinced by the priests to see their suffering in such terms, Nietzsche continues, human beings

> receive a hint, they receive from their sorcerer, the ascetic priest, the *first* hint as the "cause" of their suffering: they must seek it in themselves, in some *guilt*, in a piece of the past, they must understand their suffering as a *punishment*. (GM III:20)

Nietzsche's introduction of the idea of "a piece of the past" here is crucial for our purposes. For it is connected with the search for a meaning that is thought to inhere in history—in our own history in this case—and which is there to be discovered by us if we go about it in the right way. This piece of the past, according to Nietzsche, is nothing other than our inevitable engagement in acts and immersion in desires all of which—sensual, ambitious, self-serving, egoistic—are, as he believes, characteristically human and which, therefore, we cannot possibly avoid.

Yet morality, interpreting such desires and actions as sinful, enjoins us to distance ourselves from them as much as is humanly possible. Its effect is twofold. In the first instance, it offers suffering a meaning—it is God's punishment for the fact that we are (there is no other word for it) human. Morality therefore makes suffering, to the extent that it accounts for it, tolerable. In the second instance, however, and in the very same process, it "brings fresh suffering with it, deeper, more inward, more poisonous, more life-destructive suffering" (GM III:28).

This, in turn, is brought about in two ways. First, because the forbidden desires, impulses, and actions can be fought against only by the same sort of desires, impulses, and actions, we can curtail our cruelty toward ourselves only by acting cruelly toward ourselves. The effort to curtail them, therefore, secures their own perpetuation: it guarantees that suffering will continue. Second, because if this sort of behavior is, as Nietzsche believes, essentially human, then the effort to avoid it and not to give expression to the (equally essential) impulses on which it depends perpetuates the suffering caused by any obstacle to the tendency of instinct to be "directed outward." In a classic case of the double bind, the moral approach to suffering, in its interpretation of it as sin, creates more suffering the more successfully it fights it and the more tolerable it makes it.

Now the reason why morality is for Nietzsche an interpretation of suffering is that it gives suffering a meaning and a reason ("reasons relieve") and accounts for its persistence by means of attributing it to some *agent*. "Every sufferer," Nietzsche claims,

> instinctively seeks a cause for his suffering; more exactly, an agent, still more specifically, a guilty agent who is susceptible to suffering—in short, some living thing upon which one can, on some pretext or other, vent his affects, actually or in effigy.

Suffering is taken as the result of someone's actions. Whose actions? Here is the answer to this question:

> "I suffer: someone must be to blame for it"—thus thinks every sickly sheep. But the shepherd, the ascetic priest, replies: "Quite so, my sheep! Someone must be to blame for it: but you yourself are this someone, you alone are to blame for it—*you alone are to blame for yourself!*" (GM III:15)

This moral account of suffering, in contrast to Nietzsche's explanations, is an interpretation, I now want to claim, because it appeals to intentional vocabulary, because it construes suffering as the product or result of someone's actions—in this case, of the actions of the sufferers themselves and of God's—because it says, in effect, "What you feel is as it is because of who you are and of what you have done."

In my opinion, what is essential to interpretation is to construe a particular phenomenon as an action and thus to attribute to it some agent whose features account for the features of that action.[16] And if I am right in claiming that the connection between interpretation and intention is essential, then Nietzsche's account of human suffering—at least what we have seen of it so far—is not interpretative. The reason is that Nietzsche is careful to avoid the description of suffering as a general phenomenon in intentional terms. We have seen that, in general, he attributes it to physiological or social causes and that he believes that, at least in one sense of that term, suffering is meaningless. There is no reason, no agent, no purpose, no "For the sake of what?" in it.

This allows me to return to my discussion of UDH. For it may be tempting to suppose that just as in that earlier work Nietzsche believed that in reality history is meaningless, so in the *Genealogy* he believes that suffering is meaningless and that this is a brute fact with which we shall simply have to live from now on. This is actually the view of Arthur Danto, who has argued that the main point of the *Genealogy* is the idea that "suffering really is meaningless, there is no point to it, and the amount of suffering caused by *giving* it a meaning chills the blood to contemplate." Danto continues:

> The final aphorism of the *Genealogy*, "man would rather will the nothing than not will," does not so much heroize mankind, after all: what it does is restate the instinct of *ressentiment*: man would rather his suffering be meaningful, hence would rather will meaning onto it, than acquiesce in the meaninglessness of it. It goes against this instinct to believe what is essentially the most liberating thought imaginable, that life is without meaning. In a way, the deep affliction from which he seeks to relieve us is what today we think of as hermeneutics: the method of interpretation primarily of suffering.[17]

This is in many ways a wonderful interpretation. The meaning it attributes to the *Genealogy*, that exemplary book of interpretation, is that there is no meaning anywhere for anyone. Danto's interpretation of Nietzsche's interpretation of the moral interpretation of suffering says, in effect: "Stop interpreting immediately; don't even begin." But since, of course, Danto's view *is* an interpretation, it does just what it says we shouldn't do, and thus instantiates, in a manner Nietzsche would have been only too happy to acknowledge, the execution of the impossible task it proscribes. In addition, by attributing to Nietzsche the view that only the uninterpreted (or unexamined) life is worth living for a human being, it establishes him in yet another dimension as Socrates' antipodes. The trouble, however, is that ultimately this interpretation will not stand.

I agree with Danto that Nietzsche believes that suffering has no meaning—it has, after all, only causes, social or physiological. But this is a view to the effect that no one has already given suffering a meaning, a point (say, as punishment for sin) which is the same for everyone and there for us to discover and live with. *In itself,* suffering has no meaning—in itself, as we have seen in connection with every thing in itself, it just stands there, stupid to all eternity. But the consequence that follows from this is not necessarily the idea that since in reality there is no meaning, we should give up the goal of trying to create meaning altogether. This would be the view of *The Birth of Tragedy* and of the second *Untimely Meditation* minus Nietzsche's insistence that we should still try to accomplish something with our lives despite the knowledge that nothing is thereby accomplished. It would be to hold the metaphysics of those works without the aesthetic justification of life they demand.

But what separates these works from the *Genealogy* is Nietzsche's realization that the fact that suffering or history is meaningless in itself does not force the conclusion that any attempt to give it a meaning would necessarily falsify it. Instead, it implies that *in themselves* both suffering and history are irrelevant to us. And this is precisely what allows the conclusion that if one were to succeed in making something out of one's own suffering or one's own history (and, on my reading, Nietzsche offers himself as his favorite example[18]), then the suffering that that individual life, like every life, is bound to have contained will also thereby have acquired a meaning.

This meaning will be its contribution to the whole of which it will have then become a part—and this is true, in my opinion, not only of life but of all meaning, particularly of the meaning of texts. In this way, if a life has had a point, if it has made a difference, if it has changed something, then everything in it, everything that happens or has happened to the person whose life it is becomes significant. It becomes part of a work whose author is the person in question and, as we should have expected, it becomes something we can describe in intentional terms. It becomes something for which one is willing, "*a posteriori,*" to accept responsibility, something that one in a very serious sense of the term *is.* This idea, that even events in our past can in this manner become things we did and therefore things we are, becomes explicit in *Thus Spoke Zarathustra,* where it is applied specifically to suffering and to punishment:

"No deed can be annihilated: how could it be undone by punishment? This, this is what is eternal in the punishment called existence, that existence must eternally become deed and guilt again. Unless the will should at last redeem itself and willing should become not willing." [This is the aim of asceticism.] But my brothers, you know this fable of madness.

I led you away from this madness when I taught you, "The will is a creator." All "It was" is a fragment, a riddle, a dreadful accident [it is meaningless]—until the creative will says to it, "But thus I willed it." Until the creative will says to it, "But thus I will it; thus I shall will it."[19]

This passage shows that Nietzsche cannot possibly be the enemy of hermeneutics Danto describes. He is, however, a relentless enemy of the view that the significance of the events in a life, of the components of history, of the parts of a text, is given to them antecedently, that it inheres in them, and that it is therefore the same for everyone. If, indeed, we want to find out what anything means to everyone, the answer is bound to be "nothing," and the inference we may be tempted to draw from it will be that nothing is meaningful in itself, or in reality, and that all meaning is therefore illusory. This is not unlike Nietzsche's early view. In the late works, when he no longer believes in anything in itself, when history is all there is, he comes to believe that what the events in each life mean differs according to what, if anything, one makes of one's life. This, in turn, can be seen to be connected with his turn away from the effort directly to influence the culture of his time.[20] Whereas the second *Untimely Meditation* seems to envisage that all the "young" have the ability to accomplish something great and different, the later works start from the observation that most people are not at all capable of anything remotely like this. Since, then, most people do not succeed in making a difference, the events in most people's lives turn out not to mean very much at all—in which case, people might as well believe that they are a punishment: Christianity is not to be abolished, and a new culture is no longer called for. It is difficult enough to organize "the chaos one is" for oneself.

The crucial difference, then, between Nietzsche's early and late works on the question of our relationship to our past and of its interpretation is that in the *Genealogy* Nietzsche does not believe that the establishment of meaning must falsify history or the text. There is no order of events in themselves which do, or do not, have a significance of their own. Only what is incorporated into a specific whole has a meaning, and its meaning is nothing other than its contribution to that whole. How the value of that whole is to be in turn established is a question as difficult to answer as it is independent of the view of interpretation put forward here.

NOTES

1. *On the Uses and Disadvantages of History for Life*, in Friedrich Nietzsche, *Untimely Meditations*, trans. R. J. Hollingdale (Cambridge: Cambridge University Press, 1983). I shall give references by section number. "F" indicates Nietzsche's foreword.

2. *Philosophy in The Tragic Age of the Greeks*, trans. Marianne Cowan (Chicago: Henry Regnery Company, 1962), p. 30.

3. *On the Genealogy of Morals*, trans. Walter Kaufmann, in *The Basic Writings of Nietzsche* (New York: Random House, 1968), Third Essay, section 9. I shall refer to this work by means of essays and sections.

4. See Mark Warren, *Nietzsche and Political Thought* (Cambridge, Mass.: The MIT Press, 1988), chap. 3.

5. Jonathan Culler, *The Pursuit of Signs: Semiotics, Literature, Deconstruction* (Ithaca: Cornell University Press, 1981), p. 5. Leaving aside the question of whether "yet another" interpretation of *King Lear* is as easy to come by as this statement suggests, it is important to note that such an approach does not really abandon interpretation as such, but only the interpretation of literary works in favor of the interpretation of those interpretations of literary works which we already possess.

6. Jorge Luis Borges, "Funes the Memorious," in *Labyrinths* (New York: New Directions, 1964).

7. Borges, *Labyrinths*, p. 66.

8. Arthur C. Danto, "The End of Art," in his *The Philosophical Disenfranchisement of Art* (New York: Columbia University Press, 1986), pp. 114–115. Compare UDH 8: 104.

9. *The Birth of Tragedy*, trans. Walter Kaufmann, in *Basic Writings of Nietzsche*, section 7.

10. Paul de Man, *Allegories of Reading* (New Haven: Yale University Press, 1979), pp. 79–102.

11. For a criticism of de Man's interpretation of *The Birth of Tragedy*, see Maudemarie Clark, "Deconstructing *The Birth of Tragedy*," *International Studies in Philosophy* 19 (1987): 69–75. Robert L. Anderson has made a strong case for de Man's reading of the work but against his broader conclusions in his unpublished "Deconstruction and Metaphysical Realism: Paul de Man's Interpretation of *The Birth of Tragedy*" (1989).

12. De Man, *Allegories of Reading*, p. 100.

13. *The Gay Science*, trans. Walter Kaufmann (New York: Vintage Press, 1974), section 54.

14. *The Twilight of the Idols*, trans. Walter Kaufmann, in *The Viking Portable Nietzsche* (New York: Viking Press, 1968), "The 'Improvers' of Mankind," section 1.

15. *Beyond Good and Evil*, trans. Walter Kaufmann, in *Basic Writings of Nietzsche*, section 202.

16. I have made an argument for this claim in my essay, "Writer, Text, Work, Author," in *Literature and the Question of Philosophy*, ed. Anthony J. Cascardi (Baltimore: Johns Hopkins University Press, 1987), pp. 267–291.

17. Arthur C. Danto, "Some Remarks on *The Genealogy of Morals*," *International Studies in Philosophy* 18 (1986): 13. (Reprinted in this volume—ED.)

18. This is the central thesis of my *Nietzsche: Life as Literature* (Cambridge, Mass.: Harvard University Press, 1985).

19. *Thus Spoke Zarathustra*, trans. Walter Kaufmann, in *The Viking Portable Nietzsche*, Book II, section 20, pp. 252–253.

20. An interesting connection between Nietzsche's and Overbeck's attitude toward this issue is established in Lionel Gossman's "Antimodernism in Nineteenth-Century Basle," *Interpretation* 16 (1989): 359–389.

SIXTEEN

Genealogies and Subversions*

Alasdair MacIntyre

In the first of my Gifford Lectures I argued that, if and insofar as we are still able to ask and to answer questions about God and the good that Adam Gifford would have been willing to recognize as legitimate successors of his own, it has to be from some standpoint alien to his and that of his 19th-century Edinburgh contemporaries precisely in its rejection of their unitary conception of reason as affording a single view of a developing world within which each part of the inquiry contributes to an overall progress, and whose supreme achievement is an account of the progress of mankind—or (to rewrite Walter Bagehot's remark about Adam Smith's view) of how man, having been originally and still being in remote colonial parts of the globe a biologically evolved savage, had risen to the height of being a Scottish professor of the 1880s. The canonical books of those who gave their allegiance to this *Weltanschauung,* so I suggested, were the volumes of the Ninth Edition of the *Encyclopedia Britannica.* The encyclopedia article was the genre whose form perfectly matched that particular content. But it was not the only such genre. Many of the writers of the Ninth Edition were the professors of a university establishment dominant in Scotland, Germany, and those other countries from which the contributors to the Ninth Edition

*This essay is the second of MacIntyre's 1988 Gifford Lectures, which were delivered at the University of Edinburgh, and were subsequently published in 1990 under the title *Three Rival Versions of Moral Inquiry* by the University of Notre Dame Press (in the U.S.) and by Duckworth (in the U.K.). The first lecture/chapter, which precedes this essay, is entitled "Adam Gifford's Project in Context," and deals with such matters as the intentions of the founder of the lecture series, the character of the series and of moral thought in the past, and "the canonical expression of the Edinburgh culture of Adam Gifford's day, the Ninth Edition of *The Encyclopedia Britannica*" (p. 18). This explains some of the backward-looking references in this essay. Interested readers may wish to consult the previous and subsequent lectures/chapters; but most of what MacIntyre has to say here can be understood independently of them—ED.

were drawn. And just as in their encyclopedia articles they gave written form to the type of lecture in which they spoke *ex cathedra*, so their university lectures were spoken encyclopedia articles. This type of lecture was thus a genre very different either from its medieval predecessors or from what a lecture can be today.

The medieval lecturer shared with his audience a background of beliefs concerning which texts were authoritative. The lecture as interpretative commentary upon such texts appealed to an authority beyond itself and had as its sequel the disputation in which the lecturer's theses were tested dialectically and demonstratively. It was just because both audience and lecturers accepted standards of truth and rationality independent of either that each could summon the other to test any particular thesis in the forum of disputation, the intellectual equivalent of trial by ordeal. In the late nineteenth-century lecture, by contrast, it was the lecturer who himself was the authority upon the standards in constituting himself as the voice of the *Weltanschauung*; authority resided in the lecturer himself and in the lecture. The audience came to hear and to learn from authoritative, encyclopedic pronouncements, not to dispute. Deference on the part of the audience was one of the defining marks of the late nineteenth-century university.

For us in the contemporary university the nineteenth-century lecture is a genre as impossible as the medieval, for we no more share the agreements presupposed by the deference of the nineteenth-century audience than we do the acknowledgment of authoritative texts by the twelfth or thirteenth century. For us in our situation of radical disagreements a lecture can only be an episode in a narrative of conflicts; sometimes it may be a moment of truce or negotiation between contending parties, or even a report from the sidelines by a necessarily less than innocent bystander, but nonetheless it is always a moment of engagement in conflict. And this is why it is not only the intellectual content of Adam Gifford's will which is so alien to us that the implementation of his intentions has become problematic but also the very form of performance which he prescribed for that implementation, the lecture. For content and form were matched perfectly. The lectures were to be, so the will declares, "public and popular, open . . . to the whole community" because they were to convey "real" knowledge of a kind which "lies at the root of all well-being." A summons to the hearing of such a lecture is very different from a summons to participate in a conflict over what the reality of knowledge consists in, if anything.

It is therefore unsurprising that one of the two most notable nineteenth-century rejections of the encyclopedists' conception of knowledge and of rationality should have been accompanied, indeed preceded by an abandonment of the lecture itself as a genre. Nietzsche's breaking away from the university, his abandonment of both professorial chair and professorial stance, was an integral part of his preparation for the assumption of a new role, that of genealogist. No one had been more thoroughly educated into the orthodoxies of nineteenth-century academia than had Nietzsche. He was both the pupil and the protegé, first at Bonn and then at Leipzig, of Friedrich Wilhelm Ritschl, who died in 1876, in time for his work to be celebrated in volume 20 of the Ninth Edition by the Cambridge classical scholar James S. Reid. Ritschl's great work on Plautus had played its part in the development of a view of *Altertumswissenschaft* in which the philological study of texts united with the study of ancient institutions and art and archeology to provide a portrait of the ancient world serviceable for the culture of the nineteenth century, a view developed most fully by Nietzsche's younger contemporary at Bonn, Ulrich von Wilamowitz-Moellendorf, who in 1877 was chosen to deliver an address *On the Splendor of the Athenian Empire* to celebrate the birthday of the German emperor. And when Nietzsche was appointed to the chair of classical philology at Basel in 1869 at the age of twenty-four, those who recommended and appointed him clearly had the same expectations that they were to have of Wilamowitz.

Nietzsche's repudiation of the whole ethos of *Altertumswissenschaft* derived from his perception of a very different relationship between classical antiquity and nineteenth-century modernity from that taken for granted by his teachers and contemporaries. Were the classical philologists in fact to understand classical realities, he was to remark, they would recoil horrified. And they would do so in part at least because they would have to acknowledge that their own academic purposes had alienated them from their object of study and concealed it from them. The initial offense which separated Nietzsche from academia was his discovery in archaic Greece of a standard by which to judge the inadequacies and distortions of the present, a discovery expressed in 1872 in *Die Geburt der Tragödie aus dem Geiste der Musik,* a book whose lack of respect for academic boundaries was integral to its judgment upon modernity. The outrage of the scholarly and literary establishment was unambiguous, ranging from Ritschl's public silence—his private comment was "*geistreich Schwiemelei*" ("clever giddiness")—and the rejection of a favorable review by Erwin Rohde by the *Literarisches Zentralblatt* to Hermann Usener's "Anyone who has written a thing like that is finished as a scholar" and the twenty-two-year-old Wilamowitz's savage pamphlet *Zukunftsphilologie!*[1]

Nietzsche did not finally resign his Basel chair until 1879. But he had previously been absent on sick leave for part of the time and his departure not only from the university but from *bürgerlich* society into the self-imposed exile of one without any fixed home expressed in his life the thought that much earlier he had uttered in a letter to Erwin Rohde: "No genuinely radical living for truth is possible in a university."[2] Yet it was not long before not only the university but truth itself had to be put in question.

By 1873 he was asking, "What then is truth?" and replying, "A mobile army of metaphors, metonymies, anthropomorphisms, a sum, in short, of human relationships which, rhetorically and poetically intensified, ornamented and transformed, come to be thought of, after long usage by a people, as fixed, binding, and canonical. Truths are illusions which we have forgotten are illusions, worn-out metaphors now impotent to stir the senses, coins which have lost their faces and are considered now as metal rather than currency."[3] In this short passage there are already to be found four key aspects of Nietzsche's later developed thought, psychological, epistemological, historical, and literary.

Psychologically what is taken to be fixed and binding about truth—and Nietzsche would of course have said the same about knowledge and duty and right—is an unrecognized motivation serving an unacknowledged purpose. To think and speak of truth, knowledge, duty, and right in the late nineteenth-century mode, the mode in fact of the Ninth Edition, is to give evidence of membership in a culture in which lack of self-knowledge has been systematically institutionalized. To be, and not to rebel against being, a member of the professoriate or of its disciples is to be a deformed person, deformed by whatever drive it is whose inhibition and distortion have led to an unacknowledged complicity in a system of suppressions and repressions expressed in a fixation whose signs and symptoms are the treatment of highly abstract moral and epistemic notions as fetishes. That drive turns out to be what Nietzsche was later to characterize as the will to power.

Epistemologically what this lack of self-knowledge and the arguments which are assembled in its support sustain is a blindness to the multiplicity of perspectives from which the world can be viewed and to the multiplicity of idioms by means of which it can be characterized; or rather, a blindness to the fact that there is a multiplicity of perspectives and idioms, but no single world which they are of or about. To believe in such a world would be the illusion of supposing that "a world would still remain over after one subtracted the perspective!" (WP 567).

Such a passage cries out for commentary and the cry has been more than sufficiently responded to. Nietzsche has surely committed himself, it has been argued, for example, to the thesis that all claims to truth are and can only be made from the standpoint afforded by some particular perspective. There is then no such thing as truth-as-such, but only truth-from-one-or-other-point-of-view. But this is of course itself, so the commentators go on, a universal nonperspectival theory of truth. And such commentators have then gone on further to debate whether Nietzsche's theory of truth is or is not some kind of pragmatic account. But it is not the outcome of such debates at the level of commentary that I wish to examine; it is rather the status of such commentary. Is such commentary no more than a spelling out of Nietzsche's own intentions and presuppositions? If so, it is presumably what Nietzsche himself would have asserted, had he only made those intentions and presuppositions fully explicit.

There are passages in Nietzsche which perhaps lend support to understanding him in this way, especially perhaps in his denials rather than in his affirmations. The denials of truth to Judaism, to Christianity, to Kant's philosophy, and to utilitarianism do seem to have the force of unconditional and universal nonperspectival denials. And insofar as Nietzsche's affirmations are the counterpart of such denials they too may seem to have the same kind of force. So the assertion that there *are* a multiplicity of perspectives as a counterpart to the denial that there is one world, "the world," beyond and sustaining all perspectives, may itself perhaps seem to have an ontological, nonperspectival import and status. If this is so, Nietzsche thus understood will have been restored to conventional academic philosophy, an apparent radical at one level but not at all so at another.

Yet if this way of understanding Nietzsche—as someone who speaks and writes at two distinct levels, as not only the author of but also implicitly at least the earliest academic commentator upon his own works, predecessor to such as Arthur Danto and J. P. Stern and Alexander Nehamas—can find some apparent support in the texts, it is nonetheless wholly at odds with what Nietzsche himself says about the relationship of any interpreter to any text: "Ultimately, the individual . . . has to interpret in a quite individual way even the words he has inherited. His interpretation of a formula at least is personal, even if he does not create a formula: as an interpreter he is still creative" (WP 767). And it is not just that all interpretation is creative, but also that all commentary is interpretation; Nietzsche held of utterances what he held of things: "That things possess a constitution in themselves quite apart from interpretation and subjectivity is a quite idle hypothesis" (WP 560).[4]

From this point of view to comment upon Nietzsche's texts is not to move to another level of discourse, one at which covert conventional ontological commitments can be identified; instead it is to rewrite and to extend Nietzsche's texts as texts of one's own. This creative action has two aspects. It is not freed from the constraints required by accuracy in reproducing Nietzsche's or anyone else's words. On this point the classical philologist in Nietzsche survived: "What is incorrect [in a particular text] can be ascertained in innumerable cases,"[5] although Nietzsche goes on to insist that even in this respect in many cases lack of evidence ensures the multiplication of interpretations. But within the constraints imposed by such accuracy each interpretation brings to bear its own metaphors. For metaphors are the currency of interpretation just as they are of the texts interpreted. The notion that we can escape from metaphor to some other conceptual mode—especially to the idiom of ontology—is a mistake, although those who apparently commit that mistake may in fact covertly be using their own metaphors in some more-or-less successful attempt to preempt the possibility of rival interpretations.

So it is perhaps with the metaphor of levels of discourse to which I referred earlier; it and kindred metaphors may be read as expressions of an academic attempt to reduce Nietzsche's thoughts to a certain kind of systematic order, metaphors which, rightly understood, reveal the parallel between the way in which analytical philosophers attempt to reduce the hitherto conceptually unsystematic to order and that in which an alien occupying power may reduce to order the hostile inhabitants of a territory which it has attempted to annex. Thus such metaphors express partisanship in a struggle to make Nietzsche safe territory for analytical philosophy. Hence we find in the conflicting texts concerning the interpretation of Nietzsche's texts just that "play of forces" which Gilles Deleuze has taught us to look for in those texts themselves. And each side in this conflict, in which French interpreters such as Deleuze, Jean Granier, and Sarah Kofman are matched against English-speaking analysts, can claim with some justice to be extending Nietzsche's own thought. But this points us toward what is in part ambiguity and in part instability in that thought itself, features that can be illuminated by a comparison with the encyclopedic mode of utterance so decisively rejected by Nietzsche.

The difference between that mode of utterance and Nietzsche's is not merely a matter of the latter's multiplicity of perspectives and relativization of truth to those perspectives, as against the former's underlying conception of the unity of truth and reason and of the comprehensiveness of the encyclopedic framework. Nor is it even only a matter of the latter's stress upon the conflict between perspectives and the struggle between rival interpretations as against the former's emphasis upon synthesis and development toward an agreed truth. It is also a matter of the contrast between utterance intended to express what is taken to be a warranted fixity of belief and utterance construed as a moment in the development of one position against others, a moment doubtless to be superseded in the shifting play of forces and use of metaphors. Yet Nietzsche did not entirely deliver himself over to this new or newly revived mode. What he partly withheld was the self as commentator upon and therefore external to both modes—a self who provided the grounds for finding in Nietzsche (as Danto and others have done) anticipations of doctrines advanced within analytic philosophy, but who (as those analytic commentators have failed to notice) both comments and, by then further abstracting himself, escapes from his own commentary. It is the movement between this abstracted commenting self and the self whose only voice and view is that of some perspective which is the source of the instability in Nietzsche's writing; it was his failure to demarcate any consistent boundary between those selves which is the source of the ambiguity. But "failure" may be the wrong word. For it remains to be asked whether such demarcation is in fact possible. That question must however be postponed to a later point in the argument at which its full importance can be made clear. What matters for the moment is to consider the implications of Nietzsche's complex stances for the genres through which he gives expression to those stances.

Nietzsche understood the academic mode of utterance as an expression of merely reactive attitudes and feelings, their negative, repressed, and repressive character disguised behind a mask of fixity and objectivity. It was therefore the perfect form of expression for the fetishistic morality of its culture, a morality which at the level of academic exposition provided the subject matter for debate between Kantians or neo-Kantians and utilitarians of various kinds. Nietzsche in directing his aphorisms against both parties not only undermined their moral and their philosophical theses but also mocked their style and their genre. By contrast the Nietzschean aphorism is active, a place and a play of contrary forces, the medium through which a current of energy passes. "An aphorism," Deleuze has said, "is an amalgam of forces that are always held apart from one another."[6] It is in uttering and responding to aphorisms that we outwit the reactive, academic mode. And what is true of the aphorism is true in another way of the poetic, prophetic mode of *Also Sprach Zarathustra*. But if this is so, then certain other of Nietzsche's works themselves become problematic by reason of their genre and none more so than *Zur Genealogie der Moral*, the book which is, as Deleuze points out, neither a collection of aphorisms nor a poem but "a key for the interpretation of aphorisms and the evaluation of poems."[7] It is in fact, as Nietzsche recognized (GM P:7), an academic treatise. And if Nietzsche was to carry through the task he had set himself, it had to be. What was that task?

It was to exhibit the historical genesis of the psychological deformation involved in the morality of the late nineteenth century and the philosophy and theology which sustained it, the type of morality, philosophy, and theology shared equally by Nietzsche's teachers and by Adam Gifford and his Edinburgh contemporaries. So the task of the genealogist more generally was to write the history of those social and psychological formations in which the will to power is distorted into and concealed by the will to truth, and the specific task of the genealogist of morality was to trace both socially and conceptually how rancor and resentment on the part of the inferior destroyed the aristocratic nobility of archaic heroes and substituted a priestly set of values in which a concern for purity and impurity provided a disguise for malice and hate.

There have recurred in the course of this history, as Nietzsche recounts it in *Zur Genealogie der Moral*, revivals of the archaic idea: in classical Rome, at the Renaissance, even in debased form in Napoleon, "that synthesis of the brutish with the more than human." But in this conflict between the aristocratic polarity of good against bad and the herd polarity of good against evil it was the latter which had prevailed, embodied most importantly first in Judaism and then in that "new Judaic Rome," the Church. What emerged was the victory of a life-denying ascetic ideal which issues in those conceptions of sin, of duty, of conscience, and of the relationship of virtue to happiness which have perpetuated both resentment and rancor and the denial of life. The ascetic ideal, as Nietzsche understands it, assumes many different forms, among them those of nineteenth-century academic scholarship. That scholarship prided itself on its freedom from those theological and other transcendental illusions which had imprisoned inquiry prior to the Enlightenment. Yet that pride was, according to Nietzsche, a mark of the reestablishment of the ascetic ideal in one more unacknowledged, life-destroying form. What Christianity had once purveyed had become the stock in trade of anti-Christianity.

Among those so indicted were the academic historians. Nietzsche had particularly in mind French and German scholars. But his view of nineteenth-century academic history is recognizably a view of the same terrain as that surveyed by the contributors on historical subjects to the Ninth Edition, although from a very different angle of vision. Where they saw a solid progress which displaced the past's understanding of itself in favor of their own understanding of it as an inadequate precursor of their own institutional, legal, and moral arrangements and views,[8] Nietzsche pilloried what he took to be the false claims to objectivity of those who had rejected the teleology of their predecessors and boasted of their own value-neutrality.

Nietzsche thus presents his own narrative in *Zur Genealogie der Moral* as superior to those of the academic historians precisely in that it enabled him to identify limitations and defects in their writing of which they themselves were unable to become aware. But this claim to superiority is easily misunderstood. For it may well be read, and Nietzsche from time to time gives us some reason to read it, as a straightforward claim to have defeated the academic historians, and indeed the philosophers too, in the light of standards of truth and rationality which may not perhaps be those actually appealed to within academic history and philosophy but which differ from them only in being a corrected and improved version of them, standards that provide a neutral court of appeal for Nietzsche, his adversaries, and his readers. And certainly Nietzsche was gratified by the sympathetic reading which he took himself to have received from such orthodox academics as Jacob Burckhardt and Hippolyte Taine,[9] while at the same time voicing again and again in his letters the thought that his views would have to be unpalatable to the vast majority of the reading public. What he never quite brought himself to say, and perhaps never quite brought himself to think, was that, if his views were not in fact almost universally rejected, they could not be vindicated, that on his own account assent by those inhabiting the culture of his age could only be accorded to theories infected by distortion and illusion.

What Nietzsche could not quite bring himself to think about his own views Adam Gifford and his contemporaries would have found completely unintelligible about theirs: that what is in fact the truth about the nature of God and the foundations of morality and about the forces at work in the formation of beliefs concerning those subjects might be such that, were it to be presented in Gifford Lectures to the late nineteenth-century academic and lay public, it could not but appear to them both incredible and offensive. Their inability even to entertain this type of thought was a sign of the depth of their commitment to a belief in the unity of truth and reason which excluded any possibility of the existence of radically incommensurable standards. Yet it is only in the light of such standards that Nietzsche's claim for the superiority of the narrative of *Zur Genealogie der Moral* can be rightly understood.

For Nietzsche all theorizing, all making of claims occurs in the context of activity; and it is from the standpoint afforded by and emerging in and from different modes of participation in and response to activity—some reactive and repressive, others open to the biologically vital possibility of activity—that different perspectives upon the variety of subject matters defined within each perspective become available. So it is not by reasoning that at a fundamental level anyone moves from one point of view to another. To believe that reasoning can be thus effective is to express allegiance to that dialectic of which Socrates was the initiator and in so doing to reaffirm one's inability to escape from the inhibiting and repressing reactive formation to which the repressing and reactive habits of activity exhibited in dialectical reasoning bind its adherents. Nietzsche did of course assert that the most skillful dialectical reasoning had in fact failed by its own standards as well as by his, especially in ethics, in theology, and in antitheology. He had nothing but scorn for both Kant and Mill. But in pointing this out Nietzsche was once again mocking the pretensions of dialectic, not turning it against itself in a way which would have made of him only one more dialectician.

So we have matched against each other two antagonistic views. The encyclopedist's conception is of a single framework within which knowledge is discriminated from mere belief, progress toward knowledge is mapped, and truth is understood as the relationship of *our* knowledge to *the* world, through the application of those methods whose rules are the rules of rationality as such. Nietzsche, as a genealogist, takes there to be a multiplicity of perspectives within each of which truth-from-a-point-of-view may be asserted, but no truth-as-such, an empty notion, about *the* world, an equally empty notion. There are no rules of rationality as such to be appealed to, there are rather strategies of insight and strategies of subversion. Correspondingly in ethics there is on the encyclopedist's view a set of conceptions of duty, obligation, the right, and the good which have emerged from and can be shown to be superior to—in respect both of title to rational justification and of what is taken to be genuinely moral conduct—their primitive, ancient, and other pre-Enlightenment predecessors. Problems there may indeed still be, even after Spinoza and Kant and Mill, and progress still has to be made; this is one reason why lectureships such as Lord Gifford's need to be established. But these problems are posed from within, and progress is expected from within, the enclosing framework of a unified, encyclopedic rationality. By contrast a genealogical view requires of us sufficient insight to understand that allegiance to just such a view is always a sign of badness, of inadequately managed rancor and resentment. The conduct of life requires a rupture, a breaking down of such idols, and a breaking up of fixed patterns, so that something radically new will emerge.

Each of these two rival views, the encyclopedist's and the genealogist's, contains within itself a more or less spelled-out representation of the other, indeed cannot dispense with such a representation as a counterpart to its representation to itself of itself. From the standpoint of the encyclopedist the genealogist is reproducing familiar irrationalist themes and theses; so the genealogist's perspectivism is characteristically understood as merely one more version of relativism, open to refutation by the arguments used by Socrates against Protagoras. From the standpoint of the genealogist the encyclopedist is inescapably imprisoned within metaphors unrecognized as metaphors. And from both standpoints any attempt, such as my own in this lecture, to produce a characterization of this antagonism from some external, third vantage point is doomed to failure; there is no idiom neutral between the encyclopedist's affirmations and distinctions and the genealogist's subversions.

One can indeed, as I have tried to do, learn the idiom of each from within as a new first language, much in the way that an anthropologist constitutes him or herself a linguistic and cultural beginner in some alien culture. In so doing one can come to recognize that the only capacity which the adherents of each standpoint possess for translating the utterances of the other would always result in what some adherent of that other standpoint who had learned the rival language would have to characterize as mistranslation, as misrepresentation. Of course within both conceptual schemes it is possible for each to recognize the concepts of the other as in some ways variants upon his or her own. So those genealogists who speak only of "true-from-a-point-of-view" recognize in utterances about *the* truth, or what is "true as such," a mystifying reified extension of their own concept, while the encyclopedist understands "true-from-a-point-of-view" as a diminished, misleading, and self-undermining reworking of "true as such."

And a similar understanding extends to a whole range of epistemological and practical concepts, so that we have two radically different alternative and rival conceptual schemes, recognizable as such only by those who have learned the language of each and of both as two first languages and who are able to speak each as those who inhibit that scheme speak it, but necessarily unrecognized by those who insist that to understand the language of the other it must be translatable into their own. But it is just this insistence which the standpoint of the encyclopedist requires, for a blindness to the possibility of genuine alternative conceptual schemes is a necessary part of the encyclopedist's point of view, while an openness to that possibility is equally necessary on the part of the genealogist. So here is one more way in which the two are at odds, exemplifying the truth that in philosophical controversies of any depth what divides the contending parties is characteristically in part how to characterize the disagreement.

Yet it is just at this point that the question of genre becomes urgent once again for the genealogist. In assuming the role of genealogist Nietzsche had had to repudiate that of professor and along with it those modes of public utterance which presupposed and expressed the academic establishment's encyclopedic allegiance. The lecture as understood by that establishment, whether in Germany or in Scotland, the article in the scholarly and increasingly to be professionalized journal, and the magisterial treatise all provided forms which could not contain Nietzsche's content, any more than the Nietzschean aphorism—and along with it the paragraph of commentary—so well adapted to Nietzsche's purposes, could have become the common currency of academic life. And yet it is quite difficult *not* to read *Zur Genealogie der Moral* otherwise than as one more magisterial treatise, better and more stylishly written indeed than the books of Kant or Hermann Cohen, of Leopold von Ranke or of Adolph von Harnack (a contributor to the Ninth Edition), but deploying arguments and appealing to sources in the same way, plainly constrained by the same standards of factual accuracy and no more obviously polemical against rival views. Did Nietzsche then simply relapse into being once again a professor, albeit one now without a chair, and could he indeed have done otherwise if he was to elaborate and defend the central positions of *Zur Genealogie der Moral*? If so, then genealogy in the course of defending itself has both relapsed and collapsed into encyclopedia.

The genealogist's answer is that it may indeed seem to be so, if any one piece of writing is considered in isolation from what precedes and follows, if it is abstracted from that movement through time of which it is a part and in terms of which alone it is rightly to be understood. Every piece of writing, like every spoken word—and in this at least writing and speech have more in common than what distinguishes them—is utterance on the move, in which the utterer is actively responding to what has gone before and actively expecting both others and him or herself either to react or to act in further response, so that he or she may move beyond it to something else. So the genealogical genre is one in which present theses about what has been are presented in a genre open to what is not yet. Such theses cannot have either the type of fixity or the type of finality to which the encyclopedic mind always aspires and which it sometimes, as recurrently in Adam Gifford's writings and in the Ninth Edition, believes itself to have achieved. But this answer by the genealogist raises a further difficulty.

For the genealogist who has put the academic stance in question by writing and publishing his or her book is addressing whom? Someone presumably to and with whom he not only puts in question the objects of his critique, but to whom he opens up the possibility of in turn putting the genealogist in question, either in respect of particular theses or in respect of his or her overall project. Yet this cannot be done without adopting a fixity of stance, a staying in place, a commitment to defend and to respond and, if necessary, to yield. A piece of writing, whenever it confronts a reader—or indeed a set speech, when it is reuttered to a new hearer—does so at a time which is not only "now" for that reader or hearer, but becomes the author's coincident "now," no matter how long previously the work was written or spoken. In that shared time, exempted in some respects, although not in others from the temporal separation of the "now" of utterance from the "now" of reading or hearing, the timelessness extends to the standards of reason-giving, reason-accepting, and reason-rejecting, in the light of which alone the genealogist and his or her reader can put each other to the question. This appeal to impersonal, timeless standards, so often taken for granted in the post-Enlightenment world by those who take themselves to have rejected metaphysics, is itself only to be understood adequately as a piece of metaphysics.

The possibility of such an appeal is inseparable from the possibility of that atemporal "now" at which writer and reader encounter each other, that "now" at which both can appeal away from themselves and the particularity of their own claims to *what is* timelessly, logically, ontologically, and evaluatively, and is only thereby and therefore the property of neither writer nor reader. And Nietzsche recognized the force of this objection. "In order to think and infer it is necessary to assume beings: logic handles only formulas for what remains the same," he was to write (WP 517), anticipating the need to respond to this point; and he replied that the beings so assumed are fictitious, among them the being of the ego or of other individuals (WP 517–520). But it is nonetheless necessarily presupposed by the act of writing for a particular reader or readers that the ego of writer and that of reader have enough fixity and continuity to enter into those relationships constitutive of the acts of reading-as-one-who-has-been-written-for and of writing-as-one-who-is-to-be-read.

The claim that I am making is a modest, albeit metaphysical one, not to be confused, for example, with Jürgen Habermas's neo-Kantian thesis that allegiance to one specific set of ideal norms is a necessary condition for acts of communication. All that writer and reader must presuppose is enough of logical, ontological, and evaluative commitment—and the commitments of the one need not be in all respects the same as those of the other—to ensure the continuities and fixed identities and differences without which each cannot by his or her own standards, even if not yet or not at all by those of the other, convict that other of inconsistency, falsity, and failure of reference. Yet even this is enough to engage both parties in the kind of metaphysics which Nietzsche and a variety of post-Nietzscheans have tried to proscribe. It is one sign of the inescapable character of this metaphysics of reading that those who proscribe it so often fail nonetheless in the eyes of their post-Nietzschean colleagues to eliminate all traces of it from their own work. Thus Martin Heidegger has accused Nietzsche of retaining in his thought an unacknowledged metaphysical remnant and so Jacques Derrida has in turn similarly accused Heidegger.

It is not of course that some forms of writing and reading cannot occur without this metaphysical dimension; but its absence makes of the encounter of writer and reader one in which each can be no more than and no other than the other's intentional object, cast for whatever role that particular intentional stance requires, victim to the other's victimizer. So perhaps the vigilant suspicion of a completely consistent Nietzschean antimetaphysician, always on the watch for distorted expressions of the will to power, would find its self-confirming justifications in a type of situation which it itself had created and sustained. But to all this there is of course a Nietzschean reply, one which in its strongest and most plausible version recognizes (as Nietzsche himself did) that at the moment of writing for a reader and at the moment of a reader confronting that writer in his or her writing, something very like what I have been describing—a now of the present and of at least apparent ontological presencing—must occur and endure for a time: but *only*, so the reply runs, for a time. It is its temporariness which disengages us and which enables us to regard once more as a fiction this apparent momentary metaphysical disregard of the temporality of flux and perspective.

So the genre of the academic treatise is, it may be conceded, the apparent genre of Nietzsche's writing in *Zur Genealogie der Moral*, but only apparent, not real, because it represents no more than a temporary stance, a mask worn only for the purposes of certain particular addressings of certain particular audiences. "Metaphysical theories are masks," said Oscar Wilde, and Nietzsche would have added that our apparently cognitive attitudes toward them are no more than modes of putting on, displaying, and discarding such masks. The problem then for the genealogist is how to combine the fixity of particular stances, exhibited in the use of standard genres of speech and writing, with the mobility of transition from stance to stance, how to assume the contours of a given mask and then to discard it for another, without ever assenting to the metaphysical fiction of a face which has its own finally true and undiscardable representation, whether by Rembrandt or in a shaving mirror. Can it be done? The research program of the post-Nietzschean enterprise, so prodigally endorsed by Nietzsche for his intellectual heirs, is to find out by trying and either failing or succeeding in a systematic attempt to carry through that program. No such attempt in terms of systematic implementation or erudition or honesty is likely to be more impressive than that to which Michel Foucault devoted so much of his life.

Yet this way of understanding Foucault's project as a continuation of Nietzsche's—and it was for much of the time Foucault's own understanding of that project—requires a response to the objection that Nietzsche's thought was not, and indeed could not have been, as radically alien to conventional modes as Foucault and Deleuze and I, following them, have taken it to be. For certainly Nietzsche not only drew upon, but at times identified himself with positions which found a place within the encyclopedists' scheme. Karl Jaspers spoke of Nietzsche's engagement with theses from nineteenth-century physics and biology as his positivist phase. Nietzsche wrote history on occasion much as some other nineteenth-century historians wrote it, even while disowning his kinship with them. And he reserved some of his most radical remarks either for unpublished texts or for the characterization of conceptions such as that of the Eternal Recurrence, which he may later have rejected.

So it is possible by excision and reinterpretation and change of emphasis to construct an alternative account of Nietzsche's development in which Nietzsche did indeed attempt to break systematically with conventional modes of thought but failed to do so. Nor on this alternative view could it have been otherwise. The attempt to spell out the consequences of the death of God by moving beyond the constraints of grammar and logic and of all established values was bound to end in tragic failure. For what Nietzsche may have aspired to say moves beyond intelligible speech. Incommensurability with what both the encyclopaedists and their academic heirs have taken to be the necessary features of *any* intelligible thought and discourse, the type of incommensurability with such thought and discourse which I and others have ascribed to Nietzsche, cannot occur. If Nietzsche did envisage it as a possibility, *we*, so it is suggested, know better.

It is indeed from the standpoint of such a "we" that this objection is advanced, a "we" who insist that intelligibility is nothing other than translatability into "our" language and conceptual idiom. So Nietzsche, having been translated into "our" terms and evaluated by "our" standards, turns out to be after all not so different from "us." The objection fails of course for everyone unwilling to equate intelligibility with translatability into one's own initial language and conceptual idiom. And what its attempt to coopt Nietzsche cannot reckon with is his subordination of the elucidatory academic treatise to the poem and the epigram, a subordination designed to enable us finally to dispense with elucidatory treatises altogether in favor of a mode of discourse and a way of life in which mockery, celebration, and disruptions of sense make use of assertions only in order later to displace them.

Hence the argument that Nietzsche could not have propounded a set of statements which put him at such radical variance with traditional ways of understanding the place of logic and grammar in our discourse, because *any* set of statements *must* presuppose to some large degree just that kind of understanding, misses the point. Nietzsche's final standpoint, that toward rather than from which he speaks, cannot be expressed as a set of statements. Statements are made only to be discarded—and sometimes taken up again—in that movement from utterance to utterance in which what is communicated is the movement. Nietzsche did not advance a new theory against older theories; he proposed an abandonment of theory.

Notice that I am not claiming to be able to refute this type of objection by appeal to Nietzsche's writings. What is at issue between those who understand Nietzsche in the one way and those who understand him in the other is in key part how those writings are to be interpreted and how the development from one text to another is to be construed. Nietzsche's writings do not provide us with a set of neutral data, appeal to which will resolve the disagreement. And this is precisely what we should expect if this disagreement is, as I judge it to be, one in which incommensurable standpoints are at odds.

Notice also that I am not at this point claiming that the Nietzschean project, as I have understood it, has been or can be carried through successfully. All that I am claiming is that it must be understood and judged initially in its own terms and that in these terms it is not evidently and at once self-defeating. Whether it can in fact be carried through successfully is a question posed by the history of Foucault's thought.

Nietzsche's progress was from professor to genealogist, Foucault's from being neither to being both simultaneously. And hence for him the problem of academic presentation as a mask assumed by the genealogist exerted pressures perhaps even more intense than those felt by Nietzsche. He confronted that problem directly in his contribution to the *Festschrift* for Jean Hyppolite,[10] published within a year of his inaugural lecture at the Collége de France. In that essay he addresses in Nietzschean terms not so much the question of what history is and achieves—that is the question to be answered by the whole Nietzschean research program—but the question of who the historian is and how he or she must be transformed by engagement with history if the work of history is to be informed by genuinely Nietzschean insights. History thus understood turns out to have three uses, all of which sever the connection of history with memory and with memorial veneration of the past by creating a disruptive countermemory.

The first of these uses is to understand official academic history—the history propounded by professors of history—as itself a kind of parody of the past, so that instead of taking the identities of the significant figures of the past as solid, we understand them as masks and ourselves as the producers of a charade, producers whose own illusory self-conception has been put in doubt by this understanding. Second, we go on to comprehend them and ourselves, not as persons, as identities, but as complex patterns of elements representative of their various differing cultures. So that the identity of the historian, like that of his or her subjects of study, is dissipated, a dissipation which makes visible the discontinuities concealed by the continuities of academic history. The third of these uses of history is to reveal in the consciousness of the historian a rancorous will to knowledge, shared with other modern inquirers, a will which does not in fact issue in any progress toward truth and reason, but which, because it does not recognize limitation, demands destructive and self-destructive sacrifices.

There is of course for Foucault a self-endangering paradox here: the insights conferred by this post-Nietzschean understanding of the uses of history are themselves liable to subvert the project of understanding the project. Consider in this regard *Les Mots et les choses,* published five years earlier. This is at one level a conventional academic treatise, even if a somewhat radical one. It is a recognizable extension of the thought of Gaston Bachelard in its emphasis upon the place of discontinuities and incommensurabilities in intellectual history and it could be read—has been read, for example, by Ian Hacking—as doing for immature sciences, and notably for the human sciences, something akin to what Thomas Kuhn achieved for our understanding of the mature physical and chemical sciences. But this kind of reading of *Les Mots et les choses* undervalues or ignores two key aspects of that book. The first is emphasized by Foucault himself in his preface.

His interest in the immature sciences, he makes it clear, is not or not only for their own sake; it is because they tend to exemplify a middle area, always of some obscurity and confusion, between the fixed codes of a culture, on the one hand, and the well-ordered enterprises of the mature sciences on the other, an area in which what underlies those determinate orders can be identified, an area in which we can be liberated into a perception of what is anterior to the modes of being of order, an insight into sets of coherences, resemblances, and correspondences, capable of being organized in alternative, incompatible, and incommensurable modes of classification and representation.

A second relevant aspect of *Les Mots and les choses* only seems to have become visible to Foucault later. In *Les Mots et les choses* Foucault distinguished three successive styles of thought, each with its own standards in respect to classification and the use of signs, divided historically by moments of rupture, one in which the Renaissance period is displaced by the Classical at the beginning of the seventeenth century, and another in which the Classical in turn loses its place at the end of the eighteenth. But this book about incommensurable ordered schemes of classification and representation is itself organized as an ordered scheme of classification and representation, a scheme not identified or justified within its own pages except by implication in the recurrent methodological remarks, which have the surface qualities—from the standpoint of genealogy—of all such methodological remarks. It thereby, unlike standard texts in academic history, puts itself in question—notice that it is the text which does this, not the author—requiring us to supplement and perhaps correct, how radically we cannot know in advance, our first-order understanding of *Les Mots et les choses* by a second-order understanding of what underlies and orders the ordering of *Les Mots et les choses*. Foucault's threefold Nietzschean indictment of history has become self-referential.

When I say that it is the text which puts itself in question, and not the author, I do not of course only mean that *Les Mots et les choses* could not but be read as a self-subverting text, whatever Foucault's actual intentions at the time of writing. I mean also, and perhaps more importantly, that as Foucault had argued in "Qu'est-ce un auteur?"[11] "the author" for him names a role or function, not a person, and the use of a particular author's name discharges this function by assigning a certain status to a piece of discourse. Hence any possibility of moving beyond and behind the text to authorized intention is already ruled out by authorized intention. Text-and-author, text-as-authored, this is the self-presenting unit. It was of course in part because Foucault thus concurred in the liquidation of the conventional conception of the author that he was, much to his own annoyance, sometimes described as a structuralist. But if he agreed with some of the structuralists in what he, as a genealogist, denied, he disagreed fundamentally with them over what they affirmed.

Structuralisms have been of different and incompatible kinds, diminishing in intellectual power and interest as they moved further away from their sources in the anthropology of Georges Dumézil and the mathematics of Nicolas Bourbaki. But what they have all shared is the appeal to some set of elements, structured in this or that way, as fundamental to explanation and understanding, as that in terms of which all else is to be explained. That there are any such fundamental sets or structures Foucault consistently denied. And so when he moved from *Les Mots et les choses* to *L'Archéo-logie du Savoir* (1969) it was not in order to disclose some single fundamental level of the ordering of sciences, even of immature sciences, for that too would be an order whose underlying principle would need to be identified and itself put in question, but a movement toward the preconceptual, the presystematic, and the prediscursive which itself necessarily cannot but be comprehended in terms that are conceptual, systematic, and discursive. So very different and heterogeneous regularities and levels of discourse are disclosed, through which are generated a variety of incommensurable bodies of claims assigned in their assemblage the status of a science. To the set of relations which in any given time and place unify the discursive practices underlying any one such body of claims Foucault gave the name *episteme*, mocking Plato's and Aristotle's uses of that word in so doing.

Sciences then, as conventionally understood in the history of science or by natural scientists themselves, have become secondary phenomena. The ruptures in that history, as identified by Bachelard or Kuhn, moments in which a transition is made from one standardized understanding of what it is to be rational to some other, sometimes incommensurable standardized understanding of rationality, are also secondary phenomena. For they, like the standardized orders which they divide and join, are the outcome of assemblages and confluences in the making of which distributions of power have been at work, in such a way that what appear at the surface level as forms of rationality both are and result from the implementation of a variety of aggressive and defensive strategies, albeit strategies without subjects. Truth and power are thus inseparable. And what appear as projects aimed at the possession of truth are always willful in their exercise of power. In so exposing them Foucault thus discharges the third of the genealogist's tasks as characterized by Nietzsche and recharacterized by Foucault himself. But what now about the discourse in which and through which the genealogist performs his or her tasks? I have described Foucault's development in my terms; but what would it be to describe it in his? Could they be so very different? The question arises once again: How far can the genealogist, first in characterizing and explaining his project, to him or herself as much as to others, and later in evaluating his or her success or failure in the genealogist's own terms, avoid falling back into a nongenealogical, academic mode, difficult to discriminate from that encyclopedist's or professorial academic mode in the repudiation of which the genealogical project had its genesis and its rationale?

Certainly Foucault himself became a professor of professors, restoring Nietzsche's project to the professoriate from which Nietzsche had rescued it. I do not mean by this only that whereas Nietzsche began as a professor but became a homeless wanderer in the lodging places afforded by Nice and Marienbad and Stresa and Genoa, Foucault began as a transient, moving from Lille to Uppsala to Warsaw and later between Clermont-Ferrand and both Brazil and Tunisia, but ended with nearly fifteen years speaking *ex cathedra* from the Collége de France; but also that this inversion symbolizes Foucault's movement toward and final arrival at the plain academic style of the *Histoire de la sexualité* and the even plainer explanations of his explanations offered in that wearisome multitude of interviews in which the academic deference evident in the questions is never rejected by Foucault in his answers.

This final Foucault was in one aspect at least a twentieth-century Hobbes, replying, when asked by Jacques Alain Miller and Alain Grosrichard in a discussion in 1977[12] to identify the subjects who oppose each other in those exercises of power which constitute social, cultural, and intellectual life, that it is "all against all. . . . Who fights against whom? We all fight each other. And there is always within each of us something that fights something else." When Miller asked whether the components of the transitory coalitions formed by participants in those struggles would be individuals, Foucault replied, "Yes, individuals, or even subindividuals." So there is even internalized Hobbesian struggle in this war of each against all. And in the portrayal of this struggle ironic distance, unmasking, self-unmasking, and all the other features of those essentially temporary stances which mark the genealogist's historical disclosures are quite absent. So Foucault regressed into academia. But did this regression from Nietzsche to Hobbes have to happen? Could the genealogical enterprise have been sustained in its integrity? The answers to these questions depend upon those to two others.

I noted earlier that the relationship which *Zur Genealogie der Moral* requires to hold between reader and text involves a mode of reading and of argumentative debate in the light of certain impersonal and timeless standards of truth, reference, and rationality, standards enduring allegiance to which would be inconsistent with the genealogical project. To this however it was possible to reply that this relationship need only be temporary and provisional, an allegiance to be sustained not by the genealogist him- or herself, but only by one of his or her potentially many *personae*, masks, and thus one not committing the genealogist him- or herself as that elusive figure moves from stance to stance. Whether this reply could be sustained, so I have suggested, depends upon the success or failure of genealogy, not as a single set of claims in a single text, but as a research program of the kind undertaken, but in the end almost, if not quite, abandoned by Foucault.

Yet now the question arises as to whether what even Foucault's partial implementation of that program may not have revealed is that the successive strategies of the genealogist may not inescapably after all involve him or her in commitments to standards at odds with the central theses of the genealogical stance. For in making his or her sequence of strategies of masking and unmasking intelligible to him- or herself, the genealogist has to ascribe to the genealogical self a continuity of deliberate purpose and a commitment to that purpose which can only be ascribed to a self not to be dissolved into masks and moments, a self which cannot but be conceived as more and other than its disguises and concealments and negotiations, a self which just insofar as it can adopt alternative perspectives is itself not perspectival, but persistent and substantial. Make of the genealogist's self nothing but what genealogy makes of it, and that self is dissolved to the point at which there is no longer a continuous genealogical project. Or so I am suggesting.

Is this indeed so? If we press this question, we find ourselves asking another closely related question. In narrating the systematic development and recurrent reworking of Foucault's strategies, it is not just that we have to ascribe a unity of project to a deliberating, purposeful self with its own unity as agent, if that project is to be intelligible. We also have to recognize the parts played by logic, by the identification, for example, of contradiction, by appeals to evidence, by the practical reasoning exhibited in the actions through which Foucault's inquiries progressed or failed to progress toward a from time to time reformulated *telos,* and by his reevaluations of their success and failure. The standards in the light of which such reevaluations are made and such reasoning conducted are independent of the particular stages and moments of the temporary strategies through which the genealogist moves his or her overall projects forward, and the recognition accorded to them is necessary for the genealogist to find his or her own actions and utterances intelligible, let alone for them to be intelligible to anyone else. Hence once again it seems to be the case that the intelligibility of genealogy requires beliefs and allegiances of a kind precluded by the genealogical stance. Foucault's carrying forward of Nietzsche's enterprise has thus forced upon us two questions: Can the genealogical narrative find any place within itself for the genealogist? And can genealogy, as a systematic project, be made intelligible to the genealogist, as well as to others, without some at least tacit recognition being accorded to just those standards and allegiances which it is its avowed aim to disrupt and subvert?

The inadequacy of responses so far to these questions may suggest that the history of genealogy has been, and could not have been other than, one of progressive impoverishment. It is not of course so much that Foucault's later scholarly enterprises suffered from impoverishment but that they avoided it only by drawing less and less covertly upon nongenealogical sources and methods. Yet if genealogy now confronts problems for which it does not at least as yet seem able to devise solutions (a resourcelessness which may of course be only temporary), the surviving adherents of the encyclopedist's mode of moral inquiry can take no comfort from this for two reasons. First, the particular genealogical diagnoses of the moral, metaphysical, and theological attitudes typified by the Ninth Edition of the *Encyclopedia Britannica* retain a great deal of cogency independent of the fate of the genealogical project in general. If genealogy has not, or not yet, overcome those difficulties which must be overcome if its claims to sovereignty in the realm of moral inquiry are to be vindicated, it has at least succeeded in impugning the encyclopedist's form of moral inquiry.

Second, any defects in the developed genealogical treatment of the incommensurability of rival fundamental moral, scientific, metaphysical, and theological standpoints do nothing to lessen the existence and the importance of that incommensurability and of the presently unresolvable disagreements and conflicts which stem from it. The transformation of the moral inquirer from a participant in an encyclopedic enterprise shared by all adequately reflective and informed human beings into an engaged partisan of one such warring standpoint against its rivals is an accomplished fact, any adequate recognition of which results in the dissolution of the encyclopedist's standpoint, a dissolution evident in the current Fifteenth Edition of the *Encyclopedia Britannica*. In the Ninth Edition the editor's overall standpoint and scheme was widely, if not quite universally, shared by his contributors, and the structure of particular entries, especially in such key entries as those on "Ethics" and "Theology," was consonant with the structure of the encyclopedia as a whole. But with the Fifteenth Edition it is quite otherwise. Heterogeneous and divergent contributions, which recognize the diversity and fragmentation of standpoints in central areas, are deeply at odds with the overall scheme, insofar as that scheme presupposes any real unity to the work, rather than merely providing some organization for a massive work of reference. Mortimer J. Adler, chairman of the board of editors of this edition,[13] recognizes this when he allows at the close of his introductory account that what the Encyclopedia embodies is no more than "faith in the unity of knowledge."[14] The encyclopedic mode of inquiry has become one more fideism and a fideism which increasingly flies in the face of contemporary realities.

Since the presuppositions of the encyclopedist's standpoint and mode of inquiry are, as I argued earlier, the same presuppositions which underlay the endowment of such distinctively academic institutions as the Gifford Lectures, it may well seem that to continue to appoint Gifford lecturers can itself be no more than a similar act of unwarranted faith. Whether it is so or not depends upon whether there is any third alternative to the encyclopedic and genealogical modes of moral inquiry. It is therefore toward an investigation of the possibility of just such a third alternative that I shall turn in the next four lectures.[15]

NOTES

1. See, more generally, *Nietzsche and the Classical Tradition*, ed. J. C. O'Flaherty, T. F. Sellner, and R. M. Helm (Chapel Hill: University of North Carolina Press, 1976).

2. 15 December 1870.

3. *Über Wahrheit und Lüge im Aussermoralischen Sinn*, I.

4. See also GS 374.

5. Letter to Claus Fuchs, 26 August 1888.

6. Gilles Deleuze, "Pensée Nomade," in *Nietzsche aujourd'hui* (Paris: Union Generale d'Editions, 1973).

7. Gilles Deleuze, *Nietzsche et la philosophie* (Paris: Presses Universitaires de France, 1962), pp. 3, 7.

8. See, for example, "History," by J. Cotter Morrison, volume 12.

9. Letter to Jacob Burchhardt, 14 November 1887.

10. Michel Foucault, "Nietzsche, la genealogie, l'histoire," in *Hommage a Jean Hyppolite* (Paris: Presses Universitaires de France, 1971).

11. Or, "What is an Author?" First published in *Bulletin de la Societe Française de Philosophie* 63 (July–September 1969): 73–104.

12. *Ornicar* 10 (July 1977).

13. Chicago: Encyclopedia Britannica, Inc.: 1974.

14. *Propaedia*, p. 446.

15. The following four lectures (chapters) are: "Too Many Thomisms?"; "The Augustinian Conception of Moral Enquiry"; "Aristotle and/or/against Augustine: Rival Traditions of Enquiry"; and "Aquinas and the Rationality of Tradition." Four more follow: "In the Aftermath of Defeated Tradition"; "Tradition against Encyclopedia: Enlightened Morality as the Superstition of Modernity"; "Tradition against Genealogy: Who Speaks to Whom?"; and "Reconceiving the University as an Institution and the Lecture as a Genre"—ED.

SEVENTEEN

The Question of Genealogy*

Eric Blondel

While the idea of genealogy relates to a problem posed and developed in the main (and made famous) by Nietzsche, he was not the first to use the term. This is a sign, perhaps, that in spite of his reputation for originality, Nietzsche locates himself within the framework of an already established inquiry that he follows and revives, yet does not truly initiate.

To which problems does the notion of Nietzschean genealogy respond? Complementing his critique of the dominant Platonic-Christian culture, the goal and general orientation of his thought and his constant concern are the search for "new paths for culture." Nietzsche adopts a genealogical perspective to render problematic the "ideals" of our culture as they are revealed in our morals, science, religion, and philosophy and in the political assumptions that have been dominant for more than twenty centuries. He seeks to establish the two-thousand-year-old underlying unity and permanence behind these diverse manifestations. Thus described, the analysis might seem traditionally Platonic: a search for the unity and permanence of a hidden essence that is discovered behind multiplicity and is then perceptible. What could be more typical of Plato and the philosophical and religious traditions that followed him than the search for a hidden foundation, for a deeper nature, or for the primal essence of diverse appearances?

It is an old reproach (touching upon a problem of philosophical interpretation) to say that Nietzsche would be paradoxical, even irresponsible, if he merely borrowed a Platonic schema for evaluating and diagnosing the institutions, values, and ideals of a culture, while at the same time condemning that culture as being deeply influenced, through its Christianity,

*Translated by David Blacker and Annie Pritchard, revised by the author and the editor.

by the dualism, essentialism, intellectualism, and rationalism that one customarily attributes to Plato. If the basis of his interrogation is classical, and if his critical gesture is itself characteristic of the Western philosophical tradition, then what does Nietzsche bring that is truly novel to the analysis of culture and values?

This apparent analogy with Plato reveals, first and foremost, Nietzschean genealogy's connection with a quite well-defined tradition. It is necessary to recognize that Nietzsche's very critique, which is directly inspired by Schopenhauer, represents a continuation of a debate begun by Kant. More precisely still: insofar as genealogy seeks to discover the hidden principles of morality, metaphysics, and religion, and to examine Western science by revealing its origins, meanings, and worth, it charges itself with the search for essences—as might a "Kantian" critical tribunal, which inquires into the conditions of possibility and of criteria and then renders a verdict. Furthermore, Nietzsche adopts a Kantian attitude of attempting to end previous errors and illusions once and for all, and of challenging not only its philosophical predecessors—heralding a new and definitive philosophy (critical philosophy)—but also previous attempts to diagnose, ground, and engender metaphysical thought. Like Kant, he combats metaphysical dogmatism. But he substitutes mistrust and suspicion for "critique," thereby substituting genealogy for transcendental philosophy.

This is the viewpoint from which to comment on the occurrence of the word "genealogy" in Kant's preface to the first edition of the *Critique of Pure Reason* to designate—and impugn—potential Lockean criticisms. According to Kant, it is Lockean empiricism that seeks to establish a "physiology of human understanding" and to discover the origin and foundation—and thus the worth and validity—of our concepts. But this "pretended Queen" (to follow the Kantian metaphor) fails in her "pretensions," since the birth of our metaphysical ideas can be neither legitimized nor justified by genealogy. Similarly, in Nietzsche's work, the fine phrases and exalted ideals of morality will reveal themselves to be of a most base extraction—indeed, from a "birth" of "shameful origin [*pudenda origo*]" (D 42, 102). One might also note that, in order to challenge what seems to him a most illegitimate conception, Nietzsche opposes his "genealogy" to the term "origin," which his rival Paul Rée employed toward the same end (in *The Origins of Moral Feelings*).

As a follower of Schopenhauer, however, Nietzsche strays from the purely Kantian critical path with respect to genealogy. Schopenhauer affirms that the thing in itself—*qua* ultimate reality, the founding basis of all phenomena, the truth hidden by appearances (and especially by representation)—is the will, the "will to live"; that is, desires and affects (which Nietzsche calls the "body"), whose principle is the "will to power." Thus Nietzsche's genealogy grafts a Schopenhauerian problem onto a Kantian question, becoming a critique and assessment that determines and evaluates ideals by exposing their hidden origins in the affects, drives, body and "will (to power)." Furthermore, in order to counter the "fixity" of Schopenhauer's Platonic "Ideas," Nietzsche's genealogy considers the contributions of Darwinian *evolutionary* theory. He thereby brings forward the *historical* questions of becoming, change, development, homology and reproduction— that is, of "natural history."

In other words, Nietzsche *diverts* the Kantian critique by applying it from a Schopenhauerian perspective. This critique (and this is the reproach addressed to Kant) makes a kind of "short circuit" or takes a "shortcut," thereby rendering reason its own ground and judge: but "an instrument is incapable of judging itself" (D P:3). Nietzsche then substitutes a detour of his own: a circuitous route that must of necessity pass through the body whose instrument reason is. In this way, Nietzschean genealogy is not just an extending or surpassing of the Kantian critical question that would merge philosophical theories into an all-embracing unity (and allow them to go beyond philosophies into Philosophy). Genealogy on the contrary implies that, through this detour—this *return* of philosophy to its hidden self—philosophy becomes *itself and its other* (which displaces or decenters its concepts), and restores not only homogeneous reason but also the *heterogeneity* of the "body."

As evidence, consider the enigmatic phrase that opens the *Genealogy*: "We are unknown to ourselves, we men of knowledge—and with good reason (*Grund,* foundation)" (GM P:1). Behind the apparent tautology, this phrase leads to a paradoxical contradiction that opens a chasm between knowledge and itself, between the "will to truth" and its real foundation in the will to power (of the affects), and between knowledge and the unknown body's need to know. This chasm divides thought from itself and philosophy from itself—as if it were its other: genealogy is situated in this open, unexplored, and almost unfathomable space. Kantian critique (in Kant's words) invites "reason to tackle anew the most difficult of all its tasks, that is, the knowledge of itself." Genealogy, by setting reason aside, brings reason and knowledge to know and recognize themselves in one another, and in (or as) their other.

Hence an impossible enterprise (divided, contradictory, and unfathomable) that interminably tries in vain to heal the rupture that it produces and yet maintains between reason and itself, between language and the drives, and between the body and itself as "great reason." Genealogy will inevitably be *heterology* (i.e., discourse of or on the other) insofar as it uncovers the other hidden in the same. Because it concerns culture and the body, Nietzsche's thought is radically ambiguous and impossible: it is between thought and body, between reason and unreason, between "philosophy" and Philosophy, and between the last avatar of metaphysics and the "new philosophers." As Nietzsche says, this is a thought of the (at)tempt(ation), of *Versuch* and *Versuchung* (BGE 42).

Genealogy thus develops as

—(natural) history
—psychology
—philology-interpretation
—evaluation.

Before detailing this development, one should note a second point of view: Nietzsche the genealogist inherits a tradition to which he lays claim, assumes, and even claims to prolong. Although genealogy is innovative, Nietzsche as "psychologist" on the one hand, and as "evaluator" on the other, is and remains a *moralist*. What we understand by this, as he does, is certainly *not* the philosophical preoccupation of imposing judgment, criteria, and norms. That type of "moralist" is, on the contrary, the main target of his notably anti-Christian attacks. But, as in the classical French literature Nietzsche admired, the writer-thinker is at bottom concerned with describing and reflecting upon the *customs*, thoughts, and general behavior of certain human *groups* (sexes, peoples, nations, occupations, religions, and so forth). Moreover, the writer-thinker unveils these hidden or secret psychological motives in order eventually (explicitly or implicitly) to subject these groups' psychological characteristics and mores to evaluative or axiological (not to say moral) judgment.

La Rochefoucauld and Chamfort, as well as Montaigne and Pascal—the so-called "moralists" of the eighteenth century—and Stendhal, in their wide-ranging analyses, aphorisms, and apothegms, are the models of moralists for Nietzsche (*qua* author of psychological and moral maxims and aphorisms). Like them, he observes *the* Women, *the* English, *the* Christians, *the* Priests, *the* Jews, and the like, and means to show the unity and secret motives of their ways, thoughts, and impulses, describing and evaluating them according to the disparity between their facade and their deeper psychology. Toward this end, he is fond of employing a concise, paradoxical, and spirited style of pointed maxims. This is made evident by the fact that his admonitions, which take the form of maxims and aphorisms, imitate classical French authors. Furthermore, the numerous passages and aphorisms in which he makes his points are sprinkled with psychological and evaluative generalizations—from *Human, All Too Human*[1] to *Twilight of the Idols*.[2] "The psychologist speaks": this formula of *Nietzsche contra Wagner*[3] designates the moralist-genealogist Nietzsche in one of his most characteristic works.[4]

This moralist background allows us to outline the general problem and project of genealogy: (1) On the one hand, (a) as a "psychologist" and as one who "trieth the reins and the heart,"[5] Nietzsche seeks to discover (in the body, affects and passions) the (psychological) origin of the ideals of *culture*—not to mention his preferred object, the symbol of the whole of Western culture: *morality*. Psychological genealogy unmasks, reveals, uncovers, and denudes. Upon it are grafted (b) as far as the body is concerned, a *natural history*: inquiry into physiological origins is a result of, evolves from, and is inspired by models of *transformism* (Lamarck) and evolutionary theory (Darwin); and also (c) since culture is an enigmatic text, a cryptic discourse, a *philology* that attempts a reading, decoding, and interpretation of the hidden meaning of the *Zeichenrede* (encoded language), of the *Symptomatologie*, of the *Semiotik* which morality is. This *philology* is at once a physiology, a medicine (semiotics means: the science of the interpretation of signs and of diagnosing maladies), a natural history of *evolution* and at the same time a *psychology* (the unveiling of affects).

(2) On the other hand, genealogy evaluates: drawing on the aforementioned disciplines, it refutes, judges, or confirms moralities in their pretensions. With regard to their ideals, genealogy assays the content, quality, and value of the affects which constitute, ground, and engender them; and it measures their value in terms of their relation to negation or affirmation. It finds their value in their meaning; that is to say, in their rapport with the "will," body, and drives. It eventually undermines the autonomy or absolute character of a morality by detecting and evaluating in it the need to dominate or to submit, the strength or weakness of the will to power, affirmation or negation, joy or *ressentiment*, hatred or vengeance. To interpret as a psychologist is to evaluate, according to its strength or weakness, the quality of the will required by an ideal, a belief, a conviction, a behavior, or an institution.

Hence in genealogy, the famous typology of strong/weak, noble/slave, affirmative/reactive (or negative) appears, which separates two types of culture: for example, the culture of Tragic Greece and the morals of Manu on the one hand, and Christian morality, Platonic-Christianity, and Socratic theoretical optimism on the other. At stake for Nietzsche is genealogy both as an instrument of a negative and affirmative critical description and as an instrument with which to evaluate Platonic-Christian culture.

Genealogy can evaluate and categorize only on the condition that it *interrogates* ideals—especially as they pretend to be compelling and absolutely obvious. Genealogy, well before taking this name in *On the Genealogy of Morals*—qua (natural) history and psychology—turns up as mistrust and suspicion,[6] as interrogation, "seeing behind" (A 47), even demystification: remember to mistrust [*memnes' apistein*] "the worshippers of the miraculous in morality" (HH I:136). For one must admit that dissimulation and disguise necessarily characterize the more fundamental "reality" or "truth" of the ideals of morality and culture (even if every "foundation" proves to be merely interpretive). Now, does genealogy—which breaks "confidence in morality" (D P:4) under its various "disguises," and which works as an "underground 'being' of those who bore, who sap, who undermine" (D P:1)—aim to recover the grounding, the ultimate soil, the real basis of the ideals of a culture? Is not this hidden foundation, for all that Nietzsche says, the *true essence* of the real behind appearances? The *origin* as the *originary* principle?

This suspicion of Nietzsche's secret return to Platonism allows one better to draw out the issues and methods of genealogy. Thus posed, the question of the origin develops as was indicated above:

—(natural) history
—psychology
—interpretation-philology
—evaluation.

But these disciplines—which in Nietzsche's works constitute schemas for reflecting on the problems of foundation, grounding, interpretation, and the body—are employed by genealogy in a way that sidesteps the accusation and snares of "metaphysical" Platonism. Indeed, the problem of the origin—*Ursprung, Herkunft, Vorgeschichte*—is connected to genealogical inquiry at many levels.

(1) It refers first and foremost to *history* or *prehistory,* to the zero point of birth, to the first moment, and to the past: to the temporal, biological, and social origins of an individual or species. Nietzsche names this enterprise the "history of moral feelings" (HH I, part 2), the "natural history of morals" (BGE, part 5), or the "history of morals" (GM P:7), as a return to ancestors, to *genos,* "back through the generations" (HH I:47); it tries to define itself with regard to the sexual, social, and biological status of an ideal "offspring." But Nietzsche is not so much concerned with assigning a place or time of birth as he is with pointing out—through both history and the biological theory of evolution—historicity, development, and evolution. He is concerned with "knowledge of the conditions and circumstances under which the values grew, under which they evolved and changed" (GM P:6): the terrain and the soil,[7] but also the terms indicating change. Together with the grammatical forms marking the passage of time (the preterit tense), they schematize the occurrence and not the exact specification of a temporal or essential origin; and they indicate the *Entwicklung* (development) and the *Herkunft* (derivation) rather than the *Ursprung* (origin, grounding). It is not at all a matter of indicating the essence, nature, proper place, or certificate of nobility [*lettres de noblesse*] but of indicating a development and a derivation.[8] Genealogy is a discourse on the *genesis* and not on the *principle*; on the growth of life, on the soil, the tree, the birth, the living and death, on the passage, engenderment, heritage, atavism, origins, and the father. It combats "Egypticism":

You ask me about the idiosyncrasies of philosophers? . . . There is their lack
of historical sense, their hatred of even the idea of becoming, their Egypticism. They think they are doing a thing *honor* when they dehistoricize it, *sub
specie aeterni*—they make a mummy of it. (TI III:1)

Therefore genealogy is properly the language of the *life* of the body. The
Nietzschean considerations and metaphorics founded on these schemes
are: soil, family, engenderment, history, becoming, life/death, evolution,
ancestors, noble/base, vegetation, and growth (with a curious absence of
sexual metaphors). This is the story of the *phusis* as it issues from a *phuein*.

(2) Similarly, genealogy—as a suspicion of a *hidden* soil, a dis-covery, a
deciphering—relates the symptoms of morality to that which, dissimulated,
engenders it: "Morality, as consequence, as symptom, as mask, as tartufferie, as illness, as misunderstanding; but also morality as cause, as remedy,
as stimulant, as restraint, as poison" (GM P:6). Is there an essence behind
appearances that causes the ideals of morality? Is genealogy truly a physiology, a medicine diagnosing causes and effects, essential origins, and the
body (as the material cause of ideals)? If genealogy stands in opposition to
idealist dogmatism, is it at bottom a mechanistic and materialist doctrine?

Here the psychological metaphorical schemas and philological interpretations intervene: it is precisely the body, the drives, and the affects that
genealogy tries to make manifest and dis-cover [*entdecken*]. But insofar as
they evaluate, judge, name, and impose labels like "good" and "evil," "noble" or "base," and the like—insofar as they *interpret*—they thereby constitute the *text* of culture and morals (compare GM I:2). It is revealing that,
speaking about meaning and interpretation in *Genealogy*, Nietzsche wonders: "What do ascetic ideals signify [*bedeuten*]?"—a question he gives as
an example of the art of "interpretation" (*Auslegung*), of "reading elevated
to the level of an art," and of "commentary" (GM III:1,2). In other words,
genealogy does not bind a text (an ideal) to a body (the drives) that conceals it; rather, it interprets a text as a bearer of meaning, as a hidden
(affective, corporal, and psychological) *signification*. Moreover, this "body"
should not be merely "seen," but deciphered and interpreted *as a text*.
Genealogical "medicine" and physiology are *readings* oriented toward a
semiotic (or symptomatology) as a science of the *signs* of sickness.

This is why "for the genealogist of morals, the color *gray* should be one
hundred times more important . . . , that is to say, the long, difficult-to-
decipher hieroglyphic record of human morality's past!" (GM P:7).[9] Genealogy is interpretation of an interpretation, of a text as interpretation of
a body, of a body interpreting and being interpreted. One suspects, from
this moment on, that it will be a double interpretation: both physiological
and philological—and, in both, *distrustful* and *suspicious* (GM P:6)—bring-

ing out the "shameful parts,"[10] the *"pudenda origo,"* which "devalues the thing thus coming into the world."[11]

But in this double capacity, genealogy is most of all an interpretation that confronts ambiguity, the signs' obscure enigmas and their illegibility; the hidden *invisible* grounding it searches for is not what it finds behind appearances. And although it brings things to light, because of the text's ambiguity genealogy multiplies significations and renders it nearly *illegible.* The genealogical Trophonios does not descend underground in order to find the soil of truth—a mere inversion of the Platonic cave—but rather enters into an "incomprehensible, secret, and enigmatic element," the text; it digs into the grounding and the soil only in order to "mine" it (D P:1). Nietzsche is quite intent, in his genealogical philology, upon avoiding the dualism of "true world" and "apparent world":[12]

> What is the meaning of the act of evaluation itself? Does it point back or down to another, metaphysical world? (As Kant still believed, who belongs *before* the great historical movement.) In short: where did it originate? Or did it not "originate"?—Answer: moral evaluation is an *exegesis,* a way of interpreting. The exegesis itself is a symptom of certain physiological conditions, likewise of a particular spiritual level of prevalent judgments: Who interprets?—Our affects. (WP 254)[13]

Within a monistic framework, interpretation is a plural play of appearance and truth—a riddle of the united plurality of the text of the body and of morality. Nietzsche as genealogist is not foundational (*gründlich*) but abyssal (*abgründlich* or *untergründlich*) (D 446), since he mines the soil even of the perceptible, clear, obvious, and essential truth. His suspicion is "incessantly more radical," his skepticism (*Skepsis*) "incessantly more profound" (GM P:5). Now there is an interpretation precisely insofar as no meaning-founding *essence* or truth is to be found. Interpretation is reading without being able to fix the origin, proper place, code, or principle of the text. It is to suppose that meaning is always external and that the text does not contain its code in and of itself, but *depends,* like Plato's orphan (*Phaedrus,* 275), upon what is outside of itself. With neither origin nor proper place, the interpretation of the text is plural and errant.

Therefore genealogy is obscurity, mystery, and chance. "Mistrust" signifies not only that there is something hidden, suspect, and double in the thing but also that the thing unfolds and distances itself as a *sign,* and becomes enigmatic, opaque, confused, plural, and deceptive. The genealogist-interpreter will therefore have to shift the signifiers back to the signified(s) and open up a path through ambiguity and arbitrariness. Each time Nietzsche must interpret morals and culture, his use of quotation marks or italics and his recurring glossaries and translations testify to his repudiation of the "appellations" and "fine phrases" of morality. One must add here that the enigma of history's "past" is so tangled that genealogical interpretation finds itself faced with plural and successive significations, which Nietzsche metaphorizes with images of hieroglyphs (GM P:6), palimpsests, and overwritten scrawlings (BGE 230). Thus antiquity and enigma together oppose themselves to the "primal eternal text" of *homo natura*—itself a text to restore and decipher.

History, in genealogy, is therefore not a quest for the origins, for a primal fact, but rather a scheme for interpretation—less "*Geschichte*" (history) than "*Vorgeschichte*" (prehistory) (GM P:4; HH I:45). The etymologies of the *Genealogy* do not at all constitute facts, but they schematize the necessity of retranslation in order to recover a lost meaning or text (GM I:5). Yet as a discipline that *interprets* facts and documents, history is merely a metaphor for *interpretation*. For instance, when Nietzsche attributes the "beginning" of the "slave revolt in morality" to the Jews (GM I:7), he does not situate his genealogy as a necessary historical fact, but as an interpretation: "But you do not comprehend this? You are incapable of seeing something that required two thousand years to achieve victory?—There is nothing to wonder at: all *protracted* things are hard to see, to see whole" (GM I:8). And indeed, this interpretation must establish the genealogy of a "hatred creating ideals," paradoxically engendering "a new love, the deepest and most sublime of all the forms of love."

Genealogy proceeds from one interpretation to another; it discovers new meanings without ceasing. It is interminably translation and transposition,[14] as indicated by the quotation marks, equivalences, and phrases like "in my language,"[15] "I mean," "I understand," "that is to say," and "translated into German."[16] It is a *retranslation* [*Zurückübersetzung*] into the "primal" language of reality (BGE 230). "*Die Realität heißt*," "reality says or means"—such is the "last word" of Nietzsche the genealogist-translator (A 26). Genealogy is interpretation as a singular-plural conflict and as a conflict of interpretations.

It thus schematizes itself along two fundamental metaphorical axes: medicine (natural history, semiotic/symptomatology, physiology) and philology (interpretation, psychology, history, translation, etymology). But we will see that these two axes, evoking the two "sides" genealogy tends to unite (i.e., the body and the text of the ideal), come together again in philology's unique metaphoric, which wants to incorporate physiology as a reading of the body. Yet insofar as genealogy is considered to be interpretation, it seems that Nietzsche, in order to define it, employs a linked chain of metaphors which proceed from interpretation to the body—but return, as in a circle, to interpretation.

Since genealogy relates the ideal back to the body as a discourse on its origin and as a production of the ideal by the body (the ideal as lack, diversion, and error of the body), it must reflect upon what the body is, and upon the nature and status of interpretation (idealist or, by contrast, genealogical). The body's thought must also reflect upon itself in terms of a dualist yet monist discourse, where negation and denial always threaten the thought of the Same as Other. How can one be a genealogist without also being a dualist?

Such are the questions that lead to Nietzsche's interrogation of the body and which genealogy tries to resolve. A plurality of drives—of multiple, contradictory, and fluctuating centers of power—appear and disappear.[17] But with respect to what are they ordered? It is remarkable that Nietzsche gives neither a mechanistic nor physiological type of explanation or description of them, but instead gives an interpretation in which interconnected metaphors reciprocally interpret one another.

The body [*Leib*], in Nietzsche, is "a great reason" [*grosse Vernunft*]: a plurality of drives which refuses the separation of *Geist* (spirit) and *Körper* (physiological body), and is therefore the psychosomatic ensemble envisaged in unitary or monist thought. For Nietzschean genealogy, spirit (consciousness) is but the name of a certain configuration or equilibrium among the drives and their respective "wills." Nietzsche at first presents this conflict of the drives' forces in terms of the metaphor of the assimilation (i.e., appropriation, incorporation, reduction) of a foreign plurality into a unity-identity. Thus the body-spirit is first of all digestion, an assimilating stomach or metabolism whose equilibrium rests between indigestion and a too-rapid expulsion—both diverse effects of a bulimic voraciousness. The body-spirit is, as assimilation, a mastery of absorption, a selective and even fastidious choice or a discriminating taste, rather than an imperialistic, gluttonous, and undiscriminating desire to exercise the power of devouring.

This discrimination leads Nietzsche to present the body in terms of a second series of metaphors: that of the body politic, "a fantastic collectivity of living beings," "fighting or collaborating among themselves," the drives submit and control themselves, eventually "choosing" a leader—a "reigning aristocracy"—in accord with the psychopolitical image of "decisions" or of relations of forces (which implies an "always fluctuating delimitation of power"),[18] with "obeisance, assiduousness, mutual aid, and vigilance."[19] Thus "we are a multiplicity *which constructs itself,* through consciousness, as an *imaginary unity.*"[20]

This multiplicity, which chooses, governs and obeys, selects, excludes, divides, and controls according to rules—and this is the third series of metaphors—points toward interpretation. The drives are a ruling collectivity that offers to the conscious intellect a choice of interpreted, leveled down, and simplified experiences. But to interpret is to reduce plurality to unity of meaning or to an ensemble of significations. The body, as an ensemble of drives expressing themselves through one consciousness and one reason, is thus interpretation. "The organic process presupposes a continuous interpretive activity."[21]

One understands, then, how Nietzsche presents genealogy as the interpretation of an interpretation (of a text), and not as a resort to a mechanistic, physiological causal account. But also, if one wants to avoid the redoubled tautology of a genealogical interpretation of an interpretation (the body), what is interpretation, in genealogy and in the body?

One is forced to admit that Nietzsche's response locks him into a circle. Interpretation is not defined by him, but is presented according to metaphors of political struggle and (especially) of digestion: to interpret is to assimilate, to digest, to reject, to "ruminate" (GM P:8). And insofar as he does this, he produces a reduction of plurality to unity and a repluralization of the simple. To interpret is to select and simplify. But it is also to pluralize, disintegrate, and multiply the text—to render it in accordance with the erratic nature and infinitude of interpretations. To do genealogy is to let the text (of culture, morals, world) go back to its infinity, even to its indefiniteness, to its *Versuch* (attempt, try, experimentation); it is to make the "concepts quake" (UM II:10) and to set out onto the open sea toward adventure: "philosophers, embark!" (GS 289).

But one might justly wonder if there is a true circle in the "definition" of interpretation as the digesting (and conflicting) body, and in the "definition" of the body as a conflict of interpretations. As interpretation, genealogy's status is such that it can only interpret, and cannot explain itself in order to ground itself. The only way it can do this is on the basis of metaphors of the body and of interpretation—*that is to say*, on the basis of interpretations of the body and of interpretation. Genealogy, as interpretation of the text in rapport with the body, implies that there can be only interpretations—as such, endless ones—of the body and of interpretation.

Now the metaphors have the task of exhibiting the following: on the one hand, they are interpretive—as they are partial, simplifying, and multiple. On the other hand, they reciprocally and circularly interpret one another— as if one could never justly place a definite and final concept alongside genealogy (interpretation and the body), and should on the contrary endlessly and plurally refer from interpretation to digestion, from digestion to struggle, from struggle to selective and interpretive reading, and so on to infinity. More precisely: to interpret is to suppose that there is no *ananke stenai* (necessity to stop), no rightful term, no end or limit to interpretation, but rather an infinitude of the *text* (Penelope's complex)—an unceasing report of conflict in the *life* of the *body*. Because life is conflict, plurality, and ambiguity. And genealogy wishes to return to life.

Genealogy appears neither as an investigation of causes, nor as physiological medicine (and rather "medicynical"[22] than medical), nor as ascending to an origin (chronological, logical, or spatial), nor as revealing an essential grounding, but rather as an unstable mix, a plural monism, and a metaphorical and *displaced* (meta-phor) play of many disciplines: psychology, physiology, and philology. It is, if one dares to use a concoction as monstrous and disparate as the idea of genealogy itself, "psychophysiophilology." Because of this, it is rightly of an uncertain, endless, and metaphoric standing. And as we have seen, genealogy is best articulated by the three schemes that govern all of Nietzsche's thought: assimilation, conflict, and text (as interpretation and body, which infinitely refer to one another). But this ambiguous, metaphorical, mixed, and uncertain status of genealogy, which has neither origin nor grounding, neither essence nor concept—this new critical thought, whose unknowable thing in itself is the body, and whose transcendental is interpretation—this status, according to Nietzsche, is no other than that of philosophy.

NOTES

1. For example HH I:36, 50, 377–437, and so on.
2. For example, the first part, "Maxims and Arrows."
3. Echoing BGE 269.
4. Compare H. P. Balmer, *Philosophie der Menschlichen Dinge.*
5. Jeremiah 11:20—TRANS.
6. Compare D P:4, HH I:P:1, GM P:6.
7. KGW, VIII, 3, 14 [76] and HH I:99.
8. Compare Michel Foucault, "Nietzsche, la généalogie, l'histoire," in *Hommage à Jean Hyppolite,* PUF, despite a few hesitations.
9. "Gray" is an allusion to Goethe's *Faust* (v. 2037)—ED.
10. HH, posthumous fragment 23 (4).
11. KGW, VIII, 1, 2 [189].
12. "How the 'True World' Finally Became a Fable" (TI IV).
13. Trans. Walter Kaufmann and R. J. Hollingdale (New York: Vintage Books, 1967). KGW, VIII, 1, 2 (190).
14. Compare BGE 21; GM I:9, 13, 14.
15. In GM and A.
16. In GM, TI, and EH.
17. Compare Müller-Lauter, *Nietzsche. Seine Philosophie der Gegensätze und die Gegensätze seiner Philosophie* (Berlin: de Gruyter, 1971).
18. KGW, VII, 40 (21).
19. *Nietzsches Werke: Grossoktaveausgabe,* 2d ed. (Leipzig: Kröner, 1901–1913), vol. XIII, 394 (KGW, VII, 25 [426]).
20. Ibid., vol. XII, 1st part, 307.
21. KGW, VIII, 1, 2 [148].
22. *Ecce Homo,* "Why I Write Such Good Books," section five (EH III:5).

EIGHTEEN

Genealogy and Critical Method

Daniel W. Conway

INTRODUCTION

The question of validity haunts Nietzsche's critical philosophy as a whole, but especially the genealogical interpretations that inform his later writings. In light of his formidable critique of foundationalism, whereby he calls into question all claims to objectively valid knowledge, how can he claim for his genealogical interpretations the validity that they confidently presuppose? Is Nietzsche's familiar swagger simply a rhetorical pose, or do his genealogies constitute valid interpretations of the historical phenomena they investigate?

In this essay, I argue that Nietzschean genealogy gains access to the meaning of historical phenomena only via the dominant interpretations of those phenomena. If successful, Nietzsche's genealogies not only account for the historical phenomenon in question, but also reveal the hermeneutic inadequacies of rival interpretations. Nietzsche is therefore warranted in claiming for his genealogies a validity relative to the authoritative interpretations they discredit and supplant. Beyond the terms of this relation, however, he is entitled to stake no further claim to the validity of his genealogies, though he may occasionally do so; as a hermeneutic strategy, genealogy is entirely parasitic on the interpretations it challenges. The relative validity of Nietzsche's genealogies thus contributes to his revised critical method, whereby he formulates immanent criticisms of historical phenomena. Only on the basis of some such immanent critique are we philosophically justified in preferring the "immoral" vocabulary Nietzsche recommends to the moral vocabulary that it supplants.

GENEALOGY AND SYMPTOMATOLOGY

In order to appreciate Nietzsche's idiosyncratic adaptation of genealogy to the history of morality, we must situate genealogy in the shifting context of his critical philosophical project. In *Beyond Good and Evil,* Nietzsche claims as his critical task the preparation of a typology of morals (BGE 186).[1] In *Toward a Genealogy of Morals,* he explains that "all the sciences have from now on to prepare the way for . . . the solution of the *problem of value,* the determination of the *order of rank* [*Rangordnung*] *among values*" (GM I:17n.). Nietzsche apparently understands this ambitious typological project as a prelude to the revaluation of values to be executed by the "philosophers of the future" (BGE 44).

Yet Nietzsche's devastating critique of objective validity calls into question the possibility of completing the normative component of the typological project he describes. If all values are simply infra-objective moral prejudices, then how can he place them in a defensible order of rank? Among the moral prejudices to be ranked (and those of most interest to Nietzsche) are the metaphysical commitments that moral judgments express—for example, estimations of the value of life. But even if we grant Nietzsche that these metaphysical commitments are simply ossified moral prejudices, how can he possibly judge any estimation of the value of life to be better or worse than its negation?

Acknowledging the self-imposed epistemic restrictions within which he must prepare this typology, Nietzsche avers that "the value of life cannot be estimated" (TI II:2). He later explains that

> one would require a position *outside* of life, and yet have to know it as well as one, as many, as all who have lived it, in order to be permitted even to touch the problem of the *value* of life: reasons enough to comprehend that this problem is for us an unapproachable problem. (TI V:5)

Despite his recognition of the epistemic difficulties involved in any attempt to estimate the value of life, Nietzsche nevertheless informs his typology of values with an order of rank. He argues, for example, that "for a philosopher to see a problem in the value of life is thus an objection to him, a question mark concerning his wisdom, an un-wisdom" (TI II:2). In order to complete this typology, critics claim, Nietzsche must presuppose access to a privileged Promethean perspective, an epistemic gambit that he expressly disallows. Although he admits that no one can verify the validity of moral prejudices, he nonetheless presumes to pass judgment on their value.

As Nietzsche explains, however, he does not establish this order of rank by appealing to the objective validity of the metaphysical commitments he investigates. In order to discern the relative value of moral prejudices, while circumventing altogether the question of their (objective) validity, we must view them semiotically:

> Judgments of value, concerning life, for it or against it, can in the end never be true: they have value only as symptoms, they are worthy of consideration only as symptoms; in themselves such judgments are stupidities. (TI II:2)

Although epistemically illegitimate and therefore "stupid" in themselves, estimations of the value of life assume paramount philosophical importance when reinterpreted as symptoms of an underlying physiological condition. Nietzsche's typological project thus leads him to semiotics, as a means of establishing a defensible order of rank.

Nietzsche's interest in semiotics arises in conjunction with his campaign to emigrate "beyond good and evil." Although his distaste for morality is well known, the precise focus of his enmity is perhaps less clear. His attack on Western morality is specifically directed not toward its normative character *per se* but toward its metaphysical foundation—that is, its reliance on the metaphysical apparatus of free will, responsibility, blame, and guilt. In the *Genealogy*, Nietzsche identifies the voluntarist and intentionalist vocabulary of Western morality as a vestige of its origins in the slave revolt. In *Twilight of the Idols* he grounds his critique of morality in an insight into "the four great errors," all of which contribute to the transformation of human animals into *moral agents*—that is, causally efficient, endowed with free will, and responsible, both factually and counterfactually, for their actions. As a consequence of its propensity for these errors, the moral mode of evaluation not only is ill-suited to an analysis of the problem of modernity but also exacerbates the problem.

Nietzsche's deconstruction of the metaphysical foundation of morality thus exposes the moral mode of evaluation as not only hermeneutically deficient but also decadent: predicated on an egregious misinterpretation of certain physiological conditions, Western morality actually compounds the suffering it purports to ease.[2] Arthur Danto has drawn a helpful distinction between "extensional suffering and intensional suffering, where the latter consists of an interpretation of the former."[3] Although Nietzsche can do little to reduce the level of extensional suffering in the world, and in no event exhibits any inclination to do so, he can perhaps eliminate some degree of intensional suffering by providing an alternative, nonmoral interpretation of extensional suffering. Drawing on Danto's distinction, we might characterize the goal of Nietzsche's critical philosophy as the elimination of the surplus suffering engendered by Western morality.

As he matured as a philosopher, Nietzsche realized that his initial attacks on morality succeeded only in reinforcing the authority of its categories and vocabulary. In *The Birth of Tragedy*, for example, while attempting to implicate modernity in the hyperrationalism of Socratism, he unwittingly endorsed the moral mode of evaluation by *blaming* Socrates for the "death" of tragedy. In blaming priests and moralists for introducing blame into the vocabulary of Western morality, Nietzsche perhaps succeeded in discrediting *them*, but only at the expense of validating their enterprise. His early attacks on Western morality may have defaced its edifice, but they failed to demolish (and in fact reinforced) its metaphysical foundation. Hoping to purge his critical philosophy of its residual metaphysical taint, and thus avoid the moralizing into which his youthful fulminations often degenerated, Nietzsche attempted to fashion a critical method that neither relies on the moral mode of evaluation nor reinforces its metaphysical foundation. To do so, he required an alternative critical vocabulary.

The typological project that occupies Nietzsche's later works thus sanctions his campaign to subject moral prejudices to a further, more rigorous, psychological interpretation. He vows, for example, to penetrate to "the *origin* of our moral prejudices" (GM P:2).[4] He consequently recommends that we interpret moral prejudices as symptomatic of the underlying drives and affects they manifest, proposing, in effect, a naturalistic reduction of morality: "In short, moralities are also merely a *sign language of the affects*" (BGE 187).[5] In *Twilight*, Nietzsche "officially" announces his adoption of symptomatology as his new model for critical philosophy:

> My demand upon the philosopher is known, that he take his stand *beyond* good and evil and leave the illusion of moral judgment beneath him. . . . Moral judgments are therefore never to be taken literally: so understood, they always contain mere absurdity. Semiotically, however, they remain invaluable: they reveal, at least for those who know, the most valuable realities of cultures and inwardnesses which did not know enough to "understand" themselves. Morality is mere sign language, mere symptomatology: one must know what it is all about to be able to profit from it. (TI VII:1)

Although Nietzsche never articulated his means of achieving this unprecedented emigration beyond good and evil, his repeated attempts to equip philosophers with a nonmoral critical vocabulary suggest his route of passage. He came to interpret moral prejudices as symptomatic of varying degrees of health and decadence, and to rank them accordingly. "A condemnation of life by the living remains in the end a symptom of a certain kind of life: the question whether it is justified or unjustified is not even raised thereby" (TI V:5).

Nietzsche thus moves beyond good and evil by translating his critical philosophy into the vocabulary and categories of symptomatology: "healthy" versus "sick" replaces "good" versus "evil" as the governing frame of philosophical evaluation. In *Twilight*, for example, he returns once again to "The Problem of Socrates." But in contrast to the argument of *The Birth of Tragedy*, he no longer *blames* Socrates for the death of tragedy, or for anything else. No decadent, whether modern or premodern, can help but enact his physiological destiny. Socrates no more chose to privilege reason than a sick man chooses to run a fever: "neither Socrates nor his 'patients' had any choice about being rational: it was *de rigueur*, it was their last resort . . . ; there was danger, there was but one choice: either to perish or—to be absurdly rational" (TI II:10).

Nietzsche's symptomatological turn thus enables the *immoralism* that characterizes his later philosophy: because all values—even those that promote asceticism—further the interests of a form of life, no constellation of values deserves to be singled out as "evil." Operating free of the distractions of nausea and pity, Nietzsche is able to interpret signs of physiological decay without resorting to moral evaluations of the pathogenic agents he isolates. Symptomatology thus replaces morality; the sick are not to blame for their sickness. But Nietzsche's emigration "beyond good and evil" does not preclude the possibility of philosophical criticism. The "immoral" philosopher must continue to formulate normative judgments, preferences, and orders of rank, although no longer on the basis of moral criteria.

Having exchanged morality for symptomatology, Nietzsche now describes the crisis of modernity in strictly physiological terms, as the mutual clash of instinctual systems: "Our instincts contradict, disturb, destroy each other; I have already defined what is modern as physiological self-contradiction" (TI IX:41). Nietzsche thus concludes that, like the desperate hyperrationalism prescribed by Socrates, the governing values and sustaining institutions of modernity are symptomatic of physiological decay. He defines this decadence as the "instinctual preference" for "what disintegrates, what hastens the end" (TI IX:39). In the *Genealogy*, of course, Nietzsche locates the source of this physiological self-contradiction in the checkered career of the ascetic ideal.

Nietzsche's alleged emigration "beyond good and evil," and his concomitant turn to symptomatology, have generated little enthusiasm among philosophers. Even if we disregard the disturbing ease with which Nazi ideologues seized upon his "immoral" vocabulary, we still find it difficult to take seriously, much less implement. Surely the least Nietzsche must supply in his own defense is an account of the superior explanatory power of his revised critical method. Nietzsche's symptomatological turn may enable him to avoid various epistemological snares, but it raises equally vexing hermeneutic problems. For example, what philosophical advantage do we gain by exchanging a traditional moral account of "evil" for Nietzsche's "immoral" account of "sickness" or "decadence"? Does "immoralism" actually eliminate the surplus suffering inflicted by morality? These questions, I believe, lead us to the more basic question of the validity of Nietzschean genealogy; for Nietzsche's turn to symptomatology as a critical method makes sense only as presupposing the validity of genealogy.

GENEALOGY AND RELATIVE VALIDITY

By attending closely to Nietzsche's later books, and to the critical project they purport to execute, we can reconstruct with some confidence the relation of genealogy to his revised critical method. Because genealogical interpretations figure so prominently in his later books—*Twilight* offers a (revised) genealogy of modernity, *The Antichrist(ian)* genealogies of Christ and Christianity, and *Ecce Homo* a genealogy of Nietzsche himself—it seems plausible to assume that Nietzsche intended his genealogies to contribute to the critical standpoint that these books confidently presuppose. Genealogy, I propose, supplies the empirical "case history" that enables the "immoral" philosopher to detect and interpret physiological symptoms, and to do so more accurately than priests and moralists. Genealogy thus informs Nietzsche's later writings with the validity that he is entitled to claim for them.

Some commentators attempt to "solve" the problem of validity by construing Nietzsche's occasional appeals to "life" as conferring some measure of objective validity: interpretations are better or worse (healthier or sicker) to the extent that they promote/impugn life itself. Nietzsche's rhetoric certainly suggests some such strategy, for he often denounces philosophers and philosophies as "hostile to life," as if this *ad hominem* were sufficient to vanquish his enemies.[6] But in taking him to be summoning "life" as an objective standard of validity, this strategy effectively convicts Nietzsche of illicit recourse to a privileged perspective.[7] If his sole defense of his genealogies rests on their (unspecified) fidelity to "life," then he simply begs the question of their validity as interpretations.

A more promising strategy would be to claim for Nietzsche's genealogies a relative validity. Kant's defense of the postulates of pure practical reason provides an instructive example here. Although Kant denied the possibility of objectively valid knowledge of metaphysics, he did not conclude that all metaphysical commitments are therefore equally valid. According to Kant, beliefs in the existence of God, freedom of the will, and the immortality of the soul, although objectively insufficient for theoretical knowledge, are nevertheless subjectively sufficient for rational faith. As Kant explains, the antinomy of pure practical reason yields the following dilemma, which defies resolution by theoretical reason: if the *summum bonum* (that is, the coincidence of perfect virtue and earthly happiness) is unattainable, "then the moral law which commands that it be furthered must be fantastic, directed to empty imaginary ends, and consequently inherently false."[8]

In order to avoid the contradiction involved in believing the moral law to be false, Kant recommends that we postulate the existence of God and the immortality of the soul as necessary conditions of the *summum bonum,* even though we cannot objectively determine that it depends upon them.

Our rational faith in these postulates of pure practical reason, although objectively insufficient, thus facilitates our pursuit of happiness. In fact, only by virtue of one's belief in these postulates can one avoid what Kant calls the *absurdum practicum*, the life of the scoundrel who chooses to disobey the moral law.[9] He apparently believed that a practical advantage would accrue to a life informed by the postulates of pure practical reason, as evidenced by a comparison of the (potentially) happy lives of the faithful and the *absurdum practicum* that falls to the infidels.

Kant's reasoning here is somewhat obscure, for he defends the postulates of pure practical reason only negatively, by appealing to the consequences of *failing* to embrace them.[10] A life uninformed by the postulates cannot intelligibly aspire to the *summum bonum*, and consequently issues in an *absurdum practicum*. The validity of the postulates therefore obtains only in relation to the *absurdum practicum* itself, and is in no sense objective; we might say (although Kant himself did not) that Kant claims for the postulates a subjective or relative validity.

Although Nietzsche rejects the voluntarism that Kant's account of the postulates presupposes,[11] he adopts the strategy of grounding the validity of his genealogies in relation to those rival interpretations that issue in an *absurdum practicum*. Hence a Nietzschean genealogy is successful not if it achieves or approximates objective validity, but if it effectively supplants or discredits the dominant interpretation of the historical phenomenon in question. The relative validity of a genealogy is therefore dependent upon its success in calling into question the authoritative interpretation it challenges. Unless we understand Nietzsche's genealogies as enabling an immanent critique of rival vocabularies, his turn to symptomatology is impossible to defend.

Was bedeuten asketische Ideale?[12] The title of the Third Essay of the *Genealogy* identifies Nietzschean genealogy as a hermeneutic strategy that demands close attention to the historical traces and details of our moral development. In the course of this essay, while reminding us (and himself) of the task at hand, he outlines his hermeneutic project:

> It is my purpose here to bring to light, not what this [ascetic] ideal has *done*, but simply what it *means*; what it indicates; what lies hidden behind it, beneath it, within it; of what it is the provisional, indistinct expression, overlaid with question marks and misunderstandings. (GM III:23)

Nietzsche's genealogy reveals that the checkered history of the ascetic ideal is overdetermined with meaning.[13] He consequently attempts to sort out these meanings and determine how a single constellation of meaning gained ascendancy and authority.

In order to secure access to the meanings of the historical phenomenon under investigation, Nietzschean genealogy parasitically inhabits the dom-

inant interpretation of that phenomenon.[14] The aim of Nietzsche's genealogies is to provide a compelling interpretation of the historical phenomenon in question that includes an account of the genesis of the rival
interpretation. His genealogies therefore comprise (relatively) more complete interpretations, insofar as they explain the genetic limitations of the
authoritative interpretations in question. Whatever its other merits or de-
merits, a successful Nietzschean genealogy is thus hermeneutically superior
to the interpretation it supplants.

Because Nietzsche's genealogical interpretations are logically dependent upon the authoritative interpretations they seek to supplant, they are
entirely parasitic and cannot stand independently. Genealogical interpretations are always abnormal and reactive, preying upon the normal, authoritative interpretations they challenge. Whatever degree of validity a
genealogy acquires is therefore entirely relative to the interpretation it discredits.[15] Nietzsche harbors no delusions (or at any rate in his most sober
moments he does not) that his genealogical interpretation might be somehow objectively better than the dominant interpretation it supplants. His
own genealogy of morals will eventually be rendered obsolete by the greater
relative validity of a rival interpretation. Here we recall Nietzsche's fasci-
nation with the Homeric *agon*: his reliance on genealogy reflects his conviction that all hermeneutic victories are relative to a specific context of
contest. Only an objectively valid interpretation could secure a final victory,
and no such (context-independent) interpretation exists.

GENEALOGY AND IMMANENT CRITIQUE

As we have seen, Nietzsche's emigration beyond good and evil contributes
to his campaign to eliminate the surplus suffering engendered by Western
morality. For an example of his "immoral" critical method in practice, let
us turn now to the *Genealogy*. Before interpreting the ascetic ideal and Western morality as symptomatic of a certain form of life, Nietzsche must first
gain access to an empirical "case history." He thus sets out in the *Genealogy*
to articulate a more detailed account of the history and development of
our values within the framework of justification that asceticism provides.

As we have seen, Nietzschean genealogy gains hermeneutic access to the
historical phenomenon in question via its parasitic inhabitation of the dominant interpretation of that phenomenon. Rather than import some external or transcendent standard of evaluation, Nietzsche takes as his starting
point the dominant interpretation of Western morality, as reflected in the
history and practice of Christianity.[16] Central to the self-understanding of
Christian morality is the voluntaristic conviction that anyone and everyone
could have acted otherwise. Christian morality thus takes as originary for its
enterprise a freely determined choice to cultivate the virtues of humility

and submission. Christians *could* choose to pursue a life of evil, but have determined that their own morality affords them greater prospects for flourishing. Christian morality therefore rests on a familiar metaphysical foundation of free will, bolstered by a sustaining apparatus of blame, guilt, and accountability.

Nietzsche's genealogy of morals proposes an alternative interpretation of the genesis of Christian morality: contemporary Christians may choose a life of humility and submission, but the practice of Christian morality could not have arisen as the result of an original free choice.[17] According to Nietzsche, the dominant, voluntaristic interpretation of Christian morality cannot account for the distinctly reactive orientation of its mode of evaluation. He hypothesizes that Christian morality must have originated as a reaction or countermovement against a prior, and oppressive, moral order. He thus locates the origins of Christianity in a "slave morality,"[18] which he identifies as the simple negation of a logically and historically prior "noble" morality. Hence his famous distinction between noble and slave moralities:

> While every noble morality develops from a triumphant affirmation of itself, slave morality from the outset says *No* to what is "outside," what is "different," what is "not-itself"; and this *No* is its creative deed. This inversion of the value-positing eye—this *need* to direct one's view outward instead of back to oneself—is the essence of *ressentiment:* in order to exist, slave morality always first needs a hostile external world; it needs, physiologically speaking, external stimuli in order to act at all—its action is fundamentally reaction. (GM I:10)

Whereas the nobles' assessment of the slaves, arising from an original *pathos* of distance (GM I:2), acknowledges the slaves as other, as bad [*schlecht*], the slaves condemn the nobles not simply as other, but as evil [*böse*], that is, as accountable for this otherness.

According to Nietzsche, then, the originary moment of Christian morality is marked not by a free choice, but by a surfeit of *ressentiment,* which distinguishes the "slave" from the "noble," and explains the difference of orientation in their respective acts of creation. This surfeit of *ressentiment* furthermore attests to the suffering of the slaves, for, like all powerful, consuming passions, *ressentiment* serves an anaesthetic function: "The actual physiological cause of *ressentiment* [is] a desire to *deaden pain by means of affects*" (GM III:15). In order to anaesthetize the pain of the bad conscience, the slaves' *ressentiment* welled up as an involuntary physiological reaction. Nietzsche's genealogy of morals thus locates the genesis of Christian morality in the physiological need of the slaves to combat their seemingly meaningless suffering.

"The slave revolt in morality begins," Nietzsche contends, "when *ressentiment* becomes creative and gives birth to values" (GM I:10). The "external stimuli" that triggered the creative expenditure of *ressentiment* constitutive of slave morality were initially provided by the nobles, whose self-affirmation contributed to the slaves' perception of a "hostile external world." But an explosive expenditure of *ressentiment* directed against the nobles would have proved suicidal for the slaves. At this point, Nietzsche speculates, the ascetic priest intervened, identifying the slaves as responsible for their suffering, and redirecting *inward* the slaves' *ressentiment*:

> "I suffer: someone must be to blame for it"—thus thinks every sickly sheep. But his shepherd, the ascetic priest, tells him, "Quite so, my sheep! someone must be to blame for it: but you yourself are this someone, you alone are to blame for it—*you alone are to blame for yourself!*" This is brazen and false enough: but one thing at least is achieved by it, the direction of *ressentiment* is *altered*. (GM III:15)

By means of a moral (and therefore metaphysical) interpretation of the bad conscience, the ascetic ideal transforms the slave from sufferer to sinner: "he must seek [the 'cause' of his suffering] in *himself*, in some *guilt*, in a piece of the past, he must understand his suffering as a *punishment*" (GM III:20). Under the aegis of the ascetic priests, the slave assumes full responsibility for his suffering, and the internalization of his *ressentiment* brands him as a sinner.

Their embrace of the ascetic ideal thus enables the slaves to transform their suffering into the cornerstone for a new brand of morality. In a creative act of unprecedented *ressentiment*, the slaves announce that they deserve to suffer, and that they therefore prefer humility and submission to the apparent prosperity and flourishing of the nobles. By thus interpreting the slaves' sense of guilt as sin, "the ascetic ideal offered man meaning! . . . In it, suffering was *interpreted*; the tremendous void seemed to have been filled; the door was closed to any kind of suicidal nihilism" (GM III:28).

Nietzsche thus identifies the invention of "free will" as the metaphysical catalyst of the slave revolt in morality: "No wonder if the submerged, darkly glowering emotions of vengefulness and hatred . . . maintain no belief more ardently than the belief that *the strong man is free* to be weak and the bird of prey to be a lamb—for thus they gain the right to make the bird of prey *accountable* for being a bird of prey" (GM I:13). Hence the slaves could not have chosen their morality, for the physiological precondition of their morality antedates the invention of "free will."

According to Nietzsche, however, the priestly preoccupation with "sin," upon which Christian metaphysics rests, is merely an interpretation of an underlying physiological condition: "Man's 'sinfulness' is not a fact, but merely the interpretation of a fact, namely of physiological depression— the latter viewed in a religio-moral perspective that is no longer binding on us" (GM III:16). More to the point, Nietzsche views sin as an inferior and dangerous interpretation of the sense of guilt that "naturally" attends the bad conscience. As he indicates in the Second Essay, he believes that the sense of guilt originates in the bad conscience, and thus "as a piece of animal psychology, no more" (GM III:20). The bad conscience is "simply" the physiological price human animals pay for having strayed from their instincts and entrusted to consciousness the regulation of their natural economy. Nietzsche therefore prefers (and advances) a strictly physiological interpretation of our sense of guilt, and claims for it a relative validity.

As I have suggested, the relative validity of Nietzsche's genealogical interpretations depends on their success in discrediting the interpretations they challenge. Nietzsche therefore attempts to establish not simply that Christian morality is wrong about its origins, as if by accident or oversight, but that it *necessarily* cannot account for its genesis. He consequently maintains that the contemporary practice of Christian morality depends on a willful ignorance or denial of its debt to the slave revolt. Whereas Nietzsche's account of *ressentiment*, bad conscience, and guilt may eventually be rendered hermeneutically obsolete, some such explanation of the reactive orientation of Christian morality is surely in order. So although Nietzsche's genealogical interpretation of the genesis of Christian morality *may* be wrong, Christianity's voluntaristic account of its origins *must* be wrong—hence the relative validity of the former, and its hermeneutic advantage.

But even if Nietzsche's genealogy of morals were relatively more valid than the standard, voluntaristic account of the origin of Christianity, what possible relevance could it have for the current practices of Christianity? Like the British psychologists whom Nietzsche lampoons in the preface to the *Genealogy*, Christian apologists treat their current practices as logically unrelated to their origins. Nietzsche's genealogy of morals is ultimately uninteresting to them because their alleged "slave heritage" exercises no causal influence over their current, voluntary practices; their lives certainly bear no traces of this dubious legacy. If Nietzsche intends this unflattering genealogy to apply to them, it would seem that his own *ressentiment* has occasioned an egregious instance of the genetic fallacy.

In an attempt to defend him from these and related charges, several commentators have suggested that his critical evaluations operate only at the narrative level and therefore appeal exclusively to general, formal criteria such as consistency, transparency, completeness, and internal coherence.[19] Although this defense of Nietzsche squarely situates genealogy within the domain of hermeneutics, thus reflecting his opposition to dogmatic critique, these commentators tend to assume that Nietzsche's critical method is reducible to genealogy.

Perhaps Nietzsche *should* have restricted the scope of his critical evaluations to the narrative structure of rival interpretations—but he did not.

An appeal to the formal criteria of hermeneutic analysis remains light years removed from the emphatic, dogmatic, extranarrative criticism that Nietzsche formulates of Christianity: "I *condemn* Christianity. I raise against the Christian church the most terrible of all accusations that any accuser ever uttered. . . . I will call it the one immortal blemish of mankind" (A 62). From Nietzsche's ante-postmodernist point of view, no interesting critique of Christianity (or any other historical phenomenon) can be derived from an exclusive attention to the formal properties of its autobiographical narrative.

Nietzsche therefore does not present his genealogies as free-standing interpretative exercises, as if he were content to best Pauline theologians in a hermeneutic contest. In order to advance a critical evaluation of Christianity or slave morality, he must translate the findings of his genealogy of morals into an extra-genealogical critical framework. This genealogy shows "only" that Christian morality originated in a slave morality; his critical interpretation of this slave heritage is delivered not by genealogy itself, but by the immanent symptomatological critique that genealogy enables.[20]

As I have suggested, genealogy contributes to Nietzsche's revised critical method by supplying the "case history" that enables him to detect and interpret symptoms of cultural decay. His readers therefore could accept his genealogy of morals without necessarily endorsing the critical method it serves. Nietzsche advertises the *Genealogy* as a *polemic* [*eine Streitschrift*]; it contains both a genealogical interpretation and elements of a symptomatological critique. Many of the book's confusions are attributable to Nietzsche's failure (or unwillingness) to distinguish clearly between his genealogy of morals and the critical method it enables.

For Nietzsche, the enduring value of a (relatively) valid interpretation lies in the strength of the larger critical apparatus that it informs and enables. More important than any hermeneutic gaffe is the practical error that Christian morality embodies, for it has actually compounded the suffering that it originally sought to reduce. As we have seen, the slaves' sole creative power is reactive; slave morality thus requires a hostile external world, upon whose otherness it is logically dependent and practically parasitic. Yet in order to prevent the slaves from lashing out against their perceived enemies, the ascetic priests effectively relocate this "hostile external world" *internal* to the slave's consciousness; guilt lends meaning to the suffering of the bad conscience, but only by compounding it. Because Christian morality denies its genealogical debt to the slave morality, insisting instead on an original moment of free choice, it cannot acknowledge its creative acts as products of a self-destructive expression of *ressentiment*.

The hermeneutical "blind spot" of Christian morality—its insistence on an original free choice—ultimately issues in an *absurdum practicum*: we heirs to the slave revolt have embarked upon (and have progressed dangerously

toward completing) an ascetic campaign to destroy the source of our suffering. Every "victory" of Christian morality further sickens its adherents,
weakening them to the point of physiological exhaustion: "It goes without
saying that a 'medication' of this kind, a mere affect medication, cannot
possibly bring about a real cure of sickness in a physiological sense; we may
not even suppose that the instinct of life contemplates or intends any sort
of cure" (GM III:16). In short, Christian asceticism exemplifies a self-destructive form of life; in destroying the source of its suffering it ultimately
destroys itself as well. Despite the apparent triumph of Christian morality
in the West, it can claim for itself only a Pyrrhic victory.

Nietzsche's diagnosis of guilt, as the trace we all bear of our slave heritage, provides the basis for his immanent critique of Christian morality.
Blind to the costs and consequences of its moral interpretation of the bad
conscience, Christian morality fails on its own terms: it promises an ideal
of human flourishing that is incompatible with the methods it prescribes
for attaining it. Nietzsche concedes that the "priestly medication" of Christianity has *improved* its adherents; but he hastens to explain what this means
for him: "The same thing as 'tamed,' 'weakened,' 'discouraged,' 'made
refined,' 'made effete,' 'emasculated' (thus almost the same thing as
harmed)" (GM III:21). Contemporary Christians are therefore mistaken in
their belief that their current practices bear no debt to their slave heritage.
That contemporary Christians appear to *choose* their morality simply indicates the degree of domestication needed (and accomplished) to breed an
animal for whom a "free choice" of humility and submission becomes possible.

The *absurdum practicum* of Christian morality is difficult to detect, and
can be established only indirectly by a careful and clever reader of signs.
Nietzsche presents himself as one such reader, and, armed with the "case
history" provided by his genealogy of morals, proceeds to read the symptoms of physiological decadence inscribed into our bodies and the tormented affective lives they enact. Here, in our ascetic self-flagellation, the
slave heritage of Christianity is most visible; for the surplus suffering of
Christian sinners far outstrips the bad conscience that Christian morality
originally attempted to interpret and justify. Hence the *absurdum practicum*
of Christian morality: the treatment it prescribes is deadlier than the condition it purports to treat.

The "victory" of Christian morality consequently ushers in the "last will
of man," the will to alleviate suffering via self-annihilation. "Man would
rather will nothingness than not will" (GM III:28), Nietzsche claims, and
the advent of nihilism marks the historical space in which the release promised by this last will once again looms attractive. The will to nothingness is
engaged when the sole remaining goal capable of inducing anaesthesia is

that of self-annihilation: the will never to will again. Buckling under the physiological burden of two millennia of sin, we are delivered to the brink of a suicidal nihilism known all too well to our slave ancestors. "What is nihilism today if it is not *that?*" Nietzsche asks; "We are weary of *man*" (GM I:12).

Nietzsche's genealogy of morals thus enables the immanent symptomatological criticism he delivers of Christianity and of the culture it informs. Based on the "case history" provided by his genealogy of morals, Nietzsche pronounces modernity to be decadent, by virtue of its continued reliance on and identification with the decaying institutions of slave culture. If he has successfully completed his emigration "beyond good and evil," then he offers an immanent critique of Christianity that does not rely on the metaphysically freighted vocabulary of morality. As I have suggested, however, even if we do not accept Nietzsche's symptomatological critique of modernity, we need not reject the genealogy of morals that enables it.

But what of Nietzsche himself? Whence his credentials as a physician of culture? Here it is important to note that in the *Genealogy* Nietzsche neither commands nor claims the privileged perspective of the Promethean benefactor.[21] He identifies himself as operating within slave culture itself, and accepts the *absurdum practicum* of Christianity as his inheritance as well.[22] Nowhere in the *Genealogy* does he pretend to liberate his readers from their decadence; nor does he indicate that we are free to avoid the *absurdum practicum* of European nihilism. In fact, the most consistent (if not the most liberating) reading of the *Genealogy* would require us to treat Nietzsche's description of the ascetic priest—a "physician" who is himself sick—as self-referential in scope.

We should therefore not confuse Nietzsche's hermeneutic triumph in the *Genealogy* with a triumph of liberation or emancipation. Nietzsche claims as a genealogist of morals "only" to replace one set of prejudices with another set. In no event does he pretend that his genealogies liberate us *überhaupt* from our past.

NOTES

1. With the exception of occasional emendations, I rely throughout this essay on Walter Kaufmann's editions/translations of Nietzsche's works for Random House and Viking Press.

2. For example, Nietzsche observes that "good conscience is indistinguishable from good digestion" (TI VI:6), leaving us to conclude for ourselves how foolish it would be to praise (or blame) someone for good (or bad) digestion. Virtue is not the cause of happiness; the dispositions associated with virtue are caused by the physiological conditions (for example, good digestion) of happiness.

3. Arthur Danto, "Some Remarks on *The Genealogy of Morals*," in *Reading Nietzsche*, ed. Robert C. Solomon and Kathleen M. Higgins (New York: Oxford University Press, 1988), p. 21. (A version of this essay may be found in this volume.—ED.)

4. As Michel Foucault points out, Nietzsche refers here to origin not in the sense of *Ursprung*, but of *Herkunft*. The latter sense is concerned not with unearthing Archimedean foundations, but with tracing a descent. "Nietzsche, Genealogy, History" in *Language, Counter-Memory, Practice*, ed. and trans. D. F. Bouchard and S. Simon (Ithaca: Cornell University Press, 1977), pp. 140–148.

5. On the subject of Nietzsche's "moralistic naturalism," see Richard Schacht, *Nietzsche* (London: Routledge & Kegan Paul, 1983), pp. 440–444.

6. See BGE 4; TI 5:1; A 62.

7. For example, see Stephen Houlgate, *Hegel, Nietzsche and the Criticism of Metaphysics* (Cambridge: Cambridge University Press, 1986): "Nietzsche may not set up truth as his highest goal, but in being biased towards the strong *he is in fact being 'true' to life as he sees it*" (p. 72, emphasis added). Houlgate thus concludes that Nietzsche's appeal to "life" serves as both a "concrete foundation" for his philosophy and an "external standard" of criticism (p. 99).

8. Immanuel Kant, *Critique of Practical Reason*, trans. Lewis White Beck (Indianapolis: Bobbs-Merrill, 1956), p. 118.

9. In my discussion of Kant's moral philosophy, I have relied on Lewis White Beck's *Commentary on Kant's Critique of Practical Reason* (Chicago: University of Chicago Press, 1960); and Allen Wood's *Kant's Moral Religion* (Ithaca: Cornell University Press, 1970).

10. As Allen Wood observes, "[Kant's] moral arguments depend for whatever force they may have on my regarding the conclusion that I am (or am committed to be) a scoundrel as an unwelcome and unacceptable conclusion, an *absurdum practicum*" (p. 33).

11. Kant's essay, *Religion Within the Limits of Reason Alone*, trans. T. H. Greene and H. H. Hudson (New York: Harper and Row, 1960), furnishes an instructive example of the scope of his voluntarism (see pp. 32–36).

12. Kaufmann's translation—"What is the meaning of ascetic ideals?"—obscures the hermeneutic moment of genealogy, insofar as it suggests that there is only one meaning of ascetic ideals. Nietzsche asks a similar (and I would argue a related) question about the meaning of nihilism in his notebooks.

13. In order to give us "an idea of how uncertain, how supplemental, how accidental the 'meaning' of punishment is," Nietzsche provides a long list of the various meanings punishment has acquired over the years (GM II:13). The example is designed, I think, to exhibit the extent to which historical institutions are overdetermined with meanings.

14. As Foucault observes, "The search for descent [*Herkunft*] is not the erecting of foundations: on the contrary, it disturbs what was thought unified; it shows the heterogeneity of what was imagined consistent with itself" (p. 147).

15. This view of genealogy as parasitic, as successful relative only to an established interpretation, is consonant with Nietzsche's view of himself as a debunker and destroyer of idols: "No new idols are erected by me; let the old ones learn what

feet of clay mean. *Overthrowing idols* (my word for 'ideals')—that comes closer to being part of my craft" (EH P:2).

16. In *The Antichrist(ian)*, Nietzsche explains, "In my *Genealogy of Morals*, I offered the first psychological analysis of the counter concepts of a *noble* morality and a morality of *ressentiment*—the latter born of the No to the former: but this is the Judeo-Christian morality pure and simple" (A 24). See also EH III:GM.

17. Gilles Deleuze offers an insightful account of the interplay of active and reactive forces in chapter 2 of *Nietzsche and Philosophy*, trans. Hugh Tomlinson (New York: Columbia University Press, 1983), pp. 39–72.

18. It is important here to bear in mind that the designation "slave morality [*die Sklaven-Moral*]" is historical rather than evaluative. The designation reflects Nietzsche's belief that such morality could arise only in a community of slaves, for whom no viable alternatives exist.

19. Alexander Nehamas, for example, claims that Nietzsche's interpretations announce themselves as such, and are therefore superior to dogmatic interpretations, which masquerade as truths. See his *Nietzsche: Life as Literature* (Cambridge: Harvard University Press, 1985), p. 32. David Couzens Hoy claims that Nietzsche attributes the superiority of his genealogies to their "defeasible" character. "Nietzsche, Hume, and the Genealogical Method," in *Nietzsche as Affirmative Thinker*, ed. Y. Yovel (Dordrecht: Martinus Nijhoff, 1968), pp. 20–38. (This essay is reprinted in this volume.—ED.)

20. Mark Warren argues that genealogy comprises a critical method that incorporates three moments: logical criticism, genetic criticism, and functional criticism. Warren thus collapses genealogy and symptomatology into a single critical method. *Nietzsche and Political Thought* (Cambridge: MIT Press, 1988), pp. 104–110.

21. It is difficult to confer a privileged epistemic status to an author who begins by announcing that "we are unknown to ourselves, we men of knowledge—and with good reason" (GM P:1).

22. As he readily volunteers, "We godless men and antimetaphysicians, we too still derive *our* flame from the fire ignited by a faith millennia old, the Christian faith, which was also Plato's, that God is truth, that truth is divine" (GS 344; cited in GM III:24).

NINETEEN

Perspectivism in Nietzsche's
Genealogy of Morals

Brian Leiter

I. INTRODUCTION

Since the 1960s, much of the scholarly interest in Nietzsche has focused on the complex of issues surrounding his "perspectivism" and, more generally, his theory of knowledge and truth.[1] In the interval, one particular reading of "perspectivism" has attained the status of near-orthodoxy among commentators.[2] This "Received View" (or RV as I shall sometimes refer to it) attributes to Nietzsche the following four claims:

(i)   the world has no determinate nature or structure;
(ii) our concepts and theories do not "describe" or "correspond" to this world because it has no determinate character;
(iii) our concepts and theories are "mere" interpretations or "mere" perspectives (reflecting our pragmatic needs, at least on some accounts);
(iv) no perspective can enjoy an *epistemic* privilege over any other, because there is no epistemically privileged mode of access to this characterless world.

As epistemological pictures go, this is surely not a very appealing one. It seems wildly skeptical at best and perhaps incoherent at worst.[3] Moreover, by attributing this view to Nietzsche, commentators undertake a double burden: first, because they must make it out as an epistemological position worthy of serious attention; and second, because they must show how it could be compatible with the rest of his philosophical corpus, which seems unaffected by this radical epistemological doctrine.

Yet interpreters needn't undertake these daunting tasks; for the Received View, notwithstanding its remarkable currency in the secondary literature, is simply *not* Nietzsche's. Or so I shall argue. In particular, the Received View can not be sustained by a close reading of the central text in the work Nietzsche published in which he actually discusses perspectivism: section 12 of the Third Essay of *On the Genealogy of Morals*.

In challenging the Received View, of course, I am not entirely alone. In broad outline, the position I will defend below has affinities with those defended by John Wilcox, Richard Schacht, and, most recently, Maudemarie Clark.[4] My aim here is to make three concrete contributions to articulating a viable alternative to the Received View: first, to state with some precision the interpretive difficulty presented by the Received View (section II); second, to sketch an alternative interpretation of the passages often thought to support it (section III); and third and most important, to present an extended analysis of the "perspectivism" metaphor as it figures in GM III:12, as the key to Nietzsche's actual epistemological position (section IV).

Before turning to these tasks, I should put two interpretive scruples on the table. First, I proceed on the assumption that no position should be attributed to Nietzsche on the basis of passages that *only* appear in the *Nachlass*; this material (including that in *The Will to Power*) should only supplement, rather than constitute, the core of an interpretation.[5]

Second, I take "Nietzsche's position" to mean the *mature* Nietzsche. While I shall have things to say about the "immature" Nietzsche (and the *Nachlass* Nietzsche), it seems to me that the later Nietzsche's work should ultimately be decisive in his interpretation. This aligns me with Clark's recent work on the development and *progress* in Nietzsche's thought. According to Clark, Nietzsche's view of truth moved through three stages.

Stage I: In the oft-quoted early essay "On Truth and Lie in an Extra-Moral Sense" (1873), he accepted the "metaphysical correspondence theory, the conception of truth as correspondence to the thing-in-itself" (Clark, p. 22). Under the influence of Schopenhauer, he thought we can have no knowledge of things-in-themselves, and so accepted the Falsification Thesis (FT): our merely "human" knowledge necessarily falsifies what the world is really like in itself.

Stage II: By the early 1880s, Nietzsche rejected the idea of the thing-in-itself as incoherent—but, owing to the pernicious influence of certain other Schopenhauerian doctrines, continued to accept the FT.

Stage III: Only in his final six works—beginning with the *Genealogy* in 1887—did Nietzsche leave Schopenhauer behind, and come to realize that his earlier rejection of the thing-in-itself should lead him to abandon the FT and accept the possibility of (nonmetaphysical) truth and our knowledge of it (see Clark, chapters 1–4).

I find myself in basic agreement with Clark here. Much more remains to be said about the last stage, to which I shall return in section IV. To anticipate, however, I take the "mature" Nietzsche to be the Nietzsche of this third stage—and to be the wiser for having reached it. This mature Nietzsche, moreover, is not the Nietzsche of the Received View—and that, as I shall argue, is a great virtue, given his other philosophical commitments.

II. THE PROBLEM WITH THE RECEIVED VIEW

If the Received View were really Nietzsche's, then his work simply would not make any sense: first, because his philosophical corpus contains numerous themes that presuppose the possibility of privileged modes of epistemic access to a world with determinate contents; and second, because the Received View seems to entail at least one philosophical position he explicitly rejects. In sections A and B, I shall illustrate these difficulties; in section C, I will consider the possible ways in which one might try to escape this interpretive dilemma.

A. Criticism and Epistemic Privilege

On the Received View, the world (we might say) is like a piece of infinitely malleable clay, whose contours and determinate lines are all of human making. Such a world would impose no independent constraint on our interpretations of it. The first problem for the Received View is this: Nietzsche criticizes certain views on their *epistemic* merits, and takes his own view to enjoy an epistemic privilege over those he criticizes. The *epistemic* merits of a view are those bearing on its claim to count as *knowledge*; at a bare minimum, then, an epistemically privileged view must be capable of being true or false. Truth carries an implicit requirement of objectivity: what counts as being the case (as true) must be independent of our predilections. But on the Received View, what is the case about the world is not independent of our predilections; and there is nothing about the world that constrains us in interpreting it. Hence on this view there appears to be no room even for Nietzschean criticisms (let alone positive claims) having anything to do with epistemic merits.

That is the problem baldly stated. It seems undeniable, however, that Nietzsche does indeed make such criticisms—along at least two dimensions, which I shall briefly indicate.

1. *Empiricism/Verificationism.* Nietzsche often levels his harshest comments at views which are, in some respects, strikingly close to his own. This is certainly true of his vitriolic attacks on the works of Renan and Carlyle; but it applies equally in the case of his remarks on positivism. His differences with nineteenth-century positivism are real enough (see section III below); but throughout his mature work, he remains committed to the most basic and general empiricist criterion: experience—in particular,

sense experience—is the source of all genuine knowledge. (Thus BGE 134: "All credibility, all good conscience, all evidence of truth come only from the senses.") Like the logical empiricists of the second quarter of this century, he is relentless in wielding this standard against various contenders for cognitive discourse: morality, religion, metaphysics. Consider three examples:

(a) In a passage that sounds more "positivist" than "deconstructionist," Nietzsche writes:

> Today we possess science precisely to the extent to which we have decided to *accept* the testimony of the senses—to the extent to which we sharpen them further, arm them, and have learned to think them through. The rest is miscarriage and not-yet-science—in other words, metaphysics, theology, psychology, epistemology. . . . In them reality is not encountered at all, not even as a problem. (TI III:3)

Note that Nietzsche's point here is not simply that neglect of empiricist epistemic standards leads to "bad science"; it is rather that failure to observe such standards deprives one of access to "reality" at all.

(b) Another of the central themes of *Twilight*—that the metaphysically maligned "apparent" world is, in fact, the only *real* world—is defended by Nietzsche on unabashedly verificationist grounds. As he remarks: "Any other kind of reality [than the world of the senses] is absolutely indemonstrable" (TI III:6)—and therefore, he implies, nonexistent. Similarly, in his history of the *error* of a "true [i.e., verification-transcendent] world," the turning point comes with "the first yawn of reason. The cockcrow of positivism" (TI IV). Not long thereafter, the "true world" is, accordingly, abolished.

(c) *The Antichrist* mounts much (though certainly not all) of its attack on Christianity on broadly empiricist grounds. For example, Nietzsche claims that "in Christianity neither morality nor religion has a single point of contact with [empirical] reality" (A 15); and he even commends Buddhism—which "is a hundred times more realistic than Christianity"—for its adherence to a "strict phenomenalism" (A 20).[6]

Let us set aside for now the problems confronting empiricist epistemology. What is important to note here is that an empiricist critique depends precisely on the existence of an epistemically privileged class of claims about the world (the claims based on sense experience). Nietzsche's empiricism thus would be unintelligible on the Received View.

2. *Naturalistic Critiques.* Nietzsche seems to embrace two distinctively naturalistic views:

Explanatory Primacy of the Natural: The primary causal/explanatory facts are natural facts; and

Explanatory Continuity: Explanatory Primacy holds across all domains of explananda (physical, moral, social, and so on).[7]

So he holds that the best explanation of humans and human values is couched in terms of natural facts about agents—in particular, physiological facts (compare BGE 230; A 14). For example, he repeatedly attacks interpretations of phenomena in moral or religious terms for appealing to "imaginary causes" while misconstruing the *real* natural phenomena (TI VI:6; compare D 83, 86, 119; WP 670). As he puts it in *Twilight*: "Moral judgments agree with religious ones in believing in realities which are no realities" (TI VII:1). Yet for these criticisms to be intelligible—for it to be the case that "reality" is being construed in "imaginary" terms, that moral causes are not *real* causes—the naturalistic claims must enjoy an epistemic privilege over the moral and religious ones. On the Received View, this too would be impossible.

B. Appearance, Reality, and the Received View

The Received View generates a paradox when juxtaposed with Nietzsche's well-known rejection of the appearance/reality (A/R) distinction: that is, his rejection of the idea of an unknown and unknowable world, transcending the world of experience (compare TI III:6 and IV). On his view, the world of "appearing" is just all the world there is—though it is, of course, no longer a *merely* "apparent" world.

Yet the Received View, by holding that no view gives "a better picture of the world as it really is" than any other,[8] reinstates the distinction. For on this account there are, on the one hand, epistemically equivalent "mere" perspectives, and on the other, the indescribable (and hence unknown) world "as it really is," a world to which no perspective is adequate.[9] Hence the paradox: Although Nietzsche rejects the A/R distinction, on the Received View "mere perspectives" seem to have the same status as the metaphysician's "mere appearances" that Nietzsche sought to abolish.

Admittedly, some RV-minded commentators (e.g., Alexander Nehamas) do make a point of saying that perspectives for Nietzsche are not "mere" perspectives. The difficulty, however, is that as defenders of the Received View, it is not clear on what grounds they can do this, and what they might mean. Nehamas, for example, ends up saying: "Perspectivism does not result in the relativism that holds that any view is as good as any other [which would surely make them "mere" perspectives]; it holds that one's views are the best for oneself without implying that they need be good for anyone else" (p. 72). Putting aside such questions as whether this interpretation is fair to relativism and whether there are any texts in Nietzsche to support such a reading, this account still hardly seems an adequate response to a worry about the "mereness" of perspectives: if anything, it would seem to reinforce it!

C. Resolving the Problem

These two general themes—epistemic privilege and rejection of the A/R distinction—are central to Nietzsche's mature philosophical thought; yet both appear inconsistent with the epistemological commitments of the Received View. I shall suppose, for the sake of focusing the argument, that the problem presented by the A/R distinction could be avoided by a more perspicuous formulation of the Received View. How then might one reconcile the Received View with the claim of epistemic privilege implicit in Nietzsche's empiricism and naturalism? Three strategies suggest themselves.

Denial. One might simply deny that Nietzsche criticizes other views and promotes his own on *epistemic* grounds, and hold rather (as some proponents of the Received View are fond of saying) that he simply commends his view (his "perspective") over others because, for example, it is better suited to a stronger or more vital life. Now Nietzsche may indeed have thought that (see IV A, below); but he surely wants to make an epistemic point too. Recall, for example, the hardly atypical claim that "in Christianity neither morality nor religion has even a single *point of contact with reality*" (A 15, emphasis added; compare with EH IV). Any interpretation that can do justice to passages like this has to allow, it seems, that Nietzsche entertained the possibility of an epistemically privileged mode of access to reality—a reality which, in turn, functions as an epistemic standard.

Rhetorical Device. One might grant that Nietzsche makes criticisms with epistemically loaded language (truth, lie, reality, false, and so on), but dispute that it should be interpreted literally. It might be argued that he uses this language for rhetorical effect only (it helps persuade to have "truth" and "reality" on one's side).[10] Such a reading might emphasize the possible Sophistic pedigree of Nietzsche's epistemological views, and claim that, in best Sophistic fashion, he appreciates the rhetorical value of epistemically loaded—but semantically empty—language. This, it seems to me, is an important possibility, and one that awaits an able defender; but the textual burden is heavy. The "rhetorical" reading must explain away all of Nietzsche's naturalistic and empiricist themes in these terms. Until the case for such extensive revisionism is persuasively made, we ought to discount the rhetorical reading.

Concession. Finally, one might simply concede that the problem is a real one, and that the best hope is in finding a different set of epistemological commitments in Nietzsche than those ascribed by the Received View. This is the course I shall pursue.

III. SEVEN INTERPRETIVE PROPOSALS

That the Received View is incompatible with Nietzsche's actual philosophical practice—his empiricism and naturalism—has largely escaped the attention of its defenders. They have built their case instead on particular
remarks scattered here and there throughout his corpus. At the same time,
these remarks pose an obstacle to the concession strategy recommended
above. Rather than review in detail the standard catalogue of evidence for
the Received View,[11] I want to proceed directly to a sketch of seven interpretive proposals for reading these passages that will show them *not* to entail
the Received View—and thus clear the way for its replacement. In the accompanying notes I indicate some of the major passages to which each
proposal speaks.

All of the passages typically enlisted in support of the Received View are
more properly construed, I suggest, in one or more of the following seven
ways, as:

(A) *Attacks on the Thing-In-Itself.* Of a piece with Nietzsche's attack on the
A/R distinction is his rejection of the Kantian idea of a thing-in-itself, conceived as something that transcends, as well as underlies or undergirds, all
possible perspectives on it. The upshot of this critique, however, is not the
Received View, but rather the vindication of the reality—and not merely
the transcendentally ideal reality—of the world of experience.[12]

(B) *Attacks on Particular Beliefs About the World: Metaphysical, Moral, Religious, Commonsensical.* Nietzsche's empiricist and naturalistic critiques underlie the passages most often enlisted as evidence of his rejection of truth
and the possibility of knowledge. Yet, as I argued in section II, none of this
commits him to the Received View as a general epistemological picture.
On the contrary, all of these critiques are only possible on the assumption
that some claims can enjoy an epistemic privilege over the claims targeted
by Nietzsche's attacks. Their point is not that *no* belief is epistemically warranted (or that there is no truth), but rather that a particular (admittedly
large) *class* of familiar beliefs or supposed "truths" are in fact false. To
infer from Nietzsche's denial of the existence of epistemic standards in
some particular region—for example, morals—to the conclusion that he
denies *all* epistemic standards is simply a gross error. Yet this error surprisingly has fueled much of the enthusiasm for the Received View.[13]

(C) *Socioempirical Observations.* Nietzsche frequently remarks that numerous interpretations of the world have actually been proffered, and that
these reflect diverse needs and interests. Yet he does so (at least in the
passages at issue) without passing positive judgment on the epistemic merit
of the various interpretive needs and interests at work.[14] While it may indeed be a socioempirical fact that the world is populated with a remarkable
plethora of views—a phenomenon that presumably admits of naturalistic

explanation—his harsh judgments concerning the epistemic merit of the vast majority of them is a recurring theme in his empiricist and naturalistic critiques.[15]

(D) *Accounts of the Pragmatics of Belief Acquisition and Retention.* One consequence of Nietzsche's relentless critical assaults is that most people turn out to believe false things—a phenomenon that he rightly thinks requires some explaining. Thus he frequently offers accounts of the *pragmatic* influences on belief acquisition, formation and retention that would explain the fact that people believe so many sundry lies and simplifications. Yet in none of this is there a denial that his own claims are justified, or a suggestion that all beliefs admit of the same pragmatic explaining away.[16] To the contrary, as any careful reader of his texts should know, Nietzsche insisted on distinguishing beliefs that are *true* from those that were merely useful (compare, e.g., GS 110, 121; BGE 210; WP 172, 455, 487).

(E) *Attacks on Overestimating the Value of Truth.* Nietzsche sometimes disparages the value of truth, but only in a carefully circumscribed respect: he disparages the "*overestimation* of truth" (GM III:25, emphasis added), that is, the tendency to treat "truth" as an "absolute value" (GM III:24). He objects to this "overestimation" essentially because there is an important sense in which we *need* to believe various simplifications and falsifications in order to get by in the world at all (see section II D); and the sanctimonious pursuit of truth has long obscured both the ulterior *moralistic* motivations of philosophers, and the respects in which their "truths" have, in fact, simply stood "truth itself on its head" (GM III:24; compare BGE P).[17] So Nietzsche rejects the "overestimation" of truth—as characteristic of the philosophical tradition—in part out of a concern to stand the "truth" right side up. At no point does he suggest that "truth" should be abandoned *altogether* as an *epistemic* ideal.

(F) *Remarks on the Necessity of Interpretation (in a Nonpejorative Sense).* Nietzsche *does* think that all knowledge of the world involves "interpretation"; but he plainly does *not* intend anything pejorative by that appellation. It is only when we read a disparaging tone into his remarks on the necessity of interpretation—when we read it as "mere" interpretation—that we are drawn to the Received View. Yet as an inveterate "old philologist," he believes in "the art of reading well—of reading facts without falsifying them by interpretation" (A 52). Such an art, however, requires that one be able to "interpret" while at the same time reporting the "facts" truthfully.[18] Similarly, in the oft-quoted passage in which Nietzsche criticizes mechanistic cosmology but concedes that his own view is "interpretation" too (BGE 22), he explicitly calls the physicist's interpretation of the world a "perversion of meaning," involving a "bad mode of interpretation" and "bad 'philology.'" He refers contrastingly to his own preferred view (of the world in terms of will to power) as an "opposite . . . mode of interpretation"—

presumably meaning that it involves both opposite interpretive assumptions and "good" interpretation and "good" philology. But as we have seen, good philology just involves interpretation that does not falsify the matters at issue. In none of this is there a suggestion that, because knowledge requires interpretation, the justification of the conclusions of *good* "philology" is undermined.[19]

(G) *Attacks on Positivism.* Why then does Nietzsche persist in the use of the word "interpretation"? The answer, I think, is that it is the word he chose to emphasize his opposition to the positivist assumption that "unmediated" access to the world was possible. The famous passage, for example, in which he asserts that "facts is precisely what there is not, only interpretations" is explicitly a critique of "positivism, which halts at phenomena" (WP 481). But as a host of philosophers have shown since—from philosophers of science like Russell Hanson and Paul Feyerabend to critics of confrontationalist epistemologies like Wilfrid Sellars and Donald Davidson—no such simple epistemic access to phenomena can be had. By talking about the inescapability of "interpretation," Nietzsche underlines the point that what the facts are is always conditioned by particular *interpretations* of what the facts are.[20]

Yet accepting that we can never confront "any fact 'in itself' " (WP 481), and that the positivist aspirations are untenable *in this quite specific respect,* does not necessarily entail an epistemological nihilism *of the sort envisioned by the Received View.*[21] That result only follows with the addition of a (generally suppressed) skeptical premise: namely, the premise that once linguistic (or theoretical or perspectival) mediation enters the picture, the "facts" must vanish altogether, with the consequence that the world is (in Rorty's famous phrase) "well lost." Justification then becomes nothing more than a certain sort of socially sanctioned practice.[22]

But does the rejection of positivism lead us straight to pragmatism? As I will argue in section IV, there is a middle ground to be staked out by challenging this skeptical premise. On this alternative picture, we should: (a) give up the crude confrontationalist foundationalism that would have us (quite implausibly, as Sellars and others have shown) picture "justification" as a matter of comparing particular propositions with nonlinguistic items in the world; but (b) retain the thought that there can still be some form of epistemic hierarchy. To hold both views simultaneously will require showing that the "mediation" of interpretive perspectives does not foreclose an epistemically robust sense of knowledge or truth. Since these issues go to the very heart of Nietzsche's epistemological view, their full treatment will have to await section IV. If I am successful there in making my case, this will effectively defuse WP 481, one of the most important sources for the Received View.

I believe I have shown both that the Received View is inconsistent with

Nietzsche's philosophical practice; and that the Received View is not required by the texts typically enlisted to support it. (The issues raised in (G), above, of course, await resolution.) But what then *is* his epistemological position? I shall attempt to answer that question in the context of a reading of his central published discussion of perspectivism.

IV. A READING OF GM III:12

Although Nietzsche uses the language of "interpretation" freely throughout the material published during his lifetime, discussions of "perspectivism" and "perspectives" are far less frequent. The primary text in his mature work in which he does offer a sustained discussion of these topics in an epistemological context occurs in the Third Essay of the *Genealogy*, section 12. This passage begins with an attack on any metaphysics that posits the truth as essentially unknowable, with Kant's thing-in-itself as a paradigmatic case in point. Nietzsche then continues that " 'objectivity' " should be:

> understood not as "contemplation without interest" (which is a nonsensical absurdity), but as the ability *to control* one's Pro and Con and to dispose of them, so that one knows how to employ a *variety* of perspectives and affective interpretations in the service of knowledge.
>
> Henceforth, my dear philosophers, let us be on guard against the dangerous old conceptual fiction that posited a "pure, will-less, painless, timeless knowing subject"; let us guard against the snares of such contradictory concepts as "pure reason," "absolute spirituality," "knowledge in itself": these always demand that we should think of an eye that is completely unthinkable, *an eye turned in no particular direction* [emphasis added], in which the active and interpreting forces, through which alone seeing becomes seeing *something*, are supposed to be lacking; these always demand of the eye an absurdity and nonsense. There is *only* a perspective seeing, *only* a perspective "knowing"; and the *more* affects we allow to speak about one thing, the more complete will our "concept" of this thing, our "objectivity" be. But to eliminate the will altogether, to suspend each and every affect, supposing we were capable of this—what would that mean but to *castrate* the intellect?—

Let us characterize the two central epistemological doctrines of this passage as follows:

(i) *Doctrine of Epistemic Affectivity (DEA)*:
   (a) all knowledge necessarily presupposes some "interest" or "affect"; as a result,
   (b) knowledge can never be disinterested; and
(ii) *Doctrine of Perspectives (DP)*: as a consequence of the DEA, the knowledge situation is analogous to the optical situation in that both are essentially dependent on "perspectives"; so,

(a) just as knowledge always presupposes an "interest"; so too,

(b) seeing always presupposes seeing from some particular direction, under some particular conditions, and so on.

It is the DP, then, that explains Nietzsche's choice of the optical-sounding "perspectivism" to characterize his view; and it is the DEA, in turn, that underwrites the DP. My interpretive proposal, then, is this: If knowing is like seeing (DP), and if the Received View really represents his considered epistemological position, then an analysis of the optical situation ought to show that an optical analogue to the epistemic doctrine of the Received View holds there as well. Conversely, if no such analogue does hold in the optical situation—and given that Nietzsche invites us to employ the optical analogy—then we should return to the epistemic situation to see whether it might be construed such that it preserves the relevant analogy with the optical case, while not entailing the Received View. I will, of course, be arguing that no optical analogue to the Received View is required by reflection on the ordinary features of the optical case. After having offered that argument (in section A below), I will turn to some of the issues raised about epistemic hierarchy (in section III(G) above). In particular, I will consider whether the DEA, on its own, entails something like the Received View.

A. Knowing and Seeing: An Exploration of the DP

Nietzsche holds that knowing is like seeing in that both are essentially dependent on perspectives: interests or affects in the former case; distance, angle, background conditions, and so on in the latter. The Received View allegedly characterizes how the DP plays out in the case of knowledge; does it characterize how the DP plays out in the case of seeing?

In the case of our visual grasp of an object, it seems that the following four claims are (uncontroversially, I hope) true:

Necessarily, we see an object from a particular perspective: for example, from a certain angle, from a certain distance, under certain conditions (perspectivism claim).

The more perspectives we enjoy—for example, the more angles we see the object from—the better our conception of what the object is actually like will be (plurality claim).

We will never exhaust all possible perspectives on the object of vision[23] (infinity claim).

There exists a catalogue of identifiable factors that would distort our perspective on the object: for instance, we are too far away or the background conditions are poor (purity claim).[24]

Now what is striking about these four claims is that they do *not* appear to entail any optical analogue of the Received View. That is, we do not seem committed to claims like:

(i)   the object of vision has no determinate nature; or
(ii) all visual perspectives on the object are equivalent in terms of their access to the object.

To the contrary, the plurality claim tells us that:

(i′)   the more perspectives we take on an object, the more we will know about its actual nature.

Though of course, as the infinity claim notes, we will never exhaust the possible perspectives, and thus will never have a final and complete view of the object's actual visual nature. Similarly, the purity claim permits us to say:

(ii′) some visual perspectives do not give us access to the object at all because of the influence of identifiable distorting factors.

Thus we *can* maintain some sort of "visual hierarchy": some visual perspectives will simply be better than others—better, that is, in virtue of their adequacy to the real visible nature of the object. And surely that conclusion is perfectly in line with our intuitive understanding of the optical case.

Now if seeing does *not* entail any optical analogue of the Received View, and if we are to take Nietzsche at his word—namely, that *seeing is like knowing*—then we should not be committed in the epistemic case to the Received View either. Yet since the optical case is the perspectivist paradigm, we must preserve the analogy between the epistemic case and the defining features of the optical case: thus, we must specify the epistemic analogues of the perspectivism, plurality, infinity, and purity claims. If we can do that without slipping into the Received View, then we will have shown both *what* Nietzsche's doctrine of perspectivism really is *and* that it does not entail the Received View.

Here, then, are the epistemic analogues of the defining claims of the optical case:

Necessarily, we know an object from a particular perspective: that is, from the standpoint of particular interests and needs[25] (perspectivism claim).

The more perspectives we enjoy—for example, the more interests we employ in knowing the object—the better our conception of what the object is like will be (plurality claim).

We will never exhaust all possible perspectives on the object of knowledge (there are an infinity of interpretive interests that could be brought to bear) (infinity claim).

There exists a catalogue of identifiable factors that would distort our knowledge of the object: that is, certain interpretive interests and needs will distort the nature of objects (purity claim).

Plainly, the epistemic version of the purity claim is the most contentious, and I will return to it momentarily. But note the epistemological picture we get from pursuing the analogy with the optical case: we do indeed have knowledge of the world, though it is never disinterested, never complete, and can always benefit from additional nondistorting perspectives. As long as we can make out the purity claim, this epistemology is not egalitarian, though it is certainly pluralistic.[26] It is also plainly an epistemology that permits the sort of philosophical practice that actually characterizes Nietzsche's mature philosophical work.

Yet there remain two difficult tasks: first, showing that we can have something like the purity claim in the epistemic case; and second, showing that the perspectivism claim itself—the concession that knowing is always "interested" (in essence, the DEA)—does not already undermine any claim of epistemic privilege. I will take up the first issue now, and the second issue in the next section.

If we are to have the epistemic purity claim then we must be able to make out something like the following thought: certain interpretive needs and interests distort the nature of objects. We require, then, some criterion for distinguishing nondistorting and distorting needs and interests. How can we have one?

Nietzsche's general view, put somewhat crudely, is something like this: (i) the truth about the world is "terrible";[27] (ii) only certain sorts of people can tolerate knowing this truth—call them the "strong"; (iii) the vast majority—call them the "weak"—prefer various and sundry lies and falsifications (though they persist in calling these "truths"); (iv) the strong and weak differ, in part, in terms of their respective interests and needs; (v) the strong can know (at least some aspects of) the "terrible truth" precisely because they possess the right sort of constitutive interests and affects; (vi) that is, (at least some of) the interpretive interests of the strong will not distort reality, while those of the weak will and do.

Unusual as it may be, this view would seem to me to be Nietzsche's (compare BGE 39, 43; EH III:BT:2 and CW:2; and IV:4–5). So if he is right in thinking that the "terrible truth" about reality will only be cognizable by agents with sufficiently robust interpretive interests—namely, the "strong"—then those interests just will be the nondistorting ones, and the "terrible truth" about reality will be our criterion for vindicating the purity claim. More precisely, given the "terrible truth" about reality, we should be able to extrapolate from it to those interpretive interests that will be ill-disposed to recognizing it: for example, those interpretive interests that are moralistic, seduced by the metaphysics of grammar, and the like.

But let me be clear about what I am saying here. The mark or criterion of a nondistorting interest, for Nietzsche, is that it is adequate to the "terrible truth" about the world.[28] But that "terrible truth" must be established on other grounds: for example, empirical adequacy, explanatory potency, coherence, and the like. Note, of course, that there is no sense in which these grounds can be truly interest "independent." (That is the final upshot of perspectivism, as I discuss in the next section.) Yet Nietzsche plainly takes his terrible-truth-view of the world to have many of these epistemic virtues. Before dismissing his criterion one needs to show why his view of the world is untenable *on the merits of the case.* Note, too, that even if one were to do so, one still would not have shown that Nietzsche's epistemology is really that contemplated by the Received View. For if his terrible-truth-view of the world is wrong, it would follow only that his *basis for discriminating* between differing interpretive interests is unsound. His epistemology would be unaffected; at issue would only be the particular assignment of epistemic privileges that he envisions.

My conclusion, then, is that we *can* make sense of the purity claim in the epistemic case, and that the only obstacle to Nietzsche's particular use of the purity claim is that we may dispute the account of reality that grounds the discrimination among competing interpretive interests. This may, indeed, be a contestable account, but that fact in no way touches the structure of his epistemology, which is both pluralistic *and* hierarchical.

B. Knowledge and Interests: A Consideration of the DEA

A final worry remains: namely, that by conceding that all knowing is mediated by particular interpretive needs (interests, affects)—that there are no "facts," only (affective) "interpretations"—Nietzsche effectively holds that reality exercises no epistemic constraint on our interpretations of the world (the "facts" themselves turning out to be simply our affective projections). Without any such constraint, however, it is not clear what room there could be for the idea that interpretations could have differing *epistemic* (as opposed to, e.g., pragmatic) merits.

This problem is the one we encountered earlier (III(G)) in the form of the "suppressed skeptical premise" in certain forms of the challenge to empiricist epistemology—namely the premise that once any human mediation enters the picture, the world is "well lost." Hilary Putnam has explained how the problem arises this way:

> The mind never compares an image or word with an object, but only with other images, words, beliefs, judgments, etc. The idea of a comparison of words or mental representations with objects is a senseless one.[29]

This is so because we never get hold of objects (themselves) but simply "other images, words, beliefs, judgments" about objects. If this sort of objection is on target, then what sense can be made out of the empiricist demand—as formulated by Nietzsche (BGE 134)—that "all evidence of truth come only from the senses"? And does not his introduction of the DEA effectively cut off any intelligible answer to this question?[30]

We may get a first sense of an answer here by way of considering a related problem from Wittgenstein. There are two well-known strands in Wittgenstein's thought that are important in this context. On the one hand, he famously tells us that philosophy "leaves everything as it is."[31] Yet on the other, his remarks on rule-following seem to alter radically our understanding of meaning, normativity, and objectivity.[32] That is, he shows us that our idea of the objectivity of meaning, of a normative *constraint* that is independent of human judgment or opinion on the matter, is simply unintelligible: that, in fact, normativity is parasitic on *our* actual dispositions to use words certain ways. It looks, then, as if Wittgenstein's conclusions are profoundly revisionary of our ordinary understanding of the objectivity of rules and meanings—and threatening to our commerce with both.

We needn't saddle Wittgenstein with a deep inconsistency, however; for, as some writers have suggested, there is another way of taking the upshot of his remarks on rule-following.[33] On this alternative reading, the suggestion is that he has identified something like a "transcendental" *condition* on notions like meaning: that is, a condition without which semantic facts wouldn't be possible. That condition is simply that there be a community of human language-users with particular dispositions of use. It is only against a background of such dispositions that it is possible to employ any intelligible idea of a constraint on meaning.

On this view, all that would have to be revised is the *metaphysical* gloss (either realist or idealist) that we would give to our meaning-talk. That is, we would be forced to abandon the realist thought that meaning could transcend *every possible* human disposition (that violates the condition-requirement); and likewise, the idealist thought that meaning is nothing other than a matter of consensus (that construes the dispositions as constituting meaning-facts, rather than being conditions of them). But our commerce with meaning itself—our practice of asking about, fixing, and correcting meanings—would be left "as it is."[34]

To make the connection with Nietzsche clearer, let us reformulate this Wittgensteinian point in terms of objectivity. On one plausible understanding, for facts about the world to be objective—to be capable, in other words, of exercising some constraint on our interpretation of them—they must not depend on our beliefs about them or our evidence for them. Call this the "independence" requirement. The independence requirement admits of at least two construals, strong and modest, corresponding to two different sorts of objectivity. According to "strong objectivity," it is *global* independence from human evidence or belief that is the mark of objectivity. Thus, a fact is strongly objective only if everything we believe about it and all the evidence we have about it—even at the ideal limit—could prove mistaken. Strong objectivity, then, requires that global error be an intelligible possibility.

Wittgenstein's arguments challenge the viability of this strong independence requirement. On the Wittgensteinian view, we simply have no intelligible idea of what a feature of the world could be that would satisfy *this* independence requirement, since what is the case is necessarily parasitic on our dispositions and practices. As John McDowell has nicely put it, "We have no vantage point on the question what can be the case, that is, what can be a fact, external to the modes of thought and speech we know our way around in."[35] Yet from within these "modes of thought and speech," we can and do still avail ourselves of the notion of objectivity—what we might call "modest objectivity."

Modest objectivity does not require us to deny Davidson's "platitude"—"believing something does not in general make it true"[36]—nor even its corollary: the community's believing something doesn't make it so either.[37] It requires only that we abandon the Strong Objectivist's thought that there is some sense to be made of (as Nietzsche puts it) a "fact-in-itself," that is, a fact that would transcend any and all human beliefs, evidence, and so on. At the limit, the modest objectivist claims, distinctively human beliefs, sensibilities, practices, and dispositions are a condition of the very possibility of anything being true or knowable—but this does not mean that what is the case or what beliefs are justified depends directly on what *any particular* person or community believes, is sensitive to, has evidence for, or is disposed to talk about. We can keep asking our mundane questions "Is this true?" and "Am I justified in believing that?" without supposing that the requisite objectivity demanded for proper answers is one that could transcend the human point of view altogether.

My suggestion, now, is that it is within this epistemological framework that we should locate the mature Nietzsche's perspectivism. For on the one hand, he avails himself of the distinction between truth and falsity, and of the idea of epistemic merits and epistemic hierarchy (section II). Yet on the other, he tells us that all knowledge is, in some sense, interest- or need-bound. The right reading of these remarks, I suggest, is to see them as identifying a trivially necessary *condition* of all our knowledge claims: namely, actual human interests and needs. But as with Wittgenstein, the specification of what is essentially a *condition* on any epistemic practice is not supposed to be revisionary of the practice itself—makes possible a practice that the use of such notions as true/false and better/less well justified.

What we must give up, however, is the metaphysical construal of the epistemic notions in our practice: for example, the idea that truth might be explicated in a metaphysically realist sense, as that which is available from no perspective at all (i.e., independent of *all* human interests); or, conversely, the vulgar idealist gloss that it is nothing other than what particular human interests take it to be. A metaphysical realism of this sort is rendered unintelligible because human interests are *conditions* of anything being true or knowable (whereas the metaphysical realist would have truth transcend *all* human interests). And crude idealism is avoided because: interests are *only conditions* of our knowledge of objects; hence particular interests are not *constitutive* of objects. So just as it is a condition of seeing a thing that we see it from some perspective, so too it is a condition of knowing it that we do so from the perspective of some interest (need, affect). Similarly, this epistemic interest—like the analogous visual perspective—determines what piece of the object of knowledge we pick out. But the object of knowledge is never constituted by that or *any other particular* interest. In that sense, it remains an independent object.

Yet it is not—and this is the key point—a *transcendent* object, a thing-in-itself. For the thing-in-itself is the thing that would transcend *all* possible perspectives on it; but the thing—the object of knowledge—as conceived by Nietzsche would not be left over after all possible perspectives were taken. It would just be the *thing itself* (*not* in-itself). As the perspectivist infinity claim tells us, however, we *never* reach this point: there is only epistemological plurality, not finitude, in the offing.

The real thrust of the claim that there are no facts, only interpretations (where these too are always expressions of various interests and needs) is simply that our knowledge is always a knowledge of an interpreted world, not a world of naked facts (what Nietzsche in GM III:24 calls "the *factum brutum*")—and that it could not be otherwise, since the positivist ideal of a "naked fact" is an unintelligible one. Yet this sort of interpretive mediation should only undermine any metaphysic—either realist or idealist—of knowledge or truth; as with Wittgenstein's related point, this mediation does not entail that we revise (or even jettison) our mundane questions "Is this true?" and "Am I justified in believing that?" So the object of knowledge, to repeat, can be and is known, if never fully and if always from some particular interested human angle. That it is human knowledge, however, is not an objection to its being knowledge!

We might summarize the preceding as follows. Nietzsche's two related claims—the DEA and the claim that there are only (affective) interpretations (not unmediated "facts")—have three upshots: an antimetaphysical thesis, a nonrevisionist thesis and a perspectivist thesis. The antimetaphysical thesis:

> The object of knowledge neither can transcend human interests (as realism would have it) nor is simply constituted by particular human interests (as idealism would have it).

The nonrevisionist thesis:

> Within our epistemic practices, we can still ask our mundane questions about truth and knowledge, and aspire towards modest objectivity in the answers; only our meta-epistemological and metaphysical views about these epistemic categories require revision.[38]

Finally, the perspectivist thesis (proper):

> Knowledge of objects in any particular case is always conditioned by particular interpretive interests that direct the knower to corresponding features of the object of knowledge.

Together these three theses define the Nietzschean response to the skeptical challenge in section III(G) and the nihilistic challenge seemingly embodied in the DEA.

In sum, Nietzsche's perspectivism is the epistemological position characterized by the perspectivism, plurality, infinity and purity claims, and by the antimetaphysical, nonrevisionist and perspectivist (proper) theses. On this position knowledge is possible, though never complete, and it always requires a plurality of interpretive perspectives. It is a condition of knowing objects that we do so from the standpoint of particular interpretive interests and needs, and against the background of the profusion of human interpretive interests. If they are not to distort the real (but nontranscendent) nature of objects, however, these particular interests must be adequate to relevant aspects of the "terrible truth" about reality.

V. CONCLUSION

I have argued that we may preserve the relevant analogy with the optical case—the one that Nietzsche tells us is essential to his understanding of perspectivism—without any commitment to the Received View. On this reading, his doctrine of perspectivism turns out to be much less radical than is usually supposed: we get, as one writer has recently put it, "a Nietzsche who is merely rehashing familiar Kantian themes, minus the rigor of Kant's exposition."[39] There is something to both points (even though the themes are not *exactly* Kantian). Yet this is not a problem, particularly since Nietzsche's primary concerns lie elsewhere. Like Wittgenstein, Nietzsche does break significantly with the philosophical tradition here; but unlike

Wittgenstein, Nietzsche attaches far more significance to other breaks he sought to effect with those who preceded him.

Under the influence of the Received View—and its analytic and post-modernist proponents—Nietzsche has become best known as the precursor of deconstruction and the "end of philosophy."[40] If, as recent work suggests, the Received View may finally be waning, then we may discover a different Nietzsche: one with philosophical theories of agency and value, with a commitment to a certain brand of naturalism, and with an interest in assessing competing views along many dimensions—including their truth.[41]

NOTES

1. I will cite Nietzsche's works using the acronyms of their standard English-language titles. Roman numerals refer to major parts or chapters; Arabic numerals to sections (not pages). Translations, with occasional very minor emendations, are by Kaufmann, Kaufmann/Hollingdale, or, in the case of D, Hollingdale alone.

2. The account originated, in the English-speaking world, with Arthur Danto's *Nietzsche as Philosopher* (New York: MacMillan, 1965), especially chaps. 1 and 3. Typical of Danto's reading is the following: "We score the blank surface of reality with the longitudes and parallels of concepts, but the concepts and ideas are ours, and they have not the slightest basis in fact. This is his doctrine of Perspectivism" (Columbia University Press edition, 1980, p. 67). Among the other authors who either defend (often independently of Danto) or simply take for granted the same basic view are: Sarah Kofman, *Nietzsche et la Metaphore* (Paris: Payot, 1972); Ruediger Grimm, *Nietzsche's Theory of Knowledge* (Berlin: de Gruyter, 1977); Jacques Derrida, *Spurs: Nietzsche's Styles*, trans. B. Harlow (Chicago: University of Chicago Press, 1978); Bernd Magnus, *Nietzsche's Existential Imperative* (Bloomington: Indiana University Press, 1978); Paul de Man, *Allegories of Reading* (New Haven: Yale University Press, 1979); Alexander Nehamas, *Nietzsche: Life as Literature* (Cambridge, Mass.: Harvard University Press, 1985), cited in the text by page number; Tracy Strong, *Friedrich Nietzsche and the Politics of Transfiguration*, expanded edition (Berkeley, Los Angeles, London: University of California Press, 1988); Alan Schrift, *Nietzsche and the Question of Interpretation* (New York: Routledge, 1990); Mary Warnock, "Nietzsche's Conception of Truth," in *Nietzsche: Imagery and Thought*, ed. M. Pasley (Berkeley, Los Angeles, London: University of California Press, 1978); Nicholas Davey, "Nietzsche's Doctrine of Perspectivism," *Journal of the British Society for Phenomenology* 14 (1983): 240–257; Bernd Magnus, "Nietzsche Today: A View From America," *International Studies in Philosophy* 15/2 (1983): 95–103; Alexander Nehamas, "Immanent and Transcendent Perspectivism in Nietzsche," *Nietzsche-Studien* 12 (1983): 473–490; Daniel Conway, "Perspectivism and Persuasion," *Nietzsche-Studien* 17 (1988): 555–562.

Nehamas's work provides a good illustration of the uncritical orthodoxy now reigning in the treatment of perspectivism. In his book, Nehamas makes a Danto-esque version of perspectivism one of the two organizing themes of his study, without engaging in any sustained textual defense of this reading. (Nehamas does reject Danto's attribution of a pragmatic theory of truth to Nietzsche [pp. 52–55].) Similarly, in his 1983 article, Nehamas writes that according to Nietzsche "no *particular* way of representing the world is privileged" (p. 486). This tendency to see Nietzsche's epistemological views in Dantoesque or perhaps Derridean terms is even more pronounced outside the community of Nietzsche scholars: for example, Richard Rorty, *Contingency, Irony and Solidarity* (Cambridge: Cambridge University Press, 1989). Rorty has done more than many others to saddle Nietzsche with the "orthodox" view.

3. Incoherence looms when the question arises of the epistemic status of the perspectivist thesis itself—a problem discussed at great length in the secondary literature. See, for example, Nehamas, *Nietzsche: Life as Literature,* chap. 2, and Magnus, *Nietzsche's Existential Imperative,* chap. 7.

4. John Wilcox, *Truth and Value in Nietzsche* (Ann Arbor: University of Michigan Press, 1974); Richard Schacht, *Nietzsche* (London: Routledge, 1983), chap. 2; Maudemarie Clark, *Nietzsche on Truth and Philosophy* (Cambridge: Cambridge University Press, 1990). See also, Robert Nola, "Nietzsche's Theory of Truth and Belief," *Philosophy & Phenomenological Research* 47 (1987): 525–562; Kenneth Westphal, "Nietzsche's Sting and the Possibility of Good Philology," *International Studies in Philosophy* 16/2 (1984): 71–90, and "Was Nietzsche a Cognitivist?" *Journal of the History of Philosophy* 22 (1984): 343–363. My differences with Wilcox concern the paradoxical position Wilcox's Nietzsche ends up holding: for example, Nietzsche's "human truth" turns out on Wilcox's reading to be " 'erroneous' truth" (p. 156). For some of my differences with Clark, see my review in *Journal of the History of Philosophy* 31 (1993): 148–150.

5. This view is warranted by doubts about the canonical status of the *Nachlass* raised in Mazzino Montinari, "Nietzsches Nachlass von 1885 bis 1888 oder Textkritik und Wille zur Macht," in *Nietzsche Lesen* (Berlin: de Gruyter, 1982), and Bernd Magnus, "The Use and Abuse of *The Will to Power,*" in *Reading Nietzsche,* ed. R. Solomon and K. Higgins (New York: Oxford University Press, 1988). I disagree with Magnus, however, that the "postmodern, nonrepresentational" Nietzsche can survive without reliance on the *Nachlass.*

6. The distinctively Nietzschean move—which sets him apart from other empiricist-minded philosophers—is to follow the broadly empiricist critique of metaphysical or religious claims with speculation about the real explanation for belief in these manifestly untenable claims; in particular with speculation about what *types* of people would hold such beliefs. A 15 is again typical in this respect.

7. I discuss the contours of Nietzsche's naturalism at greater length in my "Nietzsche's Metaethics: Value and Naturalism in the Philosophy of Nietzsche" (manuscript).

8. Nehamas, *Nietzsche: Life as Literature,* p. 49. See also, Conway, "Perspectivism and Persuasion," p. 555 for similar remarks. Nehamas does suggest that "some perspectives are, and can be shown to be, better than others" (p. 49), but his sense of "better" has no epistemic force: views are better for particular agents, given their ways of life, not because they are better in virtue of some epistemic property. See the further discussion in the text.

9. A defender of the Received View may wish to object that *there is no way* the world "really is"; rather the world as it "appears" from different perspectives is just *all there is.* There is a sense in which I find this formulation more palatable, as I discuss in section IV; but most defenders of the Received View are not entitled to it. For example, Nehamas (whom I quote in the text) puts the point in such a way that it invites the charge as it stands. Other defenders of the Received View (for example, Danto, *Nietzsche as Philosopher,* p. 35) maintain a distinction between perspectives on the one hand and the in-itself characterless flux of the world on the other—a distinction sufficient, as far as I can see, to also warrant the challenge in the text.

10. I owe the general suggestion here to Michael Forster.

11. Much of which is helpfully collected in Wilcox, *Truth and Value in Nietzsche,* chap. 1.

12. Passages to which this interpretive proposal should apply include GS 354, 374; BGE 11, 16; TI III and IV; WP 481, 553, 555, 567, 568. (These passages should also be read with the account of Nietzsche's positive view given in section IV in mind.)

13. Passages to which this interpretive proposal should apply include BGE 24; TI III; WP 497, 552, 589, as well as many of the passages cited in chap. 1 of Wilcox, *Truth and Value in Nietzsche.* A good example of the faulty inference criticized in the text is Nehamas, "Immanent and Transcendent Perspectivism in Nietzsche," p. 473.

14. Passages to which this interpretive proposal should apply include GS 374; WP 481, 540, 600. It is important that these passages also be read in light of the other interpretive suggestions above and below. They also support what I call in section IV the "plurality claim," which is one aspect of Nietzsche's perspectivism.

15. See especially the emphasis on "truth" versus "lies" that Nietzsche invokes in summing up his work in EH IV.

16. Passages to which this interpretive proposal should apply include GS 110, 121, 354; BGE 11, 24; WP 493, 507, 584, 589. These points are explored in Nola, "Nietzsche's Theory of Truth and Belief."

17. Passages to which this interpretive proposal should apply include BGE 1–6; GM III:24–25. The first point in the text is an important one. Nietzsche's concern with the value of the *superficial, ignorance,* and *forgetting* (for example, GS P:4)—in other words, his concern with the *desirability* of knowledge—should not be confused with the topic of this paper: namely, Nietzsche's views on the *possibility* of knowledge. Knowledge could be both possible and yet not always desirable—which seems to me to be precisely Nietzsche's view, though I do not explore this issue here.

18. In GM III:24, Nietzsche describes "falsifying" (*Umfälschen*) as being "of the essence of interpreting." Here, however, the context of this (hyperbolic) remark is extremely important. Nietzsche is in the midst of a polemic against those scholars who manifest that positivist "*desire* to halt before the factual, the *factum brutum*" (compare WP 481) and who thus seek a "general renunciation of all interpretation." From their standpoint, interpreting would seem to involve "falsifying" because it can never be the case—as Nietzsche contends and as I discuss below—that we ever get a hold of "any fact 'in-itself' " (WP 481). *In that sense,* we would necessarily falsify in interpreting the facts. But once we realize—as Nietzsche would have

us do—that the positivist aspiration is untenable, then interpretation needn't "falsify" just because it does not capture "facts-in-themselves." (The hyperbolic character of the remark derives also from the fact that he is attacking those who overestimate the value of truth and thus presumably overstates his case in order to mock their pretensions to possess only the factual and truthful.)

19. As Westphal notes ("Nietzsche's Sting"), Nietzsche's thought here is surely also that the possibility of good philological practice is precisely the means by which one guards against the falsifying tendencies built into ordinary language. In addition to the passages cited in the text, passages to which this interpretive proposal should also apply include GS 374; BGE 34. Compare with my criticism of Nehamas in "Nietzsche and Aestheticism," *Journal of the History of Philosophy* 30 (1992): 276–277.

20. Passages to which this interpretive proposal should apply include BGE 34; WP 481. Note that Nietzsche conceives the "mediation" or "conditioning" differently from some of the critics of positivism and empiricism mentioned in the text. As he says in WP 481: "It is our needs that interpret the world." I shall return to these issues in section IV. My discussion does not do justice to the full scope of Nietzsche's critique of positivism: for example, his attack on positivism as simply the latest form of Platonism, in which final authority is assigned to "facts," rather than "forms."

21. A point typically missed by defenders of the Received View. For example, Alan Schrift writes that "perspectivism is the Nietzschean doctrine that asserts there are no uninterpreted 'facts' or 'truth' " (*Nietzsche and the Question of Interpretation*, p. 145). This conflates Nietzsche's antipositivism (antifoundationalism) with his views on the possibility of truth. This confusion is, in fact, the trademark error of postmodernism: to infer epistemological nihilism from the untenability of epistemological foundationalism. Compare Larry Laudan, *Science and Relativism* (Chicago: University of Chicago Press, 1990), p. 86.

22. For this pragmatic reading of the upshot of the Sellarsian arguments see Richard Rorty, *Philosophy and the Mirror of Nature* (Princeton: Princeton University Press, 1979), pp. 182–192. The heart of the Sellarsian critique appears to be this: that we can't both construe the "confrontation" with experience as nonpropositional *and* at the same time have this experience play a role in the *justification* of belief. "Confrontations" with experience must, it seems, enter the "logical space of reasons" in order to *justify* belief; but allowing that entry undercuts the noninferential warrant of the "given"—which must now itself, like all other propositional claims, be justified as well. Put simply, and in more Davidsonian terms, objects may *cause* beliefs, but only other beliefs (e.g. about objects) can *justify* beliefs. Compare Donald Davidson, "A Coherence Theory of Truth and Knowledge," in *Truth and Interpretation: Perspectives on the Philosophy of Donald Davidson*, ed. E. LePore (Oxford: Basil Blackwell, 1986).

23. Consider, for example, the following perspectives that could be taken on a chair: viewed from a distance of five feet, viewed while sitting upon it, viewed closely so as to reveal its texture, viewed from underneath, viewed with a magnifying glass, viewed from a third-floor window, and so on. Note that it needn't be the case that we need all these perspectives in order to have a perfectly adequate visual grasp of

the object; all that is being claimed is that we could never exhaust these perspectives and the corresponding possible interpretive interests.

24. I call this the "Purity Claim" because it holds that we can "purify" our vision by identifying the "distorting" factors. David Hills has pointed out to me that, strictly speaking, perspectives—understood, for example, as "vantage points"—cannot be "distorted," but rather may be "limited," "impoverished," or "blinkered." I think, though, that there are other familiar uses of "perspective" in which it is closer in meaning to "view"; and with respect to the latter, we often speak of a "distorted view" of things. In any event, substituting the "impoverished" metaphor for the "distorted" metaphor throughout the remainder of my discussion would not affect my substantive conclusions.

25. See GM III:12, quoted above; compare WP 481: "It is our needs that interpret the world."

26. A useful analogy, originally suggested to me by Frithjof Bergmann, is that of maps. Think of what our intuitive "epistemology" of maps claims: (i) a map always presupposes some interest—that is, it is a certain sort of map (topographic, road map) because of what we are interested in knowing; (ii) the more maps we have of an area, the more we will know about it (e.g. from one we will learn about the roads, from another about the "lay of the land"); (iii) yet we have no difficulty with the idea that some maps of an area will simply be wrong: our commitment to plurality (ii) does not prevent us from ruling out some maps as misleading. Nietzsche, in a sense, is saying that while there is no doubt an infinity of good maps of the world, some maps—like the "Christian map"—just aren't about the world at all.

27. When Nietzsche says this (for example, EH IV:1) he has in mind aspects of his worldview such as the following: that the world has the fundamental character of will-to-power; that the world is essentially amoral; that the terrible aspects of reality are indispensable (for certain outcomes).

28. Note that the case of the object of vision is similar: from a conception of what the object of vision is really like we can work out the conditions under which this visual nature is available and those under which its character will be distorted.

29. Hilary Putnam, "Introduction," *Realism and Reason: Philosophical Papers, Volume III* (Cambridge: Cambridge University Press, 1983), p. viii.

30. The DEA of course is not framed in linguistic terms.

31. Ludwig Wittgenstein, *Philosophical Investigations*, 3d ed., trans. G. Anscombe (New York: MacMillan, 1953), part 1, section 124.

32. A useful summary of the philosophical issues raised by the rule-following remarks can be found in Crispin Wright's review of Colin McGinn's *Wittgenstein on Meaning*, *Mind* 98 (1989): 289–305, especially pp. 298–305. See also Paul Boghossian, "The Rule-Following Considerations," *Mind* 98 (1989): 507–549. The relevant sections in Wittgenstein are *Philosophical Investigations*, part 1, sections 84–87 and 185–242.

33. I am thinking especially of John McDowell, "Anti-Realism and the Epistemology of Understanding," in *Meaning and Understanding*, ed. H. Parret and J. Bouveresse (New York: de Gruyter, 1981), especially p. 248. There is a paradoxical element in McDowell's view, which I ignore in the text. On the one hand, he acknowledges the force of antirealist criticisms; but at the same time, he claims that

from within our linguistic practice "the possibly verification-transcendent world [of the realist] is certainly in the picture" and that such a picture is an "ineradicable necessity . . . in our making sense of ourselves." One wants to reply, though, that if the antirealist criticisms are sound, then the metaphysically realist image of the world is simply a false one, no matter how embedded it may be.

34. See *Philosophical Investigations,* part 1, sections 241–242. As Wittgenstein says in rejecting a crude communalism about truth: "It is what human beings *say* that is true and false"—and Wittgenstein's remarks do not try to dislodge that ordinary understanding.

35. "Projection and Truth in Ethics," Lindley Lecture, University of Kansas Department of Philosophy (1987), p. 11.

36. Donald Davidson, "The Structure and Content of Truth," *Journal of Philosophy* 87 (1990): 305.

37. But for a different view of the upshot of Wittgenstein's view on this score, see José Zalabardo, "Rules, Communities and Judgments," *Critica* 21 (1989): 33–58; Sabina Lovibond, *Realism and Imagination in Ethics* (Minneapolis: University of Minnesota Press, 1983), p. 37 (discussing "our lack of access to any distinction between those of our beliefs which are *actually true,* and those which are merely *held true by us*").

38. Note, though, that Nietzsche respects no such nonrevisionary constraint with respect to the *specific content* of what is true or what can be justified.

39. Ken Gemes, "Nietzsche's Critique of Truth," *Philosophy and Phenomenological Research* 52 (1992): 49.

40. Nietzsche, it should be recalled, thought that it was *with him* that philosophy might finally begin on the right foot, not that philosophy was coming to an "end." Compare BGE P; also 42–44, 203.

41. I would like to thank the following people for their comments on earlier drafts of this essay: Elizabeth Anderson, Frithjof Bergmann, Stephan Burton, Michael Forster, Ken Gemes, David Hills, Harold Langsam, Alexander Miller, Richard Schacht, William Schroeder, and Sheila Sokolowski. I am especially grateful to Bergmann and Schacht—to the former for much help and encouragement early on, to the latter for the same in connection with preparing the final version. I should also like to acknowledge my debt—both intellectual and personal—to Maurice Leiter.

TWENTY

Debts Due and Overdue
Beginnings of Philosophy in Nietzsche, Heidegger, and Anaximander

Gary Shapiro

What sort of text is *On the Genealogy of Morals,* this work that Nietzsche called the "uncanniest" of all books? Is it only a book about morals, as the title might indicate? Even the superficial reader will see that much more is at stake, since questions concerning politics and aesthetics are prominent. But could we also read more attentively and with an ear to hearing a certain diagnosis of the metaphysical condition and its tradition that are necessarily implicated in the genealogy of morals? Certainly Nietzsche begins to suggest ideas of this sort quite early in the text, as in his account of the way in which the morality of *ressentiment* is responsible for the invention of the metaphysical fiction of free will by which the doer is separated from the deed.

In this essay I want to suggest that there is a confrontation with the metaphysical tradition on an even larger scale that emerges in Nietzsche's account of the economy of guilt, debt, and credit that forms the subject especially (but not only) of the book's second essay " 'Guilt,' 'Bad Conscience,' and the Like." In order to see this it will be necessary to place Nietzsche's *Genealogy* in the context of two other texts—*Philosophy in the Tragic Age of the Greeks* and *Thus Spoke Zarathustra*—that speak of penance, guilt, and redemption as themes characteristic of philosophy as we know it.

This contextualization can be made plausible, I think, by taking a look at Martin Heidegger's essay on Anaximander, who seems to have spoken of debt at the very beginning of the philosophical tradition, and so to have placed us all in his debt despite ourselves. Heidegger's essay, I want to suggest, is to a great extent a determined polemic with Nietzsche on the meaning of a sentence—and so on the sense of the tradition that harkens back to that sentence. Considering these two methods of Western philosophical bookkeeping involves writing at least some initial promissory notes toward a final accounting of the ways in which Nietzsche and Heidegger succeed in marking a difference with and posing an alternative to the metaphysical economies of the tradition they articulate.

One of Heidegger's strangest and uncanniest readings of Western philosophy is his encounter with the saying reputed to be that of Anaximander, supposed to be its earliest surviving sentence. To read that saying, Heidegger thinks, requires nothing less than the destruction of the metaphysical tradition. The point of the destruction is to uncover what is unsaid and unthought in metaphysics in order to think of the beginning and the end that lie at the margins of the tradition, and to think in a way more attuned to origins than the tradition allows.

That the very beginning—that which might serve as an *arche*, an origin, or a principle—is available only in the form of a fragment, in fact a scrap from Simplicius's physics textbook dating from a thousand years after Anaximander's lifetime, is itself odd enough. Of course Heidegger cautions us that mere antiquity is not a proof of significance or profundity.[1] Yet as Simplicius notes, Anaximander was the first to speak of the *arche*; so what makes his saying a potential *arche* for philosophy is not only his place at the beginning but his having brought the beginning, or *arche*, into the world of thinking that we now take to define ourselves. Let us recall the saying in the same form in which Heidegger cites it initially, that is in the translation by the young Nietzsche.

Soon we'll see that the citation of this "conventional" translation is a crucial hinge in Heidegger's strategy, and that the confrontation with Nietzsche is a major theme of his essay *"Der Spruch des Anaximanders."* What seems to be Heidegger's confession of a debt to Nietzsche, his owning up to an I.O.U., is in fact an attempt to free himself from any such obligation. To serve as a beginning is at the same time to open oneself to translation: the beginning must always be carried forward or carried over into another context. So in the "young Nietzsche's" translation from the posthumously published *Philosophy in the Tragic Age of the Greeks* (Heidegger emphasizes Nietzsche's youth: does that help to free from debt or does it reinforce it? Anaximander is in one sense the most youthful, and *we* are the oldest):

> Whence things have their origin, there they must also pass away according to necessity; for they must pay penalty and be judged for their injustice, according to the ordinance of time.

This of course is an English version of Nietzsche's

> *Woher die Dinge ihre Entstehung haben, dahin müssen sie auch zu Grunde gehen, nach der Notwendigkeit; denn sie müssen Büsse zahlen und für ihre Ungerechtigkeiten gerichtet werden, gemäss der Ordnung der Zeit.*[2]

And that is based on the young philologist's reading of the Greek:

ἐξ ὧν δὲ ἡ γένεσίς ἐστι τοῖς οὖσι καὶ τὴν φθορὰν εἰς ταῦτα γίνεσθαι κατὰ
τὸ χρεών διδόναι γὰρ αὐτὰ δίκην καὶ τίσιν ἀλλήλοις τῆς ἀδικίας κατὰ τὴν
τοῦ χρόνου τάξιν.

According to Heidegger, Nietzsche's translation is not sufficiently thoughtful; the youthful scholar, he implies, has all too easily assumed his own debts to the philological and philosophical traditions. He makes this point in a number of ways throughout the Anaximander essay. He does so at the outset by juxtaposing Nietzsche's translation to one by Hermann Diels that appeared in the same year (1903) as the posthumous publication of Nietzsche's book. The two versions, Heidegger says, "arise from different intentions and procedures. Nevertheless they are scarcely distinguishable."[3] The implicit claim is that, metaphysically speaking, the aberrant young philologist (who was at the time of his translation being excluded from the charmed circle of his profession because of *The Birth of Tragedy*) and the more conventional scholarly translator are operating on the basis of a common set of assumptions and beliefs.

These assumptions and beliefs in fact add up to the culmination of Western metaphysics. For Heidegger this conclusion or "*Vollendung*" accomplishes itself in a twofold manner. It is expressed in the later Nietzsche's doctrines of the will to power and eternal recurrence, which assert the absolute presence of beings. Modern science—and this would include the philological science of a Diels or a Nietzsche—is also part of this development, for it claims to make all beings present and accessible, retrieving even the oldest and darkest sayings of the beginning for a comprehensive and intelligible history of the tradition.

The very enterprise of translation, then, is metaphysical insofar as it supposes universal standards of intelligibility and rules of transformation and correspondence that guarantee equivalence of meaning from one language to another. While Nietzsche sometimes voiced doubts about the possibility of translating the philosophy of one language family into that of another, he does not seem to see any essential obstacle to the translation of Greek into German—a translation that would allow us to assume our debt to the Greeks. In the era of the global will to power and its information network, Heidegger says, a translation may be perfectly "correct" by prevailing standards, and yet everything in it may be "embroiled in equivocal and imprecise significations."[4]

Let us notice that we have begun to describe the activity of translation in economic terms that are hardly alien to the (usual) translation of the Anaximander "fragment" itself; remember that the "fragment" seems to say that there is a fundamental law of equivalence among things that renders justice possible. (My quotation marks indicate a caution, to be developed in what follows, as to whether we do justice to the phrase in question by calling it a fragment.) But it will also be precisely and importantly just these aspects of the usual translation that Heidegger will be concerned to eliminate. For Heidegger it is apparent that Diels and Nietzsche, as well as Hegel before them, were working under the spell of Plato and Aristotle. Under that spell (or shouldering that enormous debt) the Anaximander "fragment," like the rest of what is called "pre-Socratic" thinking, can appear only as an attempt to think of nature (in the later sense of that word, not as the coming into being that is *physis*), and as a confused attempt at that. The alleged confusion would be the transference of moral and political notions, such as punishment and justice, to the natural or physical world.

Already in the sixth century Simplicius had said that Anaximander spoke in a poetic manner that was difficult to understand; and before that Aristotle had read the earlier thinkers as natural philosophers who dimly anticipated his conceptions of substance and cause. We could hear in these responses to the saying of Anaximander the double register of all desire: as the oldest it is that to which we are most indebted; as poetry or confused speculation about nature we scarcely owe it anything.

On Heidegger's view it is profoundly anachronistic to read the saying in terms of the distinctions made between logic, ethics, and physics in later philosophy. To establish a thinking conversation with Anaximander that is not restricted by these divisions, Heidegger must bracket the entire story of philosophy from Plato to Nietzsche—a story whose common thread is the need to make beings present in their being. Payments on the debt to this tradition must be suspended and perhaps rescheduled. Heidegger's translation will operate on the principle of incommensurability rather than on the supposition of universal equivalence that he finds so misleading in Diels and Nietzsche.

The outline of Heidegger's metahistory of philosophy as the metaphysics of presence are well known, so I will recall it here only in the most telegraphic fashion. Beginning with the form or *eidos* that is supposed to be eminently present in contrast to the changing things of sense, Plato sets the stage for further refinements in the conception of what is truly present. Christian theology finds such intrinsic presence in God, despite the fact that we see only through a glass darkly in this life. The modern, Cartesian turn takes the present to be subjective, that which is revealed to the thinking subject reflecting on itself. Leibniz, through his thesis concerning the identity of perception and appetition, begins the development that culminates in the German idealists who take the present to be will—either in the rational form of the Kantian moral will or in that of the blind, raging will of Schopenhauer or the Nietzschean will to power.

To read Anaximander against this tradition, rather than through it, requires that we question almost all the usual assumptions concerning the saying. In particular it means being vigilant with regard to the notion that Anaximander confuses physics and ethics, by viewing natural things under the categories of justice and economics. By the time Heidegger is done with his reading, all the language of debt, exchange, reparation, penalty, and of justice and injustice found in the usual translations has disappeared. In fact over half the text of what, following Simplicius, has been taken to be the "fragment" itself has been deleted, so that at the end we are left with just this:

> along the lines of usage; for they let order and thereby also reck belong to one another (in the surmounting) of disorder.

But the English is hardly adequate to Heidegger's German which is pervaded by a deliberate *Entfremdungseffekt*:

> *entlang dem Brauch; gehören nämlich lassen sie Fug somit auch Ruch eines dem anderen (im Verwinden) des Un-Fugs.*

Heidegger has fragmented the supposed fragment even further in order to make it speak. In his removal of all references to debt, penalty, and the like, we may be tempted to see an injury that he has inflicted on the beginning itself, a kind of primal wounding or marking of the *arche* itself; or perhaps it is an attempt to restore the *arche* so far as that is possible, by following traces of language and meaning that have been shoved back into the indefinite by the workings of the later tradition.

This may be the point at which to note that Heidegger does not call the text in question a fragment (as we tend to do in English, and as the otherwise excellent English translation of his essay does). Rather, he refers to it in the essay's title as a *Spruch*, that is as a saying, a maxim, a dictate, or an aphorism. While Heidegger does not speak explicitly of restoring or redeeming the saying, he does speak of rescue (*Rettung*) at the very conclusion of the essay, immediately after he has provided the translation we have just read. We must talk of rescue, he says, because we cannot know what it would be like to enter into a conversation with the earliest thought unless we think of the current devastation of the earth, a devastation that takes the form of a universal technologism expressing "a singular will to conquer." "Is there any rescue? Rescue comes when and only when danger is."[5]

The question of rescue remains a question; but at least it has been stated, and the suggestion has been made that there is some relationship between the rescue of early Greek thinking and the rescue of our technological civilization from what we might call the universal translation machine. It is worth noting that the issue of rescue also attaches in the doxographic tradition to Anaximander's own thought. As Charles Kahn suggests in his book on Anaximander, we can ask: "Did Anaximander envisage an even greater cycle, in which the appearance of this differentiated universe out of the Boundless would itself be periodically balanced by the return of all things, including the elements, back into their original source?"[6]

As Kahn notes, this talk of rescue from the injustices and reparations of the many things is not supported by our most reliable sources. Rescue, as with Heidegger, is conjectural. Nietzsche seems not to have had any doubts about this part of the doxographical tradition, for he explicitly links Heraclitus to Anaximander, saying that the former "believes, like Anaximander, in a periodically repeated end of the world, and in an ever-renewed rise of another world out of the all-destroying cosmic fire."[7]

The thematics of rescue and redemption are also associated with Anaximander and what he stands for in Nietzsche's thought, as we shall see. Eventually I will articulate three significant places where Nietzsche confronts Anaximander directly or by allusion. In each of these passages Nietzsche emphasizes and articulates the themes of debt, penalty, and punishment that Heidegger wants to eliminate. The most comprehensive treatment of the economy of thought, practice, and culture in these terms is, of course, that in *On the Genealogy of Morals.* But the *Spruch* or saying itself is not in need of rescue, for the first thing that Nietzsche says about Anaximander in *Philosophy in the Tragic Age of the Greeks* is that his sentences are quite in order as they are. He is described as "the first philosophical author of the ancients," who

> writes exactly as one expects a typical philosopher to write when alienating demands have not yet robbed him of his innocence and naiveté. That is to say, in graven stylized letters, sentence after sentence the witness to fresh illumination, each the expression of time spent in sublime meditation.[8]

This is a remarkable claim to make on the basis of one surviving sentence (if indeed we have that much). From this perspective the text that we are dealing with is not a fragment in need of rescue, but a sentence hanging over our heads. To the image of Anaximander as first to speak of the *arche* we can now add that he is the first to put philosophy into writing, and to inscribe it with a force such that later thinkers will necessarily be indebted to it.

This lapidary inscription forever marks the body of philosophy. Like the marks of punishment that Nietzsche describes in the *Genealogy,* they provide a forced and perhaps a painful memory that seems inescapable. After quoting the sentence—a sentence that Nietzsche says speaks with "lapidary impressiveness"—he wonders how we are to read it: "Enigmatic proclamation of a true pessimist, oracular inscription [*Orakelaufschrift*] over the boundary stone of Greek philosophy: how shall we interpret you?"[9]

At this point Nietzsche makes a significant gesture—a gesture that Heidegger does not mention in his own brief reference to Nietzsche's translation and interpretation. For in order to interpret Anaximander, Nietzsche recalls Schopenhauer, who as "the only serious moralist of our century charges us with a similar reflection":

> The proper measure with which to judge any and all human beings is that they are really creatures who should not exist at all and who are doing penance [*Büsse zahlen*, the same words that appear in Nietzsche's translation] for their lives by their manifold sufferings and their death. What could we expect of such creatures? Are we not all sinners under sentence of death? We do penance for having been born, first by living and then by dying.[10]

Several things are notable here when we compare Nietzsche's presentation with Heidegger's reading. Although Heidegger claims that from Aristotle and Theophrastus down to Hegel and Nietzsche the saying has been interpreted as a principle of natural philosophy (in the narrow sense), it is clear that Nietzsche (by way of Schopenhauer) takes the saying to apply to human beings as well as to natural things. It may be "extracted from man's life" and projected onto all existence, but it does not cease to pertain to men and women. More significantly, in associating Anaximander and Schopenhauer, Nietzsche seems to be doing something remarkably similar to what Heidegger does in stressing the continuity of the metaphysical and hermeneutical traditions from Plato to Nietzsche. It is as if Nietzsche is saying that from Anaximander to Schopenhauer philosophy has been saying and thinking the Same. He would be sketching a metahistory of philosophy that could be taken to be both a model for and a rival of the one that Heidegger deploys. Just as Heidegger sees Nietzsche providing one more version—albeit an *in*version—of Platonic metaphysics, so Nietzsche comments that Kant's thing in itself is simply a transformation of the *apeiron* (the indefinite or boundless), and that Anaximander was dealing with the "profoundest problem in ethics . . . : How can anything pass away which has a right to be?"[11]

Of course one might wonder whether these are indeed the themes that define the philosophical tradition. But notice how both Nietzsche and Heidegger, in dealing with the thinker of the *arche*, maintain that the tradition as a whole must be brought into play, and that in order to enter into conversation with the earliest it is necessary to know the late position from which we speak. If Heidegger owes Nietzsche a debt here, it is one that he has carefully obscured by associating him, via Diels, with the will to power of the scientific and technological world—the scholarly form of *Gestell*, in which the oldest sayings of the Greeks become mere material or resources (*Bestand*) for the translation industry. Yet there are obviously important differences between the two metahistories of philosophy, differences that become clearer in the second of Nietzsche's confrontations with the thought of Anaximander.

This second *Auseinandersetzung* occurs in a major chapter of *Thus Spoke Zarathustra* entitled *"Von der Erlösung"* or "Of Redemption" (Z II:20).[12] Let us note immediately that *Erlösung* is a multifaceted word that can designate either religious or spiritual redemption on the one hand or the redeeming of a debt on the other. And in this chapter redemption is considered on several levels. The issue is introduced by a spokesman for a number of cripples who says that Zarathustra cannot persuade the people unless he also persuades those who are blind or deformed. If he could correct or redeem their bodily excesses and defects he would be a more plausible teacher. But, Zarathustra asks, would this in fact be a great redemption? Even the people say that to take away the hump from the hunchback is to destroy his spirit.

This thought leads to a consideration of bodily and spiritual fragmentation that now appears to be almost universal, extending far beyond the obvious cases of deformity. Some people are nothing but particular bodily organs in a monstrously enlarged state with a corresponding atrophy of others; such an inverse cripple might, for example, be an "ear as big as a man" with "a tiny envious face." So most people are nothing but fragments and severed limbs (*Bruchstücken und Gliedmassen*). Those who appear to be whole are actually fragments; while ancient sayings, like those of Anaximander that appear to be fragmentary, are in fact lapidary utterances whose inscriptions remain hanging over us for millennia.

In fact the inscriptions themselves may help to account for the human fragmentation. For the essential question of redemption has to do not with the blind and the lame but with the woundings, scarrings, and divisions effected by time—and especially by the time of the inscription of revenge, a time that Nietzsche here calls madness (*Wahnsinn*). Because the will cannot will backward, because it is bound to the law of time and time's "it was," life is a perpetual process of fragmentation in which the past seems to be nothing but a collection of dispersed and shattered ruins. In this situation the will can be nothing but an "angry spectator" who sees "man in ruins and scattered as over a battlefield or a butcherfield" (*zertrümmert und zerstreuet wie über ein Schlacht- und Schlächterfeld*) (Z II:20).

But these fragments can also be seen as "fragments of the future"—if redemption is possible. Already Nietzsche is appearing to speak in the language of Anaximander: the fragments (men or men-parts in this case) suffer by being cut off from the whole, perhaps simply for coming into separate existence "according to the ordinance of time." The doxographers, even if unreliable, spoke of the possibility of a redemption through the collapse of the individuated things and elements back into the whole. Zarathustra now defines what he sees as the only possible form of redemption:

> To redeem those who lived in the past and to recreate all "it was" into a "thus I willed it"—that alone should I call redemption. (Z II:20)

Redemption would be redemption from the spirit of revenge. Zarathustra at this point distinguishes "revenge" and "the spirit of revenge" in a way that will help in explaining the significance of Anaximander's saying:

> Verily, a great folly [*Narrheit*] dwells in our will; and all men are under a curse insofar as this folly has acquired spirit. (Z II:20)

The folly of revenge is one thing, but it becomes malevolent and dangerous when it acquires spirit. How did revenge acquire spirit? Zarathustra's answer is that thought and reflection have been preoccupied with suffering and punishment, and that "madness" (*Wahnsinn*, a step beyond *Narrheit*) has produced a law, a formula, and an inscription that has marked the will. Now this fateful inscription, I want to suggest, is the lapidary utterance of Anaximander as it has been carved and engraved in the stones and monuments of philosophy: when madness comes to preach and inscribe, then revenge passes from its simple state to one in which it has acquired spirit. We need to read Zarathustra's comments on the spirit of revenge (at some length) so that we hear in them the resonance of the thinker and speaker of the *arche*. For the *arche* here is the principle of philosophy, the tradition from Anaximander to Schopenhauer:

> The *spirit of revenge*, my friends, has so far been the subject of man's best reflection; and where there was suffering, one always wanted punishment too.
>
> For "punishment" is what revenge calls itself; with a hypocritical lie it creates a good conscience for itself.
>
> Because there is suffering in those who will, inasmuch as they cannot will backwards, willing itself and all life were supposed to be—a punishment. And now cloud upon cloud rolled over the spirit, until eventually madness preached, "Everything passes away; therefore everything deserves to pass away. And this too is justice, this law of time that it must devour its children." Thus preached madness.
>
> "Things are ordered morally according to justice and punishment. Alas, where is redemption from the flux of things and from the punishment called existence?" Thus preached madness. (Z II:20)

The passage continues, but let us stop here. The Anaximander saying or fragment, at least in the translation of the "young Nietzsche," is clearly recognizable in the preaching of madness. Here the Schopenhauerian heritage of the saying has been made explicit so that philosophy itself is the voice of madness, preaching in sentences that compel over the centuries. Madness is the very name of philosophy here, and its history and development are interpreted as indebted to the initiator of the *arche*, to the first inscription of universal indebtedness. No redemption is possible within this world of madness, unless it is that, in the last subjective form of the madness, the philosophy of the will, that the will should cease to will. If existence is a debt, the debt can be paid off and marked "paid in full" only by the self-destruction of the debtor.

Is some other form of redemption possible? This would have to be a redemption from the preachings of madness; one might say that it would have to be a redemption from redemption as madness understands it. The name of this redemption is the eternal recurrence of all things. Taken in a simple and preliminary way, that teaching would speak of "the innocence of becoming"; it would declare that nothing is owed and no debt is to be paid.

But should we read Anaximander in Nietzsche's translation? Although Heidegger says that the words *dike, tisis,* and *adikia* "resound" in the saying, he also maintains that we translate them as justice, retributive payment, and injustice only because of our own "juridical-moral notions."[13] If we listen to "what comes to language" in the fragment, Heidegger tell us, we will hear something else (I quote selectively from some of the work of Heidegger's translation):

> We hear that wherever *adikia* rules all is not right with things. That means something is out of joint. . . . To presencing as such jointure must belong, thus creating the possibility of its being out of joint. . . . Coming to presence in the jointure of the while, what is present abandons that jointure and is, in terms of whatever lingers awhile, in disjunction. Everything that lingers awhile stands in disjunction. To the presencing of what is present, to the *eon* of *eonta, adikia* belongs. . . . [So contrary to Nietzsche and Diels] the fragment says nothing about payment, recompense, and penalty; nor does it say that something is punishable, or even must be avenged, according to the opinion of those who equate justice with vengeance.[14]

Heidegger reads the other words of the fragment in a similar fashion, following what he calls "the way of translation."[15] *Tisis* is not "penalty" for him but "esteem" (*Schätzen*). "To esteem something means to heed it, and so to take satisfactory care of what is estimable in it."[16] Such esteeming is related to the sense that Heidegger finds in *didonai diken*: "gives jointure." Here we are very close to the Heideggerian thematics of the "*es gibt*" to which we must return. But what should be evident now is that Heidegger's translation is a way of substituting an economy of giving for that of penalty and debt. So we need to consider carefully what Heidegger says about giving here in order to ask whether his economy of the gift is in fact a critical alternative to the economy that the tradition (which he represents by Nietzsche and Diels) has found in the Anaximander fragment. He asks:

> What does "give" mean here? . . . How should what is present as such give the jointure of its presencing? The giving designated here can only consist in its manner of presencing. Giving is not only giving-away (*Weggeben*). More

originally, giving is acceding or giving-to (*Zugeben*). Such giving lets something belong to another which properly belongs to him.[17]

We will return to the "*es gibt*," but for now let us note that the giving that Heidegger finds in Anaximander, a giving that would in some sense be outside the metaphysical tradition, is a giving oriented toward providing the recipient with his or her own. Is this so far from saying that it provides the recipient with what he or she is owed? And so how far is it from that discourse that Heidegger finds to be an illegitimate projection of concerns with restitution and setting things right? Notice that Heidegger specifically relegates giving in the sense of giving-away (*Weggeben*) to a secondary or peripheral status. The *es gibt* does not refer to an economy of excess or expenditure.

It should be noted, by the way, that historical etymology provides little support for Heidegger's readings. (Of course Heidegger is able to acknowledge this, and to contest scientific philology on the grounds that it simply acts out the imperatives of the metaphysical tradition.) For even in Homer *tisis*, for example, frequently seems to have the sense of "vengeance" or "retribution," as in the *Illiad* where Achilles tells Apollo that, being divine, the latter cannot possibly fear any *tisis* or retribution from a mortal.[18] In the *Odyssey* Telemachus warns the suitors who are indulging themselves with the goods of his father's estate that if they were to eat up the flocks altogether, *tisis* would have to be made one day.[19]

In fact the conventional lexicon would find more indications of the complex of debt, credit, punishment, and justice in the language of Anaximander's saying than occurs even in the Nietzsche and Diels versions. Consider *chreon*, which Nietzsche translates as "necessity" (*Notwendigkeit*), and which Heidegger reads provocatively as "usage" (*Brauch*). Either is lexically possible, and Heidegger's complaint that "necessity" seems indebted to Platonic and Aristotelian conceptions is not implausible. But as Kahn points out, Anaximander's *chreon* could also be taken to be related to *chreos*, or debt, which comes from the same root.[20]

Are these the teachings of a madness all too solidly inscribed on the boundary stone of philosophy, as Nietzsche would have it, or have they been distorted by a later deviation, by that history which Heidegger equates with error? Kahn's more recent reading is congruent with the tradition of interpretation that Heidegger rejects. In the *Genealogy* Nietzsche returns to the double theme of indebtedness and redemption. It is perhaps with reference to the "teaching of madness" that Nietzsche writes there of the "*redeeming* man of great love and contempt," a redeemer who will lift the "curse of the hitherto reigning ideal" (GM II:24).[21] Here at the end of the second part of the *Genealogy* Nietzsche speaks repeatedly of redemption and of a redeemer—just after he has attempted to demonstrate that the

Christian notion of redemption, tied as it is to the economic complex of debt and credit, makes the earth into a madhouse.

Now among the principle themes of the *Genealogy* are guilt, debt, punishment, justice, and redemption. Nietzsche's treatment of these themes is usually read (by Michel Foucault, for example) as an account of those sociopolitical formations that eventually produce the aberrations of Christianity and other forms of asceticism.[22] Yet the analysis goes further, for Nietzsche claims that such notions are so rooted in human beings that they constitute "thinking *as such*" (*das Denken*): "Setting prices, determining values, contriving equivalences, exchanging—these preoccupied the earliest thinking of man to so great an extent that in a certain sense they constitute thinking *as such*" (GM II:8; Nietzsche's emphasis).

The *Genealogy* is, among other things, a text about interpretation. We are told in the preface, for example, that the entire Third Essay is an *Auslegung* of a single aphorism from *Zarathustra*. We can now suggest that the Second Essay, " 'Guilt,' 'Bad Conscience,' and the Like," is an interpretation of the saying of Anaximander. Just as in Heidegger's essay, there is a sequential treatment of the significant words or concepts of the saying, and an attempt to trace the way in which the tradition inscribes its translations of these words and of the saying itself. In the course of his analysis Nietzsche, too, proposes a number of translations or equivalences—for example that between *Schuld* (guilt) and *Schulden* (debts). A similar relation obtains between the English "owe" and "ought." The principle here, Nietzsche says, is "the idea that every injury has its *equivalent* and can actually be paid back, even if only through the pain of the culprit" (GM II:4). And he gives this observation an Oedipal, genealogical, and tragic twist by noting that this is the way that "parents still punish their children." Not far below the surface of Nietzsche's analysis is the contextualization of these debtor-creditor relations in terms of social structures such as those of the commercial Milesian world in which Anaximander flourished.

At this point it would be possible to note Nietzsche's translation and analysis of a number of key terms in the Anaximander saying that he takes to characterize "thinking *as such*." Without repeating that analysis here, we can take note of the fact that philosophy does often, if implicitly, confess its own indebtedness. Plato's *Republic* opens with the warning that telling the truth and paying one's debts may not be an adequate account of justice. At its philosophical center stands the story of the cave, the sun, and the divided line—a story, Socrates says, which stands in place of a completely adequate presentation of the truth. It is simply the best he can do in the circumstances. To quote the dialogue:

"It's a debt I wish I could pay you in full, instead of only paying interest [*tokos,* which can also mean 'child,' hence the frequent translation 'child of the

Good'] on the loan," I replied. "But for the present you must accept my description of the child of the Good as interest. But take care I don't inadvertently cheat you by paying in bad money."[23]

Is the debt ever paid? Or is it internalized and made infinite? This is the question that Nietzsche poses for the philosophical tradition.

Should we say, with Heidegger, that Nietzsche does not enter into a "thoughtful dialogue" with early Greek thinking because he takes over the metaphysical sense of being that has dominated our tradition? For Heidegger the key is how we are to think and translate the *ta onta*, the "beings" of which Anaximander's saying speaks. Although he admits that it will sound exaggerated to say it, Heidegger says it anyway: "The fate of the West hangs on the translation of the word *eon*, assuming that the translation consists in *crossing over* to the truth of what comes to language in *eon*."[24]

Nietzsche agrees, in a way. His genealogical or archaeological project of unearthing the sense of "thinking *as such*" and of "man" is directed precisely at overcoming a careless and hasty assimilation of the customary sense of man and thinking. Yet Heidegger, at the beginning of his discussion of the *onta* of which the fragment speaks, again finds it necessary to distinguish himself from Nietzsche, and to demonstrate that Nietzsche is still enclosed within metaphysics. After stressing the importance of *onta* and its translation, Heidegger abruptly introduces Nietzsche again without any obvious preparation:

> At the summit of the completion [*Gipfel der Vollendung*] of Western philosophy these words are pronounced: "To *stamp* Becoming with the character of Being—that is the *highest will to power.*" Thus writes Nietzsche in a note entitled "Recapitulation."[25]

We might note that Heidegger takes Nietzsche's fragment (a posthumous note) to be a significant utterance, while he treats the Anaximander *Spruch* as in need of severe editing. In any event, he says here that Nietzsche and Anaximander would *seem* to be saying the Same (*das Gleiche*) even if what they say is not "identical." And this conjunction of the Same and the nonidentical would seem to be "the fundamental condition of a thoughtful dialogue between recent and early times."[26]

This is the point at which Heidegger wants to distance himself from Nietzsche's and the tradition's merely correct translation of *onta*. Should we see in this gesture an assertion of his own freedom from indebtedness? Heidegger does not consider the possibility that Nietzsche might also be challenging the "correct" translation by using the language of being and becoming against itself. In fragments like this one, or in the much more subtle and complex published texts dealing with the eternal recurrence, Nietzsche can be read as deforming the metaphysical language of being and becoming, and time and eternity, precisely in order to establish an altered relation to the "teachings of madness" or to what has hitherto constituted "thinking *as such.*"

The question is whether the sort of thinking embodied in Anaximander's saying is inside or outside the metaphysical tradition. In his efforts to place it outside, Heidegger is forced to eliminate or retranslate a whole set of terms—*chreon, tisis, dike, taxis*—that have to do with what we may generally call the economic: the world of valuing and evaluation. For Nietzsche the position represented by Anaximander is the earliest form of civilization to which we have access, and is at least as old as the concept of "legal subjects" (*Rechtspersonen*) (GM II:4). Eventually, of course, we will have to ask whether there is anything more archaic than this "prehistory." We could see the claim about "thinking *as such*" as an extension of Nietzsche-Zarathustra's view of what madness preaches. As in the latter account, there is a distinction to be made between an unreflective thinking in terms of guilt, punishment, debt, and credit and the appearance of specific ideals and doctrines based on that thinking.

According to the narrative given in the *Genealogy,* the latter result from a cataclysmic event brought on by the needs of organized social life, and the self-inflicted transformations that warriors unwittingly incur when they bind themselves to a world of law. This is a crisis of internalization, in which guilt, debt, and punishment are no longer inscribed merely on the bodies of men and women, but in their consciousness. Restricted to their consciousness, the instincts of aggression turn inward and generate an internal economy of debt and credit. Part of such an internal economy is the development of explicit religious and philosophical teachings—that is, the internal inscription of what madness preaches from Anaximander to Schopenhauer. The internalization of guilt and debt is followed by its infinitization when the community comes to seem all powerful and is metaphorically represented by an infinite and omnipotent god.

What requires emphasis is that Nietzsche sees *both* external and internal inscriptions as variants of "thinking *as such.*" Such thinking coincides with man's self-definition as the evaluating or esteeming animal. So far Nietzsche is in agreement with Heidegger that there is a profound correspondence among the earliest conceptions of being, thinking, and man. As Heidegger puts it: "What is Greek is the dawn of that destiny in which Being illuminates itself in beings and so propounds a certain essence of man: that essence unfolds historically as something fateful, preserved in Being and dispensed by Being, without ever being separated from Being."[27] Nietzsche too thinks that the essence or concept of man is hardly accidental or adventitious, as he suggests in this genealogical sketch of the appearance of "man":

The feeling of guilt, of personal obligation, had its origin, as we saw, in the oldest and most primitive personal relationship (*Personen-Verhältnis*), that between buyer and seller, creditor and debtor: it was here that one person first *measured himself* against another . . . ; here it was that the oldest kind of astuteness developed; here, likewise, we may suppose, did human pride, the feeling of superiority in relation to other animals, have its first beginnings. Perhaps our word "man" (*manas*) still expresses something of this feeling of self satisfaction: man designated himself as the creature that measures values, evaluates and measures, as the "valuating animal as such." (GM II:8)

We know what Heidegger would say about Nietzsche's identification of man as the valuer or esteemer. He would see Nietzsche as simply projecting back into the origins of thought the value thinking that is typical of the metaphysical era in its completion, but that is also the destined culmination of that era, already implicit in the metaphysics of presence. It is just such projection, he would maintain, that prevents Nietzsche from entering into thoughtful conversation with the early Greeks. And he would add that it is just this adoption of valuational thinking as the norm that also prevents Nietzsche from thinking beyond the tradition, and in fact locks him into it.

But is it so clear that Nietzsche has trapped himself in that way? Consider for a moment the role that *man* plays here. The identification of man as the esteemer is one that had already been made in *Zarathustra* in the chapter "On the Thousand and One Goals," where it is said:

Verily, men gave themselves all their good and evil. Verily, they did not take it, they did not find it, nor did it come to them as a voice from heaven. Only man placed values (*Werthe*) in things to preserve himself—he alone created a meaning for things, a human meaning. Therefore he calls himself "man," which means: the esteemer (*Schätzende*). (Z I:15)

This would be the supreme instance of what Nietzsche early in the *Genealogy* calls "the lordly right of giving names" (GM I:2). For here men name themselves precisely as those who give such names in so far as they esteem and create (*Schätzen ist Schaffen*). The attempt to bolster this interpretation of man by reference to the Sanskrit *manas* seems no better or worse by conventional philological criteria than other such etymologies in Nietzsche and Heidegger. Esteeming and disdaining are listed in Sanskrit dictionaries as among the senses or cognates of *manas* but not as the word's primary sense. But to say that Nietzsche sees no other possibility than valuative thinking, and sees man as nothing but the evaluator, would be to ignore the very important point that man is a *limited* concept for Nietzsche. One might say, following Foucault, that he is the first thinker to attempt to expose and explore the limits of the concept man, and that the texts just cited are contributions to discerning those limits. "Man" Zarathustra announces in his very first speeches "is something that must be overcome."

And if, as Nietzsche suggests, we are to translate man as "the evaluator," how then ought we to understand and translate "*Übermensch*"? As "meta-evaluator," as "man beyond evaluation," as "post-man" or as "posteval-uator"?

In *The Birth of Tragedy* Nietzsche had spoken of the truth as that which lies beyond measuring when he said of the Dionysian (but not only of the Dionysian) that "excess (*Übermass*) reveals itself as truth."[28] The *Übermensch* is the excessive one who goes beyond the measure, which means that he goes beyond man as the measure or as the measurer. This way of under-standing the *Übermensch* may, incidentally, help to distinguish Nietzschean thinking from the sophistic or Protagorean relativism with which it is often all too hastily associated. To the extent that man is not ultimate, the force of "man is the measure of all things" is drastically undercut.

Like Heidegger, then, Nietzsche interprets the Anaximander fragment and its heritage in order to establish a site beyond the economy and con-straint of the metaphysical tradition. He is not bound to valuational think-ing in the way that Heidegger suggests; but he is engaged in a project of tracing the limits of that thinking. In his *Introduction to Metaphysics* Heideg-ger says that Nietzsche's commitment to valuative thinking is a sign of his acceptance of the metaphysics of presence:

> At *bottom* this being [of values] meant neither more nor less than the presence of something already there, though not in so vulgar and handy a sense as tables and chairs [the "furniture of the earth" of that form of the metaphysics of presence which is Anglo-American empiricism]. . . . How stubbornly the idea of values ingrained itself in the nineteenth century can be seen from the fact that even Nietzsche, and precisely he, never departed from this perspec-tive. . . . His entanglement in the thicket of the idea of values, his failure to understand its questionable origin, is the reason why Nietzsche did not attain to the true center of philosophy.[29]

Now in the *Genealogy* Nietzsche does think this questionable origin. It could be said that Heidegger and Nietzsche both attack the metaphysics of presence by circumscribing the limits of valuative thinking and offering an alternative to it. Heidegger's critique and alternative are economic, con-sisting in a vertical perspective according to which the *es gibt* ("it gives/it is") takes precedence over the circulation of values. Heidegger inscribes appropriation within *Ereignis*. Nietzsche's alternative is a horizontal one that juxtaposes to the economy of debt and credit one of excess, circulation and gift giving. It is this economy of the gift that is invoked in Zarathustra's first address to the sun—"You great star, what would your happiness be had you not those for whom you shine" (Z I:P)—and which is formulated in his (first) farewell address to his disciples "On the Gift-Giving Virtue" (Z I:22).

By reading the structures of gift giving in *Zarathustra* against the analysis of "thinking as such" in the *Genealogy*, it is possible to see the outlines of an economy of excess that would contrast strongly with that of debt and credit. This would bear some remarkable affinities to the economy of the gift and the potlatch as they have been articulated by Marcel Mauss and then rediscovered in Nietzsche by Georges Bataille.[30] In such an economy presents (as opposed to values) are precisely what is not present. They circulate, so that they are not property (and therefore perhaps not substances) in our metaphysical terms. They may be squandered or destroyed in the potlatch (as in the festival or banquet in the last part of *Zarathustra*) rather than preserved as investments.

Read against such an economy of the gift, Heidegger's *"es gibt"* appears both thin and transcendental. Moreover, Heidegger seems blind to the gift giving theme in Nietzsche's texts. For example, in the long analysis that he devotes to a passage from *The Will to Power,* which he takes to be Nietzsche's emblematic statement concerning the question of nihilism, Heidegger totally omits any consideration of the beginning of this notebook entry, in which Nietzsche presents nihilism as "the recognition of the long squandering (*Vergeudung*) of strength, the agony of the 'in vain,' the insecurity, the lack of any opportunity to recuperate and regain tranquility" (WP 12). Nihilism can see squandering only as a defect, a marginal corruption of the metaphysical economy of debt; while Zarathustra, we remember, describes himself as a squanderer, and in the beatitudes that he speaks in the marketplace (that is, in the heart of the metaphysical economy of exchange) he says, "I love those who squander themselves" (Z I:P:4).

Just as we may need to think of the *Übermensch* as the post-evaluator, we may need to give some more thought to Nietzsche's talk of an *"Umwertung aller Werthe,"* which we have been accustomed to translate as a "transvaluation of all values." Is it simply a question of reversing or inverting the values that attach to various items and concepts? Or is it more a matter of using the language of valuation against itself, in order to suggest the possibility of economies that may not be completely recuperable within the thinking we have practiced for so long, and which so far has had a claim (although only a claim) to be considered as "thinking *as such*"?

NOTES

1. Martin Heidegger, *Early Greek Thinking,* trans. Frank Capuzzi and David Farrell Krell (New York, 1985), p. 16; hereafter cited as EGT.

2. Friedrich Nietzsche, *Philosophy in the Tragic Age of the Greeks,* trans. Marianne Cowan (Chicago, 1962), p. 45; *Kritische Studienausgabe,* vol. 1, p. 818. The former hereafter cited as PTG, the latter as KSA.

3. EGT, p. 14.

4. EGT, p. 23.

5. EGT, p. 57.

6. Charles H. Kahn, *Anaximander and the Origins of Greek Cosmology* (New York: Columbia University Press, 1960), p. 185.

7. PTG, p. 60.

8. PTG, p. 45.

9. PTG, pp. 45–46.

10. PTG, p. 46.

11. PTG, pp. 48–49.

12. That is, section 20 of the Second Part. Quotations from "On Redemption" are taken from *Thus Spoke Zarathustra*, trans. Walter Kaufmann (New York: Viking, 1966), pp. 137–142; KSA, vol. 4, pp. 177–182.

13. EGT, pp. 39, 41.

14. EGT, pp. 41–42.

15. EGT, p. 28.

16. EGT, p. 45.

17. EGT, p. 43.

18. Homer, *Iliad* 22.19.

19. Homer, *Odyssey*, 2.76.

20. Kahn, *Anaximander and the Origins of Greek Cosmology*, p. 180.

21. GM refers to Friedrich Nietzsche, *On the Genealogy of Morals*, trans. Walter Kaufmann (New York: Vintage, 1967).

22. Michel Foucault, "Nietzsche, Genealogy, History" in *Language, Counter-Memory, Practice*, trans. Donald F. Bouchard and Sherry Simon (Ithaca: Cornell University Press, 1977), pp. 139–164.

23. Plato, *Republic* 507a, trans. H. D. P. Lee (Baltimore: Penguin Books, 1967).

24. EGT, p. 33.

25. EGT, p. 22.

26. EGT, p. 23.

27. EGT, p. 25.

28. Nietzsche, *The Birth of Tragedy*, trans. Walter Kaufmann (New York: Vintage, 1967), p. 46.

29. Martin Heidegger, *An Introduction to Metaphysics*, trans. Ralph Manheim (New Haven: Yale University Press, 1959), pp. 166–167.

30. See my book *Alcyone: Nietzsche on Gifts, Noise and Women* (Albany: State University of New York Press, 1991), especially the "Prelude" and "On Presence and Presents: The Gift in *Thus Spoke Zarathustra*."

TWENTY-ONE

Reading Ascetic Reading
Toward the Genealogy of Morals and the Path Back to the World

Bernd Magnus, Jean-Pierre Mileur, Stanley Stewart

> *The ascetic ideal springs from the protective instinct of a degenerating life* which tries by all means to sustain itself and to fight for its existence; . . . life wrestles in it and through it with death and *against* death; the ascetic ideal is an artifice for the *preservation* of life. . . . (GM III:13)[1]

GENEALOGY OF GENEALOGY[2]

In *Beyond Good and Evil,* Nietzsche claims that every great philosophy constitutes "the personal confession of its author and a kind of involuntary and unconscious memoir" (BGE 6). This assertion leads, naturally enough, to two questions expressible as one: What does the greatness of Nietzsche's philosophy consist in and what is it confessing? Further, of what—or in what sense—is it an involuntary and unconscious memoir? And does the declaration that "philosophy" is "personal confession" not undermine its purported aim to voice impersonal truth arrived at through lucid, disinterested reflection? Isn't an involuntary and unconscious memoir the very opposite of the God's-eye-view to which philosophy aspires?[3]

We shall be turning some time-honored philosophical analyses inside out by refusing to read Nietzsche's written sentences as "the expression" of "his ideas," vehicles for the transcription of thought, embodiments of prior philosophical convictions. We shall refuse to read the written grapheme as the body of thought. This reversal may instead be read with greater profit as an attempt to pose and answer a different question: How would one expect someone who writes like this to think?

Such a reading does not replace more conventionally philosophical readings. Rather, it supplements them at precisely those points where philosophical discourse fails to connect satisfactorily with what and how Nietzsche actually wrote. Our goal is not to prosecute a project of literary *ressentiment* against philosophy but to establish a mode of intimacy that does not ultimately require us to make a choice between satisfying the disciplinary requirements of one or the other, that allows us to say something of value to both without trivializing either. Whether this succeeds or not will de-·

pend, in part, upon our success in rendering no longer interesting or appropriate the question, Is it philosophy or is it literature?

At the end of *Thus Spoke Zarathustra,* Zarathustra turns away from the higher men to his "work," perhaps even to go in search of the "laughing lions" whose sign he has just seen. Yet it is not clear what this means or where Zarathustra can go from here, since the materials of quest, pastoral care, and gospelizing have already been used up (as it were) in order to yield their ultimate product, the higher men.[4] Zarathustra/Nietzsche's "work"[5] could be the writerly task of composition; but it is still unclear what comes next when so much—almost a whole gospelizing and literary tradition—has been used to arrive where he is. "My work," in its vagueness, bespeaks a certain solipsistic sublimity—but threatens a kind of impasse, too.

It is against this background that *Toward the Genealogy of Morals*—as the culmination of the movement down from Zarathustra's mountaintop had begun with *Beyond Good and Evil* and as the presumptive manifestation of his "work"—assumes particular importance. That Nietzsche's succeeds in finding his way back to the world (and in externalizing in some sense his concluding stance in *Thus Spoke Zarathustra*), and that this helps to explain Nietzsche's importance for his critical heirs, is our initial thesis here.

As a project of externalization, an attempt to define a path back to the world, the *Genealogy* is also of particular importance for the argument we will be exploring here: that it is useful to read the significant context and immediate referend of Nietzsche's philosophy, in both its negative and positive aspects, as his own practice as a writer. It is one of the canards most frequently leveled at Nietzscheanizing literary critics—critics like Bloom and de Man (who see works of literature as commenting on their own origins and status as works of fiction)—that their emphasis on self-referentiality somehow undermines or excludes the very possibility of referentiality, of significant address to the world. In the case of Nietzsche, this accusation might well take the form of a complaint that the claim that he is constantly referring to his own practices and identity as a writer undercuts, even makes impossible, readings that would see him as a philosopher, engaged with and attempting to make his own contribution to the philosophical tradition. This is not the case, either in general, or for Nietzsche.

We think that the *Genealogy* shows not only that Nietzsche was aware of the problem but that he can usefully be read as rationalizing, if only implicitly, his dependence on his writer's self-experience as the origin/referend and necessary complement both of his parabolic fictionalizing in *Zarathustra* and of his philosophizing. And it can be argued that it is precisely his success in forging this link between self and world, in demonstrating the general significance of internal self-experience that authorizes and releases the outpouring of (mock) autobiography and reflexive commentary that mark the final stage of Nietzsche's career.

These later works develop Nietzsche's interest—frequently expressed in the *Genealogy*—in the physiological origins of moral evaluations and act out the supercession of the Romantic conception of writing/thinking as "expression" by what might be called "embodiment." Tracy Strong has remarked that Nietzsche

> wants us to encounter these texts as we would encounter another person, with the assurance of his presence. As with other people, we can never start or end by claiming to know what they mean—we do not mean the statement "I know John" to be equivalent to "I know what John means." We do not, therefore, if Nietzsche be correct, learn from them by determining what they mean, as if they were a container for his "message." We learn from them by finding ourselves in them.[6]

In contrast, our reading of *Zarathustra* IV[7] suggests that the focus of Nietzsche's interest is not only in how this sense of "finding ourselves" in the text is frequently an illusion but in how exploiting this illusion is the writer's stock in trade. And Strong's sense that Nietzschean embodiment also offers "the assurance of his [or any] presence" similarly strikes us as wide of the mark. Our point is not that the writer's embodiment of his or her ideas is a superior guarantee of genuineness; rather, embodiment represents a reconceiving that constitutes both a challenge and an addition to the philosophical tradition of how meaning happens. After all, actors also "embody," and few philosophers have been more alert to the variety of dramatic possibilities than Nietzsche, the theorist of tragedy and comedy alike. And, in this connection (on the subject of embodiment), it is often said that the *Genealogy* is the most "digestible" of Nietzsche's major works, the one that looks most like an "argument." Perhaps for that very reason, it makes sense for us to pay more careful attention than is frequently done to the details of its unfolding.

"We are unknown to ourselves, we men of knowledge" (GM P:1), Nietzsche begins, because we are concentrating too much on the object of our knowledge for self-knowledge to set in. Like critics intent on literature, Nietzsche's men of knowledge—and he does not exclude himself—are for the most part blind to the nature and origins of their own practices.[8] The comparison is particularly appropriate for a book culminating in a chapter that presents itself as a "commentary" on a few lines from *Zarathustra*. The peculiar function of the genealogist, Nietzsche implies, is to alert us to the ground we stand on and which, for that very reason, we cannot normally see. Not that our "ground" is hidden from view, however; it hides in plain sight. As the ground we stand on, nothing is farther from us than our own practices; yet somehow, Nietzsche's stance gives him—and, through him, us—access.

The origins of the present attempt to examine the origins of our moral prejudices go back, we are told, to before the aphoristic work *Human, All Too Human.* In that book, Nietzsche tells us, he was able "to pause as a wanderer pauses and look back across the broad and dangerous country my spirit had traversed up to that time" (GM P:2). The ideas contained here, however, are even older. But not only does Nietzsche still cling to them, "they have become in the meantime more and more firmly attached to one another, indeed entwined and interlaced with one another . . . arisen in me from the first not as isolated, capricious, or sporadic things but from a common root, from a *fundamental will* of knowledge, pointing imperiously into the depths, speaking more and more precisely, demanding greater and greater precision" (GM P:2). Over time, largely in and through the medium of writing, an immanent intentionality or necessity has emerged, manifested in the way that diffuse ideas have revealed their underlying interrelatedness. The affinities between this "fundamental will of knowledge" and will to power are clear enough, and invite in the midst of this discussion of origins the speculation that the self-experience hyperbolically becomes the origin of the idea, without defining it sufficiently.

But the origins of this project go even farther back, to childhood, to "a scruple peculiar to me that I am loath to admit to—for it is concerned with *morality,* with all that has hitherto been celebrated on earth as morality—a scruple that entered my life so early, so uninvited, so irresistibly, so much in conflict with my environment, age, precedents, and descent that I might almost have the right to call it my '*a priori*' " (GM P:3). What is this scruple that sets Nietzsche apart, made him different from all that one would expect from a bookish young German, the son of a clergyman? this scruple so early, uninvited, irresistible? this "already" or "before" that makes him the genealogist he is?

Paul Bové has commented on this very passage in his essay, "Mendacious Innocents, or, The Modern Genealogist as Conscientious Intellectual: Nietzsche, Foucault, Said." According to Bové, the Nietzschean genealogist is the type of modern "oppositional critic," who here "identifies his difference from his age as the enabling factor of his insight and practice":

> Nietzsche gives us in this passage the scene of instruction of the conscientious intellectual. The violent penetration of consciousness by a "scruple" antagonistic to the shell of public sentiment is the initial weighing of Nietzsche's peculiarity. The cutting edge of this uninvited guest frees the intellectual's curiosity to examine a common phenomenon, morality, in an uncommon light, free of societal preconceptions. In fact, this irresistible scruple guides this curiosity in a struggle against family, nation, and religion—evils which must be overflown. The genealogist is "born" in a revolt against the given;

the sharp edge of the liberating scruple which tears the obscuring veil of the hegemonic figures of morality becomes a pointed weapon not only goading the conscientious intellectual along in his process of research and individuation, but also fracturing the dynastic edifice against which the genealogist defines himself. This originary scruple, this "a priori" which enables genealogical research and individuation, is also a measure of success. . . .

But this scruple exists nowhere but in the system of research, individuation, and liberation. It "enters," but from no "outside." Its "entrance" is merely a penetration pricking consciousness, announcing a "choice" of "identity" to be struggled for in the rhetorical and research struggle of the conscientious intellectual against the hegemonic mediation of meaning and value in his culture.[9]

In the end, Nietzsche's "*a priori*," which allows him to challenge the "hegemonic figures of morality" and fracture "the dynastic edifice" of his culture, comes down to "merely a penetration pricking consciousness." And this scruple "exists nowhere but in the system of research, individuation, and liberation." We have argued ourselves that it is in writing that Nietzsche's self-knowledge originates and emerges, that Bové's "nowhere but" is troubling, as is the vagueness of "a penetration pricking consciousness." Neither formulation quite seems adequate to the question that Bové shares with Nietzsche: "How *does* one get free of societal preconceptions?" Moreover, even this formulation leaves unclear its precise relationship with the far more specific story that Nietzsche claims to be telling: "How I became a genealogist/I have always been a genealogist."

And nothing in Bové's argument, which accommodates Nietzsche so neatly to the right-mindedness of Said and Foucault, gives even a hint as to why Nietzsche would be "loath to admit" to his scruple. Certainly no modern conscientious intellectual, no oppositional critic, hesitates for a second to do so. Make no mistake about it: there is much in Nietzsche that we do not approve of, much that makes us uneasy, much to make us doubt the ease of this accommodation.

Perhaps Bové does put his finger on something when he says that the "genealogist is 'born' in revolt." If we dispose of the quotation marks and take the figure seriously—this is, after all, what is at stake in one's genealogy—we begin to see that although the *a priori* emerges in the writing, the work, it is in relation to the work that it serves as a "before" or "already." In other words, what is at issue here is where and in what manner the project of writing, Nietzsche's work, touches the person, the life, the world—on what terms self-experience has been generalized, translated into concept and commentary. For instance, of the origins of "evil," Nietzsche writes:

My curiosity as well as my suspicions were bound to halt quite soon at the question of where our good and evil really *originated*. In fact, the problem of the origin of evil pursued me even as a boy of thirteen: at an age in which you have "half childish trifles, half God in your heart," I devoted to it my first childish literary trifle, my first philosophical effort—as for the "solution" of the problem I posed at that time, well, I gave the honor to God, as was only fair, and made him the *father* of evil. (GM P:3)

Here Nietzsche's italics suggest that the father's death is connected with the scruple that entered his life "so early, so uninvited, so irresistibly" as to put him in conflict with "environment, age, precedents, and descent." "Fortunately," he "learned early to separate theological prejudice from moral prejudice and ceased to look for the origin of evil *behind* the world" (GM P:3).

The separation that imparts the genealogist's perspective arises from this point of view, from the loss of the father. Nietzsche's first attempt to conceptualize that loss results in accusing the God whose death he will later simply announce. That form allows him, by examining, questioning, and revising, to veer away from literal origins toward autonomous self-creation. Nevertheless, he suggests, his writing, and therefore "Nietzsche" himself, are about the loss of the father. His externalization, conceptualization, and generalization are rational and justified insofar as the loss of the father and its consequences are of collective concern. Yet this origin, like the Freudian primal scene, is incurably ambiguous. Nietzsche cannot "know" that this narrative of origin is "true." He can only choose it or, perhaps to capture the quality of the thing more precisely, consent to be chosen by it.

To choose an origin or literality, to speak it, however indirectly, is to give up the would-be writer's dream, the illusion of originality as autochthony, or at least to mitigate it severely. Nietzsche recalls: "At length I had a country of my own, a soil of my own, an entire discrete, thriving, flourishing world, like a secret garden the existence of which no one suspected.—Oh! how fortunate we are, we men of knowledge, provided only that we know how to keep silent long enough!" (GM P:3). This secret garden, this private, compensatory Eden in which the man of knowledge "rules" and dwells apart, playing at infinite potential, requires silence. It cannot survive formulation or exposure. In order to speak, to externalize, it is necessary to accept reduction, limitation, specificity—to accept the literal origin that is at one with a distinctive voice or style. But this still leaves us short of a satisfying explanation of why Nietzsche is "loath" to admit his scruple.

The fictional character Zarathustra, who comes from nowhere in particular and goes nowhere in particular, is the center of a work addressed to everyone and no one. This infinite power of making, of evading, of feigning, of now being, now merely using Zarathustra—the same mobility and plasticity that moved Plato to banish poets from his Republic—Nietzsche is loath to forego. He is reluctant to remove the mask of Zarathustra, even though the Nietzsche behind it can only be a mask of Nietzsche. This is because the genealogy, which now accepts or emanates from an origin, is far from unambiguous—it is not even, contra Bové, unambiguously "oppositional." What Derrida will call "the name of Nietzsche," which must bear responsibility for what "the ear of the other"—including the Nazi ear—will make of it, which is the only conceivable recipient of the fame which the dead man himself cannot inherit, is given here.

Nietzsche names himself "fatherless" (or perhaps even better, since Wordsworth uses this same term to describe the imagination, "unfathered"). Whether this name is the end or origin of Nietzsche's quest is not clear. The writer's work of self-construction/discovery is irreducibly ambiguous, as uncertain as the literality of the Freudian primal scene or as obscure as the distinction between questing after the name one desires and questing to desire the name one has already been given, as in Browning's "Child Roland to the Dark Tower Came." Nevertheless, the founding gesture of Nietzsche's genealogy can with profit, we think, be construed as this reaching out toward the world, toward "literal" origins, which sites and embodies the heretofore unembodied power of making and conceiving everywhere at play in *Zarathustra*, which opens it to responsibility and guilt and above all, returns it to a world everywhere infected with the awareness of mortality.

Of course, not every fatherless child is a Nietzsche. While Nietzsche could not have named himself "fatherless" in this way without a real father who really died, this literal fact fails to help us much here. The denomination retains a connection with the fictional, asserts a mythic specialness, calling to mind as it does Oedipus, whose father's death is at once a contingent fact, an accident, and a structural necessity of his fatality—the central, exemplary figure of the tragic vision of the West. So if the literal fact of his father's death makes of the genealogy a history, or at least an interpretive history, the mythic dimension of his fatherlessness, its representation as self-presentation, also makes of the genealogy the story that requires Nietzsche as its authoritative commentator, the history that needs him as its last man or decadent as well as the avatar of its self-overcoming.

Nietzsche's immediate claim is that the fact of his fatherlessness freed him from the automatic investment in and identification with the received ideas and prejudices of his culture, deprived him of the automatic identification with received authority that is the patrimony of the fathered, and thus made possible the oppositional stance of the genealogist. But this singularity, this power of standing aside, is also a loss of patronymic, which is to say "natural," authority: authority that is never questioned because it is transmitted in the guise of biology, with mortality in the blood. Authority, wrapped in the awesome power of society and culture, fuses its own arrangements with the "natural," thus eliciting a tenuous sense of security.

But such assurance (or "legitimacy," a term that resonates with the Socratic connection between the authority of the father, the claim of truth, and the activity of philosophy) can never be restored; its absence is the wound or limp that makes the genealogist and requires from Nietzsche the writer the assertiveness, the élan, the gaiety, the hyperbole that aim less at authority than at assurance. In this sense, then, "fatherless" names the lack that makes him a writer and that, furthermore, makes him the writer he is.

A GENEALOGY OF COMPOSITION/DECOMPOSITION

Nietzsche was first moved to publish his ideas on the origins of morality, he tells us, by Paul Rée's *Origins of the Moral Sensations,* not as an instance of academic "hypothesis mongering" but as an opportunity to raise the question of "the *value* of morality"—a question all but unposed because the value of the phenomenon is simply assumed. In those rare instances where this has not been the case, as with Nietzsche's "great teacher," Schopenhauer, the value attributed to morality and particularly to pity, is the opposite of Nietzsche's estimation:

> What was especially at stake was the value of the "unegoistic," the instincts of pity, self-abnegation, self-sacrifice, which Schopenhauer had gilded, deified, and projected into a beyond for so long that at last they became for him "value-in-itself," on the basis of which he *said No* to life and to himself. But it was against precisely *these* instincts that there spoke from me an ever more fundamental mistrust, an ever more corrosive skepticism! It was precisely here that I saw the great danger to mankind, its sublimest enticement and seduction—but to what? to nothingness?—it was precisely here that I saw the beginning of the end, the dead stop, a retrospective weariness, the will turning *against* life, the tender and sorrowful signs of the ultimate illness: I understood the ever-spreading morality of pity that had seized even on philosophers and made them ill, as the most sinister symptom of a European culture that had itself become sinister, perhaps as its bypass to a new Buddhism? to a Buddhism for Europeans? to—*nihilism?* (GM P:5)

"Pity" names the bad conscience infecting the individual's relationship with the gifts—beauty, strength, vitality—that life has bestowed. In a world filled with the sick, pity argues, how can the healthy help but feel guilty? Yet pity deprives us of the basis for a *positive* attachment to life, which makes no sense when appreciation of its compensations is repressed. Pity, Nietzsche implies, is the temptation to renounce (as opposed to valuing) the good because it is so unevenly distributed. The tainting of life's compensations with guilt creates the permanent imbalance between loss and compensation which constitutes nihilism, weariness: a turning against life arrested only by the invention of an imaginary existence elsewhere—that is, by Christian morality and eschatology.

The first problem with this account of pity and nihilism is the similarity it suggests between self-overcoming and pity, or even nihilism. How are they to be distinguished? Perhaps it can be argued that the self is overcome in the name of what is best in us, whereas in pity, what is best is overcome out of a loyalty to the condition of the majority. Such an analysis may cast light on structuralist and poststructuralist deconstructions of the self, which follow Nietzsche in the critique of a particular structure or ideology of selfhood, but diverge from him in an attack on the self in the name of a leveling politics, if not of pity then of equality. For Foucault and Derrida,[10] the deconstruction of the self takes the form of questioning the role of the author as the "sovereign" origin of his or her own text.

It is worth noting that Nietzsche's analysis of pity is first and foremost intertextual: as reader, he finds his own fate in Schopenhauer's. Part of the problem seems to be what Schopenhauer says, and part to be the position of reader itself. In one sense, Nietzsche's rejection of pity (somewhat like Blake's) is a rejection of the claims of a consumerist conception of the legitimacy of the reader's demands; still more precisely (and perhaps less "elitist") it might be seen as an argument against the author's preemptive capitulation to the imagined needs and demands of an absent readership. For an author, the audience is as much a fiction as author is for a reader. And if the "being" written is as unstable, as much a projection as the "sovereign" being who writes, then the benefits derived from renouncing authorial authority belong to the same imaginary space as the powers attributed to authorship.

As we have already noted, Nietzsche also seems to suggest that nihilism is the reader's disease. The reader, like Nietzsche—like Western civilization—is somehow "unfathered." Nietzsche knows—at least after *Zarathustra* IV—that however much he is prepared to claim for himself as author in the face of the claims of the reader, his own "corrosive skepticism" as a reader undermines the author/father, drives a wedge between the two functions, and leaves the fatherless reader exposed to the nihilism, the sense of futility that attends this unlooked-for loss. As Nietzsche argues, God is not merely dead, we have killed him (GS 125). When he acknowledges his fatherlessness as the origin of his unusual perspective on morality, he not only acknowledges his father's antecedence, he *chooses* it. This positive choice of what is "true" allows him not only to judge but to kill this antecedence—"delicate, good, and morbid" and so to reduce it to "a being destined merely to pass by." Nietzsche's relationship to Schopenhauer here is equally instructive. Schopenhauer is his antecedent; in him, he discovers himself. Schopenhauer is also the prime example of the author who, in renouncing the predecessor's authority, exposes readers (including Nietzsche) to the nihilism of the unfathered. But how is Schopenhauer, whose pity unfathers the reader, any different from Nietzsche, whose corrosive commentary also undermines the author and unfathers the reader? A crucial distinction seems to exist between commentary, in which authorship or writing is reinscribed within reading, and a readership that remains totally exposed to the death of the author as father. To put it differently: Nietzsche, the genealogist/commentator, chooses the identity "unfathered," whereas fatherlessness merely befalls the normal reader. It is no accident that this motif echoes Nietzsche's famous formulation at the end of Essay Three, "man would rather will *nothingness* than not *will*" (GM III:28). That choosing fatherlessness is better then simply being fatherless accounts for the profound affinity that Nietzsche and commentary in general have for asceticism. At the same time, that fatherlessness and nothingness are not the same helps to account for his rejection of asceticism. In this context, the choice of "fatherlessness" is linked to the actual hyperbolic "what if?" that begins Nietzsche's project and defines its antithetical method:

> One has taken the *value* of these "values" as given, as factual, as beyond all question; one has hitherto never doubted or hesitated in the slightest degree in supposing "the good man" to be of greater value than "the evil man," of greater value in the sense of furthering the advancement and prosperity of man in general (the future of man included). But what if the reverse were true? What if a symptom of regression were inherent in the "good," likewise a danger, a seduction, a poison, a narcotic, through which the present was possibly living *at the expense of the future?* (GM P:6)

There is nothing more worth taking seriously, Nietzsche tells us, than the problem of morality, and he marks this valuation by a dramatic reversal. Perhaps our valuations are the opposite of our true interests. Perhaps our malaise results from our mistaken valuations:

> Among the rewards for it being that some day one will perhaps be allowed to take them *cheerfully*. For cheerfulness—or in my own language *gay science*—is a reward: the reward of a long, brave, industrious, and subterranean seriousness, of which, to be sure, not everyone is capable. But on the day we can say with all our hearts, "Onwards! our old morality too is part of the comedy!" we shall have discovered a new complication and possibility for the Dionysian drama of "The Destiny of the Soul"—and one can wager that the grand old eternal comic poet of our existence will be quick to make use of it! (GM P:8)

It is now "the eternal comic poet of our existence" and not the father or God the Father with whom we must deal. He is a comic poet in part because he mocks our tendency to see ourselves as the culmination and end—and to despair accordingly—instead of as a mere stage in the march of our kind. Even more, the unfolding spectacle of existence, seen from the genealogist's antithetical perspective, mocks all our solemn pretensions to knowing where we are or what we are actually doing. It is impossible to estimate the value of life or to justify it by aesthetic means—or by any others for that matter.[11]

Indeed, the "economic" imbalance that motivates the *Genealogy* to begin with, challenges the totalizing claims of the aesthetic/tragic vision of *The Birth of Tragedy*. The "tragic" apprehension of *Zarathustra*, for example, is a sign of the limits of fictions, their irreducible difference from the world and betrays a certain temptation to see this as a "thing-in-itself." The cheerfulness, the gaiety of Nietzsche's new "science" stems from the fact that we no longer need to feel that everything depends on frail and inadequate *us*. Again, the contrast is between a tragic vision, in which the author is doomed to fall short in his attempts to convey a message of urgent, even salvific, importance, and a comic one, in which the author recognizes that everything is not up to him, that there is plenty going on (perhaps even in his own text) to which he may be blind and over which he may have no control.

In this context, self-overcoming is more a self-affirmation of the authorial self in its finitude than a self-hating rejection of the self for its failures or imperfections. Kathleen Higgins argues that "the central, 'tragic' message of Zarathustra is that meaning in life is to be found in simply loving life for its own sake."[12] The "eternal comic poet" of the *Genealogy* suggests that we can also love life for what it engenders and makes possible, even out of its errors. Whether we view life tragically or comically, we are doing something with life and to it, not just apprehending a "thing-in-itself." The problem posed by Nietzsche's comic vision, like that posed by his tragic vision, is thus one of identification. In the former case, it is the capacity of a yearning, finite being to identify with a temporal extensiveness that is indifferent to its desires but, for that reason, liberating. In the latter case, it is the capacity of a being with unlimited desires to identify with a finite and therefore absolutely limited existence. The way toward the comic vision is blocked by the complexities and challenge of eternal recurrence; the way to the tragic vision is blocked by the logic of asceticism. Again, the analogy is literary: on the one hand, the book that we are writing must be good enough to justify it and us; on the other, we need no justification, and it is only one book among many.

The importance of commentary is confirmed in the conclusion to Nietzsche's preface, which not only calls attention to the fact that Essay Three is an "exegesis" of a single aphorism, but recommends the aphorism as a form whose essence is that it requires exegesis. It draws the reader into an askesis fundamentally different from contemporary standards of "readability." Nietzsche makes demands on his readers, but these demands are anything but paternal. For instance, Nietzsche's First Essay aims to show how the familiar distinction between "Good and Evil" actually overlays and intends to obscure a far more archaic and fundamental distinction between

"Good and Bad" (like corpus over corpse, perhaps). Nietzsche derides "English psychologists" for an ahistorical method that merely imposes their own prejudices on the question of morality. The true origins of judgments of the good, he argues, were not with those benefited but with the "good" themselves. The noble called themselves "good," the lower orders "bad," not out of some utility but out of a "pathos" of distance—a distance somewhat reminiscent of the reader/writer relationship we have been discussing. Appropriately, the essay, an etymological investigation, reveals a consistent connection between words designating " 'noble,' 'aristocratic' in the social sense" (GM I:3) and " 'good,' in the sense of 'with aristocratic soul,' 'noble,' 'with a soul of a high order,' 'with a privileged soul' " (GM I:4). Indeed, "through the words and roots that designate 'good' shines the most important nuance by virtue of which the noble felt themselves to be men of a higher rank" (GM I:5). Typically, they refer to themselves as "the truthful," not in our conditional and moralistic sense, but in the sense of "one who *is*, who possesses reality, who is actual, who is true." By contrast, the common man "lies" in that he is at a greater distance from being (GM I:5).[13]

This redefinition of the truthful/lying distinction, like the argument of the *Genealogy* as a whole, undercuts the authority of a readership inclined to measure a writer by the standards of its "reality." Revealing this reality to be constituted by fictions more egregious and less aware of themselves than those of many writers, Nietzsche not only puts readership at a disadvantage but projects the problem of authorship and the fictional onto the stage of morality and of society. But according to him, this alternative system of valuation has been suppressed (though imperfectly, since its traces can still be read), by means of etymology, on the body of language. For Nietzsche, it is through etymology that language speaks for itself in a voice apart from conscious use, apart from the impositions of prejudice and ruling concept. In fact, his reading presents the moral point of view as the repression of what reappears (or persists) in the body of language like the symptoms of hysteria on the body of a patient. This link between hysteria and etymology as the symptom of a language which serves—at times unwillingly—as the body of thought is more than casual. In a long note to the concluding section of the First Essay, Nietzsche calls for the interests of "philologists, historians, and philosophers" on the one hand, and "physiologists and doctors" on the other to converge on the question of the origin and evolution of moral concepts (GM I:17n.). And he closes the section itself emphatically:

> The well-being of the majority and the well-being of the few are opposite viewpoints of value: to consider the former *a priori* of higher value may be left to the naiveté of English biologists.—*All* the sciences have from now on to

prepare the way for the future task of the philosophers: this task is understood as the solution of the *problem of value*, the determination of the *order of rank among values*. (GM I:17)

At the end of the twentieth century, we may well prefer the naiveté of English biologists to that of German philosophers; but what is striking is the convergence between this large clash of social (and even biosocial) values and the problematic of author/reader relations. The interests and authority of the one are pitted against the claims and demands of the many. And yet neither the archaic equivalence of "truth" and "proximity to being," nor the ideal of an order of rank among competing values, describes the actual evolution of moral concepts under the influence of religion in general and Christian asceticism in particular. The key figure in this evolution is the priest, whose appearance as part of the noble class does not necessarily contradict the rule that political superiority resolves itself into superiority of soul. The priestly opposition between "pure" and "impure" is initially taken quite literally by ancient folk whose notions were essentially unsymbolic. Nevertheless, though they still designate a difference in station, these concepts introduce something that is not entirely concerned with station—an abstract, qualitative distinction that creates the possibility of an alternative form of valuation. Despite the initial innocuousness of their appearance, these new concepts are pernicious:

> It is clear from the whole nature of an essentially priestly aristocracy why antithetical valuations could in precisely this instance soon become dangerously deepened, sharpened, and internalized; and indeed they finally tore chasms between man and man that a very Achilles of a free spirit would not venture to leap without a shudder. There is from the first something *unhealthy* in such priestly aristocracies and in the habits ruling in them which turn them away from action and alternate between brooding and emotional explosions, habits which seem to have as their almost invariable consequence that intestinal morbidity and neurasthenia which has afflicted priests at all times. (GM I:6)

Indeed, Nietzsche's treatment of the priest's "intestinal morbidity and neurasthenia" forcefully recall his own chronic ailments; and the antithetical valuations of the priest are echoed and (perhaps) even parodied in Nietzsche's own antithetical method. By their bad health we shall know them. And could the author by his askesis to some degree be acknowledging his alignment with the valuations of the priests?

Be that as it may, on one point Nietzsche distinguishes himself. The priest, he says, sought to remedy this morbidity by means of asceticism, which "has ultimately proved itself a hundred times more dangerous in its effects than the sickness it was supposed to cure." And so the species goes on, but goes on impaired:

[It] is still ill with the effects of this priestly naiveté in medicine! Think, for example, of certain forms of diet (abstinence from meat), of fasting, of sexual continence, of flight "into the wilderness" (the Weir Mitchell[14] isolation cure—without, to be sure, the subsequent fattening and overfeeding which constitute the most effective remedy for the hysteria induced by the ascetic ideal): add to these the entire antisensualistic metaphysic of the priests that makes men indolent and overrefined, their autohypnosis in the manner of fakirs and Brahmins . . . and finally the only-too-comprehensible satiety with all this, together with the radical cure for it, *nothingness.* (GM I:6)

The suppression and paralysis of the senses and the consequent distance from being is explicitly characterized as a hysteria that even now we try to treat with more asceticism—a hysteria whose symptomology the etymologist finds apparent in the body of language, which is, in turn, confined and silenced in part by the tyranny of moral ideas. Still, Nietzsche adds, it is only "on the soil of this *essentially dangerous* form of human existence, the priestly form, that man first became *an interesting animal,* that only here did the human soul acquire *depth* and become *evil*—and these are the two basic respects in which man has hitherto been superior to the beasts!" (GM I:6).

Nietzsche's intertwining of the state of language and the state of the body allows inspection of the pathology of conceptualization in the West, in which the suppression of the senses and devaluation of the body, on the one hand, are answered by the limitation and restraint of language, on the other hand. This asceticism of language and of the body makes conception possible by giving humanity *depth.* The relevance of this analysis to the philosopher as, in some sense, the priest of truth, should be apparent. Less obvious perhaps, but equally important, is that this discovery of depth also sets the stage for interpretation, for the hermeneutics of texts.

It was inevitable, Nietzsche maintains, that the priestly mode would branch off from and become antithetical to the knightly/aristocratic. And faced with their own relative impotence in the face of the knights' physical superiority, it was inevitable that priests, with their hatred of life, would grow to "monstrous and uncanny proportions" (GM I:7). For Nietzsche, the Jews of the Bible are the priestly people *par excellence,* whose thirst for spiritual revenge begins and sustains a "slave revolt in morality" culminating in the stunning victory of Christianity, in which hate triumphs by donning the antithetical guise of love:

The slave revolt in morality begins when *ressentiment* itself becomes creative and gives birth to values: the *ressentiment* of natures that are denied the true reaction, that of deeds, and compensate themselves with an imaginary revenge. While every noble morality develops from a triumphant affirmation of itself, slave morality from the outset says No to what is "outside," what is "different," what is "not itself"; and *this* No is its creative deed. This inversion of the value-positing eye—this *need* to direct one's view outward instead of back to oneself—is the essence of *ressentiment*: in order to exist, slave morality always first needs a hostile external world; it needs, physiologically speaking, external stimuli in order to act at all—its action is fundamentally reaction. (GM I:10)

Here the No to the "other" or "outside" and the "imaginary revenge" connected with it offer disturbing suggestions about the ambiguity of fiction making, with its at least qualified rejection of what "is," its urge to be elsewhere, and its implied revenge on reality. The noble mode of evaluation, for which the reverse is true, may also recall the self-sufficiency of the authorial imagination. There is, Nietzsche points out, not hate but forbearance in the contempt of the masters; they are happy, present in themselves and not in relation to others. They are fully present in their own lives. Of course, as he later admits, the behavior of nobles to those outside their groups was barbarous. But their "joy in destructiveness" can be seen as corresponding to the iconoclasm and insistence on the self, the necessary ruthlessness and indifference of an author to the claims of others.

And yet there is an ambiguity here. We can think of *ressentiment* as the "revenge of the reader," which Susan Sontag[15] associates with interpretation grown arrogant, hateful, usurpatory. Nietzsche links this revenge of the reader with a self-serving morality on the basis of which the reader tries to bend the author to the reader's needs and prejudices. The lesser instinctively desires to bring the greater, the luckier, down to its level. This leveling down is tantamount to a social disease. "Supposing that what is at any rate believed to be the 'truth' really is true," argues Nietzsche, then the meaning of culture is the domestication of the human beast. And *ressentiment* is one of its prime instruments, the resentful its prime bearers. Not only, he insists, is "the reverse not merely probable . . . today it is *palpable.*" *Ressentiment* and the resentful are now regressive, restraining a new overcoming. Now we suffer from endemic malady: "We *suffer* from man" (GM I:11). Humanity is ill-constituted, sick, weary. This domesticated species—hopelessly "mediocre and insipid"—has been deluded into thinking itself the goal of history. But unlike the nobles they have displaced, the resentful cannot afford to take joy in the worthiness of their enemies; they seek to exclude all but themselves. They are amputees, who call up the specter of nihilism by their attempts to make their own incompleteness serve as the *ne plus ultra* of humanity.

Nietzsche thinks of this weariness in human consciousness as a symptom of nihilism. The mechanism at work here concerns "love" and "fear." In his account, it is humankind's sublimity, the "pathos of distance" between love and fear, that gives the project of humanization its impetus and underlying sense—but which also makes it deeply contradictory. For how can the sublime be rationalized and brought to heel by democracy? In effect, we have two versions of culture: domesticated, humanized; and demonic, sublime. These correspond to Thomas Weiskel's[16] distinction between humane and sublime critics: those who subordinate themselves to the humane values they find immanent in the text and those who try to bring out and manifest a power, however problematical and ambiguous. This is very much a difference about what people want and need—perhaps even about which values actually sustain and compensate the project of writing and the writer, as opposed to those values that make writing and writers acceptable to the mass of readers and, behind them, to society as a whole.

After all this, the question of "the *other* origin of the 'good,' of the good as conceived by the man of *ressentiment*" still remains to be answered (GM I:13). In a famous passage, Nietzsche likens resentful people to sheep, whose understandable dislike of birds of prey for bearing off little lambs leads them to condemn the birds and the characteristics associated with them as evil. The opposite of the bird of prey, the lamb, then becomes the embodiment of good. What is hurtful or disadvantageous to lambs is condemned and branded evil. This may be easy enough to comprehend. Less obvious is the intervention of "likeness," an abstracting figure of similitude by means of which predatory qualities are detached from the bird of prey. More fundamentally, "likeness" is a means of creating that aphasia, that discontinuity or gap which, once crossed, obscures from the sheep the origin of their judgment of evil in simple disadvantage *to them.*

Not even the fundamental judgments of value are above or beyond perspective. Clearly, the birds of prey not only see things differently. Since things are arranged very much to their advantage, they have no need of such an antithetical, "good-evil" morality; they are perfectly happy to regard tasty little lambs as "good." In fact, then, morality itself seems to belong to the particular perspective of the weak or disadvantaged. It must serve as their chief weapon against the strong. Implicitly, Nietzsche raises here the questions that will occupy all of Essay Two: How are the strong subverted? How do they subvert *themselves?* By what means are they induced to play this game of morality? Implicitly, he answers, the major source of human vulnerability is language. An underlying implication of the passage (the secret appropriateness of the bird of prey image) is that humans can be transported by words. And it is not just the moralist but the philosopher, Plato himself, who is "carried away" by language:

> For just as the popular mind separates the lightning from its flash and takes the latter for an *action,* for the operation of a subject called lightning, so popular morality also separates strength from expressions of strength, as if there were a neutral substratum behind the strong man, which was *free* to express strength or not to do so. But there is no such substratum; there is no "being" behind doing, effecting, becoming; "the doer" is merely a fiction added to the deed—the deed is everything. The popular mind in fact doubles

the deed; when it sees the lightning flash, it is the deed of a deed: it posits
the same event first as cause and then a second time as its effect. Scientists
do no better when they say "force moves," "force causes," and the like—all
its coolness, its freedom from emotion notwithstanding, our entire science
still lies under the misleading influence of language and has not disposed of
that little changeling, the "subject" (the atom, for example, is such a changeling, as is the Kantian "thing-in-itself"); no wonder if the submerged, darkly
glowering emotions of vengefulness and hatred exploit this belief for their
own ends and in fact maintain no belief more ardently than the belief that
the strong man is free to be weak and the bird of prey to be a lamb—for thus
they gain the right to make the bird of prey *accountable* for being a bird of
prey. (GM I:13)

The "seduction of language (and of the fundamental errors of reason
that are petrified in it)" points first to similitude as a principle of mobility
that dissolves identities into qualities and makes differences equally accessible to judgment; second, it points to a hardening of language effects into
identities, capable of being called to account and of receiving judgment.
It is in language that all persons are created equal, in the sense of being
rendered equally accessible to the law and its judgments. "The fundamental errors of reason petrified in language" are, in fact, the errors of philosophy and its epigone, science, whose founding gestures, Nietzsche implies, are to hypostasize effects of language.[17] The particular error that
concerns him here is that of the "subject," a cause added to the effect in
order to make this effect available to judgment (or analysis) by creating
the illusion that it could have been otherwise if the subject had been otherwise ("*the strong man is free* to be weak and the bird of prey to be a lamb").
The view that " 'the doer' is merely a fiction added to the deed" can be
deployed in still another context than the standard philosophical one: that
of authorship and of Nietzsche's own writing. Clearly, the author (or, as
Foucault would have it, the "author-effect") is a kind of subject, constructed of "authorial" choices, which, in turn, open the work to interpretation and judgment—by creating the illusion that it could have been otherwise.

But one has to wonder if the conviction that "it could have been otherwise" *is* an illusion. If so, in what sense? The scathing irony of Nietzsche's
own "*the strong man is free* to be weak" seems to point to an "elsewhere" or
"otherwise"—a language-effect that appears to open up the possibility of
a choice. Also, Nietzsche's own "bird of prey" metaphor appears to exploit
the abstracting power of similitude in the same way that moralists do. After
all, is "the strong man" really like a bird of prey? In Nietzsche's analogy,
the bird's "strength" manifests itself in a single way. Can the same be said
of "man's"?

We are arguing, then, not that Nietzsche's logic is flawed, but that his central concerns can be read equally well as somewhat other than those expressly stated. We need not think of his attack on "the subject" as an attack on "the self" or "identity" as such. After all, the bird of prey has an identity that is completely expressed and comprehended in the act of predation. Even if the same could ever have been said of the strength of "the strong man," we have long since lost touch with the relevant sense of the word "strength" (perhaps as the result of the genealogy that Nietzsche describes).

But this *can* be said of an author: that one writes as one does because one cannot do otherwise, and that the effects of that writing (that is, the texts) express and comprehend (or establish) a particular identity *as author.* And here is the problem. This selfsameness involves the reduction of an empirical to an immanent self, creating the possibility of the author who "writes" reading his or her own "authorship," and so of the reinscription of the "writer reading." The bird of prey suffers no such "residue." Disanalogy is also a "language effect," and there is no perspective from which the selfsameness of authorial identity is not also a language effect, seen from the opposite end of the reader-writer relationship. Authorial selfsameness, then, may be thought of as the complement of a readerly "otherwise" in a relationship that is portrayed here as a struggle for power and authority. And one of the stories that Nietzsche tells is of the subversion of authorial authority by readers (in a consumerist society); it is also the story of how authorship is infected by readership. *Ressentiment* is, in at least this sense, also the reader's disease, something directed against the author's apparent selfsameness. Inherent in this dynamic is the all-too-human impulse to disguise motives:

> "We weak ones are, after all, weak; it would be good if we did nothing *for which we are not strong enough"*; but this dry matter of fact, this prudence of the lowest order which even the insects possess (posing as dead, when in great danger, so as not to do "too much"), has, thanks to the counterfeit and self-deception of impotence, clad itself in the ostentatious garb of the virtue of quiet, calm resignation, just as if the weakness of the weak—that is to say, their *essence,* their effects, their sole, ineluctable, irremovable reality—were a voluntary achievement, willed, chosen, a *deed,* a *meritorious* act. This type of man *needs* to believe in a neutral independent "subject," prompted by an instinct for self-preservation and self-affirmation in which every lie is sanctified. The subject (or, to use a more popular expression, the *soul*) has perhaps been believed in hitherto more firmly than anything else on earth because it makes possible to the majority of mortals, the weak and oppressed of every kind, the sublime self-deception that interprets weakness as freedom, and their being thus-and-thus as a *merit.* (GM I:13)

Creation of a "subject" that could be otherwise allows the resentful to represent what they must in any case be—quiet, calm, resigned—as virtue, "as if the weakness of the weak . . . were a voluntary achievement, willed, chosen, a *deed*, a *meritorious* act." There is an almost parodic relationship here between the representation of what is, as chosen, and Nietzsche's own descriptions of eternal recurrence as a kind of retrospective willing. From this perspective, the abstracting power, the mobility of similitude, allows the weak to act the role of strength, to embody falsely. Yet they do not so much embody strength as assume it as a cloak or dress up, which fools even themselves. Perhaps the main difference is that the weak believe their morality and forget its interested origins in precisely the sense that Nietzsche, as we have argued, does not believe in eternal recurrence or present himself as its embodiment.[18] The resentful ones represent the hardening of the figural, and of the hyperbolic in particular, into the literal.

For writers like this, authorship, or fiction making, is a kind of auto-illusion. As weak readers themselves, they mistake their incapacity to sustain the tensions and contradictions inherent in figuration for strength. Against an author's identification with the writing itself, weak readers offer a "judgment" based on the illusion that the "same author" could somehow have written "otherwise"—a judgment that sustains the illusion of a unified and stable self, a self, in principle, incapable of "authorship." Weak readers are simply unable to sustain the contradictions of an author's role. On the one hand, the author is identical with the text; on the other hand, the "self-same" writer is fragmented by that text, torn apart like Orpheus (or Pentheus) by the multiplication of authorial words. This scattering in language is a real Dionysian revel, corresponding to the self-disseminating movement of will to power, with the fragmentation of the aphoristic style, extending even to the body itself.

In a sense, then, selfsameness of an author corresponds to the idea of eternal recurrence, corresponds to this lack of "otherwise" or "else-where"; however, its complement is the scattering in language that corresponds to the will to power, at once everywhere and nowhere. This ineluctable doubling effect invites the resentful dream of creation without alienation. Samuel Coleridge's famous definitions of primary and secondary imagination speak to such a dream. His primary imagination internalizes the "eternal act of creation in the infinite I AM"[19]—the convergence of "I am" and "It is" in the single word that suffices for God to create and sustain the world in perpetuity. This divine will to power disseminates itself everywhere while subtracting nothing from itself, Coleridge suggests—a miracle reflected in the way that language as well emanates from and at the same time remains answerable to a single word.

But humankind is not God. So Nietzsche enacts a self-harrowing, or rather forces his reader, "Mr. Rash and Curious," to repeat it. Looking into "the secret of how *ideals are made* on earth," in a prosopopoeia echoing that by means of which the poet speaks for the dead, he speaks the original transvaluation of all values—putting noble names on weakness in the original antithetical criticism, devising figures that fail to recognize themselves as such, and holding his nose as we might expect to have to do among the dead and their decaying morality. Among the central mysteries addressed in the *Genealogy* is an inversion of high and low, healthy and sick. It speaks to an even more fundamental sense of "economic" imbalance, of indebtedness that, try as he might, Nietzsche cannot entirely put off onto asceticism, with its vague sense that this debt can be redeemed, perhaps even at a profit, by scourging and sacrificing "this" life.

Essay One can be read as providing the what and why of the slave revolt in morality and its successful subversion of noble values. But the how of this subversion—how it is that the weak manage to overcome the better and stronger masters—is left unanswered. How do the masters internalize the slave's unspeakable thirst for universality and neutrality—the slave's self-deceptive will to power—and in the process *become* weak, *become* slaves themselves? In Essay Two, as Nietzsche attempts to answer these questions, his earlier account of slave morality as pathological begins to converge with a new account, in which this pathology is increasingly difficult to separate from "normal" socialization and from culture itself. By moving a sense of inversion, imbalance, and indebtedness from contingent pathology to aspects of civilization, he begins to challenge in a fundamental way notions of balance, equilibrium that extend even to the body in the moral/intellectual tradition derived from Plato. But his sense of the fluid, idiosyncratic, and even indeterminate relationship between mind and body (which we have already begun to trace) is no less a challenge to the Christian ascetic's ideal of delicately balanced imbalance. The problem of reappropriating the body to the self through language is complicated by the way that language scatters the body—a complication echoed in and intertwined with the ambiguity of style.

Nietzsche begins this essay on " 'Guilt,' 'Bad Conscience,' and the Like" by defining "the paradoxical task that nature has set itself in the case of man": "To breed an animal *with the right to make promises*" (GM II:1). This project is opposed by an equally natural and necessary *forgetfulness*—an active faculty of "repression" or inhibition, determining that "what we experience and absorb enters our consciousness as little while we are digesting it . . . as does the thousandfold process, involved in physical nourishment" (GM II:1). This active forgetfulness closes consciousness off, for example, from "the noise and struggle of our underworld of utility organs working with and against one another" (GM II:1). For the "animal" in whom this capacity is damaged, there can be "no happiness, no cheerfulness, no hope, no pride, no *present*." Why? Because this creature has "bred in itself" a memory, which abrogates "robust health" in cases where promises are made:

This involves no mere passive inability to rid oneself of an impression, no mere indigestion through a once-pledged word with which one cannot "have done," but an active *desire* not to rid oneself, a desire for the continuance of something desired once, a real *memory of the will*: so that between the original "I will," "I shall do this" and the actual discharge of the will, its *act*, a world of strange new things, circumstances, even acts of will may be interposed without breaking this long chain of will. (GM II:1)

In order for this situation to occur, this "animal" "must first have learned to distinguish necessary events from chance ones, to think causally, to see and anticipate distant eventualities, to decide with certainty what is the goal and what is the means to it." Indeed: "Man himself must first of all have become *calculable, regular, necessary,* even in his own image of himself, if he is able to stand security for *his own future,* which is what one who promises does!" (GM II:1).

This primitive capacity to make promises also appears to be one of the necessary attributes of the author of books. An author must be able to sustain a narrative or an argument, to fulfill a formal and creative "contract," to fulfill a "promise." But then the world of things can come between this promise and its fulfillment; by which we mean to say that, subject as it is to duration (say, of writing), it is necessarily open to intrusions from the outside. If all this is necessary to the *completion* of a project, a complementary forgetfulness is required to create the perpetual present that sustains writing from moment to moment. Otherwise, a dyspeptic inability to let go can fix the writer's gaze on the past; in retrospect, the writer frets and tinkers, anxiously recoiling from the expanse ahead. Dyspepsia is, for Nietzsche, a symptom of disorder in the body of the text as well as of disorder in the body as the physiologist thinks of it.

"Our organism," Nietzsche argues, "is an oligarchy," in which an "active" forgetfulness—"like a doorkeeper, a preserver of psychic order, repose, and etiquette"—makes room "above all for the nobler functions and functionaries, for regulation, foresight, premeditation" (GM II:1). He implies, too, that the organism of the text is an oligarchy. Such a characterization speaks to style as selectivity, continuity, an impression of harmony and unity typically based in a dominant key or keys. Yet "style" also rebounds upon oligarchy: the complement of this forgetfulness, the memory of will which may require cruelty, may base itself in indebtedness, may go beyond mere dyspepsia, and tends toward an illness indistinguishable from civilization itself. This points to style as idiosyncratic. Individual in a way testifying to the distorting power of the "memory of will" as character, it may testify to the distorting power of life. More pointedly, we may still be left to wonder whether Nietzsche's style is an expression of his askesis, or of his chronic illness.

The result of this project of calculability, Nietzsche claims, then, is the "sovereign individual," who (like the "sovereign author") possesses "free will," and has the "right" to make promises. For that reason emancipated and thus imbued with value, this creature is "a proud consciousness, quivering in every muscle, of *what* has at length been achieved and become flesh in him, a consciousness of his own power and freedom, a sensation of mankind come to completion" (GM II:2). The "*sovereign individual,*" "this emancipated individual," embodies "what has at length been achieved" (GM II:2). Indeed, this being sounds very much like the nobles of Essay One—which may be the more remarkable considering what Nietzsche will have to say about the role of asceticism in creating memory, and what he will imply about the continuity between conscience and the bad conscience exploited by slave morality:

> Looking out upon others from himself, he honors or he despises; and just as he is bound to honor his peers, the strong and the reliable (those with the *right* to make promises)—that is, all those who promise like sovereigns, reluctantly, rarely, slowly, who are chary of trusting, whose trust is a mark of distinction, who give their word as something that can be relied on because they know themselves strong enough to maintain it in the face of accidents, even "in the face of fate"—he is bound to reserve a kick for the feeble windbags who promise without the right to do so, and a rod for the liar who breaks his word even at the moment he utters it. The proud awareness of the extraordinary privilege of *responsibility*, the consciousness of this rare freedom, this power over oneself and over fate, has in his case penetrated to the profoundest depths and become instinct, the dominating instinct. What will he call this dominating instinct, supposing he feels the need to give it a name? The answer is beyond doubt: this sovereign man calls it his *conscience.* (GM II:2)

Above all, conscience carries with it the "*right to affirm oneself*" (GM II:3). But what an ordeal of preparation was endured for this to be achieved! Extreme cruelty was required to create memory in a forgetful animal. Pain has proved to be the most powerful aid to mnemonics. "In a certain sense, the whole of asceticism belongs here" as "ascetic procedures and modes of life" are the means of freeing a few ideas "from the competition of all other ideas, so as to make them 'unforgettable' " (GM II:3). The archaic codes of punishment used by the Germans testify to "the effort it costs on this earth to breed a 'nation of thinkers' " (GM II:3)—and, through the connection with asceticism, to the violence of the psychodrama required to generate intellectual/creative activity. The odd leap here from "the right to make promises" to "a nation of thinkers" also tends to confirm the connection we have been pursuing between "genealogy" and Nietzsche's own work.

Conscience, created out of punishment and ascetic self-torture, is transformed through internalization into habit and made instinctual by a kind of forgetting. But can pain be forgotten in this way, and transformed into instinct? How great are the transformative powers of thinking and writing? It is a curious aspect of Nietzsche's discourse here that he insists on the "right" (*Recht*) to make promises, to affirm oneself, when it seems that the less moralistic/legalistic term "capacity" (*Vermögen*) would have done just as well—better perhaps, since less suggestive of residual anxiety. Strictly speaking, he is describing the origin and evolution of a capacity to keep promises more than of a "right to make them." The nobles assume their right; for them, it is not a question. They feel no need to establish or insist on their rights. The key question is "where does the 'right' to claim rights come from?" Nietzsche's answer is that it comes from pain—an answer that not only links pain indirectly to writing but also suggests that we write in order to establish rights, that is, to be "more" than others. Writing (at least of a certain kind) carries with it the burden of inequality, imbalance, disequilibrium, and distinction. It also requires and testifies to a pain that is never entirely subsumed or transformed into "instinct."

But how did the "consciousness of guilt," "bad conscience" come into the world? It evolved, not from some prior notion of the freedom of the will (a relatively late development in any case), but from the debtor/debtee relationship (in German, the word for "guilt" and "debt" is the same: *Schuld*). Furthermore, the injury of a broken contract could be compensated for by the pleasure of giving pain, as in the case of Shylock. In contrast, we moderns see pain and suffering as arguments against existence only because we have forgotten how powerful a seduction to life inflicting pain can be.[20] The pessimist's disgust at and weariness with life is not characteristic of the most "evil" epochs of what Nietzsche calls "the human race" (GM II:2); instead, it arises from the "morbid" softening and moralization that occurs when humankind becomes ashamed of "all his instincts" (GM II:7).

The "true"[21] object of humanity's indignation is not suffering but the *senselessness* of suffering. Gods were invented to make sense *out of* suffering. Hence, the Greeks represented both pleasure and pain as divine diversions: "What was at bottom the ultimate meaning of Trojan Wars and other such tragic terrors? . . . they were intended as festival plays for the gods; and, insofar as the poet is in these matters of a more "godlike" disposition than other men, no doubt also as festival plays for the poets" (GM II:7). The invention of gods to bind suffering to sense—but also to express a positive enjoyment of cruelty—resonates strangely and yet inevitably with the relationship between poets and readers. Poets delight in cruelty attributed to the gods; they enjoy the unease that they cause their readers. Likewise, Nietzsche seems to revel in the disorienting effects of his iconoclasm. He delights in making readers squirm, in exposing and rejecting them. But this is not all. The gods, God, constituted a necessary audience:

It was in the same way that the moral philosophers of Greece later imagined the eyes of God looking down upon the moral struggle, upon the heroism and self-torture of the virtuous: the "Herakles of duty" was on a stage and knew himself to be; virtue without a witness was unthinkable for this nation of actors. Surely, that philosopher's invention, so bold and so fateful, which was then first devised for Europe, the invention of "free will," of the absolute spontaneity of man in good and in evil, was devised above all to furnish a right to the idea that the interest of the gods in man, in human virtue, *could never be exhausted.* . . . The entire mankind of antiquity is full of tender regard for "the spectator," as an essentially public, essentially visible world which cannot imagine happiness apart from spectacles and festivals.—And, as aforesaid, even in great *punishment* there is so much that is festive! (GM II:7)

Suddenly, in this unexpected reversal, the reader reappears in the position of the gods, without whose spectatorship being itself would seem empty of significance. But the modern author must make do with imagining a spectatorship composed of readers, not gods. The implicit contrast makes the point. The peculiar satisfaction of taking the gods for one's audience concerns their capacity to serve as spectators of internal struggles, to testify to a purely internal heroism; the European invention of free will decisively privileges this internal drama over all others, and provides a compensation for the suffering it involves.

Here we might read "free will" as analogous to "artistic freedom" or "dramatic license," as the autonomy of art that frees creator and audience from determinism: the certainty of boredom. At the same time, this autonomy frees art to serve as a vehicle for self-expression, the privileged mode of the inwardness comprehended (if not invented) in the notion of free will. But, again, readers are not gods. Above all, as spectators they lack the "aesthetic" detachment of the gods. Not only is the reader's insight less penetrating and less complete, but it stubbornly confuses its inwardness with that of the author. Unlike the emotionally involved reader, the gods are not frightened or disgusted by suffering. For them, there is no need to worry that they will turn away. The imposition inherent in authorship, which so concerns Derrida in his reading of Nietzsche,[22] cannot touch these gods; indeed, what makes them gods is the fact that they find us endlessly interesting and have all the time in the world to expend on the "festival" of existence.

Guilt, we have said, originates for Nietzsche in the creditor/debtor relationship. Punishment begins as one of the creditor's recourses, and the pleasure of inflicting pain is one means of reconciling both parties to life by making suffering meaningful, even pleasurable. Does this mean, then, that the phenomenon of punishment has been explained? Are origins and purpose one and the same? Nietzsche thinks not. The explanatory narratives change, as do their interpreters, until previous notions of " 'meaning' and 'purpose' are necessarily obscured or even obliterated" (GM II:12). Beyond a disclaimer regarding the dynamism of punishment, this section on "will to power" also suggests an implicit account (or defense) of writing. In it, we suggest, Nietzsche approaches a philosophical poetics, a theory of reading, and a response to positivist nightmare/fantasies of an infinite regress of interpretation. Here he contrasts will to power with "adaptation" as active against merely reactive:

> Indeed, life itself has been defined as a more and more efficient inner adaptation to external conditions (Herbert Spencer). Thus the essence of life, its *will to power,* is ignored; one overlooks the essential priority of the spontaneous, aggressive, expansive, form-giving forces that give new interpretations and directions, although "adaptation" follows only after this; the dominant role of the highest functionaries within the organism itself in which the will to life appears active and form-giving is denied. One should recall what Huxley reproached Spencer with—his "administrative nihilism": but it is a question of rather *more* than mere "administration." (GM II:12)

Here, in one sense, we might construe will to power as the vital principle in life, an instinct for growth and durability; but in another, textual sense, will to power defends against a reduction to determined reactivity. In this sense, will to power is like style: not determined by (and therefore not reducible to) utility. It is not an "adaptation" to conception.

And here Nietzsche also distinguishes what is enduring in punishment (custom, act, drama, a sequence of procedures) from what is fluid (meaning, purpose, expectations) in a way that could be applied to the traditional fictions and tropes that he borrows, and the new meanings they acquire, in *Zarathustra.* "Punishment" is for us a crystallized synthesis of meanings; it is now impossible to say exactly *why* people are punished, since "all concepts in which an entire process is semiotically concentrated elude definition; only that which has no history is definable" (GM II:13). Overdetermined by utilities of all kinds, punishment cannot be specified as the origin of guilty conscience. No, Nietzsche argues, "bad conscience" actually originates as the "serious illness man was bound to contract under the stress of the most fundamental change he ever experienced . . . when he found himself enclosed within the walls of society and peace," when "instincts were disvalued and suspended" and his behavior could no longer be guided by his drives. Then, he had to seek "new and, as it were, subterranean gratifications" (GM II:16). Accordingly, he concludes: "All instincts that do not discharge themselves outwardly *turn inward*—this is what I call the *internalization* of man: thus it was that man first developed what was later called his 'soul' " (GM II:16). The inner world, "originally as thin as if it were stretched between two membranes," is enlarged and deepened by this inhibition and internalization (which can be read as commemorated and repeated in the inward turn of writing).

Deprived of an external theater of action and instinct, man "had to turn himself into an adventure, a torture chamber, an uncertain and dangerous wilderness." That man is now sick of himself is the result of this sundering from the animal instincts on which "his strength, joy, and terribleness had rested hitherto." The animal soul turned against itself. And this self-induced malady made humankind "among the most unexpected and exciting lucky throws in the dice game of Heraclitus's 'great child' " (GM II:16). In other words, "the human race" *is* a "throw" or hyperbole; "hyperbole," as we are using the term, names not just a trope or element of style but the mode of our existence, the shape of our project as well. Here is a striking advantage of the convergence of trope and world which is itself a trope for the whole of the *Genealogy.*

If then "the human race" is not a "goal" but a "great promise," it follows that the value of the inward turn (including Nietzsche's inward turn of writing) can be construed in this "arena of instincts." This radical change in our mode of existence was not gradual or organic. Like the discontinuity that typically begins a book, it was a break, a leap, a disaster. It was a hyperbole made possible by violence, by the "blow" of the tyrant subduing. The originary violence of these ruler/organizers is explicitly equated with ("exemplifies," not "is exemplified by") "that terrible artist's egoism that has the look of bronze and knows itself justified to all eternity in its 'work,' like a mother in her child" (GM II:17).

It was not *in* these archaic figures but *because* of them that bad conscience developed. The instinct to freedom was forced into latency; this turning-in-upon-itself of "will to power" Nietzsche calls "*bad conscience*" (GM II:17). But out of the "secret self-ravishment," which is the literary analogue of this internal dynamic, comes the violent hyperbole representing the human estate, and with it the imaginary construct of its opposite, namely, "beauty and affirmation, and perhaps beauty itself" (GM II:18). As we can see, Nietzsche here equates "bad conscience" with that original malady afflicting the human animal. As a writerly illness ("as pregnancy is an illness" [GM II:19]), ascetic self-torture involves a debt owed to ancestors, to parents, and to God. So the debt can never fully be requited, the guilt never fully expiated. The perfect text will never be finished. In Christianity, humanity's guilt before God—the creditor who sacrifices himself for his debtors—raises self-torture to its highest pitch. This God is the ultimate antithesis of instinct and his invention expresses a perversely hyperbolic *will* to be guilty beyond atonement: "What *bestiality of thought* erupts as soon as he is prevented just a little from being a *beast in deed!*" (GM II:22). Even here, Nietzsche imagines the danger of a resurgent nihilism—that "*sickness,* beyond any doubt, the most terrible sickness that has ever raged in man" (GM II:22).

What is "invincibly" horrifying here is the specter of the ultimate perversion of love. What if it is simply too late for divine love to be naturalized or humanized as that sensation of being loved *by life?* But the real abyss lies in the possibility that love—of our kind, of life—is irredeemably perverted by ascetic ideals, and is so fraught with hidden conditions, so given over to compensating for self-hatred, as to be little more than the most seductive version of the ascetic desire to be somewhere else, to be someone else.[23] From this possibility Nietzsche himself must draw back, lest he become frozen in place by an "unnerving sadness," reminiscent of Freud's account of melancholia. Indeed, Nietzsche suggests, nihilism is essentially a form of melancholia: humanity's unresolved grief at the loss of the primary object of its affection—the self.

And yet, he insists, none of this had to be. The Greeks did not use their gods for self-torture. They used their gods to absolve themselves of evil, to characterize themselves as foolish rather than sinful. And when one of their "foolish" number did something terrible, they argued that the sublimity of evil was beyond them, that it could only come from the gods. The ascetic ideal and culture are not necessarily one and the same. But if this is so, how are we to extricate ourselves from "bad conscience"? From our present position within the culture and emotional economy of the ascetic ideal, any attempt to erect a new "temple" necessarily appears to be wantonly, if not apocalyptically destructive. (" 'What are you really doing, erecting an ideal or knocking one down?' I may perhaps be asked. . . . If a temple is to be erected *a temple must be destroyed*" [GM II:24].) Nietzsche's self-directed question might almost be taken as a reply-in-advance to such later commentators on the "end of philosophy" as Heidegger and Derrida.[24] Nietzsche's point is that from within a culture of millennial duration, any fundamental change assumes—for reasons having to do with our perspective—an apocalyptic aspect. We are no more able to judge the meaning (or "value") of such changes in advance than we are able to estimate the value of life. In the case of the ascetic ideal, we read:

> Man has all too long had an "evil eye" for his natural inclinations, so that they have finally become inseparable from his "bad conscience." An attempt at the reverse would *in itself* be possible—but who is strong enough for it?— that is, to wed the bad conscience to all the *unnatural* inclinations, all those aspirations to the beyond, to that which runs counter to sense, instinct, nature, animal, in short all ideals hitherto, which are one and all hostile to life and ideals that slander the world. To whom should one turn today with *such* hopes and demands? (GM II:24)

Here Nietzsche amplifies the interrogative mode: Who indeed—when these hopes and demands look so much like the ascetic wish to be elsewhere, when the hyperbolic "what if?" so closely resembles the ascetic rejection of what we are—is strong enough? How *are* we to take such an

exhortation to overcome what we are in the name of what we are? to choose
between nature and culture, as if they were not one and the same?

Our own "decaying self-doubting present" is probably incapable of producing such a "*redeeming* man of love and contempt" who will

> redeem us not only from the hitherto reigning ideal but also from that which
> was bound to grow out of it, the great nausea, the will to nothingness, nihilism;
> this bell-stroke of noon and of the great decision that liberates the will again
> and restores its goal to the earth and his hope to man; this Antichrist and
> antinihilist; this victor over God and nothingness—he must come one day.
> (GM II:24)

As often elsewhere, so here Nietzsche echoes a biblical prophet—in this
instance St. John at Patmos: "Even so, come quickly."[25] In fact, he very
nearly transgresses this limit, failing to fall silent at the appointed moment:

> But what am I saying? Enough! Enough! At this point it behooves me only to
> be silent; or I shall usurp that to which only one younger, "heavier with fu-
> ture," and stronger than I has a right—that to which only *Zarathustra* has a
> right, *Zarathustra the godless.* (GM II:25)

We noted earlier in our discussion that, although Zarathustra "dies,"
this does not prevent him from speaking—before the end of the book.[26]
What does it mean here, when Nietzsche "falls silent," with Essay Three
yet to come? Announcing the future and being part of it are not the same;
the two may even be incompatible. But having announced the imminent
pregnancy of the future, what remains but to wait silently for parturition?[27]
Jonah discovered that announcement can alter the future, but announcing
it and making it happen are still not the same. In the end, Nietzsche returns
to the split between himself and Zarathustra. It seems that the individual
of his own time, the one sufficiently of the temple to bring it down, cannot
also be the emergent individual—no more than the Moses of the wilderness
could become the "suburban" Moses in the promised land. At this limit,
which is also the limit of what thinking and writing can in and of themselves
do in the present, we come upon the discontinuity (Nietzsche/Zarathustra)
at the heart of the "work." The "work" can be—must be—completed in
the "other." So Nietzsche creates a Zarathustra to serve that purpose; Zarathustra imagines "laughing lions"—disciples unlike any disciple he has
ever had, readers unlike any readers Nietzsche has or has had.

What, we might ask, is this "writing in the mode of silence"? In one
sense, writing *is* a mode of silence, an inwardness that some mistake for
solipsism (in the literary, not the philosophical sense). However, that mode
is in fact (at least in Essay Three) *commentary*, which Nietzsche treats not as
a "safe" mode, a way of "hugging the shore" in Updike's metaphor, but
as a writing at the limit where thought and imagination recoil from the
obduracy of the future. It is the ambiguous mode—Nietzsche and Zarathu-

stra, speech and silence, writing and reading—a "play" at or about the limits. In this mode, hyperbolic "excess" finds expression in the paradoxical task of prophesying what has already been done, which is to say, of investing in the past our own prophetic awareness and of attributing to the past an efficacy with regard to a desperately desired future. In the context of this analysis, Nietzsche's commentary can be seen as a commentary on himself, on himself as Zarathustra, one which internalizes a complex relationship. He attributes to that earlier work a prophetic awareness of what is to come, must come in the *Genealogy*. At the same time, his commentary marks the limits of that work: its need for the supplement of the *Genealogy* to advance and fulfill its prophetic promise.

FIGURES OF FIGURATION FIGURING: ASCETICISM AND COMMENTARY

"What is the Meaning of Ascetic Ideals?"—the final essay in the *Genealogy*—offers itself as a commentary on this passage from the chapter "On Reading and Writing" in *Zarathustra*: "Unconcerned, mocking, violent—thus wisdom wants *us*: . . . she is a woman and always loves only a warrior" (GM III:Epigraph).[28] We do not want wisdom. She wants us, but only on the condition that we are "unconcerned, mocking, and violent," which is to say, that we cast off concern, seriousness, and restraint in a gesture that seems at least to be the opposite of ascetic denial, a kind of Nietzschean sublime. But what does *this* mean? The initial problem in determining the meaning of ascetic ideals is that they have meant so many things:

> In the case of artists they mean nothing or too many things; in the case of philosophers and scholars something like a sense and instinct for the most favorable preconditions of higher spirituality; in the case of women at best one *more* seductive charm, a touch of *morbidezza* in fair flesh, the angelic look of a plump pretty animal; in the physiologically deformed and deranged (the *majority* of mortals) an attempt to see themselves as "too good" for this world, a saintly form of debauch, their chief weapon in the struggle against slow pain and boredom; in the case of priests, the distinctly priestly faith, their best instrument of power, also the "supreme" license for power; in the case of saints, finally, a pretext for hibernation, their *novissima gloriae cupido*, their repose in nothingness ("God"), their form of madness. (GM III:1)

This variety of manifestations is "an expression of the basic fact of the human will, its *horror vacui: it needs a goal*—and it will rather will *nothingness* than not will" (GM III:1). The assertiveness of the will, like an errant hyperbole, wanders in so many directions that we are forced to wonder what the difference between not willing and willing nothingness actually is.[29] "Not willing" cannot merely name a quietism, the most pervasive mask the ascetic ideal wears, for this is no more than the nihilism of an unmitigated human condition. Nietzsche thinks of this, too, as a mask: nothingness in disguise. Perhaps "not willing" is in this context the litotes to the hyperbole of willing "nothingness." As we argue elsewhere,[30] litotes and hyperbole mark perspectival differences at best, and, at worst, mark a distinction that makes no difference. Is the contrast then perhaps to be understood as a pure play of perspectives, like the difference between merely being the fool and laughing at *oneself*, only in this case emptied of all contents—a simple but saving shift in point of view? Will is represented by Nietzsche as a movement that leaves itself open to interpretation as an ascetic transformation, a sublimation: this for that, this into that, flesh into spirit, lower into higher, here into there.

Nietzsche is particularly concerned with the artist, for whom ascetic ideals mean "nothing or too many things," and the philosopher or scholar, for whom they are "a sense and instinct for the most favorable conditions of higher spirituality" (GM III:1). His exemplary artist (at least early on) is of course Wagner, who "pays homage to chastity in his old age," prompting Nietzsche to ask: Why this unnecessary antithesis between chastity and sensuality? and why the failure of *Parsifal* to laugh at itself, to transcend Wagner's own art and overcome the ascetic ideal in self-directed laughter? This "secret laughter of superiority at himself" would have marked the "triumph of his ultimate artist's freedom and artist's transcendence" (GM III:3). As we see here, Nietzsche's own tendency is to separate the artist from the art work. He is, after all, "the womb, the soil, sometimes the dung and manure on which, out of which, it grows" (GM III:4). This origin must be forgotten "if one is to enjoy the work itself. Insight into the origin of a work concerns the physiologists and vivisectionists of the spirit; never the aesthetic man, the artist!" (GM III:4). But, one might ask, who is who here? Earlier, Nietzsche presented himself as a "physiologist" of the spirit. And what is a genealogist but an investigator of origins? But here he seems to be siding with the "aesthetic man" or "artist," who refuses to be concerned with such things and focuses instead on the work like a good (later) formalist. In these terms, however, Wagner is no artist; moreover, his failure is "typical." What are we to make of this?

Literality, the impulse to "real-*ize*" the work through some kind of reduction to world, might usefully be read as a key. Accordingly, the physiologist, like those historians who insist (mistakenly, we would say) that past origins define the present utility of customs and practices, becomes the critical equivalent of a vivisectionist by asserting a literal equivalence of origins and work. The aesthetic individual (one who perceives the world in such and such a way as distinct from one who produces such and such a "thing") becomes a "mere" artist by literalizing the product, that is, by identifying it with the consciousness (or "quality of perception") which produced it. This was Wagner's error:

The poet and creator of *Parsifal* could no more be spared a deep, thorough, even frightful identification with and descent into medieval soul conflicts, a hostile separation from all spiritual height, severity, and discipline, a kind of intellectual *perversity* (if I may be pardoned the word), than can a pregnant woman be spared the repellent and bizarre aspects of pregnancy—which, as aforesaid, must be *forgotten* if one is to enjoy the child. (GM III:4)

Wagner mistakenly identifies with himself, and so literalizes the asceticism he must think and feel in order to write *Parsifal*. For that reason he cannot enjoy the work. He suffers from it, and identifies that suffering with the art he thinks of as its cause. Similarly, the pregnant woman may identify the misery attending pregnancy with the child and consequently be unable to enjoy it. In this way, as Nietzsche sees it, the work is at once a source of the creator's suffering and of its audience's joy. It suggests why almost anyone is better qualified than the creator to appreciate the art work. But does the metaphor work? Is almost anyone better qualified than its mother to enjoy the child?

This metaphor, we suggest, calls attention to its own pregnancy. It casts the whole question of the conception of bodies into the realm of the aesthetic. The child is "taken away" from the mother and appropriated to the "aesthetic man" who confuses it with nothing outside itself. What is at stake here is autochthony—freedom—a growing away from origins sufficient to cancel their authority. More radically, the figure points to the *potentially* autochthonous, self-creating nature of an author, a capacity that extends even to the creation of the artist's body (*the distinct body of the work*), since even the mature sense of one's own body is a creation of sorts.[31] But in Nietzsche's account the artist fails to realize this potential independence. Having created a freedom he is unable to exploit, Wagner chooses (through a fatality the dynamics of which we will discuss momentarily) to re-create his own enslavement. The artist re-creates, in other words, the body of ascetic suffering. What we have in these remarks on Wagner, we think, is a truncated version of Nietzsche's critique of Romantic ascetics/ aesthetics—his account of its power and failure, including (we would add) his own *Zarathustra*.

Generalizing, then, the artist is only prone to confuse the creation with the self that created it, and so to forget what *fiction* is: "If he were it, he would not represent, conceive, and express it: a Homer would not have created an Achilles nor a Goethe a Faust if Homer had been an Achilles or Goethe a Faust" (GM III:4). For the artist above all, fiction is not enough, for no one knows better than the artist how alienating, how self-defeating it can be: "One can understand how he may sometimes weary to the point of desperation of the eternal 'unreality' and falsity of his innermost existence—and that he may well attempt what is most forbidden to him, to lay hold of actuality, for once actually to *be*." Such is "the typical velleity of the artist" (GM III:4). And yet, for Nietzsche, there seems to be a loophole: "Whoever is *completely* and *wholly* an artist [emphasis added] is to all eternity separated from the 'real,' the actual" (GM III:4). Is this to say that whoever is ambiguously, partially, and with reservations an artist may achieve contact with the real *and* preserve some elements of the artist's unrealized freedom of self-creation? Even as Nietzsche seems to envision the possibility of being a physiologist with regard to origins and an "aesthetic man" with regard to present practices and customs, a gap opens up that the genealogy crosses and recrosses by means of the "leap" of hyperbole/litotes. A bridge is provided, and hyperbole and litotes are prevented from canceling each other out. By means of asceticism, they become part of the same structure, which is at once a "historical" origin and the structure of the aesthetic: the figure of figuration figuring.

Why then, in the case of artists, do ascetic ideals mean nothing or so much that it amounts to nothing? Either their identification with them is false, based on a desire to evade the fictional (as in the case of Wagner), or it is a fiction. Such beings as artists cannot stand "independently enough in the world and *against* the world for their changing valuations to deserve attention *in themselves!*" (GM III:5). They need some kind of prop, something outside their relationship with fictions. For Wagner, this prop was Schopenhauer, whose influence raises the more serious question of what it means "when a genuine *philosopher* pays homage to the ascetic ideal." For it was Schopenhauer—"a man and knight of steely eye who had the courage to be himself, who knew how to stand alone" (GM III:5)—whose elevation of music moved Wagner to value it over drama, to see the musician as the mouthpiece of a metaphysical "in itself"—until finally, inevitably, he offered ascetic ideals as the (dis)embodiment of this transcendent otherness.

In Nietzsche's account, "Kant, like all philosophers, instead of envisaging the aesthetic problem from the point of view of the artist (creator), considered art and the beautiful purely from that of the 'spectator,' and unconsciously introduced the 'spectator' into the concept 'beautiful' " (GM III:6). Kant's spectator was no enthusiast devoted to the immediacy of "vivid, authentic experiences, desires, surprises, and delights in the realm of the beautiful," but one above all disinterested, an observer with nothing at stake. (Kant defined the beautiful as that "which gives us pleasure *without interest*" [GM III:6].) In contrast, Stendahl (and Nietzsche) argue that there is no beauty without interestedness. By interpreting the words "without interest" in an extremely "personal" way, on the basis of "one of his most regular experiences" (GM III:6), Schopenhauer becomes an important revisionist of Kant. For him, aesthetic experience counteracts "*sexual* interestedness" and so provides liberation from the "will." Schopenhauer's famous conceptions of will and representation, Nietzsche suggests, were generalizations from his sexual experience:

Schopenhauer described *one* effect of the beautiful, its calming effect on the will—but is this a regular effect? Stendahl, as we have seen, a no less sensual but more happily constituted person than Schopenhauer, emphasizes another effect of the beautiful: "the beautiful *promises* happiness"; to him the fact seems to be precisely that the beautiful *arouses the will* ("interestedness"). And could one not finally urge against Schopenhauer himself that he was quite wrong in thinking himself a Kantian in this matter, that he by no means understood the Kantian definition of the beautiful in a Kantian sense—that he, too, was pleased by the beautiful from an "interested" viewpoint, even from the very strongest, most personal interest: that of a tortured man who gains release from his torture?—And, to return to our first question, "What does it mean when a philosopher pays homage to the ascetic ideal?"—here we get at any rate a first indication: he wants *to gain release from a torture.* (GM III:6)

Nietzsche's view of Schopenhauer's generalization from his sexual experience may indirectly pose the question of his own dependence on the immediacy of the writing experience—and, by analogy, the still more obscure question of the link between writing and sexuality. Kant's definition of the beautiful, with its stress on the pleasures of the spectator, empties life of personal meaning in precisely the same movement in which it renders it most available to philosophical scrutiny. From a writerly point of view, this disinterested spectatorship seems to correspond to the philosopher's assumption of the transparent or disposable nature of the stylistic "supplement" of ideas; what Frege was (more than a century later) in the habit of calling "[mere] coloration" *(Farbung).* Kant's focus on the spectator's point of view to the exclusion of the creator's, inclines toward a devaluing of the creative act, which is not only excluded as a criterion of "meaning," but virtually removed from Kant's scheme.

Nevertheless, Schopenhauer's "interested" disinterestedness raises a fundamental question about the accessibility of personal experience to general statement. What does Schopenhauer say about the beautiful? Is he, in the end, just talking about Schopenhauer? For the moment, Nietzsche leaves the question unanswered. But, as in the case of Wagner, his identification with and critique of Schopenhauer begins to forge a path back to the world from "mere" expressionism. This point is twofold: the philosopher's "objective" contemplation/reading is always interested, always sited, even when this interestedness corresponds with the partialities of philosophy itself; and there is no automatic convergence (or divergence) of self-experience and the general or typical. That relationship must be worked out and worked over. But "interest" is no simple matter. If Schopenhauer *is* any indication, when a philosopher pays homage to the ascetic ideal it means that he wants to gain release from torture. No one, Nietzsche insists, needs to become "gloomy" at the word "torture." Rather, Schopenhauer needed enemies, for all that he deplored them: Hegel, woman, sensuality.

Without them, "Schopenhauer would not have persisted, one may wager on that; he would have run away: but his enemies held him fast, his enemies seduced him ever again to existence; his anger was, just as in the case of the Cynics of antiquity, his balm, his refreshment, his reward, his specific against disgust, his *happiness*" (GM III:7).

So much for Schopenhauer personally. What is typical is his philosopher's "irritation at and rancor against sensuality: Schopenhauer is merely its most eloquent and, if one has ears for this, most ravishing and delightful expression" (GM III:7). But this pose, Nietzsche suggests, masks the underlying meaning of this prejudice and affection for the ascetic ideal: "Every animal—*la bête philosophe*, too—instinctively strives for an optimum of favorable conditions under which it can expend all its strength and achieve its maximal feeling of power" (GM III:7). For the philosopher, marriage and other forms of sensuality are impediments. Ascetic ideals reveal to the philosopher "bridges to *independence*," the "optimum condition for the highest and boldest spirituality. . . . He does not deny 'existence,' he rather affirms *his* existence and *only* his existence" (GM III:7). In Schopenhauer's case (and in Nietzsche's case too), this solipsism is the means of converting asceticism into a mode of strenuous self-affirmation or egotistical sublime, not an "ideal" but an aspect of being.

Similarly, the ascetic ideals of poverty, humility, and chastity are characteristic of "great, fruitful, inventive spirits"—not as virtues!—but as the "most appropriate and natural conditions of their *best* existence" (GM III:8). That *desert*, "where the strong, independent spirits withdraw and become lonely," is not as commonly imagined:

> A voluntary obscurity perhaps; an avoidance of oneself; a dislike of noise, honor, newspapers, influence; a modest job, an everyday job, something that conceals rather than exposes one; an occasional association with harmless, cheerful beasts and birds whose sight is refreshing; mountains for company, but not dead ones, mountains with *eyes* (that is, with lakes); perhaps even a room in a full, utterly commonplace hotel, where one is certain to go unrecognized and can talk to anyone with impunity—that is what "desert" means here. (GM III:8)

This "desert" is, of course, the life out of which Nietzsche—like John, like Jesus—now prosaically emerges. That is the point. This is the desert, not of the extravagances of fiction, but of commonplaces. It is not writing but fiction that conspires with the distractions of sensuality. It is the urge to be elsewhere implicit in the fictional, with its irreducible difference from the real, that prevents Nietzsche from affirming his and only his existence, and yet which answers to its own narcissistic discipline:

> One should listen to how a spirit sounds when it speaks: every spirit has its own sound and loves its own sound. That one, over there, for example, must

be an agitator, that is to say, a hollow head, a hollow pot: whatever goes into him comes back out of him dull and thick, heavy with the echo of great emptiness. This fellow usually speaks hoarsely: has he perhaps *thought* himself hoarse? That might be possible—ask any physiologist—but whoever thinks in *words* thinks as an orator and not as a thinker (it shows that fundamentally he does not think facts, nor factually, but only in relation to facts; that he is really thinking of *himself* and his listeners). A third person speaks importunately, he comes too close to us, he breathes on us—involuntarily we close our mouths, although it is a book through which he is speaking to us: the sound of his style betrays the reason: he has no time to waste, he has little faith in himself, he must speak today or never. A spirit that is sure of itself, however, speaks softly; it seeks concealment, it keeps people waiting. (GM III:8)

There are several things happening and happening to each other in this passage. First, there is the emphasis not on *what* but on *how* something is said as a guide to the inner imperatives that constitute meaning by giving it impetus. There is also the reversal of the immediacy of speech and distance of writing. The orator's "closeness" is aimed at disguising but nevertheless expressing separation from fact; it tells us that everything is mediated by the orator's awareness of the audience, and of the self before that audience. In the third example, not even the distance of reading can disguise the writer's fervent closeness. Here, there is thought without words—a thinking *before* words, Nietzsche seems to imply, a thinking in "facts." All is not "mere" language; and the distinction between "words" and "facts" remains useful, not just because one can think closer or farther from fact, but because "words" and "thoughts" are both aspects of language. Furthermore, to insist on a thinking before words, in facts, is to insist on the continuing possibility of distinguishing between ambiguity and confusion. Nonetheless, it is the "sound of [the] style" that betrays the quality of that thinking, even of thinking in facts. Style brings out the texture, the "interestedness," of the thought.

A philosopher, in Nietzsche's caricature based on Schopenhauer, shuns fame, princes, and women; they do not need to avoid him. His "humility" is an expression of his "maternal" instinct, "the secret love of that which is growing in him," which "directs him toward situations in which he is relieved of the necessity of thinking of *himself*; in the same sense in which the instinct of the *mother* in woman has hitherto generally kept woman in a dependent situation" (GM III:8). This is simple enough: a recurrence of the pregnancy figure. What the philosopher carries within himself—his project and preoccupation—preempts his participation in the things of the world, and places him at a disadvantage like that of the pregnant woman:

They ask for little enough, these philosophers: their motto is "he who possesses is possessed"—*not,* as I must say again and again, from virtue, from a laudable will to contentment and simplicity, but because their supreme lord demands this of them, prudently and inexorably: he is concerned with one thing alone, and assembles and saves up everything—time, energy, love, and interest—only for that one thing. (GM III:8)

So now the matter is not so simple. Who is this "supreme lord" who sounds so much like the "lord and master," father, husband, and husbander of "time, energy, love, and interest"? It would seem that he is, at once, the child being carried, the cherished object loved by life herself, and the begetter of himself on himself. In short, Nietzsche's philosopher makes *himself* pregnant. But how? We might helpfully ask the generative question in rhetorical terms: Is it dominance or subjection that matters here, hyperbole or litotes?

This kind of man does not like to be disturbed by enmities, nor by friendships; he easily forgets and easily despises. He thinks it in bad taste to play the martyr; "to *suffer* for truth"—he leaves that to the ambitious and the stage heroes of the spirit and to anyone else who has the time for it (the philosophers themselves have something to *do* for the truth). They use big words sparingly; it is said that they dislike the very word "truth": it sounds too grandiloquent. (GM III:8)

It would appear, Nietzsche argues, that the philosopher is not merely aping, playacting at female pregnancy, but actually competing with it in a serious way. We take the sign of this seriousness to be his restraint. But is this—Nietzsche's poker-faced protestations aside—a species of self-dramatization? Is "pregnant with truth" less "grandiloquent" than "suffering for truth"? For Nietzsche, the philosopher's "restraint" will seldom appear as an unequivocal value:

As for the "chastity" of philosophers, finally, this type of spirit clearly has its fruitfulness somewhere else than in children; perhaps it also has the survival of its name elsewhere, its little immortality (philosophers in India expressed themselves even more immodestly: "Why should he desire progeny whose soul is the world?"). There is nothing in this of chastity from any kind of ascetic scruple or hatred of the senses, just as it is not chastity when an athlete or jockey abstains from women ["No sex before a fight?"]: it is rather the will of their dominating instinct, at least during their periods of great pregnancy. Every artist knows what a harmful effect intercourse has on states of great spiritual tension and preparation; those with the greatest power and surest instincts do not need to learn this by experience, by unfortunate experience [?!]—their "maternal" instinct ruthlessly disposes of all other stores and accumulations of energy, of animal vigor, for the benefit of the evolving work: the greater energy then *uses up* the lesser. (GM III:8)

Here withholding and propagation appear as false opposites. Restraint is a practical means of accumulating energy for the moment of ruthless and total discharge in giving life. So Nietzsche interprets Schopenhauer's aestheticism as an explosion of sexual energy:

> the sight of the beautiful obviously had upon him the effect of releasing the chief energy of his nature (the energy of contemplation and penetration), so that this exploded and all at once became the master of his consciousness. This should by no means preclude the possibility that the sweetness and plenitude peculiar to the aesthetic state might be derived precisely from the ingredient of "sensuality" (just as the "idealism" of adolescent girls derives from that source)—so that sensuality is not overcome by the appearance of the aesthetic condition, as Schopenhauer believed, but only transfigured and no longer enters consciousness as sexual excitement. (GM III:8)

So it could be said that the "saving up" of the "supreme lord" nevertheless culminates in this ejaculatory "explosion" by means of which the energy of "contemplation and penetration" masters Schopenhauer's consciousness. Indeed, not only are the woman-hating Schopenhauer's powers of penetration exposed, but Nietzsche also implicitly represents him as an adolescent girl and pregnant mother. Perhaps our impulse may be either to look askance at this extraordinary passage or (defensively) to make clear what Nietzsche is "really" saying—in effect, to rescue him from hyperbolic excess. Neither response seems quite right, however; for although the passage is violently parodic, it is also quite serious. Nietzsche succeeds in breaking through to the "fantasia" of a certain kind of philosophy that underlies its "style."

The ambiguity of Nietzsche's figurative treatment allows, and even demands, that while abstaining from women does make a difference, it is nonetheless not asceticism—because philosophers are not abstaining from what they really want. And what *do* they want? and what *is* this progeny whose birth must be indefinitely postponed by refusing to beget it on woman (who is, in any case, already pregnant)? Nietzsche's description of sexuality seems to be dominated by a sense that there is only so much, and not enough to go around; that only by storing up and accumulating can "time, energy, love, and interest" somehow exceed itself; that it can be more by being saved rather than spent.[32] "Enough" is enough to complete a circuit, a system of self-begetting, self-conception, an economy of perpetual dissemination—all of which point to a fundamental unwillingness to accept the limits of bodies, the limits that sexual differentiation imposes even on "conception."

If this way of reading Nietzsche presents his discourse as a usurpatory metaphorics of maternity, one might ask what a metaphorics of paternity would look like. As we have already seen in our discussions of "fatherlessness," he came to see his project at least partially in this light. In the *Genealogy,* commentary as begetting is opposed to conceiving (as in the fictional *Zarathustra*); indeed, it appears that he "begets" this essay parthogenetically in the form of commentary on his own work. Here Nietzsche is ambiguously one of the philosophers—an ascetic—and a commentator upon them at the same time: as it were, a fertile and fecund hermaphrodite of the spirit. That "a certain asceticism, a serene and cheerful continence with the best will, belongs to the most favorable conditions of supreme spirituality, and is also among its most natural consequences" helps to explain why "philosophers have always discussed the ascetic ideal with a certain fondness" (GM III:9). However, further investigation reveals that, for historical reasons, this bond is even closer than this passage would suggest: "It was only on the leading-strings of this ideal that philosophy learned to take its first steps on earth" (GM III:9). Without such a disguise, Nietzsche argues, the philosopher would have been unable to be himself; his objectivity and neutrality would have contravened the demands of morality and conscience. What we value today is, in a sense, the reverse of what was valued before: "All good things were formerly bad things; every original sin has turned into an original virtue" (GM III:9). For most of human history, under the sway of the "morality of mores," values were different, even antithetical.

Contemplation, Nietzsche argues, had to disguise itself to avoid being either feared or despised; it had to appear in ambiguous form "with an evil heart and often an anxious head" (GM III:10). The contemplatives of the "frightful ages" understood that by controlling pain, even as it was inflicted upon themselves, they could turn even the social stigma against them to their advantage, finally arrogating to themselves powers that once belonged only to the gods: "As men of frightful ages, they did this by using frightful means: cruelty toward themselves, inventive self-castigation—this was the principal means these power hungry hermits and innovators of ideas required to overcome the gods and traditions in themselves, so as to be able to *believe* in their own innovations" (GM III:10). Thus, on this view, asceticism was a means of securing a belief in oneself by stimulating awe in others. Belief in one's own innovations is always blocked by internalized contemporary mores and values. How can our creations, our "innovations," be promoted and valorized as the verities we receive from without? How can they be "naturalized"? Ascetic self-punishment, so much at odds with the typical attachment to ease and sensual pleasure, is understood as a sign of "possession" by a higher power or force—of "inspiration" in a literal sense.

If the philosopher uses asceticism as a means to an end without *really* being ascetic, however, the case of the genuine priest is quite different. For him the question of asceticism is deadly serious; his very existence depends upon it. The key to priestly asceticism is the valuation placed on life. The priest opposes life—nature, the world, becoming—to something else that opposes life, and demands that life oppose or deny itself. He treats life as the wrong road; and wherever he can, he "compels acceptance of *his* evaluation of existence" (GM III:11).

What does such a "monstrous" mode of evaluation mean? According to Nietzsche, since the ascetic priest is antipropagative yet repeatedly crops up throughout history, it can only mean that asceticism is, all appearances to the contrary notwithstanding, somehow in the *interest of life itself*:

> For an ascetic life is a self-contradiction: here rules a *ressentiment* without equal, that of an insatiable instinct and power-will that wants to become master not over something in life but over life itself, over its most profound, powerful, and basic conditions; here an attempt is made to employ force to block up the wells of force; here physiological well-being itself is viewed askance, and especially the outward expression of this well-being, beauty and joy; while pleasure is felt and sought in ill-constitutedness, decay, pain, mischance, ugliness, voluntary deprivation, self-mortification, self-flagellation, self-sacrifice. All this is in the highest degree paradoxical: we stand before a discord that *wants* to be discordant, that *enjoys* itself in this suffering and even becomes more self-confident and triumphant the more its own presupposition, its physiological capacity for life *decreases*. "Triumph in the ultimate agony": the ascetic ideal has always fought under this hyperbolic sign; in this enigma of seduction, in this image of torment and delight, it recognized its brightest light, its salvation, its ultimate victory. (GM III:11)

This passage might call to mind Harold Bloom's adaptation of Nietzsche's thought to the task of describing the poetical character.[33] Bloom holds that the poet is distinguishable from other people by a greater rebellion against the necessity of death. Here, we suggest, the origin of the ascetic negation of life seems apposite to the poet's obstinate denial of death's final dominion. If the poet is denied this one thing (that is, to be an exception to the rule of death), then the ascetic, by rejecting all else, forces the surrender of what is withheld. In this context, the "ultimate" agony of deprivation is the "hyperbolic sign" that the "ultimate victory" of satisfaction is at hand. On this view, ultimacy is radical, absolute, and the essence of sublimity, in which ultimate dearth and ultimate plenitude are essentially the same. It is here, at the heart of ascetic psychology and practice, that hyperbole and litotes are linked, and become rhetorically interchangeable.

The ascetic refuses the "gift" of life until a certain condition is met. Perhaps this stance invites characterization as "regressive." It may be reminiscent of the child who, by refusing substitute satisfactions, tries to coerce parent into meeting a particular desire. The child tries to seduce authority into a contract. But who, in the case of the adult ascetic, is the authority to be seduced? Perhaps, Nietzsche suggests, God (the cosmic "cause"), who appears at times to be seduced into covenants by—not in spite of—the excesses of humankind. And in at least one of its aspects, the ascetic "contract" resembles the "agreement" imposed by the writer on the unseen, unconsenting reader.

Perhaps the foregoing discussion may help to explain Nietzsche's interest in distinguishing the priest's ascetic attempt to master *life* itself from the philosopher's more comprehensible attempt to master something *in* life. For the former, "mastery" of life means changing the rules; for the latter, it means learning to accept them as one's own. The priestly ascetic, by embodying a sublimity based on a capacity to endure pain and suffering, seeks to make them the locus of value. Why, Nietzsche asks, should sublimity not be based on a superior capacity to accept and affirm—even revel in—pleasure as well as suffering?

Previously established religious types of the ascetic ideal—sorcerer, soothsayer, priest—served as the necessary masks of the philosopher, as the very precondition of his existence. His withdrawn and world-denying pose is the result of the conditions of philosophy's emergence, of a necessary "ascetic self-misunderstanding." But it is by no means clear that the butterfly philosophy is yet ready to emerge fully from the priestly/ascetic caterpillar form it has long taken. Indeed, if philosophy is tied to asceticism both by a disposition to higher spirituality and by history, it is not easy to imagine what a non-ascetic philosophy would look like; nor is it apparent, even if we could find some other way to believe in what we ourselves have made, that we would be inclined to call it "philosophy."

We have tried to suggest that the litotes/hyperbole connection made here may provide a helpful basis for considering the reversibility of perspectives, including the inside-outside of Romantic internalization. In this very connection, it is significant that the next section of the *Genealogy* is on internalization. What, Nietzsche wonders there, if such a will to contradiction, to the antinatural, is moved to philosophize? It looks for error where the will to life posits truth; it renounces the senses, even reason, in order to conclude: "There is a realm of truth and being, but reason is excluded from it" (GM III:12). This recognition of ascetic reversals should not, however, be taken as an opportunity to achieve an impossible "contemplation without interest." Rather, the future "objectivity" of the intellect will reside in the "ability to control one's Pro and Con and to dispose of them, so that one knows how to employ a variety of perspectives and affective interpretations in the service of knowledge."

> Henceforth, my dear philosophers, let us be on guard against the dangerous old conceptual fiction that posited a "pure, will-less, painless, timeless knowing subject"; let us guard against the snares of such contradictory concepts as "pure reason," "absolute spirituality," "knowledge in itself": these always demand that we should think of an eye that is completely unthinkable, an eye turned in no particular direction, in which the active and interpreting

forces, through which alone seeing becomes seeing *something*, are supposed
to be lacking; these always demand of the eye an absurdity and a nonsense.
There is *only* a perspective seeing, *only* a perspective "knowing"; and the *more*
affects we allow to speak about one thing, the *more* eyes, different eyes, we can
use to observe one thing, the more complete will our "concept" of this thing,
our "objectivity," be. But to eliminate the will altogether, to suspend each
and every affect, supposing we were capable of this—what would that mean
but to *castrate* the intellect? (GM III:12)

It has been observed repeatedly that Nietzsche is not claiming that the
accumulation of perspectives adds up to a definitive picture of "the thing
in itself."[34] He is still pleading for partiality, sitedness, interestedness as
valuable and necessary components of knowledge. There is, he argues, no
individual insight, observation, or formulation that escapes the limits of
perspective. Nevertheless, certain aspects of the formulation suggest the
same kind of underlying certainty of reference, buried in a discourse of
perspectivism, for which we (elsewhere) challenge Alexander Nehamas.[35]
In this passage we find something evasive in its dependence on eye/object
terminology; that is, on its own perspective. Sight is a sense intrinsically
dependent on perspective, and invoking it lends strong support to a perspectival view of knowledge; but sight is hardly the only sited sense. Other
senses might well support different conceptions of knowledge.[36]

Even more fundamentally, the perspective of the passage is that of sur-
veying an object from without. This serves the purpose of forestalling the
otherwise very difficult question: "How do we know how or even that various perspectives are related?" The answer is so simple that the question
need not arise: "With reference to the same object." Perspectives, in this
self-consuming rhetoric, are always *of* something, always views directed toward an object independent of perspectives—the very thesis perspectivism
contests, displaces, or seeks to set aside.

But Nietzsche is also moving here toward a further consideration of the
relationship between philosophy, asceticism, and the body for which the
question of perspectivism is potentially very important. The privileged, will-
less, external perspective of philosophy's "old conceptual fictions" was designed to secure a certain idea, image, or "experience" of the body as quasi-
object. If, rather than a spatial and external perspective, one were to adopt
a temporal or internal perspective (whatever that might mean[37])—as one
views from within, for instance—the unfolding work of literature, the unity
of the body as object, is challenged: and with it, the dependence of classical
philosophy (for its own coherence in disposing of that body in a certain
way). The multiplicity of perspectives that specify an object may fragment
the self thought to have all of them. The nature of the control that we
exercise over the play of perspectives, and its relationship to the nature of
our perception and control over the body, emerges, we think, at this point.

For the moment, however, Nietzsche is content to explain how it is that a nonpropagative asceticism can appear over and over again in the course of history. The appearance in asceticism of "life against life" can only be that: an appearance. In fact, "*the ascetic ideal springs from the protective instinct of a degenerating life*"; it points to a "partial physiological obstruction and exhaustion against which the deepest instincts of life, which have remained intact, continually struggle with new expedients and devices" (GM III:13). The ascetic ideal is one of these: "The case is therefore the opposite of what those who reverence this ideal believe: life wrestles in it and through it with death and *against* death; the ascetic ideal is an artifice for the preservation of life" against disgust, exhaustion, the desire for the end (GM III:13). Like Bloom's poet, the ascetic priest incarnates the "desire to be different, to be in a different place." The strength and intensity of this desire "is the chain that holds him captive so that he becomes the tool for the creation of more favorable conditions for being here and being man." This power enables him "to persuade to existence the whole herd of the ill-constituted, disgruntled, underprivileged, unfortunate, and all who suffer of themselves" (GM III:13). It is not clear whether it is the ascetic priest's self-understanding or our complacent expectations that get overturned here.[38] Nietzsche's readers, including the higher men, are drawn on by his "promise," "persuaded to existence" by the appearance of a new, iconoclastic "gospel."

"Man," Nietzsche tells us, "is *the* sick animal." "Man" is at once the most daring and the sickliest of animals, vexing himself so that his "own restless energies never leave him in peace, so that his future digs like a spur into the flesh of every present" (GM III:13). Sickliness has become the norm, he insists; and he emphasizes the need to honor and protect from infection those few who are still healthy. It is not the fear of man, of "evil" (which is to say, of strength, health, and confidence), that is the greatest danger. It is *nausea* that threatens the species (a nausea which, interestingly enough, has been identified by Sontag and others with *interpretation,* that most modern of writerly activities). In Nietzsche's account, if nausea and pity were to unite, it would beget a "last will," or nihilism. "Where," he laments, "does one not encounter that veiled glance which burdens one with a profound sadness, that inward-turned glance of the born failure which betrays how such a man speaks to himself—that glance which is a sigh! 'If only I were someone else,' sighs this glance: 'but there is no hope of that. I am who I am: how could I ever get free of myself? And yet—I *am sick of myself!*' " (GM III:14). Here nausea, figuration, and the urge to originality (which so often masquerades as a desire to be fully oneself) are all knotted together. But now not even the urge to be elsewhere can sustain itself; for even that requires a measure of faith in oneself.

These sufferers, bearers of *ressentiment* and "physiologically unfortunate," hate the well-constituted and desire revenge; they try to poison the consciences of the fortunate with their misery by making them feel shame. Nor should the well-constituted allow themselves to be seduced by the lure of pity into becoming nurses and physicians to the sickly. The higher should not be reduced to an instrument of the lower. Indeed, Nietzsche suggests, the situation requires doctors who are themselves sick: the priests. "Dominion over suffering" is his; he too must be sick of himself, profoundly related to the sick. He despises rather than hates; he knows how to feign superiority, to make fear look like restraint. He makes the healthy sick and the sickly tame. In addition to protecting the herd against the healthy, he protects the herd against itself. It is natural to seek a cause for suffering in order to vent affect on the "guilty"; this effort aims to establish a cause and effect relation. But the priest answers: "You yourself are to blame," and thus alters the direction of *ressentiment* (GM III:15). In Nietzsche's view, then, sinfulness is not a "fact," but rather an "interpretation of a fact—namely of physiological depression" (GM III:16). That someone feels guilty is no more proof of guilt than feeling good is proof of health:

> When someone cannot get over a "psychological pain," that is *not* the fault of his "psyche" but, to speak crudely, more probably even that of his belly (speaking crudely, to repeat, which does not mean that I want to be heard crudely or understood crudely).—A strong and well-constituted man digests his experiences (his deeds and misdeeds included) as he digests his meals, even when he has to swallow some tough morsels. If he cannot get over an experience and have done with it, this kind of indigestion is as much physiological as is the other—and often in fact, merely a consequence of the other. (GM III:16)

Just how "crudely" should Nietzsche be understood here? Is he suggesting that perhaps we cannot so simply reduce psychology to physiology after all, and that they are complementary as well as antithetical? And if we can attribute psychological pain to the belly, it is indeed in part as a corrective. It is not a "materialism" (Nietzsche's cryptic aside: "With such a conception one can . . . still be the sternest opponent of all materialism"), because this "physiology" is actually a "textualism" or a "tropology" or a "style."

In any case, the priest is not a true physician, because he treats only the discomfort and not the cause. His gift for the alleviation of suffering, his refinement and subtlety, is in guessing what stimulant affects will—at least for a time—overcome depression, exhaustion, and melancholy. The main concern of religion has been to fight an epidemic weariness. The priest combats the "physiological inhibition" (GM III:17) affecting his flock first, by reducing life to its lowest point, bereft of love or hate—to a selflessness akin to self-hypnosis. Renouncers of life may actually free themselves from physiological depression, but the crucial point is that this state is not attained by moral means: "For the man of knowledge has no duties" (GM III:17).

A more common means for dealing with displeasure is mechanical activity, or petty pleasure—including, in some cases, the pleasure of giving pleasure: "good deeds." The priest's "love thy neighbor" is a small dose of will to power, allowing a slight, compensatory sense of superiority (GM III:18). These are the priest's "innocent" means of dealing with displeasure; his "guilty" ones all involve some kind of "orgy of feeling," or enthusiasm, achieved by exploiting the sense of guilt. Thus the invention of sin was the greatest event in the history of the "sick soul," and the most dangerous artifice of priestly interpretation. The sufferer must see that he causes his own suffering, and "he must understand his suffering as a *punishment*" (GM III:20). This will to misunderstanding (to misreading) makes life interesting again; it creates a hunger for the pain of contrition, for conscience.

Later, such orgies of feeling make the sick sicker. They lead to physiological and mental disturbances. We know that the priestly treatment has not worked because the sickness—not just spiritual sickness but physiological debility (hysteria, epilepsy, and venereal disease) continue to spread (GM III:21): "The ascetic priest has ruined psychical health (which is also physiological health) wherever he has come to power; consequently he has also ruined taste *in artibus et litteris*" (GM III:22). Nietzsche complains of the vanity of the early Christians, who said "we have no need of the classical tradition, we have our own book"—one which Nietzsche sneeringly describes as a book of "legends, letters of apostles, and apologetic tracts" (GM III:22). The bumptiousness of Christianity is typified by Luther, whom Nietzsche thinks of as a "lout" with no comprehension of good manners (GM III:22). Despite its apparent digressiveness, the point being made is an important one. It makes the leap from physiology to a "body of books" or canon, and implies a connection between the Christian ascetic's disregard of the body and his lack of appreciation for the canon or body of culture.

The ascetic ideal, then, is a totalizing interpretation—a closed system that not even science can counter: indeed, of which "science" is itself an instance. Yet, Nietzsche insists, science is the noblest form of the ascetic ideal. Where it is not, it is self-narcosis (GM III:23). Even those unbelievers among philosophers and scholars, the would-be counteridealists who fancy themselves the enemies of the ascetic ideal, are merely the ascetics of "truth." Their faith and strength of self-denial remains absolute: "*They still have faith in truth*" (GM III:24).[39] No European has yet confronted and known from experience the Minotaur represented by the idea that "nothing is true, everything is permitted" (GM III:24). Like science, modern scholarship, viewed in this light, is renunciation, refusing as it does to affirm or deny, to interpret. This turning away is also a mode of sensual denial. Scholars and philosophers alike are constrained by their faith in truth as a metaphysical value. The question of how to "justify" truth does not arise,[40] because ascetic religion will not allow it any more than it will allow the question of how to "justify" God. Deny God, however, and the problem of "truth"—at least experimentally—is called into question (GM III:24). Asceticism and science thus rest on the same foundation: the overestimation of truth—the belief that its value is inestimable, that it can be universally and objectively attached to states of "the self" and "the world."

Art, however, in which "the *lie* is sanctified and the *will to deception* has a good conscience" (GM III:25), is, as Plato recognized, much more opposed to the ascetic ideal than science. Putting oneself at the disposal of the ascetic ideal is the greatest corruption for an artist; but, as we saw in the case of Wagner, it is common—for no one is more corruptible than the artist (GM III:25). "Physiologically" speaking, science requires the same "impoverishment of life" as does asceticism. Science belittles humankind; it holds up this self-contempt as its most serious claim to self-respect (GM III:25). The only *real* enemies of the ascetic ideal today are its "comedians," who "arouse mistrust of it" (*GM* III:27). Even atheism contains a remnant of the will to truth; in fact, it is the culmination of two thousand years of asceticism that denies itself the lie involved in a belief in God. For atheism emerges out of the privileging of "truth" and "truthfulness," which the Judaeo-Christian tradition sponsored. Thus, it could be said that Christian morality has conquered the Christian God. Nietzsche attributes this apparent paradox to "the confessional subtlety of the Christian conscience translated and sublimated into the scientific conscience, into intellectual cleanliness at any price." This has been Europe's "longest and bravest self-overcoming" (GM III:27).

Now, however, it remains for Christian morality to be overcome—which can only happen when it finally comes to pose for itself the question: " 'What is the meaning of all will to truth?' " (GM III:27). It may well be not only that Nietzsche's uncanny suggestion is that "truth" once understood—that is, "conscious of itself as a *problem*" (GM III:27)—will not only undermine morality itself over the next two hundred years, but moreover that this prospect is both terrible *and* hopeful:

> As the will to truth thus gains self-consciousness—there can be no doubt of that—morality will gradually *perish* now: this is the great spectacle in a hundred acts reserved for the next two centuries in Europe—the most terrible, most questionable, and perhaps the most hopeful of all spectacles.—(GM III:27)

This perspective may refigure the shape of "moral philosophy" after the

Holocaust. Philosophers as diverse as Bernard Williams and Michel Foucault, Martha Nussbaum and Jean-François Lyotard, Walter Benjamin and Richard Rorty have begun to suspect that "the moral point of view" *simpliciter* may be *the* problem rather than a solution. It is not merely that morality—conceived as the search for action-guiding principles—is too "thin" to do any useful work. Rather, the suspicion is now emerging that *im*morality may well be morality's Siamese twin, just as the irrational may be the flip side of rationality. The suspicion (that is, the "truth") is now dawning that we cannot have the one without the other. The horrific insight is dawning that whatever gave us the electric light bulb *necessarily* also gave us the electric chair! Our will to truth virtually assures—as we are beginning to learn from fetal viability technology—that whatever *can* be thought *will* be thought; that whatever *can* be tried *will* be tried; that whatever *can* be done *will* be done. For "someday, if there is a someday, we will have to learn that evil thinks of itself as good, that it could not have made such progress in the world unless people planned and performed it in all conscience."[41]

All of this is captured quintessentially in the image of that man in the glass booth in a courtroom in Jerusalem in 1962, who appealed—and we mean *thoughtfully*—to Kant's *Critique of Practical Reason* to justify his actions: Adolf Eichmann explaining his *duty* to carry out "the final solution to the Jewish question."

Nietzsche's claim that "morality will *perish* now" through "a hundred acts reserved for the next two centuries in Europe" is "terrible," of course, for those who think that without the moral point of view there is no defense against encroaching madness, no defense against nihilism. However, for those who have come to see "through those hundred acts" that morality itself has been invoked, necessarily, for the slaughter of millions of innocents, for them liberation from the moral point of view may well be "the most hopeful of spectacles." Indeed, as Milton passionately argued two centuries before Nietzsche, "good" and "evil" cannot be separated by edict, but rather only through the most excruciating and painstaking exertion of all that we are:

> Good and evil we know in the field of this world grow up together almost inseparably; and the knowledge of good is so involved and interwoven with the knowledge of evil, and in so many cunning resemblances hardly to be discerned, that those confused seeds which were imposed on Psyche as an incessant labor to cull out and sort asunder, were not more intermixed. It was out of the rind of one apple tasted, that knowledge of good and evil, as two twins cleaving together, leaped forth into the world.[42]

Nietzsche addresses his "readers," as yet unknown (perhaps yet to be born), in order to say that in us, "will to truth" becomes conscious of itself as a problem. However, "will to truth" also names Nietzsche's desire to find a path back to the world from the fictions of *Zarathustra*. The *Genealogy* is the process in and by which that desire is problematized and embodied as self-questioning—problematized as an aspect of his own project that answers to the will to truth.

In his conclusion, Nietzsche argues that "apart from the ascetic ideal, man, the human *animal*, had no meaning so far" (GM III:28). He suffered from this lack of meaning, the absence of an answer to the question "why man?" But humanity found meaning in suffering by inventing guilt to answer the question: "Why do we suffer?" Humankind created meaning, and hence a capacity to will, thus closing the door on suicidal nihilism. Despite the fact that the species suffered even more deeply from guilt, the will itself was saved; humankind could at least will *something*:

> We can no longer conceal from ourselves *what* is expressed by all that willing which has taken its direction from the ascetic ideal: this hatred of the human, and even more of the animal, and more still of the material, this horror of the senses, of reason itself, this fear of happiness and beauty, this longing to get away from all appearance, change, becoming, death, wishing, from longing itself—all this means—let us dare to grasp it—*a will to nothingness*, an aversion to life, a rebellion against the most fundamental presuppositions of life; but it is and remains a *will*! . . . And, to repeat in conclusion what I said at the beginning: man would rather will *nothingness* than *not* will.—(GM III:28)

We see the circularity of the *Genealogy* in this final observation, which suggests (among other things) the repetitive nature of commentary, its nature as a rebounding from limits. Indeed, we would say, it suggests a will to write against a silent void—to write over rather than to write nothing at all. For silence is the literary equivalent of death, an acquiescence to nothingness. In this context, the invention of guilt involves many things, many of which concern the philosopher/writer. It necessarily involves an "otherwise" or "elsewhere," and implies a someone or something that punishes, with whom a contract or bargain or act of identification can be made. Death in particular and suffering in general, are understood as punishment; and asceticism is a means of identifying with the punisher.[43] Will springs up as the measure of a human excess beyond life, the hyperbolic complement of the litotic "elsewhere" of death.

Viewed in this way, asceticism exhibits a hyperbolic inherent in mimesis. It is not just an attempt to imitate, but to exceed the punisher in harshness—and Nietzsche's project in the *Genealogy* is as much a critique of mimesis as a definition of our mode of contact with the world as it is a critique of philosophy (which it purports to be as well). "Metaphysics" can be viewed as acting or speaking or thinking as if there were someone or something out there with whom or with which the author might strike a bargain. Nietzsche persistently explores this "blind" relationship, using all means at his command of the reader/writer relations. Writing for "no one," or for friends as yet "unknown," he denies that there is anyone out there whose assent can be purchased by a self-imposed limitation. However, in writing as he does, he willingly risks becoming the avatar of nihilism; for the moment in which we are stripped of our traditional defenses, however injurious they have become, is also the moment in which the chances of our succumbing are greatest.

NOTES

1. A different, fuller version of this essay appears as chap. 5 of our *Nietzsche's Case: Philosophy as/and Literature* (New York: Routledge, Chapman and Hall, 1993). A great deal of the discussion that follows is parasitic on the pages and chapters that function as the silent backdrop for this essay.

2. There is a feature of undecidability which tethers thought inseparably to style in Nietzsche's published writings, an undecidability that challenges closure at every turn. In the case of *Zur Genealogie der Moral* Nietzsche's subtitle will give the careful reader pause; for one might still wonder what to make of the fact that it is subtitled "a polemic" (*Eine Streitschrift*) when it is the one work of his whose drift and argument is recognizable, even a touch familiar. Even the title itself is often mistranslated simply as *The Genealogy of Morals*. Yet Nietzsche's title does not begin with the definite article. Had he wanted to convey *the* genealogy of morals, the book's title would have been *Die Genealogie der Moral*. Instead, *zur* in the title functions at the same time as a preposition and an article. The *zu* of *zur* suggests either the English preposition "toward" or the preposition "on" (in some specific contexts even "to" or "for"); and the concluding letter "r" is a contraction of the German definite (dative case) "*der*" ("the"). It is undecidable in principle, therefore, whether the preposition "toward" or "on" was intended by Nietzsche. At best the title of Nietzsche's text thus might be either *Toward the Genealogy of Morals* or *On the Genealogy of Morals*, but certainly not *The Genealogy of Morals*. Walter Kaufmann, incidentally, seemed to be quite conscious of this difficulty, for he translated the title *On the Genealogy of Morals* in his *Basic Writings* edition of some of Nietzsche's works, having earlier translated the same title as *Toward the Genealogy of Morals* in the selections he included in the *Viking Portable Nietzsche*. This undecidable difference between the prepositions "toward" and "on" in Nietzsche's title is not without significance, because "on the genealogy of morals" suggests a topic upon which one is remarking; whereas "toward the genealogy of morals" does not imply the prior existence of the subject upon which Nietzsche is remarking. The one preposition ("toward") suggests that Nietzsche is working in the direction of the genealogy of morals in a way that the preposition "on" does not suggest. Indeed, the preposition *zu*, which always takes the dative case, implies direction as often as not, as in *zum Bahnhof*, when one is going "to the railroad station." But to repeat and underscore the two points made here: (1) whatever the prepositional intent of *zu* in *Zur Genealogie der Moral*, the title cannot bear the substitution of the definite article ("the"); and, (2) it is undecidable whether *zur* means to convey "toward" or "on" the genealogy of morals. The pro-

visional, tentative, and future-directed character of some of Nietzsche's other sub-
titles during this period lead us to prefer "toward" to "on."

3. The book from which this essay derives considers these questions yoked as
one. The title of our book, *Nietzsche's Case: Philosophy as/and Literature*, is itself intended to capture, underscore, and reinscribe these essential tensions, the essential
ambiguity inscribed in the expression "Nietzsche's Case." By "Nietzsche's case" we
mean both the case Nietzsche prosecutes, his critiques of our shared tradition, as
well as the case Nietzsche himself *is*. In the first sense, "Nietzsche's case" points
beyond the philosopher's brief, beyond even its author, to the objects the brief
interrogates—traditional religion, philosophy, and morality. In the second sense,
"Nietzsche's case" is token-reflexive; it interrogates its subject, the proper name
"Nietzsche." Put differently, if Nietzsche has given us a new sense of the genealogy
of our shared tradition, then he has also insinuated a genealogy of that genealogy,
one which points us back to its origin. So, while unraveling the greatness of
Nietzsche's philosophical achievement we aspire at the same time, by interrogating
its voice, its authority, its authorship, to unravel the unconscious and involuntary
memoir it constitutes.

4. This is our conclusion in chaps. 1–4 of *Nietzsche's Case*.

5. For purposes of exposition and analysis, we are treating Zarathustra's *Werk* as
Nietzsche's "work." The primary textual basis for conflating Nietzsche and Zarathustra here is that Nietzsche has Zarathustra say in "The Sign"—the closing "chapter" of *Thus Spoke Zarathustra*: "My suffering and my pity for suffering—what does
it matter? Am I concerned with *happiness*? I am concerned with my *work* [*Werk;* in
italics]." These words precede the book's inverse epiphany: his animals draw near,
his hour has come (he says), *his* morning, *his* day, is breaking: "Rise now, rise, thou
great noon!" (which, we could remember, is the moment of the briefest shadow,
end of the longest error, Nietzsche will later tell us in *Twilight of the Idols*).

What is remarkable in the conclusion of "The Sign" is Nietzsche's use of the
German *Werk* for "work." Ordinarily, "my work" is "*meine Arbeit*." Work, in the more
standard German usage, is *Arbeit*, not *Werk* (compare *Arbeit macht frei*, the horrific
slogan that greeted all "newcomers" to Germany's death camps)—although in
some idiomatic contexts the noun *Werk* is appropriate. God's work alone is *Werk* that
is not *Arbeit*; and, importantly for our purposes, Zarathustra's *Werk* may be regarded
as his "work" in the sense of producing a literary corpus, the other standard sense
of the word *Werk*. His (i.e., Zarathustra's) work is his literary production, or, alter-
natively, it is his creation of a new world. This shift from "readerly" to "writerly"
perspectives is discussed by us in chap. 4 of *Nietzsche's Case*.

6. Tracy B. Strong, "Nietzsche's Political Aesthetics," in *Nietzsche's New Seas: Ex-
plorations in Philosophy, Aesthetics, and Politics*, ed. Michael Allen Gillespie and Tracy
B. Strong (Chicago: University of Chicago Press, 1988), p. 167.

7. See *Nietzsche's Case*.

8. Compare BGE 6.

9. Paul Bové, "Mendacious Innocents, or, The Modern Genealogist as Conscientious Intellectual: Nietzsche, Foucault, Said," in *Why Nietzsche Now?* ed. Daniel T.
O'Hara (Bloomington: Indiana University Press, 1985), pp. 371–372.

10. They touch on this matter in many places, but see, for instance, Michel

Foucault's "What Is an Author," *Language, Counter-memory, Practice: Selected Essays and Interviews*, ed. Donald F. Bouchard, trans. Donald F. Bouchard and Sherry Simon (Ithaca: Cornell University Press, 1977), pp. 115–138; and Jacques Derrida, "Otobiographies: The Teaching of Nietzsche and the Politics of the Proper Name," in *The Ear of the Other: Otobiography, Transference, Translation*, ed. Christie McDonald, trans. Peggy Kamuf (Lincoln: University of Nebraska Press, 1988), pp. 1–40, respectively.

11. Nietzsche addresses this point directly in "The Problem of Socrates" (TI II:2): "*The value of life cannot be estimated.* Not by the living, for they are an interested party, even a bone of contention, and not judges; not by the dead, for a different reason."

12. Higgins, *Nietzsche's Zarathustra* (Philadelphia: Temple University Press, 1987), p. 241.

13. This discussion, in Nietzsche, prefigures later discussions in Heidegger and Sartre of "authenticity" (*Eigentlichkeit*).

14. For a discussion of Weir Mitchell, proprioception, and the connection of bodily identity with authorial and textual identity, see chap. 6 of *Nietzsche's Case*.

15. See her essay "Against Interpretation" in *Against Interpretation and Other Essays* (New York: Noonday Press, 1966).

16. Thomas Weiskel, *The Romantic Sublime* (Baltimore: Johns Hopkins University Press, 1976).

17. For an acute "summary" of this view, see "Reason in Philosophy" in *Twilight of the Idols*.

18. For a discussion, see *Nietzsche's Case*, chap. 1, "A Fish Story: Self-Consuming Concepts."

19. Samuel Taylor Coleridge, *Biographia Literaria*, ed. John T. Showcross, 2 vols. (Oxford: Oxford University Press, 1907), I:202.

20. Of course, this forgetfulness is on the whole true primarily of "writers"— that is, of the writerly we are discussing here. Charles Manson, Jeffrey Dahmer, systemic child abuse, not to mention the Holocaust, My Lai, Katyn Woods, and Vietnam, are eloquent testimony that "we moderns" have *not* forgotten how powerful a seduction to life inflicting pain can be. Indeed, some would argue, cruelty has *become* "our" narcotic!

21. We use scare-quotes to flag the peculiarity of Nietzsche's genealogical method, the assurance it claims for itself in the fame of Nietzsche's proclaimed perspectivism.

22. See Jacques Derrida, "Otobiographies," and *Spurs* (Chicago and London: University of Chicago Press, 1978).

23. See our more extended discussion of eternal recurrence in *Nietzsche's Case*, chap. 1.

24. From a literary point of view, the metaphor of the temple is itself crucial, since the inferiority of the second temple to the first was taken by Dryden and others as a sign of the inevitable running-down of the literary tradition, of the coming end of poetry.

25. "He which testifieth these things saith, Surely I come quickly. Amen. Even so, come, Lord Jesus" (Rev. 22.20).

26. See *Nietzsche's Case,* chap. 4.

27. Note our discussion of the subtitle of *Beyond Good and Evil: Prelude to a Philosophy of the Future* in chap. 1 of *Nietzsche's Case.*

28. For different readings of these same passages see Alexander Nehamas's *Nietzsche: Life as Literature* (Cambridge, Mass.: Harvard University Press, 1985), and Arthur C. Danto in Robert C. Solomon and Kathleen M. Higgins, eds., *Reading Nietzsche* (New York: Oxford University Press, 1988). (A version of Danto's essay appears in this volume.—ED.)

29. We are aware that some commentators, for example, Danto, mark this distinction as relevant to the contrast between active and passive nihilism; but it is hard to see how that will help, and is to be cashed out.

30. See chaps. 1 and 4 of *Nietzsche's Case.*

31. For further discussion see chap. 6 of *Nietzsche's Case.*

32. Compare this discussion with the suggestion, in "What the Germans Lack" (TI VIII), that all energy is finite, and that whatever is spent in one direction will be unavailable for expenditure in another.

33. Harold Bloom, *The Anxiety of Influence: A Theory of Poetry* (New York: Oxford University Press, 1973), especially chaps. 2–4.

34. See, for example, Maudemarie Clark, *Nietzsche on Truth and Philosophy* (Cambridge: Cambridge University Press, 1990); Nehamas, *Nietzsche: Life as Literature;* Bernd Magnus, *Nietzsche's Existential Imperative* (Bloomington: Indiana University Press, 1978); Richard Schacht, *Nietzsche* (London: Routledge and Kegan Paul, 1983); and John Wilcox, *Truth and Value in Nietzsche* (Ann Arbor: University of Michigan Press, 1974).

35. See *Nietzsche's Case,* chaps. 1 and 4. For further discussion of this important matter, see authors cited in the previous footnote.

36. Compare, for example, Richard Rorty's suggestion—in his discussion of "Antipodeans" in his *Philosophy and the Mirror of Nature* (Princeton: Princeton University Press, 1979)—that if the tactile sense had achieved the dominance in our tradition assumed by the visual the "problem" of mental representation might never have arisen; we might all "naturally" have been eliminative materialists in our philosophy instead, in this scenario.

37. We note, without further comment, that the history of recent philosophy is strewn with examples of instructive failures that attempt this "internal" perspective—from Bergson to Husserl to Heidegger.

38. For further discussion, see Bernd Magnus, "Jesus, Christianity, and Superhumanity," in *Studies in Nietzsche and the Judaeo-Christian Tradition,* ed. J. C. O'Flaherty, T. F. Sellner, and Robert M. Helm (Chapel Hill: University of North Carolina Press, 1985), pp. 295–319.

39. Compare "I fear we are not rid of God because we still have faith in grammar" (TI III:5, "Reason in Philosophy").

40. In addition, of course, attempting to "justify" truth presupposes it—like a snake attempting to devour itself.

41. Stanley Cavell, *Must We Mean What We Say: A Book of Essays* (New York: Charles Scribner's Sons, 1969), p. 136.

42. John Milton, *Areopagitica,* in *Complete Poems and Major Prose,* ed. Merritt Y. Hughes (New York: Odyssey Press, 1957), p. 728.

43. Compare "On Redemption" in *Thus Spoke Zarathustra* (Z II:20).

TWENTY-TWO

Of Morals and *Menschen*

Richard Schacht

Sitting in moral judgment should offend our taste. Let us leave such chatter and such bad taste to those who have nothing else to do but drag the past a few steps further through time and who never live in the present—which is to say the many, the great majority. We, however, *want to become those we are*—human beings who are new, unique, incomparable, who give themselves laws, who create themselves. To that end we must become the best learners and discoverers of everything that is lawful and necessary in the world: we must become *physicists* in order to be able to be *creators* in this sense—while hitherto all valuations and ideals have been based on *ignorance* of physics or were constructed so as to *contradict* it. Therefore: long live physics! And even more so that which *compels* us to turn to physics—our honesty! (GS 335)[1]

Thus spoke the Nietzsche of the first edition of *The Gay Science* in 1882. As the subtitle of *Ecce Homo* ("How One Becomes What One Is") shows, Nietzsche held on to the idea of "becoming those we are" to the end. By the time he published the second edition of *The Gay Science* and *On the Genealogy of Morals,* however, he had come to realize that something more than "physics" was also necessary in this connection, and indeed even more crucial. A knowledge of something the natural sciences alone do not suffice to enable us to comprehend is indispensable if we are to position ourselves for this sort of "becoming." We must come to know our already attained "no longer merely animal" humanity. It too is something that has "become"; and as this relatively early passage shows, Nietzsche was convinced even at that time that we must comprehend what we already are, and how we came to be that way, in order to discern what we might yet become, and to take stock of what we have to work with as we set about to realize this possibility.

To achieve such comprehension, however, a kind of inquiry is required that is appropriate to the historical transformation of our initial merely natural existence into our present humanity (our "disanimalization," as he had earlier put it). Five years after writing the above passage,[1] Nietzsche had a new name for it: "genealogy." And he also had come to recognize that, while such inquiry is quite different from "sitting in moral judgment," attention to "morals" was an important part of it, owing to their role in the emergence and shaping of our humanity. More than "genealogical"

427

inquiry focusing upon morals is also necessary in this connection. So Nietzsche reaffirmed his earlier characterization of his larger endeavor as *"fröhliche Wissenschaft "*[2] by publishing an expanded edition of his book bearing that title at that time, in the newly added fifth book of which he addresses a variety of other matters from other perspectives, to the same end.[3] But the importance he attached to such a "genealogical" effort is clear from his devotion of an entire book to it—*On the Genealogy of Morals*—published in the same year (1887).

The same "honesty" that had earlier prompted Nietzsche to extol "physics" now led him to turn to genealogy. While he had earlier held that "we must become physicists" in order to come to know ourselves well enough to go on to "become those we are," he became convinced that we must become "genealogists" as well. He did not thereby abandon the idea that "to that end we must become the best learners and discoverers of everything that is lawful and necessary in the world," but rather extended it, with appropriate modifications, to take account of the historical as well as natural character of our humanity. We must also "become the best learners and discoverers" of everything that has contributed significantly to our historical development, and so of how we have come to be "those we are," actually as well as potentially.

It was in this spirit, I suggest, that Nietzsche engaged in the project that resulted in the *Genealogy*, as well as in its companion work, the fifth book of *The Gay Science*. His larger task, of positioning ourselves to "become those we are," requires "genealogy"—and more. For it involves an assessment of the various possibilities that our attained humanity opens up to us—and this requires not only interpretation but also evaluation. So we find Nietzsche from this time onward (in his prefaces of 1886 and after, as well as in his subsequent books) making much of "the problem of value," and of the need for a "revaluation" and "rank-ordering" of values. Such value inquiry goes beyond anything that can be "learned" about how we have come to be what we are, and about how prevailing modes of valuations have come about. Nietzsche's recognition of this point is reflected in his repeated insistence that the value of something is by no means settled by a knowledge of how it originated, as well as by his frequent reiteration of the point that the task to which his other inquiries have led him is to take up the problem of value and the "revaluation of values." At the same time, however, he recognized that these tasks must be pursued in conjunction with inquiry into the nature of our fundamental and attained humanity, which must be reinterpreted by drawing upon a variety of perspectival investigations of aspects of our humanity and the conditions under which they have taken shape.

I

In his preface to the *Genealogy* Nietzsche not only discusses how his thinking in the *Genealogy* relates to his earlier concerns and efforts but also reflects upon these very points. Observing that he had long been interested in "the *origin* of our moral prejudices" (GM P:2), he then remarks that this interest eventually gave rise and gave way to other questions, both interpretive and evaluative:

> *What value do they themselves possess?* Have they hitherto hindered or furthered human prosperity? Are they a sign of distress, of impoverishment, of the degeneration of life? Or is there revealed in them, on the contrary, the plenitude, force, and will of life, its courage, certainty, future? (GM P:2)

Nietzsche recognizes that his early efforts left a good deal to be desired, as he proceeded "ineptly," but nonetheless with a determination, "as becomes a positive spirit, to replace the improbable with the more probable"—even if this may then often have been only to replace "one error with another," while he was "still lacking [his] own language for [his] own things" (GM P:4). Quite clearly, however, the picture he is painting of the kind of philosopher he was coming to be is the picture of such a "positive spirit," engaging in this task of "replacing the less probable with the more probable" to the best of his ability.

As Nietzsche immediately goes on to observe, his concerns further extended to evaluation as well as to interpretation. He summarizes the relation between these sorts of inquiry—all encompassed within and characterizing his kind of philosophy—as follows:

> Let us articulate this *new demand*: we need a *critique* of moral values, *the value of these values themselves must first be called in question*—and for that there is needed a knowledge of the conditions and circumstances under which they grew, under which they evolved and changed . . . , a knowledge of a kind that has never yet existed or even been desired. (GM P:6)

It is this kind of preparatory "knowledge" that his genealogical inquiries are intended to provide; and it is this further "demand" that his larger philosophical enterprise is (among other things) intended to meet. I say "among other things," because this "revaluation of values" is not the whole of it. His enterprise is also a response to other such "demands" that he elsewhere articulates, extending to a reckoning with the nature and significance of phenomena as diverse as the varieties of art, religion, social organization, science, and humanity itself—all of which Nietzsche touches upon in this book. And it further extends to questions pertaining to the character, scope, pursuit, and value of the varieties of humanly attained and attainable knowledge.

Looking at these matters in light of their relation to "morals" and their development is not the only way to look at them, and is not by itself decisive with respect to their nature or their significance; but this affords a perspective upon them that illuminates them. Looking at them from other perspectives illuminates them in other ways—just as looking at moral phenomena from a variety of perspectives likewise is necessary for one to do justice to them. And this is the very point Nietzsche makes next, availing himself of the image of "new eyes" he so often employs in characterizing the perspectival manner of engaging in his kind of philosophy. Having recognized how profoundly problematic morality is, he writes:

> Let it suffice that, after this prospect had opened up before me, I had reasons to look about me for scholarly, bold, and industrious comrades (I am still looking). The project is to traverse with quite novel questions, and as though with new eyes, the enormous, distant, and so well hidden land of morality—or morality that has actually existed, actually been lived; and does this not mean virtually to *discover* this land for the first time? (GM P:7)

Nietzsche's "genealogical" inquiries are often taken to have a kind of reductionist intent, as though he believed that the manner in which something originated *settled* the questions of its nature and of what is to be made of it. In fact, however, while he does believe (and here tells us) that one does well to *begin* by considering how something may have originated, he is equally insistent that this settles nothing on either score. For what is of decisive importance in both respects, he repeatedly insists, is what thereby has emerged and become possible. It is above all *by their fruits*— and not merely *by their roots*—that he would have us "know them," whether it is morals or "the type *Mensch*"[4] or ourselves as "men of knowledge" that is at issue. And to this end, he suggests that a variety of kinds of questions must be posed and investigated, from a variety of different perspectives.

It seems evident to me from Nietzsche's remarks in this preface that he considers not only the interpretive but also the evaluative parts of his discussion in the *Genealogy* (as elsewhere) to be concerned with matters in which *comprehension* is possible. Indeed, he regards them as objects of possible "knowledge," and as proper concerns of philosophy. This is the clear implication, for example, of the following passages from several of its early sections:

> *That* I still cleave to [the ideas that I take up again in the present treatises] today . . . , that they have become in the meantime more and more firmly attached to one another, strengthens my joyful assurance that they might have arisen in me from the first not as isolated, capricious, or sporadic things but from a common root, from a *fundamental will* of knowledge, pointing imperiously into the depths, speaking more and more precisely, demanding

greater and greater precision. For this alone is fitting for a philosopher. (GM P:2)

A certain amount of historical and philosophical schooling, together with an inborn fastidiousness of taste in respect to psychological questions in general, soon transformed my problem into another one: under what conditions did man devise these value judgments good and evil? *and what value do they themselves possess?* Have they hitherto hindered or furthered human prosperity? . . .

Thereupon I discovered and ventured diverse answers . . . ; I departmentalized my problem; out of my answers there grew new questions, inquiries, conjectures, probabilities—until at length I had a country of my own. . . . Oh how *fortunate* we are, we men of knowledge, provided only that we know how to keep silent long enough! (GM P:3)

The fact that Nietzsche begins this preface by observing that "we are unknown to ourselves, we men of knowledge" (GM P:1) does not detract from the significance of his approving references to "knowledge" in such other passages as these. He clearly does mean to shed light upon himself and ourselves as "men of knowledge" in the course of his discussion of the ways in which morals (and in particular "ascetic ideals") have influenced our development as such a peculiar human type. But he also distinguishes fruits from roots, and allows for the possibility (which he explores in the very first section of the First Essay) that very "human, all too human" dispositions and motivations *may* issue in the attainment of genuine comprehension—if they come to be configured and transformed in a certain manner—*despite* the fact that none of them may constitute anything like a "will to knowledge" to begin with. So he conceives of the possibility of "investigators and microscopists of the soul" emerging from a particular development of this sort with the capacity as well as the determination to come to understand much about it that most people do not know, and would rather not know—

brave, proud, magnanimous animals, who know how to keep their hearts as well as their sufferings in bounds and have trained themselves to sacrifice all desirability to truth, *every* truth, even plain, harsh, repellent, unchristian, immoral truth.—For such truths do exist. (GM I:1)

An interesting and significant parallel may thus be observed between the outcome of his genealogical and other reflections on morals and morality, on the one hand, and of his related genealogical and other reflections on ourselves as "knowers" and on the knowledge we may attain, on the other. As he observes at the end of the First Essay, he trusts that it should be "abundantly clear what my *aim* is," and more specifically "what the aim of that dangerous slogan is that is inscribed at the head of my last book *Beyond Good and Evil.* —At least this does *not* mean 'Beyond Good and Bad' " (GM I:17). This aim is a double one: both to take us to the point that we understand and are emancipated from the all-too-human "herd" and "slave" morality of "good and evil" and to awaken us to the possibility and preferability of a different mode of valuation and "higher morality" along the lines of his contrasting polarity of "good and bad."

Similarly, I would suggest, the aim of his reflections on "knowers" and knowledge is likewise a double one, and their outcome is positive as well as negative. One might take some of his pronouncements to be variants of an analogous "dangerous slogan" in this context, along the lines of "Beyond True and False." But to this it must be added that his larger aim should be "abundantly clear" to readers of this same book—and that "at least this does *not* mean 'Beyond Truths and Lies, Errors and Illusions.' " For his double aim is both to enable us to comprehend and free ourselves from all-too-naïve and all-too-metaphysical ideas and ideals of truth and knowledge and to show us *that* and *how* a different sort of thinking is humanly possible, for which there is more to be said than there is for others, in terms of honesty and insightfulness. His investigations in the *Genealogy* serve both of these purposes.

In the next few opening sections of the First Essay Nietzsche goes on to indicate a number of the sorts of sophistication and sensitivity that he considers to be needful if such "investigators of the soul" are to be equal to their task and subject. Their eyes and thinking must be sharpened and attuned to historical, psychological, linguistic, sociological, and cultural phenomena and developments (GM I:2–5); for all these perspectives yield insights into aspects of what "the soul" has come to be in the course of human events.

All of this is stage-setting for the particular investigations with respect to "morals" that Nietzsche proceeds to undertake, beginning shortly thereafter. Yet these opening remarks obviously have a considerably broader applicability—to the investigation of other such phenomena that also are encountered when one turns one's attention to the varieties of human experience, and to our attained humanity in which they figure along with them. Genealogical inquiry, of the sort Nietzsche here undertakes with respect to "morals," and involving their exploration by bringing the various sorts of sensitivity indicated above to bear upon them, is here advocated— and not only with respect to them. It is commended with respect to "the soul" more generally as well—that is, to "the type *Mensch,*" the "no-longer-merely-animal animal" that has acquired what came to be called a "soul," both as a general "type" and in its considerable diversity. It is thus commended (and practiced) not only for the purposes of Nietzsche's kind of moral philosophy, but also in connection with what may correspondingly be called his kind of "philosophical anthropology."

II

The *Genealogy* is therefore more than an elaboration of what Nietzsche (in his preface) calls "my ideas on the *origin* of our moral prejudices," even though he goes on to say that "this is the subject of this polemic" (GM P:2). As has been observed above, he is also and just as deeply concerned with *our* origin and genealogy as "men of knowledge." But this is not all. The *Genealogy* is further a companion piece to the fifth book of *The Gay Science* (published, as has been noted, in the same year). It is an extension of his *fröhliche Wissenschaft*, and has the same fundamental focus. In *The Gay Science* Nietzsche deals with many topics and issues; but his fundamental concern is to carry out the project of what he calls " 'naturalizing' our humanity," in terms of a "de-deified" and thereby "newly redeemed nature" (GS 109).[5]

That is a project he pursues in the *Genealogy* as well. His general and underlying concern, in both works, is with *our human* nature and possibilities. And in the *Genealogy* he is offering us further suggestions pertaining not only to the genealogy of morals and of knowers but also to the genealogy of the humanity we exemplify, as it has come to be and may yet become. He obviously seeks to shed light on the origin of our "moral prejudices" and of our commonplace ways of "knowing," with a view to attaining a perspective upon them by means of which we might go beyond them. But he further desires to shed light on the origins of our humanity, in general and also in some of its more remarkable forms, with a view to attaining a more comprehensive perspective upon them by means of which we might at once arrive at a better understanding of what he calls "the type *Mensch,*" and also discern "what might yet be made of man."

I shall not deal here with what Nietzsche has to say in the *Genealogy* about the "moral prejudices" he discusses, "slave" and "master" moralities, the "bad conscience" and "ascetic ideals," and about the relation of these phenomena to scholarly ideals and related ways of construing and esteeming truth and knowledge—important and central to this work though his discussion of these matters certainly are. I shall instead be concerned with the *Genealogy* as a contribution to Nietzsche's development of his "philosophical anthropology," and with the ideas he seeks to advance and substantiate in it with respect to our emergent human nature.

My general claims are these: that Nietzsche's enterprise in this work is to be understood in the context of his philosophical anthropology, which it also helps to illuminate; that the inquiries he pursues here are intended fundamentally to contribute to this larger enterprise, no less than to an assessment of the particular phenomena with which he deals; that part of what he does in this work is to advance certain important claims specifically

addressed to the issue of how our human nature is to be understood; and
that what he has to say sheds important light both on how he conceives of
our nature (what sort of nature he believes it to be appropriate to attribute
to ourselves as human beings) and also on how he believes it is best approached and dealt with.

It is no objection to my interpretation and argument to observe that
Nietzsche rejects the idea of "man" as an "eternal truth" possessed of a
timeless and ahistorical essence. This observation is certainly correct; but
it leaves open the possibility that he proposes to replace *this* conception of
our nature with one of another sort, which nonetheless is (at least to his
way of thinking) still deserving of the name. And it is likewise no objection
to observe that he makes much of contingencies that have influenced our
development, and have given rise to differences among various types of
human beings. For while this observation too is correct, it is entirely consistent with the view that he intends all of this to contribute to our understanding of the *sort* of nature we as human beings have, and does not rule
out the idea that we *have* any such nature of which it is meaningful to speak.

Nietzsche makes it clear at the outset in his preface that his concern
with "the type *Mensch*" underlies his more immediate investigations in the
three essays of the *Genealogy*. So he frames them by expressing his motivat-
ing suspicion that "precisely morality would be to blame if the *highest power
and splendor* actually possible to the type man was never in fact attained"
(GM P:6). And it may further be observed that, in order to be able to carry
out a critique and revaluation of "morality" in the terms suggested here,
the attainability of a comprehension of "the type *Mensch*" (taking account
of this "type" both as it has come to be and as it has the potential to
become) is presupposed. This is something of which Nietzsche shows himself to be well aware—for example, in a well-known passage from the fifth
book of *The Gay Science:*

> "Thoughts about moral prejudices," if they are not meant to be [mere]
> prejudices about prejudices, presuppose a position *outside* morality, some
> point beyond good and evil to which one has to rise, climb, or fly. . . . That
> one *wants* to go precisely out there, up there, may be a minor madness, a
> peculiar and unreasonable "you must"—for we seekers for knowledge also
> have our idiosyncrasies of "unfree will"—the question is whether one really
> *can* get up there.
>
> This may depend on manifold conditions. In the main the question is how
> light or heavy we are—the problem of our "specific gravity." One has to be
> *very light* to drive one's will to knowledge into such a distance and, as it were,
> beyond one's time, to create for oneself eyes to survey millennia and, more-
> over, clear skies in these eyes. (GS 381)

As I read him, Nietzsche is attentive, in the *Genealogy* as well as elsewhere,
to the fact that it is thus incumbent upon him to supply the anthropological

foundation or context for the assessment of morality to which his "genealogy of morals" is intended to contribute. So, on numerous occasions along the way, he pauses to indicate and sketch relevant features of the conception of the nature of "the type *Mensch*" with which he is working, upon which he is drawing, and to which he also means his examination of the moral phenomena to contribute. My picture of Nietzsche's procedure is thus that of a double movement. On some occasions he draws upon general anthropological considerations to illuminate various moral phenomena. On others he avails himself of the insights thus attained into these phenomena to refine the interpretation of our nature he is attempting to develop and substantiate.

This procedure has its dangers, and invites the charge of circularity; but I believe that Nietzsche would respond (as would Heidegger, and with equal justice) that one can do no better—and that any circularity here is not vicious but hermeneutical. Further, interpreters we are, and cannot but be, in dealing with both "morals" and "the type *Mensch*"; but this does not mean that we therefore are not and cannot be "knowers." It only means that it is in the manner and spirit of conscientious interpreters and would-be "good philologists" that we must proceed if we are to have any prospect of doing something approaching justice to our "text." As I read him, Nietzsche does not repudiate this hope as a vain and impossible dream, but rather embraces it as a coherent and legitimate aspiration. Nothing less is worthy of his "new philosophers" who are to be "men of knowledge" and "lovers of knowledge" as well as "legislators of values" on that newly open sea of which he speaks so evocatively at the conclusion of the fifth book of *The Gay Science*.

III

This double movement may be seen in each of the three essays in the *Genealogy*. At the outset of the First Essay, he insists upon the importance of "the *historical spirit*" (GM I:2), if moral phenomena and our nature more generally are to be properly understood. It may not suffice for their understanding; but they certainly may be *better* understood if approached in a manner attentive to their historical development. A little further on, after having introduced his conceptions of the different modes of valuation "good and bad" versus "good and evil," and linking the latter to the influence of "priestly" activity, he remarks:

> It was on the sort of this *essentially dangerous* form of human existence, the priestly form, that man first became *an interesting* animal, that only here did the human soul in a higher sense acquire *depth* and become *evil*—and these are the two basic respects in which man has hitherto been superior to other beasts! (GM I:6)

Nietzsche goes on to observe: "Human history would be altogether too stupid a thing without the spirit that the impotent have introduced into it" (GM I:7). Much of what he has to say in the following sections is intended to elaborate on how this came about, and what occurred as the immediate result of this process. He sums it up in the suggestion that "the *meaning of all culture*," at least to date and broadly speaking, "is the reduction of the beast of prey 'man' to a tame and civilized animal, a *domestic animal*" (GM I:11).

Nietzsche next proceeds to advance a sketch of part of a psychological theory—a *general* theory, clearly intended not only to apply to the understanding of the origin of the phenomenon of *ressentiment* (his immediate topic) but also to pertain to the understanding of our nature more generally. It is cast in terms of a general model of events, treating human actions as a class of such events. Here I merely draw attention to it, as an illustration of my general thesis. It is at this juncture that he contends that "a quantum of force is equivalent to a quantum of drive, will, effect—more, it is nothing other than this very driving, willing, effecting," rather than something "caused" to occur by some sort of underlying "subject" entity— for "there is no substratum; there is no 'being' behind doing, affecting, becoming; 'the doer' is merely a fiction added to the deed" (GM I:13). Nietzsche then goes on to apply this sketch of a part of a picture of our nature to the interpretation and understanding of the phenomenon of *ressentiment* and the associated moral ideals—at the same time deriving support for his generalized hypothesis from the plausibility of the account it enables him to give of them.

Finally, it is of no little interest and relevance that he concludes this First Essay with a "Note" in which he calls not only for attention to be given to the light linguistics and etymology may "throw on the history of the evolution of moral concepts" but also for an "amicable and fruitful exchange" between "philosophy, physiology, and medicine," so that questions relating to "the problem of value" and "the determination of the order of rank among values" may be approached and dealt with in their proper general and fundamental context. For this context is clearly implied by these suggestions and his other remarks to be that of human life more generally, and of our human nature and possibilities, both in their general outlines and in what might be called their "human type-specificity."

Nietzsche opens the Second Essay by posing a question about our human nature in the very opening lines of the first section: "To breed an animal *with the right to make promises*—is this not the paradoxical task that nature has set itself in the case of man? Is it not the real problem regarding man?" And he concludes this section, which goes on to deal with the general usefulness of "forgetting" in healthy animal life (thus generating this "paradox"), with the observation that "man must first of all have become *cal-*

culable, regular, necessary, even in his own image of himself, if he is to be able to stand security for *his own future,* which is what one who promises does!" (GM II:1).

In the next section Nietzsche goes on to spell out the general significance of this "tremendous process" for the understanding not only of moral phenomena such as "guilt" and "bad conscience" but also of our attained humanity—and further, of a higher humanity that it has made possible, of which account must likewise be taken in an adequate interpretation of our humanity. So he remarks that "society and the morality of custom at last reveal *what* they have simply been the means to: . . . the *sovereign individual*" (GM II:2). By what he terms "the labor performed by man upon himself during the greater part of the existence of the human race, his entire *prehistoric* labor," we have made ourselves into the type of creature we now are, with this prospect of further enhancement. It is this above all that Nietzsche seeks here to comprehend and elaborate, with the specific topics of the moral phenomena he discusses serving chiefly as points of departure and clues, evidence, and means of confirmation.

So too, in the next section, his guiding question is the more general one: "How can one create a memory for the human animal?" (GM II:3). In the same vein, when he returns to the genealogy of morals in the following section, his remarks are couched in terms of his more general concern with our attained humanity, as when he writes that "a *high* degree of humanity had to be attained before the animal 'man' began to make the sorts of distinctions" that attributions of guilt and responsibility involve (GM II:4). In subsequent sections Nietzsche has a great deal to say about how all of this may have come to pass, which is as much material for a "genealogy of humanity" as it is elaboration of a "genealogy of morals." Along the way, he even brings in his "theory that in all events a *will to power* is operating" (GM II:12). He does so, once again, because he is concerned to relate his genealogy of morals to its larger interpretive context, and to his larger interpretive enterprise.

Nietzsche's whole discussion in this Second Essay culminates in his famous "provisional statement" of his "hypothesis concerning the origin of the 'bad conscience'," which is actually a much more comprehensive hypothesis concerning the way in which "man first developed what was later called his 'soul'." It involves his contention that "all instincts that do not discharge themselves outwardly turn inward—this is what I call the *internalization* of man," and that this "fundamental change . . . which occurred when he found himself finally enclosed within the walls of society" transformed the "semi-animals" we once were into the "humanity" we now are (GM II:16). This for Nietzsche was the crucial step in what might be called "the birth of man." The *Genealogy* is in effect his attempt to make a case for the decisive importance of this development, and for the associated interpretation of our nature it suggests. The remainder of the Second Essay is devoted chiefly to working out an account of the "moral" phenomena of "guilt" and the "bad conscience" that both draws upon this interpretation and supports it by demonstrating its explanatory power and sense-making usefulness. (In the next section I will offer a closer reading and more detailed discussion of the points in the Second Essay sketched above, which are of particular interest and importance in their own right as well as for my purposes here.)

In the Third Essay, on the question "What is the Meaning of Ascetic Ideals?," Nietzsche carries his inquiry a step further, seeking not only to answer this question but to make use of his investigation of this topic to add further detail to his portrait of our nature. Thus, in the first section, he states: "*That* the ascetic ideal has meant so many things to man . . . is an expression of the basic fact of the human will, its *horror vacui: it needs a goal—and it will rather will nothingness* than *not* will" (GM III:1). And it is with this same reflection that he concludes this essay, with the observation: "Apart from the ascetic ideal, man, the human *animal,* had no meaning so far" (GM III:28).

Nietzsche's basic question in this essay is: How is the phenomenon of the ascetic ideal possible, and what light does it shed upon our nature? And he clearly takes this light to be considerable. In the course of his discussion he draws upon his general view that "every animal," ourselves included, "instinctively strives for an optimum of favorable conditions under which it can expend all its strength and achieve its maximal feeling of power" (GM III:7); and he employs the phenomenon of "ascetic ideals" to show how this general disposition has taken on particular form in our own case, which the developments discussed previously have greatly complicated. Thus he likens the ascetic priest and kindred types to a "caterpillar" form, and contemplates the extent to which "that many-colored and dangerous winged creature, the 'spirit' which this caterpillar concealed," has begun to be "unfettered at last"; and he looks to the further realization of this salient possibility our attained humanity harbors within it (GM III:10).

Throughout this essay, Nietzsche repeatedly asks: What does all this *mean?* And his attempts to answer this question are conducted in the spirit of his reflections on the possibility and conditions of attaining "knowledge" here, of the sort of creature we ourselves are, in one of the most notable passages in the entire book. "Precisely because we seek knowledge," he contends, we must avail ourselves of many perspectives; and so, he goes on to observe, "the *more* affects we allow to speak about one thing, the *more* eyes, different eyes, we can use to observe one thing, the more complete will our 'concept' of this thing, our 'objectivity,' be" (GM III:12).

In the course of his discussion, Nietzsche dwells upon the point that "man is more sick, uncertain, changeable, indeterminate than any other animal . . . —he is *the* sick animal," and upon the questions of "how that has come about" and where it all may lead (GM III:13). His ideas concerning this "sickness" that has come to characterize us and concerning the possibility of a new and greater "health" beyond it (as well as beyond mere animal vitality), both require and are intended to help elucidate a conception of the sort of nature we have that now presents both possibilities. And much of what he has to say about the shortcomings of various remedies to which human beings have resorted presupposes the possibility of a comprehension of our nature, in relation to which it makes sense to assess them and find them wanting. Here again, his examination of moral phenomena and his elaboration of a philosophical anthropology thus go hand in hand, each serving to contribute to the other.

IV

Perhaps the best way to make my case is to look more closely at one of these three essays.[6] I shall focus upon the Second Essay, for he develops several ideas in it that are of the greatest importance not only to his understanding of the attained humanity of "the type *Mensch*" as it has come to be, but also to his conception of the sort of humanity that has thereby come to be humanly attainable. Both of these interrelated concerns had long preoccupied him—they are arguably the twin basic themes of *The Gay Science*, for example—and quite clearly do so here as well; and in this Second Essay in particular, his developing thinking about them is deepened and extended. Nietzsche addresses himself to these matters at some length twice in this essay: in the opening sections, and then again shortly after its midpoint. I shall consider the latter discussion first, because it is the more fundamental of the two.

It is Nietzsche's general view that, while the eventual outcome is still very much in doubt, nature is making a unique experiment in us. In our social and conscious life, a complex alternative to the general kind of instinct-structure operative in other forms of life has emerged. Indeed, he considers certain aspects of the conditions imposed upon us by our social life to have played an important role in the breaking down of our former instinct-structure, as well as in the filling of the resulting void. This may be seen in his discussion relating to the emergence of "the bad conscience" in the *Genealogy*. He takes this phenomenon to be a "serious illness" marking the onset of a larger "sickness," which

> man was bound to contract under the stress of the most fundamental change he ever experienced—that change which occurred when he found himself finally enclosed within the walls of society and of peace. The situation that

faced sea animals when they were compelled to become land animals or perish was the same as that which faced these semianimals, well adapted to their
wilderness, to war, to prowling, to adventure: suddenly all their instincts were
disvalued and "suspended." From now on they had to walk on their feet and
"bear themselves" whereas hitherto they had been borne by the water: a
dreadful heaviness lay upon them. . . . In this new world they no longer possessed their former guides, their regulating, unconscious and infallible drives:
they were reduced to thinking, inferring, reckoning, coordinating cause and
effect, these unfortunate creatures; they were reduced to their "consciousness," their weakest and most fallible organ! (GM II:16)

Nietzsche goes on to refer to this departure from our instinctive "former
guides," in favor of conscious processes better attuned to the different and
variable circumstances of social life, as "a forcible sundering from [man's]
past, as it were a leap and plunge into new surroundings and conditions of
existence," involving a "declaration of war against the old instincts upon
which his strength, joy and terribleness had rested hitherto." At the same
time, however, he is quick to draw attention to the potentiality and promise
implicit in this development. Thus he considers it important to "add at
once" that this spectacle of "an animal soul turned against itself," depart-
ing from the life its old instincts marked out for it, and having to oppose
and disengage them by means of and in favor of a very different sort of
life-regulating and guiding process, "was something so new, profound, un-
heard of, enigmatic, contradictory, *and pregnant with a future* that the aspect
of the earth was essentially altered" (GM II:16).

As these remarks indicate, it is not Nietzsche's intention to suggest that
our old instincts have simply vanished altogether and without residue, leaving the field entirely to the socially conditioned conscious processes that
thus came to the fore. On the contrary, he contends that in the circumstances described, even while no longer possessing their former sovereignty, "the old instincts had not suddenly ceased to make their usual demands!" And although with the breaking of their hold upon the course of
life their structure too is suggested gradually to have broken down, he holds
that the basic drives once finely articulated in this structure can by no
means be supposed to have disappeared. They may in a sense be said to
have been "reduced" from the highly differentiated and specialized state
characteristic of other complex forms of life, and presumably also of that
which was ancestral to our own. The drive-reduction presumed thus to have
occurred here, however, is suggested to be qualitative rather than quanti-
tative.

Moreover, Nietzsche suggests that this drive-reduction has not been carried to completion in the interval. Strong residues of our old instinct-structure are held to have survived the "fundamental change" he describes in
the passage cited above. And their survival is purported to have played a

profoundly important role in the specific direction taken in the development of major portions of our spiritual life, as well as serving (together with the more generalized forces released through drive-reduction) to fuel and inform the whole range of our conscious processes and activities. Thus in this same context he advances one of his central ideas touched upon briefly above:

> All instincts that do not discharge themselves outwardly *turn inward*—this is what I call the *internalization* of man: thus it was that man first developed what was later called his "soul." The entire inner world, originally as thin as if it were stretched between two membranes, expanded and extended itself, acquired depth, breadth, and height, in the same measure as outward discharge was *inhibited*. (GM II:16)

Instincts so inhibited by the pressure of circumstances from discharging themselves "naturally" do not (as Freud was also to observe) simply dissipate. Rather, Nietzsche suggests, they "seek new and, as it were, subterranean gratifications." When they take such modified and sublimated forms as "the bad conscience" or that broader class of phenomena with which he deals later in the same work under the rubric of "ascetic ideals," their impact upon human life tends to be negative and even self-destructive. But this phenomenon can also take a very different turn. Thus Nietzsche regards this process of "internalization" and sublimation as the key to the emergence of all the life-enriching and -enhancing phenomena of human spiritual life as well, from the political to the emotional, artistic, and intellectual. If he considers it appropriate to term this too a form of "sickness" in relation to the "healthy animality" of a kind of life governed by an undisrupted, smoothly functioning, and comprehensive instinct-structure, he is far from supposing that the latter is inherently preferable to it. Thus he remarks elsewhere that we would do well to consider whether "the will to health alone is not a prejudice, cowardice, and perhaps a bit of very subtle barbarism and backwardness" (GS 120).

Nietzsche further contends that a great many of the major constituent features of our mental life are *social* rather than either purely intellectual or merely biological phenomena, owing their very origins to circumstances associated with our social existence. He is particularly concerned to establish that this is so with respect to those that have long been regarded as operations of special faculties of "the mind"—of which, after "reason," two of the most prominent examples are memory and conscience. He identifies the context in which their development received the most powerful stimulus as the practical one of action. Thus he links the phenomenon of memory to that of *promising*; and his answer to the question "How can one create a memory for the human animal?" is developed with reference to this social practice (GM II:3). He approaches the matter by rhetorically asking: "To breed an animal *with the right to make promises*—is not this the paradoxical task that nature has set for itself in the case of man?" (GM II:2). The thought he expresses here is deserving of attention in its own right, owing to its implications for the issue of our human nature. What engages his attention is not the normative question of whether one is morally obligated to keep one's promises, but rather the larger and more fundamental one of what the possibility of promising (and keeping one's promises) presupposes, and the ramifications in human life of the establishment of this possibility.

The establishment of this possibility, Nietzsche contends, required the development of a kind of memory going beyond the (basically animal) capacity to absorb and retain things experienced. Where the latter alone is operative, such experience "enters our consciousness as little while we are digesting it . . . as does the thousandfold process involved in physical nourishment" (GM II:1). For promising to be possible, a further sort of more explicit memory had to be developed, involving the partial abrogation of what he terms the overt "forgetfulness" characteristic of this basic retentive capacity. "A real *memory of the will*" had to be attained, enabling one to "ordain the future in advance," despite the intervention of many other events and the continuous alteration of circumstances (GM II:1). And "it was only with the aid of this kind of memory," he suggests, "that one came at last" to be capable of "reason, seriousness, mastery over the affects, the whole somber thing called reflection, all those prerogatives and showpieces of man." He goes on to observe, moreover, that "they have been dearly bought," at the price of "much blood and cruelty."

The account Nietzsche goes on to provide of how this came about—in terms of debt, punishment, and cruelty—is highly speculative, and its details may certainly be questioned. All he requires for his larger purposes, however, is that the phenomenon of overt remembering may plausibly be accounted for in an entirely naturalistic manner, in terms of *some such* social-psychological etiology—and thereby, along with it, the various forms of spirituality and conscious activity of which it is the precondition, and for which it prepares the way. The only essential point of the story he tells here is that it was the social necessity of rendering human beings reliable that was the original and primary impetus to its development. Without this necessity there would and could never have emerged the phenomenon of a "long chain of will" sufficing to override our natural condition of being "attuned only to the passing moment."

Nietzsche takes the consequences of this development to have been (and to continue to be) of the greatest importance, both for our manner of relating to our surrounding world and for our own identity. With regard to the former, our immersion in and preoccupation with the "passing moment" is thereby at least partially broken; we are impelled to learn to "see and anticipate distant eventualities," to operate in terms of ends and means, to "think causally," and "in general to be able to calculate and compute." And with regard to the latter, Nietzsche observes that something of profound significance had to occur: "Man himself must first of all have become *calculable, regular, necessary,* even in his own image of himself, if he is to be able to stand security for *his own future,* which is what one who promises does!" (GM II:1).

This is "the long story of how *responsibility* originated"; but there is more to the matter as well. For it thus may be seen further to have direct and important bearing on the nature of *personal identity,* which is suggested by this account to be a function and consequence of this socially induced transformation, rather than attaching to some sort of substantial (and individual) "self" each of us has, or is, innately and on our own. What is here at issue is not the sort of identity we each possess by virtue of the spatio-temporal continuity and discreteness of our bodily existence (which is equally attributable to animals generally, and thus falls short of personal identity or selfhood). Rather, it is what is purportedly characteristic of each human being as a single *person* persisting as the same thinking, feeling, choosing, acting, responsible subject throughout the course of life. Nietzsche does not dispute that there is something to this idea of personal identity. But he maintains that it must be fundamentally reinterpreted.

On a rather rudimentary level, one may be said to have (acquired) such an identity to the extent that one has come to have a relatively settled set of rather specific behavioral dispositions. But such identity is insufficient by itself to insure the degree and kind of reliability required in order for social institutions to develop and function. Assurance is needed of reliability in courses of action reaching far beyond the present, even if one's dispositions change or incline one otherwise, and independently of the desires one might have or come to have. It is only if one learns to think of oneself as having an identity transcending one's desires, dispositions, immediate circumstances, and momentary condition—which remains the same even though all of these may vary, and extends from the present back into the past and on into the future—that one becomes fit for social life.

As long as one's existence is little more than a succession of episodes in which one responds in an immediate way to situations with which one is confronted, in accordance with whatever dispositions and desires are dominant at the moment, this social requirement is not met. A kind of consciousness needs to be established which transcends the immediacy of absorption in these circumstances of the moment, bringing both past and future into view, and forging links of identification between episodes in one's life such that one can feel bound in the present by performances occurring in the past, and bound in the future by what one does in the present. One must learn to *think of oneself,* rather than merely acting and reacting as one is moved in the moment to do—and moreover to think of oneself as somehow being the *same* now as previously, and as being the same in the future as now, notwithstanding changes in one's states and situation.

The purpose of such self-consciousness and self-identification becomes clear only when the idea of agency with respect to one's performances and actions is added to them. It is only with this addition that the social requirement is satisfied of rendering human beings reliable in their dealings with each other beyond the extent to which settled dispositions render them predictable. Our personal identity, according to Nietzsche, may thus be seen to originate in this socially induced self-identification, as unitary agents in relation to our conduct through time. And while fundamentally a fiction, the acceptance of this idea (under the pressure of our being treated as though it were fact) has the consequence that we not only apprehend ourselves accordingly, but also to a considerable extent cease to *be* creatures of the moment, and *become* such "selves"—at least in a functional sense, if not substantially. Thus Nietzsche concludes the passage cited previously by observing that, "with the aid of the morality of mores and the social straitjacket, man was actually *made* calculable" (GM II:2). One is brought to *take on* the sort of identity "even in his own image of himself" that is the basis of such calculability, and so is rendered fit for society.

But this is not all: one also takes a crucial and indispensable developmental step in the direction of becoming capable of that more exceptional, extrasocial sort of undertaking Nietzsche has in mind when he speaks of the "great tasks" to which exceptional human beings may apply themselves. Thus he suggests that, even though the process of transforming human beings in such a way that they may be said to come to have personal identities is a socialization phenomenon in which the "social straitjacket" is employed to render them reliable members of society, it prepares the way for a further development that transcends this result. For "at the end of this tremendous process," there emerges its "ripest fruit," which is "the *sovereign individual,* like only to himself, liberated again from the morality of custom, autonomous and supramoral," who "has his own independent protracted will," and whose "mastery over himself also necessarily gives him mastery over circumstances, over nature, and over all more short-willed and unreliable creatures" (GM II:2).

In this way, Nietzsche seeks to show how the foundation is laid for the possibility of those he elsewhere calls "higher men," through a process he considers to have come about in response to certain very fundamental demands, and which initially has a considerably different sort of result. Even the personal identity of such a "sovereign individual," however, is not to be construed as the "being" of an unchanging spiritual substance. Yet it is no mere illusion either, but rather a genuine attainment. It radically transcends the merely spatiotemporal identity of a living creature; and it further differs qualitatively from that which human beings typically develop under the circumstances described above.

The socially induced development under consideration also has important implications for the nature of human action. The behavior of a mere creature of the moment, doing what it does in accordance with whatever impulses and dispositions happen to be dominant on any given occasion, may no more appropriately be considered *action* than such a creature may be ascribed personal identity. And the same sorts of social impositions that engender the latter also serve to establish the context in which the former emerges, through the disruption of this immediacy that occurs when one learns and is compelled to take the past and the future into account. Human action involves at least a minimal degree of what Nietzsche terms "mastery over the affects" (GM II:3), even if it never occurs in their absence or without their influence; and it is by means of the "social straitjacket" that a degree of such mastery is first achieved.

A fundamental distinction between human action and animal behavior is therefore clearly implied, and is held to be bound up with the development of this cluster of social practices and with the transformation of one's manner of comporting one through one's initiation into them. The acquisition of language is only the first step in this process, albeit an important and indispensable one. The decisive step is a matter of coming further to be able to operate in terms of promises, agreements, rules, values, and, in general, to frame and act pursuant to *intentions*. The social character of the conditions of human action by no means implies that all such intentions are but the internalization of general social influences. This should be clear from Nietzsche's remarks about the possibility of "the sovereign individual." But even the very "autonomy" and "independent protracted will" of which he speaks in characterizing an individual of this sort are represented as outgrowths of what is basically a social phenomenon, rather than attributes assignable to some special nonnatural and extrasocial faculty of the individual as such. He does not consider all human action to be completely determined by prevailing social institutions together with our general human and particular individual biological endowments, let alone by these latter endowments exclusively. But he does hold that it is grounded in the social transformation of our fundamental biological nature; and he takes the more exceptional forms of action to which autonomy and independence may legitimately be ascribed to be a matter of the individual transformation of a previously established social nature.

V

I certainly would not maintain that this way of reading the *Genealogy* is the only appropriate way of doing so, or that Nietzsche is doing nothing more in it than what I have been talking about. But I *would* maintain that he is doing *nothing less* than this in it, and that reading him as doing this is being unfaithful neither to his text nor to his intentions. To my way of thinking, this work, along with *The Gay Science* and a good many others, provides clear evidence that he considers it appropriate and philosophically important to think about "the type *Mensch*" as well as about various particular human types—and further, that he believes there to be a good deal to be said along these lines, which he is intent upon saying, toward the development of what I have been calling a philosophical anthropology.

I further would not maintain that his thinking on this topic is set out whole and complete in the *Genealogy*. On the contrary, in it he approaches this topic only from certain angles. He approaches it from others elsewhere, to equally good effect. But I *would* maintain that Nietzsche's *Genealogy* constitutes a good example of the kind of investigation he believes to be called for in order to make progress in this larger project of comprehending our nature, in terms of its development, attained general character, variability, and prospects. As *some* might conceive of the ideas of human nature and of the project of a philosophical anthropology, he clearly will have no part of them. *He* conceives of them differently, however; and his *Genealogy* is a significant contribution to his attempt (and ours) to deal with them. I consider it important to the understanding of what he sought to do to read him, and this work, with these eyes, if also with others as well.

In *The Gay Science* Nietzsche makes the interesting remark that, while his scientific and scholarly knowledge is lacking in a good many respects, this does not greatly matter for his purposes, since "we need more, we also need less" than such knowledge for the questions that concern him (GS 381). He calls what he is doing *fröhliche Wissenschaft*, and what he is after "knowledge"; but his point is that something other than natural- and social-scientific inquiry is involved and required in order to deal best with the main issues with which he is concerned. And one of my points is that, in the works like *The Gay Science* and the *Genealogy*, he shows us what he has in mind. For Nietzsche, they enable one to get further with these matters than one can get in other ways, shedding more light upon them than the kinds of inquiries pursued by scientists and different types of philosophers and scholars.

This is an important and interesting suggestion about philosophical *method*, in certain areas at least, which we would do well to take seriously ourselves, as well as reckon with in interpreting Nietzsche. But what are the kinds of issues and questions which Nietzsche says "concern *him*," to which this suggestion is meant to apply?

Clearly "the origin of our moral prejudices" is one of them—as is his analysis and revaluation of moral "values" and other "values" more generally. Clearly what he calls his "psychology of philosophers"—and also of scientists, scholars, priestly types, "herd" and "master" types, and the like—are others. So also is the status of the various forms of what commonly passes for "truth" and "knowledge." But so too, and more fundamentally, is what he calls "the type *Mensch*," and therewith also both the "all-too-human" and the possibility of exceptions to the human rule.

Even if this point is granted, however, and even if it is further agreed (as I would hope) that this too is an important and interesting suggestion about the *agenda* of philosophy, which we also would do well to take seriously ourselves, as well as reckon with in interpreting Nietzsche—even then, it may still be asked: Why call this *philosophical anthropology*?

For some reason, this label seems to make many people uncomfortable. By contrast, labels like philosophical psychology, theology, biology, and even cosmology seem unobjectionable to most. Why not "philosophical anthropology" too? What better could one call inquiry into "the type *Mensch*" of the sort Nietzsche undertakes in these and other works? As his remark about needing less and also more than science suggests, it is clearly a philosophical rather than a merely biological or social-scientific endeavor. As his repeated references to "the type *Mensch*" and our "humanity" make clear, its focus is upon *anthropos* rather than upon some otherwise deline-ated object of inquiry. "Anthropology" is the least artificial and most com-monplace coinage to designate such inquiry. It may have associations with ways of thinking we and Nietzsche do not embrace and wish to disavow; but so does "psychology," which he and we nonetheless are ready enough to appropriate and retain. Why balk at "anthropology," then, and at "phil-osophical anthropology"?

This expression does a better job than any other of conveying what is under investigation here, and its investigation is to be understood as "need-ing less and also more" than human-scientific inquiry (even if perhaps some of that as well) in order to be carried out at all adequately. In the end, of course, the important thing is not what this endeavor is called, but rather that its possibility and importance are recognized, and that it is pursued. I would suggest, however, that appropriate labels have their uses in the directions and focusing of attention and effort, and that no other at hand does the job better than "philosophical anthropology."[7] In any event, this is an important part of the task, whatever it may be called, that Nietz-sche sets for himself and his type of philosopher; and I believe that task to be an important part of the agenda of philosophy today, thanks in no small measure to Nietzsche.

NOTES

1. By 1887, when *On the Genealogy of Morals* was published.
2. The German title of (*The*) *Gay Science*.
3. The second (expanded) edition of *The Gay Science*, in which Nietzsche added

a fifth book and preface to the four "books" making up the original edition, was completed in 1886 and published in 1887, just prior to *On the Genealogy of Morals*.

4. The use of the term "man" to render Nietzsche's term *Mensch* is virtually unavoidable; but I shall often use the German term as a reminder that this rather more gender-neutral term—which is properly understood in the sense of "human (being)" rather than "male"—is the one Nietzsche actually uses. He may well be deserving of criticism for at least some of his views with respect to men and women; but it is not his use of the term *Mensch* that invites such criticism. Whether it is objectionable on other grounds (e.g., that there is no such thing as human nature or "the type *Mensch*") is a different matter, that must be differently addressed and settled. It is Nietzsche's commitment to notions of the latter sort and his thinking with respect to them that are the issues in this essay; and they neither stand nor fall with his ideas about "men and women." (Indeed some of the latter may even be inconsistent with them, and so may be subject to internal criticism and correction; but that is a topic for another occasion.)

5. See my "Nietzsche's *The Gay Science*, Or, How to Naturalize Cheerfully," in *Reading Nietzsche*, ed. R. C. Solomon and K. M. Higgins (New York: Oxford University Press, 1988), pp. 68–86.

6. This section is derived from chap. 5 of my book *Nietzsche* (London: Routledge & Kegan Paul, 1983), pp. 274–277 and 291–295. Interested readers may find it helpful to consult this entire chapter.

7. See my "Philosophical Anthropology: What, Why and How," in *Philosophy and Phenomenological Research* 50 (Fall 1990): 155–176.

TWENTY-THREE

The Rationale of Nietzsche's
Genealogy of Morals

Claus-Artur Scheier

"You are not able to invent one page of this work, let alone its form."[1] Nietzsche wrote this in a draft of a letter to Carl Spitteler[2] at the end of December 1888, judging the literary endowments of the author of *Prometheus and Epimetheus*[3] by the artistic qualities of *On the Genealogy of Morals*. In view of the *style* of his books published after *Thus Spoke Zarathustra*, there can be little doubt that Nietzsche's assessment was right after all; at least German readers had to wait for the later essays of Gottfried Benn to enjoy such dashing prose once again. But concerning the *form*—what is the distinguishing feature of the *Genealogy*, which Spitteler had suggested to have been written in a hurry heedless of the rules of literary composition?[4]

Since the score of the *Hymn to Life*—finished with the help of Heinrich Köselitz (his Peter Gast)—was published only some twenty days before the *Genealogy*, Nietzsche evidently had not despaired of cutting a figure as a composer; and he moreover was a conscientious classical philologist, well versed in the problems of good reading and writing.[5] Though in a hurry, why should he forget his métier altogether in the case of a book which, it may be noted, he wanted to be printed exactly in the same fashion as *Beyond Good and Evil* with respect to "the lay out, letters, *number of lines*, etc."?[6] Furthermore, he claimed to have invented "a new gesture of language for these utterly new things,"[7] which the somewhat overtaxed Spitteler had taken for shoddy style. And finally, it appears that Nietzsche had thought of a subtle enough arrangement of the aphorisms.

For note that the *Genealogy* is divided into three parts containing seventeen, twenty-five, and twenty-eight aphorisms respectively, the sum total thus amounting to seventy—precisely the number of chapters of *Zarathustra I–III* (including the ten sections of the *Prologue*). At first glance this might seem to be accidental or, in any case, irrelevant. But there are many examples of the fact that Nietzsche loved to count his books and their parts, chapters, aphorisms, and, in the case of *Zarathustra,* even the verses. Notoriously, his favorite numbers were ten and seven—the latter presumably because of the New Testament book of *Revelation,* the former because of the Old Testament Decalogue and the Dekas of the Pythagoreans. In this light it is not farfetched to discover that the rationale of the seemingly irrational division of the *Genealogy* is the **golden section,** first applied to the complex as a whole and then to its greater part[8]—a device Nietzsche might have thought of before, but had never used in print.

This division possibly may provide for a certain kind of indirect aesthetic satisfaction; but it is nonetheless a little surprising. Why should anyone, let alone a philosopher, busy himself with such an exotic geometrical contrivance? As far as I know none other ever did. The golden section was well known to the Greeks, of course, and it played an important role in Renaissance mathematics and art—but not in philosophy.[9] Traditionally, the simplest way of not leaving a philosophical text to the unpremeditated flow of the pen seems to be that of cutting it up into two symmetrical halves, to stress the "middle term" (or conversely the absence of the middle term)— a method Plato had used with supreme art in many of the dialogues, and which sometimes was also adopted by Nietzsche. The divisions of the classical texts of philosophy typically reflect the backward and forward movement of thought. It was Hegel (of all philosophers!) who in his *Science of Logic* had stressed the distinction between division and method, allowing for the concealing of the progress of pure reflection behind a variegated and even impenetrable screen of sections, subsections and sub-subsections.

But then method in the strict sense of the Greek word *methodos* belongs to the belief in a *kosmos* or *systema mundi*; and Schopenhauer's renunciation of this belief in favor of the idea of a "one and only thought"[10] marks a turning point in the history of philosophy. Henceforth the division of a philosophical book was not employed to reflect and amplify the methodological procedure of clarifying the objective (natural) architecture of its subject matter in order to gain acceptance for it. Rather, it was designed to facilitate the presentation of the philosopher's experience of a reality that was no longer to be justified by any metaphysics whatever. The most famous as well as most influential example in the nineteenth century is Marx's account of the world of capitalism.

So the problem of an adequate division could not but accompany Nietzsche's continual pondering of the most efficient form of conveying his judgments to hoped-for disciples, after he had come to realize that the books to be published after *Zarathustra* had to be "fishhooks."[11] Like all his earlier books, these would not be written in the manner of methodical development. They were compiled out of a basically amorphous mass of spontaneous notes on the most diverse subjects. Thus the whole process of preparing this bric-à-brac for publication could only be one of selecting, combining, rewriting, gathering-under-heads, and so on. This, in its turn, clearly had to be guided by a self-conscious judgment of what in each case was indispensable concerning the context, as well as what would be digestible—and, moreover, alluring—to the reader. Above all, though, Nietzsche was an artist, who was proud of his "taste," early equated with Greek *sophia*;[12] and he had his secrets of craftsmanship, just as the greatest of his literary contemporaries did. So it was not at all unnecessary or even idiosyncratic that he should remind us time and again of his being "a teacher of slow reading" (D P:5).[13]

> An aphorism, honestly coined and cast, is not yet "deciphered" simply by being read off; this is only the starting point for its *interpretation*, which is in need of an art of interpretation. (GM P:8)

This may be taken for granted. But then it is more than merely a generally applicable rule for getting to the core of the books of a philologist-philosopher, who used to describe himself as a "friend of riddles," and who confessed to a deeply rooted aversion against allowing the "stimulus of the enigmatic character" of the world be taken away from him.[14] For Nietzsche provides a hint, which is missed easily enough, but which may strike a reader already familiar with his *Genealogy* as rather perplexing:

> In the third essay of this book I have presented a paradigm of what I call "interpretation" in a case like this:—this essay is preceded by an aphorism, the essay itself is its commentary. (GM P:8)

This "aphorism" runs:

> Careless, mocking, violent—such it is that *we* are willed by wisdom; she is a woman, she always loves only a warrior. (GM III)

Again, there might seem to be nothing special in this to worry about. The part of the *Genealogy* in question deals with the meaning of ascetic ideals, with their presence in modern science, with scientific truth as a means of degeneracy, with decadence as the way to final peace of mind, and with the hidden essence of the ascetic ideal or with the will to nothingness. (So much for wisdom, woman, war.) Yet science is but one of the many aspects of the power of the ascetic ideal—and not the foremost one, since the figure looming largest in these twenty-eight aphorisms is neither the scientist nor even the priest, but the artist-priest (or artist-philosopher). And for Nietzsche the contemporary paradigm of *the* artist is, of course, Richard Wagner.

To be sure, this was so from the beginning of their acquaintance, which at first (not surprisingly) had been characterized by devotion, love, and adoration on the side of the younger of them. Richard Wagner was thirty-one years older than Nietzsche, and Cosima (Baroness Bülow, when he first came to know her), seven years older. But the halcyon days of Triebschen proved to be the constellation of a tragedy (which Nietzsche for peculiar reasons of his own would later on prefer to call a parody[15]). The Bayreuth affair of the Wagners could not but result in the end in a more or less creeping disillusionment with hopes *The Birth of Tragedy* had proclaimed as the *task* of Bayreuth: that the tragedian Wagner and the philosopher Nietzsche together would revoke the fateful error of the philosopher Socrates and tragedian Euripides—namely, the introduction of logical optimism into the history of European mankind (BT 18), changing its course in the fatal way fundamentally revised and retold in the *Genealogy*.

So there is a deeper reason why Nietzsche was so eager to present the *Genealogy* as the exact twin of *Beyond Good and Evil*. In the case of this first book after the publication of *Zarathustra*, Nietzsche also had taken great pains to make it as far as possible akin to an earlier one both in content and form—namely, to *Human, All Too Human*.[16] A *déjà vu*, it would seem; yet there is an important difference. Even if Nietzsche wanted *Beyond Good and Evil* to be exactly like *Human, All Too Human*, and the *Genealogy* to be exactly like *Beyond Good and Evil*, he clearly did not want the *Genealogy* to have the same structure as *Human, All Too Human*—apparently because it had such a different subject. Thus he saw to it that *Beyond Good and Evil* should be divided into ten parts, the headings of which would even at the first glance show a parallelism to the ten parts of the earlier book. But the subject of the sequel to *Beyond Good and Evil* was European history conceived as the coming-to-be of a certain (nihilistic) type of soul—evidently the same subject with which he had first come to grips in *The Birth of Tragedy*. So why not model the new book on his first one from the outset, saving the trouble of the detour? At least, if *Beyond Good and Evil* had been anything like a commercial success. But it hadn't been—and in any event, Nietzsche had something else in mind. What he wanted to make sure of was that "his" reader should himself *take* (and not only recognize) the decisive step back, which the author of the new book had ventured upon before.[17] It was a case of "fishhooks" again.

In this perspective it becomes clear why Wagner plays such an important (even if superficially not at all conspicuous) role in the *Genealogy*. It would no doubt be an exaggeration to maintain that the Third Essay (let alone the other two) has merely to do with the originary relation between *the* artist (Wagner) and *the* philosopher (Nietzsche). These twenty-eight aphorisms have—as all of Nietzsche's final work has—a textural polyphony comparable only to that of the score of Wagner's *Tristan*. But note, after lengthy preparation, the introduction of the theme giving the colors and, in a way, the clue to the preceding parts, by the at once innocent and portentous "Or" after the dash in the second aphorism:

What is the meaning of ascetic ideals?—Or, to take up one single case, concerning which I have often enough been asked for advice, what does it mean,
for instance, when an artist like Richard Wagner in his old days runs into
worshipping chastity? (GM III:2)

Wagner's conversion from Feuerbach to Schopenhauer became, retro-
spectively, a spur to Nietzsche's conversion from his "educator" Schopenhauer to himself. The way was a long one, counting by books. Planning
Nietzsche contra Wagner, he writes to Spitteler: "In fact I've been waging war
for the last ten years—as Wagner himself knew best."[18] This "war" had at
least two phases. The first phase, from *Human, All Too Human* to *Zarathustra
III,* was the recognition, rumination, and subsequent digestion of his initial
error in estimating the role Wagner was to play in revolutionizing the reigning European mentality in the way Nietzsche had outlined previously in
The Birth of Tragedy. The second phase, beginning with *Zarathustra IV,* had
its first exacerbation (as it were) in the course of the prefaces to his pre-
Zarathustra works in 1886. Nietzsche realized, in fact, that he could not do
without Wagner; that the composer of *The Twilight of the Gods* was indeed a
destiny; and that the success of the Zarathustrian project was in an ominous
manner dependent on the creator of "that poor devil and boor Parsifal"
(GM III:3)—not as an ally (as a matter of fact, there seemed to be none
left), but as the very paradigm of the antipode. It is in this mood that he
must have thought of himself as Zarathustra in relation to this former idol:

> I was not asked, I should have been asked, what precisely in my mouth, in the
> mouth of the first immoralist, is the meaning of the name of *Zarathustra.*
> Zarathustra *created* this most baneful error, morality: consequently he must
> also be the first to *recognize* it. (EH IV:3)

Zarathustra IV[19] is the mythopoeic constellation of the "new problem"
(HH I:P:7). *Beyond Good and Evil,* "the school for the *gentilhomme,*"[20] is
perceptibly reconnoitering the terrain.[21] The prefaces of 1886 are an open
declaration of war;[22] and in answering the question of the meaning of ascetic ideals, the *Genealogy* commences full battle. No wonder that the next
book, characterized as "a little relief,"[23] is devoted exclusively to "the case";
and *Twilight of the Idols* will be a parody, as if in remembrance of *Philology
of the Future,* Ulrich Wilamowitz-Moellendorff's attack on *Birth,* already rid-
iculed in Zarathustra's speech "On Scholars" (Z II:16).

It is one of the most curious and intriguing phenomena of Nietzsche's
philosophical "psychology" that the traditional linguistic limits between
the professional and the private existence of the author, or between his
private life and his public teaching, gradually disappear in the course of
his development. This was not because Nietzsche came to be more and
more involved in certain private problems (such as, for instance, his relations to the Wagners). On the contrary, it was rather because he became

increasingly aware that there were no "private" problems of his apart from the "public" ones. Not only was he a *destiny* (not necessarily quite in the sense he imagined)—*he* was a destiny: whatever his experiences, they were paradigmatic. Subtracting Nietzsche's philosophy from what we arbitrarily deem not his philosophy but "only" his life (or, to make matters worse, his psychopathological condition) will leave us with a rather barren thing, despised by those who think they know once and for all what philosophy is, and what science is, and that philosophy is a science. Nietzsche, for his part, thought of his philosophy as "wisdom."

Therefore, for Nietzsche, Wagner is also more than the famous composer whose operas everybody is free either to like or not. Wagner is, in truth, a philosophical "case"[24]—and whatever Nietzsche chose to write with regard to *that* is something we had better take as part and parcel of Nietzsche's *philosophy*. This leads to the philosophical reason why he maintained that "What is the Meaning of Ascetic Ideals?" (the Third Essay of the *Genealogy*) should be read as a basic text in the school of interpretation. This reason is the idea to which the lines to be interpreted originally belonged. *Zarathustra* had just been recalled in the last aphorism of the Second Essay; and it follows naturally that the "aphorism" recommended in the preface for close inspection by any "good" reader is to be found (with some minor differences) in Zarathustra's speech "On Reading and Writing," which begins:

> Of all that is written I love only what one writes with one's blood. Write with blood: and you shall experience that blood is spirit. (Z I:7)

This entire speech is the literary program of the philosopher Nietzsche;[25] but what is of special interest here is its clandestine relation to the later book. For Nietzsche picks out the fourteenth verse, the first one of the second half, of a set of twenty-six; and since "On Reading and Writing" is the seventh speech of Zarathustra's, one may suppose that Nietzsche was counting even in looking for some lines he could pretend to have interpreted in the last part of a book divided by the golden section. In a sense the verse is the gist of the whole speech, ending with an astonishing outburst, which raises the question of how it is pertinent to the subject of reading and writing at all:

> Now I am light, now I fly, now I am seeing myself below myself, now a god is dancing through me. (Z I:7)

But this is again in need of a reader possessing the art of "rumination" (GM P:8), connecting this final verse instinctively, as it were, with Zarathustra's prayer on behalf of beauty, "that an image might not remain a mere image" (Z II:15), and also with the last three sections of *Zarathustra III*.[26] All this seems to show that the speech prefigures the fulfillment of

Zarathustra's mission. This mission, his repeated "catastrophe" or "going under" (Z I:P:1), is the breeding and cultivation of "life" for eternal recurrence, hinted at as early as the tenth section of *Zarathustra's Preface*, or (as will unobtrusively appear in the course of the second part[27]), the education of Zarathustra's soul[28] to the knowledge of itself as the Bride of Dionysos. All of Nietzsche's writings are more or less overtly of a dialogic character,[29] exemplifying Feuerbach's comprehensive post-idealistic postulate that "true dialectic is no monologue of the lonesome thinker with himself," but a "dialogue between I and You."[30] Nietzsche will remember this well in Zarathustra's verse: "Meanwhile I speak as one who has time to myself. Nobody tells me of new things: so I tell myself of myself" (Z III:12:1)—a lonesomeness finally transfigured into the remembrance of the originary You: "And so I tell myself of life."[31] But this is only the next to the last stage of his continual dialogue with his soul.

The last stage will be reached as soon as the program of *Ecce Homo* is put to the test. It is in this sense that we ought to rank the postcards and letters of *Sanctus Januarius* 1889 with the previous works as the *disjecta membra* of an impossible book: its title would be *Ecce Deus*. Here the vanishing of persons into their *personae* has come to its close—the equation of individuals with eternal forces, of Nietzsche with Dionysos, of Wagner with Theseus, of Cosima with Ariadne, is perfect. For it is in the texts after *Zarathustra*, though long prepared for, that the Dionysian connotation of the name of Wagner will be Theseus, and of the name of Cosima, Ariadne.[32] The sense of this *triple alliance*[33] is generally behind Nietzsche's purposefully leading the reader astray,[34] as it is behind the calculated "rationalization" of the intense relation between the verse from "On Reading and Writing" and the third part of the *Genealogy* as the ingenuous interpretation of an "aphorism." The inquiry into the origin of the power of ascetic ideals leads up to their first and only alternative as the anti-ideal of Zarathustra; and Zarathustra and the ascetic ideal are both competitors in the war Nietzsche had waged for the last decade,[35] the *spolia opima* of which would be "life" itself. To be sure, "wisdom" is a woman, as the verse from "On Reading and Writing" tells us; but "life" is also a woman, as the whole speech will tell us. And then she is the more beloved one (Z III:15:2), since "wisdom" knows of creation, whereas "life" is creation itself—or might be, if only. . . . So the soul as creative life is the essential aim of a "psychological" interpretation in the Nietzschean sense of "psychology," and the virtual task of the "aphorism" is to give the hint to the ruminative reader.

Now, after more than a hundred years' lapse of time and the collapse in two world wars of the Nietzschean world (as well as of the one by which it was immediately succeeded),[36] we may be prompted to ask what all this means—with Nietzsche himself reminding us that he should have been asked for the meaning of the name Zarathustra.[37] At the risk of being all-too-brief, I would like to venture upon an answer, referring Nietzsche's concept of life to the notion of representation he had taken over from Schopenhauer. The principal subject of German idealism was *self-consciousness*, whether as the synthetic unity of apperception (Kant) or the absolute ego (Fichte) or the absolute spirit (Hegel). These and other such notions within this horizon (like the early romantic concepts of "nature") mean *reflection*; and it is owing to the nature of (methodical) reflection that Hegel is justified in saying: "The *Begriff*, insofar as it has ripened to such an *existence*, which itself is free, is nothing but *I* or the pure self-consciousness."[38] Thus the transcendental Ego is conceived of as the *bright* point of existence.

But when Schopenhauer in the second volume of *The World as Will and Representation* defines the Ego as the *dark* point in consciousness (comparing it to the point of entrance of the optic nerve on the retina),[39] then the concept of *reflection* is already replaced by the notion of *intentionality*, which was to enjoy such a triumphant advance since the times of Brentano and Husserl. By introducing the essence of intentionality into the very heart of metaphysics, Schopenhauer naturally did not absolutely dismiss reflection. It survives on the one hand as a faculty of consciousness, and on the other as the "thing in itself"—no longer the Kantian one, to be sure, but "will" willing itself or hungry "will to life," the first in the nineteenth and twentieth centuries' series of realities no longer justified by metaphysics.

Since in Schopenhauer "will" is the anti-value *par excellence*, the sounding of the depth of the interdependence of "will" (reflection) and "representation" (intentionality) must result in a clash; and consequently Schopenhauer's answer to the problem of existence is "neither/nor"—the *Nirvana* or nothingness preached in the fourth book of *The World as Will and Representation*. But it remains to consider the third book on "the object of art," the true birthplace of Nietzsche's philosophy. Whereas the doctrines of Schopenhauer's older idealistic contemporaries construed art as the aesthetic appearance or revelation of truth itself, in Schopenhauer art becomes the appearance of a mere appearance, that is, of the "Veil of the Maja"—with the result that aesthetic satisfaction, in itself transitory between pain and boredom,[40] is no real satisfaction either.

It is precisely this "pessimistic" outlook, even in matters of art, to which Nietzsche, his pupil, will eventually object. Roughly speaking, the aesthetic moment had to be *eternalized* to escape existentially both from the Scylla of "will to life" devouring itself and the Charybdis of "will to nothingness." Thus Nietzsche in his turn had to become aware of the abysmal connection between reflection and intentionality—or, in his own words, "life" giving perpetual birth to itself by perpetually surmounting itself on the one hand, and "thought" loving "life" and educating it to its task of creation on the other. His own answer to the problem of existence, in short, is quite the reverse one of Schopenhauer's—namely "both/and"; and in this sense he was right in emphasizing that he and Schopenhauer were antipodes.

This, at last, yields the reason for Nietzsche's as yet unexplained pride concerning the *form* of the *Genealogy*. "Dionysos is notoriously also the God of Darkness" (EH III:GM); but in the first place he is a Greek god,[41] and the bridegroom of Ariadne at that. Musing afresh over the subject of Zarathustra's speech "On the Three Transformations" in the spring of 1884, Nietzsche notes: "Higher than 'Thou shall' is 'I will' (the heroes); higher than 'I will' is 'I am' (the gods of the Greeks)."[42] The following note reads: "Regarding Zarathustra: 'the golden beings' as the highest step."[43] When in 1887, after having finished the prefaces and "We Fearless Ones" (the fifth book of *The Gay Science*), Nietzsche wanted the reader to accept "What is the Meaning of Ascetic Ideals?" as the interpretation of a verse in a speech of Zarathustra's, dealing itself with interpretation (of Life, that is), and leading up to the anticipation of Dionysos, he was intimating that what is at stake in waging war against the Ascetic Ideal and its contemporary artist-priest are precisely "the golden beings." For the "*enkrateia* and *askesis* is only one step to the height: higher is the 'golden nature'."[44] What *form* then would be more appropriate to the division of a book aiming at the "golden nature" higher than all ascetic ideals, even the philosopher's, than the golden section? Since, to quote one of his last messages, "I, together with Ariadne, have to be but the Golden Equipoise of all things [. . . .]"[45]

NOTES

1. Quotations refer to the *Kritische Gesammtausgabe: Werke* (KGW) and *Briefwechsel* (BW), ed. G. Colli and M. Montinari, Berlin 1967ff (KG); translations are my own, and so are any blunders. I want to thank Richard Schacht for his careful reading of the first draft of this essay, and for kindly disencumbering it of a rather heavy load of rough English.

2. Carl Spitteler (1845–1924), a Swiss journalist and prolific writer, who had reviewed Nietzsche's books in the New Year's supplement of *Der Bund* in 1888. Compare *Ecce Homo*, "Why I Write such Good Books," § 1. For the rather involved personal connections between Nietzsche and Spitteler, see Curt Paul Janz, *Friedrich Nietzsche Biographie* (München: Hanser, 1981 [1st ed. München/Wien, 1978/79]).

3. Published in 1880 under the pseudonym of Felix Tandem. Spitteler was convinced that his poem had a decisive influence on *Thus Spoke Zarathustra* (compare his engaging remembrances *Meine Beziehungen zu Nietzsche*, München 1908), but this has proved not to be very likely (compare Janz, *Nietzsche*, vol. 2, pp. 224–228). He would finally publish his *Weltanschauung* in the form of a long epic poem, *Olympic Spring*, in 1900. As it appears, it is Nietzsche's olympic autumn, "his many-coloured tendernesses and fifty yellows and browns and greens and reds" (BGE 296), which represent the genuine season of the *fin de siècle*.

4. Compare Nietzsche's letter to Spitteler, 10 Feb. 1888.

5. Compare for instance the notes on "the perfect book" from autumn 1887, KGW VIII.2, 9[115].

6. Letter to the publisher, 29 July 1887, compare the letter of 17 July 1887.

7. Letter to Spitteler, 10 Feb. 1888.

8. In mathematical strictness the double division marks out the last aphorism of the first part and the beginning of the second aphorism of the third part.

9. The term "golden section" for the *proportio continua* seems not to have been used before the second third of the nineteenth century, compare the relevant passage s.v. "golden" in *Deutsches Wörterbuch von J. und W. Grimm*, 4 Bd., I. Abt., 5. Teil (Leipzig, 1958). I am indebted to my linguistic colleague Professor Helmut Henne for the reference, and to Dr. Claudia Frenzel and Dr. Regine Nahrwold for valuable information on the role of the golden section in mathematics and the history of art.

10. A. Schopenhauer, Preface to the first edition of *The World as Will and Representation* (1818).

11. EH III, "Beyond Good and Evil," 1.

12. HH II:1:170.

13. That is, *Daybreak*, Preface, section 5. In this and other such references, the works in question will be identified by the acronyms of their standard English titles, followed by indications of the relevant parts and/or sections.

14. KGW VIII.1, 2[162] and VIII.1, 2[155].

15. Compare GS P:1.

16. See the letter to the publisher, 12 April 1886; for the practice, see the letters regarding the layout of *The Birth of Tragedy*, which was to be like that of Wagner's *Über die Bestimmung der Oper* (1871).

17. This is already the intention of the series of prefaces of 1886; compare my introduction to *Friedrich Nietzsche. Ecce auctor. Die Vorreden von 1886* (Hamburg: Felix Meiner, 1990).

18. Letter to C. Spitteler, 11 Dec. 1888.

19. In which Wagner appears as the sorcerer, whom Nietzsche first met with in Horace's *Epistles*: "Ille per extentum funem mihi posse videtur/ire poeta meum qui pectus inaniter angit,/inritat, mulcet, falsis terroribus inplet,/ut magus, et modo me Thebis, modo ponit Athenis" (II.1.210–213).

20. EH, "Beyond Good and Evil," 2.

21. Compare BGE 47, 229, 240, 244f, 254, and particularly 256.

22. Compare above all the Preface to HH II.

23. Foreword to *The Case of Wagner*.

24. That "Wagner" was the aesthetical gathering together of basic modern tendencies formulated above all by Kierkegaard and Marx is a thesis I have tried to elucidate in the chapter on Wagner in *Nietzsches Labyrinth. Das ursprüngliche Denken und die Seele* (Freiburg/München: K. Alber, 1985).

25. Compare the remarks *On the Doctrine of Style* for Lou Salomé, August 1882 (KGW VII.1, 1[109]).

26. For the assessment of Nietzsche's philosophical development as well as of his art of literary composition it is important to see that *Zarathustra* both as a thematic and a structural unit comprises only *Zarathustra's* Preface plus the parts I–

III. *Zarathustra IV* is in both aspects independent of the first three parts ("the Higher Man" will be the subject of the post-Zarathustrian phase) and introduces, in fact, quite another Zarathustra.

27. Compare for instance the thirty-fifth verse of *On the Sublime Ones* together with the note in KGW VII.1, p. 453.

28. Compare the letter to C. Spitteler, 10 February 1888: "[My Zarathustra is] the deepest and most decisive event—of the *soul*, by your leave!—between two millennia. . . ."

29. For the several levels of the Nietzschean dialogue, see my remarks on "Contemporary Consciousness and Originary Thinking in a Nietzschean Joke," *The Southern Journal of Philosophy* 27 (1989): 549–559.

30. L. Feuerbach, *Principles of the Philosophy of the Future*, trans. Manfred H. Vogel (Indianapolis: Hackett, 1986), section 62. (Originally published in 1843.)

31. EH, prefatory note, "On this perfect day. . . ."

32. According to the development of the thought through the several stages of "going under" in *Zarathustra I–III* the very last word Zarathustra says to Life must be her name (Z III:15:2).

33. Foreword to *Nietzsche contra Wagner.*

34. Compare EH III:GM.

35. See note 18 above.

36. See my "I am no Human, I am Dynamite. Nietzsche's Historical Moment," *Journal of Nietzsche Studies* 2 (1991): 78–94.

37. Heidegger addressed this question in his lecture on "Who is Nietzsche's Zarathustra?" in *Lectures and Essays (Vorträge und Aufsätze,* Pfullingen: Neske, 1954). Heidegger's answer has the merit of being the answer of one of the three or four unquestionably inescapable philosophers of our century; but nevertheless there are reasons in Nietzsche not to subscribe to it.

38. G. W. F. Hegel, *Science of Logic,* trans. W. H. Johnson and L. G. Struthers (New York: Macmillan, 1956), vol. II, *Subjective Logic,* Introduction, "The Doctrine of the Notion: On the Notion in General." (Originally published 1812–1816.)

39. A. Schopenhauer, *The World as Will and Representation,* trans. E. F. J. Payne (New York: Dover, 1969), II:41.

40. Schopenhauer, *World as Will,* I:57.

41. Compare GS P:4.

42. KGW vol. VII.2, 25[351].

43. KGW vol. VII.2, 25[352].

44. KGW vol. VII.2, 25[351].

45. Letter to J. Burckhardt, 4 January 1889.

TWENTY-FOUR

"Have I Been Understood?"

David B. Allison

Have I been understood? . . . *"Not at all, my dear sir!"* (GM III:1)

On many occasions Nietzsche claimed a positive thematic unity between *Beyond Good and Evil* and *On the Genealogy of Morals*. Specifically, both were held to inaugurate the "revaluation of all values," and to serve as a "critique of modernity." Negatively, both texts were framed to overcome the stylistic and poetic excesses of *Zarathustra*. In the letters from this period, Nietzsche repeatedly lamented that his works were not understood, that no publisher wanted to touch them, and that even Heinrich von Stein—whom Nietzsche considered to be one of his three intellectual peers—could understand only twelve sentences of *Zarathustra*.[1]

What is at stake, then, is the question of communication. Nietzsche's attempts to invoke music and the dithyramb in *The Birth of Tragedy*, as well as a sustained poetic effort in *Zarathustra*, didn't prove to be effective vehicles by which to communicate his insights, his critique, and his teaching. He therefore felt compelled to return to the fundamental rhetorical strengths of his own tradition, and to find *in them* the communicative resources he so needed. In *Beyond Good and Evil* and the *Genealogy*, for example, Nietzsche specifically borrows the discourse of an unlikely ally: Martin Luther. Nietzsche had repeatedly declared that belief and faith subtend the axioms or principles of traditional thought. What better model should he turn to for the tropes of figurative language than to Luther himself—that *feste Burg* of German popular culture?

To examine the agency of this newfound *pensée domestique*, I'd like to focus on Nietzsche's rhetorical use of *aposiopesis*, which he explicitly borrows from Luther. Now, aposiopesis, or "becoming silent," designates a rhetorical halt, a narrative arrest or incompleteness, by which the speaker seems unwilling or unable to say anything—but, while the *idea* is literally unexpressed, it *is* clearly perceived. I'd like to point out how this figurative usage is effective in communicating to an audience—without itself, of course, being a logically proper form of expression; how, by reflecting on the means of its operation, Nietzsche devises the notion of what he comes to term "retrospective inference" in *Beyond Good and Evil*—a notion that will enable him to lend new coherency to his metacritical analyses; and how his reflections on these issues will ultimately have a most practical venue: they will provide his audience with an accessible means of understanding, and thus overcoming, *bad conscience*—which for him was precisely Luther's legacy. The overcoming of bad conscience is surely one of Nietzsche's principal teachings, and is widely regarded as one of the most difficult to communicate. More specifically, its teaching is the task—set forth so enigmatically in *Zarathustra*—of the Eternal Return.

Nietzsche draws two examples of aposiopesis from Luther. In one of his earliest published references to Luther, he first cites Luther's celebrated little philippic on faith: "This you have to decide for yourself, for your life is at stake." "With this cry of 'spiritual assault'," Nietzsche explains, "Luther *springs at us* and thinks *we feel the knife* at our throat."[2] This certainly reflects an awareness of the agonistic extremes Luther was prepared to take in the teaching of his "faith." Yet it seems that at the time Nietzsche perhaps confused the person with the doctrine, failing to appreciate the performative effect of Luther's rhetoric; for just a month earlier, he had written to Peter Gast:

> Dear friend, as for Luther, I have for a long time been incapable of saying honestly anything respectful about him. . . . Luther's hideous, arrogant, peevishly envious abusiveness—he felt out of sorts unless he was wrathfully spitting upon someone—has quite disgusted me. . . . I grant that *you* have the more charitable attitude toward him. *Give me time.*[3]

Only a year after Nietzsche's denunciation of this "spiritual assault," which lays the threat of perdition itself so heavily upon the reader, all the while *leaving it to the reader* to discern the content and validity of this faith, he would himself employ precisely the same rhetorical strategy—in the same context, perdition, and for a quite similar end: namely, for eternal salvation.

The later reference, of course, is to one of Nietzsche's most dramatic passages, section 341 of *The Gay Science*, entitled "The Greatest Weight" or "The Heaviest Burden." The same scene is again dramatically played out in *Zarathustra*, especially in books three and four, where the Eternal Return emerges as a teaching to overcome *ressentiment* and guilt (that is, *bad conscience*) through the expedient of accepting—of *willing*—the factual past along with the train of events continuous with it: namely, the present. Thus the Eternal Return is framed precisely to *counter* the attitude of bad conscience, brought about by the Christian worldview in general, and by Luther in particular. This will be Nietzsche's principal charge against Luther in *Beyond Good and Evil,* and will in turn serve to orchestrate the three essays of the *Genealogy.*

In the *Genealogy* Nietzsche explicitly invokes Luther once again, borrowing a second example of rhetorical aposiopesis from him—namely, Luther's own defense at the Diet of Worms: a discourse practically *without* any semantic content, without reason, without explanation; in short, a kind of *proffered silence,* fully ambiguous and infinitely transformable—according to the intentions of the audience. The example is Luther's famous remark to the Diet, on 28 January 1521: "Here I stand, I cannot do otherwise." What *is* this discourse of Worms? What was it *meant* to say, and precisely to whom? Was Luther simply being *humble?* As Nietzsche remarks in *Twilight of the Idols,* "When stepped on, a worm (*Wurm*) doubles up. That is clever. In that way, he lessens the probability of being stepped on again. In the language of morality: *humility*" (TI I:31). Or was Luther admitting his own *heretical* tendencies, and, thereby, his guilt? Or is this discourse of Worms the kind that Nietzsche attributed to Pascal—a "wormlike reason" (*wurmhaften Vernunft*)—which itself possesses an obstinacy and perdurance, ever vigilant and critical? All of this, perhaps. Nietzsche himself, however, was especially attentive to the undermining and destructive *effects* of such a rhetoric, turned against the foundations of proper discourse itself—a rhetoric directed against the systematic, ontotheological order as such. Hence Nietzsche's attribution—already in *The Gay Science*—of such a wormlike discourse to Luther:

> An edifice like Christianity that had been built so carefully over such a long period—naturally, it could not be destroyed at once. All kinds of earthquakes had to shake it, all kinds of spirits that *bore, dig, gnaw, and moisten* have had to help. But what is strangest is this: Those who exerted themselves the most to preserve and conserve Christianity have become precisely its most efficient destroyers—the Germans. . . . Luther's work, his will to restore that Roman work became, without his knowing or willing it, nothing but the beginning of a work of destruction. (GS 358; my emphasis)

When Nietzsche thus comes to criticize the Christian moral order of the New Testament in the *Genealogy,* he employs Luther's own rhetoric to do so, claiming: "I have the taste of two millennia against me: but there it is! Here I stand. I cannot do otherwise." There it is. No argument. A question of taste—taste against Luther, the "lout (*eines Rüpels*) who could not stomach the good etiquette of the church, that reverential etiquette of hieratic taste." A question of taste principally, however, against the ascetic ideal itself—which includes the inheritor of and successor to the Christian ascetic ideal, namely, modern science. He will say, in the following section, that "even when it is not the latest expression of the ascetic ideal . . . science today is a hiding place for every kind of discontent, disbelief, gnawing worm (*Nagewurm*), *despectio sui*, bad conscience" (GM III:22).

These and other passages of the *Genealogy* are an interesting *development* of Nietzsche's thought, for several reasons: they constitute a rhetorically informed agency—ironically so, by drawing upon Luther's own rhetoric— to bring about the demise of the traditional order (of thought and of morality), with its attendant metaphysics. These passages also show a marked tendency to approach the question of totality and system from its effects: namely, from the *inertial force* of the tradition—at once ideological, cultural, and psychological—which constituted the *codes* and the individual human *subjects* of that tradition. It is the analysis Nietzsche makes of Luther's *rhetoric* in *Beyond Good and Evil*, however, that enables him to characterize it as one of "bad conscience":

> In Germany ... there really was (until quite recently) only one species of public and *roughly artful rhetoric*: that from the *pulpit*. In Germany, the preacher *alone* knew what a syllable weighs, or a word, and how a sentence strikes, leaps, plunges, runs, and runs out. He alone had a conscience in his ears, and often enough a bad conscience.... The masterpiece of German prose is therefore, fairly enough, the masterpiece of its greatest preacher.... Compared with Luther's Bible, almost everything else is mere "literature"— [that is,] something that did not grow *in* Germany and therefore also did not and does not grow *into* German hearts—as the Bible did. (BGE 247, my emphasis)

If, for Nietzsche, bad conscience is the projection of *ressentiment* to the entire domain of the cultural—when resentment becomes creative to the point of instituting an entire "moral metaphysics" of good/evil, God/devil, and so on, (and Luther's *reform* of this tradition is striking in its almost Mannichean hyperbole)—the characteristic attitude of this resentful man of bad conscience is *silence* (or, as Erik Erikson would insist, passivity[4]). It is silence that serves as a shield and protection for bad conscience, which stands opposed to naiveté—a silence that loves hiding places, secret paths, and back doors. As Nietzsche would remark in the *Genealogy*: "Everything covert entices [such a person] as his world, his security, his refreshment. He understands how to keep silent, how not to forget, how to wait, how to be *provisionally self-deprecating and humble*" (GM I:10). Again, "Here I stand, I cannot do otherwise."

Aposiopesis is an especially effective figure, since it forces the reader, the auditor, to supply additional cognitive, emotional, and semantic material to complete what was initially written or spoken.[5] More than most tropes, which demand a similar obligation on the part of the audience, the figure of aposiopesis is incomplete in a dramatically temporal fashion. It capitalizes on the inertia of expectation, the demand for propositional completeness: namely, that the semantic content of the utterance be expressed or acknowledged completely. As initially uttered or written, it is not complete, since it must be *supplemented* by the audience to be rendered complete. The incompleteness may in many cases be sustained by a narrational inertia which is suspended, which pauses or stops abruptly—even by raising a question. But in every case, the audience feels itself *obliged* to complete the utterance, to make sense out of what was only partially or incompletely expressed. Incompletely expressed: that is, only indicated. It is the indicative utterance *par excellence*, similar in form to a hint, a pointing, an impulse or gesture. Since aposiopesis (like figurative discourse in general) presupposes the extant field of signs, the semantic field of custom, value, habit, codes, and so forth, *communication is* (to all appearances) *effective*, but *expression proper* is not. *Effective, affective* communication does occur; but it is not necessarily true, not necessarily referential, that is, according to truth, conventionally understood as *adequatio*.[6]

Nietzsche could only marvel at the fact that Luther's rhetoric concerning an inner faith, an inner dialogue with God himself, would effectively incite 150,000 German peasants to be slaughtered by their princes in the Peasant Revolt of 1526. He saw a terrifying circuit here: because Luther was of the people, spoke their language, rhetorically intensifying the only book available to them—precisely by translating it into German, circulating it widely, and preaching endlessly from it—it was clear that *they* would be of *his* mind. A kind of communication, then, by induction, by inference, at a distance. Thus, for Nietzsche, the "founders" of religions—specifically Luther—are really "finders" of a yet to be fully articulated and pronounced doctrine: the articulation is theirs, the semantic foundations are everyone's.

Since aposiopesis also relies upon the dialogical stratum of language, its effectiveness testifies to a temporally constitutive (or recollective) *consciousness* on the part of the reader or auditor—precisely to fill in the lacuna of discourse become silent. It is with this recognition in mind that *Beyond Good and Evil* (especially) begins to assemble a *positive* account of what had been, until then, variously scattered theses and themes, concerning epistemology, ontology, language, and culture. In *Beyond Good and Evil*, all these issues owe their respective coherence not to Dionysian rhapsody or to poetic embellishment, but to a broadly construed structure of concept-formation—an operation Nietzsche will now call "retrospective inference" (*Rückschluss, Rückbeziehung*). And "retrospective inference" or the "retrospective force" (*rückwirkende Kraft*), or "connection," as he also terms it, stands as the collective response and supplement to the rhetorical figure of aposiopesis.

This retrospective force operates as the structuring at once of memory, of association and habit; it draws upon and continually augments the screen of familiarity and semantic reference, in terms of which anything comes to consciousness at all and is re-cognized as such. In retrospective inference, the new is always explained in terms of the old, the different in terms of the same; and this means that to *be* cognized, the object is always *re*cognized; that communication itself—with all its strata, with all that it presupposes—subtends every knowledge and truth claim.

Obviously, the degree of generality covered by such a notion as retrospective inference is enormous: it would be the cognitive and semantic equivalent of that "single force" or "hypothesis" otherwise known as the "Will to Power." In any case, Nietzsche first explicitly characterizes this "activity" of retrospective inference in BGE 16, showing that the very foundation of metaphysics—namely, the possibility of any immediate certainty—is the *result* of this operation, and thus hardly merits the name (much less the place) accorded it by tradition. The example given initially criticizes the axiom of the ego subject:

When I analyze the process that is expressed in the sentence, "I think" ..., if I had not already decided within myself what it is, by what standard could I determine whether that which is just happening is not perhaps "willing" or "feeling"? In short, the assertion "I think" assumes that I compare my state at the present moment with other states of myself which I know, in order to determine what it is; on account of this *retrospective connection* (*Rückbeziehung*) with further "knowledge," it has, at any rate, no immediate certainty. ... In place of the "immediate certainty" [one rather] finds a series of metaphysical questions ... : "From where do I get the concept of thinking?" "Why do I believe in cause and effect?" "What gives me the right to speak of an ego?" etc. (BGE 16; my emphasis)

The tasks set forth by this "retrospective connection," this interminably mediated, interminably reinterpreted character of understanding and knowledge, will govern the majority of Nietzsche's analyses for the rest of *Beyond Good and Evil*: for example, his accounts of the ego subject, the will, free will, determined will, causality, objectivity, the nature of predication and the copula function, the notion of "being" as a derivative grammatical function, faculty and ego psychology, as well as knowledge and truth. In raising the preconditions for the very axioms of thought, that is, the information that subtends axiomatics itself, Nietzsche also sets forth the tasks for the *Genealogy*, his very next work, where he will say:

Whatever exists, having somehow come into being, is again and again *reinterpreted* to *new* ends, taken over, transformed, and redirected by some power superior *to* it; all events in the organic world ... involve a *fresh interpretation*, an *adaptation* through which any previous "meaning" and "purpose" are necessarily obscured or even obliterated. ... The *entire history* of a thing, an organ, a custom, can in this way be a continuous sign-chain of ever new interpretations and adaptations. ... The form is fluid, but the "meaning" is even more so. (GM II:12; my emphasis)

What is striking here, for Nietzsche, is that "reality" (so called: that is, "being," "truth," and "reference"), insofar as it makes any sense at all, or has any meaning whatsoever, is itself a *product* of this retrospective inference. What becomes the object *of* this generalized procedure is thereby understood to have been produced *by* it: historically, culturally, linguistically, and morally—and, invariably, "herdlike." Nothing can be properly expressed as such, since the *as such* is itself precisely part of the signifying, or as Nietzsche says, of the interpreting. Thus, he remarks, "all concepts in which an entire process is semiotically concentrated, elude definition; only that which has no history is definable" (GM II:13). Or, to borrow a phrase from Spinoza, *natura naturata* is always *natura naturans*.

Thus, for Nietzsche in the *Genealogy*, "good," "bad," and "evil" are always understood to be evolving concepts. The very *first* analysis *begins* with a "transformation" of preexistent value formations. Likewise the notion of "punishment"—to which Foucault's analysis owed so much—is *so* malleable and ductile as to be "fluid." "Bad conscience"—which emerges out of "conscience," and that in turn, out of a "trained memory" and an acquired "sense of responsibility," prompted in turn by "fear"—also entails a series of grafts, causal reversals, and cultural imputations, doggedly lost to antiquity. Auguring multiple future "uses," "senses," and "adaptations" of bad conscience, Nietzsche suggests that these will be subject at least in part to the manipulative wits of our latter-day "priests, administrators," and self-styled "great communicators." Finally, the "ascetic ideal" itself emerges as a veritable *constellation* of practices, valuations, and beliefs. Discursively, it would seem successively to embrace practically every formation from obscure Cappadocian heresies to modern-day scientific and scholarly inquiry. In fact, this is part of Nietzsche's amazement at the outset of the Third Essay. "*That* the ascetic ideal *has meant so many* things to man," he exclaims, must reflect "the basic fact of the human will," which would appear to be "its *horror vacui*" (GM III:1).

That one learn to recognize *how* retrospective inference works upon the past (which, after all, no longer is), thereby perpetually reworking it, recreating it and us with it—this is perhaps Nietzsche's strongest general claim in *Beyond Good and Evil* and the *Genealogy*, as well as in the immediately following texts. To tie this series of operations into a teaching, the Eternal Return, which would overcome the tradition of bad conscience—that tradition which, precisely *by* retrospective inference, had turned the "world" into a moral and metaphysical indictment, a place of opprobrium, in which every entity and act is judged accordingly (Luther: "*Scatet totus orbis*"[7])—to overcome *all that*, precisely by returning to the *same rhetorical strategy*, would for Nietzsche constitute a fully liberated past and an open future for humanity. It would constitute the long-awaited *cure*. As he would remark in

Ecce Homo, "To redeem those who have lived in the past and to turn every 'it was' into a 'thus I willed it'—that alone I should call redemption."[8]

Following the reception of *Zarathustra* (and in deference to von Stein's insistence), however, Nietzsche realized he could no longer freely express his teaching of the Eternal Return in such grandiose and poetic terms. Henceforth, he would reformulate his "most enigmatic" teaching in other terms: he would recast the constituent and interrelated elements of the teaching into an extended series of particular analyses, generally structured according to "retrospective" forms of interpretation, of concept-formation. This strategic rhetorical move would have the double advantage of permitting a great deal more specificity in his discourse, and of inducing the *reader* to recognize, precisely within himself, the existence and cognitive operation of these formations—thereby lending them a more effective purchase. In turn, what Nietzsche had to say about these matters (ultimately leading to the hoped-for elimination of bad conscience, to a cure, indeed, to "redemption") would no longer appear to be so directive or dogmatic, so suggestive of that very tradition with which he took such issue—"moral metaphysics."

As a postscript: Nietzsche's texts would henceforth appear to be far more conventional; yet they would also be characterized—due to his newly found appreciation of aposiopesis—by a marked element of indirection, of *silence,* about the "grand" teachings, the oftentimes overembellished "doctrines." It is not at all surprising, then, that the balefully enigmatic and poetically overcharged term "Eternal Return" (*die ewige Wiederkehr des Gleichen*) is *not itself mentioned a single time* in *Beyond Good and Evil* or in the *Genealogy.* In his unpublished drafts, however, right through 1888, Nietzsche would continue to describe the Eternal Return at length, in quite specific (and variant) detail. Nonetheless, it is *not mentioned* in *Beyond Good and Evil,* nor in the *Genealogy,* nor in *The Antichrist.* When it is explicitly discussed in his "autobiographical" *Ecce Homo* of 1888, it is still held to be "the highest formula of affirmation that is at all attainable"—attainable, perhaps, by Nietzsche alone.

"—Then let us start again, from the beginning."

NOTES

1. Letter to Gast, 2 October 1884. In *Selected Letters of Friedrich Nietzsche,* ed. and trans. C. Middleton (Chicago: The University of Chicago Press, 1969), p. 269. Four years later, recounting this very incident, in *Ecce Homo* (*On the Genealogy of Morals and Ecce Homo,* trans. W. Kaufmann [New York: Vintage, 1969]), "Why I Write Such Good Books," section 1, p. 259, von Stein is credited with understanding only *six* sentences of the entire work.

2. Compare *Daybreak*, trans. R. J. Hollingdale (Cambridge: Cambridge University Press, 1982), book 1, section 82, p. 84.

3. Letter To Gast, 5 October 1879 in Middleton, *Selected Letters*, pp. 169–170. My emphasis. By the time of GM, however, he is clear to separate the individual from the work. Having just compared Wagner to Luther at the opening of the Third Essay of GM ("What is the Meaning of Ascetic Ideals?"), Nietzsche remarks "that one does best to separate an artist from his work, not taking him as seriously as his work. He is, after all, only the precondition of his work, the womb, the soil, sometimes the dung and manure, out of which it grows—and therefore in most cases something one must forget if one is to enjoy the work itself" (pp. 100–101). The allusion to Luther is hardly to be missed by the German reader: Luther's central insight, the doctrine of the justification by faith—occurred to him in the Wittenberg privy. N. O. Brown would later devote an extensive analysis to this "excremental vision," as he termed it, in his *Life Against Death: The Psychoanalytical Meaning of History* (New York: Random House, 1959), chap. 13, pp. 179–201.

4. Compare E. Erickson, *Young Man Luther: A Study in Psychoanalysis and History* (New York: Norton, 1958).

5. Compare especially Nietzsche's Basel lectures on rhetoric, "Description of Ancient Rhetoric (1872–73)," sections 7 ("The Tropical Expression") and 8 ("The Rhetorical Figures"), in *Friedrich Nietzsche on Rhetoric and Language*, ed. and trans. S. Gilman, C. Blair, and D. Parent (New York: Oxford, 1989), pp. 51–83.

6. "The power to discover and to make operative that which works and impresses, with respect to each thing, a power that Aristotle calls rhetoric, is, at the same time, the essence of language; the latter is based just as little as rhetoric is upon that which is true, upon the essence of things. Language does not desire to instruct, but to convey to others a subjective impulse and its acceptance," Gilman, Blair, and Parent, eds., *Nietzsche*, p. 21.

7. In Brown, *Life Against Death*, p. 226.

8. EH, "Zarathustra," 8, pp. 308–309. Affirmatively, such a task would result, precisely, in the reformation of Luther's Reformation.

NOTES ON CONTRIBUTORS

DAVID ALLISON is Professor of Philosophy at the State University of New York at Stony Brook. He is editor of *The New Nietzsche* and author of *Psychosis and Sexuality*, and has recently completed a book on the Marquis de Sade.

FRITHJOF BERGMANN is Professor of Philosophy at the University of Michigan. His publications include *On Being Free* and essays on Nietzsche and ethics. He is writing a book on the transformation of work and its place in our lives.

RÜDIGER BITTNER is Professor of Philosophy at the University of Bielefeld. He is the author of *What Reason Demands* and essays in recent European philosophy, moral philosophy, and action theory.

ERIC BLONDEL is Professor of Philosophy at the University of Paris (Pantheon-Sorbonne). He is the author of *Nietzsche, le cinquièine évangile?*, *Nietzsche: The Body and Culture*, and *Le Risible et le Dérisoire*, and has translated a number of Nietzsche's books into French.

MAUDEMARIE CLARK is Associate Professor of Philosophy at Colgate University. She is the author of *Nietzsche on Truth and Philosophy*, and is writing a book on Nietzsche's critique of morality.

DANIEL W. CONWAY teaches philosophy at the Pennsylvania State University, where he is also Codirector of its Center for Ethics and Value Inquiry. His publications include essays on Nietzsche and other developments in European philosophy.

ARTHUR C. DANTO is Johnsonian Professor of Philosophy Emeritus at Columbia University. His many books include *Nietzsche as Philosopher, The Transfiguration of the Commonplace, The Politics of Imagination, Connections to the World*, and *Encounters and Reflections: Art in the Historical Present*.

PHILIPPA FOOT is Griffin Professor Emeritus at UCLA, and now resides in Oxford. Her publications include *Theories of Ethics, Virtues and Vices,* and many essays dealing chiefly with topics in ethics.

KATHLEEN MARIE HIGGINS is Associate Professor of Philosophy at the University of Texas at Austin. She is the author of *Nietzsche's Zarathustra* and *The Music of Our Lives,* and coeditor (with Robert Solomon) of *Reading Nietzsche* and *The Philosophy of (Erotic) Love.*

DAVID COUZENS HOY is Professor of Philosophy and of the History of Consciousness at the University of California, Santa Cruz. He is the author of *The Critical Circle: Literature, History, and Philosophical Hermeneutics,* and is editor of *Foucault: A Critical Reader.*

SARAH KOFMAN is Professor of Philosophy at the University of Paris (Sorbonne). Her many books include *Nietzsche and Metaphor, Nietzsche et la scène philosophique,* and *Explosion I: de l'Ecce Homo de Nietzsche.* Others published in English translation are *The Childhood of Art, The Enigma of Woman, Freedom and Fiction,* and *Literary Theory Today.*

BRIAN LEITER teaches philosophy at the University of San Diego School of Law. He holds a law degree as well as a Ph.D. in philosophy, and has published in journals of both law and philosophy.

ALASDAIR MACINTYRE is McMahon/Hank Professor of Philosophy at the University of Notre Dame. His recent books include *Against the Self-Images of the Age, After Virtue, Whose Justice? Which Rationality?,* and *Three Rival Versions of Moral Enquiry.*

BERND MAGNUS is Professor of Philosophy at the University of California, Riverside and Director of its Center for Ideas and Society. He is the author of *Heidegger's Metahistory of Philosophy* and *Nietzsche's Existential Imperative,* and is coauthor of *Nietzsche's Case: Philosophy as/and Literature.* He was cofounder and the first executive officer of the North American Nietzsche Society.

JEAN-PIERRE MILEUR is Professor of English at the University of California, Riverside. His publications include *Vision and Revision: Coleridge's Art of Immanence, Literary Revisionism and the Burden of Modernity,* and *The Critical Romance;* and he is coauthor of *Nietzsche's Case: Philosophy as/and Literature.*

ALEXANDER NEHAMAS is Professor of Philosophy and Carpenter Professor of the Humanities at Princeton University. He is the author of *Nietzsche: Life as Literature* and essays on ancient philosophy, the philosophy of art and literary theory, and (with Paul Woodruff) has translated Plato's *Symposium* and *Phaedrus.*

MARTHA C. NUSSBAUM is David Benedict Professor, Professor of Philosophy and Classics, and Adjunct Professor of Comparative Literature at Brown University. She is editor of several volumes on Greek philosophy, and is author of *The Fragility of Goodness: Luck and Ethics in Greek Tragedy and Philosophy* and *Love's Knowledge: Essays on Philosophy and Literature.*

RICHARD SCHACHT is Professor of Philosophy and Jubilee Professor of Liberal Arts and Sciences at the University of Illinois at Urbana-Champaign. He is the author of *Alienation, Classical Modern Philosophers: Descartes to Kant, Hegel and After, Nietzsche,* and *Making Sense of Nietzsche,* and is Executive Director of the North American Nietzsche Society.

CLAUS-ARTUR SCHEIER is Professor of Philosophy at the University of Braunschweig. He is author of *Nietzsche's Labyrinth* and editor of *Ecce Auctor* (a volume of Nietzsche's prefaces of 1886). Other publications include *Kierkegaard's Ärgernis, Die Selbstentfaltung der methodischen Reflexion als Prinzip der neuren Philosophie,* and commentaries on Hegel's *Phenomenology* and on Wittgenstein's *Tractatus.*

GARY SHAPIRO is Tucker Boatwright Professor in the Humanities at the University of Richmond. He is the author of *Hermeneutics: Questions and Prospects, Nietzschean Narratives,* and *Alcyone: Nietzsche on Gifts, Noise, and Women.*

IVAN SOLL is Professor of Philosophy at the University of Wisconsin-Madison. He is the author of *An Introduction to Hegel's Metaphysics* and essays on Nietzsche and other European philosophers from Kant onward. He is writing a book on Nietzsche and the transformation of philosophy.

ROBERT C. SOLOMON is Quincy Lee Centennial Professor of Philosophy at the University of Texas at Austin. He is the author of *From Rationalism to Existentialism, The Passions, In the Spirit of Hegel, About Love, Continental Philosophy Since 1750,* and *A Passion for Justice;* editor of *Nietzsche: A Collection of Critical Essays;* and coeditor of *Reading Nietzsche* and *The Philosophy of (Erotic) Love.*

STANLEY STEWART is Professor of English at the University of California, Riverside. He is the author of *The Enclosed Garden: The Tradition and the Image in Seventeenth-Century Poetry, The Expanded Voice: The Art of Thomas Traherne,* and *George Herbert.* His novel, *The King James Version,* was published by Random House. He is coauthor of *Nietzsche's Case: Philosophy as/and Literature.*

RICHARD WHITE teaches philosophy at Creighton University. He has published essays on Nietzsche and other developments in recent European philosophy, and is writing a book on Nietzsche and the idea of sovereignty.

BERNARD WILLIAMS is White's Professor of Moral Philosophy at Oxford and Monroe Deutsch Professor of Philosophy at the University of California, Berkeley. His books include *Problems of the Self, Moral Luck, Ethics and the Limits of Philosophy,* and *Shame and Necessity.*

YIRMIYAHU YOVEL is Professor of Philosophy at the Hebrew University of Jerusalem, and is founder and chairman of the Jerusalem International Spinoza Institute. His publications include *Kant and the Philosophy of History* and his two-volume *Spinoza and Other Heretics*.

BIBLIOGRAPHY

EDITIONS AND TRANSLATIONS OF NIETZSCHE'S WRITINGS

Kritische Gesamtausgabe: Werke (KGW), ed. Giorgio Colli and Mazzino Montinari, 30 volumes (Berlin: de Gruyter, 1967–1978).

Kritische Gesamtausgabe: Briefwechsel (KGBW or BW), ed. Giorgio Colli and Mazzino Montinari, 24 volumes (Berlin: de Gruyter, 1975–1984).

Sämtliche Werke. Kritische Studienausgabe (KSA), ed. Giorgio Colli and Mazzino Montinari, 15 volumes (Berlin: de Gruyter, 1980).

Werke in drei Bänden, ed. Karl Schlechta, 3 volumes (Munich: Carl Hanser, 1954–1956), with an index in a fourth volume (1965).

The Birth of Tragedy (Die Geburt der Tragödie, 1872). Trans. Walter Kaufmann, with *The Case of Wagner* (New York: Vintage, 1966); Trans. Frances Golffing, with *The Genealogy of Morals* (Garden City, N.Y.: Doubleday, 1956).

Philosophy in the Tragic Age of the Greeks (Die Philosophie im tragischen Zeitalter der Griechen, 1870–1873). Trans. Marianne Cowan (South Bend: Gateway, 1962).

"On Truth and Lie in a Nonmoral Sense" (*"Über Wahrheit und Lüge im aussermoralischen Sinne,"* 1873). Trans. Daniel Breazeale, in Nietzsche, *Philosophy and Truth,* ed. Breazeale (Atlantic Highlands, N.J.: Humanities Press, 1979); Trans. Walter Kaufmann, in *The Portable Nietzsche,* ed. Walter Kaufmann (New York: Viking, 1954).

Untimely Meditations (Unzeitgemässe Betrachtungen, 1873–1876). Trans. R. J. Hollingdale, as *Untimely Meditations* (Cambridge and New York: Cambridge University Press, 1983); ed. William Arrowsmith, as *Unmodern Observations* (New Haven: Yale University Press, 1990).

David Strauss, the Confessor and the Writer (David Strauss der Bekenner und der Schriftsteller, 1873). Trans. R. J. Hollingdale, in *Untimely Meditations*; intro. J. P. Stern; Trans. and intro. Herbert Golder, in *Unmodern Observations,* ed. William Arrowsmith.

On the Uses and Disadvantages of History for Life (Von Nutzen und Nachteil der Historie für das Leben, 1874). Trans. R. J. Hollingdale, in *Untimely Meditations;* Trans. Gary Brown, as *History in the Service and Disservice of Life,* in *Unmodern Observations;* intro. Werner Dannhauser; Trans. Adrian Collins, as *The Use and Abuse of History* (Indianapolis: Liberal Arts Press, Bobbs-Merrill, 1957); Trans. Peter Preuss, as *On the Advantage and Disadvantage of History for Life* (Indianapolis: Hackett, 1980).

Schopenhauer as Educator (Schopenhauer als Erzeiher, 1874). Trans. R. J. Hollingdale, in *Untimely Meditations;* Trans. William Arrowsmith, in *Unmodern Observations;* intro. Richard Schacht; Trans. James W. Hillesheim and Malcolm R. Simpson (South Bend: Gateway, 1965; intro. Eliseo Vivas).

Richard Wagner in Bayreuth (Richard Wagner in Bayreuth, 1876). Trans. R. J. Hollingdale, in *Untimely Meditations;* Trans. and intro. Gary Brown, in *Unmodern Observations.*

We Classicists (Wir Philologen, 1875). Trans. and intro. William Arrowsmith, in *Unmodern Observations.*

Human, All Too Human (Menschliches, Allzumenschliches, first volume, 1878; first part of second volume, *Assorted Opinions and Maxims,* 1879; second part of second volume, *The Wanderer and his Shadow,* 1880); intro. Erich Heller; Trans. R. J. Hollingdale (Cambridge and New York: Cambridge University Press, 1986); Trans. Marion Faber, with Stephen Lehmann (Lincoln: University of Nebraska Press, 1984, first volume only).

Daybreak: Thoughts on the Prejudices of Morality (Morganröthe, 1881). Trans. R. J. Hollingdale (Cambridge and New York: Cambridge University Press, 1982; intro. Michael Tanner).

The Gay Science or *Joyful Wisdom (Die fröhliche Wissenschaft,* books I–IV, 1882; second edition with Preface and book V, 1887). Trans. Walter Kaufmann, as *The Gay Science* (New York: Vintage, 1974); Trans. Thomas Common, as *Joyful Wisdom* (New York: Frederick Ungar, 1960).

Thus Spoke Zarathustra (Also Sprach Zarathustra, parts I and II, 1883; part III, 1884; part IV, 1885). Trans. Walter Kaufmann, in *The Portable Nietzsche;* Trans. R. J. Hollingdale (Harmondsworth: Penguin, 1961); Trans. Marianne Cowan (Chicago: Gateway, 1957).

Beyond Good and Evil (Jenseits von Gut und Böse, 1886). Trans. Walter Kaufmann (New York: Vintage, 1966); Trans. R. J. Hollingdale (Harmondsworth: Penguin, 1973); Trans. Marianne Cowan (Chicago: Gateway, 1955).

On the Genealogy of Morals (Zur Genealogie der Moral, 1887). Trans. Walter Kaufmann and R. J. Hollingdale, with *Ecce Homo* (New York: Vintage, 1967); Trans. Francis Golffing, with *The Birth of Tragedy* (Garden City, N.Y.: Doubleday, 1956).

The Case of Wagner (Der Fall Wagner, 1888). Trans. Walter Kaufmann, with *The Birth of Tragedy* (New York: Vintage, 1966).

Twilight of the Idols (Götzen-Dämmerung, completed 1888, first published 1889). Trans. Walter Kaufmann, in *The Portable Nietzsche*; Trans. R. J. Hollingdale, with *The Anti-Christ* (Harmondsworth: Penguin, 1968).

The Antichrist (Der Antichrist, completed 1888, first published 1895). Trans. Walter Kaufmann, in *The Portable Nietzsche*; Trans. R. J. Hollingdale, with *Twilight of the Idols.*

Nietzsche contra Wagner (Nietzsche contra Wagner, completed 1888, first published 1895). Trans. Walter Kaufmann, in *The Portable Nietzsche.*

Ecce Homo (Ecce Homo, completed 1888, first published 1908). Trans. Walter Kaufmann, with *On the Genealogy of Morals* (New York: Vintage, 1967); Trans. R. J. Hollingdale (Harmondsworth: Penguin, 1979).

SELECTIONS AND COLLECTIONS

The Will to Power (Der Wille zur Macht, a selection of notes from Nietzsche's notebooks made and arranged by his sister and others, published in several editions of increasing size in 1901, 1904 and 1910–1911). Trans. Walter Kaufmann and R. J. Hollingdale (New York: Vintage, 1967).

Basic Writings of Nietzsche, ed. and trans. Walter Kaufmann (New York: Modern Library, 1968).

The Portable Nietzsche, ed. and trans. Walter Kaufmann (New York: Viking, 1954).

Nietzsche Selections, ed. Richard Schacht (New York: Macmillan, 1993).

A Nietzsche Reader, ed. and trans. R. J. Hollingdale (Harmondsworth: Penguin, 1977).

Philosophy and Truth: Selections from Nietzsche's Notebooks of the Early 1870s, ed. and trans. Daniel Breazeale (Atlantic Highlands, N.J.: Humanities Press, 1979).

The Philosophy of Friedrich Nietzsche, ed. and trans. Walter Kaufmann (New York: Modern Library, 1968).

Nietzsche: A Self-Portrait From His Letters, ed. and trans. Peter Fuss and Henry Shapiro (Cambridge: Harvard University Press, 1971).

Nietzsche: Unpublished Letters, ed. and trans. Kurt F. Leidecker (New York: Philosophical Library, 1959).

Selected Letters of Friedrich Nietzsche, ed. and trans. Christopher Middleton (Chicago: University of Chicago Press, 1969).

SELECTED STUDIES IN ENGLISH OR ENGLISH TRANSLATION

Ackerman, Robert. *Nietzsche: A Frenzied Look.* Amherst, Mass.: University of Massachusetts Press, 1990.

Alderman, Harold. *Nietzsche's Gift.* Athens, Ohio: Ohio University Press, 1977.

Allison, David B., ed. *The New Nietzsche: Contemporary Styles of Interpretation.* New York: Dell, 1977.

Behler, Ernst. *Confrontations.* Trans. Steven Taubeneck. Stanford: Stanford University Press, 1991.

Bergmann, Peter. *Nietzsche: The Last Antipolitical German.* Bloomington: Indiana University Press, 1987.

Blondel, Eric. *Nietzsche, the Body and Culture: Philosophy as a Philological Genealogy.* Trans. Sean Hand. Stanford: Stanford University Press, 1991.

Clark, Maudemarie. *Nietzsche on Truth and Philosophy.* Cambridge: Cambridge University Press, 1990.

Cooper, David. *Authenticity and Learning: Nietzsche's Educational Philosophy.* London: Routledge & Kegan Paul, 1983.

Copleston, Frederich. *Friedrich Nietzsche: Philosopher of Culture.* New York: Barnes and Noble, 1975.

Crawford, Claudia. *The Beginnings of Nietzsche's Theory of Language.* Berlin: Walter de Gruyter, 1988.

Danto, Arthur C. *Nietzsche as Philosopher.* New York: Columbia University Press, 1980.

Darby, Tom, et al., eds. *Nietzsche and the Rhetoric of Nihilism.* Ottawa: Carleton University Press, 1989.

Del Caro, Adrian. *Nietzsche Contra Nietzsche: Creativity and the Anti-Romantic.* Baton Rouge: Louisiana State University Press, 1989.

Deleuze, Giles. *Nietzsche and Philosophy.* Trans. Hugh Tomlinson. New York: Columbia University Press, 1983.

Derrida, Jacques. *Spurs: Nietzsche's Styles.* Trans. Barbara Harlow. Chicago: University of Chicago Press, 1979.

Detwiler, Bruce. *Nietzsche and the Politics of Aristocratic Radicalism.* Chicago: University of Chicago Press, 1990.

Gilman, Sander L. *Conversations with Nietzsche.* Trans. David Parent. New York: Oxford University Press, 1989.

Graybeal, Jean. *Language and "the Feminine" in Nietzsche and Heidegger.* Bloomington: Indiana University Press, 1990.

Grimm, Ruediger Hermann. *Nietzsche's Theory of Knowledge.* Berlin: Walter de Gruyter, 1977.

Haymann, Ronald. *Nietzsche: A Critical Life.* New York: Oxford University Press, 1980.

Heidegger, Martin. *Nietzsche,* four volumes. Trans. David Farrell Krell. New York: Harper and Row, 1979–1984.

Heller, Erich. *The Importance of Nietzsche.* Chicago: The University of Chicago Press, 1988.

Heller, Peter. *Studies in Nietzsche.* Bonn: Bouvier, 1980.

Higgins, Kathleen Marie. *Nietzsche's Zarathustra.* Philadelphia: Temple University Press, 1987.

Hollingdale, R. J. *Nietzsche*. London: Routledge & Kegan Paul, 1965.

Hollingdale, R. J. *Nietzsche: The Man and His Philosophy*. Baton Rouge: Louisiana State University Press, 1965.

Houlgate, Stephen. *Hegel, Nietzsche, and the Criticism of Metaphysics*. Cambridge: Cambridge University Press, 1986.

Hunt, Lester H. *Nietzsche and the Origin of Virtue*. London: Routledge, 1991.

Jaspers, Karl. *Nietzsche: An Introduction to the Understanding of His Philosophical Activity*. Trans. Charles Walraff and Frederick J. Schmitz. Tucson: University of Arizona Press, 1965.

Jaspers, Karl. *Nietzsche and Christianity*. Trans. E. B. Ashton. Chicago: Regnery, 1961.

Jung, C. G. *Nietzsche's Zarathustra*. Ed. James L. Jarrett. Princeton: Princeton University Press, 1988.

Kaufmann, Walter. *Nietzsche: Philosopher, Psychologist, Antichrist*. 4th ed. Princeton: Princeton University Press, 1974.

Koelb, Clayton, ed. *Nietzsche as Postmodernist: Essays Pro and Con*. Albany: State University of New York Press, 1990.

Krell, David F., and David Woods, eds. *Exceedingly Nietzsche: Aspects of Contemporary Nietzsche Interpretation*. London: Routledge, 1988.

Lampert, Laurence, *Nietzsche's Teaching: An Interpretation of Thus Spoke Zarathustra*. New Haven: Yale University Press, 1987.

Love, Frederick. *The Young Nietzsche and the Wagnerian Experience*. Chapel Hill: University of North Carolina Press, 1963.

Magnus, Bernd. *Nietzsche's Existential Imperative*. Bloomington: Indiana University Press, 1978.

Magnus, Bernd, Jean-Pierre Mileur, Stanley Stewart. *Nietzsche's Case: Philosophy as/and Literature*. New York: Routledge, 1993.

Martin, Glen D. *From Nietzsche to Wittgenstein: The Problem of Truth and Nihilism in the Modern World*. New York: Peter Lang, 1989.

May, Keith M. *Nietzsche and Modern Literature*. New York: St. Martin's Press, 1988.

May, Keith M. *Nietzsche and the Spirit of Tragedy*. New York: St. Martin's Press, 1990.

Moles, Alistair. *Nietzsche's Philosophy of Nature and Cosmology*. New York: Peter Lang, 1990.

Morgan, George A. *What Nietzsche Means*. Westport, Conn.: Greenwood, 1975.

Nehamas, Alexander. *Nietzsche: Life as Literature*. Cambridge, Mass.: Harvard University Press, 1985.

O'Hara, Daniel, ed. *Why Nietzsche Now?* Bloomington: Indiana University Press, 1985.

Parkes, Graham, ed. *Nietzsche and Asian Thought*. Chicago: University of Chicago Press, 1991.

Pasley, Malcolm, ed. *Nietzsche: Imagery and Thought.* Berkeley, Los Angeles, London: University of California Press, 1978.

Pettey, John Caron. *Nietzsche's Philosophical and Narrative Styles.* New York: Peter Lang, 1991.

Pfeffer, Rose. *Nietzsche: Disciple of Dionysus.* Louisburg, Pa.: Bucknell University Press, 1972.

Pletsch, Carl. *Young Nietzsche: Becoming a Genius.* New York: Free Press, 1991.

Podach, E. F. *The Madness of Nietzsche.* Trans. F. A. Voigt. New York: Gordon, 1974.

Rickels, Laurence A., ed. *Looking After Nietzsche.* Albany: State University of New York Press, 1990.

Sallis, John. *Crossings: Nietzsche and the Space of Tragedy.* Chicago: University of Chicago Press, 1991.

Sautet, Marc. *Nietzsche for Beginners.* New York: Writers and Readers Publishing, 1990.

Schacht, Richard. *Making Sense of Nietzsche.* Urbana: University of Illinois Press, 1994.

Schacht, Richard. *Nietzsche.* London: Routledge & Kegan Paul, 1983.

Schrift, Alan. *Nietzsche and the Question of Interpretation.* New York: Routledge, 1990.

Schutte, Ofelia. *Beyond Nihilism: Nietzsche Without Mask.* Chicago: University of Chicago Press, 1984.

Scott, Charles E. *The Question of Ethics: Nietzsche, Foucault, Heidegger.* Bloomington: Indiana University Press, 1990.

Shapiro, Gary. *Alcyone: Nietzsche on Gifts, Noise, and Women.* Albany: State University of New York Press, 1991.

Shapiro, Gary. *Nietzschean Narratives.* Bloomington: Indiana University Press, 1989.

Silk, M. S., and J. P. Stern. *Nietzsche on Tragedy.* Cambridge: Cambridge University Press, 1981.

Sloterdijk, Peter. *Thinker on Stage: Nietzsche's Materialism.* Trans. Jamie Owen Daniel. Minneapolis: University of Minnesota Press, 1989.

Solomon, Robert C., ed. *Nietzsche: A Collection of Critical Essays.* Notre Dame: University of Notre Dame Press; originally published by Doubleday, 1973.

Solomon, Robert C., and Kathleen M. Higgins, eds. *Reading Nietzsche.* New York: Oxford University Press, 1988.

Stack, George J. *Lange and Nietzsche.* Berlin: Walter de Gruyter, 1983.

Stack, George J., *Nietzsche and Emerson: An Elective Affinity.* Columbus: Ohio State University Press, 1992.

Stack, George J. *Nietzsche: Man, Knowledge and Will to Power.* Wolfeboro, N.H.: Hollowbrook Publishers, 1991.

Stambaugh, Joan. *Nietzsche's Thought of Eternal Return*. Baltimore: Johns Hopkins University Press, 1972.

Stambaugh, Joan. *The Problem of Time in Nietzsche*. Philadelphia: Bucknell University Press, 1987.

Staten, Henry. *Nietzsche's Voice*. Ithaca: Cornell University Press, 1990.

Stern J. P. *Friedrich Nietzsche*. New York: Penguin, 1978.

Stern, J. P. *A Study of Nietzsche*. Cambridge: Cambridge University Press, 1979.

Strong, Tracy B. *Friedrich Nietzsche and the Politics of Transfiguration*. Berkeley, Los Angeles, London: University of California Press, 1975.

Strong, Tracy B., and Michael Gillespie, eds. *Toward New Seas: Philosophy Aesthetics and Politics in Nietzsche*. Chicago: University of Chicago Press, 1988.

Thiele, Leslie Paul. *Friedrich Nietzsche and the Politics of the Soul: A Study of Heroic Individualism*. Princeton: Princeton University Press, 1990.

Warren, Mark T. *Nietzsche and Political Thought*. Cambridge, Mass.: MIT Press, 1988.

White, Alan. *Within Nietzsche's Labyrinth*. New York: Routledge, 1991.

Whitlock, Greg. *Returning to Sils-Maria: A Commentary to "Also Sprach Zarathustra."* New York: Peter Lang, 1990.

Wilcox, John T. *Truth and Value in Nietzsche: A Study of His Metaethics and Epistemology*. Ann Arbor: University of Michigan Press, 1974.

Young, Julian. *Nietzsche's Philosophy of Art*. Cambridge: Cambridge University Press, 1992.

Yovel, Yirmiyahu, ed. *Nietzsche as Affirmative Thinker*. Dordrecht: Martinus Nijhoff, 1986.